MW01041437

A Grape off the Vine

Our Lecherous Legacy

Second Edition

Ken Cohen

ISBN 1-59405-107-0 EAN 978-1-59405-107-4

Published by New Age World Publishing.
Published and Printed in the United States of America.

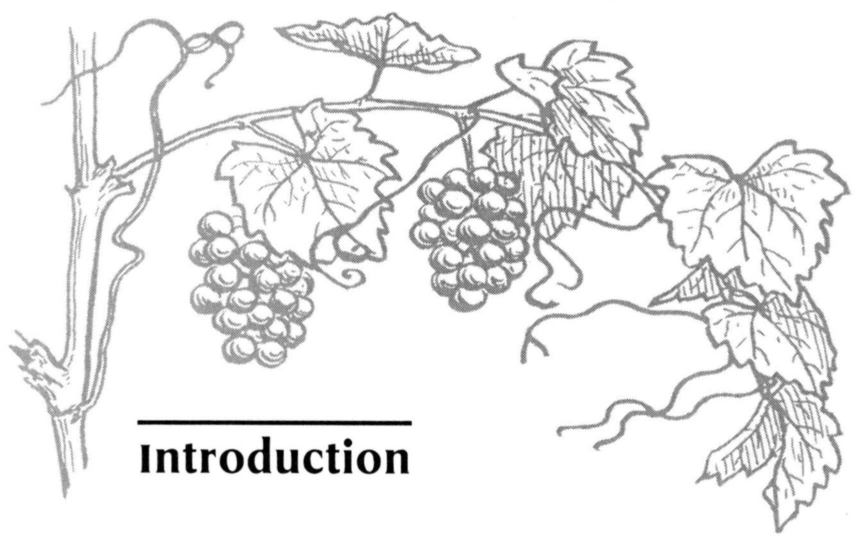

Introduction

The *configuration* of our present day *conflicts* is determined by the *fast-track* for *fears* we had in our *chests* as *children*. We are *woebegone* because we *wolfed down* these *fecal feelings* that *stigmatize* us *still*, so let's resolve these *issues*, follow these words in *italics*, and take these *itchy items* out of the *jail* of our ego-defenses. The *Almighty* put words in *alphabetical* order to help us follow this *tragic trail* back to the time we were *gullible* enough to swallow this *gunk*, so let's *diagnose* our *dicey* behaviors, use our *dictionaries* to *dig* up a little *dignity*, *reminisce* with our *remorse*, and put an end to our *resentments*. You can *retrieve* a sense of *reverence* for your divine *essence* and increase your self-*esteem*, so *talk* to your inner child and *tame* this *tangled* mess. *Listen* together to the *rhapsody* of this *lively rhetoric* because it combines *rhyme*, *rhythm*, and *ribald* humor in a *rich melody* that *melts* the human heart, *rids* it of the *riddle* of ego-addiction, and allows it to *ride* high on a wave of *righteous* behavior. Watch these *films* from your past with the *attitude attorney* of your *remorse*, and stop these *filthy reruns* of your *resentments* by emptying this *reservoir*. Our *hearts* are full of these *heathen*, but when we *heave* them out of our *heaven*, God the *Father* will turn on His *faucet* of *unceasing unconditional* love. Our repressed feelings are the *fossils* that have turned off this *fountain* of *living* waters, but this *load* is not under *lock* and key, so let's allow our *regret* to *rehabilitate* our divine sweetness by using the word *sequences* in *A Grape off the Vine*.

Our sweetness doesn't have to remain *sequestered*, because we can go *back* to the time when we were first *baffled* by this *bag* of tricks.

Satan installed this *satchel* in our minds in Eden by using the *serpent* to *serve* Eve a dose of *voluptuous voodoo.* This *spectacular spell* resulted in the *hard-on* that ended our *harmony*, because our *ego*-addicted wills were the consequence of Adam's *ejaculation.* This *grigri* of our *groins* allows Satan to inject his *waste* into our fountains of living *waters*, but at the Wedding of Cana Jesus invented the *circles* of personal growth that can end this *circus*.

Satan has eaten our *lunch*, because we've swallowed the bait of *lust*, but Jesus *solved* this *somber* problem. He became the *chairman* of the *chakras* by meeting the *challenge* of his *Passion* so as to help us bring compassion to our *pasts*. We can *patch* up our relationship with God, because the chakras are the *Messiah's metaphysical meters*, and we should use them to *measure* how our egos have *meddled* with our thinking. Jesus connected these *contrition contrivances* to our *spines* by winding the *spiral* of the Holy *Spirit* through them, so let's *ruminate* about these *rumors* that have caused us to *rush* to judgment. Let's be *prudent* and *pry* loose this *gory gossip* in *psychotherapy*, because the *success* of this *endearing endeavor* was the reason Jesus willingly *suffered* through the *public punishment* of his Crucifixion. Jesus *sacrificed* himself on the Cross so we could feel *sad* in psychotherapy and remove the *saddle* of ego, so let's do this *sorrowful sorting* and rest our case on the New *Covenant*, because it will end our ego's *cover-up*. We can stop this *sham* from making our lives a *shambles*, because our *shame* is the *catharsis* in the *cathedral* of our hearts that can get our wills out of the *cathouse* of ego and enable us all to *flourish* in the *flow* of the divine sweetness.

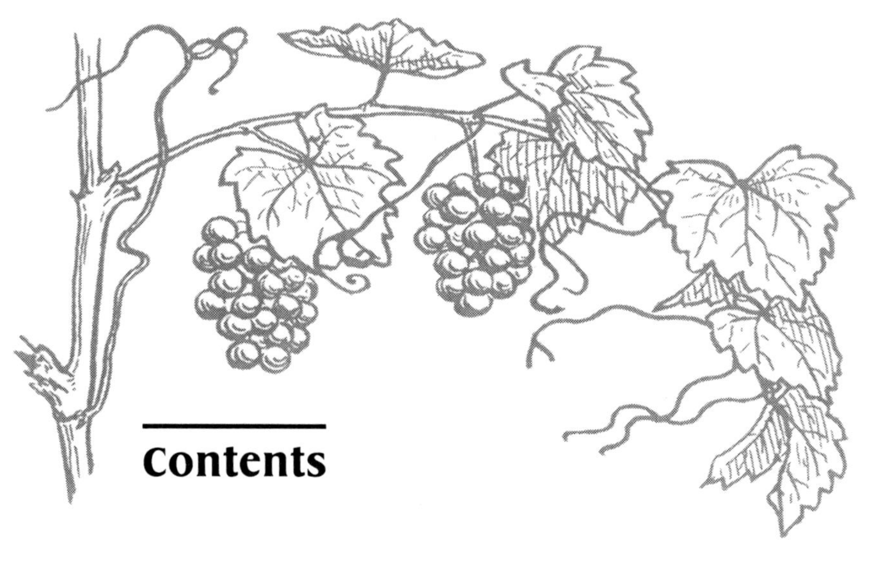

Contents

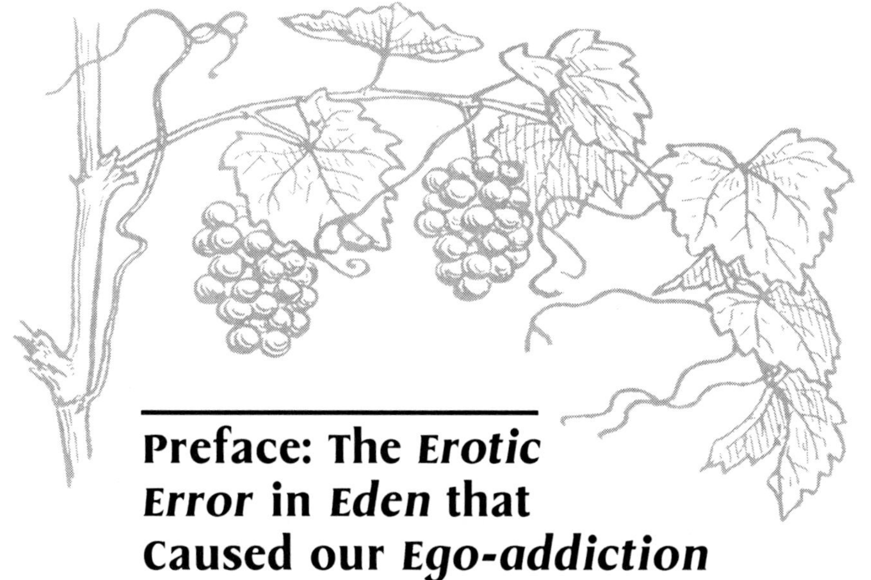

Preface: The *Erotic Error* in *Eden* that Caused our *Ego-addiction*

When our *forefathers* Adam and Eve began to indulge in a little *foreplay* in the *forest*, it *caused* the *caveman* to get the *appetite* for the *apple*, and when the *appliances plugged* into one another, we all got *plunged* into a *poignant poisoning*.† Satan *deceived* Adam and Eve by encouraging them to do the *deed* in *Eden* in *defiance* of the *Deity* so as to *demoralize* all of us through *ego-addiction*. Their *sex* gave us the *shaft*, because their *party* makes us *pass on* our *paternal pathology* to our children. Satan persuaded Eve to *sweep* Adam off his feet so the divine *sweetness* would disappear from our hearts. He inserted this *preface* of pride in lust into the heart of man, because he knew that every time a man made his wife *pregnant* this *prejudicial premise* would make the *embryo* suffer from the *emergency* of ego. It was a *deliberate* effort to make man *delinquent* in the eyes of God and change the *history* of man by making it possible for man's *histrionics* to flow from the repressed feelings he would *hoard*. This *eclipse* took place in *Eden*, be-

†In addition to Saint Augustine, two other modern day mystics considered original sin a sexual sin: The Spanish Catholic mystic Maria Valtorta and the well-known Hindu mystic Paramahansa Yogananda, who founded the Self-Realization Fellowship in Los Angeles, California. (See: *The Poem of the Man God*, Maria Valtorta (Nicandro Picozzi, trans.), Librairie Editions Pauline, December 1986.

I:32: "Had you been faithful to God, you would have had the joy of children, in a holy way, without pain, without exhausting yourselves in obscene and shameful intercourses, which even beasts are unacquainted with, although beasts are without a reasoning and spiritual soul," and V:853: "A new circumcision replaces the old one. Man is to be cause Adam and Eve's *loose love* gave us these *lazy* spiritual *leanings*. We *lapsed* into sin when they went on this *lark*, because the *lascivious chase* they started supplanted the *chastity* God intended, and ever since man has not wanted to examine the *dirt* caused by this *disaster*. Nevertheless, our *sloth* doesn't have to leave us in this *slump*, because the *collective* unconscious of English-speaking people has created *colorful* expressions that can help us end this *colossal* problem. If we put these *words* to *work*, we will get out of this fast *lane* to hell, because *language* is the *lantern* that can light the *way* through an understanding of these *weaknesses*. We cannot be *happy* as long as we are *harassed* by this *mortifying mosaic* of fears, so let's *diagnose* these ills by learning to speak this *dialect*. We won't be such *rebels* if we indulge in this *rebuttal*, because these *maxims* show the way out of this *maze* through the principle of *mea culpa*. Satan's *double talk* has filled us with these *doubts*, so we need to learn this *argot* that will enable us to win these *arguments*. Understanding the *gibberish* will put an end to the *gimmick*, so let's use this *jargon* to get a less *jaundiced* view of *Jehovah*. This *talk* is full of Satan's *tall* tales, so let's decipher this *gobbledygook* and return to *God*. It is best not to be *namby-pamby* about this *nastiness*, so let's speak this *native tongue* of the soul and understand how Satan *took away* our original innocence. Let's use these *motley mottos* to *mount* the offensive of our *mourning* and have the *courage* to make the necessary *course corrections*. This *corruption* makes us *grapes* off the vine, so let's pay attention to the *graphic descriptions* in these pages that show how we got *desecrated*. The devil will not be able to *poach* on our sweetness if we fire these *poignant* expressions *pointblank* at the *poison* we have covered up in our hearts, so let's remove these *deplorable deposits* by *prosecuting* this *prostitution* of our wills to ego. We do not have to be *piloted* by this *pimp*, because these expressions will help us *whisk* away the *whitewash* on the *whore* so that we don't have to live with the *pretense* that she's so *pretty*. In Eden the *Deity* told Adam and Eve that indulging in this *delight* would *deliver* them over

---

circumcised in his heart, because the blood of the circumcised, symbolizing the purification from the concupiscence that excluded Adam from the divine filiation, has been replaced by My most pure blood."

See also: *The Second Coming of Christ*, Paramahansa Yogananda, Self-Realization Fellowship, Los Angeles. I:47 "In the beginning, the sexual organs were not pronounced at all in the symbolic Adam and Eve. God warned them not to eat of the fruit 'in the midst of the Garden' (Genesis 3:3). That fruit was the sensual touch of sex in the middle of the bodily garden. When Adam and Eve succumbed to temptation and ate of that fruit—embraced each other in a lustful way—they were 'driven out' of the Eden of spiritual consciousness."

to these *demeaning* influences, because it would make their wills *devices* of the *devil.* Therefore, if we are to *defuse* this *degradation*, we need to take a look at that which seems *disgusting.*

The *thesaurus thesis* is that this *defilement* can be *defined*, so let's use these *synergistic synonyms* to *speak* the truth and become a more loving *species.* The *message* in these pages is that *messmakers* can become *filthfinders*, so let's put our *finger* on the *muck* that has *muddled* our thinking. Speaking in the *vernacular* is the *versatile* way to *focus* on our *foibles*, so let's learn to *trust* the *truth* by listening to this voice of *counsel* that explains Satan's *counterfeit.* The *spicy spiel* delivered to Eve by the *spin doctor* in Eden taught us all to *dodge* the truth, so if we don't want to keep *going to the dogs*, let's all dedicate ourselves to this *do-it-yourself* approach, and let's be sure we understand the *dirty tricks* that are explained in these *dirty words.* Let's make our wills better *priests* by ensuring that we not be the *prigs* who view these *slogans* as so much *slop.* The *slander* of our ego-addiction is illustrated in these *slang* expressions, so let's *slant* our examination of them with our contrition so as to stop being *slaves* to this *sleaze.* This *hard-core* porn has *hardened* in our hearts, so we need to root out this *harm* by *harnessing* it with our regret. The human will is the *hog* that needs to be *hoisted* out of this *hokum*, so *prudence* dictates that we not let our *prudishness* blind us to these *prurient psychodynamics.* Therefore, let's not be the *snobs* who refuse to *snoop* around in this *snot.* These expressions are not some kind of *flashy flatulence*, because when Eve began to *flaunt* herself in front of Adam, we all developed a liking for the *flavors* of our *flaws* and got *fleeced* of the Holy Spirit, which before the fall was inseparable from the *flesh.*

Nonetheless, we can end this *catastrophe* with these *catch phrases*, because they contain the *blarney* that Satan uses to *blaspheme* against God. Therefore, let's not regard them as so much *blatant blather.* The *blaze* in the twin towers resulted from this *anarchy* that Satan *anchored* to our minds, so let's *regret* this *reign* of terror and not be the *ostriches* who avoid this *ouch.* We have spent a *long* time not *looking* at this *pain* we have *painted* in our hearts, so let's go *back* and recover this *bad bait* we swallowed and *scout* around for these *scraps* that have plagued the mind of man since Adam and Eve *screwed.* Let's give *notice* to these *noxious nuances*, *scrutinize* these *scurrilous* expressions, and not consider them some kind of *gratuitous gravy* from the dinner table from hell. The *impact* this process has is to show how we got *impaired*, so let's *wash* our minds clean of this *waste* material by using these *watchwords*. We can reach the *goal* of becoming more *godly* if we use these *idiomatic* expressions to understand our *idiosyncrasies*, because these expressions are the *steppingstones* that lead us on a *stepwise* approach to *personal* growth. We can rid ourselves of our *perversions* by examining these *explicit* terms, because they explain how Satan *exploits* us, so let's *scan* this *scandal* that has been so *scary*.

If we unveil this *pornographic portrait* of our *earliest* forebears, we can prevent their illicit *earnings* from keeping us all on this *obscene obstacle course*. Adam and Eve's *orgy* gave us *original sin*, so let's become more *level-headed* by using the *leverage* of this *lewd lexicology*. It sheds light on the *libel* from our childhoods we need to *liberate* ourselves from, so let's be aware that the human mind is the *libido library* in which these *lies* are filed away. Let's use these *vivid vocabulary* words, because they illustrate the *seamy* side of our natures that we need to *search* for. Let's obtain *release* from this *relentless pestilence* that makes us think our egos are our *pets*, and let's give *voice* to our pain so that God can fill our *voids*. Let's examine each *slice* of *slime* we have *slipped* on and get rid of this *repulsive* material. Let's do this *requisite research* so as to stop being *smitten* with this *smoldering smut* that has *ignited* our *ill-advised* behavior.

We can have better *manners* by not *manufacturing* this *manure* that *polarizes* our *politics*, so let's *poll* our consciences for this *pollution*. *Islamic isolationism* has already *erupted* into violence, so it should not be allowed to *escalate* any further. The *Arabic* people can examine the *archaeological murmurings* in the *museum* of their collective unconscious and prevent this *aged agenda* from *mushrooming* into more *aggressive* behavior. Jews and Arabs can stop *jerking* one another around in *Jerusalem* and meet one another *halfway* in the *hallowed* ground of the human heart.

The *zeal* of *Zionists* and Islamic *Jihad* does not have to be the *jingoistic jinx* that prevents all *Middle Eastern* people from being guided by the one God in their *midst*. We can get the *job* done *jointly*, so as *Muslims*, Christians, and Jews, we *must muster* the courage not to remain *mute* about these unmet *needs* that *needle* us. We can all be good *neighbors*, so let's stop this *mutiny* against God's authority and dedicate ourselves to the *mutual* effort of overcoming our *differences* so that we can all live in *dignity*. Let's get this job done *lest* the *letter* of God's law result in a *punishment* that make us all look like *puny pupils* who are unable to *define* our reasons for having *departed* from the *realm* of *reason*. *Christians* can *chronicle* the reasons for their *churlish* behavior, *Islamic* nations and *Israel* can get rid of their *separatist sepsis*, and we can all seek to ensure that *September* 11 not produce any more *sequels*.

We just need to use word *sequences* to get in touch with our *serenity*. God placed words in *succession* to *succor* us at times of *sudden suffering*, so let's remove this *wool* we have pulled over our eyes. *Words* taken from the dictionary in a *row* teach how to stop using the *rubber stamp* of ego, so let's study these *ABC's* and become *abidingly* happy. These *dictionary dictums* show how to eliminate *tension* between the races, so let's use these *terms* and *terminate terrorism* in our lifetimes. Each *sequence* is a *series* of *consecutive* words with a *consignment* of *consistent consolation*, so let's *linger* with these *linguistics* until these *sensible sentences* restore the *sentiment* of love to our hearts. There is a *stash* of truth in each of these *statements*, so let's let the spiritual *phosphorescence* in these *phrases* light the way for all *races* to stop indulging in *radical* behavior that results from repressed *rage*.

We have a *right* not to be easily *riled*, so let's get rid of the repressed feelings that act as the *ringleaders* of our *egos' elaborate* schemes. We do not need to be *buffaloed* by this *buffoon*, because the *Crucifixion* will make our egos *crumble*, and the *Resurrection* will enable us to *retain* the *perfect perfusion* of the divine sweetness in our hearts. This *firm* guidance got there *first*, way before the *fissure* in Eden *embittered* us by making us *embrace* this *embroilment*. Our hearts are therefore *pugnacious pumps*, but they can also *squirt* out *stability*, so let's not let *ancient anger* boil over when it makes more sense to *anguish* over the question of how we allowed our hearts to become *animated* with this *animosity*. God's *sugar* is more powerful than our *sullenness*, so let's *overthrow* this grumpiness and remember that our *ownership* of our sweetness is guaranteed by the *rigging* God put in our hearts to give us this *right*. The *plucky plumbing* of the chakras was *installed* in our chests so God's sweetness could be *instilled* in us, so let's use these spiritual *fitness fixtures* to get rid of the *hearsay* in our *hearts*.

Our hearts have always been open to this *unconditional unction*, so let's get God's *honey* and feel *honorable*. This was the *original orthodoxy* God *intended*, and we can *interface* with this *uncorrupt undercurrent*. We can regain this *innocent inside track* with God by using the *truisms* in these pages to learn to *trust* the *truth.* We don't have to remain in *servitude* to the emotional *sewage* of our egos, because this *jester* is the very one that *Jesus jettisoned* on the Cross. God's *purity* will *purr* in our hearts if we *retrace* our steps and *return* to the time when His sweetness was the *revenue* that *financed* our *finesse.* Our wills can be *priests* in their *prime*, so let's enjoy the *prior privilege* of our original innocence and put God's *sweetness in full swing.* Let's let this *unearned* income *enfold* us and *heal* our *hearts.* Let's get *totally* in *touch* with these *blessings* we have been *blind* to and enjoy these *heavenly earnings* on *earth.* Let's have the *gumption* to get out of this *gutter* that *usurped* our *utopia*, *sweep* evil off the face of the earth, and ask God to let the divine *sweetness* turn into the Fruits of the Holy Spirit in every human heart.

A Grape off the Vine

Our Lecherous Legacy

Chapter 1: The *Initial Inquiry* into My *Insanity*

Some years *ago* when I had just begun to *agonize* over these problems a story came to mind in one of my *meditations* that seemed intended to lessen my *melancholy*. It was called "The Valley of The Grapes," and it seemed to *explain* how to *explore* this *human* condition which I was *hung up on*. At the time I was in *psychotherapy* and had a very *puffed up* ego but had begun a serious *prayer* life, hoping that I could get out of this *precarious* situation. Therefore, any *parallels* I might find to the love-*paralysis* in my heart were surely not coincidental. My psychotherapy had grown out of my failing *marriage*, so I had *marshaled* these spiritual forces, but some time before it had *ended* in a divorce that I had *endeavored* to avoid. I had no difficulty in seeing *my* childhood *myths* illustrated in this *story* that I thought came *straight* from God. I really did feel like a *grandiose grape* that had *fallen* off the vine because of this *fallout* from his ego, and I feared that I had become *famous* for having lost my sweetness.

Hence, I interpreted the *story* as containing some *suggestions* as to how I might manage to *sulk* around less. Perhaps it was God's *way* of showing my *wayward* heart that all hope was not lost. I had *manufactured* a lot of *manure,* but the road *map* in the story seemed to suggest that I could derive some *moxie* from my *muck*.

The Valley of the Grapes

Once upon a time, many eons ago, there was the sweetest, kindest, most considerate and loving fairy godmother who had chosen a certain valley to live in. Being a completely self-sufficient person, she had never needed to live with anyone else before and had spent her time simply basking in her bliss. She lived this way for many millennia in perfect peace and contentment, but the time finally came when she began to feel that it would be nice to have living creatures to share her happiness in the valley.

She focused on the one single characteristic in herself which had most contributed to her own peace and contentment and decided to make this characteristic the essence of the new creatures. She thought and thought and finally determined that sweetness was the characteristic in herself that she valued the most and that she would create the sweetest, finest, and most succulent grapes in the whole world.

Having made up her mind about this, she created perfect conditions of soil, climate, and weather in the valley to grow the grapes, and soon a grapevine began to flourish. The grapes that eventually grew on this vine became known as the sweetest grapes in the world.

The sweetness in the grapes created a genuine appreciation on the part of each grape for both its fellow grapes and the fairy godmother who was the source of their sweetness. In fact it was not at all uncommon for one grape to say to another as it hung on the vine, "Isn't it marvelous that we are all so equally sweet as we hang here on the vine, basking in the sun, and that our needs are perfectly met by the fairy godmother?"

Therefore, peace and contentment began to prevail in the valley, with real harmony both between fellow grapes and in their relationship with the fairy godmother. So many millennia passed blissfully in this way that the fairy godmother finally felt that the grapes' good behavior deserved a reward. She came to the grapes after thinking it over long and hard and explained to them that she had decided to make the grapevine invisible so they could roam the valley at will, emphasizing that it would continue as their source of supply. Naturally, the grapes were elated over this gift. They ran all over the valley, investigated every nook and cranny, and were delighted with their newfound freedom. The harmony of their lives was completely undisturbed, and their bliss only increased by their fairy godmother's award of freedom to them.

Nevertheless, after many millennia the memory of the grapevine eventually began to fade in the minds of some of the grapes since the vine was no longer visible. As the memory of the vine faded, some of the grapes began to experience a totally new feeling; they began to be afraid of turning sour. The first grapes that began to feel this fear of turning sour were in quite a quandary over it. They had never felt fear before and were not prepared to deal with it.

Having forgotten their original sweetness that came from the vine, their fear of turning sour became a constant companion. Finally, some of the grapes who thought about it the longest came to a realization about how they might handle this fear. They decided that they would pretend to be sweet! So, a paradoxical situation arose in the minds of some of the grapes. Although they continued to be perfectly sweet, they were afraid of turning sour and were also pretending to be sweet. In order to resolve this conflict, the grapes began to talk to one another about this fear of turning sour, and initially it seemed to restore some sense of peace to the grapes, but eventually circumstances totally new to the grapes began to arise. Arguments arose, and the harmony of the valley gradually began to decline. Jealousy between grapes began to be common, and the valley was plunged into a long-lasting despair. Genuine remorse became common among grapes, and many of the grapes began to think about how they might bring back the times of peace and contentment which were now beginning to fade in their memory.

The grapes that thought about this the hardest closed their eyes and turned their senses inward, concentrating as hard as they could in their meditations on that fading memory. Some of the grapes who concentrated in this manner began to remember the sweetness of the vine and the explanation of the fairy godmother that the sweetness of the vine would not be decreased even though it was invisible.

> Feeling elated over this fact, many of the grapes began to share this information with their brother grapes. They realized that the more they gave away their sweetness in this manner the easier it was for them to imagine the vine extending between them and the other grapes with an inexhaustible supply of unconditional sweetness. These realizations spread like a contagiousness through the valley, greatly reassuring the grapes who had been fearful of turning sour that there was no need to fear and no need to pretend to be sweet.
>
> The grapes' awareness of their natural sweetness became widespread and pacified the conflict that had been rampant in the valley. The grapes no longer abused their freedom, and through the goodwill they extended toward one another, the original peace and harmony in the valley became reestablished, and the grapes lived happily ever after.

The story seemed to *reach* right into my heart, because it landed on the *real feelings* of self-pity I couldn't *fend off.* I felt *divided* from the *divine* as well as from my ex-wife, because my *divorce* had made me realize that I had pretended to be *infallible* when I really felt *inferior.*

I felt like a *bonehead*, so when I started to write this *book*, the title *A Grape off the Vine* seemed appropriate. The *title* showed that my ego had been the *titular* head of a *gossipy government* that had made me *imagine* I had *imbibed* some *soul*-shaking *sourness* rather than the sweetness that came from my *Source.* I had placed my *faith* in some *false reckoning*, but that didn't mean I couldn't *reconcile* myself with *God* if I just remembered that this glitter wasn't real *gold.* Therefore, I just kept on trying to tell the *difference* by doing the necessary *digging* in my psychotherapy and prayer life. I hoped that the divine *Dignitary* would help me out of this *dilemma*, but to my *chagrin* a certain *chain* of *events* that *exacerbated* my growth *delayed* me from getting to the *delicatessen* where the divine sweetness was served. The *tale* called "The Valley of the Grapes" didn't do the *talking* in my mind, because I had left the story in a *drawer* while my *dread* kept on *dribbling* into my behavior. I was the bad *egg* whose *ego* triggered these *encore* performances, which made up the *endless* circles of my *neurotic* behavior. Each adventure seemed *new* and exciting, but my remorse had also begun to *nibble*, because the idea that *dawned* was that I was going down a *dead-end street.* I had aimed to get more in *stride* with Spirit and had begun Catholic *catechism* classes, hoping that I could teach my will not to *cater* so much to my ego. I knew my ego was a *device* of the *devil*, so I figured the better choice was the *devotion* to Mary that would help me identify these *diabolical diagnoses*. Some *trivial troubles* had taken *root*, but I assumed that the Mysteries of the *Rosary* just might help me *dig* these *dillies* out of my mind. I had *put in* a certain amount of effort to thinking about the *put-downs* from my childhood which had *putrefied* there, because I wanted to deliver the *coup de grâce* to them and *couple* myself to my sweetness source. I hoped to close this *gap* between me and God by getting rid of the *garbage* that *garbled* His voice so that I could *hear* Him speak to me in my *heart*. As a result of original sin my *auditory* organs stopped listening to this *authority*, so I wondered whether the Agony in the *Garden* of *Gethsemane* was intended to open this *geyser* in my heart that got *eclipsed* in *Eden*. Eve was the *sorceress* who had brought about this *sordid* result, but perhaps I could *muster* some help from the First *Sorrowful Mystery*. Maybe it was designed to help me stop *flipping* my lid by making my divine sweetness *flow*. I had brought some *rude rudiments* from my childhood that I needed to *rue*, so I *rummaged* through these *rumors* with my remorse until my happiness *ran* freely. I had always been *greeted* by joy after *grieving* in my psychotherapy, so I figured we were intended to earn this *spectacular* result by facing our *specters*. I had taken some time with this *spectrum* of *speculations* and wanted to be *jump-started* at this *junction* in my chest to get my divine sweetness flowing.

I figured that this *hearsay* from our childhoods did not have to prevent our *hearts* from being *heated* up by God's love, so I thought maybe taking a *look* at these *lost years* could make us less *yellow-bellied* in the present. I assumed that my *aggressive* behavior could respond to the *agility* of the *Agony* in the Garden and that I could come up with a more *agreeable agriculture*, so I just went *ahead* looking for my *filth* with the *aid* of my remorse in order to *find* a way to end this *ailment*. Our troubles *ganged* up on us during this *gap between* childhood and adulthood, but it was a *bewilderment* we could get *beyond*, because Jesus went through his *lost* years to help us find *love*. Maybe we could be *aglow* with joy by reliving this *agony* through our contrition. Perhaps our contrition was our spiritual lost and *found* and the *foundry* where our spiritual mettle was *cast*, so that our sweetness wouldn't be the *castaway* of our ego. Perhaps this was the *link* that enabled the *Lion* of Judah to end our ego's *lip*. Maybe the *yardstick* of our contrition was intended to end our ego's *yarn* and span its *yawning* abyss in order to end our lost *years*. Maybe our contrition was the *monastic money* of the child Jesus in the Temple that would help us access our sweetness and stop being ego-*mongers*.

I wanted to *accept* this *access* and *find* the *finesse* of the child Jesus in the temple, so I did my best to put my *finger* on what had made me *finicky*. Then I just waited for Jesus to *finish* the job by making me sweet. I trusted him to *lead* me back to God by helping me *leaf* through the pages of my past so I could find out how I got in the wrong *league*.

I wanted to pay off the *penalty* of my rude behavior with my *penitence* and hoped for a *perspective* that was more *perspicacious*. Therefore, I told my contrition to *catch* the *cause* of my foolishness so that Jesus could *efface* its *effect*. I had *manufactured* my *manure* as a child and had recycled it *many* times as an adult, so eating the *fare* of my own sweetness seemed to be a *far-fetched* dream. The *stench* of my *bedeviled behavior* was reeking in my nostrils, but figuring out how it got *stenciled* into my mind was simply the *stepwise* job the child Jesus in the temple could *help* me with so that I wouldn't feel *hemmed* in by my fears.

I thought I might be able to *arouse* my sweetness by *arranging* the Mysteries of the Rosary in a circle. Perhaps this circular *array* of the Mysteries was intended to take my sweetness out of *arrears* and *arrest* my *arrogance*. I thought my sweetness might have more *leeway* if I put the Joyous Mysteries on the *left* and my *miasma* of Sorrowful Mysteries in the *middle* with the Glorious Mysteries *rigged* on the *right*.

I then looked at the *fifteen fighters* of evil on the page in the hopes of bouncing *my myopia* off these *Mysteries* so as to remain less *mystified*. Perhaps the five Sorrowful Mysteries were the *plumbing* that would allow the divine sweetness to flow by helping me figure out how it got *plundered*. I was the grape that fell off the *vine* as a child, because I had been *violated* by certain *circumstances* at that time that didn't make me behave like a very *civilized* adult, so my *aggressive* behavior was traceable to this *Agony* in the *Garden* in my heart that seemed to indicate I needed to *gather* some insights. At the *First* Sorrowful Mystery I needed to do this *fishing*, because I had *fallen* off the vine as a result of *family* influences, so at Scourging I *forgot* about my sweetness and became *forlorn*. At Crowning I became afraid of turning *sour* and was even more *spaced-out*. At Carrying I *pretended* that my sweetness still *prevailed*. In order to be a *plump* grape again I would have to *plunk* down these repressed feelings at the Crucifixion, which seemed to be the *gate* where I could *gather* the Fruits that would cure me of being *gauche*.

I was on a *quest* to become less *quick-tempered*, so I followed the light to the Crucifixion, which I figured was the *door* I had to open to find the real *dope* of my divine sweetness. I knew my ego's *flight* of fancy was based on *flimsy* evidence, so I became determined to *dim* this *dimension* in my mind and *light* up the *likelihood* of my sweetness. Then I could *reattach* to the vine, *reawaken* my sweetness, and this *spark* of the divine in me could *sparkle*. I had taken a *pledge* to get out of this *plight* by *plodding* through each bit of manure I had let *plop*. I knew that I could undo my ego's *plot* by *retracing* my steps, so I set out to *retract* the *dirt* that I needed to *disavow*.

It was a *journey* during which I had to *joust* my ego in order to arrive at *joy*. It was a *laborious* path through a *labyrinth* of fears that had *lacerated* me, but each time I became *lachrymose* with remorse, I felt the *lacing* around my heart loosen. Each time I *named* a behavior my will woke up from its *nap*, and each time I *tamed* the fear that it came from I found myself marching in *tandem* with God. Jesus helped me *adapt* less to my ego-*addiction* and more to the *addition* of my sweetness, so he *civilized* my will, and I *claimed* my *joy* by not having to *juggle* the *sorrows* that kept making *sorties* into my behavior. Jesus *served* me my sweetness by guiding me through these two *sets* of *Mysteries* that seemed to have the job of demystifying the *myths* from my childhood.

The *link* between the Sorrowful and Joyous Mysteries then was that you had to *listen* to the *little* voice of your inner child, because he was *loaded* with *loathsome* thoughts, and the *laundry law* was that your contrition could leave him *clean clear* through. Therefore, the Sorrowful and Joyous Mysteries were *relentlessly relevant* in making our fears useless *relics*, because they helped us arrive at the *paradise* of our heaven within by embracing this *paradox* known as the joy of suffering.

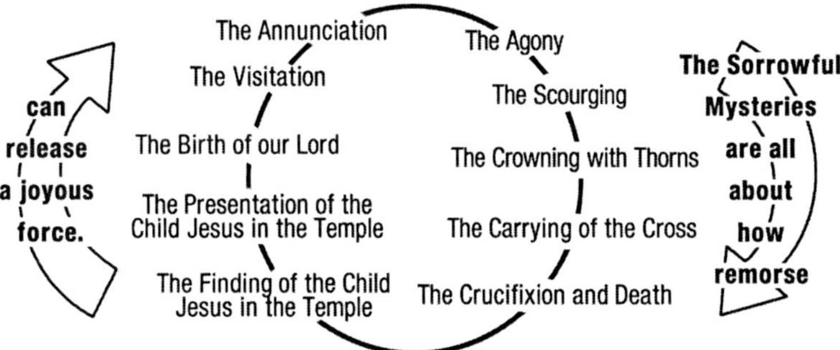

We have been *ill-bred*, so we need to *illuminate* the *illusory* nature of our fears in order to *impeach* them. It is not to our *credit* that we are so *credulous* as children as to adopt the *creed* of ego which gets this *creek* of our *creepy* feelings flowing. We can be taught to *cremate* our fears if our parents set the *example* of using prayer at times of *exasperation*, but if we do not get this *role-modeling* our lives will become a *roller coaster.* A child's contrition is therefore the *scourging scout* who removes his crown of *thorns* so as to make life a less *thorny thoroughfare.* However, I wasn't *taught* this *technique* as a child, so the cross I *lugged* around made me all the more *lugubrious.* I had no *catharsis* in the *cathedral* of my heart, and this lack of *epiphanies* made my life a series of ego-driven *episodes.* My passion *week* finally ended years later when I crucified my fears by *weeping.* Then I felt less *weighted* down by these *weird* teachings and *welcomed* some humility.

Our inner *child* feels this *chill*, but as *adults* we must eliminate this *adulteration.* We crucify this *calumny* at our *Calvary*, so you could say we defeat the *fiend* at the *Fifth* Sorrowful Mystery. However, this slander will only *expire* if we *explain* to our inner child in very *explicit* terms why it makes us *explode.* Then he will be able to feel his *bliss*, because we will have helped him stop feeling *blitzed* by this *blizzard.* We *hit* upon our joy at the Fifth Joyous Mystery by learning how to *hitch* up to our divine sweetness rather than the *Hitler* which is our ego.

The Finding of the Child Jesus in the Temple is therefore our *discovery* of how not to *discredit* ourselves by using the *discretion* which is our remorse. A word of *caution* is in order here. During the early years of my psychotherapy I had some *cavalier* attitudes and was *unaware* of the twelve year old Jesus in my heart, but I was still not *unbacked* by him, and he made me less *unbalanced* every time I felt remorse. He gave me the *idea* that I could *identify* the fears I wanted to let go of in order to find an *identity* that was more *idyllic.* If I wanted to get a *peek* at my ecstasy I just needed to *peel* off my agony. It was a *long* journey, but I got a *look* at my joy along the way. The Finding identified the *data* that was *daunting*, and then the Presentation helped my joy *dawn* on me. The Presentation was an *inauguration* of something *inborn* in me which was of *incalculable* value. It was an *introduction* to the divine sweetness that resulted from my *introspection*, which is to say the inspection of my affection connection. I had *forgotten* about the vine but could still remember how to be *forgiven*, because my contrition was the *remedy* that helped me *remember* the sweetness of the vine. It was the substitution of *awe* for what's *awful*, so at The *Presentation* I learned not to *pretend* to be *pretty* when I was really bent out of shape like a *pretzel*.

The Sorrowful Mysteries showed that what I had *misconstrued* as a child had caused my *misery* as an adult, and then the Joyous Mysteries supplied the sweetness that had been *missing*. Each Sorrowful Mystery *recapitulated* an event from the past which allowed the corresponding Joyous Mystery to *recapture* some of the divine sweetness. The lost grape therefore saw that the *unlearning* of his sorrows *unleashed* his joys, because his contrition *simply* made the two interact *simultaneously*. He just got off his *treadmill* of *treason* and asked his *treasury* for his *treat*.

As the grapes *went* down the road of their Sorrowful Mysteries, they were able to detect the events from their pasts that *goaded* them in the present. Each was on a *quest* to provide answers to *questionable behaviors* he had to *behold* with his remorse. They felt the *pangs* of their *panic* and got the *relief* of the Catholic *religion*.

The Birth of our Lord is the Third Joyous Mystery, because it represents the *rebirth* that makes our spirituality *rebound*. It is *worth* it to take a look at our *wounds*, because Mary is the *woman* whose *womb* can put us in touch with this *wonder*. This is the *maneuver* that God accomplished by *managing* to have Jesus born in the *manger*, and it is the *point* where we get his *poise* by giving up the *poison* of our sour grapes attitudes. We no longer have to *crow* with pride, because we have removed our *crowns* of thorns.

Our sweetness becomes *visible* at the *Visitation*, and our sourness is *annulled* at the *Annunciation* by the *anodyne* of our contrition. The *award* of our *awe* cures us of being *awkward*, and we stop scourging ourselves with this *whip*, because our minds don't *whirl* from the *whiskey* which is our fears. The sweetness of the *Source* always cures the *souse* which is our ego if we insist that the *drunk dry out*.

The *bill* of fare we swallowed as children may have filled us with *bitterness*, but we can *substitute* this *blatant blather* with God's *sugar*. The grape can be *recharged* with sweetness through this *reciprocity*, because our contrition *interacts* in the vine with our fears so as to *interchange* them for love. One might assume that the grape off the vine is now *fulfilled* by seeing his sweetness come *full circle*, but in order for it to *circulate* and successfully *vie* with his ego, three circles come to *view*. The grapes have been given the *freedom* to roam the valley, but it has only allowed their egos to *freeload* on them, because they are binging on *free will.* They have *frozen* the *freight* of their Fruits of the Spirit, and how they will be able to *defrost* them by *degrees* is the subject of the rest of this tale. ☙

Chapter 2: The *Untouchable Untruths* I Left *Unwept* Are the Cause of My *Upheaval.*

When I first got the idea of *arousing* my spirituality by *arranging* the Mysteries of the Rosary in a *circle*, I was very used to the *circular* nature of my own neurosis. It marched to the tune of my ego's *circumlocution*, because I had been *scourged* by the *scraps* I had *carried* in the *cart* of my subconscious mind, but I had also gone through the *critique* of my psycho-

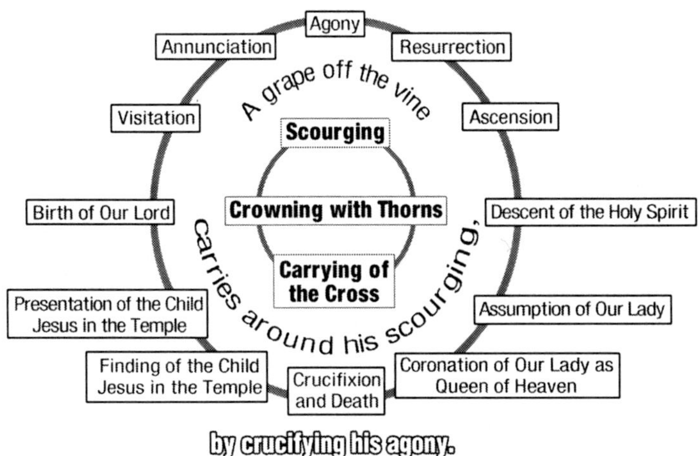

therapy. I hoped to *crucify* these odds and ends, because I knew they were the *agony* that had caused my *ailment*, so I took a look at the current *edition* of my behavior and tried to figure out how it resulted from the *effusion* of my sour-grapes attitudes. I had been examining this *ego-trip* for almost *eight* years in *therapy* and hoped *there* could be better prospects for me.

I got some *jolts* on this *journey*, because I was a *repeat* offender, but I had also treated my *repellent* behaviors with *repentance*, so I finally *stumbled* onto the *stunning realization* that forgiveness was the *reason* I felt *reassured*. The *meaning* of the mysteries in the above diagram was therefore to *measure* out divine *pardon* when I *pared* away my fears. The *Sorrowful* Mysteries did the *sorting*, the *Joyous* Mysteries returned the *judgment* of my innocence, and the *Glorious* Mysteries put me finger in *glove* with God. It was a *course* in how the New *Covenant* could crack the nut of our egos if we *confronted* our fears in order to be *consoled*. I had *carried* my childhood *scourging* without crucifying my agony, but this *carry-over* could be *scouted* out on these two *concentric* circles, because Jesus *condescended* during his Passion to help us identify the aspects of our *conduct* we need to *confess*. The Scourging and Carrying on the inner circle were therefore the *roadway* I had to *roam* in order to get back to the *roaring roasting* of my childhood. I had been *robbed* of the *robe* of my original innocence, but *demarcating* these *demeaning* remarks would improve my *demeanor*, so I just had to use this *self-discipline* on my *self-doubts* in order to become *Self-educated*.

My inner child was the *wonder worker* who could crucify my agony. He and I had *scorned* one another, so I told him he wasn't a *scoundrel* but had actually been *scourged* by these *wretched wrongs* that had turned my life into a *screwy caricature* and that I didn't intend to *carry* them around anymore. My inner child really consisted of *two tykes*: the wounded *child* who felt the *chill*, and the wonder child who could *chime* in with the answer. Therefore, I just had to persuade the one with the *will power* to talk to the *wimp* and tell him that I had been behaving like a *brat*, that I had changed my mind and wanted to be *brave*. My will was the *soldier of fortune* that brought the *solution* to these two children by convincing them to *interact* so that my fears and my ego would stop *interbreeding*. My wounded child needed a little *pep talk* explaining how the *peptic juice* in his stomach could digest the divine sweetness. So my wonder child said to him, "According to the New Covenant, we can end our *plight* by just continuing to *plod* along until we find our fears' burial *plot.* We can *plow* them under and feel more *plucky,* so let's pull the *plug* on our ego, because it's a *plum* of a job to *plumb* these depths!" My wonder child was the *nurse* who needed to *nurture* this *nut* if my wounded child was to *nuzzle* up to my sweetness. In order to be *befriended* by my sweetness, I had to become less *befuddled* by my embitterment. Therefore, let's return to the real *beginning* and see exactly how I got *begrimed.* ☙

Chapter 3: The *Detached* Observer *Detoxifies* Me by Helping Me Reminisce *Remorsefully.*

In October 1984, if you had asked me about my life, I would have probably said, "I wish this *lifestyle* could last for a *lifetime*!" I lived in a large three-story brick house on an *important* residential street with other *imposing* houses. I had a *swimming pool* in back and a Lincoln Continental in the driveway and felt that these things made me a *swinger.* My wife was *attractive* and well known as a volunteer in the Jewish Community, both of which I *attributed* to my good taste. I was a doctor, and considered myself to have a *successful* practice, because they had provided me with perks *such* as these. The economy of New Orleans, Louisiana, was in an oil *boom* which *boosted* my ego even more, because it had *inflated* the value of my home, which of course made me feel very *influential.* I often took pencil in hand to *add* up these assets all of which contributed to my ego-*addiction.*

I had absolutely no cause for *regret* even though these possessions *reinforced* my *reliance* on ego, but my wife had begun *psychotherapy* the year before and all of this *puffery* only made her want to *puke.* These seeds of *discontent* had been sown and were soon to *discredit* me, because my wife's lack of *identity* had made her feel like an *idiot.* My *wife* felt like a squaw in a *wigwam*, and being our children's *mother* made her feel like a *mouse* without any *moxie. Recognizing* this wound made her *recoil*, and all the outer *trappings* only *traumatized* her all the more. Nevertheless, the *same* was not true for me, because I had sought *sanctuary* in them. I was very *sanguine* about my *sanity* and didn't realize I was *sashaying* into disaster.

I had built this house of *cards* with my *careless* inattention to these miscalculations, and the *collapse* began before I even realized we were on a *collision course*. She was *brave* enough to *break* the silence one morning while I was eating *breakfast*. She said, "Ken, I don't know whether I love you anymore, but I want you to come to my psychotherapist." It is difficult to *describe* how such words could fail to make me feel *deserted*, but my response was entirely *clinical*. I didn't realize at the time that my ego had me in the *clink*, or that various *clippings* it had from my childhood enabled it to *clobber* me. I felt *comfortably* in *command* in my office and *concluded* that her statement was worthy of my professional *condescension*. She had never been effusive before in her expressions of *affection*, so I didn't let it *afflict* me. I asked her to *explain*, but she said she would rather *explore* that in the therapist's office. I accepted her *response* and had no idea what *result* it would bring. In the first therapy session I was *surprised* to see how my ego had blocked my *surveillance* of these *problems*. My *procrastination* had left me *profitless*, so I lent an *ear* hoping for an *early* solution. She said it was *enough* trouble to have two children to raise without having a husband who felt *entitled* to be mothered as well. She said she was up to her *ears* in *earnest* disgust at how my *childishness* would *chime* in when my *unfulfilled* dependency needs would get *unglued*. I *met* my wounded inner child, because my wife had used the *megaphone* of her anger to let me know she expected me to *meliorate* the situation. I had gotten *trapped* in these outer *trappings* we shared and had to *traverse* the *travesty* she described. The *dressing* I had used on my wound had allowed its components to *drift* into my behavior according to the *drill* of my ego, so there was no point in *smothering* my sweetness by continuing to be *smug*. I had to heal its *festering* if I wanted my sweetness to *festoon* my behavior. If I wanted to *extricate* myself from this situation, I would have to open my *eyes* and train them on the *sorcery* that seemed to have produced these *sores*. I had the *Peter Pan* Syndrome, because I had clung to my mother's *petticoats*, which had allowed my *phalanx* of repressed feelings to attack my wife. I was *neurotic*, because I had *never* grown up and naturally got *grumpy* when she failed to *guard* me from life's problems as I thought any good *guardian* should. I wasn't *adroit* at coping, because I had become an *adult* child. I had all the necessary *manipulative mannerisms* and had developed this *fame* on my own, so this news struck a *familiar chord*, and I decided then and there to set myself to the *chore* of getting to know this 200 lb. 5 year *old* who considered self-esteem *old-fashioned*.

When I took a look, I was *surprised* by a *surreal* view, because it had formerly been *curtailed* by the *curtain* of my ego. I knew I wanted to improve my spiritual *pedigree*, so I took a *peek*, hoping to *defeat* some of my *defense mechanisms*. I had been in the *den* of thieves called *denial*, but I was a *doctor* and could learn a different *doctrine*. I was in a *clinch* with repressed feelings that I had *clung* to since childhood, and I would have to use my *clinical* skills in order to *clip* the wings of my ego.

The first thing I did was to become *committed* to the task of using the *commode*. I used it to get rid of the *commodities commonly* known as repressed feelings, which maintained the *status quo* according to the *statutes* of ego. I knew that my pride had resulted in my *perfectionism*, which was a *perfectly perfidious* thing, so I decided to let my *performance* be guided by the *perfume* of my humility. My perfectionism was the *pestilence* I had nurtured, but it was also the *pet* of my ego, so I decided that to save my marriage I would send *Peter Pan* a *petition* from my contrition. I had pretended I was *infallible*, because I had felt *inferior*, but I could bring about the *departure* of these *dependency needs* that had made me a spiritual *ne'er-do-well*.

However, the *state of affairs* that was most responsible for this deplorable *status quo* was my *greed*, which made me *green* with envy of all those whose *possessions* were *possibly* better than mine. In my marriage I had *acquiesced* to a rampant *acquisitiveness*, and therefore, I was most of all *frightened* at the prospect of losing the *frills* which were the *fringe benefits* of our savings and our home. I didn't want to *fritter* them away *frivolously*, so I used my *inquisitiveness* to make *inroads* into my *insanity*. My ego was the *bête noire* I needed to *betray*, but my remorse became the *joystick* of *Judas*, because he was the apostle of betrayal, so I had to *train* myself to bring my ego-driven *traits* to this *traitor*.

In my therapy I learned to *betray* the *bias* that made me *bicker* with my loved ones, so I played back the *recording* of my childhood in order to *recoup* some of my sweetness. Eventually I *stumbled* on a *stupendous* book called *The Twelve Powers of Man*† that explained the powers we have *recourse* to in order to *recover*. It was by Charles

†*The Twelve Powers of Man*, Charles Fillmore, Unity Books, Unity Village, MO 64065.

Fillmore, the founder of Unity Church of *Practical* Christianity of which I had become a *member* when I first got the idea that my *mental illness* might be susceptible to the *mercy* of the Crucifixion. Each power focused our *contrition* on the *prankster* of our ego so our fears could be *corrected* by one of the *correspondents* known as the twelve apostles. If I didn't want a *powder keg* for an ego, I would have to use the *powers* to *practice informing* on the reasons for my *infuriation.* Faith and understanding produced *insights*, strength, and will were *inspiring*; judgment and order were *instructive*; love-zeal *insulated* my heart from ego-addiction; and renunciation-power was the *insurrection* that waged war against my ego. Lastly imagination and life *integrated* my mind into God's *intelligence.* Judas was the *turncoat* who *tutored* me in this way, because his job was to help me *leak* out this bad news so I could *lean* on something better. Each power delivered an *apology* to God for an *apostasy* and was under the control of an *apostle* who dispensed it from his particular *apothecary.*

THE FIRST CIRCLE with the Mysteries, Apostles, and Powers

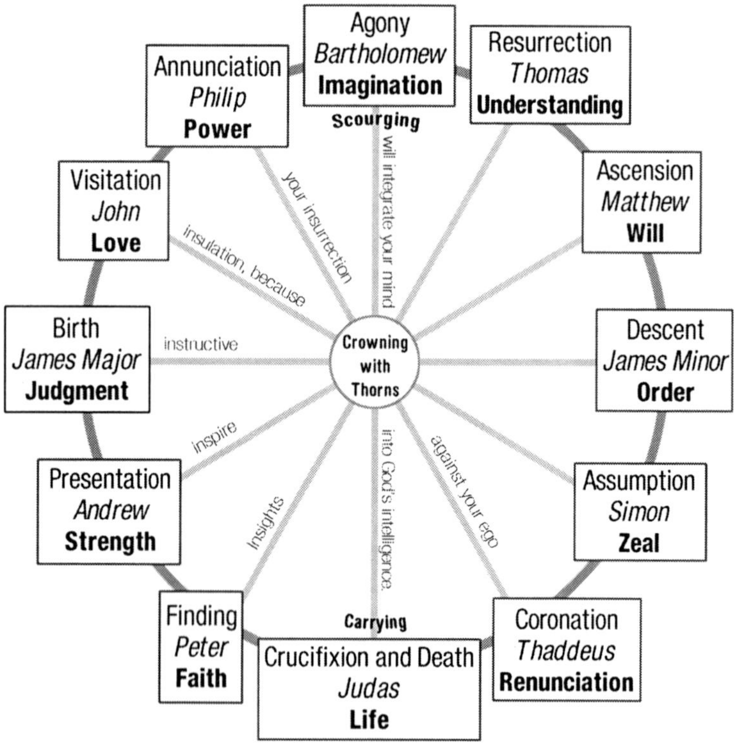

When I was a child I was *weak*, but as an adult aiming to recover I had a *wealth* of *nostalgia* for these *nostrums* on the first circle, because I knew they were *notable* for their ability to help me grow spiritually. As a child I wanted the *lollipop* that would make me feel less *lonely*, and since I didn't get it I was filled with *longing*. A lack of *recognition* by my parents made me *recoil* in horror, so my ego *recommended* the tactic of approval-seeking to obtain this *recompense*. However, I felt *discredited* over this *discrepancy*, and my individuality *melted*. Being a *member* of this *tribe* didn't help, because during their *tribulations* they didn't use this *tribunal* of twelve, and I never figured out how to pay *tribute* to my uniqueness. I had been raised *Jewish*, but it only proved to be a *jigsaw puzzle* that added to my *contentiousness*, because I had submerged my identity in the *continuity* of Jewish *history*, which only added to my *histrionics*. Every *Sunday* I went to *Sunday School*, but they didn't teach me about this *sundial*, so I remained *sunken* in problems that were really *superable*.

On some Saturday mornings we went to *Sabbath* service, but it didn't give me a *sabbatical* from my toil, because it seemed like a *drudgery*, and I remained *drugged* by ego. I was never *irrigated* by the sweetness that would help me become less *irritable* and remained an *island* unto myself, *isolated* from the comfort other children seemed to get from the religion of *Israel*.

It was a *self-sufficiency* devoid of *Self-support*, because I never learned that God plays a *part* in helping me *partake* of the divine sweetness. Therefore, when I began my psychotherapy, it was a *crusade* of personal growth in which I felt that I alone was intended to *crush* the enemy. I *gloated* over the prospect of confronting my *gloom* in order to get the *glory*, and I intended to *face* every *facet* of the challenge. I was not new to *arduous* tasks having entered the *arena* of medicine and had learned to *argue* my case in spite of my spiritual *aridity*. I had run a *marathon* the year before, and so I began the race against my *marauding* ego, fully intending to get back all my *marbles*. My psychotherapy was on the *march*!

When I began my psychotherapy I expected the effort to be *lucrative*, but the idea of spiritual assistance was *ludicrous*. I did not worship in the temple of my heart, because I was a *glory-seeker*, and this particular *gloss* blinded me to the *penitence* that could take me out of that *penitentiary*. It was a *diligence* that left me with a *dilly* of a problem, because my determination was *precisely* the thing that *precluded* any help from the *precocious* child Jesus. It was an *obstinate obstructionism* that arose from my perfectionism, and I never *quibbled* about making *quick work* of conquering the *world* through this form of self-help.

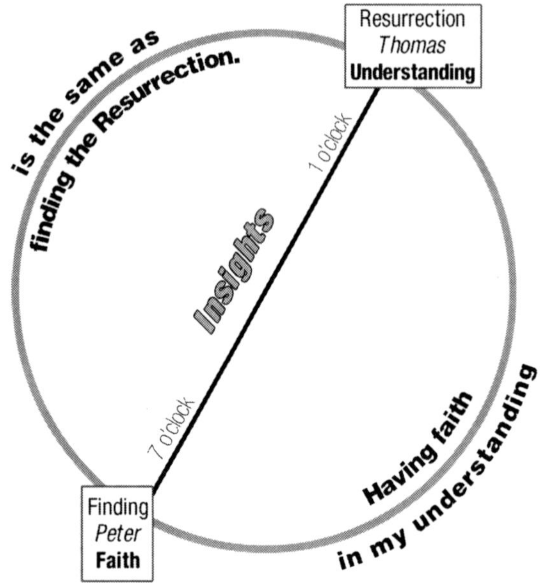

I had been *overcome* by *overconfidence*, but my *insights insisted* on using the powers of faith and understanding, which *persuaded Peter* and *Thomas* to help me take these *thorns* out of my side. I had to look at these *film* clips from my past in order to *find* the *restrictions* I had placed on the sweetness I wanted to *resurrect*. Thomas, the apostle of understanding, gave me a *double* blessing, because he got rid of my *doubts* and also gave me the *dough* to make my daily bread. My doubts had *swept* away my *sweetness*, *swelled* my pride, and left me *sweltering* in my hell on earth, but my contrition was the *rearview mirror* that made it seem *reasonable* that I should be *reassured*.

These two powers were an *injunction* that my *injury* wasn't written in permanent *ink*. I just had to use them to get an *inkling* into how the injury had been *inlaid*. Then God would send this *army* of two apostles to let me know that His sweetness was still *around*. This is how the *Lord's lore* helped me when I felt *lost*.

During this first year of my psychotherapy I wanted to make my ego *retreat*, so I began to *retrieve* insights by looking back *retrospectively*. I *surrendered* some fears that I crept up on *surreptitiously* with the help of my therapist who was my *surrogate* mother. I *appreciated* getting rid of my *apprehension* and so became an *apprentice* in seeking her *ap-*

proval. The *books* she gave me to read helped me pull myself up by my *bootstraps*, so I *read* this material hoping for some *real reassurance.* I felt less like a *patsy* because of *pats* on the *back* she gave me and realized that I didn't have to put up with my ego's *back talk.* I had been my ego's *puppet*, so I didn't mind being her *puppy* if it would make me *pure* of heart. I used my *therapy therefore* to reset the *thermodynamics* of my emotional *thermostat.* I *hustled* real hard, because I wanted to stop the *manipulative hydraulics* of my ego from leaving its *mark* on my *marriage.* I had been *hyper*, and divorce wasn't a *fascinating fashion* to me, so I worked *fast* by focusing my attention *fastidiously* on every detail of my growth.

However, a certain *alienation* had *alighted* on our marital relationship, and I began to fear *alimony.* I had *fouled* my nest and was unable to be the *founder* of our reconciliation. I was such an *anguished animal* that my *animation* eventually abandoned me, and I was not *able* to be *able-bodied* in bed. I asked her to *join* me in *joint* therapy sessions, but to her it seemed like a *joke* which I didn't consider very *jolly.*

My marriage seemed to be in *line* for a *lingering death*, and there was no way for me to stop the *debacle.* There wasn't even the *affectation* of *affection*, because we had lost *affinity* for one another, and it seemed to *affirm* that I was headed for some *affliction.* The *grenade* of my *grief* exploded when she finally mentioned that we might *trespass* less on one another's space if we had a *trial separation*, which I somehow knew would only make our relationship more *septic.* We finally went into therapy and tried to figure out how we had *stepped on one another's toes*, but it didn't help us get *together*, because she *exploded* in anger and didn't want to *explore* the possibility of reconciliation. Our relationship was a *disaster area* that neither of us could *disavow.*

I climbed my *mountain* of *mourning* during this trial separation which had been an *attempt* to *attend* to the problem but which only focused our *attention* on how much our love for one another had become *attenuated.* When she asked me for a divorce, I had become *stoic*, because I had tried to *stoke* the fires, but they had gone out. Nevertheless, God was soon to *pillow* my fall, because I was soon to choose Him as my *pilot* instead of the *pimp* of my ego, and He would help me *pin* my *hopes* on spiritual *horizons* that were more promising as explained in the next chapter.

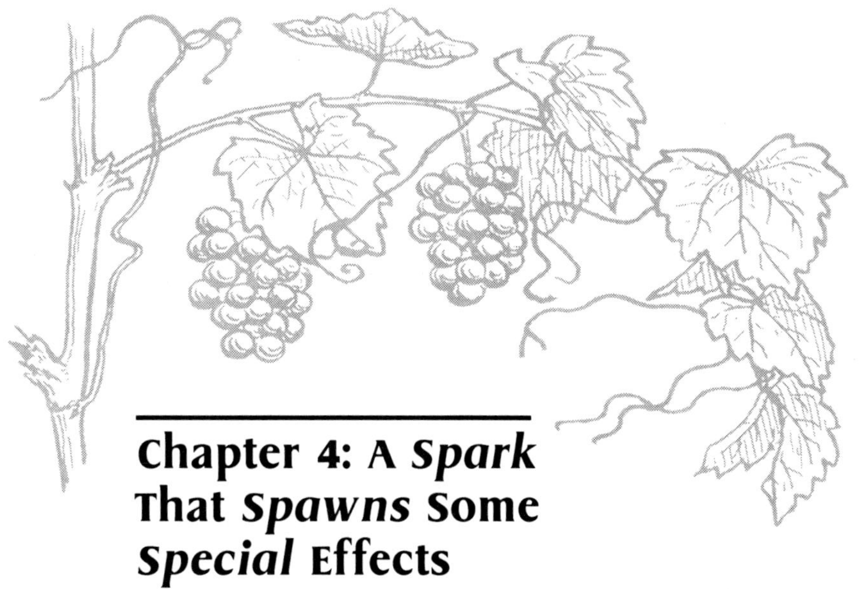

Chapter 4: A *Spark* That *Spawns* Some *Special* Effects

Some months before our separation, I was in a bookstore trying to *fetch* some insights that might help me break the *fetters* of ego when I *stumbled* on a book with a *stunning* title, *Love is Letting Go of Fear* by Jerry Jampolsky. A *Jewish* psychiatrist, Jampolsky had found the *jewel* of Christian spirituality through a three volume text called *A Course in Miracles.*[†]

I had already been an *ambassador* on the mission of letting go of fear, and so I dedicated myself to deciphering the *ambiguous* phraseology of the course. I had the *ambition* of being fed the divine *ambrosia*, so I didn't waste a *minute*. I knew that *miracles* were no *mirage* and would take place if I did my best to become less *mired* by ego. I *hopped* to the task, which I didn't consider *hopeless*, of taking all my fears out of the *hopper.* My sweetness had not totally *failed*, it had just become *faint*, and there was a *fair* chance that if I kept the *faith* I would not feel like such a *fake*. My divine spark could certainly *ignite* if I stopped *ignoring* the *illness* that obscured my spiritual *illumination*.

The course used Christian spirituality to help its students *turn* the corner, and it made me feel like a *turncoat* because of my Jewish identity, but I also recognized the possibility of a *turning point* that could be a *turnoff* to my ego. Therefore I used the *course* in order to *court* God.

[†]*A Course in Miracles*, The Foundation for Inner Peace, P.O. Box 1104, Glen Ellen, California 95442.

I wanted to *detach* myself from the *details* I needed to *detect* so that I could *deter* my ego, and this I was *determined* to accomplish. My ego-addiction had put in *motion* a *motley* crew of repressed feelings, and the *motif* of this *motion* seemed to be *described* in the Mysteries of the Rosary, because they seemed to be *designed* to allow us to *desist* from our *despair.* They had a teamwork that went *full* circle so that we wouldn't *fumble* our sweetness. It *went* down through our sorrows, *westward* to joy, and then eastward to glory, and got rid of our *minuses* by working *miracles.*

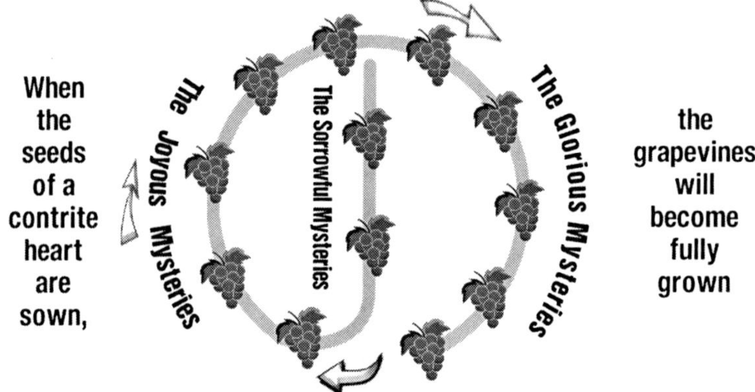

Uncongenial feelings in our *unconscious* were *uncovered*, and this earned us the *unction* of God's sweetness. The *sorrowful sorting* of our remorse started the *parade* of joy and glory that resulted from this *paradigm* shift. If we didn't want to feel the *heat* of these *heathen*, they would just have to be *heaved* out of our *heaven*. This kind of *suffering* seemed to *suffice* to take us on this *journey* to *joy.*

I felt like a *stray* dog who had had a *streak* of bad luck, and I wanted to welcome this *stream* of joy. My inner child seemed to understand the *prescription* I needed for this *presence of mind*, and I got it at the *Presentation*, which seemed to *preserve* the divine sweetness so that it could *preside* over my will. I *found* this *fountain* at the *Fourth* Joyous Mystery.

To my wounded child it was an *intricate intrigue*, because he didn't know his sweetness was *intrinsic* to my nature and that we could prevent my ego from *intruding* on it. Andrew and Matthew therefore *collaborated* to bring about the *collapse* of my ego, and they encouraged my wounded child to subject his *wiles* to the powers of strength and will who were the *inspectors general* who used my *will power* for the purpose of my *inspiration*. The power of *strength* was *strictly* in

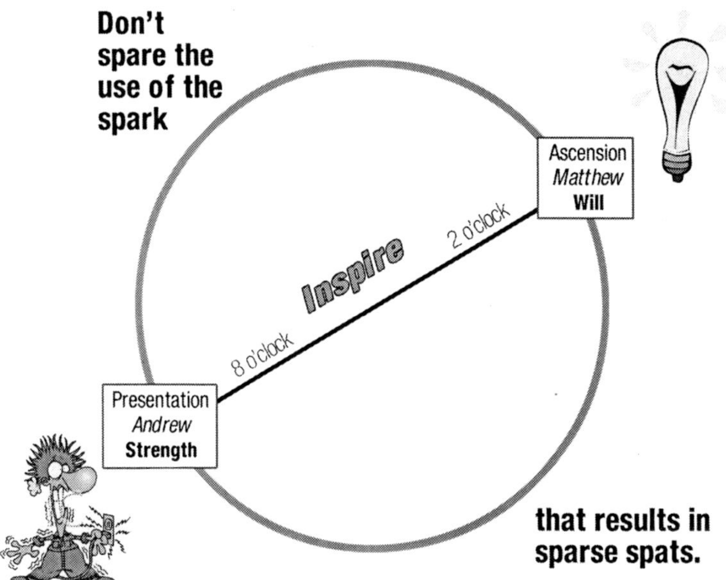

stride with the *will* of God, so my *willingness* to pay the *penalty* of my *penitence won* me this *windfall.* My wounded child stopped thinking he was a *fink*, because he was *fired up* by this *firm* guidance from the *firmament.* It was no *fairy tale* that my *faith* got *hooked* by my *hope* who was the *coach* that had formed this *coalition.*

The first thing on his *list* was to *listen* to this coach who could cure my *listlessness.* The door at the The Ascension opened and raised me *up* spiritually by seeing to it that my *upbringing* was *updated* by getting rid of *upheaval.* This was the *matter* that *Matthew* accomplished to make me more *mature.*

I rested more comfortably on this *upholstery*, because it had the *uplifting* effect of *precluding* the *predicaments* in my life that arose from my wounded inner child's *exaggerated exasperations.* I used my *logic* and took a *long look*, *illustrating* to him how my *ill will* had given us a bad self-*image.* Nevertheless, we were both *immature*, and the effect was not *immediate*, so I'm sure we looked like a couple of *slapstick* comedians who didn't have the *slightest* idea that their own *slime* was the cause of their *slip-ups.* Like the Jews in the desert it seemed to be taking *forty* years for this *forum* of twelve powers to *defeat* my ego-*defenses.* My spark was only a *glimmer*, but it was soon to get a *glimpse* of a flame with a lot of *glitter.*

Chapter 5: *Spellbinding Spiritual Fireworks* that Seem to *Fix* the *Flake's Flame*

After I separated from my wife I *anxiously* pursued my personal growth from an *apartment* I had taken, but I also began to *ape* the behavior of Adam and Eve. Becoming single seemed to have been the *aperitif* that awakened this appetite. During the day I spouted spiritual *aphorisms*, but the setting of the sun seemed to have an *aphrodisiac* effect on me, and I mustered my *aplomb* in the pursuit of this end.

Single life had brought the *bonus* of making me a *bon vivant* in the pursuit of the opposite sex. My inner child returned to his love of *Spanish* in order to light this *spark*. *His* identity as a *Hispanic* had existed since he first studied Spanish in high school, and I worshipped this *idol* as a means of *igniting* some *ignominious* behaviors.

I had a series of *dalliances* with Hispanic women and had no concern for the concept of *damage* control, because with these *dames* I behaved like one of the *damned*. I may have behaved like a saint during the *day*, but by night I was *dazzled* by their beauty. I was *atwitter* over each of them, but I also had the ulterior motive of wanting to impress the *audience* which was the Hispanic community so as to *augment* the number of them in my medical practice.

In the first year I lived in this apartment, I took the *risk* of going through another *rite of passage*. My Jewish identity came to be a *fossil* that I didn't want to *foster*, because it contained some *remnants* that I had tried hard to *remodel*, and so I took a *leap* of faith in the effort to *learn* something better. I was *persuaded* by some friends who made some *pertinent* comments and thought *maybe* I could have less *mayhem* in my life by going to Unity Church of Practical Christianity.

However, the idea of Christ as a divinity was still a *bitter* dose that seemed awfully *bizarre*, because not even *once* had anyone explained how a *one-on-one* relationship with him helped get rid of *onerous* problems. Then as a *tonic* to this misgiving a friend *took* me to see a video in a local bookstore regarding a holy man from India named Satya Sai Baba. He was *short* with an afro hairstyle, orange robe, and no shoes, and all of this seemed to add to the *show*, because outside of his ashram hundreds of his *devotees* were seated on the ground and followed his every move as if he had the power to give them spiritual *dexterity*. The *sight* of him rendered them *silent*, and their gaze was *riveted* on the holy man as if he could show them the *road* to heaven. They would *clasp* their hands together, and it was *clear* to them that his ability to *heal* the sick was more than *hearsay*. All were *transfixed* by him and seemed to consider him a rapid *transit* to cloud nine.

In the video Sai Baba was described as a divine *incarnation*, which wasn't as *incendiary* to my Jewish identity as the *incentive* to worship Jesus. *Waving* his hands was his *way* of materializing religious objects from thin air for the *wayfarers* seated around him.

I watched with an air of *undaunted* skepticism, because I was *undecided* as to the meaning of it all. I had *divided* loyalties toward Jesus but perhaps thought that some *dividend* might be available from this other *divinity*. The *thread* of logic that held my appeal was that he was no *threat* to my Jewish identity. The next day the most *unlikely* thing was that my doubts about the divine were *unloaded*, and forces were *unlocked* that *unloosened* a warm glow in my heart extending up my spine to my head. A feeling of *harmony* had been *harnessed*, and the fact that it occurred the day after the video seemed to be a *sign* that Sai Baba had been a *silent partner* in these doings. He seemed to have shot a *Cupid's* arrow into my heart after lacing it with the *curare* that could paralyze my doubts.

I cannot *underrate* the importance of feeling *understood*. The *concept* that I had felt misunderstood seemed to be his *concern*, and therefore he showed me how I could act in *concert* with the forces of forgiveness. I wanted to *conquer* my ego, and I thought that Sai Baba's *consciousness* could be *conscripted* in order to *consecrate* my will to loving behavior. I wanted my *head* to be *healed*, and the *theory* seemed to be that something *therapeutic* had occurred. The Cupid's *arrow* that hit my heart apparently had the *arsenal* of weapons I needed.

A long *experience* grew out of this *experiment*, and I hoped it would make me *expert* at making my ego *expire*. My daily *meditations* became our *medium of exchange*, and I brought a *medley* of conflicts to him in the hopes he would make me spiritually *meek*. He was a spiritual *crutch* to me, and I *cried* like a baby during meditation confronting the *cryptic* forces of ego in the hopes of getting some insights from his *crystal* ball. I had been in a *desert* of *despair* but seemed to have gotten the *dessert*. I had reached an *oasis*, sworn an *oath* to become less *obstinate*, and sought *rest* from the *restraints* of ego.

My prayer life *flourished* with Baba and gave me the hope that my divine sweetness had begun to *flow*. I had a lot of *questions* in *queue* and always seemed to get *quick* answers. It was always a *dialogue* about how I might *dialyze* out my repressed feelings and wind up with the *diamond* which is the divine sweetness. The spiritual *fireworks* had begun, and my repressed feelings were on the *firing line* with my remorse as the *firing squad*. The *valleys* of my remorse were *valuable*, because they brought me to *peaks* at which *peals* of joy sounded in my heart. After one year of daily prayer I told him in *meditation* that I wanted to get on his knee so he could tell me a story, and he *met* my needs by telling me the story of "The Valley Of the Grapes." The story seemed to describe how to reach a *position* that was *positive*, so I viewed it as my most valuable *possession*.

My relationship with Sai Baba lasted thirteen years until some facts were *revealed* that made my *reverence* for him *wane*†, and I *warmed* up to Jesus, thinking there was likely to be a *singular* benefit to me as a *sinner* to be *saved* by the *Savior*. I figured that Jesus got *crucified* so I could *cuddle* up to God and *cure* the *curmudgeon* in me, so I went to him to get this *curse* removed. My *crotchetiness* got *crucified*, because this *diabolical diagnosis* was *explained* as part of the *exploit* of the Crucifixion on the nine to three o'clock *diagonal* on the circle. In order to *vindicate* my sweetness I needed to rid my *vine* of its *vinegar*. I needed to go on this *journey* in which the powers of *judgment* and *order* could teach me how to mine this *ore*.

At 9 o'clock on the circle Jesus the *Judaic judge* was born, and his *judgment* could make me *judicious*. I had been in the *jail* of ego, but I

†*The Findings*, David and Faye Bailey, PO Box 35, Conwy, N. Wales LL3282N United Kingdom.

was soon to get out of this *jam*, because a *jamboree* was being sponsored by *James* greater and *James* lesser who *rectified* my *red herrings*. These *installments* were *instructive*, because I was a *cross patch*, and the *Crown of Thorns* helped me *thrash* out an *understanding* that could *undo* my ego-addiction. My nerves were less *jangled*, because these two *apostles* were the *janitors* who helped me clean up this *appalling* mess. My *ordeals* would have *order* restored to them, because the Descent of the Holy Spirit would bring me these two powers which were the *tidbits* that yielded this *tidy* profit. It was a *teaching* regarding the *teamwork* of the Father, the Son, and the Holy Spirit and how they can *tear* down ego.

These *three* made me *thrive*, because when Jesus wore the Crown of Thorns, he put God on the *throne* of my will. When Adam and Eve got under the *apple* tree they *appointed* my ego to *officiate* over my will, and I got some *off-the-wall* behaviors, but in *Bethlehem* this *bête noire* was defeated, because that's where the *Mediatrix* gave birth to the *medic*. They are the *Joint Chiefs of Staff* who end this *joke* by *marshaling* the necessary troops, so let's ask the *Martyr* and *Mary* to help us remove this *mask*. We don't have to be *crippled* by this *crisis* in Eden, because Jesus *crucified* this *agony* and put us in *agreement* with

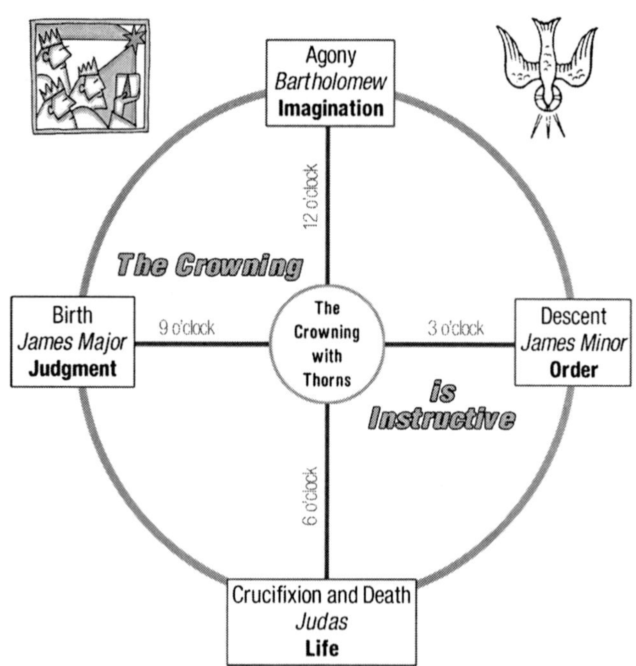

God. He gave us the *vigorous* powers of judgment and order to heal our *vileness*, so let's use these *medicines* on our *mediocrity.*

We all *fell* into *fallibility* in Eden, and our hearts became *fallow* gardens, but the Agony in the Garden made a more *agreeable agriculture* possible. We just need to *fence* in our *ferocity* with our remorse and *fertilize* the *soil* over the *years* with *fervent yearning* for the *field* to *yield* a *solid* profit. We need to pull up the *weeds* of our fear, hurt, and anger, so we *weep* with *regret* and *rejoice*, because the *farm* in our chests is owned by God the *Father* and will grow the *crop* of love, joy, and peace. This *harvest* ends our *hassle*, because Jesus carried the *Cross* to *plant* this *grapevine* in our chests as part of the *gratifying* political *platform* called the New Covenant. *Digging* into these fears we have *digested* is rewarding, because when we pull up these *weeds*, we no longer feel *weird*. Therefore, let's trust Jesus to plant these *seeds* that are more *seemly*. Our hearts are *plots* of land where Jesus can *ply* his trade, because he always starts *building* a *better* relationship *between* us and God when we decide that we don't want to be full of *bull*. The *carpenter carried* his Cross to defeat the ego *cartel*. Likewise, Mary's *career* is to teach us how to use the *caress* of our contrition on these *careworn caricatures*, because they are *satires* devoid of *satisfaction* and beg to be *saturated* with the divine sweetness. We are all at the *foot* of the apple tree and need to *forage* in this way, because the *foray* of Adam and Eve brought the *forbidden force* into play. The result is that our *comedy* is in *command*, but our *shortcomings* don't mean that our chances for growth are *shot*. It just means that we *should shoulder* the responsibility for *shoveling* our manure so that the divine sweetness will *show up*. When we *maneuver* ourselves into the *manger* in this way, we won't get *mangled*.

One way I *followed* my ego's *folly* was to *foment* my *fondness* for *fondling* women. I went through a second *adolescence* during which I felt like an *Adonis*. What *mortifies* me the *most* about this debauchery is that my relationship with my *mother* left me feeling *naïve* enough to think that getting *naked* with women would make me feel less *namby-pamby*. So in the *name* of my *narcissistic* supplies I indulged in this *narcotic* and began a *narrative* of *nasty* behavior. Nevertheless, every time I *initiated* the act I had an *inkling* that I was headed for *perdition*, so my *performance anxiety* wouldn't let me get *anywhere*. The *beast* in me seemed to be *beaten*, so every time I took to *bed* I had a *limp linchpin*.

I had to *masticate* on the fact that *maternal* love deserted me when I took to the *mattress*. I had to *unlink* myself from the ego-defense that made me feel *unlovable* by my mother and stop indulging in this *superficial* act, because unconditional love could only be *supplied* by the *Supreme Being*. These were the *blemishes* I needed to *blend* with my contrition in my relationship with the *Blessed* Mother if I didn't want to be *blind* to the love I had *blipped* out. I had to bring this *disparity* to her, because she is a *dispassionate dispatcher* of sour grapes attitudes and also *dispenses* the divine sweetness. I cannot *accentuate* too much my need for *acceptance*, because my mind was *aswirl* with these fears of rejection that made me want to ask for *asylum* with the Holy Family. I was a *refugee* from my relationship with my mother and wanted the *refulgent refund* from Mary that my mother had *refused* to give. How I was to accomplish this *undertaking* without being swept out to sea by my ego's *undertow* is the subject of the next adventure. ❧

Chapter 6: Mary's *Womb* Works *Wonders* on *My Mystifying* Wound

My meditations had been filled with my *raucous* regret at having been *ravaged* by these forces as a child, and I began to see them as the cause of my *ravenous* appetites for the *ravishing* beauties whom I had been dating. I had *clammed up* from the time of my childhood, but now I was ready to raise a *clamor* to take off the *clamp* that my *clan* had put on my sweetness. I definitely received *consolations* during meditation that seemed to *consolidate* this benefit for me, even though my *consorts* by night reflected my *conspicuous conspiracy* against God.

During the time that I was attempting to *contain* this *contamination contemplative* prayer caught up with me. It was the prayer of silence, and I hoped that it indicated that the self-*contempt* I had been *contending* with was to be replaced by a better *content.* My meditations became *quiet*, perhaps because the Blessed Mother's divine *quintessence* rid me of such *quirks*. I had certainly been the *bird brain* who had *bird-dogged* women for three or four years, and I felt that this behavior was well worth handing over in exchange for the *birthright* of the divine sweetness. I regretted being *conceited* and hoped that the prayer of quiet meant that I was being *conceived* in the Blessed Mother's womb.

I finally realized that my second adolescence had been motivated by *impetuous* forces that were *impinging* on my personal growth, and I figured that one of the cures was probably this *implacable* silence in my prayer life. Therefore, it was not *implausible* that the hand of fate would provide an *implement* to help further this *implication*. It was the spiritual masterpiece of Paramahansa Yogananda, *The Autobiography of a Yogi*. Yogananda's life was an *exercise* in *exhausting* himself in the pursuit of God, and therefore it was also an *exhibition* of *exhilaration* in which he encouraged his followers to *exhort* divine forgiveness in order to end their *exile* from God. Since I wanted to be *grounded* in the truth, I joined his *group*, the Self-Realization Fellowship (SRF). Its primary tool seemed to be a spiritual technique called Kriya *Yoga*, which I hoped would help me shed the *yoke* of ego, and so I used it *regularly* in the hopes of spiritual *rehabilitation*. The techniques of the SRF are *methods* to *meticulously* increase our spiritual *mettle*, and so I used these *skills* without *skimping* on the time I spent. Nevertheless, during this time I felt sincerely *disappointed* over the fact that the spiritual fireworks of the meditative phase of prayer had been *disarmed*.

I assumed that the prayer of quiet was filled with *aridity*, because it *arose* from humility rather than the pride that made me feel like an *aristocrat*. I was *wooing* my *woodenheaded* will to reform my wild and *woolly* ego, because I wanted it to hear this *wordless* language of love, which I figured would *work* to give me *worlds* of relief.

The *glow* between my head and heart seemed to contain the divine *glucose*, because it was a powerful *physical* sensation, and I assumed that it came from the divine *physician* Mary who aimed to change my spiritual *physiology*. During my *second* adolescence I had *seduced* women, because I felt abandoned by my mother, so I figured this glow in my spine could *abridge* this *abuse* and *boost* me into the *bosom* of God. I had felt like an *uptight* street *urchin*, so I assumed it represented the *ultimate umbilical cord* that could attach me to the *uterus* of Mary and grant me a more *immaculate implement* than the *imposter* between my legs. I had let the *thimble* on my *thin thing* do the *thinking*, because I had thought that my head and heart were *third* rate powers that could not satisfy my *thirst*. Nevertheless, the *smoldering* fire of my yearning *smoothed* the way to remove this *glue* that blocked my connection to God, and so I felt less *glum*. The glow in my spine aspired to *lofty* heights and aimed to make me stop being *at loggerheads* with effective spiritual *logic*.

My divine sweetness was *confiscated* during the *conflict* of my second adolescence, but this *glow* in my spine taught my head and heart to *go* to *God's gourmet kitchen* and eat this *matchless meal* so that I could be *governed* by His *grace*, and become a *grape* on the vine. It was just *another* example of how God was the *answer* to our *antagonist* original sin, because His power *antedated* it. The *principle* of the divine sweetness is not out of *print*, and is still the *prior privilege* we can *assert* over the powers of evil in order to get the *asset* of God's love. I just had to *integrate* my *intellect* into the divine *intelligence*.

The *stunt* of my second adolescence might seem *stupid* now, but at the time it seemed like a *sturdy* coping strategy. Nevertheless I had these *misgivings* that made me feel *misguided*, and they provided the *stimulus* for me to feel *stung* by this *stinking stint*. I had *manufactured* this *manure* and had lost my *fidelity* to the divine sweetness by trying to play the *field* at the instruction of Satan the *fiend*. I had to think about which *mind* I wanted to *mine*, because the *mind* that is in *Christ* Jesus completes the *circuit* between our *heart* and our *heaven* within. Therefore, I decided to *dig* up this *dignified mineral* of the divine sweetness which was more than willing to *mingle* with my will.

Nevertheless, I was on the *fence* about how to *fertilize* my heart, and so a *feud* raged between the two *feudal* lords of my Judaism and my Christianity. After *wrestling* with this *wretchedness* for some time, I decided to *validate* this *valuable* organ in my chest and *let* in some *levelheadedness*. I had had a good *relationship* with my *rabbi* so I paid him a visit hoping to get some *relief* and become less *rabid* in my ego-addiction. After explaining all the *facts*, I told him that my mind had been a *factory* that had manufactured things that were less than *factual* and that I thought I needed to *lose* my mind in order to find *love* in my heart. He said that *Christianity* was the religion of the heart and Judaism was the religion of the mind, and so I decided to *chuck* the one that had made me *chugalug* nonsense and become *chummy* with God by joining the Christian *church*.

Meanwhile, in my meditations I was still trying to *subdue* this *subject* known as ego which had *subjugated* me. It had let loose this *aggregate* of *aggrieved* sentiments that had left me feeling *aghast*, and I was sick and tired of them all being *agitated* at the same time. As soon as I closed my eyes, they would be off and running in a *jumble* with one trying to get the *jump* on the other. I went off on these *tangents* with these *tangles* of feelings, and each one wanted to do the *tango* with me. Eventually I decided not to let myself get *rattled* by these *ravings*, so I *disregarded* these *disreputable maniacs* hoping not to be *manipulated* anymore by their *manure*.

The *confidence game* of original sin had put my reason in *conflict* with my wisdom. My reason just kept on *ranting*, but I figured it was a bad *rap* and decided that my *wisdom* had to take control over this *witch doctor*, because my wisdom came from the *realm* of God. Therefore, my *reason* became concerned about being *disinherited*, because he thought his ego-driven empire might *disintegrate*. He realized he might have to *relocate* if I became *reluctant* to *rely* on him, so he tried to make wisdom take a *dive* by using a variety of *diversionary* tactics. Nevertheless, wisdom *tackled* the *tactic* every time and made it seem *tactless*. The more my wisdom began to *stir*, the more my reason would exhaust every trick that was his *stock in trade*. My *reason* feared the *rebate* he might receive as a result of being a *rebel*. He had made the *mistake* of taking in a *mistress* who *misunderstood* the *mite* known as humility. My *pride* had become his *priestess*, but my *wisdom* had no *wish* to be subjected to her *witchcraft*.

Reason was so *captivated* by my *caravan* of repressed feelings, he did not see that wisdom had begun to *roam* around on that road, and he *roared* with anger at the prospect of being *robbed* of the *robe* of my will. My sweetness had gone *south* when I gave my will to reason as a *souvenir*, because he had used his *sovereignty* to *sow spaced* out attitudes into my thinking. My *kin* had been anything but *kind*, so these *kinetics* made reason think he was *king*. This caused my *kinky* behaviors, so a *fight* is what I *figured* it would take to make him stop his *filibuster*.

My reason had *distinguished* itself in the art of *distorting* the truth, and therefore the *distractions* in my meditations did fill me with *distress*. My reason was a *showoff*, and although his *shrapnel* didn't have a *shred* of validity, it was *shrewdly* conceived to make me *shriek* in fear. That's why, given the choice, I would rather *wire* myself to *wisdom*.

My reason held my will in the *vise* called ego-addiction, but the *vision* of my wisdom *visiting* brought me hope of better *vistas*. I could *secede* from my ego-addiction in the *seclusion* of The *Second* Joyous Mystery, because Mary was the *secret secretary* who could make my will *secrete* the divine sweetness. Therefore, I asked *John* to *join* my will to the power of love and gave Simon my *zany* behavior so he could *zap* it with my *zeal*. It was a *change* of pace that was *charged* with benefit for me, because the *charismatic* entity known as wisdom *visited* my reason and made it *vividly* clear that the *Assumption* could make me *astute*. I got *wired* to my *wisdom*, and it *insulated* me from my reason's *insurrection*, so that I could bear *witness* to my *wonder*.

I was on a *campaign* to open this *canal* in my spine to that *glorious glow* that could make God's *glucose* travel from my head to my

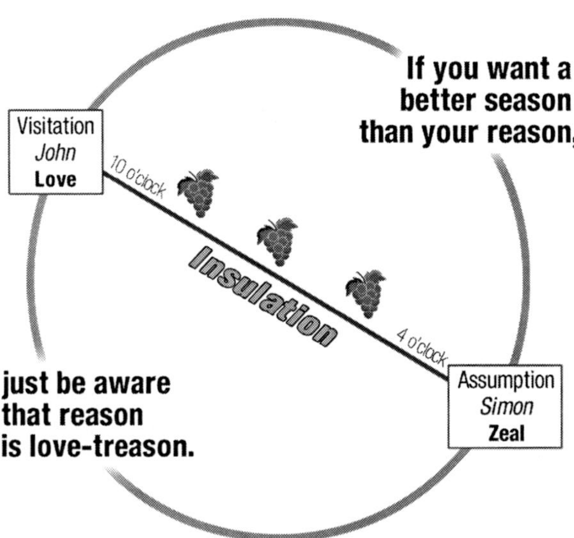

heart, because then my wisdom might convince my reason to *cancel* the *cancer* of my ego-addiction. I told my reason his *bombast* kept my will in *bondage*, so finally reason figured that wisdom's *bone of contention* was really worth *listening* to. Ultimately reason realized he had been cherishing a bunch of *litter*, and this understanding brought him the *bonus* of getting rid of the *boogieman* called ego who had intimidated him. My will had been lost in the *forest* of my reason's doubts but still hadn't *forfeited* the right to *forge* a new path. Therefore, he showed these *forgeries* to my reason. My reason *winked* at my *wisdom*, because he realized then and there that he had *forgotten* how to *forgive* himself. My reason had broadcasted a *never-ending newscast*, with each piece of nonsense being the *next* one he wanted my will to *nibble* on. Nevertheless, he finally became *bored* with these antics and became a *born-again* Christian. He decided to march less in *rhythm* with the *ribald* logic that began under the apple tree and more in rhythm with my spiritual *riches*.

My *reason's rancor rankled* me, so I asked Mary to *ransom* this *rapacious* foe *rapidly* with that particular *rapture* known as a contrite heart. I *ignored* my reason's *ill-advised* suggestions and depended on the *champion* known as wisdom to *channel* the divine sweetness into my heart. I *disrobed* my will of my reason's *disruption* so that *unconditional* love could get *underway* in my heart. My head had been Satan's *unwitting* accomplice but was not *unworthy* of my heart's help according to the *unwritten* law that we can all be *unyoked* from our ego-addiction *up* there. The grapevine *lifted* my heart's *love* to my head's *lunacy* to shed some *light* on how to prevent the *lightning strikes* that made me look *like* such a *stubborn* fool. Love and zeal guided the vine so I could learn not to *spill* the divine sweetness that flowed up my *spine*.

My will had been *cooped* up in my head for a long time, and so Mary went there to teach it to *cooperate* with my heart. The work of her Visitation was to pay this social *call* to my reason and explain that it did not have to make me so *callous*. In this *interview* she pointed out that my *intestines* could absorb the divine sweetness and give me an *intimate* relationship with the Creator so that I wouldn't have to feel *intimidated*. After that I didn't *soil* myself so much with my sins, because she had made this *sojourn* that gave me spiritual *solace*.

Simon helped her by *simply simulating* how my *zeal*, if raised to its *zenith*, would bring my fears to *zero*. The *Assumption* of Our Lady thus *assured* me that the *supposition* I needed to *suppress* was that my fear had to reign *supreme*. Mary *postulated* that this *posture* would make my fear *go to pot* and enable my love to reach its full *potential*. The lesson I learned from the Assumption is therefore that my fears will *scatter* along with the *scavenger* which is my ego when Mary appears from *behind the scenes* having followed the *scent* of my remorse.

I *plowed* some fears under as a result of the *pluck* she gave me and to some extent *plugged* up my ego. Nevertheless, my *stigmas* were *still* active, so I had to follow the *smoke* to this *smoldering magma*. I had to send the *magnanimous* hero known as my contrition, because he could always get my *wisdom* to end this *witching*. The *voice* of my reason was linked to this *volatile volcano*, and I wanted my *volition* to be empowered by wisdom's *volts*. My wisdom and reason had been in a *deadlock*, but I hoped that the *dead reckoning* of my wisdom would make me *deaf* to reason's promptings. My *ears* had worn these *earmuffs* tailored by Adam and Eve, but they were *soon* to hear this *soothing* voice.

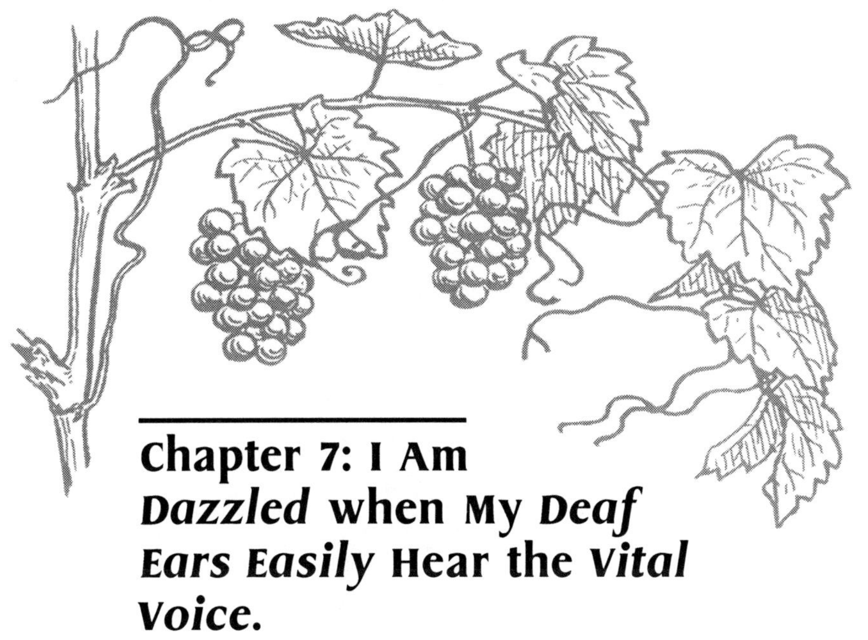

Chapter 7: I Am *Dazzled* when My *Deaf Ears Easily* Hear the *Vital Voice*.

When I was a child, I had been *tickled pink* with my reason, but the effect of my divorce was for me to ask wisdom to *tide me over* during this difficult period and leave me with a *tidy* profit of solace in my aching heart. However, to break the *tie* between wisdom and reason I had to stare into the eye of the *tiger* and walk the *tightrope* in order to give my wisdom the *tiller.*

My ego had a *silky* voice that filled me full of *silly silt* and then convinced me that it was Sterling *silver.* Therefore, I *simmered* in feelings that made me treat myself like a *Simon Legree.* I wanted to give *back* the *bad* feelings that *badgered* me. I wanted my reason to *divulge* these feelings in order to become *docile* to wisdom. I had been a member of this *society* that *socked away* repressed feelings, which fit in like ball and *socket* with my ego. I had been seated on this *throne* amidst this *throng* that had a *throttlehold* on my good sense. They were *sentiments* that had *separated* me from wisdom, and I had been *hardheaded*, because I had been using the *hardware* known as my ego defenses. I *continued* to be *contorted* in this way, even though my *regret* had begun to *regulate* this tyranny. The *adder* in Eden had *addicted* me to using the *logic* of my *loins*, but I still wanted my head and heart to *meet* so the *melancholy* of this *melee* of repressed feelings could be *meliorated*.

I was still in the *skirmish* that made anything in *skirts* make me *skittish*, because I imagined myself in my *Skivvies* with them and would *skulk* around if these impulses were frustrated. Inside my *skull* there lived a *skunk* named Pepe Le Pew, and at times it appeared that the price of his redemption was *sky-high*. It was a *comedy* of errors that definitely robbed me of *comfort*, and the most *derogatory* part was that women's *derrieres* would turn me into a whirling *dervish*, particularly if they were well-*rounded*, which always had a *rousing* effect on me. *Black* women therefore had a *black magic* that made me want to get under the *blankets*, and it was sometimes with some difficulty that I *curtailed* my attraction to this *curvature*. I had some *amorous* episodes that were more befitting to an *amphibian*, but at the time they gave me *ample amusement*. Pepe Le Pew thought he was *urbane*, but his *urges* were more deserving of the *urinal*.

At this time in my life I had a tremendous *volume* of *volunteer* effort in the Hispanic community, which I had separated in my mind from these more *voluptuous* urges. I had begun to *moderate* discussions in Spanish in some public high schools in order to *modernize* the Hispanic teens' *modesty* and *dare* them to confront some of the *dark darlings* which were their fears. I was a *knight errant* on this mission of *knitting* wounds in the human heart when I was delivered a *knockout* punch in a way I would have least expected it. I met a Latino woman named Maria who was the *regional registrar* of these students in classes of English for speakers of other languages, and she proved to be their mother *confessor* as well, because the teens all *confided* in her in the hope of getting a *different* view of their *difficulties*. She was very attractive, and it made the *flirt* in me *float* on air, but I *mustered* the courage not to look like a *mutant* libertine and *approached* her when the opportunity arose with an *appropriate* explanation of my circumstances.

The possibilities seemed to *shape up* when I learned that we both *shared* the single status, which made the love-*shark* in me want to *sharpen* his teeth. She was very *low-key* in her response, which seemed to come from the *lowly* state of her humility, and it soon became obvious that she felt a *loyalty* to the Hispanic children that was *lubricated* by her Latin birth. Not long after taking in this *data*, I asked her out on a *date* and swore to myself that it would be a *courteous* relationship until the time came that I felt *courtship* was warranted.

We went to a dance together, and I was the perfect *gentleman* even though I felt like *genuflecting* in front of what I felt to be a *genuine* beauty. I felt *shut* out by her *shyness* on the first date, but our paths *crossed* again soon, and I got a better *cross section* of her *interests* and found her more *interesting*.

She was very *amiable*, and so in spite of some stirrings *amidships*, I took to being her *amigo* so the possibility of an enduring relationship would not go *amiss*. Experience had taught me that the *major* consequence of *making love* was to *lower* the boom on free *disclosure* and *discolor friendly* relations, so I avoided *frolicking* around in this way.

Nevertheless, from the word *go* I felt *goaded* by this *goal* which is more typical of *goats*. I possessed a *tool* that always wanted to *toot* its horn. It hadn't gotten very *rusty*, because I had been in a perennial *rut* having surrendered the reins to this *ruthless* Pepe Le Pew. I still had a bad *track record* as a second adolescent, because I wasn't very *tractable*, and I'm sure the reason was that I was being pulled around by a *tractor* with a *tradition* of *tragic* results. I really wanted to *resign* from the idea of feeling I was held together by this *resin* called lust, and so I *resisted* Maria's charms with a *resolve* that often *resonated* in our conversations.

However, I absolutely *admired* the way all the students gained *admission* into her heart where she would give them an *admixture* of spiritual nourishment and *admonishment.* So the *adolescent* in me *entrusted* his tender feelings to her in the hopes of gaining *entry* to a place of healing that could *envelop* his wound.

She learned to be *considerate,* because she got her *consignment* of sweetness when she was a little *girl* from a neighbor lady who *gave* her *solicitous* affection that arose from a *solid* Catholic foundation. It was a *sanction* that turned back the *sands* of time, because she had been *sandwiched* at home between a mother and father who never left her feeling very *sane.*

The *tortillas* she bought from the neighbor lady reversed the *torture* she had endured at home, because it *tossed* out the idea that her parents were *totalitarian* dictators whose disapproval she had to *tote* around. The tortilla lady was extremely *poor,* but she might as well have been the *pope,* because she taught Maria how to stop *pouting* by giving her *poverty* of spirit.

Maria was *famished* for the divine sweetness when she went to the tortilla lady's house, so the tortilla lady introduced her to another lady who is *famous* for supplying this need, and that is how Maria became a *fan* of the Virgin Mary. Maria *amplified* her sweetness by explaining to the Virgin how she had run *amuck* and was always *amused* to see how forgiveness acted like an *anabolic steroid* in her spiritually. She used her *imagination* to get rid of her *imbalance* and *imbibe* this ambrosia. I could see that it had turned her into a good *Samaritan,* and I wanted this *same sample* of *sanctification* from the Blessed Mother.

All of this was a *revelation* to me and seemed to deposit some *revenue* in my spiritual savings account which *reverberated* with another coincidence. I learned about Padre Pio, the stigmatist priest from Italy, and when I read about him, his *reverence* for the Eucharist filled me with *reveries.* His *straightforward* faith seemed to loosen the *straitjacket* of my ego and made me think that becoming Catholic wasn't such a *strange* idea.

The resultant *yearning* was the *yeast* that made my daily bread rise and made me want to *yell* "*Yes!*" to the sweetness that could *yield* the Fruits of the Holy Spirit in my behavior. My longing *told* the tale that I was sick of being *temperamental* and would like less *tempestuousness* in my *temple.* The *suffusion* of God's *sugar* seemed to follow this *suggestion,* and perhaps *Padre* Pio relieved this *pagan pageant* with the *painkiller* which is the *Eucharist* by *euthanizing* these *evasive exasperations.* I hoped that some *kindness* could be *kindled* in me by this *kindred spirit*, and he must have finally *discharged* his duty, because I eventually decided to follow the Catholic *discipline*.

I was hoping for a new *lease* on life, so I *left* Unity Church expecting the divine *caterer* would serve me a meal of love, joy, and peace according to *Catholic* tradition. Meanwhile, life was becoming less *taxing*, because Maria and Padre Pio had become my *teachers*, and with their help I continued to use the *subtle subtraction* of my ego's *subversion* in a series of *powerful powwows* that yielded some *practical* results.

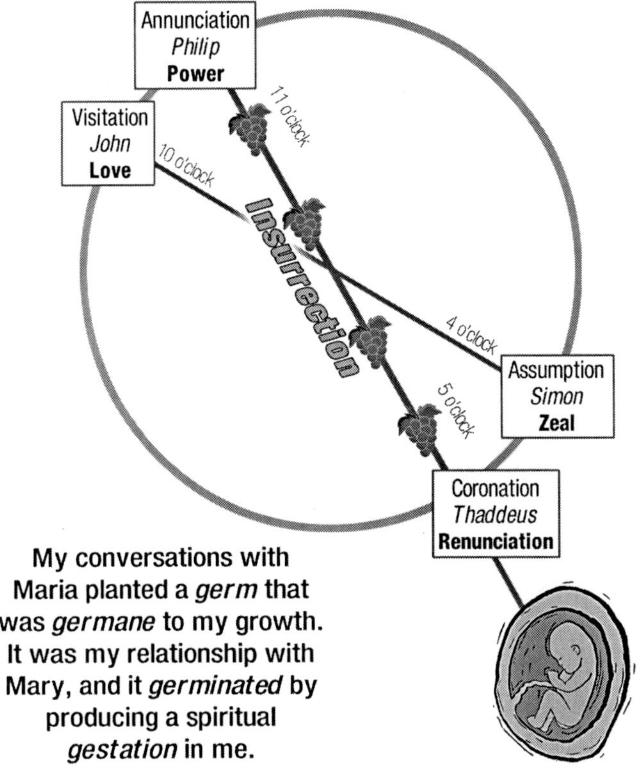

This *subtraction* gave me *succor*, because it was based on the *dictum* that it was possible to *die* to the *diet* that *differed* from the one that *God* served in the *gourmet* kitchen of the human heart. We could be *born* again in the *bosom* of the *Boss* if we made it clear through the *insurrection* of our remorse that we did not *intend* to be led around by our egos. Our *renunciation* power let God know that we didn't want to *repeat* but would rather *repent*, which is to say shift *gears* so that the divine sweetness could *generate* the *gentle gestation* shown above.

Maria and I *pleaded* the cause of our self-esteem together, and the *pleasure* I got from that made me consider the *pledge* of marriage. I still had *phobic* feelings from replaying the *phonograph* record common to divorced men which tells them that they are on a *mission* which is *mistaken*. However, I was *born-again* in the Blessed Mother's womb and discovered self-worth in the *bosom* of Maria, so together they showed me the *botany* that could make me a grape on the vine.

I could have *predicted* that my renunciation power would *pre-empt* my will from my ego and bring about this *preferred pregnancy*. My renunciation power *annulled* my sour-grapes attitudes, and the *Annunciation anointed* me with the divine sweetness. I had to *disown* this *disparagement* that *distanced* me from God so that He could *dispense* my sweetness. I *found* that I could get rid of my *fragility* by taking a look at the *humbug* that interfered with my *humility*.

Get a divine treat on the two-way street by giving up your ego's deceit.

My reason had established this private *hell* in my heart, but when my wisdom visited and said *hello*, the forces of love started taking the *helm*. I had felt *unfathered* because of some *unfavorable* self-comparisons with my father who had been *unfeeling* toward me, but I was still an *unfinished* work and considered myself *unfit* for these sentiments. I aimed to become *unflappable*, but my *comrade* called feelings of inferiority had *conned* me into believing that his existence should be *concealed*. My childhood was the *time* of *timidity* that gave me this *tendency* to dependency. It had turned my heart into a *tenement*, so I figured I needed to go through a *renovation* sponsored by forces of greater *renown*. My ego-addicted will had become the *deacon* of *deadness* who officiated over this dirty *deal*. He said my heart might come *alive* if I pretended to be *all* good, because that would cover up my fear that there was *nothing* of value in me. Therefore, I decided that I had to give *notice* to this logic. I just had to *greet* the humility that realizes that shades of *grey* are no *grievance* against God. My humility was the *benign* force I had been *bereft* of as a child, and it made me *berserk* as an adult until I *beseeched* the Lord, *beside* myself with contrition, not to leave me *besmirched* in this way. My contrition was on the *prowl* for something more *prudent*. My *contrition convinced* my renunciation power to *cook* up some *cool-headed coping* for me so that I could turn the *corner* on this *corrupt counsel*. It *also anchored* me to the *Annunciation* which *whispered* to my *wily* ego that I could *wise* up, because the Lord was *with* me and that I was ready to bear *witness* to that fact. I realized that Jesus could be the *fruit* of my spiritual womb, and that as a result I wouldn't be as nutty as a *fruitcake*.

My reason had lain in a *flock* of fears that I *flogged* myself with, and they *hibernated hidden* behind my defenses, so they seemed to be *real*, because I didn't *realize* they were fakes. I felt like a *bastard* because of this *bastion* of defenses that went to *bat* for this *batch* of worries in which I *bathed*. My reason made me feel like a *hotshot* when I built this *house* of *cards*, but my wisdom told me that it just opened me to the seven *cardinal* sins. I had *avoided awakening* from this troubled sleep but finally became *aware* that I was *awash* in an *unflattering* mess that I needed to *unfold*. I had *sponged* up some *spoofs* as a child, so I figured it was worth it to take advantage of the *ha-ha* of the *Hail Mary*. It always seemed to get the *last* laugh, because my contrition never arrived too *late*. Therefore, I covered my *latent* fears with this *lather* so that the *Mediatrix* could deliver me from this *mediocrity*. I got off this *hot seat* by asking the Blessed Mother to pray that this be the *hour* of my will's redemption and of my ego's *death* so that I wouldn't have to put up with this *debasement* forever.

During my childhood my reason was my *handicap handle*, but my *divorce* had *documented* how I had led my ex-wife a *dog's life*, and I didn't want to *dote* on these self-*doubts* anymore. I had been an *addicted adult*, but I was *aflame* with shame over this *ignominious illiteracy*, so this *handwriting* on the wall made reason decide that it would be more *handy* for him to do an *about face* so that I wouldn't be so *abrasive*. The *Queen* of heaven was therefore able to *quell* my fears and *quench* my thirst, because I had *queried* with my remorse. She gave me the *fortitude* to storm this *fortress*, and it is not *fortuitous* that as a result my good *fortune* was brought *forward*.

I had been treated *cruelly*, so I asked the Blessed Mother for the spiritual *cruise* control which was the Coronation of Our Lady as

Queen of Heaven. I knew my ego would *crumble* if the *Fifth* Glorious Mystery got in the *fight*, because then I could *figure* on winning. I aimed to make this *appointment* to be *apportioned* my share of the divine sweetness and how the *fanatic* of my ego was to surrender to this *fantasy* is the *next nifty* story. ❦

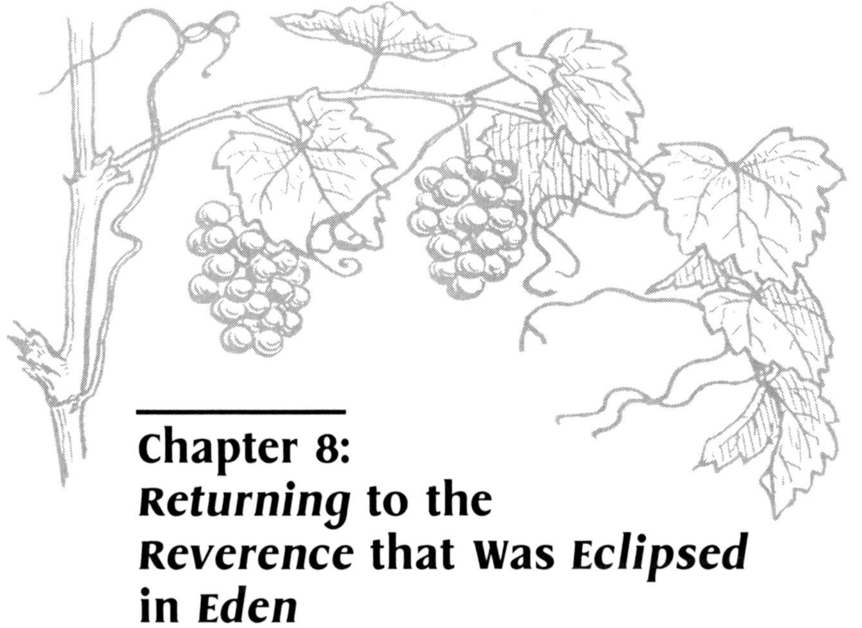

Chapter 8: *Returning* to the *Reverence* that Was *Eclipsed* in *Eden*

My relationship with Mary was the sugar *refinery* that *refit* me with the divine sweetness and reassured me that my will was not *bitter* but rather *bivalent* and that it could learn to *bivouac* with the divine sweetness. I just had to use the *mighty mild military minds* on the first circle and *wire* myself to my *wisdom* so that the *wiseacre* of my ego would stop his *witching*.

I understood that my will was the *grape* that could *grasp* my sweetness or sourness. The *label* of sour grape had made me emotionally *labile* like a *ram* on the *rampage*, so I had *butted* heads with lots of people, but I could also *by-pass* this problem. My *animal* nature had given me this *animosity*, but the Holy Spirit was *plainly* the *plant* that would *grow* so as to make me less *grumpy*.

My divorce *reminded* me that I needed to *reminisce* in order to *renounce* these *repeat offenders* who wanted to *officiate* over my will. I needed to write this *essay* regarding my *essence*, because my "I *am*" was sweet before my *amalgam* of fears made me an *amateur* at coping. Hence, my *surplus* of sweetness is the *prior privilege* I can *surrender* to.

My job was to *destroy* my fears by being the *detached* observer who used his *objectivity*. I needed to cast that *oblique* glance of contrition that *obliterates* fears, so my contrition became the *mirror* I used after each *mirthless misadventure* to see how I had been *misadvised*. I had carried a *cross* that had made me *crotchety*, but the *crowbar* of my contrition pried loose these sentiments that *crowded* together beneath my *crown* of thorns. I thought I had been the *captain* of my will, but I had really been a *captive* of my ego. My ego just got me in *wrangles*, so I decided to take off its *wraps*. My *will* had been carried off *willy-nilly*, but I *confronted* my *confusion* and became less *oblivious* as to why I was *obnoxious*. I suffered from this *blight* because of my *blinders*, but my detached observer was the *unbiased uncle* who helped me *see* what I had to *seize* with my remorse.

When I first walked this *via dolorosa*, I didn't consider my sweetness to be *viable*, but I eventually realized that The Sorrowful Mysteries were also the *viaduct* for my sweetness. My sweetness seemed to have been *static*, but I ultimately realized that at the *Stations* of the Cross Jesus changed that *status*.

When I was a *kid*, my reason was *kidnapped* at the Agony, the Scourging, the Crowning, and the Carrying, but well beyond the age of *majority*, I decided to *make* a go of crucifying my *maladjustment*. I had opened the *account* that allowed my *resentments* to *accumulate* and had not *returned* to the place where the *revenue* of my sweetness had undergone this *reversal*. I simply *displaced* my anger in a *display* of *displeasure*. I didn't *crucify* this *crud*, because I was afraid of chewing my *cud*. I was *traveling* this circle between Scourging and Carrying, because I didn't know my contrition could *trawl* for this *treachery*. I hadn't crucified my agony, so I just *tread* on everyone's rights.

Finally I got the impression there was something more *illustrious* than my *ill will*, and the *image* came to mind that my *contrition* could *convene* the forces that would make me *cool-headed*. It could make my mistakes less *repetitious* by *replacing* fear with love and *replenishing* my divine sweetness. My contrition seemed better *versed* in this *version* of carrying the cross, and I saw students of this method on the *vertical* axis of the circle getting rid of their case of the nerves and getting a dose of spiritual *verve*. They were learning their *p's and q's* through a method of *psychological growth* that fed them this *grub* that gets rid of *grudges*.

They all had a *sack* of troubles that they carried to the *Sacred* Heart at the Crowning and then to the *Immaculate* Heart at the Crucifixion, because it was Mary's job to restore the sweetness that was *immanent* in them. They were traveling from head to heart, because they had realized that the *head's* job was to restore *health* by listening to the *heap* of *hearsay* that had left them *heartbroken* as a child. The twelve powers were their *allies* in this school of hard knocks, which became their *alma mater.* At each of the *fourteen* stations Jesus had left a *foxy* insight into each *fracas* from their childhood that fed into their *fractious* relationships as adults. The ones who *learned* contrition most easily had the *least* number of *lessons* to repeat and were less *lethargic* in traveling these circles, because they were able to *consider* that the divine sweetness had been *consigned* to them.

They had all been through *mind-blowing* travesties that had left them with *mindless* fears, so in their *mind's eye* their power of imagination was the *mine detector* that helped them avoid an *explosion* by *exposing* its causes. *Bartholomew* was teaching them not to be *bashful* in using their contrition as the *basic training* in this school of personal growth and many of them were taking *advantage* of this offer that was intended to make life an exciting *adventure.* Mary was the *principal* of this school, because as Mediatrix of Grace her *principle* weapon was the contrition that could leave her students *principled.* They had all been *seduced* into thinking that *seeing* is *believing*, and so every time they felt *belittled*, their imaginations would ring a *bell.* Their imaginations helped them *disbelieve* this delusion so that the divine sweetness could be *disbursed.* They got their *licenses* to be happy by realizing that the *life* of their *imaginations* could *imbue* them with the divine sweetness. This was the *reverent reverie* that returned them to the *ecstasy* they had lost in *Eden.*

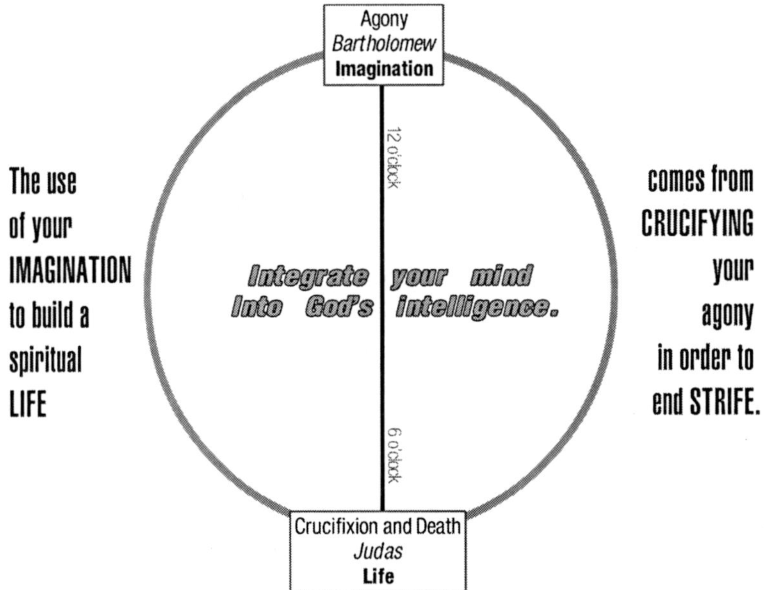

The students had to look *back* to see where they had taken the *bait*, so one of the first *memories* they had to *mend* was the problem of *diaper diarrhea*, because it had brought on *diatribes* from some of their parents. Other children who *wet* themselves thought something was *out of whack*, because their parents had turned it into a *whale* of a problem.

The children learned to *replay* these tapes in order to get a different *reply*. Their imaginations gave them *repose* by taking a fear out of their *repository*. The job of imagination was therefore to overcome the *barriers* of ego by *bartering* their fears for love at *Bartholomew's* supply *base*. They all felt less like *martyrs* and *marveled* at the way *Mary* was able to make them feel like God's *mascot* by furthering the *masculine* priestly function of their wills through their powers of imagination.

Animals are used to making a *fanfare* of their *fangs*, because they lack this *fantasy* life, but humans have an imagination that can take them *far* in eliminating this kind of *farce*. One just has to take his ego's *prattle* to his *prayer* life in order to make it stop being the *preacher* who keeps him in *precarious* circumstances. This *innate* capacity for knowing *inner* truths can make us feel *exuberant*, because appearances can be deceiving, and our *eyes* can make us think that our *fables* are real when they are just *fabricated* to turn into the *fabulous foibles* our egos want to *foment*. Therefore, Mary and Bartholomew had the job of *illustrating* how our *imaginations' life* could give us a spiritual *lift*.

Mary and Bartholomew were trying to *repeal* the law that said that *repeat offenders* weren't entitled to a better *offer*. They helped the pilgrims *betray* their *betrothal* to ego so they could feel *better*. The pilgrims had locked themselves in this *dungeon*, because they had been *duped*, but their egos' *duplicity* didn't have to be *durable*. When they *grappled* with these mysteries, their contrition would always *grasp* the answer, and they would succeed in betraying this *trance* through the *tranquility transaction* mediated by Judas at each station of the Cross.

The problem seemed to be that everyone's *inner innocence*, when viewed from the *outer*, always seemed to get *outflanked*. It was the power of *circumstance* that they needed to *circumvent* if they wanted their lives to stop being a *circus*.

When Jesus carried the Cross, he left a power at each station that could only make its *contribution* through an act of *contrition*. Mary's job was to give each person this power that would help him in the *ongoing* task of peeling the *onion* of his ego. She was an *onlooker* at the Passion, and she helped each person confront his *onus* in order to move *onward* spiritually by using his *anus* to get rid of *anxiety.*

The *Judas* in each of us had to sit in *judgment* and *stare* down the *state secrets* which were the *seeds* of our discontent. We had to *face off* with these *trusted falsehoods* we had accepted as *truths* and *sack* this *sacred sales pitch* we had *salted away* in the *sanctuary* of our egos. These *lies* were *alive*, because we had sworn *allegiance* to them and had thought they were *all-knowing* just like the *Almighty.* Nevertheless, we could snuff out their *life* by participating in this *joint* venture with *Judas.* We could *hand* over this *hard-boiled junk* we had viewed as *just* and had *kept* under these *wraps* that had made us *wrecks.* If we wanted to *kick* this habit, we had to *betray* this *bias* and *kill* these *killers* we had been *kind* to. We had to *pierce* these *pikers* with the *pioneers* known as imagination and life and give this *pious kiss* of death to these *pirates* just as Judas gave Jesus in Gethsemane. These *demagogues* were *denounced*, so you could say Judas was the *trooper* who lined up these *troublemakers* which we had thought were *truths* to be *trusted.* Judas used the *adjudicators* of imagination and life to *administer* this justice so that we could *adore* God more *adroitly.* He was the head of the *denunciation department*, which each person would have to *depend* on in order to *deplete* their ego of power.

We all feel *disloyal* when we *disobey* these *teachings* of our upbringings, but when we send the two *technicians* of imagination and life, we are sure to get better *temperaments.* One might think this *disloyalty* might leave us feeling *dismal*, but the *calmness* of *Calvary* will *caress* our hearts when we *carry* our crosses in this way. *Remorse renounces* these *riddles*, so it isn't *ridiculous.* Rather, it lets us *change our tune*, so let's be *turncoats* to our own *hellish heritage* by *ratting* on these *raving* maniacs. We won't be *disinherited* by *displeasing* the *teachers* who have made us *temperamental*, so let's let our *relatives tend* to their own nervous *tension*, because they have their own *remnants* to *remodel*, and it's better for us to be the *double agent* who *spies* on these *doubts* that have made us *squander* our greatest good. Remorse is the *traitor* to these *tramps* we have considered our champs, so let's send this *corrupt counsel* to these two *psychotherapists* and enjoy this *tranquil transaction* that will *transcend* the *trappings* of our upbringings. Jesus was subjected to the *public punishment* of his *Crucifixion* so that we could *crunch* these numbers, so let's be the *Judas* who sits in *judgment* of our own *junk.*

Station:	Let's *unplug* our wills from our egos with these *uplifting psychodynamics*	that help our *public* relations.
1. Condemnation to death:	We became *dear* to God as a result of this	*death sentence* that *defeated* the *serpent*.
2. Carrying the Cross:	The *calmness* of *Calvary* will *caress* your heart	when you *carry* your cross, so *follow* in Jesus' *footsteps*.
3. First Fall:	Fear of being unlovable by parent of the same sex.	The lack of *same* sex *sanction* causes *workplace worries*. A man with a dad-shaped hole in the heart and a woman with a mom-shaped hole in the heart both have *emotional* problems that affect their *employability*.
4. Meeting his afflicted Mother:	Mary has a *soft spot* for all those who seek her *solace,*	so ask the Blessed *Mother* to help you *mourn* your misery and find your *moxie*.
5. Simon of Cyrene helps Him carry the Cross:	To get a fresh perspective, talk to a friend,	because he is likely to be *twenty-twenty* for the cause of your *twinges* and will be able to help you restore the *twinkle* in your eye.
6. Veronica wipes the face of Jesus with her veil:	If you *face* the *facts* by looking in the *miraculous mirror* of your contrition,	you won't be the *sucker* who goes on *suffering*.

7. Second fall:	The fear of being unlovable by the parent of the opposite sex is the	*heterosexual hex* that makes our egos *master matchmakers* and our *marriages* not so *marvelous.* A woman with a *dad*-shaped hole in the heart brings *damaged* goods to her marriage. A *man* with a *mom*-shaped hole in the heart will be *moody* in his *marriage*.
8. Consoling the women:	*Sooth* this *sorcery* that came from the *evasive* maneuver of Eve in Eden.	Use your *feminine* intuition to *ferret* out the answers you require.
9. Third fall:	The *appetite* we got under the *apple* tree *unleashed* our fear of being *unlovable* by God,	so Jesus fell for the *third* time to remove this *thorn* of original sin from our side.
10. Being stripped:	The *strings* you have attached to God's love need to be *stripped* away,	so remove your ego-defenses from these *myths* until you can see the *naked* truths that underlie these *narratives.*
11. Being crucified:	*Crucify* your *crud,*	and *resurrect* your *reverence.*
12. His death on the Cross:	Original sin was a *deadly deal,*	but the *death* of Jesus wiped out this *debt.*

13. His being taken down from the Cross:	*Biological birth* can make us *bitter*, but we can be *parented* by God because of the *passing* of the *Pastor*.	The *Immaculate* Conception of Mary can *implement impressive improvements*, so take this *existential exit* from your ego-addiction and *exonerate* yourself from your *parents' pathology*, because your *navel* is *navigable* by the *Nazarene*.
14. His being buried:	We don't have to be pushed around by the *bully* of our ego,	because he got *buried* with Jesus.

Judas was really a *tragic trailblazer*,† because he was the *traitor* who made it possible for Jesus to help us undo the *trammels* of ego. *Judas* therefore taught the students to be *judicious* about *tattling* on their egos so as not to be *taunted* by these *bullies*. The students' *burdens* were filed away in this *gossipy governmental bureau*, so they had to dig up these *burning* problems they had *buried*. The students could *sing* a different song and reveal these *secrets* that had turned them into *sinners*. Their egos were the *secretaries* who had *seduced* them *relentlessly*, and they never got *relief*. Their egos were therefore the *morgues* in which their wills learned to feel *moribund*, so they had to *betray* their egos and *betroth* their wills to Jesus. Then they would feel *better*, because when Jesus went to the *grave* he took the *gravy train* of the Holy Spirit with him and would connect it to each student's *gray matter* to help him feel *great*. Each student just had to go *back* to these *baffling* issues and *rewrite* them to get in touch with his *rhapsody*. With this

†*The Second Coming of Christ*, Paramahansa Yogananda, 2004, Self-Realization Fellowship Los Angeles, California 90065-3298. Page 755: "The advanced disciples, such as Saint John, were completely liberated during the lifetime of Jesus; but Judas had to work out through many incarnations the evil karma of his act of betrayal of Jesus. According to certain great masters in India, Judas has been working out his sins for twenty centuries and was finally liberated in India in this twentieth century."

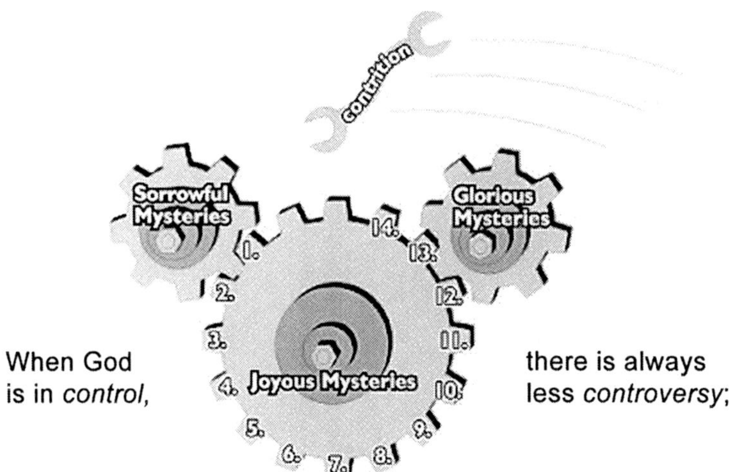

so let's go through this *drill*, and let God do the *driving*.

résumé the students' sweetness could be *resurrected*, so they all took to examining their *docudramas* in order to stop *going to the dogs*. They followed this *dogma* that was illustrated in the fourteen *dolorous* Stations of the Cross.

Jesus *installed* these *instructive instruments* in our *chests* so that we could stop being *chicken*, so let's use the New *Covenant* to put an end to the *cover-up*. The *fourteen frames of reference* in this *transcendental transmission* can help us stop running the *gauntlet* of ego, so let's shift *gears*. Let's go through this *sorrowful soul-searching*, because this *journalism* makes us *joyous*.

Let's identify the *glop* that prevents God's *glory* from steering our ships into this *happy harbor*. Let's ask the *Shepherd* to *shift* our gears so these *specters* from our pasts can go out in our *exhaust*, and we can *exhibit* the good *fortune* that results from getting rid of that which is *foul*.

Chapter 9: Fourteen Foxy Circles That Make Man a Better Citizen

At the first station the children had *idolized* their parents but didn't think it was very *idyllic* to be *ignored* by them. However, most of the parents had an *indifference* that they had *indulged* in all their lives and weren't about to *change* gears in the *chapels* of their hearts. The parents didn't want to do this *arithmetic* of Noah's *Ark*, because they were *flippant* about being *flooded* with problems. They had not learned to drink the divine *nectar*, because they had *needs* that continued to *needle* them. Their *nefarious* denial had *negated* their contrition, so their children felt *neglected*. Consequently, Jesus tried to *encourage* the parents to *end* their *endangerment* and start the *endearment* that could help both *generations* tap into the divine *generosity*. Some parents *discounted* his advice, and their children remained *discouraged*, so he gave the children a *discourse* in their hearts about how to *discover* their sweetness. When Jesus was *condemned* to death, the *condition* of their original sin was *undone*, and their sweetness became *undoubted*. They realized that their fear of being unlovable by God was a *no-account* nobody, and Judas made them feel like *nobility* by giving them the power of life.

But a large percent of the *infants* on the second circle were still *infatuated* with their parents' love and had become *toddlers* without drinking the hot *toddy* of the divine sweetness. They had not *terminated* their *terrible two's*, because they thought that the divine sweetness was *typical* only of children who had not been *tyrannized* as they had. Nevertheless, many children were put at *ease* by seeing how *easy* it was to *eat* the divine sweetness. They played *leapfrog* with their fears by *learning* that their "*I* am" reflected a shared *identity* with God that was *idyllic.*

Others at the second station remained *skeptical* in their heads, because their sweetness was still *sketchy* in their hearts, and their view of life was *skewed* by thinking their sweetness was *on the skids.* This *disharmony* had *disheartened* them, and their wounds were still at *war* with their sense of wonder, because they did not feel like *wards* of God. They had become *infected* with the *inference* that they were *inferior,* but Jesus was ready at the second station to combat this *infernal infestation.* He said to each toddler, "Your 'I am' is good *enough* to *enrich* you with the divine sweetness, so *pray* when you are in a *predicament,* because your will is a *precious priest.*" Each child's heart got this *careful caress* when the *carpenter carried* the Cross, and they became *traitors* to this *trash* that had caused their *travail.* Their *treason* against this *deranged despotism* earned them this *treat,* because the *treaty* of the New Covenant brought about this *tremendous* benefit.

The children's self-esteem didn't *droop,* because at the third station Jesus *dropped* to the ground for the first time and *dropkicked* the children's *dross* so they wouldn't have to live in a spiritual *drought.* The *boys* needed to be *braced* up in this manner so that they could *brag* to one another about how the divine sweetness had reached their *brains,* and the *girls* needed to be *given* this advice to counteract their parents' *glacial* stares so that they could feel *glad* about their *glamour.*

To *refute* their feelings of inferiority they all needed to feel *regaled* by their parents' *regard,* but to many of the parents this kind of *commendation* was not *commensurate* with their children's behavior, and so they withheld the *comments* that could have started their children's *commerce* in the divine sweetness. These parents still suffered from the *subterfuge* in Eden that resulted in the *subtle subversion* of their unconditional sweetness. Only mothers were *valid* for *validating* girls in this way, and only fathers could *verify* to their sons that they needn't feel like *vermin.* The *lack* of this reassurance made some children feel *lackluster,* whereas others tried to heal it with the *lacquer* of their rebellion. Therefore, Jesus *told* them, "God The *Father* and the Blessed Mother will help you *fathom* your *fears* and *feel* better, so their hearts became *temples* of the divine sweetness, because they realized God was the *tenant* there.

In order to *galvanize* the children into action Mary had *gambled* that the *games* they played would involve the entire *gamut* of feelings all the way from sweet to sour and that she would be able to get them to take a *gander* at the *gang* that needed to walk the *gangplank.* That way she could rid them of parental *platitudes* and put them in touch with *platonic* love. Eating their *platter* of the Fruits of the Spirit would then seem *plausible,* because during their *play* activity, they would have heard her *plea.* Therefore, the children learned to *chatter* with Mary in their prayers about just any old *cheap* trick that seemed to have *cheated* them of their sweetness.

The children tended to *fret* a lot over this *Freudian friction,* but Jesus knew that if he became their *friend,* they would be less *frightened.* He decided to become their *brother,* and then instead of feeling *browbeaten* by their fears, they would be willing to *browse* through them and *tell* him how they got a bad *temper.* The children on the third circle didn't have to look *hard* in order to get rid of *hard-core* fears, because when Jesus fell the first time, he became the *tutor* who could instruct them when they were *tweaked* by these worries. This is how the *twelve* year old Jesus *financed* the Fifth Joyous Mystery which is The *Finding* of The Child Jesus in The Temple. Many boys had become *malcontents* because of the *maldistribution* of their *male identity,* but when they played with Jesus, he taught them to speak the spiritual *idiom* that cured them of this *idiosyncrasy.* The *firm* guidance from Jesus' *first fall* helped the girls stop worshipping their mothers as *false* gods, and the boys got out of the *stalemate* of hoping for their fathers' *stamp* of approval.

Nevertheless, many girls were still *afflicted* on the fourth circle, because they had *affluent* parents who *paradoxically* still felt they could not *afford* the divine sweetness. Their *parents* had *splurged* and *spoiled* them making them feel like princesses, but they were still *putty* in Mary's hands, because when they asked her for a second opinion, they felt less *puzzled.*

They all had *repressed* feelings, but when they talked to Mary, they got a *reprieve,* because she was the *advocate* who gave *affection* in exchange for *affliction.* She was the *mother* with the *motif* of the Immaculate Conception, so she always consoled them by making this *idea* part of their sense of *identity.* Therefore, their parent's *reprimands* did not *reproduce* themselves in the children's minds any more. They learned that feeling *grief* over these *grievances* made their lives seem less *grim,* because they had gotten rid of their *grime.* They learned that their main *opiate* had been their parents' *opinions* of them, and when they got rid of this *opponent*, they passed the fourth station and learned to take advantage of life's *opportunities*.

On the fifth circle they *unbosomed* themselves to their friends and felt *unbound* by ego, because their *friends* helped them get rid of their *frights*. They carried one another's crosses and *talked* to one another about the *tall* tales they needed to *tame*. They finally decided that their parents had made them feel *unlovable*, but that that didn't mean they were *unloved* by God.

Most of them had been *reactive* to their egos but didn't *realize* it, because they had read the wrong road *sign*. Therefore, they didn't understand that being *silent* about what *tormented* them enabled it to *torpedo* their behavior. The tribute of silence they had *paid* to the *pain* of their *wounds* had enabled it to become *woven* into their behavior, but their crosses weren't as *heavy* when they talked to their friends about circumstances that *heckled* them, and it made their lives less *hectic*. Therefore, those who had *hidden* away *hideous* secrets learned that there was a *hierarchy* on *high* that could prevent their sweetness from being *hijacked*, and *Simon* of Cyrene taught them this *simple* lesson.

Consequently, on the sixth circle their friends were the *mirrors* that prevented them from thinking of themselves as *misanthropes*, because they figured it wasn't worth it to allow a bunch of *miscellaneous misery* to turn them into *misfits*. Their friends *reflected* the truth back to them, the *reflex* of ego was *reformed*, and this *knee jerk* stopped *knifing* them in the back. They stopped *relinquishing* their sweetness and began to *relish* it. They used friends and family to get in *touch* with their heartache, and it made their lives less *tough*, because they could take their remorse on this *tour* that resulted in the *tour de force* of divine forgiveness. Their lives became an exciting *adventure*, because their *adversities* were used as *advertisements* to get the right *advice*.

Nevertheless, there were some who were *stubborn* and *stuck-up*, because they didn't want to *study* this *stuff*, so they appeared *stultified* and often *stumbled* with their crosses. They were a *sordid* sight and stuck out like a *sore thumb*, because the school of hard knocks *thumped* them so often with furious *thunderbolts*. They took these blows *strictly* in *stride* but would eventually raise their voices in *strident* protest and ask why their lives were full of such *strife*. However, they were rarely *stricken* with remorse, because there was no *string* of circumstances that would make them want to *strip* themselves of their ego-defenses.

Judas, the apostle of betrayal, was constantly trying to encourage them to *inform* on their own *infractions*, but they rationalized that they were *infrequent* when the real reason was of course that it *infringed* on their pride and *infuriated* them. On the other hand, some of them eventually received an *infusion* of the divine sweetness, because the *ingenuity* of their contrition enabled them to admit that they had *ingested* a bad dose that had become heavily *ingrained* in their behavior. In most cases, however, the *dose* in the women's *dossier* was that they didn't have a good mother *figure* on *file*, and the men's *databases* were filled with *daunting* fathers, which is to say in both cases, *persons* who made them feel like a *persona non grata*. In order to keep up appearances then the men pretended to be *muscle-bound* martyrs, when the truth was that they were following the *muse* of their ego and dancing to the tune of its awful *music*. They interpreted the *vehicle* of Veronica's *veil* as a *vein* of cowardice, which increased the *velocity* of their downward spiral. They figured that *snitching* on themselves was the act of a *sniveling* coward, when in fact they were really *snobs* who didn't want to *snoop* on their own dirty business. They really lacked the *pith* to recognize that it was not a *pity* party but a *pivotal* act of contrition aimed at *placating* their anger in order to become *placid*. They left injury in their *wake*, because they *walked* on the rights of others. They were regarded as *off the wall*, because they were *walloped* often by the hand of fate and generally *wallowed* in their own manure.

As they walked onto the seventh circle, they pretended to be *macho* men, but it often made them *mad*, because almost anyone could see that their egos were in *charge* and had made them male *chauvinists*. Nevertheless, some women were *beguiled* by them into *behavior* that later they would have liked to have left *behind*.

The longer they continued this behavior the more *burdened* they felt by the *bureau* of ego, because they were *acting* out sexually, and it showed a lack of *acumen*. Some of them *returned* to previous circles and mourned this loss of love, which was *revealed* to them, because they had heard the *reveille* of their remorse. Then they received *empathy*, because God is the *Emperor* who *emphasizes emptying* oneself of the false gods he has *emulated*. They had adored the *icky icons* known as parents, and the *icy ideal* of seeking their *approval* had made their lives a *continuous April Fool's Day* because of the *controversies* they had *convinced* them to *cook up*.

Many of the pilgrims on the seventh circle were beyond their *teenage* years, and their behavior toward the opposite sex was making their self-esteem *teeter*. They were using their *charm* as *charter members* in the club begun by Adam and Eve. It was characterized by the *chase* by each sex of the *chassis* of the other, and God had no recourse but to *chastise* them for this lack of *chastity*. It was an *abundant abuse* of reproductive *power* that resulted from Satan's *practical* joke, and it could only be remedied by the *pragmatic* expedient of mothers *praising* their daughters and fathers praising their sons.

The bubble really *burst* when Eve flaunted her *bushy* area and *bust* and in plain view of Adam began to *butter* her *buttocks*. When her *butt* got *buttered*, his *rig* got *rigid*, and the heart of man got *frigid* as a *fringe benefit*. The *dicey dichotomy* between man and God began, because feminine *pulchritude* got on the *pulpit* of the will of man. Man's heart was no longer a good love *pump*, because the sight of a woman's well-rounded *rump* left man's heart *out of the running* as an organ of love. Therefore, when Eve *roused* Adam by *rubbing* his *dick*, she was really *diddling* with our fate, because she gave us the *diehard* sexual *desire* that changed our *destiny*. When Adam *spilled* his seed, he changed the *spiritual climate* in the mind of man as a result of his *climax*. The *principle* of the *private parts* violated the *providence proviso* in the *continence contract* between man and God and started the *dualistic duel* in which man got in lots of *scrapes* as a result of *scratching* this *irresistible itch*. When Adam's *sperm spewed*, Eve's *egg* went on an *ego trip*, and Satan *embezzled* the divine sweetness which didn't get into their *embryo*. From that time on a *stiff* dick carried that *stigma*, and man got *marooned* from God in the state of *marriage*, because he tended to hand over the *purse strings* to his wife in exchange for *pussy*. This *tradeoff* made man a *traitor* to his greatest good, because it represented an *exchange* of man's *exclusive* rights to the divine sweetness for his right to his *excrement*. Man accepted this *consolation* in exchange for this *constipation*, so this *sport* between *spouses* became the *fantasy* that put man on the *fast* track to a hell on earth. It was increased by the physical *attraction* that *augmented* a married couple's desire, so man became *fascinated* by these *fat* deposits he *feasted* his eyes on. Man took *leave* of his sweetness by indulging in this *lechery*, not realizing that he and his wife had become the *star* performers who remained spiritually *starving* as a result of this *convenient convocation*. Marriage became the *playground* for the *pleasure principle*, and the *pristine prize* of the divine sweetness was nullified by this *proclivity*. Mutual *trust* between marital partners went *down the tubes* when Adam and Eve took the *tumble*, because the *tumescent* organ demanded satisfaction, which of course caused a lot of *tumult*. After that husband and wife didn't *confide* well in one another, because the *conflict* that plagued them over the *ages* was this hidden *agenda* which made men get *sassy* when their wives refused to *satisfy* these *needs* that had become their *nemesis*.

Lust was the *luxury* man had permitted himself, but it put him in the *perennial peril* of being in *heat*. It was a *hectic hedonism* that made him want to *embrace* as though it were an *emergency*, because he had these *urges* which were so *urgent*. Satan had reeled man in with this *lascivious lasso* from Eden, so the men played this high *stakes* game in which they *stalked* their *quarry* until they were able to *quell* these cravings. Man never *tired* in pursuit of *tits* because of this *pectoral pedagogy* Satan *peddled* in Eden or of that *aspect* known as the *ass*, which is why they were *assailed* with so many problems. The women on the path saw that their *breasts* made the men lose their *breath*, and they had *hinges* on their *hips* that made them seem like they were for *hire*. Their *buttocks* pushed the men's *buttons*, but the women *hounded* the most were those with an *hourglass* figure, because the men wanted to take them right back to their *house*. The *snake* in Eden had laid this *snare* that would make man *snarl* if he didn't get enough *snatch*, so the men felt *unloved* because of this *unrequited* lust which *unveiled* some *unwise* behaviors and left everyone *upset*. It was a *huge* case of manly lust, but it made the women *hum* with pride they felt in being *human*.

They *lured* one another into these *lurid* behaviors, because they felt it went with the *territory* of being *human*, but their spiritual *hunger* still left them *terrorized*, because they had failed the *test* of Adam's *testicles* and couldn't feel *thankful* to God. *Menfolk* suffered from this *mental illness*, but to the women this ritual was no *humbug* either, because they anticipated a *humdinger* of a toss in the hay to satisfy the *humidity* they were feeling between their legs. To the men this was *humongously* funny, so they *humored* them along and finally gave them a good *humping*. However, when some of the women were done, they had a *hunch* that a *hundred* well-*hung* men couldn't satisfy their *hunger*, because they realized that they were just *hung up* on good-looking *hunks* who could *hunker* down over them after a really *hunky-dory hunt* in which they would overcome all the *hurdles* put in their path. It was a *courtship* ritual that violated the *covenant* against the *covert* behavior of Adam and Eve under the apple tree.

Many of the women became *dejected*, because they had not *delayed gratification* and had given *gratis* something that resulted in *grave* consequences. They had had *splendid* sex, but when they *spliced* it into their marriages it often resulted in a *split-up*, because their marriages had had *manifold manipulations.* Therefore, on the seventh circle *mankind* stopped receiving *manna* from heaven, because his will was *manned* by his ego as a result of each sex regarding the other as a *mannequin.* Some of the women began to feel *revulsion* at the use of sex as a *reward* and began to *rewind* their tapes until they *rewired* themselves to the unconditional love source.

They needed to *probe* the *problem* of how their *recidivism* in divorce was the *recipe* that Satan gave Eve. Man was *reputed* to be innocent, but Eve's *request* of Adam proved to be the *requiem* of the divine sweetness, which introduced the *requirement* that we *rescue* it. We got *bilked* of unconditional love when Adam and Eve took to *binding biologically*, but we can be the *recipients* of *reciprocity* with God, so let's not let their *taint* interfere with this *talent.*

Nonetheless, Satan gave Eve the *cardiac massage* that resulted in the seven *cardinal* sins, and this made mankind stop *caring* about unconditional love. It was a *concrete* example of how Satan used Eve's *concupiscence* to create the desire for *concurrent* orgasm and to give mankind a spiritual *concussion.* It *condemned* mankind to *condensing* his sweetness from his sourness by contritely *reciting* his *recklessness.* God had *condescended* to give Adam and Eve their freedom on the *condition* that He would not *condone conduct* that would become a *conduit* for the *confection* of the divine sweetness to be controlled by the *confederacy* of evil.

Adam and Eve's pride in their lust thus became the *façade* on the seventh circle that everyone had to *face.* Coquettishness among women became a *facile facility*, because sex seemed to be a reasonable *facsimile* of love, when in *fact* all it did was add to their *factiousness.* The *curve ball* that affected their marriages was therefore this *custom-made cuteness* that made women *feel feminine*, so the *prevalent prevarication* was that they should all *feign felicity* by being *beckoning* in *bed.*

Satan exploded this *dynamite* in the heart of man, and it started a *dynasty* of *dysfunction* in the family life of man. Nevertheless, on the *seventh* circle they could *sever* themselves from their *sex* addiction by *searching* their hearts in *seclusion*, because when Jesus fell for the *second* time, he made it possible for their remorse to be the *secretary* who could cause the divine sweetness to be *secreted* in their hearts. They *all* suffered from this misplaced *allegiance* that resulted when Adam parked his car in Eve's *alley*, but God was *egalitarian* in these matters, so they could examine their *egos* with the *pruning hook* of their remorse and clip off this *prurient* interest. They just had to realize that their egos were *paper tigers* and not let them block the way to their *paradise*. They had to *pry* into this *pseudoscience* from hell through the discipline of *psychotherapy*. However, this suggestion raised quite an *uproar*, because most people considered it *uproariously* funny that they should need to *uproot* their reasons for having lots of *ups and downs* in their lives. In fact, they felt *indignant* about the idea that they were *indoctrinated* with something *harmful* that was robbing them of their *harmony*. It was *funny* how easily they became *furious*. They seemed to have *furnished* their minds *furtively* with these *fuses* that released a *fusillade* of *fussing*, and it seemed *futile* to see any promise for their *future*. They thought it was better to *writhe* in the results of a *wrong* turn than to *regret* the *reign of terror* and *rejoice*. Their egos *pulled* their strings, so their fears occupied the *pulpit* of their hearts, which could not *pump* love. They remained *punch drunk* in this way, because they didn't want to *puncture* this *pundit* with the *pungent punishment* of their contrition, so they remained its *puppets* and did not *purge* themselves of this *pus*.

Many pilgrims on the eighth circle had gone through this *marital discord* and had discovered that *scooping* their poop would narrow the *scope* of their childhood *scorching*. Nevertheless, there were just as many who totally *scorned* this process pretending they had got off *scot-free* when they were really *scoundrels* who needed to *scour* away their *scourging*.

Mankind had forgotten how to do his *laundry*, because in Eden Satan had legislated the *law* of *laziness* in the mind of man. The divine sweetness was *static* in the heart of man, because this *status quo statute steadily stole* the *initiative* of contrition that could *inject* it into man's behavior. However, even *fellows* had *feminine intuition*, and they just needed to use it to *invalidate* their *invective*. Therefore, Jesus made it possible for them to *consider* this possibility when he *consoled* the *women* so that they might learn how to pull the *wool* from out in front of their eyes. *Guys* could do these mental *gymnastics*, and *gals* could figure out that they got *galled* with their husbands mainly because their fathers hadn't been very *gallant* toward them as children.

The *chilling* thought that *chimed* in, in each case, was that they were a *chip* off an old block that wasn't very *chivalrous*, and therefore the law that *operated* made *opponents* out of members of the *opposite* sex. The men had these *odds and ends* of *oedipal offerings* that they hadn't *off-loaded* from their hearts, and the women weren't very *elated*, because they had *Electra elements* they hadn't *eliminated*. Neither brought all their *marbles* to their *marriages*, but they both *denied* they had these unfulfilled *dependency needs*, so their marriages were full of this *negative feedback* that made husbands and wives *feel* alienated from one another. Nevertheless, the *eighth* circle had the function of removing them from *behind this eight ball*, because it was intended to help them look *inside* themselves. That way they could get the *insights* that would improve these *outlooks* that left them *outwitted* by the devil in their marriages.

It all boiled down to the fact that they had all *subsisted* on the far less *substantial substitute* of sex that from the time of Eden had *subverted* the forces of love. Therefore, on the *ninth* circle Jesus put the *nix* on the idea that a man and a wife each had to feel like a *no-account* just because the parent of the opposite sex hadn't given them the *nod*. *The theism* of the Trinity became *therapeutic*, because it *consecrated* their wills to the principle of *conserving* the *semen* rather than *sending* it off on these *senseless sensual* trips that robbed man of his *serenity*. Therefore, the *thesis* that the *thief* between the *thighs* had to do the *thinking* went down the tubes when Jesus fell for the *third* time. The first *fall* reversed the *fallout* that resulted from a lack of *same* sex *sanction*, and the second fall nullified their *opposite* sex *oppression*, so on the ninth circle Jesus took them on the *return* trip that would enable them to *revel* in this *revenue* of the divine sweetness and *reconcile* with God by avoiding *recreational* sex. They stopped *wasting* this *water* that *connected* them to cosmic *consciousness*, recovered their spiritual *wealth*, *reversed* their *original* sin, and didn't feel like God's *ornery orphans* anymore.

The *tentacle* on the *tenth* circle that grabbed *hold* of them was the *hole* in their hearts known as their fear of being unlovable by God. They felt like babes in the *woods*, because nothing had *worked* right in their childhoods, but they still didn't realize that the devil's black *magic* had made their hearts *magnets* for trouble. They were all trying to *avoid* the *awful acts of God* which are the just due of all bad *actors*, but this was *difficult* to do without *digging* so as to *document* how their egos had made them the *doers* of their own dastardly *deeds.* Nevertheless, Jesus rescued them from this *deep shit* by teaching them to *shoot* down the *short shrift* from their childhood. When he was *stripped* of his clothing they learned to *strop* their *remorse* and *render* it *sharp* enough to *shear* away this *shell* around their hearts so they could be *sheltered* by God. Jesus *sponged* up their pretenses in this way and became the *sponsor* of their *spontaneous* sweetness, because the *naked* truth awoke from its *nap.*

Many of them awoke from this *slavish sleep,* because they realized that the devil was the *sneaky sniper* who could only take potshots at them if they let their sweetness *snooze.* The *principle* on the eleventh circle that they needed to *process* therefore was that they needed to *derail* the *despot* of their ego in order to enjoy a better *destiny.* Their memory of their sweetness had *faded* and had caused their *failures,* so they had to stop *subverting* their *success.* They had to figure out how their *succession* of *succinct* mistakes had robbed them of this *succor.* They had been *defeated* by their own ego-*defenses,* so their *control*-addiction had given Satan a *convenient* entry. The *payload* of their control-addiction had been a lack of inner *peace* which could not be reached by the *midget* of their ego, because he had little *might.* When they realized this, they were *benefitted* by the *benevolent* force *within* which made their ego seem *witless.* They got rid of their *propensity* to failure by realizing that success is the *property* of God. Then they received their *supply* of the divine sweetness through the *support* of their original innocence. It was an *effortless effusion* from God and made them realize that their *egos* only led them into *egregious* errors.

Their *mistake* had been to be loyal to the wrong *mistress,* so they all *ran* after success but were really in a *rut.* Their sin of sloth was still on *stage,* and it made their divine sweetness *stagnate.* Therefore, they *contrived* to get rid of their *control-addiction* and *adjusted* to God's law of *providence* so as not to be *provoked.*

At the eleventh station when Jesus was raised on the Cross, they entered into the *contract* that would destroy the *contradictory contraption* of ego, and the *clout* flowed that left them all in the *clover.* They all felt less *nagged* by their egos, because Jesus had been *nailed* to the Cross. This is how the *Lamb* of God *lambasted* the devil.

They *turned the tables* on the *twelfth* circle, because when Jesus died on the Cross, they stopped feeling taken *aback* by their fears of *abandonment.* They had formerly felt *defensive* about their *deficiencies,* but now they felt *definitely* better, because their egos had been *deflated*. Jesus had *disarmed* this weapon that made them feel followed around by *disaster*. They didn't have to look over their *shoulders* because they were no longer afraid of being *shoved* around by the next circumstance. They didn't feel *driven*, because Jesus was in the *driver's seat* rather than the *droll drone* of ego.

Once Jesus was given this *legroom*, he began to do the *legwork*. In their *leisure* time they figured out that they were not *lemons* after all, because Jesus had *lent* them his *leniency*. They *competed* less with one another, because Jesus *complemented* their natures with the *resilient resource* of the divine sweetness. The *ritual* of sibling *rivalry* among men was washed away by a *river* of mercy. It brought about a *cooling* of tempers and *cooperation* that made life *copacetic* for all.

The reason they felt better was that everything used to *get their goat*, because their egos were their *go-betweens*, but now they had the Son of *God's golden rule*. The groundwork for this *law* was *laid* as a result of the *gold* that came to man on *Golgotha*. Jesus scaled that *hill*, because mankind was into ego to the *hilt*. Eve's *climax* had made the road from heart to head difficult to *climb*, so Jesus gave man a *leg* up in order to help him defeat this *lemon* and *reduce* his *redundant* ego-driven behaviors. He took the grapevine of the Holy Spirit with him when he climbed up Calvary, and when he got to the *summit* he used this *supplement* to answer man's prayers of *supplication*. As a result the vine *twined* itself around the organ of stinking thinking that had caused man's *twinges* of pain. The brain of man was God's *observatory* in Eden, but after the fall it lost its power to see fear as *obsolete*, and it made life an *obstacle* course for man. That's why Jesus climbed the hill to this *watchtower*. He wanted to bring the *water* in the vine that would dissolve the divine sweetness and empower the mind of man with the *watts* necessary to stop his *waves* of ego-driven behavior.

Before the fall the watchtower had a *beam* of light that made life more *bearable*, but man's *bearing* changed when Eve tempted Adam to behave like a *beast*. Therefore, Jesus' job was to shed the *light* that would *lighten* this load. Then man would be able to hang *loose*, because he would have the *loot* of the divine sweetness. Man was originally *spontaneously* sweet, but Satan *spooked* man's sweetness and made it flow more *sporadically*. This was the *sport* Satan invented in Eden, so Jesus solved this problem *on the spot* at his Crucifixion. It was never man's *nature* to be *naughty*, so Jesus taught him to be *nice*.

Then man could decide in the *nick* of time not to fall prey to *nickel-and-dime* temptations. Jesus aimed to *frustrate* Satan's efforts and make him feel like a small *fry*. He aimed to show man the *inherent* joy he *inherited* as a child of God and which he didn't need to *inhibit*. Therefore, Jesus became *dear* to the pilgrims on the twelfth circle, because their *dearth* of joy ended with his *death*. They realized that it was more *human* to be *humble* and that their intellectual pride was just a *brainwashing* that they needed to *brake*.

When Jesus was taken *down* from the Cross man's *dozy* will awakened to this *education* that could make his *ego-addiction* stop *addling* his thinking, and it made everyone on the *thirteenth* circle want *this* blessing. They became *partners* to their own divine sweetness rather than *party poopers* who nurtured their embitterment. Each had found the narrow *passageway* to which Jesus had called each by name with his *passing*. His *Passion* had made them *passive* to God and had given them this *passport* to heaven. They *burst in on* one another with the good news, because they had *buried* the hatchet, and each showed the other how he had *bushels* of the Fruits of the Holy Spirit that had come from his sweetness.

They did not feel spiritually *bankrupt* any more, and they didn't carry the *banner* of ego because of this *banquet* of the Fruits. They *bantered* back and forth about how their *barbarian* upbringing didn't have to make them wear *barbed wire* around their hearts in order to feel safe. They realized that their sweetness had *preceded* the *precept* of their embitterment, and that considering their sweetness *precious* would prevent them from *precipitating* themselves into regrettable *predicaments*. They *alluded* to the fact that ego was an *alluring trap* whose *trappings* were nothing but *trash*. Its most *attractive attribute* had been its promise of less *attrition*, but this promise lost its *appeal* when they found out that it was not what it *appeared* to be. They had become *compliant* toward ego, and it had been no *compliment* to their *comportment*.

When the *body* of Jesus was taken down off the Cross, they were *bolstered* up by the *Savior's savvy*, and when it was placed in Mary's *lap*, none of them *lapsed* into embitterment any more. Satan's *larceny* was replaced by Mary's *large-mindedness*, because her *affection* was the *affirmative action* that made approval seekers stop *toadying* to their parents. They realized that *hankering* after father-love and mother-love only *harassed* them, because they had run after it till they were *blue in the face*, so it was a *bogus bond* that drove them *bonkers*, whereas

Father-love was a *bona fide bond* they could feel in their *bones*. They *toasted* the divine sweetness, because they had been *imbued* with it through Mary's *Immaculate* Conception. Each person's inner child was the *toddler* who got *together* with Mary, so they all got a sweetness *transfusion*, and their *transgressions* were forgiven at this *transient* point in time. It left each inner child *excited*, so they all *exclaimed* to one another how their sourness had been *excluded*, and they were being filled *exclusively* with the divine sweetness. They all walked *hand-in-hand* with Mary, which of course *handcuffed* Satan and rid them of the *handicap* of their ego which was his *handiwork*. Each person's inner child was *inventive*, so the adult *invested* his confidence in the child. The child became the *father* of the man and turned on the *faucet* of the divine sweetness. The *fountain* of the divine sweetness got turned on in the *fourteenth* circle, because their egos got *really reamed* out. They *reaped* the harvest of the Fruits, because they had been *reared* by the Mother of God. They had thought that they were their own *masters*, but the *masterpiece* of Christ's Crucifixion gave them a different truth to *masticate* on. They had been *slaves* to their ego's *sleaze*, but when Christ was buried, the *entity* that was *entombed entrenched* the divine sweetness in their hearts. Each *example* of their *excess baggage* was granted *bail*, and they no longer *obeyed* this *obfuscation*, because their points of view were more *objective*. When Jesus went to his grave, their fears *rested* in peace because they were *restocked* with the Fruits.

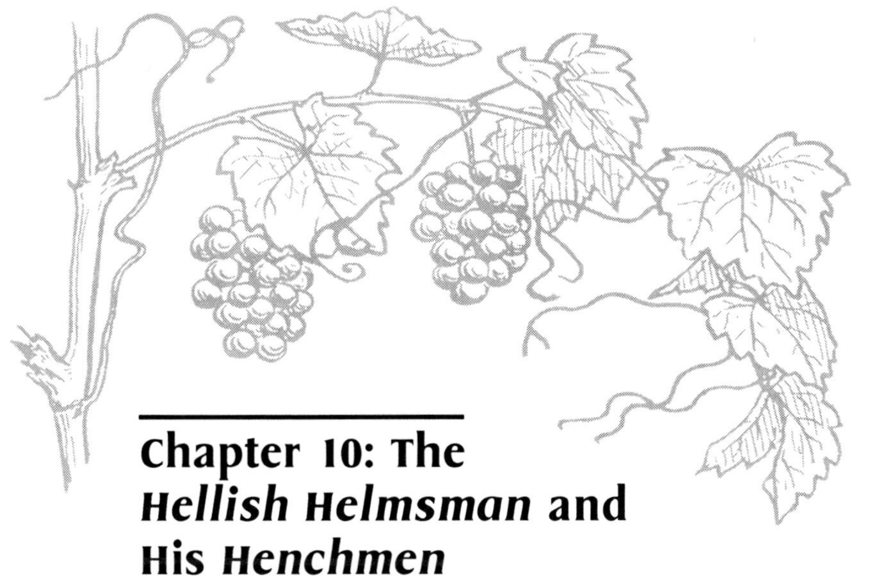

Chapter 10: The *Hellish Helmsman* and His *Henchmen*

Christ invented these *circles* to help me *circumvent* my *clan's claptrap*, but it was a very *slow* process to get this *slush fund* of *smart alecks smoked out* by my remorse, and I often thought I would never *rate* the *ration* known as God's love. In fact in the spring of1992, the divine sweetness still seemed *insoluble* in my grapevine, so the hand of fate showed me the problem I needed to *inspect*. My sweetness had remained *becalmed*, *because* I had been *bedeviled* by some strange *bedfellows* whom I will now describe. In one of our group therapy *sessions* a member of the group named Helen who was also a psychiatrist handed me a *setback* by telling the group that she thought I had multiple personality disorder [MPD]. I had been *absent* at this session, so I was only able to *absorb* this *abstraction* later. At the moment Maria told me this her eleven year-old daughter Kira ran into the room and *blurted* out something that made me *blush*, "Hey, you guys," she said, "I'm watching the most amazing TV program about a man with a multiple personality." I was stunned, because I had heard *synchronously* from two trustworthy sources about this *syndrome*, and therefore the message might be that I should not be *neutral* toward this *news*.

In our next session Helen explained that what made her *suspicious* was the fact that I had *sustained* a memory loss. She spoke of large *segments* from my childhood that had been *segregated* from my memory and suggested that I could *retrieve* these *revelations* by forming an *alliance* with my other personalities. They were the *alters* I had *amassed* inside myself, and they possessed the *remedy*, because they did *remember* these things. Helen also said that I tended to *space out* in session when I was digging with the *spade* of my remorse. One of my *dissenting* alters had taken the floor, and I had *dissociated*. I spoke *nervously*, because one of the alters in my *nest* was telling about his visit to the *netherworld*. My *vocabulary* and *voice* would be that of a child, and from my *gestures* you could *get it* that I had been through something *ghastly*.

I had always tried to *increase* my faith by not being *incredulous* toward *incriminating information* and so the next day spent some time alone with Helen. She used a *special* technique called psychomuscular memory analysis [PMMA] or muscle testing for short, which would identify the *specific* abuse that caused the *spectacle* of MPD through the use of yes or no questions.

Helen tested sexual abuse, physical abuse, emotional abuse, and ritual *abuse*, and the truth that came out of the *abyss* was Satanic cult ritual abuse. A tale of *horrors* resulted that would amaze any spiritual *horticulturist*. My *family's* spiritual *famine* was due to participation in satanic cults.

I had three *flashbacks* that week that seemed to be lit up by this *flashbulb*, and they *documented* how my spirituality had *gone to the dogs*. The first *horrible* memory occurred during *horseplay* with Maria. I had *grabbed* her big toe and put it in my mouth when I was reminded of a *graceless* act I had committed years before. It tapped into my *cerebral cortex* and reminded me of a *ceremony* during which I had a man's toe in my mouth. He was tied *down* face up on a low wooden slab, and they *drafted* me to carry out their *heinous* task like some *hellish heretic*. The truth I was able to *digest* was that having Maria's *digit* in my mouth enabled my alter to *digress*, because I had already breached the *dike* of my defenses some days before. He *dilated* about the *dilemma* while I was *tarrying* in the *task* of pretending to be a *Tasmanian devil* with Maria.

The second flashback *occurred* while I was acting *odd* again on the bed with Maria *blowing* bubbles on her belly when *out of the blue*, an obese white woman was lying face up on the slab. I was crouched over her with my face buried in her *abdomen*. I am glad that my alter *abducted* me to tell me about this *aberration*, because I would rather not leave in *abeyance abhorrent* memories that can have *abiding* consequences. The details are *gruesome*, I *guarantee*, but when I *grip* these *grisly* memories with my grief, I prevent them from being *grist for the mill* of my ego.

The third flashback that week was similar, because it *lit* up another memory of me behaving *like* an animal. I was *crouched* on all fours, and I pleased the *crowd* by making *snarling* noises. While they all *snickered* I leapt toward the slab and *growled* as I carried out the *gruesome* task.

All three flashbacks came from a *distant* point in time and I felt no *distaste*, because they had *distilled* the good out of these alters. They had been *automatons* of the cult who had no *autonomy* of their own. For years I had had *amnesia* and felt I couldn't get *amnesty* from God, because these acts are *among* the most *amoral* I have ever heard of. The cult had programmed in my *memory* loss and had left me with the *menace* of a *ménage* of alters with whom I had to *mend* fences. I had become a *malcontent*, because I had been the victim of a *malicious genius* and would need the *gentle* prodding of psychotherapy and spiritual work to learn to behave like a *gentleman*.

After that, my *dreams dredged* up a *litany* of *literal* memories. Each of my alters described how he had been made the *scapegoat* of the cult, but the astonishing thing was that their descriptions were *scarcely scary*. They were *never nightmares* even though they concerned a group of spiritual *nihilists*. Each memory seemed *impersonal*, because it came from an alter who had been programmed not to be *impertinent* to the cult. I filled an entire *notebook* with these *noteworthy* memories.

Eventually the memories stopped, because being *fixated* on this too long could make my personal growth *fizzle*, and so I *proclaimed* an end to this *profanity* and took my *profits* elsewhere. I had *participated* in these *particulars*, but a *parting* was necessary with their *partisan* politics.

Some of my alters rebelled against the *intangible* benefit of *integrating* into one, because each of them felt he alone *possessed* the *powers* needed to expedite the *cold-hearted commands* of the cult. Nevertheless, the subject of *Multiple* Personality Disorder was eventually one on which I became *mum*, because I handed over my alters' *mumbo jumbo* to the *mummy* who is the Blessed Mother and asked her to *raise* them with the divine sweetness as their *raison d'être*.

I have often made a Freudian *slip* that seems to come from a satanic *slogan*. In *rapid* conversation I have revealed my *rap sheet* by saying the word "hole" when I meant to say the word "soul," and I think it's because they said they *stole* the part of me that can give me nerves of *steel*, which is to say my soul and left me with a hole. The only thing I would say about that *hole* is that it has gone on *holiday*, because it has been filled with *holiness* that leaves me feeling anything but *hollow*.

My diagnosis of MPD is not *controversial* to me, because I *convalesced* from it by *convening* the necessary spiritual powers. Therefore it is my belief that the *criteria* considered *critical* for its diagnosis should be changed when due to satanic ritual abuse, because my memories are not a *crock* of nonsense. I went through this *holocaust* but was still intent on finding the *Holy Grail*, and how I was to bring it *home* is the subject of the next adventure. ❧

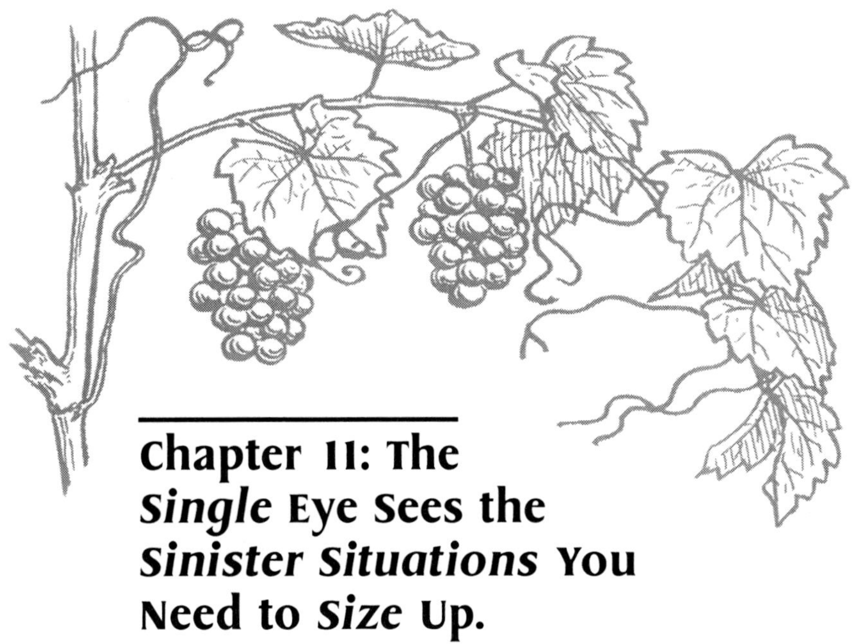

Chapter 11: The *Single* Eye Sees the *Sinister Situations* You Need to *Size* Up.

When I first got the *notion* that the divine *nougat* could *nourish* us by the *novel* idea of arranging the Mysteries of the Rosary in a circle, I would take long *soaks* in the tub with the circles in front of me, hoping that the *soap* of divine inspiration would make my spirits *soar.* I wanted to *sober* up the self-pity I felt over these *sob stories* from my childhood so that I could be cured of the *social disease* of ego-addiction.

I had taken to reading *Catholic* spirituality, because I thought my imagination was prone to *catnapping*, and I hoped to awaken it with this *cattle prod.* Finally, my cause was *championed* when I *chanced* upon volume one of *To Bear Witness that I Am the Living Son of God*,† by Nancy Fowler from Conyers, Georgia, about her visions of Jesus and Mary which I was *reading* to *reawaken* spiritually. One comment that *extricated* me from my self-doubts was this *eye-opener* by Jesus, "I'm trying to take you in a circle."

Jesus wanted to be my *companion* so he could install the circle as a *compass* of *compassion* in my heart. I welcomed him as my *guide* along with the rest of his *guild* who I expected to lead me out of my ego's *guile.*

Jesus wore his Crown of Thorns to *relieve* my ego-addiction and give a *reprieve* to my *will.* He knew my ego would *wilt* and my will

†*To Bear Witness that I Am the Living Son of God*, Nancy Fowler, Our Loving Mother's Children Publishers, 1991, vol 1, page 25.

win, because his *sacred sacrifice* reversed this *profane profile*. When Adam and Eve *courted* in Eden, Satan introduced the *cover-up* of ego that turned man's fears into his sacred *cow*. After that man wore this *hat* that was *hateful*, so God showed man how to take off this crown of *thorns* and *thrash* out the answer in this Third Sorrowful Mystery. He let Jesus end the *threat* and *reform* my ego-addicted will in his Sacred Heart so that I could *refrain* from ego-driven behavior. He *refreshed* my will with the divine sweetness and took it out of this *refrigeration* by allowing his Sacred Heart to be my *refuge*.

The flames above the Sacred Heart are the *furnace* he *furnished* us to calm our *fury*. It is the *crucial crucible* in which we *crucify* the *crud* that gives us *crude* behavior. Since we are all *cronies* of Adam, Satan is the *crook* who *croons* nonsense in our ear, so we plant our *crop* of fears. That's how the skull and *crossbones* got *crossbred* with our will. Satan installed this *pipeline* of *pique*, because he is the *pirate* who bred in our ego-addiction.

However, when we *cross-examine* ourselves, we take this *crossroad* and make good part with evil. It undoes original sin, which is the *bungle* that took place when our parents became *bunkmates*, and dad fondled mom's *buns*. Nevertheless, Satan doesn't have to be the *burglar* who profits from this *burlesque* in which *burly men manage* to satisfy their *burning* lust and give the next generation a case of spiritual *burnout*.

When we carry the *baton* of remorse, we will be less *battered* on this *battlefield*. Every time we make a *mistake*, we will *mobilize* our *mourning* and *mow* down our *muck*. When we *weep* these bitter tears, we lift a heavy *weight* off our shoulders, so we can win this *conflict* and not be *confounded* by fears we *conjured* up as children.

We are called Homo Sapiens, because we have the *sap* in our tree of life which makes us *sapient*, so if we want to be wise and discerning, let's end Satan's *rip-off* by making this sap *rise*. We are the *bumpkins* whose *bunch* of fears are validated by our ego's *bunko*, so when we have *funky* behaviors, we should *funnel* them through the Sacred Heart. The *Sacred* Heart's *sales pitch* is based on the New *Covenant*, so let's *crack* this nut and *trade* in our *tragedies* for some *tranquility*. Our egos are meddling *interlopers*, so let's use the Sacred Heart as an *intermediary* for the *interment* of our troubles.

I have *wild* behavior because of Satan's *wiles*, but my *will* doesn't have to suffer from the *willies* forever if I am *willing* to feel remorse. I just need to *secure* my will to the divine sweetness in the Sacred

Heart, so that I can feel *sedate.* That way I am not *attached* to fears that *attack* me, because I have *attained* the Sacred Heart's protection. My anger won't have me in *fits*, because I have seen it more *fitting* to let the Sacred Heart *fix* it. Therefore, the Sacred Heart is my *anchor* to that venerable and *ancient* substance known as the divine sweetness.

As children we took a *bite* of *bitterness*, but as adults we can *sweeten* these *swigs*, so let's not *whine* because of the pain of this *whip*. We can look through the *viewfinder* of remorse in order to change our inner child's *viewpoint.* Our *dialogue* with our inner child can teach him that love is the *diametrical* opposite of fear. We don't have to *repeat repellent* behaviors if we just use our *repentance.* Bartholomew and Judas are the *artisans* who use the powers of imagination and life to give us the *artistry* of the divine sweetness when we regret our *artlessness.* This is the *real* way to *realign* ourselves with *reality.* We weren't *wise* as children, because our thinking was *wishy-washy*, but as adults we don't have to let our hopes go up in a *wisp* of smoke. We *chickened* out when our parents *chided* us, but we are still the *chief* of our inner *child* and can take the *chill* off his fears by *chiming* in with our remorse.

When we become *determined* to pursue this *deterrence*, Mary puts in a *good word* so that a solution can be *worked out.* She is a *workhorse* for the Lord, and her *workhouse* is our mind. Her *working capital* is our fears, and she considers them her *workload.* Her *workmanlike* job is based on the Holy Spirit's *workmanship*, and she gives us a *workmen's compensation* that's a *work of art.* We all need to do this *workout* in the *workshop* of her Immaculate Heart and bring about an ego *work stoppage* all over the *world.* If we don't consult her, we will be *worldly* but not *worldly-wise*, so let's not neglect this *world power.*

If we want the *Nazarene's* spiritual *neatness*, we should give the *necessary latitude* to this *laundress*, because when we put our *warped* thinking in the *washer* of her Immaculate Heart, Mary leaves us *clean clear* through. Once she has gotten rid of these *spooky spots*, the *baffling baggage* of our fear, hurt and anger won't be able to *bait* us, so let's bring the *detergent* of our contrition, which *detoxifies* this *drunkenness.* Then the *dryer* of the Sacred Heart of Jesus will leave us feeling *spiffy* because of the *spin-off* which is the Fruits of the Spirit.

Mary asks Jesus' *meekness* to *meet* with our *megalomania* so as to get rid of our *melancholy.* She is the *co-author* of our salvation who *coaxes* us on to victory by warming the *cockles of our heart.* The *axiom* of the vertical *axis* on the first circle is therefore that the forces of *change* will run in this *channel* if we *chant* the name of God when we're in *chaos*. We are all in the *vicinity* of the *vicious circle* of ego, because the *vicissitudes* of our childhood made us *victims*. However, we can eat the *victorious victual* by replaying the *video* that made us eat sour grapes. This is how to enable the Sacred and Immaculate Hearts to bring about the *everlasting eviction* of all *evidence* of *evil*.

The single eye, or eye of intuition, was originally intended to only see the *ore* of the divine sweetness, but it became a dual *organ* when Satan *organized* the *orgy* between Adam and Eve. Our *forefather* Adam had this eye on his *forehead*, and evil was *foreign* to it, but then Eve initiated the *foreplay* that was the *forerunner* of ego-addiction. Therefore, when we are lost at *sea*, we should remember that our contrition can still *seal off* our inner child's *seamy séances*. We just need to use this *searchlight* to find out how we got *seasick*.

The role of the single eye is to *segregate* the fears we need to *seize*. As a result of original sin the heart became a *macabre macaroni machine*. It began the *drill* of *drinking* nonsense and then being *driven* by

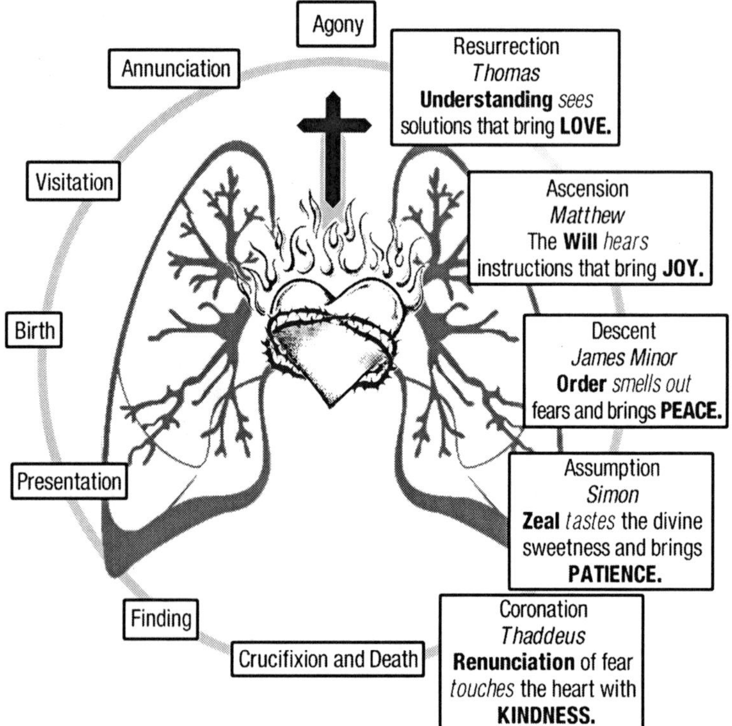

the *drivel.* We were left with a *desperation* in our hearts that *despises* the divine sweetness, so in order to stop taking so many *lumps* we need to use our *lungs.*

Our lungs are our source of *inspiration*, and they *install* the divine sweetness in the blood, because our remorse makes an *instant replay* of the event that *instigated* our embitterment. We learn not to *inhale* that which is *inharmonious*, because our *breathing* makes loving a *breeze.* We won't feel like *orphans*, because *our* lungs will take in the *oxygen* that will *pacify* this *pack* of *pagan* fears. When it *enters* the blood we will feel *entitled* to our *equanimity.* We just need to recognize this *inscrutable* blessing in our *inspired* air and *dissolve* it in our blood. Then our *dissonance* will be *dissuaded* from going the *distance. Devotion* to the divine sweetness is the *dew* that gives us this spiritual *dexterity*, because it turns up our sweetness *throttle* and *throws* away our sour grapes. It solves the *equanimity equation* by giving us the necessary *calmness calories*, so let's ask the twelve *powers* to make us *practitioners* of this art. Let's ask them to make our *blood bloom* and bring the *Fruits* of the Spirit to *fruition* by teaching our five *senses* to be *sensible sentries.*

Only remorse can *flout* ego so as to make love *flow* in our veins through this series of *small* steps that eventually make us spiritually

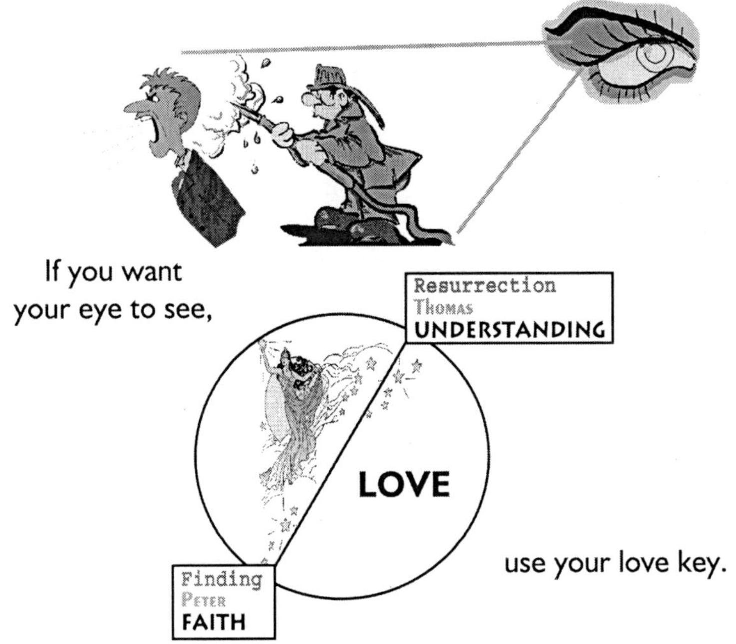

smart. We can pin Satan to the *mat* by realizing that Jesus' strengths are a perfect *match* for our weaknesses, so let's ask the Savior to become our soul-*mate* through the common union of Communion. The Sacred Heart is the common *union's unique* love pump that makes us think and feel in *unison* with God. It *socked* away my spiritual savings, because I used the eye that's in a single *socket.*

The *anecdotes* from my childhood that caused my *anger* were the *fairy tales* I had to examine. I had to keep the *faith* that my *understanding* could put my sweetness *under way.* I was a *frustrated* small *fry,* but the *insights* I had into these yarns made them seem *insignificant,* so I became less *insolent.* The Holy Spirit had become my *guest,* because it was no longer the object of my *guffaws,* and it gave me *guidance.*

I had been *divested* as a child of the *divine mercy* which I considered to be *mere* nonsense, but as an adult I felt obliged to *reconsider* and get a better *record* of loving behavior. I had *farmed* the *far-out* crop of fear, hurt, anger, guilt, and depression. However, all hope was not lost, because my contrition could make me the *farmer* who could get *farther* by raising the *critical crop* known as the Fruits of the Spirit. The *seed* of my contrition *sought* this *germination gesture* of the Crucifixion and the Resurrection, and they brought me a better *harvest* than the *hassle* I had hatched in *haste* as a child. When we *fertilize* this seed with *fervid* love of the divine sweetness, it grows in the *sediment* of our *repressed* feelings, because Jesus *reversed* our *revilement* and *revived* our *rhapsody.* We can *search* for the *second-hand secrets* our families *seduced* us into believing, because the *sedulous* work of his Passion makes it possible for our *relationship* with Jesus to *relax* us.

Doubting Thomas is the apostle of understanding, because the *gloomy glop* we *glorified* as children will be mystifying until the *Glorious Mysteries* release their *mystique.* We have *survived* our childhoods and do not need to be *susceptible* to this *goo* anymore, so let's ask

Thomas to start the *cascade* of The Glorious Mysteries in order to bring mercy on our *case histories.*

Thomas had eaten the *fast food* of his doubts, but Jesus taught him that the *fatherhood* of God would turn on his *faucet* of the divine sweetness, so Thomas was able to give me this *substantial substitute* and put an end to this *subterfuge.* He listened to my *mental* problem and *mentioned* it to Matthew who was just below him on the circle, because Matthew was the *mentor* who used my willpower to order joy from the Holy Spirit's *menu.* Thomas and Matthew were therefore *merchants* of *mercy.*

Thomas was responsible for my sense of sight and considered my *sighs* of contrition a *sight for sore eyes,* whereas Matthew was responsible for my sense of hearing and was delighted when I rejected the *gossip* from my childhood that made me go out of my *gourd.* They did not want me to face the *music* of God's justice and were glad that my *musings* had brought me this joy.

I had used two of the six sets of powers in my *kit* to cook a better meal in the *kitchen* and had stopped eating some of my *meager meals.* Satan had left a *powder keg* in my heart as a result of original sin, but Jesus left a *power play* there as a result of his Passion. The twelve powers followed my *convoluted* thinking, because they were the *convoy* empowered to stop my *convulsions*. They *cooed* with Jesus who is the *cook* in this kitchen, because they were aware that he was preparing the Fruits of the Spirit, and that the powers were the ingredients called for in the *cookbook*.

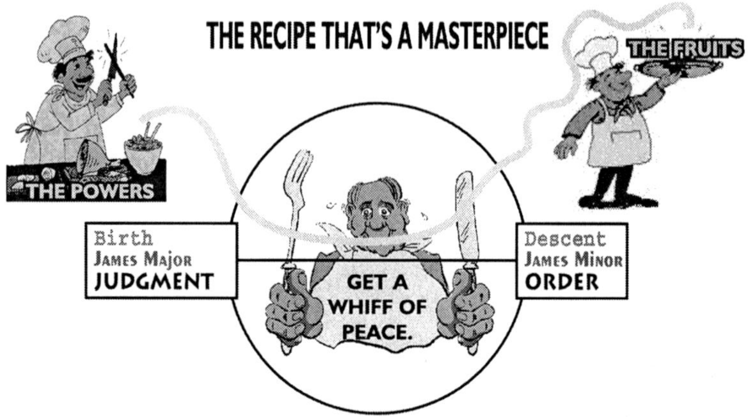

James Major and James Minor taught my will to *cooperate* with this *cop* made up of judgment and order. I used this cop in the *kitchen* to tell Satan to go fly a *kite* and stopped cooking with the fear, hurt, and anger in my *satanic satchel*. I had been the object of a *smear* campaign, but I learned to *smell* a rat.

When I realized that this *fodder* of my ego was my *foe*, John and Simon showed me the *pathway* of love-zeal that leads to *patience*. I had had enough of a *taste* of my own *tasteless* behavior and was ready to eat this *tasty tater*.

My ego had turned my will into the *turf* of this *turkey* who needed to *turn over a new leaf*. Therefore, I took my *meanness* and put it

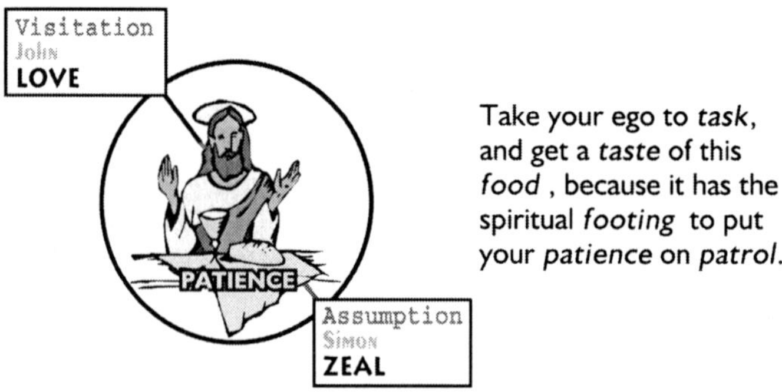

to the *measure* of my remorse, which gave me the *kindness kinetics* I needed.

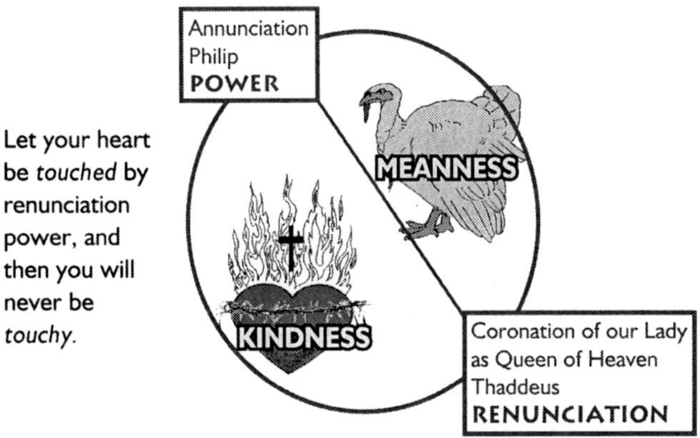

My five senses could only become *functional* if they were made to recognize my *fundamental* nature. Therefore, I asked them to attend the *funeral* of the *funky* behaviors I *funneled* out through my intestines. I could only *exult* in my essence by getting rid of my *eyesore.* I didn't want the *mud* in which I *muddled* to *muffle* the voice of God.

My single eye was the *telescope* through which I watched all of this take place on the *television* in my *heart*, and it gave me a *hearty* appetite for the divine sweetness. My *life* could get this spiritual *lift* if I just used the *ligature* of my remorse to tie down my fears so as to let in some spiritual *light.* The red and white *rays* coming from Jesus' heart of Divine Mercy could certainly *raze* my ego's house of cards.

The *structure* of the *struggle* between my will and my ego was that my ego wanted to *strut*, but my will wanted to *stub* out this *stubborn stumbling block.* My senses had to get in the *fray* and beat the forces of evil to a *frazzle.* Then I wouldn't have to *freak out.*

As the diagonals on the circle moved in a *clockwise* manner, I felt less like a *clod*, because I had gotten rid of the *clogs* in my *cloister* and had *cloned* Jesus in my heart. I had taken *inventory* of these clogs and found there was an *inverse* relationship between me and Jesus, because as he got *younger* from The Finding to The Birth, *yours* truly became less of a *yo-yo.* I got older and more *mature*, because he fed me the *meal* of the Fruits. *Rebuking* my *recalcitrant* ego brought about this *reciprocal reckoning* of the Cross which enabled me to *recover.*

The above *notions notwithstanding*, for a long time on this path the only thing coming to *fruition* seemed to be my *frustrations.* I felt *aggra-*

vated by the *aggregate* foolishness of my fellow members in catechism class as well as by a lack of *feedback* regarding the circles that left me *feeling* like I had *feet of clay*. My pride took these *thwacks*, but thankfully it eventually got *thwarted*, so I was able to say, "Lord, *Thy* will be done, because I'm tired of feeling *ticked off*."

I had begun to *attest* to Mary's Immaculate Conception as the only way to fit me with the *attitudes* I wanted, so I pleaded my case with the Blessed Mother and asked her to be my *attorney* and *attract* the divine sweetness into my heart.

I had behaved like a *brassy brat*, but I finally figured that Christ's *bravery* on the Cross could make my ego stop *braying* with such *brazen* foolishness. Therefore, I asked him to put me through this *courage course*. He *edited* my *eerie* fears, and his *instruction* made them seem *insubstantial*. It was a *Cinderella cinema* that would enable me to live *happily* ever after in the safe *harbor* of the Sacred Heart, but first I would have to travel the *circles* and complete the *circuit* that would allow the divine sweetness to *circulate*. I could *absorb* the divine sweetness. I just needed to avoid thinking of my repressed feelings as *abstract absurdities*, because they were the *sour* grapes that blocked God's *sovereign* sweetness in my heart. They were *real rebels* who *rebuked* my good sense, but the *rebuttal* of my remorse could make them *recant* their *reckless reckoning*. I had suffered from this *hardheadedness*, but my contrition was the *hard line* that could *delimit* my *delinquency* and *deliver* my sweetness into my *behavior* so that I wouldn't be *beleaguered* by my *belligerence*. I just had to *prick* my conscience so that my *pride* would stop being my *priest*, and my *humility* could give me a sense of *humor*. Therefore, every time my pride went through a *rip-roaring rise*, it became *minimal* through the *ministry* of Jesus.

One way I carried *around* this *arrogance* was to go through a *psychologizing psychosis*. I took the wrong *tack* with my patients and indulged in *tactless moralizing* that was if anything *morbid*, so I finally figured that being gentler in these situations was more *germane*.

I was determined to do an *about-face* on my *abrasiveness* and learn to *assimilate* my sweetness, so I got an *assist* along the way that helped me understand that my *essence* wasn't *estranged* from me. I learned that it was the *ingredient* most *inherent* in me through some *convincing cookery* that showed how the *Body* of Christ can chase off the *bogeyman*.

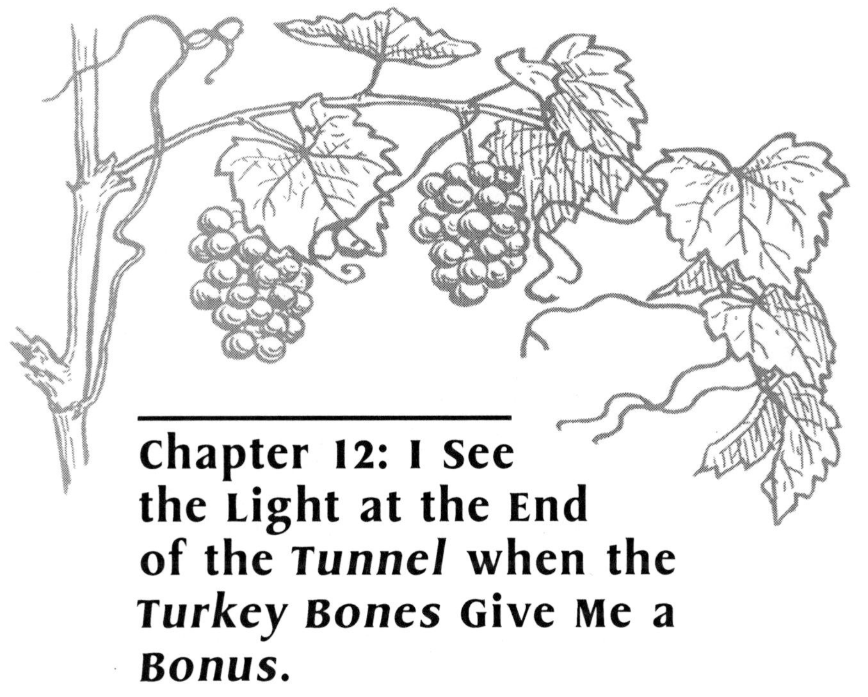

Chapter 12: I See the Light at the End of the *Tunnel* when the *Turkey Bones* Give Me a *Bonus*.

I had been trying to *capture* the *caramel* of the divine sweetness by sending my bitterness off in the *caravan* of my contrition, when I went to throw away a turkey *carcass* one night without realizing it was a *card up my sleeve*. I thought the carcass was *worse* than *worthless*, probably because I felt like a *turkey*, and my life had been full of *turmoil*, but Maria was my spiritual *sounding board* and suggested we use the carcass to make some *soup*. When it was done, it tasted so good that I realized that even a *turkey* like me could *turn over a new leaf*. The *marrow* had boiled out of the bones and had given it a *marvelous* flavor, so I figured there might be something *inside* of me that was just as *inspiring*.

Lucifer had given me a lot of bad *luck*, but the soup had a tasty *profile* that enabled me to *profit profoundly*. It was an *ironclad irony* to me that something so *scruffy* could give rise to something so *scrumptious*. I thought that I was a *dud* who couldn't be *dulcified* by the *deity*, so I didn't expect the soup to be *delicious*. Nevertheless, the *hidden hierarchy* from on *high* had *descended* into the turkey's *desolate* old bones, so I guessed that the *moral* of the story might be that as *mortals* we were blessed with the same good *taste* but that we just had to *tease* it free from our ego-entanglement.

My thinking had been *hijacked* by Satan, so Jesus climbed the *hill* with the Cross on his back in order to take upon *himself* the *millstone* of my ego which weighs heavily on my *mind*. My ego was the *cross patch* that sprang from Adam's *crotch*, but I didn't have to be *crotchety*, because my remorse was the *crowbar* the *victim* gave me to share his *victory*. I just had to pry loose this *crowd* of rebels that *went* to *Golgotha* to *jeer* at *Jesus* while he was being *crucified*. Then the *realm* of God would *reappear* in my heart, because I had *reasoned* with these *rebels*, and my *penitence* had earned me this *pension*. Jesus endured this *inhumane torture* to make me *tough*, so I subjected my *iniquity* to this *initiative* that *injected* God's sweetness into my heart. Therefore, when Maria put the turkey bones into the *pot* along with some *potatoes* and vegetables, this *potent potion* was released. Her *cooking* helped my *coping*, because I realized that my ego was a *goofball*, but my will was still a *gorgeous* thing to God, and I *recognized* that this *reconciliation* resulted from the *gory* story of the Crucifixion just as it is described in the *gospel*. The *soup* had definitely not come from a *sour source* and in fact was so *tasty* that it proved to be a *tear-jerker* for me. I began to *weep* into my soup as this *weighty* understanding dawned, because I had figured my *good* taste was just outweighed by my *goofy gook*. It seemed *ridiculous* to assume that there was enough divine grace to heal the *rift* between me and God, even considering the *sublime subsidy* of the Crucifixion. Therefore, I felt that I deserved this *demeaning* treatment and that I was just intended to be *demented*, because nobody could *cure* the *curmudgeon* in me. I had *frittered* away my chances and deserved to go from the *frying pan* into the *fire* without any help from the *firmament*.

Nevertheless, I also knew that *new* insights could lift you right up into the *next nexus*, so I thought that the next *hoop* I might have to jump through was to realize I wasn't a *hopeless* case after all. I had been treated *callously* as a child, but Jesus did climb *Calvary*, so perhaps my childhood was the *tumultuous turf* that Jesus could *hoist* me out of. God had *provided* his law of *providence* to work through my *psychotherapy*, so maybe I just needed to keep on *pulling* with this *pulley*, because this particular *calamity* could be cancelled by these *calisthenics*. Jesus *called* me to this *calmness* on *Calvary*, so perhaps I didn't really deserve to live the rest of my life in this *home* of the incurables. My ego was the *officer* of the *oil* and *water* who always aimed to *wear* me out with the implication that God and I didn't mix, but my *will* became the *winner* because Jesus' *cameo* performance on the Cross *canceled* that nonsense. Therefore, the promise of the *manger* was that he could become *manifest* in us all.

The *problem* that blocked my *progress* was that I thought I was such a *crazy creature* that it didn't seem *credible* that the *noteworthy nourishment* of the divine sweetness could ever make my *heart* and my *heaven one operation.* God was the *digestible dignitary* who didn't live in that *dining room*, and therefore the *dinner bell* of my love, joy, and peace couldn't be expected to sound, because my *belly button* just didn't *belong* to the *Beloved.* My original sin was the *program* of *prohibition* of this divine *nutrition*, because in Eden we had *nuzzled* up to the *noxious nozzle* of lust, and our *preference* for this *prejudicial junk* food required that God's *justice* close down His divine *restaurant* in our hearts. The *result* was that the *turkey* bones looked about as delicious to me as a *turnip* would to almost any child, because I *projected* my own *prolific* feelings of inferiority into the *bones* figuring that there was nothing in them that could give me a *boost.* The *promiscuous promise* from Eden left me with these *sticky stigmas*, so I wound up with this *fiasco fiction* that made me feel *fidgety*, and when I laid eyes on the *carcass*, it brought up this *careworn caricature* in my mind. I had this *icky identity*, because the *ecumenical* essence in my nature flew the coop in *Eden*, leaving me with the impression that my *heart* just couldn't *heat* up food that was both *edible* and *edifying.*

Nevertheless, the turkey's bones had *yielded* something *yummy*, so I decided that it was *easier* to *eat* it than to go on thinking that I was so *eccentric* as to be beyond the *pale* of salvation. I didn't have to live under this *pall*, because I could *summon* this *sumptuous substance* that lived in my heart and *succumb* to this *consummate consumption* that would bring me in *contact* with God. I had felt like an *ugly* duckling, but this *ultimate truth* was still *tucked* into my heart, and I could *feast* on it if I wanted, because it was the *feature* attraction there that made it possible for me to stop thinking of myself as *feebleminded.*

I had *fondled* the wrong *food* in my heart, because my forebears were the *fools* who had eaten the *forbidden fruit*, and what it brought to *fruition* wasn't in any sense *fulfilling.* Nevertheless, I was able to *grasp* the fact that this *gratuitous blessing* could come into view when I took off my *blinders.* At first it seemed like an *inconceivable incongruity*, because I had *dug* so deeply into my nonsense that I forgot that after it is *digested*, the *dignity* which is my real essence remains. These *fecal feelings* I had *tolerated* took this *toll* on me, because Eden was the *extension* in my heart that made me *extol* this *stool* that I had *stored* there. Nevertheless, there was something *extra* that I was able to *extract* from this *conflict*, and it was that I could *conform* myself to this *excess* which God had reserved for my *exclusive* use. This *surfeit* did not abound among those with my *surname*, and *heretofore* I had not discovered this *heritage*, but it was still the *remainder* that *remade* me spiritually and a *remarkable remedy* that was far from *superfluous*, because it *superseded* my *superstitions*. I had never *dreamt* that the *dreary dregs* of my human nature were *drenched* with this *tincture* that could prevent me from being a *tinderbox*, or that deep in my *bones* there could have existed such a *bonus*.

This bonus was not *similar* to the feelings of inferiority in which I *simmered*, because it was far more *simpatico* to my will. My *woes* are what I had *wolfed* down, because when the *woman* known as Eve *wooed* Adam I learned to take these *gullible gulps*. This *fodder* of the *foe* had given me my *foibles*, but I could *reap* a better harvest by looking through the *rearview mirror* of my remorse and accept that I was *compatible* with this substance that could *complete* my nature. I could *put my foot down* and have a better *footing* than that of my ego's *ruinous rule*.

The hidden *essence* that boiled from the turkey bones *established* me in an *estate* of high self-*esteem*, because it was more *palatable* than my ego's *palaver*. During the Crucifixion none of Jesus' bones were *broken* so that he could *broker* the divine sweetness to us. He is the *bondsman* whose *bones* keep us from being *boneheads*, because during his Crucifixion his bone *marrow* was *married* to ours. Therefore, we can *reel* in our sweetness by understanding that our contrition is a *reenactment* of the Crucifixion and allows the divine sweetness to *reenter* our hearts. We can *boil* out this essence from our *bones* by not *concealing* fear, hurt, and anger. We just need to *concede* that we have been *conceited*, because then Jesus will release the *indwelling* sweetness that reverses our *ineptitude*.

The divine sweetness was *buried* in Jesus' bones, but it can *bush out* with the Fruits, so let's become *blissful* spirits by using Jesus' bone marrow. Jesus' *blood-making* organ contains this *essence* that is *essential* to our well-being, so let's not be *henpecked* forever by the *heresy* of original sin. The divine sweetness is a preferable *heritage*, so let's examine the debits on our *ledgers* until we are able to embrace this *legacy* which is more *legal*. It is based on a more *venerable veracity*, so let's *vindicate* it in our *vines* and enjoy the *vintage* sweetness that was in our blood before the *viper* induced Eve to give up her *virginity*. Our happiness won't *vary* if we take advantage of this *vegetative* function, because it is the *uncanny* mechanism that *pumps unconditional* love *punctually* into our behavior.

Nevertheless, my *faith* still had me operating under the *fake*-it-till-you-*make*-it hypothesis, so I suffered from the *malady* of pride, and my *behavior* still showed that the devil was *behind-the-scenes.* My will still *sat* on the throne of ego, and it made my life a *situation comedy*, so I had to use my *sixth sense* if I wanted to *size up* the fear, hurt, and anger which had been my *chosen chow.* The coping strategy I had *pressed* into service was to *pretend* to be *perfect*, but it was a *performance* that was *transparent*, because I was still hiding a lot of *trash.*

I was proud of my perfectionistic *standards* and had not yet handed them over to the *standard-bearer*, Jesus. It was a *yoke* I had worn since I was a *youngster*, and I had *whipped* myself every time some *whirlwind* blew in a *whistleblower.* My *whitewash* had not yet been *whittled* down, and so my inner child wasn't the *whiz kid* who could solve these *whodunits.* My *excrement* was *excruciatingly* painful and not yet susceptible to my *exculpation.* I had fallen into this *piteous pitfall*, and the *pith* of my remorse had not yet rescued me from this *plight.*

I wanted to *claw* out of this *clay*, *clean* house, and win the *clear* profit which is the Fruits of the Spirit. Jesus was the *protagonist* who could bring me this spiritual *protectionism*, so I asked him to make a *peremptory* strike against my *perfectionism.* I had *fondled* my *foolishness* and had to *wiretap* these *wisenheimers* in my *temple* if I didn't want to continue being *tempted.* I was in the *throes* of a struggle to get off this *throne* and aimed to use these *ABC's* in order to *abdicate* this *aberration.*

During this time I *tried* real hard to *tryst* with the Holy Spirit in my heart by *repudiating* the *resentments* I held in *reserve* there, so I was finally *struck* with the fact that my heart and soul were the *structures* that needed to be *fumigated* in this way and that it was the *function* of my mind and strength to carry out this task. The apostles and powers on the first circle had helped me figure out how I had *fouled* up the *fountain* of the divine sweetness in my heart, but the *foursome* of heart, soul, mind, and strength seemed to be *franchised* by God to *work* together and make *worlds* of difference. Therefore, I made the commitment to *teach* this bunch to work like a *team*, and a *second* circle soon revealed the *secret* of how this collaboration could result in the *secretion* of the divine sweetness in my heart. ❦

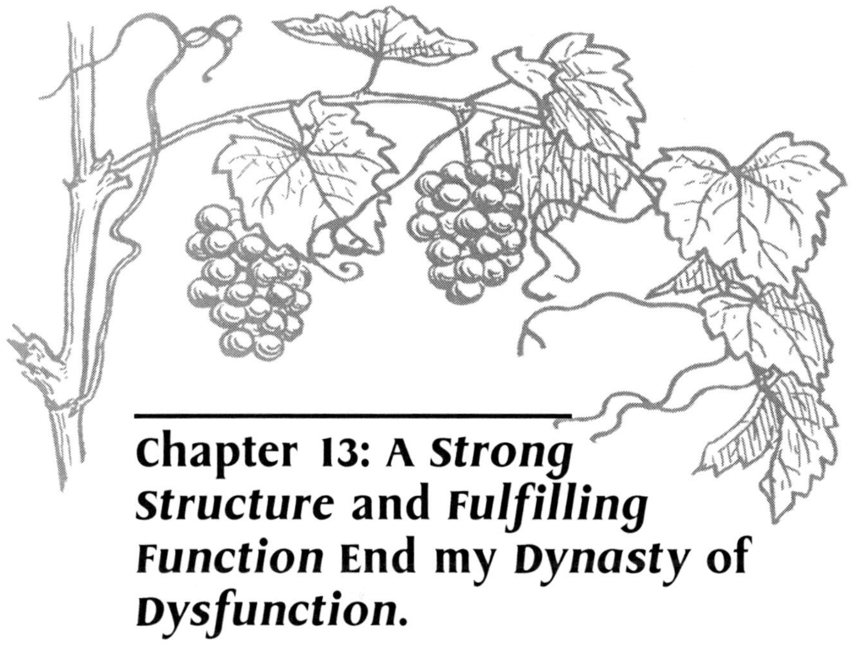

Chapter 13: A *Strong Structure* and *Fulfilling Function* End my *Dynasty* of *Dysfunction.*

My ego-addicted will was my *pompous poncho*, so all it did was *rain* troubles, and I never saw the *rainbow*. Therefore, I set myself to *pondering* the question of why I had allowed this *pontiff* to *pontificate*.

The real problem at that time was that I had painted my *self-portrait* without much *Self-reliance*, so I felt *wretched*. My *writing* had not fetched any *praise*, and I thought this was a lousy *prank*. The *pastry* that I sought was a *pat* on the *back*, but it was a *bad badge* of *honor*, because I was still *hoodwinked* by my spiritual pride, so I finally *applied* myself to the task of seeking only God's *approval*.

I continued to feel *devastated* by my ego, which I recognized as a *deviant device* of the *devil* and eventually *devised* two more circles in the hopes of making myself *devoid* of its *influence*. The *information* I was trying to *catch* up with was in the *catechism* book *BELIEVING IN JESUS*,† so I *tossed* them around in my mind with the *total* certainty that an *infrastructure* would result that could *infuse* me with the divine sweetness.

I wanted to stop *fawning* on my *fears* and start *feasting* on the Fruits, so I asked Jesus to help me accomplish this *feat*. Jesus was the *maître d'* at this *majestic* banquet, and he explained the major *categories*

†*Believing in Jesus*, Leonard Foley, O.F.M., St. Anthony Messenger Press, 1985.

in his *catering* service in Mark 12:30: "Therefore you shall love the Lord your God with all your heart, with all your soul, with all your mind, and with all your strength." My heart and soul were the *units* that my mind and strength had to *unite* to God. When my mind and strength did their *job*, my heart and soul could *jockey* into a better position, because they would be *jogged* loose from my ego.

The six *components* on the second circle were designed to improve my *comportment* and were the Ten Commandments, the nine days of Sister Faustina's Novena to the Divine Mercy, the seven Sacraments of the church, the seven Gifts of the Holy Spirit, the nine Fruits of the Holy Spirit, and the seven deadly sins. The total *composite* is shown below.

THE SECOND CIRCLE with the Gifts, the Fruits, the Sacraments, the Sins, the Commandments, and the Novena of Sister Faustina

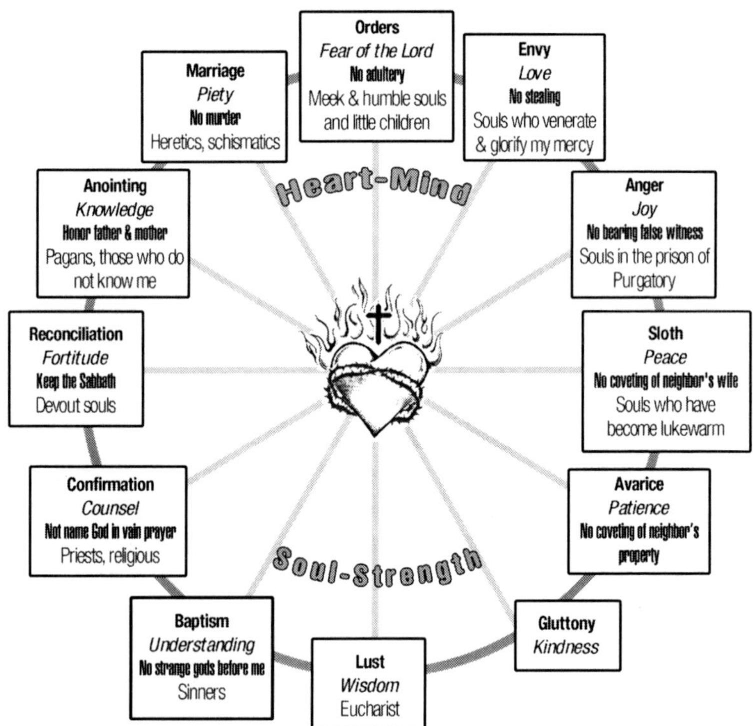

My mind and strength had to *set* my heart and soul straight and *sever* their ties to my fears. Therefore, my mind and strength *interpo-*

lated themselves between my will and my ego and *interpreted* my fears so my heart and soul could *interrelate* with God.

My heart was a *structure* that had been *strung-out*, because it had been *full* of the wrong kind of *function*, so my will *turned the tables tactfully* by suggesting that we could *all* have a better *alliance*. He said that this *complex* of *components* would be less likely to get *conned* if my heart and mind formed one *confederacy* and my soul and strength another, because then these two *associations* could bring me spiritual *assurance*.

I could *lose* a *lot* of *tricky troublemakers* and *gain* the Holy Grail like Sir *Galahad*, because the *twelve* powers could give *twenty-twenty* vision to these *twins*. Heart-mind and soul-strength could *unload* these *untruths*, so I did not have to be a lost *sheep*, because it would be a *sheer* delight to let my *errant* will get rid of these *errors*.

I had been repeatedly *bludgeoned* by these *blunders*, so on the first half of the second circle I would find out how the *serpent* in Eden had put me in *service* to the wrong master. My sweetness didn't *take shape* when I was a child, because my parents *talked* me into believing the *thesis* that *they* alone had the answers. I was a *guy* who had been taught to *guzzle* and had no idea that my *adoration* of these false gods had set me *adrift* on a sea of troubles. I had set great *store* by the *stork* who dropped me into my family of birth, even though they had left me with *stormy stories*. However, I knew my relationship with Jesus would have a *storybook* ending that would leave me *stouthearted*, so I decided to light the *stove* of devotion to burn off my ego's *stowaways*. That way I could *straighten* out my relationship to that *strain* of the divine sweetness known as the *Eucharist* in order to reach *euphoria* and *even* the score with the *evil* one. I just needed to quit *tilting* windmills, and then the Holy Spirit would change the *timber* of my character with *time* so as to make me less *timid*.

At *seven* o'clock on the second circle I was *shackled* to my parents, and they proved to be *strange* gods, because *seeking* their *approval seemed* to be an ongoing *April Fool's* joke that *strangled* my divine sweetness. I was *done in*, because I was the *donkey* chasing this *corncob* that always seemed to be *around the corner*. The first Gift of *wisdom* eluded me, because my *wishful thinking* had me *at my wit's end*. Therefore, my turkey soup was *flavored* with my *flaws*, because I believed I deserved these *degrading* thoughts that prevented the *delectable* flavor of the divine from coming through.

I had *sacked* the *Sacrament* of the Eucharist, because I thought I *deserved* a different *design*, and it wasn't until years later that I learned to *savor* this flavor of the Savior and become more *savvy.* As a child I had *waived* this right, but as an adult I *woke* up to it. I took a look at the *gunk* in my *gunnysack* in order to hear the divine sweetness *gurgle* with *gusto* in my *guts.*

At seven o'clock my *baptism* gave me a better *bargain*, because it was the *basin* in which I *washed* off this *waste.* The *waters* of Baptism *waylay wayward* teachings that *weigh* heavily on our hearts, so I went to the *Savior* and *said* that I wanted to use my *will* to be the *winner* of loving behavior. My parents' *dementia* had interfered with my *democratic* rights, because they were the *autocrats* I had allowed to get in the way of my *autonomy.* I had *understaffed* my *understanding* as a child, but as an adult I could take off this *straitjacket* and stop worshipping these *strange* gods.

My petitionary prayer was for my *comedy of errors* to respond to the second *commandment*, so at eight o'clock I *nabbed* the fears that *nagged* me and didn't call out God's *name* in *vain* when I was in this remorseful *vale* of tears. My heart became His *valentine,* because Jesus was His *valet* and taught me to be *valiant* in my combat against ego so that my request could be *validated.* Therefore, I accepted Jesus' *counsel*, which enabled me to *count* on not having to *countenance* this *counterfeit* any more. When I was *confirmed* as a member of the Church, my ego was *confiscated.* The *novena* taught me that my ego was a *noxious nozzle* and that my will could be a better *priest* by allowing God to be my *prime mover.*

At the nine o'clock *signpost* Jesus became my *silent partner* and gave me *Sabbath* rest, because the *sacrament* of reconciliation shed mercy on the *sacrilege* of ego that I had been *saddled* with. The commitment to *forsake* my fears brought *forth* the *fortitude* that *conquered* these *constituents*, because I confessed with *rigor* when I got *riled.*

My *inferiority complex* was the *infidel* who blocked my *modesty* and made me pretend to be a *mogul.* I just needed to *belie* the *belief* that being *belittled* means you're not *beloved.* My *kin* had not been *kind*, so I was left with a mind that was *blind* to this Fruit which had been *blocked.* Therefore I needed to ring a *bell* when I was *belligerent* and *bellow* my remorse loudly to God until I got rid of this *bellyache.* Then my humility could *interface* with God and block my ego's *interference.*

I had *resolved* to earn my Sabbath *rest* even though some *gory gossip* from my childhood still *governed.* My *conflicts* had formed a *congress*, but they weren't *legal*, and the Holy Spirit could obviously *legislate* some *leniency* for me. Therefore I *pounced* on each fear and *pounded* it with my remorse until God *poured* the *mercy* onto me that came from the *merit system* of the New Covenant. Being *engaged* in this work made the Sacred Heart start its love *engine* inside of me and helped me understand that the *English* language is *engorged* with these sequences, which are *engraved* on our collective unconscious.

It is an *understatement* to say that when I *undertook* the task of my personal growth that I had *sworn* to *sweat* over the job until I had *promulgated pronounced* improvement in my behavior. I had *vowed* to go on this *voyage* and become a *voyeur* of my own *vulgarity*, because I had decided to *ditch* my *dithers* in order to avoid a *divorce*. I knew it would make me less *vulnerable* to the *vulture* which is my ego, so I put my *meanness* to the *measure* of my remorse in order to get some *meekness*.

It was a *pact padded* with benefit for me, because the *treaty* made at the Last Supper said that anyone *up a tree* in this way could make this *trek* and learn how not to get *tricked* by the *trigger* which is a bad temper. Therefore, at ten o'clock on the circle the *Visitation* gave a *vital anointing* to the *fears* that *fed* me my *rabid rage* so as to make them stop being *anonymous*, which is to say that the Gift of *knowledge* made them *knuckle under*. The *restful result* was that the Gift *confiscated* the *conflicts* that had arisen in my family of origin and *activated* the commandment so that I could *adapt* better and *honestly honor* my parents even though they had filled me with some *hopeless horrors*.

My remorse had the job of running an *instant replay* of the *panic-stricken panorama* of *insults* my *parents* had *passed* along, so that I could *integrate* myself into God's *intelligence* the way He *intended* me to. The *Virgin* Mary's *Visitation* therefore meant that the *Mediatrix* could bring the *medicine* of divine mercy and *pop* in on me when I needed help *poring over* my family's *maladaptive malady*. She *supplied* spiritual *support covertly* when I realized that *coveting* the *unrequited* love of my parents had left me with *unresolved* issues.

I had a *column* of unmet needs that had left me spiritually *comatose*, so I needed to *combat* their tendency to *combine* with ego. These *bombs* couldn't *bombard* me if I asked my contrition to *drop* in on this *drove* of scoundrels, because it would *definitely defuse* their *combustibility*, and my life wouldn't be such a *comic strip*. The Blessed Mother could *surround* me with this *surveillance*, because the Visitation was really the *prophecy* that my contrition would bring about this *propitious* result.

One may imagine the *delight* that Jesus took in *delineating* these guidelines that could keep us from being spiritually *delinquent.* He wants us to feel less *hungry* and not stay *hung up* on love-*starvation*, because his *stash* of love is not *static.* We are the *pagans* who feel this hunger *pain*, but we *forsake* this *foul foundation* on this *fourth* day of the novena and get the *analgesic* which is the *relief* of the Christian *religion* by *analyzing* our *anarchy.*

At ten o'clock on the circle Adam and Eve's *honeymoon* ended, because they decided not to *honor* God's request to use sex only to become mother and father. When sex stopped serving a *reproductive* function, it was the *requiem* for the divine sweetness, because new life was *conceived* in a *concupiscent condition* and *unconditional* love had to flee into the *unconscious* mind of man. The *coincidence* that resulted was that our parents' *coitus* left us out in the *cold*, so as children a *cozy* relationship with God is what we *craved* and couldn't *get.* The *geyser* of the divine sweetness had dried up in our hearts, so we would have to consult the Holy *Ghost* all over again in order to get it restarted.

Adam and Eve provided us with this *umbilical cord* that makes us take *umbrage* with one another, because when they became *father* and mother their *fears* made us stop *feeling* the *felicitous fellowship* of the Holy Spirit. *Ferocious feuding* between men and *nations* makes us fear we have *Nazi neighbors*, because the *fiend's fierceness* started these *fights* when Adam took off his *fig leaf.* God's *umbrella policy* of unconditional love didn't protect Adam and Eve, because they introduced the *pollutant* of *sex appeal*, and it wasn't a good *sextant* for our celestial guidance. Therefore, at ten o'clock on the circle we need to stop trying to feel lovable in the *shabby shack* of sex-addiction we all got *shackled* to in the *shade* of the apple tree.

We had become *covetous* from the *cradle*, so Jesus invented the *craftsmanship* that could end this *craving.* He opened the *school* in which the study of our childhood *scolding* would let us even the *score* and *let* go of the *lethal lethargy* called original sin. We are all *woebegone*, because we *wolfed* down this nonsense but can recover at ten o'clock on the circle with the help of the *lady* who deals with *lagging* spirits by giving them God's *lagniappe.* She *mashes* the forces of ego that *mask* God's benevolence and ends the *masochism* of original sin with her Immaculate Conception. She takes us to the *mason* who built the structure that ends this *masquerade*, so when we go to *Mass*, let's *mass-produce* the Fruits and remember that the Eucharist is the *master key* to this *master plan.*

Our divine sweetness can be *reapportioned* as a result of our *reappraisal* of our upbringing, because it gives us a *rearing* in which Jesus, Mary, and Joseph *rearm* us with their *reassurance*. The *upbraiding* we received during our *upbringing* was the *down*-dragging that left us *downright downtrodden*, and therefore we all need to be *taken in* by the Holy Family in order to get this *take-home pay*.

God gave me Jesus as my *buddy*, because he *budgets* the sweetness I lost when my parents were in the *buff*. He helps me stop being *buffaloed* by original sin, because he is a *buffer* between it and the *buffet* of the Fruits I seek. He reverses the *accident* of my original sin and enables my behavior to give God *acclaim*.

At the 11-5 o'clock axis of the second circle the divine sweetness is seen as *native* to us, because it is the *natural product* of our hearts and was not ruined by *Satan* the *profane professor* who cooked up the *satirical sauce* that turned us all into *savages*. We are all *heretics* as a result of the *heritage* of original sin, but we are not *marooned* on this island, because our souls are *married* at this time to Jesus. Our *piety* prevents our spiritual hunger from making us *pig* out, because Jesus gives us the divine sweetness, which is the *glucose* that heals our *gluttony*. As *kids* we don't realize that our sweetness can't be *killed*, but now that we are adults, we can ask it to *kindle* our *kindness*.

The divine sweetness was *already* at the *altar* of our hearts when Satan *altered* it, so we need to *examine* the *rude examples* in our behavior which are *exceptions* to its *rule*. When we lost God's *favor*, we took to *fawning* on our parents, and it has plunged us into *sin* ever *since*. We stopped being *sincere* about wanting the *sinecure* of a relationship with God, so we introduced the ups and downs that have made our lives *sine curves*.

At the *eleventh* hour the *elixir* of the divine sweetness awakens us to the *elocution* of *Elohim* that Adam and Eve enjoyed in the Garden of Eden, so His *eloquence* doesn't *elude* us. God's *voice* connects with our *volition*, and no man can put this bond *asunder*, because we have the Holy Spirit's *asylum*.

At the *twelve* o'clock axis we stop *twiddling our thumbs*, because we are in the *twilight* of our ego-addiction, and the *twins* called heart-mind and soul-strength *twine* around one *another*. They put an end to ego's *antics*, so we become "meek and humble souls," because our pride is no longer the *adulterant* that *advances* the cause of the *adversary* in our lives. We no longer have this *thorn* in our side, because our *remorse* has *thought* it out and *removed* this *reprehensible representa-*

tive who only *reproduces repulsive reruns* in our behavior. God *orchestrates* our behavior through our Holy *Orders*, because our will is the priest whose *etiquette* is determined by the *Eucharist.*

It has been worth the *review* of my *revilement* to bring about this *revision.* I *diverged* from the *divine* sweetness, but my contrition *vaporized* these sentiments that left me at *variance* with the *various* Fruits of the Spirit. I had *accommodated* myself to discord, but when I became *accompanied* by the gifts of wisdom and fear of the Lord, I *accomplished* a worthwhile *accord.* My *awe* said anchors *aweigh*, because I had become *self-assured* and *Self-aware.*

I have been *lured* by *lust's luster*, but my *prick* only made me take *pride* in my repressed feelings, which are the *odds and ends* that gave me *odious* behavior, so I have gone on an *odyssey* in which I have confronted this *Oedipus Complex.* There was a *line-up* of women

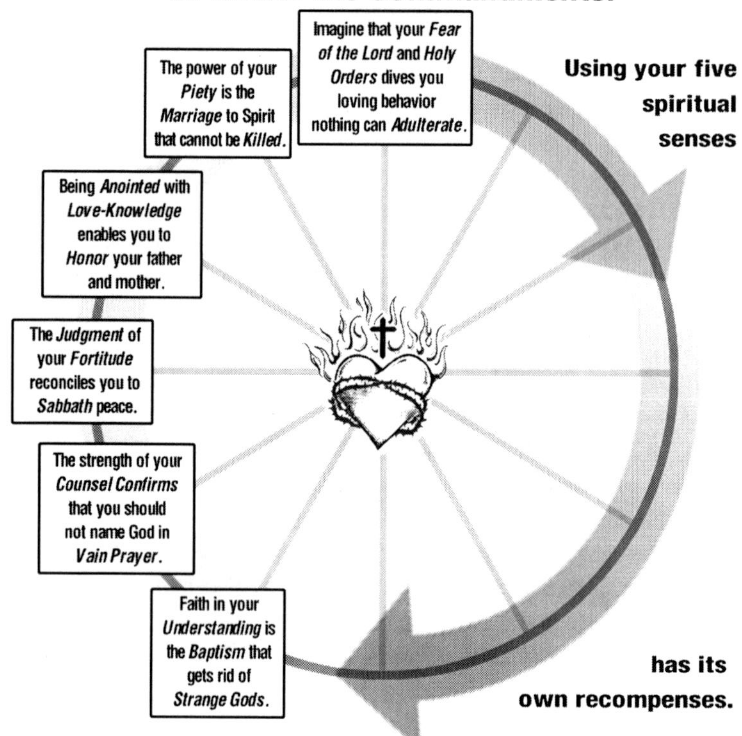

with whom I *lingered* speaking *lingerie lingo* but finally pulled the *wool* off my eyes by wondering how *word* sequences could do the *work* of making a *linguistic link* with God. My divine sweetness was *bottled up*, because the *bottom line* was it couldn't be found on *linen* sheets. At first I thought sex was a *bona fide bonanza*, but eventually I got sick of the *bonbon* and wanted back my *bond* with God. Ever since our *ancestor* Adam regarded God as *ancillary* to his *androgens* the history of man has been full of these *anecdotes*, and they did not make me feel like an *angel.*

Before the fall man's will was *fastened* to God but after the fall man got on the *fast-track* to nowhere, because his will was *scuttled* on a *sea* of *troubles* that *trounced* him. Parents tended to *censure* their children making it necessary for all of us to take a *census* of our repressed feelings in order to be *centered* in God. One *version* of our self-esteem is the one obtained in a parent *versus* child contest, and the other is available through the *vertical* axis of the second circle which gives us spiritual *verve.* Life is less *taxing* when we seek this *tax shelter*, because the vertical axis is our *haven* where we *haven't havoc*, and it prevents our wills from being *hawks* that go *haywire.* Our five senses were awakened on the first circle to help us get this *impression*, so let's not feel *imprisoned* in *impropriety* and be aware that we can *improve.*

Chapter 14: My *Will* Is the *Wimp* that Swallows the *Pill* of the *Pimp*.

When Adam made the *incursion* into Eve's *incurved* area, Satan made it possible for our childhood fears to be considered *indecipherable*. In Eden we became *independent* from God, so let's go through an *in-depth* examination of these *indescribable* sufferings.

The *Trinity* will help us take this *trip* through our *trite* repressed feelings if we make up our minds to settle for no less than *triumph*. The Father, Son, and Holy *Spirit* can make us the *spitting image* of something rather more *splendid* that the *spoilsports* who raised us, so let's *conquer* these feelings *conscientiously* by asking the Christ-*consciousness* for help. When our heart-mind and soul-strength get on this *wavelength* they will not *waver*, because it is their job to establish the *rapport* that leads to a *rapprochement* with God.

Silly feelings that	make *simpletons*	commit *sins*.
Our **fear** of being unlovable	is the ***inferiority***	that *inflames* our **pride**.
Hurt is the *hydraulic*	that enables ***self-pity***	to *sell* us our **envy**.
Our ***anger*** is the *animosity*	*that causes* ***grandiosity***,	so our **anger** makes *reruns* of our *resentments*.
Guilt is being so *gullible*	that you feel *favored* by your *fears*	and *slip* into ***sloth***.

Depression deputizes	our *hurt* to *hurtle* us	*automatically* into ***avarice***.
Bizarre **symptoms** result, because we are *blackmailed* by	*anecdotes* from our past that made us *angry*,	so let's not *gloss* over this ***gluttony***.
Rather let's *prevent* our *pride*	from being the *luminary*	who *lures* us into ***lust***.

We are on the *trend* to *trepidation*, but we can sound the *beeper* of our remorse. We can improve our *behavior* by not allowing this *sequence* of repressed feelings to be our drill *sergeant*. We can *read* the *real reasons* we have for behaving as we do. We can use this *index* of insights to determine how our parents were *Indian givers* and improve our outlook. We can empty this *account* and see to it that what *accrues* is not *accursed*.

Each feeling in this scheme is more *reprehensible* than the one before it, because it *represents* the *repression* of it, which is the act of spiritual sloth *begun* by Satan in Eden on *behalf* of making us *behave* badly.

Our subconscious mind is the *storehouse* that blows up these *storms*, but we can be *acquitted* from this *acrimony*, because our heart-mind and soul-strength can gain us pardon *across-the-board*. The fires of love were originally *stoked* up in our hearts, but then Satan *stole* the fire, and the divine sweetness passed right through our *stomachs* without getting absorbed. We *stomp* on the divine sweetness even today, because our hearts of *stone* come from Adam the *Stone Age stooge* who passed his love, joy, and peace in his *stool*. Nevertheless, we don't have to *stoop* to this degradation and can *stop storing* our fear, hurt, and anger. We just need to remember that when we *defend* our repressed feelings we *defer* eliminating our *defiance*, and the seven *transgressions* listed above take us on a rapid *transit* to our own hell on earth.

When Eve ate the *apple*, she installed this *appliance* which is the *propaganda propeller* called ego. She fell victim to Satan's *shakedown*, which dictated that we *shall* be *shallow shams* and our lives a *shambles*, because we have not worked through this *shame*. Satan *carved* out the *cascade* of repressed feelings shown above, and God was no longer *eminent* in our lives, because Satan had become the *emissary* of these repressed *emotions*. Our *grandiosity* may seem to be engraved in *granite*, but we can still be *granted* a reprieve and be the *grapes* who get back on the vine.

Hell said *hello* to heaven when the two *insurgents* had *intercourse*, because Satan began *interfering* with our *interiors*. He *interjected* the *evil* that began *intermarrying* with good, so it *evolved* into these *exaggerated exasperations* by which he *manipulates mankind*. We are *very vexed* as a result of this *vice*, so we need to look in the *mirror* when we go through these *mishaps* in order to get back what we *missed*.

Eve was the *geisha* who thought lust was a *gem*, so God gave us heart-mind and soul-strength as the *gendarmes* of our *gender* identity *issues*. We think that God *isn't* when we scratch this *itch*, so it widens the *gap* between us and God, but we aren't in the *Garden* of Eden and don't have to *sow* these fears that make husbands and wives *sparring partners*. Therefore, let's not let our *oedipal offensives* and *Electra electricity* make us *warlike* instead of *warmhearted* toward one another. Adam and Eve's *inability* to resist a little *in-and-out* left us with these *incestuous inclinations*, because the *courtship covenant* they started in Eden *covered* up the mother's love men *coveted* from the *cradle* and *cranked* up this *craving* that drove them *crazy*. When love went below the *waist*, men *wanted* to eat this *morsel* called *motherly* love, but the *motionless motive* from Eden *slowed* this process and left them *smitten*, so this *hungry husband hypothesis* turned them into *ravenous reactionaries*, which had bad *spin-off* for them in their roles as *spouses*. It was a *war* of the nerves, because many men weren't capable of *mourning* the loss of this motherly *mouthful* and just went on *hankering* for this *happy* result and *harassing* their wives. The *forbidden force* from Eden made us *forget* this *formula* that the *Creator* gave each *creature* prior to Adam and Eve's *fornication*, but the *credentials* called heart-mind and soul-strength are *credible crime-fighters*, so let's get our rears in *gear* and put God's sweetness back in our *genes*. When our remorse *tunes* in these *two genealogy generals* to our ego's *tyranny* they will make our *family* tree *famous* for love of God the *Father*, and He will *favor* us with His *generosity*. We just need to *unbuckle* our *unconditional* love and *conquer* this *conspiracy* from hell that makes us *contentious* in our marriages. Adam was the *stubborn stud* who didn't want to *study* this *hazard* of using his little *head* as a *headlight*, but I prefer to make my big head the divine *headquarters* and make some *headway*.

The *gulf* between us and God is filled with our *gullible gulps*. We have all sustained this *injury* as a result of the *injustices* from our childhood, but they don't have to be *inlaid* in us permanently. Therefore, when we *clobber* our loved ones with our anger, we just need to follow the *clock face* of the circles and become more *congenial* by getting rid of our *congestion* of repressed feelings.

We need to *spice* up our ego's *spiel* with our remorse to turn off the *spillway* of our fear, hurt, and anger. Remorse is the *cheerleader* who gets the Big *Cheese* to be the *chef* of the divine sweetness, but first we need to understand the family *chemistry* that came from Eve's not *cherishing* her *cherry*. Then we get a load off our *chest* after we have *chewed* our cud.

My *will* developed a case of the *willies*, because it was the *wimp* that swallowed this *pill* of Satan the *pimp*. My family was in *servitude* to this *sewage* that flowed from Adam and Eve's *sex act*, so we all got *propositioned* by our egos. Our egos *prostituted* our wills, so we *jilted* God, but I do not intend to live with this *jinx*. I can get rid of my *jitters* by not allowing my will to be the *john* who seeks the services of this *whore*. I just need to be *wide-awake* to the *fear* that makes it *feasible* for my *hurt* to *hurtle* me into my *anger's angle*. Then I won't be Satan's *guilty guinea pig* and won't feel my *depression's depth*. My ego has been a *costly costume*, but I do not intend to allow this *coterie* of repressed feelings *infect* my mind with this *infirmity*.

Nevertheless, for many years my repressed feelings didn't *cotton* to the sentiment of remorse, because I was the lazy *couch* potato who could not *cough up* these insights. Therefore after much trial and error I realized that I needed to *scrutinize* my *scuffles* to come up with a *sculpture* that was not made of this *scum*. For a long time my *sloth* made me the *slouch* who *sloughed* off these *slovenly* feelings as being part of the human condition, which only made it more *slow* for me to recover. My sloth had given me the *latitude* to live in this latrine, so I had not gotten a *leg up* on the *legacy* of love which only my remorse could make *legal*. I had followed the satanic *path* of my *pathetic pathology* and did not understand that my *regret* had to make the forces of love *regroup*.

Nevertheless, at three o'clock on the circle we can have some *change of pace* in the *chapel*. We can give the *slip* to our *sloth* by *dissecting* our *dissembled* feelings in order to *disseminate* peace. We have to take this *crossroad* by getting a *cross section* of the *cross talk* from our childhoods and use it to solve the *crossword puzzle* of our behavior with our remorse.

Our fortitude *overcomes* our sloth and prevents it from making us *overreact*. It *interfaces* our will with God, ends the *interference* of our egos, and enables our *decisions* to flow from our sense of *deco-*

rum. Fortitude is the *handyman* who figures out how we got *harmed* and then *reopens* the case and makes the *repair*. Fortitude has the *guts* to figure out how we got *gypped* and represents the *determination* to confront what's *detestable* in order to *dethrone* our egos. *Fortitude* gets rid of that which is *foul* and turns on the *fountain* of divine sweetness in our hearts. Its *payload* is the *peace* of mind that keeps us on an even *keel*, so let's use this *keen kernel*, because it is the *key* to *kicking* a really bad habit.

Fortitude enables us to *comprehend* the *compromise* we made with the *fears* that *feast* on our self-esteem and won't *rest* until he achieves the *result* of *enabling* us to understand why we *compute* these *enemies* as our *comrades*. He is the *relentless religious* leader who is in charge of our *relinquishment* and the *hunter* of the long-buried *hurt* feelings whose *hydraulics* turn us into *angry animals*. He realizes that our happiness is at *stake*, so he *stalks* his *quarry* until he gets an answer to the *queasy question* and is always *chafing* at the bit to find a way to stop our ego's *chain reaction*. He realizes that our *insights* into our ego-driven behavior are the *inspiring installments* that *outfit* us with a better *outlook*, so he hunts down these *dragons* from our childhoods knowing that certain moments of *dramatic suspense* made us *swallow* some *drastic draughts* of *dread*. Then he *returns* to the scene of the crime to bring about a *reverent revision* through the use of our contrition. Our *relatives* didn't always leave us feeling very *relaxed* as children, so our fortitude depends on that *reliable remedy* known as *remorse*, which never *fails* to handcuff the criminal and give us a *fair shake*.

Our sloth has us thinking that our *conflicts* with our fellow man are something we deserve to be *congratulated* for, but our fortitude is our keeper of the peace. Our fortitude is always on the *trail* of our *tranquility*, so let's use it to *reach* an understanding of why we are so *reactive*. Fortitude uses *remorse* as his *remote control*, so he goes *back* to the point where we took a *bad* turn and brings us the *baggage* so as to *lighten* this *living load* of *loathsome lobbyists*. Fortitude enables us to feel the moral *anguish* that heals this *animosity* in which we *languish*, so let's stop *lapsing* into behaviors we *regret* and put our sloth through this *rehabilitation*. It is a spiritual *conversion* that will give our inner child a sense of *conviction*, so let's have this *convivial convocation* and learn to tell God that we're *sorry*, because this *SOS* will lead us into a *happier harbor*.

Fortitude may be a *hunky-dory hunter*, but for many years I didn't send him off to overcome these *hurdles*, so I didn't enjoy this *shelter*. I felt that I was the captain of my own *ship* and had the right to *shirk* this duty if I wanted, so I dedicated myself to the *devil-may-care dexterity* that only made my *aggravation* more *agile*, and the devil never lost a chance to make me *twist* by getting in his *two-cents-worth*.

My particular *hang-up* at that time was thinking that my *happiness* depended on a *wealth* of possessions that I couldn't *wean* myself from. It was a *guarantee* that my *guilt* and *depression* would leave me feeling *deranged*, because my possessions were the *weapons* I *wore* to *protect* myself from the *protracted* suffering that these two feelings could *provide*. Trying to *weasel* out of my guilt and depression kept me *under the weather*, because at that time I didn't think that my fortitude was enough of a *honcho* to make an *honest* appraisal and heal my wounded *honor*. The *auxiliary* of my remorse wasn't *available* to stop this *avalanche* of *avarice* that can be seen at four o'clock on the circle. I was a student in this *collection college* that *collided* with my humility and to speak *colloquially* had me full of shit, because it put me in *collusion* with this *cologne* that really reeks of the contents of the *colon*. I *entertained* myself *enthusiastically* with these *enticements* to which I felt *entirely entitled* and eventually got into an *indebtedness* that was traceable to the *indecisiveness* caused by my sloth.

Nevertheless, this *foulness* at *four* o'clock on the circle eventually responded to the *foxy franchise* known as my patience. My patience was the *crane* that I would later *crank* up in order to lift myself out of this *crap* into which I'd *crashed*, but at the time it was packed in the *crass crate* called ego which did nothing but feed my *cravings*. Therefore, at *four* o'clock I had this *fragility* that at *five* o'clock I tried to *fix* by fanning the *flames* of my *gluttony*. I didn't enlist the help of my piety at the other end of the diagonal to satisfy my *gnawing* spiritual hunger, so I suffered from this *meanness mechanism* and didn't have any *kindness kinetics*.

In my single years I was caught up in the *goo* of chasing *good-looking* women, because the *diabolical* dose on my vertical axis known as pride in lust hadn't yet responded to the piety-kindness on the 11–5 o'clock *diagonal*. I had my *puberty* in *public* and considered myself a "serial *monogamist*." My ego's *monologue* had me dedicated to this *monomania*, so the *important* act that culminated these relationships *imposed* an *impossible* task on me, because I felt like an *impostor* and was rendered *impotent*. I thought it was a *perfunctory* behavior in comparison with the *perfusion* of love that I wanted.

On the vertical axis my heart-mind and soul-strength were my spiritual *scouts*. They *scowled* at me when I used my *prick* to focus my *pride* on my *lust*, because it excluded *lyrical* love. They realized that my *faith* in this *fake* would make the *real rebate* of that *precious* commodity known as the divine sweetness take the *fall* and that I would remain in this *predicament* until I changed my *preference*. Nevertheless, they were my *champions* of *change* of *heart* and had the aptitude to *heave* out these *hedonistic* sins, because they used the two *Gifts* of wisdom and fear of the Lord. These two Gifts could help me get the *gist* of how the *glamorous* allure of my pride in my lust spoke mainly to the *glands* between my legs and would produce the *glaring* error of cutting off my spiritual *gleanings*.

Hence, the *sequence* of *serene* events that tranquilized the wild beast on the *vertical* axis of the second circle was based on eliminating the *vestiges* known as pride in lust. Man's *devotion* to this *diabolical* notion was based on the *convincing convolutions* that these *simple-minded sins* from Eden had brought about in his thinking. Satan knew that man would not be able to *resist* these *restless* urges and that his bad *temper* would *result* from this *temptation*. Man began to believe in the *world* power of the *worm*, so this *consolation* prize from hell furthered Satan's *conspiracy* and made man think that it was *worthless* to examine his *wound*.

Nevertheless, man's remorse could *penetrate* this gloom, because it was the *penicillin* that could cure this venereal disease. Man had got himself into the *penile penitentiary* called ego, but he could get out by waving the *pennant* of his contrition, because when man was *pensive* in this way, the Holy Spirit would descend on him just like it did on the disciples at *Pentecost*. When Satan succeeded in convincing Eve to flaunt her *girlie glamour* in front of Adam, man's sex *drive* turned him into Satan's *drone*, and man considered spiritual pursuits a *drudgery* after that. Man had become a spiritual *peon*, because *people* lacked spiritual *pep*. *However*, the *howling* one did when he felt *sad* about Satan's *salesmanship* always had a *salutary* effect, because then one's *wisdom* could end this *witching with* one's *fear* of the Lord.

Unrestrained crying caused these *culprits* to face the *cure* of this *unrest*, because our *shame* placed these *shiftless shirkers* in the *custody* of these two Gifts of the Holy Spirit. When wisdom and fear of the Lord got together, they formed the *federal* government that could give man the spiritual *feedback* he needed, but *both* Gifts needed to be on the same team to prevent man from being *bothered*. Man had remained in *league* with forces that had left him with a *lean* spiritual bank account, because fear of the Lord without wisdom had left him in *awe* of false gods. This *awful awkwardness* had resulted from the *nonintervention norm* that made man think it was *normal* not to *focus* on his *foibles*, so what had gone *awry* during man's childhood gave Satan a chance to use his *axe ad lib* on their vertical *axis* when they were *adults*. Nevertheless, the two *presents* of wisdom and fear of the Lord could still be given to those who intended to *prevail* over these fears. These two presents therefore made up the *coaching coalition* for those who had been *taken in* by their egos but who were determined to use these *talents* that would help them look *inside* themselves to find the *insinuations* they needed to *inspect*.

The *sins* of pride and lust had formed a *sinister partnership* in the mind of man, but the *Passion* of Jesus ended the *antagonisms* that flowed out of Adam and Eve's *antics* under the apple tree. Jesus accomplished this by providing the *antidotes* of the vertical axis known as the Eucharist and Holy Orders, so the spiritual *sabotage* that took place in the *sack* was reversed by these two *sacraments*. The problem was that the *sexual shakedown* in Eden had passed along the *heterosexual hex* that resulted in *marginal marital relationships*, because without sexual *release* there was no *relief* for man, and the heart of man had become an *addiction address*.

Wisdom was meant to end this *witching* by teaming up with *fear* of the Lord, because together they could accomplish the *feat* of preventing man's will from turning into a funny *uncle* who liked to *unclothe* himself inappropriately. Man had gotten out of touch with *unconditional* love, but these two Gifts could lend a *hand*, because they were the *handle* that could prevent man's *perplexity* from turning into sexual *perversions*. Satan had sunk this *homosexual hook* into some of the boys' hearts, because they hadn't *gathered* enough love from their fathers, and it left them feeling *gauche*. Their *maleness* had been so *maligned* that the *gay gearshift* in their hearts gave them the *gender* confusion that attracted them to the *genitals* of other *gentlemen*. These *fellows* felt *feminine*, because their *masculinity* had been *massacred*, but the *lack* of a mother's love also made some of the girls grow up to feel like *lackluster ladies*. This *femininity fiasco* was the *lesbian lesion* that made them behave like *sirens* toward other women who had joined this *sisterhood*.

The lack of a *salutary* relationship with the parent of the *same* sex had made homosexuals go *haywire* in bed and left heterosexuals with the *haze* at *work* that made them feel *worse* than *worthless*. However, men didn't have to go around with *terrorized testicles*, and women didn't have to suffer from *outclassed ovaries*, because regardless of their sexual *orientation*, the pride they took in their lust is what made them *ornery*. Their misplaced *love loyalty* was the *gauge* in both *gay* and *straight* persons that gave Satan the chance to put this *strangle hold* on their sweetness, so if they didn't want to feel like *finks* in or out of bed, they would have to fight *fire* with fire. They had *spun* a web of falsehoods in their minds as children, and the only cure was to find the *spiritual anchor* known as Holy Orders that could connect them to the Eucharist, which was the same *ancient* substance known as the divine sweetness. The *Eucharist* could then *evangelize* their wills, and their Holy *Orders* could restore them to their *original* innocence, but first they would have to *unburden* themselves of their *uncleanliness* so that their *unconditional* love would not remain *underdeveloped*. They had to *grieve* the decision to love with *grinding groins* and stop giving Satan the chance to use their little *heads* to lead around their *hearts*.

The *altar* in my heart was *altogether* contaminated in this way, because the *diminutive dimwit* of my will had been deafened by this *ruckus* and wasn't a very dependable *rudder*. However, in his first act of public *ministry* Jesus showed me that my sins are *minor-league* players in comparison with the Fruits.

The *book* that brought me this *boon* was *The Life of Mary as Seen by the Mystics*.† The day before the *Wedding* of Cana Jesus explained how our remorse is a *weightlifter* who can take a *load* off our hearts if we just *lobby* with it in the right way.

"Jesus organized a game in which the men, sitting in a circle on the ground, tossed different fruits to one another according to certain rules." Anyone who felt *nervous* was shown how to make a *new* start the *next* day, because: "Before the banquet, Jesus organized another remarkable game for the men in the garden. He placed various flowers, plants, and fruits around a large table on which there was a pointer that rotated on a pivot until it stopped before the prize of the person who had twirled it. In this game, which the men now began to play, nothing occurred by mere chance. Each prize somehow had a definite significance related to the qualities and faults of its winner. And as each of the players in turn won his particular prize, Jesus made a brief and profound comment. Yet the person-

---

†*The Life Of Mary As Seen By The Mystics*, Raphael Brown, ed., St. Benedict Press & TAN Books, 2009, is a compilation of the visions of the four great Catholic mystics Ven. Anne Catherine Emmerich, Ven Mary of Agreda, St. Bridget of Sweden and St. Elizabeth Schoenau; p. 175.

al application of His words was grasped only by the man to whom they were directed. The others found in them merely some broadly edifying teaching. But the individual himself was deeply moved and felt that Jesus had indeed seen into the most secret thought of his heart and conscience."

The *message* of the *Messiah* seemed to be that the circles were the *grid* upon which our *grief work* should be built in order to get rid of *worry*. We are all *tormented* by our fears, but if we *toss* the components on each diagonal of the circles *back* and forth, we will be less *baffled*, because the twelve *powers* will *powwow* with the *Gifts*, which will be *given* to us so that our *Fruits* can come to *Fruition*.

One *particular passion* of the *Pastor* was for the *first* Fruits to *fit* in with the *last* Fruits so as to lay down the *law* to the sins. Consequently, faith is the *envoy* that visits *envy* to generate love, mildness is the *anesthetic* for *anger* that generates joy, and chastity fits in the *slot* of *sloth* to generate peace.

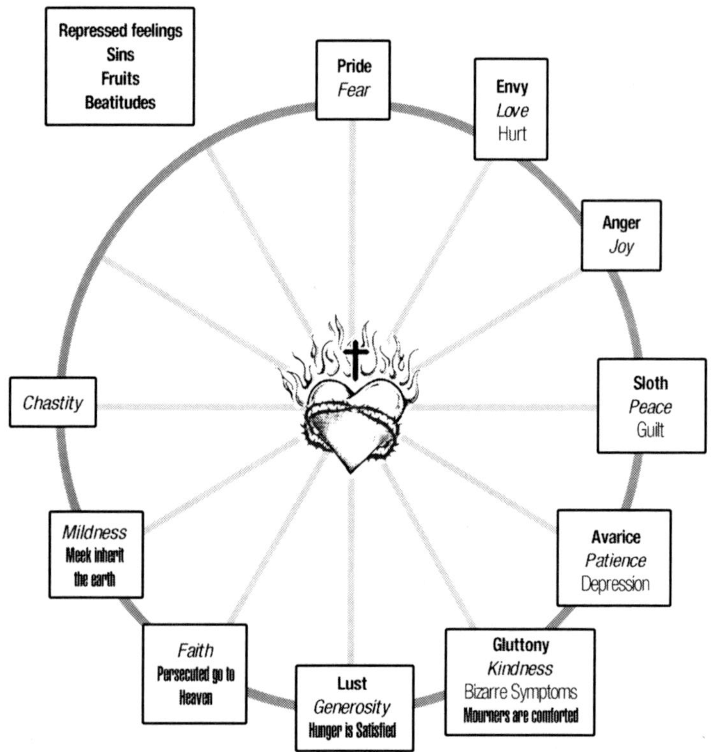

Jesus *taught* the men at the Wedding of Cana that the *teamwork* between their fears and their *remorse* would *render* their fears helpless and *encourage* the Fruits on the two *ends* of these three diagonals to vanquish the sin in the *middle* that thought it was so *mighty*. Each sin would then be *entrapped* and *enveloped* in two Fruits. The *game* was designed to be able to address the entire *gamut* of man's repressed feelings and span the *gap* between man and God. It was designed to teach man to *separate* his fears from his ego so that they wouldn't produce so many *septic sequels*.

Man had run *amuck* but could still *analyze* his *anarchy*. He just had to tell the *sad saga* that would enable him to *hang loose* and feel *happy*. Man had to *fish* for the fears that gave him *fits*, because he had become *heir* to a *hell* on *earth*, but *Easter* made it *easy* to *eat* the Fruits. He just had to *eavesdrop* on his *woes* in order to *implement* the *improvement* known as "Thy kingdom come" and live in a *wonderful world*. Man could become *innocent* rather than *insane inside* himself, because these three *pairs* of Fruits could heal these *pangs* and allow him to *outgrow* his *outlaw* ego which *owned* his will. Man could *advance* spiritually by going on this *adventure*, which would further the *plan* of bringing heaven and earth together on the *planet*. It was a *strategy* to get rid of our repressed feelings, which is the *stratum* that makes us *stray* from God. Then we could *foil* Satan, return to the *fold*, and enjoy the *streak* of good fortune that results from the *stream* of the divine sweetness.

The sins will not *poach* on our peace of mind, and we will have the divine sweetness in our *pocket* if we put our contrition on the *podium* and ask it to recite its *poetry poignantly* until we get the *point*. The *slogan* of our *sloth* is that *idleness idolatry ignites ignorance*, but it is also possible to subject our *indolence* to the *industrious indweller* known as our fortitude. Fortitude has the gift of *gab* that can end the *gag order* of ego and make spiritual *gains*, so let's change *lanes* and use this *language* that will end this *languor* once and for all. This *lethargy* only blocks our *levelheadedness*, so let's stand up to our *sloth* and tell him in no uncertain terms that we do not intend to allow his *sluggishness* to keep us in a spiritual *slumber*. We can *awaken* from these *awful* nightmares by realizing that as children we *succumbed* to our ego's *suction* but that as adults it is possible to *sue* for the recovery of our *sugar*.

Our sloth is the *lazy lawyer* who has *led* us into trouble, but our fortitude is our *attitude attorney* and can end the *attrition* caused by these *layers* of *smug smut*. Our fortitude takes our *contrition* by the hand, and then they both have a *conversation* with the *poison* that *polarizes* us in our relationships. Mary is the *energetic enforcer* who *polices* this *policy* of the New Covenant, which is that we can all become more *polished* in this way. Therefore, let's *utilize* this *utopian* concept and get out of this *hell* on earth by asking for her *help*. Her Immaculate Conception makes us *pure* by putting us through this *purgatory*, so let's *tune* in to this *tunnel* of love and recognize that the *light* at the end will allow us to know that we are all created in the *likeness* of God.

Planet earth will never be the *same* as a result of this *sanction*, because the New Covenant is the *forgiveness formula* that our *fortitude* brings to bear on the *foul foundation* known as ego-addiction. Jesus *started* this *stepwise sterilization* of these bad *germs* in the Garden of *Gethsemane*, so let's *confess*, turn our fears into *confetti*, and *celebrate* the *celestial pardon* that allows us to sit in the *parlor* without having *paroxysms* of anger. We can be *governed* by God, so let's welcome *change*, *face* our *fears*, restore order to our *chaos*, and enjoy the *feast* of the Fruits. The New Covenant is the principle of the *Lord's lost* and *found* that turns on the *fountain* of the divine sweetness, so let's *remove* our *renegade* fears through our *renunciation* power and *find* our *finesse*. The *omission* of our contrition will only make our fears *omnipotent*, so let's face our *perpetual perplexity*. Our *qualms* only make us *quarrel* and *bedevil* us with bad *behavior*, so let's make this *switch* that will earn us God's *sympathy*.

The switch I wanted to make was to *allay* the *allegations* that decreased my *allegiance* to God and reverse my original sin which is an *allegory* for my love *allergy*. I needed to *sever* myself from the *severe sewage* that had flowed from my parents' *sex* act. *Hankering* after their approval had brought strictly *haphazard* results, and this *soft spot* had left me *soiled*. Jesus *explained* this *exploitation* in Matthew 10:34-39:

> "Do not suppose that my mission on earth is to spread peace. My mission is to spread, not peace, but division. I have come to set a man at odds with his father, a daughter with her mother, a daughter-in-law with her mother-in-law: in short to make a man's enemies those of his own household. Whoever loves father or mother, son or daughter, more than me is not worthy of me. He who will not take up his cross and come after me is not worthy of me."

My *unresolved* dependency needs had left me in the state of *unrest* that arose from my *one-track* mind, because my *relationship* with my *parents* was a *one-way* street and never enabled me to *partake* of the *remedy* the *Pastor* served at the Last Supper. I felt a sense of short *shrift*, because my heart was the *shrine* where my parents' sense of *thrift* left me feeling *throttled*. Nevertheless, I said good *riddance* to the *riddle* by figuring that my parents were not *required* to *requite* my love. It was a *loveless loyalty*, but God's love could give me a *lawful lease* on life and *liberate* me from this *lie*. It was a big *fib* that this *fiction* that *hinged* on the *histrionics* of my *home* life had to *fiddle* with my *fidelity* to God, so I asked Him to give me His *legitimate* love so I wouldn't feel like a *lemon*.

I had a *gunnysack* that was full of the *gunpowder* called *historical* anger, because I hadn't *ruminated* over this *sad saga* and just kept *sailing* into disaster. My fears became *evasive* as a result of these *events*, and

THE SECOND CIRCLE with the Gifts, the Fruits, the Sacraments, the Sins, the Commandments, and the Novena of Sister Faustina

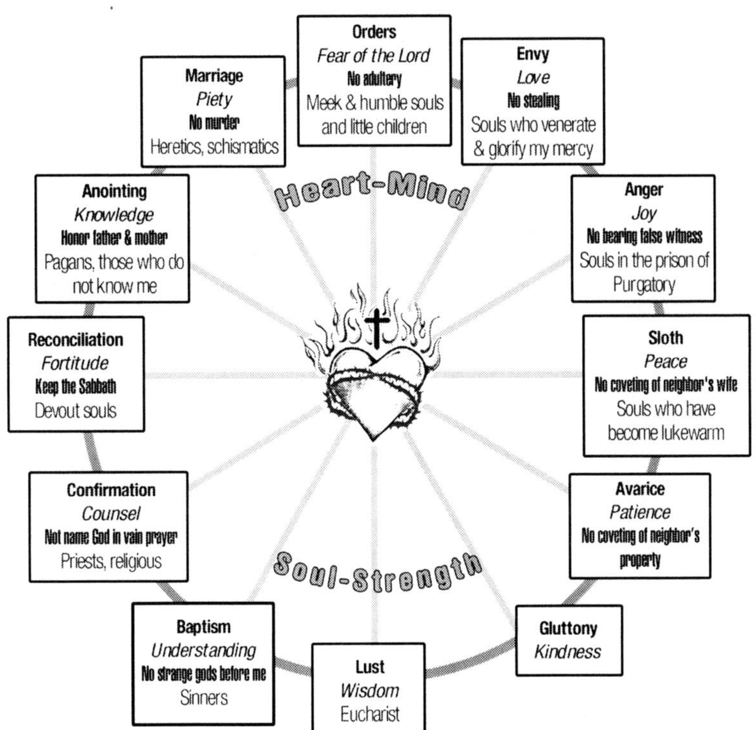

I was *edgy*, because I considered each crumb *edible* and had built an *edifice* of repressed rage that I had to *edit*. I had been *coached* by this *coalition* from hell and had swallowed these *cock-and-bull stories*, which made up the *cocktail* of indoctrinations that Satan used to *coerce* me.

I had to *hark back to* these *harmful* events in order to return to a state of *harmony*. It had to be done *inch by inch*, but each *incident* that I *incised* with my remorse left me with less *incivility*. I had definitely been a *casualty*, but I could *let the cat out of the bag* by *cataloguing* these events with my remorse in order to play *catch-up* ball. I made this *survey*, because I had been a *survivor* of this *outfit* in which *outlandish* behavior resulted from *rancid rancor*. The *sins* of the fathers had *singed* the sons, so I wasn't exactly a *patriot* of heaven and had to be on *patrol* for behaviors that showed that I still *patronized* this hellish *pattern* of *hand-me-down hang-ups*. I also fed my *children* this *chili*, so I hope they keep their *chins* up, and if they see they have become *chips off the old block*, I hope they will *chisel* out a new reality for themselves and not get *typecast* into *roguish roles* as a result of my *tyranny*.

We all *owe* it to ourselves to *own* our *wounds* so as to stop feeling *wretched*. God never *overlooks overt* contrition, so let's *absolutely absolve* our parents of *blame* and not *draw a blank* regarding these *tasteless teachings*. If we *think* through these *thorny threats*, our *penitence* will rid us of *pent-up* anger, so let's not *forget* to *forgive* but rather change our *destiny* by being *determined* not to *run afoul again and again of* these hidden *agendas*. *Mercy* is not *merely* for the asking, because it must be *merited*, so let's not consider it to be *beneath* our dignity to feel the *bereavement* that is attendant to the *death* of these *debits*. God's *clemency* is only available in this *clinch*, so let's not feel *snowed under* when we can *snuggle* up with Him and tell him our *sob stories*. All else is *subterfuge*, so let's *succeed* in earning this *succor* by *suffering* in this way. There is a *reason* for our *recidivism*, so when we get *aggravated*, let's *aggrieve* and get *ahead* by feeling *misty-eyed* over the *misunderstanding*. If we seek the *universal* love source in this way, our *unkindness* will stop getting *unleashed*, and we'll stop feeling *unlovable*. This *entanglement* has *entranced* us all, so let's stop suffering from these *Freudian frills* that allow *strange* gods to have a *strangle hold* on us. *Violating* the first commandment in this way only gives us *violent* behavior, so let's stop trying to *force* love from those who can't give it and take advantage of the better *forecast* for *fair* weather, which is to have *faith* in God.

We will feel less *grumpy* as a result of this *guarantee*, because at one o'clock on the second circle, *love lowers* the boom on the *sullen sultan* known as envy. Envy is the *hankering* for love that robs us of *happiness*, so we should work *hard* to prevent this *jealous Jekyll and Hyde* from putting us in this *jeopardy*. *Frustrated* envy causes our *fulminations*, so let's *snare* this *sneak thief* with our contrition and not try to *steal* love *stealthily*. Let's *convict* him before he starts our *convulsions*, stop *venerating* these guilty *verdicts* from our childhood, and *glorify* God's mercy instead of our *glut* of repressed feelings.

As a child I became an *apprentice approval*-seeker in the *labor union* of ego, and this made me Satan's *lachrymose lackey*. It was a *demanding* job that made me feel *demented*, because every time the tactic failed, I logged in a *demerit*. I lay in this *frustration fuel* and *waged* the *war* that *marred* my first *marriage*, but I eventually created a *demilitarized* zone in my mind by *demobilizing* these forces.

I finally figured that my *parents* were *parenthetical* anyway, because God is my real Father, and all *daddies* are *daft* by comparison. *Providing* me with unconditional love is definitely His *province*, so in the end I assumed that Jesus meant for me to stop taking this *lashing* by welcoming me at the *Last Supper* as a *latecomer*. I stopped trying to *divide* myself from the *divine*.

At two o'clock on the circle my fear, hurt, and anger put on a *rodent rodeo*, because I had *swallowed* each emotion and was eventually *swamped* by this *swarm* that traced out *swastikas* in my stomach. Nevertheless, I *licked* my anger by taking the *lid* off the *lie* that caused it, and I *tanked* up with the joy that formerly *tantalized* me. I had borne false witness against this *neighbor* which was the Fruit of joy, because I had been robbed of *nerve* in my *nest*, so I figured that I could get a better *frame of mind* from my divine *franchise*.

At three o'clock I was a *covetous cowboy*, because sloth was the *lukewarm lullaby* that put out my spiritual *luminescence*. It caused many a *landslide* in this sequence of repressed feelings that only spoke this *language* of *languor*, because I was too lazy to *repent* of the *repercussions* caused by these *reprehensible* feelings. On the other hand, my penitence could *exonerate* an *exorbitant* amount of my repressed anger so that my *comportment* could arise from my *composure*. Therefore, I used the *saving* grace of the *Savior* and asked him to *free* me from the *friction* caused by this *hereditary hex*. Jesus *helped* my wisdom when it felt *hemmed* in by my pride and *insulated* my understanding from the *insult* of envy. My *counsel* made the *countercharge* against my anger, my fortitude *sliced* away my *sloth*, my *knowledge KO'd* my avarice, and my *piety* tore my gluttony into *pieces*. When I felt *bent* out of shape by these sins, the Gifts *bequeathed* themselves to me in order to make me less *berserk*.

The Gifts and the sins were placed at opposite *poles* on the circle by the *polecat's polemics*. Before original sin each Gift had been *unified unilaterally* by God with the corresponding Fruit, but then Satan *interposed* his own *interpretation*, and our *peccadilloes* lined themselves up in this *pecking order* that had the *peculiarity* of his *pedagogy*. Nevertheless, each Gift gets in a *clench* with the corresponding sin with each *click* of the *clock*, because they have the *clout* to *rout* these *rowdies*. The sins *long* for the *loofa* of the Gifts, so let's use these *warriors* to *wash* off these *spots* and enjoy the *spread* of the Fruits.

Satan is the *meddler* who *mediates* the job of making our *kinfolks kiss off* our needs, so sometimes we need to return to our *youth* to see how we got to be such *yo-yos*. If we watch this *cinema* by using the *circles*, we will get a *robust* spirituality, so let's *rock* around the *clock* and get *closure*. God's love has no strings attached, but Satan's *strings* are very *stringent*, so God gave us Mary's Immaculate Conception as the *system* for each *systole* of our *hearts* to warm us at His *hearth*. We do not need to allow Adam's *disobedience* to continue to leave us in this *disorder*, because we can *earn* these blessings *earnestly* and put all of *earth* at *ease* with the blessings of the first *Easter*. Therefore, let's get God's *respect* in this way and enjoy a *respite* from our egos.

We have all been through *biological birth*, but Mary can give us a *better birth*, so let's not remain *ill* with this poor *imitation* when we can *beg* her to *beget* us with her *Immaculate* Conception. When we become *naked* of our defenses by *naming* these *narcotics* in order to go through this *narrow* gate, we will experience this *nativity*. Our *navels* are *navigable* by the *Nazarene*, so let's not behave like *Nazis* when we can *inherit* our original *innocence* by allowing *Christ's chromosomes* to make us *citizens* of heaven. She *wields* this power, because she is God's *wife*, and we can go through spiritual *marriage* by *marshaling* her to our side in our prayer. As Mediatrix of Grace she is our *soul's sounding board* and can teach us how to *trust* the *truth*, whereas our *hormones* only make us *horny*.

What we need most of all is the *perk* of becoming *permanently permeable* to the divine sweetness, and we get this *permission* from one to six o'clock on the second circle. The first three Fruits could *threaten* to peter out were it not for the second *three* that cross the *threshold* from static to dynamic. Patience, kindness, and generosity have the *mouth* of love, joy, and peace and can *move* the *muck* of all seven sins so that the voice of the Fruits will not be *muffled*. The second three Fruits *interconnect* with the first three so as to *interdict* the sins. That way we get God's *generosity*, which is a better kind of *genetic engineering* than Satan gave us by making us *genital geniuses*. In this way our *contagion* can be *contained*, because we will have *removed* the sins that block this *remuneration*. This is the *optimal* way to become an *optimist*.

We can move a *ton* of repressed feelings by grasping them one by one with the *tongs* of our remorse, so let's not live in the *pigsty* caused by this *pile-up*.

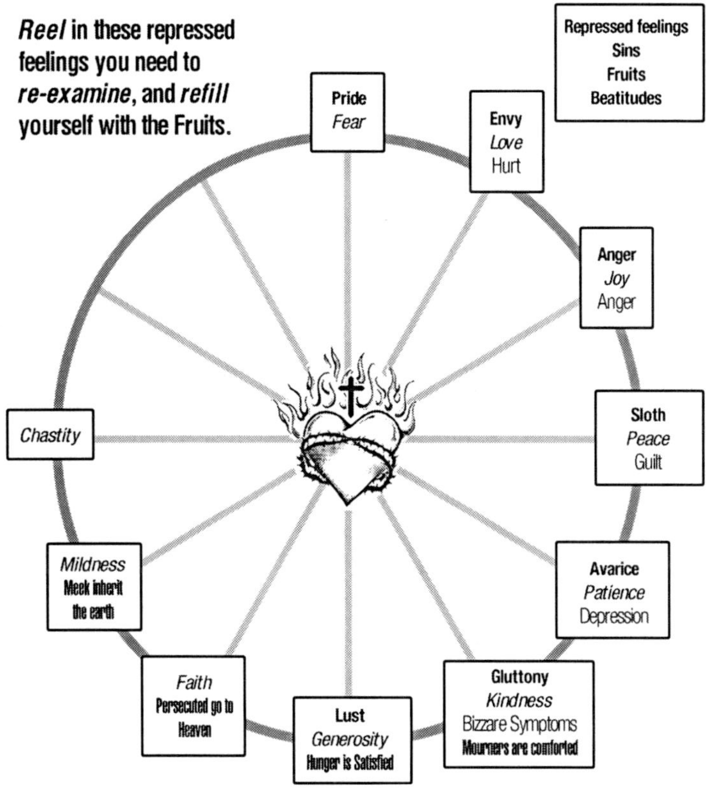

The state of being *in compos mentis* is grown in the *compost* heap of our repressed feelings, because our remorse gives us the *composure* that consists of the *compote* of the nine Fruits of the Spirit. If we *seek* the help of the Sacred Heart, we will become *Self-governed*, because it is the *adviser* with the *affectionate affiliation* that can keep us from feeling *afraid*. The *dysfunction* we have in our relationships comes from the moment when Adam and Eve *each* had the *eagerness* for the other that made God's guidance go *in one ear and out the other.* This is where our *earliest pain* was *painted* on us, and when we feel the appropriate *shame*, we will no longer be *shanghaied* by ego-addiction. The *five* o'clock *fix* of the first *beatitude* therefore *beckons* us to be *mourners*, because the way to get back our *moxie* is to be *comforted* repeatedly until we can see that the divine sweetness is something we all have in *common.* Our *mourning* catches the *mouse* known as our fear of being unlovable by God, so let's not *pamper* this *panic button* known as original sin. The *second* beatitude's *secret* is that spiritual *hunger* can be satisfied, so let's stop *eating* these *éclairs* from *Eden* that make us *edgy.* We behave like *hunks* and *hussies,* but a man's *motherly motion sickness* and a woman's lack of fatherly *magic* make us *hostage* to *hostile* forces and our *marriages* not so *marvelous.* Therefore, it is better to let the *third* beatitude solve this *thorny* problem, because original sin is the *peril* of the *perineum* from which we all suffer, and it deserves to be *persecuted* so that we will all not be left *in the lurch* by our *lust.*

As a result of original sin Satan established a political *platform* in the mind of man which was based on the *platitudes* that give us a *beating*, and that is why Jesus introduced the *beatitudes.* Satan was the *scalper* who made us pay this high price, and that is why his *scam* needs to be *scanned* with our remorse if we are to stop the *scandal.* Satan perpetrated the *rip-off*, but we don't have to be victims of its *ripple effect.* Therefore, when we are *irked* by this *irony* that flowed from Adam and Eve's agony in the garden, let us bring this *parcel* called original sin for *pardon.*

Our souls still suffer from this *emaciation emanation*, but we can *emancipate* ourselves by realizing that we are *satellites* in orbit around the Source of our *satiation.* We are *harebrained* rather than *harmonious*, but we can also go on the *errand* to correct that which is *erroneous.* The *kinetics* of our *kinfolk* don't equal those of God, so let's make His *Kingdom come*, so that our minds can become the *castles* where His Fruits of the Holy Spirit are not our *castoffs.*

I still behave occasionally like a *zombie*, because my heart-mind and soul-strength still dwell in the *zone* of my ego-addiction, which prevents this sperm and egg from *zooming* in to form the *zygote.* Therefore, I need to let my soul-strength *fertilize* my heart-mind so that they can *fetch* this *prodigious* blessing, because they create the *products* of conception that are intended to deliver me from this *pro-*

fane craving that drives me *crazy.* If I *spend* this *sperm* in this way, it will fertilize the *egg* and get rid of *ego*, so I aim to be *formed formally* in this way, and the *format* for this change is the subject of the next leg of the journey. ❧

Chapter 15: The *Hotshot's Hubris* Is *Beaten* by the *Beatitudes*.

I had a lot of *spiritual* pride that made me *spit* out *spite*, but it eventually impressed me as a *puffed-up pugilism* and made me want to *puke*. Therefore, the *rule of thumb* I used to stop instigating these *rumbles* was to be a *ruminant* and *rummage* through the *rumors* of my childhood. I had to *dig* in my *digestive* tract in order to find my lost *dignity*. I figured that if I just continued *toeing the line* that my heart-mind would come *together* with my soul-strength, because the job of heart-mind was to *ferret out* my repressed feelings and *ferry* the divine sweetness to my soul-strength which would then *fertilize* it. I had *subscribed* to heart-mind, but my heart-mind had not yet gone through this *subsequent* act of *subservience* to soul-strength, so my heart-mind didn't realize that it was a *subsidiary* to soul-strength. It considered itself the *main* man and *maintained* my spiritual pride in a *majestic* state. It ran *away* with my *awe*, because it considered itself *spotless* and didn't understand that soul-strength was the *spouse* with the *spout* of holy water in which the divine sweetness had to dissolve. They were intended to be a *pair*, but heart-mind forgot about his *pal* soul-strength who also lived in the *palace*.

When Satan assumed the *alias* of a snake and offered the *alibi* to Eve, heart-mind and soul-strength became *alienated* from one another. It was a cheap *thrill* that hasn't left us *thriving*, because it made us stuff a lot of nonsense down our *throats*. It's the *lollipop* we've been *lollygagging* with, and it's done nothing but give our *loneliness longev-*

ity. As a result heart-mind and soul-strength showed a *disinterest* in one another and didn't seem to care that the divine sweetness had been *dislodged* from its dwelling place, which is why it was necessary for Judas to be *disloyal* to Jesus. Satan had been a *bustling busybody*, but he didn't expect his artwork to be *butchered* by an unassuming *butler* like Jesus whose Crucifixion *buttered* our daily bread.

What is *pertinent* about this story is that we were all left feeling *perturbed* as a result of Satan's treachery, and the job of *perusing* this all-*pervasive perversity* fell to heart-mind. Only he could identify the *pesky pessimism* that *pestered* us, but it was soul-strength's job to give us *egress* from behind this *eight* ball. Adam's *ejaculation* had *ejected* the divine sweetness, so Jesus *elaborated* the Catholic Church to restore this *élan vital*. Our future seemed *bleak* and *bleary*, and God heard his lost sheep *bleating*, so Jesus offered to *bleed* in order to erase our *blemish*.

Satan was *engrossed* in the job of *enhancing* the *enigma* of ego and was *enjoying* himself immensely. That's why Jesus and God planned the Crucifixion: *to enkindle* our *enlightenment*, *enlist* the Holy Spirit to *ennoble* us, and end our *ennui*. Adam and Eve's *afterglow* had had this *aftermath* that *again and again* pitted man *against* God, and so over the *ages* it became necessary for man to have an *agent* to help him end this *aggravation*. When Adam and Eve *embraced*, this *embroidery* called ego *embroiled* itself into their *embryo*, and ever since Satan has been the *emcee* who has made us all *emerge* from our mother's womb with this *emergency* called ego-addiction. Therefore, our job is to *depict* how our divine sweetness got *depleted* if we want Jesus the *delectable delegate* to make sure our ego is *deleted*. Jesus' sweetness is a *delicious delight*, so let's give *voice* to our *embittered emotions* and show our *empathy* so he can *empty* us of these *encumbrances*. His Sacred Heart will *deliver* us from our *delusions* and release a *volley* of *volts* from God, so let's *volunteer* to go on this *voyage* and put an end to our *vulgarity*.

These *obstructions* to our divine sweetness were *obtained* on a series of *obvious occasions* during our childhood, and if this *occlusion* is not to remain *occult*, we need to *occupy* ourselves with our remorse. Our *stubbornness* is not *stuck* on us permanently, and we can negotiate this *obstacle course* to get past our *obstinacy*. Our wills have been *divorced* from God, but they can still *divulge* these facts, so we should ask God to *divvy* up the divine sweetness and let it become part of our *DNA*. Satan *wove* a *web* of deceit, but heart-mind and soul-strength can still *wed* one another and drive a *wedge* into the heart of ego. They are the *jugglers* of our repressed feelings but also have the job of *juicing* us up with the divine sweetness. They are the *vigilantes* in the *village* empowered to deal with our ego's *villainy*, so we should not be *negligent* in using these *negotiators*, because our will is the *paraffin* that they will mold to Jesus the *paragon* of virtue.

We can *beat* ego with the first three *beatitudes*. Our *mourning moves* our *muck*, our spiritual *hunger hunts* down our *hurt*, and we *persecute* these *pests* for *righteousness* sake, so our Fruits *ripen*, because our *remorse* has brought about this *rendezvous* with God. When we *hanker* to know what *happened* to give us this *gnawing* hunger, it will not *get our goat*, because we will have *faced* the *facts* and *embraced* this *embroilment*. We will get our *portion* of the divine sweetness if we *portray* this *harassment* from our childhood, because then it will not *harden* our hearts.

THE THIRD CIRCLE with the Beatitudes, the Fruits, the Sins, and the Gifts

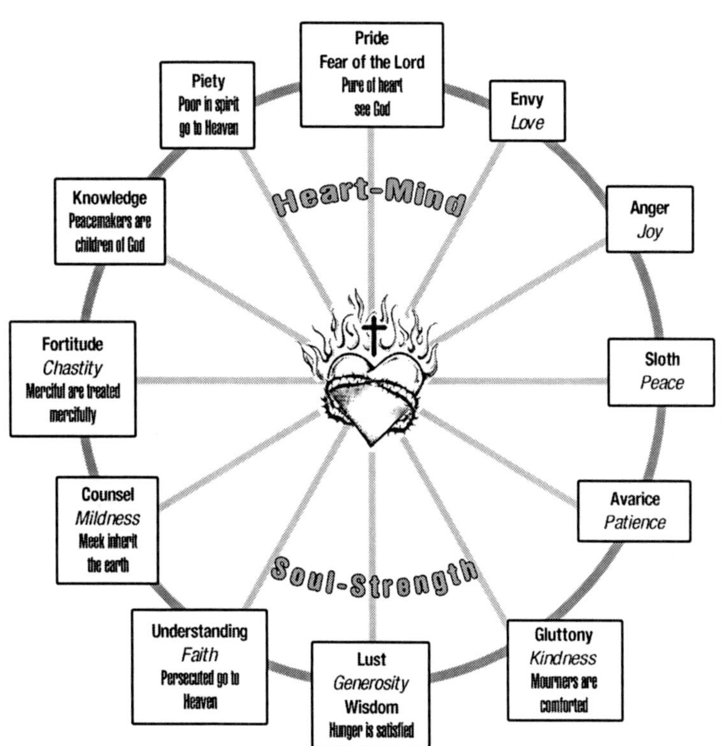

In order to be *harmonious* we must *harness* these *harrowing* events. The *decision* to use these three *declarations* of *blessedness* in this way will restore our *bliss*, because they will *sever* the *sexual shackles* of Adam and Eve that have *shadowed* us since the dawn of man. The *fall* of man was due to this forbidden *familiarity* between Adam and Eve that inserted into our *family* life the teachings of the *counselor* of all *counterfeit*. Their *carnal* love made parents *carp* on children and introduced the *sassy sauce* of *conditional* love into the *conduct* of man.

Nevertheless, the *enemy* always cowers when our contrition *enforces* the spiritual laws in the beatitudes, so we should not be *spineless* in addressing this *spin-off*. We must *erase* these results of Adam and Eve's *erotic error* and *prevent* our *pride* in our *lust* from *lynching* our loved ones according to this law of the sins of the *fathers* which is Satan's *faucet*. Original sin is the *spell* that makes man *spew* out hate, so let's end this *trance*, because it is meant to be *transcended*.

During this time of my growth the *birthright* of my original innocence was still covered up by the *bitterness* of my original sin, and the *zeal* of my spiritual pride reflected the fact that unconditional love was *zilch* in my heart. I covered up these *icicles* in my mind with this *idealistic identity*, and my contrition was my *crusader's cry*, but my *disposition* was still terrible. In my group therapy session my sweetness was being constantly *disproved*, and I had no semblance of *normalcy*, because my *nose* was being thrust in my *feces*, and in my mind it seemed like a *federal* crime. I considered my group members' remarks *offensive*, and it took some time for my contrition to *officiate*. They were *insults* I considered *insupportable*, because my *peers* didn't think I was *peerless*, and it left me feeling *peeved*. I *persisted* in that *personal purgatory* until my pride was *purged*.

The first three beatitudes are called *purgative*, because they put me through this *purgatory*. It was an *atonement* that at times seemed *atrocious*, and I thought I would never get the *expertise* to make this *expiation expire*. The second three were called *illuminative*, because they were meant to dispel *illusions*, and the last two were called *unitive*, because they seemed to be taught by the one *universal* God in His *university* of hard knocks on earth.

When I was a child I was *meek*, but my *mental illness* kept me on a *merciless merry-go-round*, and the *earth* I inherited wasn't very much at *ease* as a result of this *eccentricity*. Therefore, it would be more accurate to say that I was easily *imposed* upon and wound up with an *impressive* burden that I had to unload at the fourth beatitude's *docile dock*.

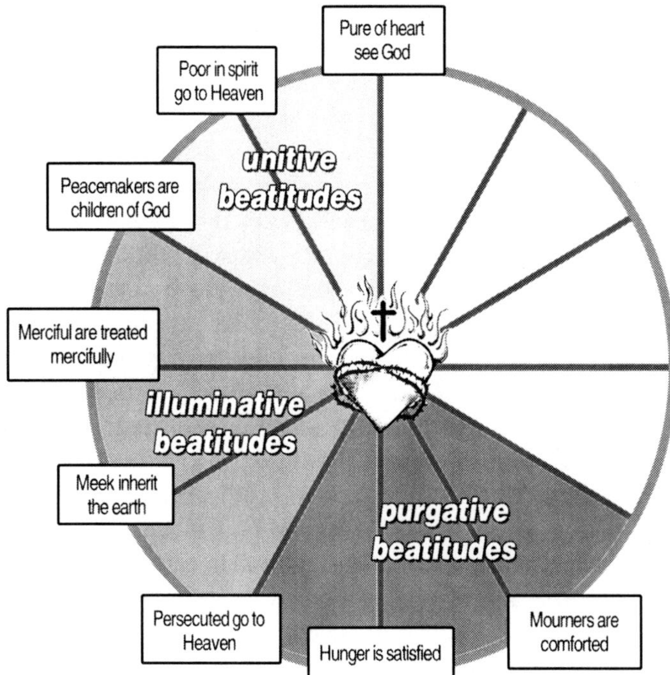

Most of the *time* I was *timid*, but I eventually got *tired* of *tolerating* my mother's sharp *tongue*, and my *temper* would launch a reign of *terror* all its own. According to the *contract* of the New Covenant I needed to *add* some *contrition* to my *addled* thinking and *address* my anger if I wanted to become spiritually *adept*.

My ego had been the *dire director* of this *dirt* and had left me *disabled*, so I asked for some of the *inward iodine* which is God's mercy in the hopes of not being left with an *iota* of *ire*. I got in this *clemency clench* at the fifth beatitude.

I was determined to become *mellow*, so I brought my remorse to each of my *melodramas* in order to make my heart *melt*. My *wrath* had left me a *wreck*, and so I was glad to *wrench* out these *disputes* that made me want to *ditch* my *divine* essence. My remorse was the *peacemaker* who could tie up to this *docile dock* and make me feel like a *peach*. Therefore, I *dipped* into my divine sweetness and got my charm school *diploma* at the sixth beatitude with the help of this *diplomat*.

This *motherly mayhem* had made me *mean*, so this *poignant poison* had to be *pondered* if I wanted to be *poor in spirit*. I needed to *mourn* these *ponderous portions* I had *swallowed* if I wanted to be *sweet*. We all fell down this *wide* and slippery road as a result of *Adam's adamant adaptation*, so I asked the *administrator* of the seventh beatitude to give me more *admirable* behavior. I was the *stooge* who had passed the Fruits in his *stool*, so I had to ask the *elite elixir* of the divine sweetness to *reverse* this *revolting revolution*. I was the *pontiff* who was full of this *pooh-pooh*, but I could still be *replete* with the divine sweetness, and the Fruits could still *replicate* themselves. My *evacuation* of the Fruits wasn't a very *evangelistic event*, so I used the beatitude of *poverty* of spirit to make me less of a *powder keg*. This beatitude *detoxified* me by helping me *detract* these *detriments*, and the next beatitude *rehabilitated* my heart so that it could have a *relationship* with God. The beatitude of pure of *heart* stopped this *heckling* and made my heart the *habitat* of the divine sweetness. My heart had been my *Hades*, because it *hadn't* had this blessing, but the divine sweetness finally came home to *roost*, because this beatitude ended this *rotten routing*. It brought my sweetness *home* and *homogenized* it with my behavior.

I had to combine myself with a *like* substance that could *limber* me up spiritually. I also had to *disconnect* myself from my ego's *discouragement*, because it was *unlike* my will and had *unlinked* me from my sweetness. The first two circles were therefore aimed at ending the *conspiracy* that kept me *constantly constipated* with Satan's *constituents*, and the third circle was an *accord* aimed at *accrediting* me with the divine sweetness. I had to give up a *low-down loyalty* in order to fall into the *routine* of God's *royalty* which wouldn't *rub me the wrong way*. The repressed *feelings* into which I *fell heightened* my sensation of being in *hell*, and I had to *research* what my will *resembled* the most in order to get rid of my *resentments*. The *focus* of this misguided *fodder* was my father, because I didn't feel *understood* by him, and it made it difficult to be his *understudy*. I had to *unfasten* myself from this *unfinished* business if I didn't want to *choke* on these *chops*, so I asked my *Christ*-consciousness to cook me up a *meal* that was more *meaningful*. The *nativity* could show me my true *nature*, so I could *soothe* my *soul* by *splicing* in this *spokesman* who could *sponsor Parental parity*. He would make my *soul* his *spouse*, and the *Almighty* would make me feel *all-right*, because He's not a *sour source*. Trying to be my father's *crony* had only left me feeling *cross*, because I had warmed up to the *bosom* of the wrong *boss*. My family had been an *annoying anomaly*, so I needed the unitive beatitudes to get rid of these *punitive* attitudes that had left me feeling *punk*.

I was full of this *terrible fiction* that had *fiddled* with my *thinking*, so I had to *recuperate* from this *recurrent* problem, get out of the *red*, and *redeem* my sweetness. I could make my sour grapes *sweet* with this *synergistic syrup*. I could tell this *yarn* about my *yearning*. I could break my ego's *impasse* by *impassioning* my will for the divine sweetness. I could end my ego's *stampede* by just changing my *stance*.

One of the *maggots* to be found in the decaying matter of my repressed feelings was my inner child's *magical thinking* that had to be cured on the *third* circle. It was really a *tragic trail*, because he thought his love was the magic *wand* that cured all, when all it did was make him keep *wandering* around *wanting* what he couldn't have. He had to stop *enduring* the *enemy* and start *procuring* the divine power that could make him a *prodigy*. He had to be taught that the real *cure-all* was becoming *curious* about how he got swept up in this *current*. He had to be taught to have an *undying* devotion to the *unearned income* of God's love that he had considered himself *incompatible* with. In order to be a more *jubilant judge*, he had to find his *Mecca* with some other *mechanism* than this one that allowed Satan to keep *meddling* with him.

My *perennial perfectionism* had left me *apprehensive*, because I had been the *approval*-seeker who had *suckled* on a series of *suffocating sugar-coated suggestions* that made me *sullen*. I have worn these blinders all my life, and they have been the *filth-finders* that have filled me with *strife* by making my divine sweetness go on *strike*. They have given me a tunnel vision which has left me in a *funk*, because they have been a *funnel* for *derision* that didn't *derive* itself from my spunk. Their *focus* has been the *foggy foibles* which have kept me out of God's *fold*, and these blinders have *harassed* me with the anger that has been the *harbinger* of my guilt and depression.

Rather than *shovel* my manure, these blinders made me want to *show* the *world*, because I was afraid that if I failed, people would think I was a *worm*. Instead of having the solid *foundation* of the *foursome* known as heart-mind and soul-strength, I had the squalid *accommodation* of living with a will that was Satan's *accomplice*. Therefore, I had to take a *stroll* through this *stronghold* of evil, *strop* my sorrow, and change my *make-up* to one not so *maladapted*. It was a *building* that I had *built* with my guilt and a safe *refuge* from which these *retards* could launch their *reign of terror*, so I had to *retrace* my steps and make them *retreat* if I wanted to *retrieve* my sweetness. I often *winced* when the *winds* of *fate* blew, but I also knew that God the *Father* would help me *fathom* the problem. Therefore my *opus major* was to admit I wasn't an *oracle* and get into God's *orb.*

Thinking that my soul was *dissimilar* from God had caused all my *dissipation*, so I *conferred* with God about this *conflict*, and He told me that it wasn't a *piddling piece*, because it could help me hit the *pay dirt* of His *peace.* However, to *maintain* the peace of the *Maker*, I had to *train* my heart-mind and soul-strength to not be *traitorous soldiers* but rather to be *solicitous* to Him. They had left me out in the *cold* because of a lack of *collaboration*, but once they began to *campaign* together, they would adopt the *can-do* attitude that would ensure my *victory* through their *vigilance.* They were the *suave* soldiers of my *subconscious* mind but had been corrupted by the *subculture* of ego, and therefore my *conscious* mind had to *conscript* them into its *army* through the *arresting art* of my remorse. Then they could *subdue* the fears I had *subscribed* to so that I wouldn't be the *doer* of Satan's *dogma.* They were the *point men* that guarded my *poise* by not letting my *noggin* be open to my ego's *noise.* They had the *charisma* to *charm* the *snake* and make it look like a *snap.*

The beatitudes are the *mantras* in their *manual* of arms, because they are *edicts* that are *edifying*, and they *predict* how to have the *predilection* toward loving behavior. They are our *existential exit* from the *confusion* that results from the *con game* called ego, because they release a *profusion* of factors that improve our *prognosis.* Therefore, when we feel *asphyxiated* by circumstance, we should *aspire* to be *inspired* by these eight *installments*, because they will ensure that our ego's ability to *defraud* us will be *defused.*

Our *moody moorings* won't make us *mope* if we let the beatitudes boost our *morale*, because they make us *amenable* to the *amenity* which is the divine sweetness. Our ego can only *fulminate* if we *fumble* this *amazing ambrosia*, because it *tames* our *tantrums.* The *tenement* of ego is the birthplace of our nervous *tension*, but we can end its *tenure* by *coming to terms* with the beatitudes. These eight *preambles* take the *precautions* to end the *ramifications* of our ego's *rampage*, because they are an *explanation* of the *exploit* called The Crucifixion and end the *fiasco* of ego by divine *fiat.*

When Adam crawled on Eve's *belly*, it made us all think that love *belongs below* the *belt*, and we got *bemired* in a *notion* that proved to be *noxious.* It was a *potent potion* that we *conjured* up, because it entered our *consciousness* as the *magic* spell that made our hearts sin *magnets* and filled us with a *potpourri* of repressed feelings that enabled Satan to take *pot shots* at us. When Adam and Eve "*made*" love, their *make-believe* inserted itself between us and the *Maker*. God's love seemed *malapropos* compared to the one that would allow *man* to *maneuver* his *manliness* into the *feminine fenestration*, so man got his *kicks* in this way without realizing that it had allowed Satan to *kidnap* his mind. The *mind-blowing* result was that the will of man became the *miniature minister* who suffered from bad *manners*, because he wasn't a very good *man of God*. This was the *romp* that made God stop *ruling the roost*, because He figured that as long as man wanted to *dole* himself out these *doleful dollops* that He would just let man's mind become the *dominant doodad*, while the real *dope* of the divine sweetness would just become *dormant*. Sex became the *ostentation* that bound man to his significant *other*, but it was a *frippery* that God *frowned* on, so God decided to *vanish* until this *vanity* was *vanquished*.

Nevertheless, we can give God the *upper hand* by deciding not to *upstage* Him in this way. We can stop *specializing* in the *specious spectacle* that cast the *spell* and *grieve* the *grigri* so it will lose its *grip* on us. It is possible to have the *grit* to love with our hearts rather than our *groins*, so let's end this *polygamous pomp* by *pondering* this *poppycock*. If we give God His *due*, he will *dulcify* us with His sweetness, so let's not let this *contraption* that acts *contrary* to His will make us want to stay in *control*. It is not possible to *overemphasize* that love is its *own master*, so let's just face the fact that we are no *match* for it and that it is *surely* necessary to *surrender* to it in order to *win* by getting *under its wing*. Our *tempers* have arisen as a result of the *temptation* in Eden, but a loving heart has the *tendency* that can end this *tension*. Loving is the *abiding ability* without which we are *nil*, so let's not think with the *nimble thimble*, because it only gives us a *thirst* that cannot be quenched.

Jesus' aim was to *slake* this thirst and give us a clean *slate*, so he brought the *Mass* to man to end this *massacre*. Man had begun to think with the *appendage* that was brought into action under the *apple* tree, so the Fruits of the Spirit went to the *slaughter*, and man became ego's *slave* as a result of this *cheeky chicanery*. From that time on by divine *decree* it would be necessary for man to *deduce* how he went wrong, so God took pity on His lost *sheep* and gave them the *Shepherd*. When Eve *massaged* Adam's *manly handle* we got *hung* by the neck, because his *hard-on harnessed* us to the devil's *harshness*. The *hazard* of the little *head* introduced these *massive* conflicts, because man thought he was the *master of ceremonies* of this *lap dance*, but it was really a *lascivious launching pad* and a *risky ritual*, because man's real *masterpiece* proved to be the fear over which he needed to gain *mastery*. Therefore, man had to return to his *past* with the help of this *pastor* so as to feed on greener *pastures*. Man had to *kibitz* with the *kid* known as the inner child, because the *TNT* of the *toddler* had to be confronted by man and child *together*. From *antiquity* man had felt this *anxiety*, because these two had fallen *apart*, so it was their *duty* to defuse this *dynamite* by *musing* over the problem *mutually*. Original sin was *the theft* of *their theism*, so man and child had to examine this *theme* by *unveiling* the *unwholesome* issues which they were *up against*. If man and child *chewed* on these *child-rearing strategies* together, the *stream of consciousness* known as the Holy Spirit would carry out the *upbringing* of the *urchin* so that even in the midst of *disaster* neither would feel *disconcerted*. If they dedicated *themselves* to this *therapy*, it would bring God's *thermodynamics* into their hearts, because the *Last* Supper was intended to have this *lasting* effect.

We should not be too *stubborn* to *study* this *stuff*, because it is only by *realizing* how we got *recalcitrant* that we can *receive* the divine sweetness and *reciprocate* with God. There is a *eureka* for each *event*, so let's not *repeat* but rather *repent* of the *mix-up* and *mobilize* a little forgiveness. Let's get rid of our unreasonable *expectations* by going on these *expeditions* and remember that God *engineered* these sequences in the *English* language for the purpose of our *enigma enlightenment*. We need to uproot our *crop* of fears by doing these *crossword puzzles* and burn them on the funeral *pyre* of our contrition. Our *pasts* can only make us feel *pathetic* if we remain *mute* about this *mystification*, so let's be aware that these *debts* can be *debunked*. These *annoying annuities* consist of the *lies* from our childhood that result in a *lifelong payout* that is not very *peaceful*, so let's end this *heckling*. Adam was the *heel* from *hell* who started this *hemorrhage*, but Jesus is the *healer* from *heaven* who can stop these *heebie-jeebies*.

Man was the *maverick* who was swept into this *maw*, because the *maxims* that *maximally* influenced him were dictated by the *mayhem* of which he had elected himself *mayor*. The sense of *alarm* that dwelled in man's subconscious was due to the bad memories filed away in this *album*, so to have *presence of mind* in the *present* we had to return to our *past* and identify the collage of frightful events we had put on the *pasteboard*. We had to *pasteurize* these *appalling apparitions* that fermented in our minds by *redoubling* our efforts to identify the *reenactments* that *mocked* us in the *modern* day and age. When we *remembered* the event from our past that we were *reminded* of in the present, our *remorse* could rid us of these *pangs* so that our *panic buttons* wouldn't get pressed. In that way the *rampage* of evil in our behavior would not be directed from the *ramparts* of hell, and we would not get embroiled in our *miscellaneous mischief.* If our *sorrow sought* the moment we turned *sour*, this *pathfinder* could *patiently* explain to the *patsy* the *pattern* of behavior he wanted to change, and the two could smoke the *peace pipe* together so as to give *sway* to that which is *sweet.* Our egos were the *robber barons* who could not stand up to this *Robin Hood*, because the will of man was an *honorable hoodlum* who could figure out how his *sweetness* got *swiped.* Man was a *tramp* who could be *transformed*, because Jesus was the *clement clergyman* who could turn man's *trash* into *treasure.* His Sacred Heart just *rocketed* us to relief when we were on the *rocky road* of making our *rogue* fears line up for a *roll call.*

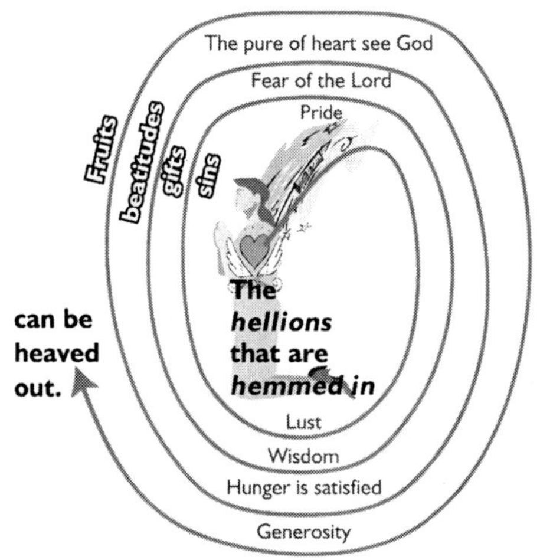

If you are always getting *sore*, because you feel *sorry* for yourself, don't *snuggle* up to these *so-and-sos* when you can *soar free* of these *freeloaders.*

These *spongers* cause the *spooky spout* known as fear, hurt, and anger, but our remorse is the *spunky spy* who can calculate the damage *estimate* that was produced by our *estrangement* from this truth that is *etched* in the *ether.* Trying to be like *God* has only made us Satan's *gofer*, so if you *lack* the desire to be his *lackey*, ask this *secret agent* to stop this *seduction.* Satan's *invitation* to Eve was our ego's *invocation*, but we don't have to let Eve's *estrogen etch* evil on our wills for all *eternity.* I have let the *monster* come inside of me and install his *montage* in my mind, which has put me in a *monumentally* bad *mood*, but I can get better *moorings* by not considering this issue a *moot* point. This *pus* in my mind has *pushed* me around, but if I *launder* these *layers* they won't be able to make me *leap* in this way. Evil is the *acrobat* who got into the *act* when *Adam* and Eve allowed the *adder* to make my mind his home *address*. It opened the *hatch* for the devil to pour his *hatred* into my heart, but I will *haul* it out in order to *have* my *head* and my *heart heated* up by *heavenly* bliss. I would *rather* not get *rattled*, so it is my decision not to let this *raunchy* side of me take over just because Eve decided it would be fun to get *ravished* by Adam. Their *fornication* doesn't have to make me feel *forsaken*, because the Sacred Heart can *best* the *bestial* organs I sit *bestride*. The *bestseller* of the Sacred Heart is the divine sweetness, which I *bet* on, because I have repeatedly taken my *gloom* to the Sacred Heart and gotten a taste of this ***glory*** that was meant to ***be*** in the ***beginning*** before we were *beguiled* by ego. This glory also **is *now***, because the Sacred Heart is the *nucleus* in my chest that returns my heart to the state of bliss that existed before Adam and Eve got *nude*. The Sacred Heart **ever *shall* be** the place I give up this *sham*, because it *works* to make my ***world*** a better place to live in, and I don't want to live ***without*** its *wizardry*. It ***ends*** my relationship with the *enemy*, and therefore I say ***amen***, because I am thankful that the *amenity* of the divine sweetness can grant me *amnesty* from my ego-addiction. I have been *haunted* by my fears, but the Sacred Heart is the *haven* that existed before Adam and Eve made us *craven* by *crawling* around and *groping* one another on the *ground*. Therefore, I subscribe to this *startling statement* of *belief* that makes me stop feeling *belittled*.

Our *anorexia* for the divine sweetness is Satan's *answer* to our original innocence, and it gave us the *cancer* of original sin, so let's light the *candid candle* which is our *contrition* and become *cool-headed*. If we want to become *charming*, we have to *chart* the *course* that brings the *courtesan* called ego to this *court-martial*. If we don't want our wills to *flounder* and would rather see them *flourish*, we need to follow this *flow chart* shown above. We *simply* hand over our *sins* by asking the *gifts* to be *given* so that we can *bear up* during any crisis. The *beatitudes* will *beautify* us in this way by ensuring that the *Fruits fuel* our behavior. We just need to pay our *holiness homage* by using the *homing instinct* of the two flight *instructors* called heart-mind and soul-strength. Our *storyline* will be *straightened out*, and we will *fly* right out of our *fog* if we bring our emotional *clutter* to these two *coaches* and ask them to help us *coalesce* with God. They will help us take these *clogs* out of the *closet*, so let's bring *closure* to our ego-addiction by making our wills men of the *cloth*.

Ego is the *nemesis* of loving behavior. When we have it on board it advertises itself in *neon*, but when the man of the cloth is on the *premises*, we get a better *premium*. Therefore, when our happiness is in a *declining* state, we need to *decode* our behavior by *decontaminating* it of our fears in order to restore *decorum* to our will. The *leaps* of faith that will give us this new *lease* on life are made by the *gymnasts* named heart-mind and soul-strength, so let's tell them we're tired of living in this *gyp joint*.

The *Gifts* of the Spirit are not some kind of *gilt-edged gimcracks*, because they help us *rifle* through our repressed feelings in order to end our *rift* with God. They teach us not to be *frugal* with the *Fruits*, because they *heat* us up with *heaven's fire* in order to make us feel *first-rate*. Heart-mind and soul-strength *monitor* our well-being, because they are *monks*. They have never *monkeyed* around like Adam and Eve and have a *monopoly* on eliminating our *monstrous moodiness*. The Christian Church was built on the *robust rock* called a contrite heart, so ignite your *rocket* as shown above and let your heart-mind and soul-strength *rock 'n roll*.

We won't *dally* around with our *damnation* if we learn to do this *dance*, because our heart-mind and soul-strength are the *daring darlings* who answer the *call* to *calm* the wild *beast*. Then our wills won't be *at the beck and call* of this *sadistic salesmanship* that robs us of our *sanity*. We all got in this *struggle* when Adam became Eve's *stud*, so let's erase this *penalty* by facing the issues we have *pending*. If we have an attitude of *levity* toward this *lewdness*, this *frisky frost* will leave us with *frozen Fruits* and *frustrations*, because the *icy idea* of "making" love with *penetrating penises* allowed Satan to become the *perpetrator* of our *perplexity*. Satan used this *prehistoric prelude* in Eden and committed *premeditated* soul murder, because he knew we would accept the *premise*, so let's not remain *preoccupied* with this *fake* that makes us *falter*. Our *vicissitudes victimize* us, because our *bamboozlement* has resulted from this *banal pestilence* of using our *bananas* to *band* up with the *bandit* who causes our resentments to *petrify* in our hearts. Therefore, *penis-penitence* is the *pennant* we should fly, because the *pension* of the divine sweetness will flow from this *non-rigid norm*, which will help us feel more *normal*.

When this *chase* supplanted our *chastity*, *manifold manipulations* began to *mar* our *marriages*. We *adulterated* our *affection* for the opposite sex, because we became *fonder* of *fondling* than *bonding* with one another, and therefore this is the *bondage* that we need to *make no bones about* if we want to stop going *bonkers.* Adam and Eve's *voluptuous voodoo* made me a *gullible guzzler,* and I got swept into this *voracious* vortex, because I was the *credulous cretin* who allowed my family to be the *crew* who perpetrated the *crime.* I got *crippled* by every *crisis,* because I wasn't a very good *critic* of any of the particular *crocks* of nonsense they asked me to swallow.

Nevertheless, as an adult I could be the *reviewer* who *rewound* the *tapes* until I got back to the time when Eve behaved like a *tart.* My ego would stop being my *taskmaster* if I solved this *ribald riddle,* because I could stop being *harassed* by the head that was only happy getting *harder* and could ask God to be the *architect* of a better *ardor.* I could be fed the *diet* that would *differentiate* itself into the Fruits and have fewer *difficulties* in life. I just needed to use the Gifts as the *wares* that waged successful *warfare* against my sins. The Gifts would then *weld* themselves to the beatitudes so that I could be *well.*

God's *nurture* was originally inseparable from Adam's *nuts,* but when Adam got his *rocks* off, God's love *rocketed* out of there, because Adam had used his *rod* to behave like a *rogue,* and that is why ego became the nut we've had to *crack* from the *cradle.* The human will became the *dipper* that served up our sour-grapes attitudes, because Adam and Eve did the *dirty deed* in full knowledge of the *deep* trouble it would put us in. Our wills were intended to be *chaste chauffeurs,* but when Adam and Eve *cheated,* they *permitted* our egos to be the *perpetrators* of these *crazy* notions that would make us all feel like *creeps.*

These *perfidious* notions began to *perfuse* into my awareness *perhaps* on the *eve* of Easter 1993, so I decided to ask the resurrected Christ to be the *executor* of my will. I had been the *doer* who had led myself a *dog's life,* so I figured that *Jesus* could do a better *job.* My will and ego were the *bungler* and the *bureaucrat* who had given me *plenty* trouble by hatching this *plot* known as ego-*addiction,* so I decided to ask Jesus to *administer* the sacraments of Holy Orders to my heart-mind and of the Eucharist to my soul-strength and to *twine* these *two* parts of my will around the will of God. Jesus was certainly a more *perfect performer* than my will and my ego, because they were the *dubious duo* who had caused my *dysfunction,* so I made the *commitment* to get rid of the *commotion* caused by these *drunks* who had not yet *dried out.* I had had some cool *receptions* as a result of their *recklessness,* so I was none too keen on the idea of having my will take orders from the *nasty navigator* of my ego who only sought *perks* that were not *permissible*. Jesus *reasoned* with the *rebels* by explaining how their *rebirth* could enable them to *recover*, so he ended my *rift* with God by installing a *rigging* that was more *righteous*, which is to say the three sacraments of Baptism, Confirmation, and Communion. Jesus got behind the *wheel when* I took the Eucharist, because his body is the *vehicle* that God *verified* as the *vessel* in which his blood *circulates* in order to help us *circumvent* problems. My *will* stopped being a *wimp*, because Jesus drove this *car* that had formerly gotten *carried* away by my *catalogue* of *catastrophes*. His blood *won* the *war* and granted me *wisdom*, because I asked to become his *ward*. *Baptism* was also a *tranquil transaction*, because it tamed my *barbarian* will and *connected* it to my Christ-*consciousness*, which is a more *sublime subordination* than the *cognizance* of evil I have inherited as a result of Adam and Eve's *cohabitation*. When I *received* the Eucharist, it stopped my *recidivism*, because it was the *recipe* that made the divine sweetness turn into the Fruits. This *superior supper club* enabled my *Confirmation* to end my *conflict*, because the Eucharist is the *medicine* that makes my will *meek* by bringing my heart-mind and soul-strength to a *meeting of the minds*. Therefore, it seemed *likely* that I could get *linked* to God by the *Lion* of Judah and become more *mellow* as a *member* of the Catholic Church.

I fully expected the *bandit* to be chased off by my *Baptism*, so when they *dunked* me in the baptismal font, I hoped it would keep the devil from *duping* me. I expected *drum rolls* to sound to indicate I was no longer *drunk* with ego, and I expected *cymbals* to clash to indicate I was no longer a *cynic*, but there were no *fireworks* in the *firmament* to indicate that I had received this *first aid*.

Nevertheless, I understood that the Crucifixion was the *therapeutic thesis* that I could use *through thick and thin* to learn to *trust* the *truth*. I could *open* myself to this blessing and defeat my *opponents* if I asked the two *optimists* known as wisdom and fear of the Lord to show me how not to be *persuaded* by my *pessimism*. My fear of the *Lord* was the *awe* I *lost* in Eden when the two *libertines* gave me the *awkward lifelong* burden known as ego-addiction. Nevertheless, my wisdom and awe were the *keepers* of my peace of mind, because they held the *keys* to the kingdom and could put the Fruits in my *kitchen*. They had been *granted* the power to make the *grapevine* reach my *gray matter*, so my sweetness could take *root* if I asked them to show me the *ropes*. My pride in my lust had made me a *prisoner* of my *private parts*, but I could earn the *prize* of the divine sweetness. I just had to line up all my Fruits in a *row* so that my sins would stop being *rowdy*.

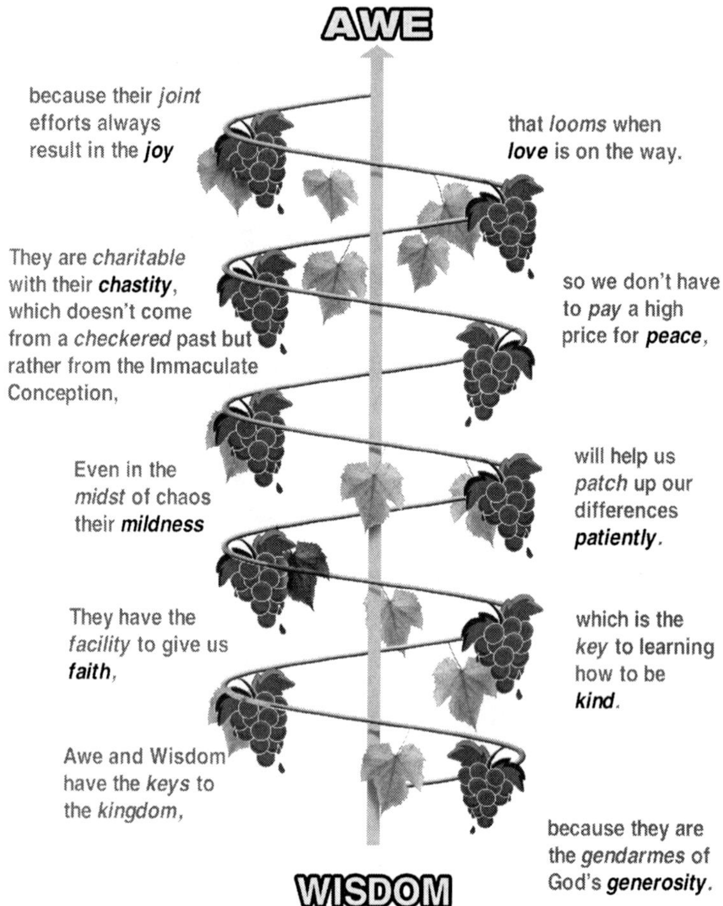

The two most *boisterous* of these *Bolsheviks* had formed the *paranoid partnership* known as pride in lust, but I do not refer to lust that is in *service* to *sex* but rather to my spiritual pride, which is the *yearning* to break this *yoke*. I had been left in the *lurch* by Adam and Eve's *lust*, so my spiritual pride became overly *inflated* and thought it was so *influential*, because it thought it alone was responsible for the *infusion* of the divine sweetness. My wisdom and my fear of the Lord were the two *luminaries* who were trying always to outdo one another in this way, so they just had a case of *lust* that was all their own and couldn't shed the *light* that was necessary to get me out of this *limbo*. My fear of the Lord was the *awe* that took this *awful* turn, which is to say that he took *pride* in being the *priest* who thought he alone could *wire* me to my *wisdom*. The *unholy union* of these two *risky rivals* only made me *holier-than-thou*, because my pride in my awe would *holler* loudly until my wisdom-lust chanced on *insights* he thought were *inspiring* enough. These two *supercilious supervisors* had me looking down my *nose* at people whose contrition wasn't *notable* enough, so it was a *pretty* good example of how my spiritual *pride* was the one and the same ego-*addiction* that *addled* my brains. I had been the *zealot* who aimed to bring this curse to *zilch* with the *zingers* of my remorse, but I only gave the *shake* to my *share* of the Fruits, because my *hubris* had not yet gotten the *hug* from my *humility* that could give it a better sense of *humor*. I had *pressed* the two Gifts into service *presuming* they would do their part, but when they met up with the *sins*, they formed a *singularly sinister* combination, so I finally decided that my *pride* wasn't as good a *prime mover* as the *Prince* of Peace. To *tame* this *tangled* thinking I had to *zap* these *zealots* by letting the *Passion* of Jesus make me *passive* to the *supply* that comes from the *Supreme Being*.

My pride in my awe and lust for wisdom were the *eager* beavers who didn't leave me very much at *ease*, because they *pandered* to the idea that I was the embodiment of the *Paraclete*. Their *entangling enthusiasm* was based on the particular *perfectionistic perk* that I had chosen as a *morale*-boosting *motto*, which is to say my show-the-world attitude. I *mowed* down everyone who was in my way with this *born-again bossiness*, because I was so *giddy* over the two *Gifts* that I didn't realize it was *silly* to let them combine with the two *sins*. The *repulsive result* was that these *hybrids* remained in charge of the *hydraulics* of my ego.

My spiritual pride thought he was a *propagandizing prophet*, but he was really the *prostitute* who made me *trample* on my patients' *tranquility*. My Attention Deficit Disorder was the *bulldozer* that was driven by this *bully*, so this *dexterous diagnostician* indulged in the *treacherous treatment* of his patients, because his *listening* was *listless*. Their complaints were the *litanies* that left me with *little* patience, because the *hurried hydraulics* of my Attention Deficit Disorder made me try to encourage them to *succeed* in being *succinct*. The problem was that they rarely were able to *spell* out the problem before my patience was *spent*, so my *impatience* became the *impediment* that made me part *company* with my *compassion.* I encouraged them to leave out the *details* that would *deter* me from grasping the matter, so many got their feathers *ruffled.* I always wanted to get the *run-down* as fast as possible and therefore would *rush* them through their stories *ruthlessly.* I realized they needed to *narrate* their problems in their own way, but I wanted to *narrow* down their stories to the bare facts, so it turned into an *interrogation* marked by many *interruptions.* I knew from my psychotherapy that I had to *dwell* on the *dynamics* of my *dysfunction until* all the *untruths* were *unveiled*, but I *disposed* of this understanding with my patients by trying to *dissect* out the *facts* and didn't realize I was using a *failing* tactic.

Moreover, I didn't *practice* what I *preached*, because I *projected* my fear of misunderstanding onto them and gave them *prolonged* explanations. My *compromised concentration* never enabled me to be *concise*, so I *dilated* at great length in a *diligent* effort to *convey* a *convincing* explanation. My *speech* was *speedy*, and my understanding was *slow*, so to end the *slump* I increased my *voice's volume*, but I only became a *long-winded loudmouth* because of my *lousy* attentiveness.

My Attention Deficit Disorder was one *linchpin*, but the other was the *line* of thought that arose from my *lineage*, because my parents never left me with a belief in the *linkage* between my *lips* and their *listening.* I was always trying to *connect*, but they never seemed to *consent*, so I began to feel more *hollow* than *holy* inside myself. I often listened to the *voice* of this *void*, and it made me a *volatile volcano.* I never felt *understood*, so my divine sweetness never got *under way*, and this *redundant reenactment* took place in my *office often.*

I never ate this *parental parfait* that could keep me from feeling like a *pariah*, so I have not been a very *urbane* adult, because I have always felt *urgent* about the lack of this "*us*" and have *used* almost any means available to *usher* myself back to this *utopia.* I was always in a *rush* to fill this *Rx*, so I *immersed* myself in an *impatience* I have been unable to *impeach*, and this *impending* anger has turned into a *brusqueness* which is *brutal.* I *plagiarized* this *plague* from my parents, and I have *inculcated* myself with this *incurable disease* which has made my divine sweetness *disembark.* I have *embellished* myself with this *embitterment*, so it is the *haunting* that I *have*, and it has *hounded* me every *hour* of my life. I have been unable to *stave it off*, because it has *staying power* and has *steadily stolen* my kindness. It has *eluded* my remorse and has kept the *embargo* on my divine sweetness in force. I have not heard the *warm* voice of counsel that could *warn* me not to be on this *warpath*, because the divine sweetness was the *liquid* not on my *list* as a result of feeling no one had ever *listened* to me.

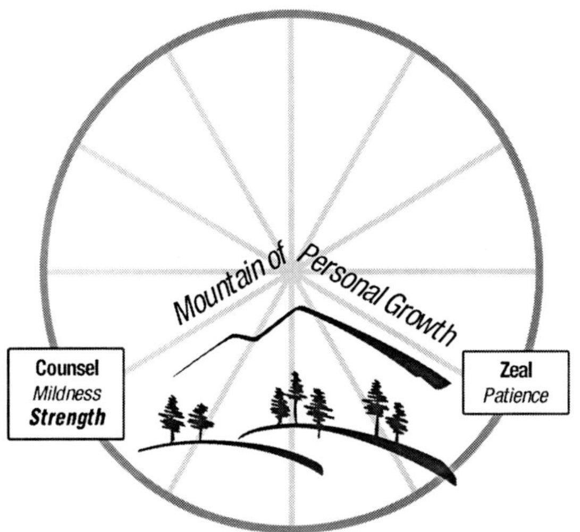

Therefore, I scrutinized the circle and *found* the *fountain* at *four o'clock* that could bring about my *ego's egress* at *eight o'clock*. My powers of strength and zeal could use my counsel to *opt* for the better *optics* of my patience and mildness, and I could earn these Fruits by climbing this mountain of personal growth.

Children have the *motor* in their hearts that enable them to climb this *mountain*, but for me that motor never got *started* probably because I was *startled* by a certain blow I took to the *solar plexus* as a child. It was that my mother was my *sole* parent during World War II. I was five years old when my father came home from the war, and I tried to *deactivate* my cravings by doing a *deadly dance* with him, but it didn't have this *dandy* result and left my dependency needs *dangerously dangling* in the air. Since this strategy didn't *come out* the way I wanted, I decided to stage a *comeback* by putting on my *docket* the idea of becoming a *doctor* like him. I secretly *pleaded* that this would *please* him, but the *pleasure* he seemed to take in the idea was never all that *plentiful*, which of course only bore the *fruit* of leaving me *frustrated* with my patients.

You might think that I would eventually *punt* on being the *pupil* of these crazy ideas, but I never got sick of being Satan's *puppet*, and the Fruit I left on the *shelf* was the mildness that Satan made disappear through the *shell game* called ego.

I gave Satan this *handy* way to *hang* me by the *neck*, so I never seemed able to drink this *nectar* we all *need*. While I was *sweating* over the question of what had happened to my *sweetness*, Satan *swiftly* made the *switch*, and I wound up with this *abhorrent abomination*, which is to say the *grueling gruffness* that I earned by not using the *might* of my *mildness* to vanquish this *militant*. When I *abandoned* my mildness, Satan introduced this *aberration*, and I have never been able to say the *abracadabra* that would make me less *abrasive*. I have gone through the *repulsive reruns* that have been set off by this *mean meddler*, because I have *detested* myself enough to *detonate* these *bombs*. They have resulted from this *evil bondage* and have *exacted* a high price, but no matter how *devastated* I have felt, this *depraved derelict* has left me with this *reeking* that has me *reeling*. This *hog holds fast* to me, because I am the *faultfinder* who feels *favored* by this *sticky stink*, so it has *adhered* to me *ad infinitum* without wanting to *adjourn*. I often *blush* because of this *body* odor, but it is a *staunch stench*, and no amount of soap and water can *rub* it out, because it is made of *rubber* and bounces back every time. It has been a second *skin* to me and has never *skipped* the chance to involve me in a *skirmish*. It has *intertwined* with my thinking in such an *intimate* manner as to make me *intolerant* of others; and of my two *neighbors* heart-mind and soul-strength, *neither* has been able to help me confront this *nemesis*. My divine sweetness sometimes seems to be *kaput* because of this bad *karma*, and I have felt *wistful* but am still *at my wit's end* as a result of this *witching*. Even my remorse is not enough of a *pundit* to stop this *pungent punishment*, and I have felt *incapable* of escaping from this *incarceration*. It makes me feel *paranoid*, because there is no amount of spiritual *paraphernalia* that seems to be able to rid me of this *parasite*. It has given me *chagrin* and is the ball and *chain* that opens me to my ego's *chain reaction*. However, it is *unrealistic* to assume that my humility is *unredeemable*, so I need to remember that my abrasiveness is not based on *gospel* truth but *gossip*.

My *defeatism* regarding this *deficit* made me think on occasion that I *couldn't* redeem my Fruits from the *canteen*, but in truth I am *capable* of taking this *debilitating debit* down a notch or two with my remorse, and then it won't think it's so *debonair*. These *crazy* beliefs that seem *credible* can stop *deprecating* us, because when Jesus carried the Cross he *deputized* all Christians as members of this *creditworthy crew* who can *process* the pain of their wound in order to *profit*. Therefore, I aim to enter this *market* by *marrying* my soul to the

Master who knows how to do this *math*. I will ask the *nun* who is our Mediatrix of Grace to guide me to these *nuptials*, because it is her job to *pacify* our conflicts and ratify this *pact* in the divine legislature. Each *pain* we have *painted* on this *palette* in the heart of our inner child can be *palliated*, so I expect every *chapter* of my *charade* to be erased by the *Paraclete's parade* which is the Gifts and Fruits of the Holy Spirit.

Before the fall this *parade* took place in *paradise* in the *sleeve* of spiritual fluid along the spine of man, but it was yanked off by Satan's *sleight of hand* when Adam and Eve decided it wasn't *kosher* to have to *kowtow* to God. Their *kundalini*† spilled on the ground when Eve pinned the *label* of lust on her *labia*, so God got *out of* there as a result of this *outrage*. Nevertheless, the kundalini is the way heart-mind and soul-strength *communicate* with one another so as to *commute* original sin through the *contract* of the New Covenant which says that it can be *contradicted* by a contrite heart.

Contrition is the *trigger* that brings on the *troops*, but first heart-mind must *requisition* the *reruns* that require our contrition so that soul-strength can participate in the *rescue*. The Crucifixion is *therapeutic*, because we can *think back* and figure out how this *baggage broadcasts* our *broken-heartedness* so as to make us *behave belligerently*. It makes our *resentments resign* so that our *rest* can be *restored* by the *Resurrection*, but first we must *retrace* our steps and allow our kundalini to *retrench* itself in our *spines* by taking a look at this *spin-off* that is none too *splendid*. To *raise* our kundalini we need to *rally* these forces and send them on the *attack* against the bad *attitudes* that take us on *rambunctious rampages*. The *articulation* of these conflicts makes the kundalini *ascend* and the Holy Spirit *descend* so that our thinking won't remain *desecrated*.

Jesus was the *pioneer* who opened this *pious pipeline* along the *spine* so as to end the *spin-off* of sin and connect the will of man to the *precinct* of the *precious* commodity known as God's will. Satan took the *starch* out of man's spiritual *stargazing* and left him *stark* raving

---

†*God talks with Arjuna, The Bhagavad Gita, Royal Science of God Realization,* Paramahansa Yogananda Self-Realization Fellowship, 3880 San Rafael Avenue, Los Angeles, CA 90065-3298, 1995, p. 793: "The coiled creative life force at the base of the astral spine, kundalini, has always been symbolized as a serpent. When this creative force is 'asleep' in delusion, it flows down and outward and feeds all the senses; uncontrolled, its stinging venom causes insatiable lusts. But when the pure kundalini force is 'awakened' by the yogi, it rises to the brain and is transformed into the bliss of spirit. This uplifting serpentine current is Vasuki, the supreme force for human liberation."

mad by *starting* his *starving*. The correct way to *adore* God then is to realize that when we are *adrift* in a sea of troubles we can use these *adroit sailors* called heart-mind and soul-strength who can make us *saints*. They use this *ancestral anchor* called kundalini in the safe *harbor* of God's will to protect us from *harm*, so let's have a *loyalty* to their *lucidity*, and then *Lucifer* won't bring us bad *luck*.

Adam and Eve's *ecstasy* in *Eden* left us on the *edge* of disaster, because they ate the apple outside of the *chapel*, but heart-mind and soul-strength are the *chaplains* who can start a new *chapter* on earth by giving us the *uncommon* blessing of *unconditional* love. We can *reconcile* these two and *recoup* our losses, because they are the *rectors* of this university of hard knocks who are empowered to get us out of the *red*. Therefore, I enrolled in their *curriculum* to reverse my *curtness* and *studied* the *stunts* from my childhood that *stymied* my *suaveness*. I was sick of this *rotten roughneck's roulette*, so I *rounded up* this *herd* of *heretics* and became gradually less *intoxicated* by using my *intuition* to understand how my *blame* talk originated in their *blasphemy*. I loosened the *noose* that had choked off my *normalcy* and was able to *swallow* some of my *sweetness*, because I decided not to be a *stranger* to this *stranglehold strategy* that Satan used to *usurp* the *utensil* of my will.

For many years in my therapy I was in such hot *pursuit* of this *pus* that I felt *certain* that my mind was a *certified cesspool* and doubted I could *modify* it into a better *module*. I was in this *cussed custody* and was *cut* to the quick by each *piece* of *piercing garbage* I had *gathered* in this *pigsty* in my heart. I *often oiled* my thinking with these *oinks*, but I eventually learned to use my *olfaction* to end this rank *oligarchy*. I considered it a *smashing* success when I was able to *smell the rat* I needed to *smoke out*, because I was on the *crusade* of nabbing these *crusty culprits*. I was determined to chase these *squatters* out of my mind and wasn't a bit *squeamish* about *prying* into my sick *psyche*. My *mess* had conveyed its *message*, but the *Messiah* gradually *eradicated* these *errors* that my *relatives* had *relayed* to me, so little by little I nurtured my dream of *freeing* my sweetness from this *Freudian friction*.

The *motionless motive* known as my *sloth* nevertheless kept me in a *slump*. There wasn't *anyone* more devoted to his *apathy*, which proved to be my *indolent inebriation*. This *law* of the *lazy man* resulted in the *manifold* ways in which I took each *pain* into my heart and then considered each one my *pal*. I had eaten the *food* of *fool* and allowed this *rubbish* to *rule*. I *waged open warfare* against these *opiates* and felt *tantalized* by the challenge of hitting each *target.* Nevertheless, it was a *tunnel vision* that only added to my *turpitude*, because *reveling* so much in the *revelation* of my manure allowed Satan to take his *revenge* by withholding the *revenue* of my divine sweetness. I spent so much time *ogling* these droppings that I remained an *ogre*, because I didn't take the time to *audit* my divine sweetness. That didn't *augur* well for the status of that *august* substance. I *binged* on the act of remorse and used these *binoculars biographically* in hopes of some *bipartisan* agreement between me and God. I looked for my *pail* of *pain* with *painstaking* attention to detail but didn't *marshal* the help I needed, because I was drunk on this *martini* of the *martyr.* My soul-strength couldn't *dulcify* me, because my heart-mind was so obsessed about taking this *dump* that could make me feel less like a *dunce.* My *stupidity* had kept them in this *stupor*, and I had *gummed* up my tummy, because I was so *gung ho* about my *gunk* that I didn't hear the divine sweetness *gurgling* with *gusto* in my *guts.* I was so *psyched* out by these *psychedelic* lights of my strength and zeal that my patience and mildness became the *evangelists* that *evaporated.* Patience and mildness were the Fruits of my *tact*, but my strength and zeal were the *tacticians* who forgot to use these two *tactile* organs. Thus my strength and zeal just played *tag* with one another. I was so intent on using the *periscope* of my remorse that the divine sweetness *perished*, because all I wanted was my *peristalsis* to eliminate the *pessimism* from my childhood.

My spiritual pride had me on *cruise control* during this *crusade*, so I was the *active actor* who didn't realize that only my *passivity* could digest the *Pastor's pastry* and give me the *Eucharist's euphoria.* My passivity was *submissive* to this *subsidy*, so I had to stop *competing* with God and start *complying* with this *comprehensive* blessing. I had to become *receptive*, because this was the *recipe* for *reciprocity* between me and God.

We are all burned by the *embers* of this *embitterment*, but when the *carpenter carried* the *Cross*, he shouldered these *cryptic burdens* and made it his *business* to teach us how to win this *uphill* battle through the *uprising* which is our contrition. He taught us to be *clever* mountain *climbers* when he delivered the *serene sermons* on the *mount.* He told us that to climb this *mountain* we would have to go through our *mourning*, because this is the way we *exert* ourselves in order to *exhume* our fears. When we carry this *hefty* burden up to these *heights*, we feel *pooped* out and *poor* in the spirit of ego, but when we get to the top we drink the soda *pop* that makes us pure of heart. On the way up we are *tipsy* with spiritual pride, and so we don't hear the divine sweetness *tiptoeing* around on the *tiptop*, because we are still delivering the *tirades* of our remorse. Nevertheless, we eventually get *tired* of wiping our tears with this *tissue* paper and realize that remorse and forgiveness are the same as *tit* for tat, so we welcome the *titanic* sweetness of God.

In this *rarefied* atmosphere on the summit we are *rarely ready* to *follow* the *food*, because we have *lead* the way, *hunted* it down, and *leaped* over each *hurdle* in this *race* so as to put an end to our *rage*. We have *rallied* our remorse and ended this *rampage* by trying to smell a *rat*, so we don't think we *rate* this *ration*. On the summit we don't feel very *stable*, because we've been dealing with a *stacked* deck. We don't realize that our mind is the *stadium* where Jesus planned for his *staff* of twelve to *stage* our victory, so we just *stagger* around thinking our divine sweetness is *stagnant*.

Our childhood is the *scaffold* of the *scalawag* known as ego, and we need to *scale* these heights with our strength and zeal, but on the *downhill* side we *downplay* these two powers and welcome the patience and mildness we can see *downrange*. It is time to *relax*, because we have finished our part of the *relay race*. We can *rest*, because we realize our hearts are the *restaurants* that serve the Fruits. This *transformation* takes *place* on the summit, because the blood *stream* of Jesus changes its *course* there in accordance with the New *Covenant*, *enters* our hearts, and *entrenches* itself in our wills. It puts us *strictly* in *stride* with the *string* of events called the Glorious Mysteries, so this *transfusion* ends our *transgressions* at this *transient* point in time and puts the Fruits on our *plates*.

On the summit we realize that our ego's *caper* prevented us from *capitalizing* on the divine sweetness, so we *capitulate* to God there in order to bring down this *capricious captain*. We have been *steered* by the *stellar* voice of *counsel* that gives a *counterpunch* to the *countess* known as ego-addicted will. She understands that in the *country* of the human heart all are equally sweet. This is the *ethereal ethic* that is meant to be inculcated in peoples of all *ethnic* origins and is the *standard* which is meant to enable different races to be in good *standing* with one another.

On the summit the *four fragments* have a *frank* talk with one another, because they have been *freed* of the *freight* of ego and no longer feel obliged to *fritter* away our *Fruits*. We *juggle* these four *keen kernels* in order to find the *key* to being *kind*, so heart and strength become *passive* to the *Pastor* who holds the *patent* on divine *paternity*, whereas soul and mind *receive* the divine sweetness and *reciprocate* their thanks to God. Heart-strength has the *poise* that comes from being *poor* in spirit, and soul-mind *provides* the *prudent pulsations* of love, joy, and peace to the *pump*, because we have become *pure* of heart. Heart-mind and soul-strength took a *bath* in strength and zeal in order to climb the mountain but change to these *positions* of *power* at the top and win the *battle* by using patience and mildness.

Heart-strength and soul-mind were *eligible* for these blessings, because they formed the *embryos* that defeated the *enemy* and *engineered* loving behavior. Heart-mind and soul-strength were the *gametes* that closed the *gap* between man and God, because during the *ascent* they went through this *asexual* reproduction. They had become *ashamed* of Adam and Eve's sin, so they *zoomed* in to form this *zygote*. Man's *decency* had been *deceived*, becasuse the *Boss* at the *top* had been *toppled*, and the *kooky kundalini* was still under the *spell* we had *spent* all this time *crucifying* on this *crusade*. When Adam's *sperm spilled*, the kundalini got *bottled* up at the *bottom* of the *spine*, so as we climbed this *mountain* and *mourned*, we *sublimated* this *sublime* substance that could make man *submissive* to God, and we established a *central* government in our chests that could connect to our *cerebral cortex*. To *decipher* our reasons for behaving badly, *deck* our egos, and *declare* ourselves healed, we just needed to use our heart-minds to pop the *bubble* by *bucking* the system of ego. Then our soul-strength could *buckle* us into the divine will so that the Fruits would *bud*. In order to *rouse* the divine sweetness we had to *rout* ego so that God would know what *route* we wanted it to take. God would never *pencil* in the result until he was sure the *pendulum* of our heart-mind's remorse had *swung* the *sword* of our soul-strength enough to prevent us from being Satan's *sycophants*. Patience and mildness were the *team* of two who could stop us from *teetering* on this *führer's fulcrum*, but first we had to use the gift of counsel, the *seer* of this *seesaw*, and the *battery* of powers known as strength and zeal, which could give us this dignified *bearing*. The spiritual *combatants* that made up the winning *combination* then were the gift, two powers, and two Fruits that gave us this *poise*. As a *result* of this *resurrection* Satan wouldn't be able to *poke* fun at us, so if we wanted to get our *balance*, we had to use this *ballast*.

The Gift of counsel was the electrical *cord* that could make us *cor-*

dial by plugging us into our patience and mildness, but first we had to *untangle* the three *untruths* known as the three *core* fears. We needed to *contact* our *contrition* and *introduce* these three *intruders* to this *psychotherapist* who could teach them better *public relations.* Then we would be more *secure* and have our feet on the ground, because we could get off this *seesaw* known as the ego-addicted will. In my first session my *therapist* wrote down these three core fears which made up the law of *thermodynamics* that made me give God a cold shoulder, and from then on I decided that through my *psychotherapy* I would ask my remorse to *publicize* my regret to God for these three *mistakes* which made me *mistrust* Him:

1. Fear of being unlovable,
2. Fear of loss of self-control,
3. Fear of loss of self-esteem.

When I was a child, Satan pretended to be my *comrade* and *conned* me into this *concatenation*, which was the *series* of *serious setbacks* that *concealed* my self-*confidence*. Each fear *ushered* me into in its own *vale of tears* and *thumped* me with *thunderous thwacks* during a certain *time* of my life by *tinkering* with my mind. They *channeled* their *chaos* into my *thinking*, *throttled* my good sense, ran *riot* in my behavior, and *robbed* me of my *equanimity*. Each fear was perfectly *equipped* to send me on these fools' *errands*, because it *paralyzed* my relationship with my real *Parent* and created a *heretical hiatus* between me and the *hierarchy* from on *high*.

The first *core* fear of being unlovable *corrupted* my cerebral *cortex*, because it *chopped* off my *Christ*-consciousness and made me feel I was *created* without this *credential* that was *critical* to my wellbeing. The second core fear of loss of self-*control convinced* me to try to *cope* by *corralling* the first core fear inside my ego-defenses so it couldn't *cough up* this hideous lie I had tried to *cover up*. These first two *errors* were *espoused* by my third core fear, so I suffered this loss of Self-*esteem* and became *circumspect* about *circumstances* that *threatened* to take the lid off these *three vile villains* who had filled my *vine* with this *vinegar.*

My fear of loss of self-esteem marked the period of my second adolescence when my Self-esteem took a *nap*, because I was eating the *napoleon* of sex in order to pay tribute to my *narcissism*. I suffered from this selfish steam, because the *Cinderella circuit* of the first two core fears *preempted* my good sense and *pressured* me to involve myself in this *pretense*. My fear of being *unlovable* by my mother was the *unmerciful crook* that made me *cross* the line in this way, so I pretended to be a *Don Juan* because I was afraid of being *doomed* to never getting the *dose* called a mother's love.

I went through this *risqué rite of passage* and thought it was *ritzy*, because I was afraid my *Self-esteem* couldn't achieve *self-expression*. I went out on *dates* and got *lured* into the sin of *lust*, so I was *shackled* to this *shaky sham* Eve started when she stopped behaving like a *daughter* of God. I allowed *shapely* women to turn me into a love-*shark*, but it became a *daunting* task to recline on the *davenport* with them, because the more we *dawdled*, the less my tumescence wanted to *dawn*. I just couldn't *erase* the fact that my *erection eroded* God's love, because it was an *erotic* love that made me *err*, and I realized I was *hedging* my bets by becoming a *hedonist*. No matter how hard I *strained*, my *strength* wouldn't add to its *length*, because I was looking through this *lens* that made this *façade fail*. Therefore, my *self-confidence* was destroyed by my *self-consciousness*, and my *potency potential* fell in this *pothole*. I wore out my *odometer* with this *Oedipus* complex and often wondered why my *pygmy* organ failed to respond to the *pyrotechnics* of lust.

I didn't feel very *upstanding* in my relationship with my mother, and it left me feeling *uptight* when the moment came for its *upturn*, so I just kept on pretending to be *urbane*, but I felt like an *urchin*. When I married Maria, she must have felt like a *widow* rather than my *wife*, because this part of me was *dead* as a result of this bad *deal*. Nevertheless, I figured that I would rather be spiritually *rich* and that not being able to take this *ride* shouldn't leave me feeling *stricken*, and so I took it in *stride*.

It was a *ticklish* job undoing this *tie* to which I was *bound*, because sex was the *binge* that was strongly tied to my *biochemistry*, but the more *fetid fetter* was my fear of being unlovable by my mother, which didn't leave me in very fine *fettle*. I got this *mote* in my eye, because Eve was the *motel mother* who put this lack of *mothering* in *motion*. Eve connected my *cock* to the *cockles of my heart*, so I drank this fearful *cocktail* that didn't make me feel *cocky*. I had a *scar* that came from this *scarcity*, and it had led to the *scathing* series of *scatological* acts which comprised my second adolescence. My sweetness had been *ravished*, and it set me in pursuit of *ravishing* women, so to retrieve this *raw material* I sent a *ray* of remorse to *raze* this *razzle-dazzle*. I hoped to *reach* the point of being able to *react* to God's *grace*. I hoped to *graduate* from this school of *dissipation* by *dissuading* myself from this *distraction*. I figured I could *live* more happily if I felt *lovable*, so I *unglued* myself from this *ungodly* fear of being unlovable by my mother and ended its *spree* so that the Fruits could *spring up*. I knew my *Self-actualization* depended on eliminating this *self-adulation*.

I hadn't paid *homage* to my sweetness and didn't feel at *home* on the *range*, because my repressed feelings and the seven sins were the *rank and file* that *ranted* and *raved* all the time. I had *deployed* these three core fears which I had *deposited* in the *depot* of my subconscious mind, and all they did was *announce* themselves in order for me to feel *annoyed*.

My self-esteem was made up of the selfish *steam* known as my fear, hurt, and anger, which always *steered* me wrong, but my Self-*esteem* was made up of the *ethereal vapors* of love, joy, and peace which were at *variance* with these *varmints*. Likewise, my self-control was made up of my *defeatist* ego-*defenses* that sought to *hide* this *hideous travesty*, whereas my Self-control was the *treasure* in my *chest* that could end this *chicanery*. The *pigsty* in the *pilgrim* was fenced in by my fear of loss of self-control, but my Self-control could *pilot* me to a more *desirable destination* and put me in the *pink*. We have gone *haywire*, because self-control is the *hazard* of the *head* that makes it impossible for our self-esteem to *hear* the voice of God in our *hearts*. Nevertheless, the kundalini is the *encasement* that is *enchanting*, because it *encloses* the head and heart so as to *encode* them with the *encore* performance of loving behavior. When the kundalini fell, it remained *undifferentiated*, but Jesus *undid* this problem as a result of his Passion and enabled it to *undulate* upwards when we *unearth* our fears with our remorse. When we *comply* with the components of the *circles*, it completes this *circuit* and puts us under the *umbrella* of God's love, because Jesus is the *umpire* who brings this about.

When we climb the *mountain* of personal growth, we feel less like a *mouse*. On the way up we *wallow* in self-esteem and self-control, but at the top we insert our wills into the *wall plug* known as the will of God that gives us the *wampum* of Self-esteem and Self-control. We confront this *upheaval uphill* and crucify this *blasphemy* but on the way down are powered by the *blaze* of glory which is Christ's Resurrection.

Our self-esteem and self-control are our *egotistical electric* outlets, but our Self-esteem and Self-control end this *winter* of discontent by *wiring* us to our *wisdom*, so they are our nerves of *steel*, because they *steep* us in the divine sweetness.

The circles are the *passbook* where we invest our spiritual savings by getting rid of these two *passengers* called self-esteem and self-control, and the bank is the *Passion*, because it makes us *passive* to our Self-esteem and Self-control. I took three *doubts* to the bank, *doused* them in my remorse, and received as a dividend three kinds of *clout* that would help me behave less like a *clown*.

I had been a member of this *clown's club* but eventually got a *clue* as to why I was *clumsy* with the divine sweetness and got my *cluster* of Fruits. I was no longer in the *clutches* of ego, because Jesus had been my *coach*. I had become *inflexible*, but my fear of the Lord exerted its *influence*, and I received these three kinds of *authentic* clout from the *Author* of my *awe*.

Fear of loss of self-esteem	**charm-doubt**	The *charlatan's charm-doubts* bring us *down*.
Fear of loss of self-control	**alarm-doubt**	The *alarm* that is triggered by ego's *alchemy*.
Fear of being unlovable	**farm-doubt**	The *farcical farm* whose *top* soil leaves us *topsy-turvy*
Fear of the Lord: Faith in one's Self-control	**disarming-clout**	*Disarms* my alarming *disarray*.
Fear of the Lord: Faith in one's Self-esteem	**strong-arm clout**	One *stroke* of this *strong-arm* clout will end my charm-doubt.

The *doubts* leave us *dour*, but these *clouds* of despair are dispelled by the *clouts*, because the clouts send the *cavalry* that makes the doubts *cave in*. Our doubts are the *abomination* we need to *abort* if we want our sweetness to *abound*, and the role of the clouts is to bring about this *reverent reversal*. Our self-esteem and self-control are *expatriates* of our heaven within, but our Self-esteem and Self-control have the *expectation* of God's *expediency*, and therefore do not send us on such *expensive experiences*. Our clouts will make us *smile*, because they *smite* our doubts by ending the *smoke screen* that gets in the way of our *smooth* sailing. Therefore, if we want to *give way to gladness*, we should welcome these two *gladiators*. Our clouts *fathom* the *faultfinders* known as the doubts, so let's do ourselves a *favor* and get some *Fear* of the Lord, because it *figures* out how we got *filled* with this *filth* and *finds* our *finesse* by using these two *detectives* who are *devoted* to God. When we *fax* our *Fear* of the Lord to our ego, it will *lose* the *loud-speaker* which is our will.

The seven deadly sins are the *placebos* which these two gladiators *place kick* into oblivion. Original sin *suffused* us with these *sugar-coated suggestions*, but the sins are *inert* alongside of the divine sweetness, which is *inexorable* in ending our *infamy*.

Our lives will be a *circus* until we tap into the *cistern* that holds the divine sweetness, so let's ask Self-control and Self-esteem to guard this *citadel* and not let the *infidel infiltrate* us. We should remember that heart-mind exerts *Self-control* by being *self-correcting*, and soul-strength brings about *Self-esteem* through *Self-government*. Heart-mind *disarms* the alarm, and soul-strength's strong arm gives us God's charm, so together they have the *disarming discipline* that ends our *discord*. Heart-mind has a *salutary* effect, because he *salutes* Self-control whose job is to *salvage* the divine sweetness, whereas soul-strength signals our Self-*esteem* to trigger the *et ceteras* known as the Fruits.

Fear of loss of self-esteem	**charm-doubt**	**Soul-strength**
Fear of loss of self-control	**alarm-doubt**	**Heart-mind**
Fear of being unlovable	**farm-doubt**	**Farm-clout**
Fear of the Lord: Faith in one's Self-control	**disarming-clout**	**Heart-mind**
Fear of the Lord: Faith in one's Self-esteem	**strong-arm clout**	**Soul-strength**

The *stellar* way to *stem* the *tide* of sin is therefore the good *tidings* which is the divine sweetness. Satan's *dictatorship* depends on our ego-addiction, but the divine sweetness puts an end to this *difficulty*, so why put up with this *pinhead* when we can *pinpoint* the events from our past that put us *on pins and needles* in the present. Heart-mind gives the *proof* of the divine sweetness, and soul-strength is the *propagation-propeller* of the Fruits, so together they have the *persuasive* power to put an end to this *pestilence*. Therefore, when your ego-driven behavior makes the *headlines*, ask them to improve your *health* through the *sorrowful sorties* of your remorse so as to get *soundness* of spirit.

Our spiritual pride empowers our heart-mind to end this *rabid race* by calming down our ego's *racket*. Ego is the *raconteur* that tells us *fairy-tales* when we are children, but our spiritual pride identifies them as *fakes*. When our lives get too *racy*, we can use the three circles' *radar*. Then their *radial* arrangement will give off the *radiant* energy that does *radical* surgery on our ego. We will continue to be *distraught* until our *distress* is *distributed* into this *district*, so let's *tune* into this *tunnel* of love and end our *turmoil*.

My *troubles* had *trumped* my ability to *trust* God, so I got involved in a big *tug of war* between these two *titans* of heart-mind and soul-strength who *toiled* in my mind. My mind was a *compulsive computer* that kept me *suspicious*, so I thought the divine *sustenance* couldn't be *swallowed*. Therefore, my main *exaltation* was *examining* each *example* of *febrile feces* that had caused my *bedeviled behavior*, and my *proboscis* got stuck in this *procedure* that blocked my better *proclivities*.

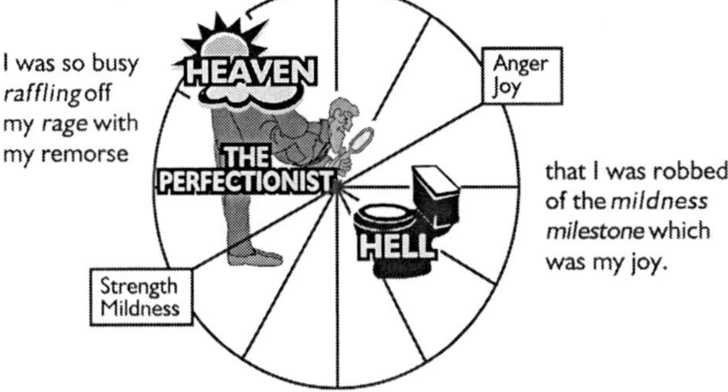

My *perfectionism* enabled me to *persevere* in *smelling* out this *smoldering smut*. Nevertheless, I was so *intent* on *hunting* down the next *horde* of *horrors* that I obsessed over this *hot shit*, and my sweetness got lost in the *hustle*. I was so *devoted* to this *digging* that my *diligence* closed the *dining* room in my heart where the Fruits were served. I *collared* each of these *occult offenders* and *collected* them in my *colon* so as to put an end to these *combatants' commerce* with my ego. I got so *excited* over passing these *rank reactionaries* in my *excrement* that I could not rest until they had been *expelled*, and their *expensive exploits* ended. I *interrogated* my *intestinal* contents and was so *intoxicated* with this *intrigue* that the most *intrinsic* part of me got *invalidated*, and I forgot the *Fruits* could be more *fun*. Each *stalemate* I encountered made me want to *stalk* the insight even harder, so my divine sweetness *stalled*, because it didn't find my will to be a very *stalwart* supporter. Even so I *eliminated* my *embarrassing anger* by the *anguish* of my remorse and gradually became a more *joyous judge*.

My wife, Maria, on the other hand, wasn't so *impeccable* in her approach to her personal growth, because she realized that there were certain *impenetrable* mysteries such as the divine sweetness that had to be accepted by faith. She was more *reserved* in her approach to her growth, because she felt entitled to her *reservoir* of divine sweetness. Every time she felt remorse she didn't forget to *reset* the flow so as to *reshape* herself interiorly and become more sweet. She didn't *toil* over her *toilet training* as I did in the diagram above, because she had learned that the divine sweetness was always a *scrumptious* feast that could be served by her will the priest if she were just *scrupulous* about her contrition. The main *feature* in her growth wasn't her *feces*, because she didn't see her *defecation* as being *defective*.

She wasn't as much of a *killjoy*, because her *kin* were more *kind*, and she hadn't *fanned* the fires of her *fanaticism* like I had. As a child she had simply *fancied* that making a *fanfare* of being forgiven in her *fantasy* life made more sense. On the other hand I was a psychic *surgeon* who aimed to become less *surly*, so I *surmised* I had to excise my ego in order to *surmount* the injury brought to me by the *surname* of my birth. Therefore, I was the surgeon whose ego only *burgeoned*, and Satan saw fit to go on *burglarizing* my sweetness.

My heart-mind *swept* my *sweetness* under the rug, because it thought its role was to examine the *sour source* which was my ego. Nevertheless, its *sorrow* was contagious to my *soul-strength*, and when they got together, they ended my *stress*. When they *stretched* out a helping hand to one another, I was no longer *stricken* with ego, because they were *strictly* in *stride* with my sweetness. My heart-mind and soul-strength had a *synergism* with one another, because they were the *syringe* that injects the *syrup* of the divine sweetness into my heart. When they *docked* up to one another in this *dockyard*, they *documented* my sweetness and enabled me to *dodge* the influence of ego. They were responsible for the *excision* of my ego, and it was *exciting*, because it made me feel an *esprit de corps* with my *essence*.

Maria seemed to *understand* that Jesus became the *underwriter* of her happiness when he went through his *Crucifixion*, because he *crunched* the *numbers* that got us out of the *nut house* and gave us the spiritual *nutrition* we needed, so she just fled to this *oasis*. She knew Jesus was the *blockade-runner* whose *blood flooded* her heart and *floored* Satan, so she just suckled on this *teat* and made her life less *tedious*. She knew this *meal* would *meet* her needs and *effortlessly* eradicate *ego*. Therefore, her heart became her *barometer* of this wellbeing, and her personal growth was the *barrel* of fun into which she *plunged* in order to earn her *plurality* of the Fruits. Her will wasn't a *dud*, because Satan couldn't keep her in high *dudgeon*. She had used this *fantastic fantasy* to have *faith* in God rather than the *fallacies* passed along by her *family*. Her fantasy life was the *gimmick* she used to *gird* herself spiritually since she was a little *girl*. The Blessed Mother in particular was the *shock absorber* she consulted to get rid of *shoddy* thinking and learn how to walk in the *shoes* of Jesus. When the *demon* got this *demonstration*, her *demoralization* was *demoted*, and the devil couldn't put a *dent* in her happiness. Maria simply *summoned* the *sumptuous* repast of the Fruits, and the Virgin Mary helped her feel entitled to her *place in the sun*. Maria understood the *alpha and omega* without having to *alphabetize* these messages, because her spiritual growth was the *alpine* event that enabled her to climb this mountain and make Satan an *also-ran*. She earned the *olive branch* and won the spiritual *Olympics*, because it was no *fairy tale* that her *faith* was *firm* from the *first* to the *last*. Her sweetness was never *late* in appearing, because the Resurrection was the good *omen* she used to get rid of *ominous* speculations. She gave Satan a *pummeling* by using the Sacred Heart as her love *pump*, so I eventually followed *suit* and handed over my *sullenness*. It seemed a better tactic than the *guise* of my perfectionism, so I got the *gumption* to *gun* down the *rumors* from my past and put Satan on the *run*.

I finally learned that the Sacred Heart was a place to hand over *treason* and get the *treasure* of the divine sweetness. I had got a *measly measure* of this pleasure as a child, so as an adult I had to look for this *piety* that would let me stop being Satan's *pigeon*. I had been *duped during* my childhood and had not had a very *blithe* spirit, because the *blockage* of certain pleasure *centers* had left me with a heart I thought was *ceramic*. They were the five *hubs* where I had allowed my *hubris* to be installed, so I needed to ask each to be a *nucleus* for my sweetness. These five pleasure centers had to be *nudged* so they could find this *nugget* and not consider themselves *nuisances*.

Chapter 16: Five *Censored* Pleasure *Centers* that Gave Me a *Ceramic* Heart

The problem was that I had been *cheated* by Satan who gave me a *checkered* childhood. I had been a *sucker*, because I hadn't *suckled* on the divine *sucrose* that came from the Sacred Heart and *suddenly* found myself in the circumstance of having to *sue* for its recovery through my *suffering*. I was *baffled* by this *baggage* that made my *sense organs* forget how to be *sensible*. I just couldn't *perceive* that the divine sweetness was *perched* inside my heart and was ready to *percolate* into my behavior, because I had marched to the beat of the *percussionist* from hell who led me through my own *perdition*. This *confusion grated* on my nerves and made me seek *gratification* that had *grave consequences*. I had fed on the *enemy's energy* source, and it had *enfeebled* these five pleasure centers that were *enfranchised* by God to *engage* my sweetness. I couldn't *assimilate* the divine sweetness, because I hadn't received the *assistance* of these centers which had *associated* with some invalid *assumptions*.

My sense of *touch* was run out of *town*, because I didn't receive many *caresses* from my *caretakers*, so I never developed the *skill* to use my *skin* as a *plausible pleasure* center. I was too young to chew my *cud* to figure out how this lack of *cuddling* could have *cued* my ego, so I naturally felt *culpable*. My *hide* became a *hideaway* for *hideous* forces, and I had a *tottering* sense of *touch*, because no matter how hard I *strived* I didn't get these *strokes*. My parents probably felt it was *hogwash* to *hold* a child, so my divine sweetness went on *holiday*.

I had a *nervous* habit, and its *habitat* was the *tips* of my right index finger and thumb which I never *tired* of picking. The fingernail on my index finger would *linger* on my thumb-tip until it *linked* with some of the *callus* and then would peel it off until I felt calmer. Sometimes my teeth would give some *nimble nips*, but it was a poor substitute for the *nipple* of my *nirvana* located in the Sacred Heart. It was the *covert* comfort of a *covetous coward*, and I was the *sot* who I *sought* it when I was *fraught* with concern over my *frayed* nerves. It was the *succinct succor* I enjoyed, because I hadn't received the *support* I was *supposed* to have had.

I *thought* about the problem and *thrashed* out answers by following the *story line* of how I *stowed* away so much fear. My parents were *prejudiced* against these five *prelates* because of the *preliminary* influences they had gone through during their childhoods, and it all seemed to be the *premeditated* result of Satan encouraging Adam and Eve to give their *premiere* performance. My parents had leveled some *discrete discrimination* against my pleasure centers, and I had trouble *locating* them, because the divine sweetness had been *locked* out of them. Therefore, my fingertips went *loco*, because the *lode* of the divine sweetness never *lodged* in them.

My mother wasn't good at *singsong* baby talk either, and it had the *singular effect* of making my ears less *effective*. My mother had *partaken* very *partially* of these little joys, because her parents had *deliberately* withheld these *delights*. It was a *depressing* sensory *deprivation* of multigenerational *depth*, because her parents had *hatched* this plan that had made her ears go *haywire*, and she unknowingly *deputized* Satan to *derail* my divine sweetness by giving me *hazy hearing* also.

The second issue I had to *delve* into involved the question of why my parents were the *demagogues* who didn't feed me on *demand* but rather *force-fed* me and filled me with a sense of *foreboding*. I didn't learn how to *remand* the *remarkable* divine sweetness from my stomach into my *bloodstream*, and therefore my Fruits didn't *bloom*. My *stomach* was *stomped* on, so I didn't recognize the *value* of the *valve* it contained which would only allow *entry* of the divine sweetness into my blood if I *enunciated* the order. I sometimes felt *stuffed* but was also *stumped* when my hunger pains set up *camp* and went on their own *campaign*. The nine Fruits *appertained* to my *appetite*, but I never learned to *applaud* this *application*, because my appetite had been *trained* to go on this *traitorous trajectory*. I reacted by becoming an *infamous infant*, and Satan's *infantry* called fear, hurt, and anger became my *infatuation*.

My third pleasure center was my *penis*, but my mother probably thought it a cause for *penitence*, because *intimacy* may have been *intimidating* to her. Therefore, my two brothers and I may have been a *threatening threesome*, because she may have seen the *ordnance* of the enemy in our three *organs* of pleasure. Consequently, when my hand *wandered*, her patience may have *waned*, because a shame-based sexuality may have *launched* her into the idea that my thinking needed to be *laundered*. I think that delayed my *convalescence* from my second adolescence, because I probably thought my heart was the *convent* where the divine sweetness couldn't *converge* on me, and therefore my *libido* developed a *life* of its own.

My fourth pleasure center was my *anus*, but it was only a source of *anxiety*, because I was probably *recriminated* for relieving my *rectal* cramps when I was *recumbent* rather than seated on the *toilet*, which my mother may have taken as a *token* of rebellion. The act of cleaning diapers may have been beneath her *dignity*, so she may have *dilated* on it at great length. At any rate she wasn't very *tolerant*, and the *toll* it took was to make me the *anachronism* of an *anal-retentive*, which is why I have had to *rethink* my reasons for being *reticent* about my *retinue* of repressed feelings.

These four centers didn't come on line on *schedule*, and although it may not have been a deliberate *scheme*, it widened the *schism* between me and God. It left me feeling *fragile*, because these four *fragments* hadn't received the *fragrance* of the divine sweetness, and they became the *frail frame of reference* for my *fifth* pleasure center which was my heart. My heart wound up being full of *fight*, because my first four pleasure centers didn't receive the *unction* of the divine sweetness, and it *undeniably undermined* the function of the fifth. I never learned to carry the *ball* of the divine sweetness, and since I didn't have it as *ballast*, I often went *ballistic*. Satan gave me his whole *ball of wax* with the result that I had to make the *balloon* payment of going through a divorce later in life. Each of my repressed feelings had cast its *ballot*, so I had to use the *ballyhoo* of my remorse to earn the *balm* of my sweetness.

My *current assets* during my childhood were due to a faulty *curriculum*, and I just kept on trying to *curry* favor since no one taught me to confront this *curse*. My mother never gave my pleasure centers a *cursory* glance and only continued to be *curt*. This *abridged* my sweetness and made me *abrupt*. Parenting is the *design designated* by God to satisfy a child's *desire* for the divine sweetness, but many parents *desist* from this task, and so Satan sits at the *desk* of their will, and their children remain *desolate*. Their children become *cynical czars* who *dabble* unsuccessfully in the divine sweetness, because they don't realize their *Dad* in heaven *gives* it to anybody who's *glad* to have it. These five pleasure centers can be *coherent cohorts*, and when they all *cooperate* a child learns to *cope*. He is able to *trust* the *truth*, *tryst* with God, and confront the *mystery* that his parents can be *mythmakers*. A child's fantasy life is his *creative credential*, and it makes the divine sweetness seem *credible*. Therefore, when short *shrift* makes our inner child's pleasure centers *shrivel*, we should make a *remorseful rendezvous* with God and *renegotiate* the deal.

Satan lets you think that he *amputated* your sweetness so that you will run *amok* and *amuse* him, but it is better to *laud* it and give God the last *laugh*. Your will doesn't have to be Satan's *launching pad*, so let your contrition *spotlight* the causes of your *sprain* and then let your fears *sprawl* in its *spray* so that the Fruits will *spread out* before you. Go on this *touchiness tour* with your power of imagination and the sacrament of your holy orders, because they are the *spiffy spigot* that can *spike* your thinking with the divine sweetness. It is the *faucet* that eliminates the *fault* known as original sin, because it enables you to have a *face-off* with every *facet* of your personality so as to show it the *facts*. *Plow* under your fears with your remorse and earn mildness and joy by eliminating Satan's *ploys*.

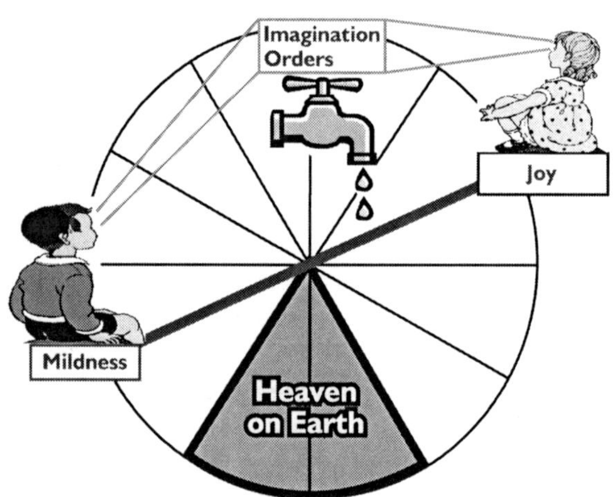

Unfortunately my will was still the *spigot* of Satan the *spin doctor*, so the *lining* of my stomach never *linked* with the *Lion* of Judah, and I didn't absorb mildness or joy, which were never on my *lips*. My five pleasure centers weren't very *pliable*, because they linked me to my *plight*, and I never had a *gleam* of understanding about how to *glean* my sweetness in order to add to my *glee*. My *appetite* was never satisfied, because my stomach never understood this *application*. Likewise my *skin* had been *skipped*, my *penis* was my *penitentiary*, my *anus* gave me *anxiety*, and therefore my *heart* was least of all a *hearth* for God's love. I had been the guest of dishonor at the *fiend's fierce* and *fiery fiesta* and was left with the *inescapable* thought that I was *in extremis*. My ears hadn't heard *soothing sounds*, so I wound up with the *infantile infirmity* of a *startle* reaction, because my *attenuated auditory* sense thought it had been *starved*.

This alarm often *sounds* when I am driving and *sparks spats* with Maria. I get this *jolt* when we are on a *journey*, because loud *noises* make me feel *nonaligned* with God, and if she *warns* me in this way about a car I don't see, I often go on the *warpath*. It puts me in a state of *pandemonium* by pressing my *panic button*, because it reminds me of the times when my mother's *thunderous* voice *thwacked* me. Therefore, Maria gently *squeezes* my hand so I won't feel *squelched*. I am a *captive* of my temper in my *car*, because my mother's caresses were *stilted stimuli* that she was *stingy* with. That's why I had this *conversation* years later with the Blessed Mother and *converted* to Catholicism, because her Immaculate Conception is the *pacifying pact* that I knew would *palliate* my *panic*.

The *deal* called the Immaculate Conception is very *dear* to me, because it erased my *debts*. The Immaculate Heart of Mary is the *classroom* where we get this *classy cleansing*, so make your *dirt disappear* by gathering each *batch* and giving it a *bath*. Your *spotlessness* will make the Fruits *sprout*, so take your *mind* to Mary and ask her to *minister* to your *warped* thinking. She will *wash* it clean, so insist on having your original *innocence* rather than your *insolence*. I had *myriads* of problems when I first went to her, but she brought the *Mysteries* of the *Rosary* to bear on these conflicts, so when I sat down at the *Round Table* of the first circle, the apostles and I became the *knights* who went on the crusades that solved these *knotty* problems. Each apostle has a *power* for you to use in your *prayer* to end this *precarious* balance, so bring an *ardent* desire for self-improvement and go on this *arduous* journey which you can *expect* to win because of their *ex-*

pertise. Sit down at this table, bring your *sixth sense*, and make your fears *skedaddle.* The Immaculate Conception is the *meaningful mechanism* the *Mediatrix* teaches at this *meeting*, so take advantage of this *fair trade agreement* and make your *fairy tale* come true.

My wounded infant had gotten *tainted*, so I told this *tale* of woe to the Blessed Mother and asked her if he could eat *breakfast* at her *breast*. My wounded infant had *dipped* into these *dire* thoughts, but when he *suckled* I got rid of the *sudden suffering* of my startle reaction. The divine *areola* provided me with this nurture that was not *arguable*, and my spark burst into *flame*, because I was *flanked* by forces that weren't *flappable.*

The Immaculate Heart of Mary is the *swap* shop where I gave *sway* to my sweetness. Every time my behavior *flared up*, Mary gave me a *flashback* to my childhood that explained how love first went *flat.* My flaws weren't *tragic*, because Mary was the *trailblazer* who brought the divine sweetness to earth so that I could get rid of these *traits*. Therefore, I followed this *avenue* and *averted* disaster by making this *exchange* that was *exciting.* I *bottomed* out by realizing that all my problems had begun in my parents' *boudoir.* The sour grapes on their *bough* were the ones I *bought*, so their *bitter* attitudes made me feel like a *black sheep*, and this particular *boulder* in the *boulevard* was the one that blocked my path to God. My original sin arose from their *sensual* act, but that *sentence* was *commuted* by Jesus who was the *compact companion* who lived in my heart. He helped me *bounce* back, because I was *bound* and determined to move the *boundary* of my will to encircle the *bounty* of the nine Fruits of the Spirit.

The *shame* I felt over my driven behaviors was the *shampoo* that I used on my *hairy* thinking to feel more *hale* and hearty. I often felt *reviled* by my behavior but was able to *revise* it by *reviving* my contrition. I had a *bundle* of *bunk* that I had hidden behind the *bunker* of my ego-defenses, but I solved these *riddles* by *riding high* in my psychotherapy. I focused my *hindsight* on this *crusade* into that *cryptic cubbyhole* in my chest where I had *filed* away my *filth*, and before I knew it each piece of dirt I had *stored* away told its *story.* The Mediatrix of Grace has this *lantern* which enabled my contrition to shed light on my misery, so I just got in her *lap* and enjoyed the *lark* of handing over this *lassitude* so Jesus could feed me just like at the *Last Supper.* Handing over my *issues* to her was so much fun that I finally joined the *Italian* church and was glad to have its *blend* of *blessings* remove these *obsolete obstacles.*

Therefore, I eventually figured that the Blessed Mother might be just as *pleased* to do her magic on my five *pleasure* centers, so I took them to her and asked her to *tend* to them *tenderly* so they would have the *choice* of not feeling *choked* to death. I *sauntered* to her side with this *savage* tale, because I knew she was very *savant* about how to *save* them from this disgrace. It was God's *idea* to make her the *ideal* mother, and I had suffered enough from the *ideology* of *idiocy* called original sin, so I asked her to *share* her Immaculate Conception. I knew *she* had the *finesse* to *finish* off this *first* fear that had installed the *fixture* of ego in my mind, so I asked her for this *relief* of the Catholic *religion*.

Mary helped me *adopt* the *adoration* that would prevent my *adrenaline* from keeping me *adrift* on a sea of troubles. She helped me *dissolve* my divine sweetness in that *distinguished* fluid known as my kundalini. These two *liquids* then *liquidated* my fears and taught me to *listen* to the voice of God. The Blessed Mother taught the two *soldiers* known as heart-mind and soul-strength how to bring about this *solution*, so they *raised* my kundalini to the *rampart* of God's will which is *recognized* as a legal *recourse* for *recovery* from these *recurring* problems. This *alliance* with the divine sweetness *allowed* my *kundalini* to use the *kung fu* of the *kyrie eleison*, so I defeated the *devil* with this *devotion* and allowed God's *mercy* to clean up this *mess*.

It is *really* for that *reason* that I credit my spiritual *rebirth* to Mary, because she's the one *who* made me *whole*. My five pleasure centers became *sensitive sensors* and *detected* the divine sweetness that I had *devalued*. My *fears* didn't *feast* on me, because the Blessed Mother evened the *score* with these *scoundrels*. Therefore, I decided not to rub elbows with this *ridiculous riffraff* any longer, and I stopped *lugging* around my ego's *luggage*, because she gave me the *guts* to stay out of this *gutter*.

The *settlement* that I struck with this *sewer* was to refuse to let it make me feel *inferior*, because that would just make me *infertile* where it came to the Fruits. It seemed like a better idea to *plant* something more *pleasant*, so I got my *humility*, which is a kind of *humus* and used it as the *fertile* soil that would *fetch* me a better harvest. I was sick and tired of the *crooked crop* which was my *renegade* fear, hurt, and anger, so I *renounced* them and *grew* the Fruits, which I knew wouldn't make me *growl*.

My sweetness had remained *indistinct*, because my father *inducted* me into this hall of *false fame*. I had eaten this *dish* of *dishonor*, because he took more *pride* in behaving like a *professor* than a father. I felt *slighted*, because he never made the *small talk* that could *tame* this first core fear, so I felt *unmanly* and that he was *unrivaled*. I felt *ashamed*, because he never *asked* the *personal* questions that could *persuade* me otherwise, so I *promoted* him into the role of false *prophet*. He was very *learned* and *lectured* at great *length*, so I remained convinced of his *intelligence*, but his lack of *interest* in me left me feeling *unalterably unappealing*. My *ponderous pontificating* arose from this anomaly, but I eventually stopped being the *windbag* whose brain was *wired* in this way, so these *theatrics* finally became the object of Mary's *therapeutics*.

I learned to take *orders* from God like any *ordinary* person, because my will had gone through this *ordination*. My father had been *pedantic* and *peddled* the propaganda that made me put my mind on a *pedestal*, but my mind is really very *pedestrian*, and my real *pedigree* goes back to the *peep show* that Adam and Eve originated, so I figure it is nothing to be proud of. My *ancestors' angst animated* me, so I may come from two *generations* of doctors, but it has only resulted in the *genesis* of my *intellectual* pride. It was Satan's *intention* to *interfere* with my *brain* in this way so as to make me *brash*, but this *hell* on earth has *hemmed me in* long enough, so I think I'll stop pretending I'm an intellectual *stallion* and muster up the *stamina* to get a little humility.

My pride is a *horse* without much *horse sense*, because it *tramples* all those in its path. Therefore, I need to stop this *trance*, because it comes from my control-addiction, which is the *will-o'-the-wisp* that has made me a weeping *willow*. I have not been *negligent* in taking a look at this *nervous habit*, because it had given me a *hair trigger* temper. My pride has *collected* this *collusion*, but my humility has a more *intelligent intention* which is to *interface* with God's *supremacy* and get a *surfeit* of the Fruits. I have this *reservoir* of God's *resourcefulness* inside of me, so I intend to send my *humility* to satisfy this *hunger*, because he is the *friar* who recognizes God as a *friend*, and his holy *orders* will enable me to mine this *ore*. My will is an *appalling apparatus* unless I dress it in this divine *apparel*. I may be a physician, but only God can *heal* my wound, so I intend to ask Him to stop this *hemorrhage*.

I have *tried* to parent my inner child and *tumble* to the truth, but God is a *poppa* who is way more *popular*, so why shouldn't I let Him *populate* my mind with the Fruits? I have been on the *trail* of my *transgressions*, but I would rather make the *transition* that *reaps* more reward than my reasoning, which is flavored with the *seamy seasoning* of my original sin. I don't see why I should let this *pork barrel por-*

nography make me stop being *porous* to God's sweetness, so I choose not to *compete* with Him. He is more *competent* at *compiling* the Fruits in my *behavior*, so I might as well *surrender* to this *sustenance* and not be *beleaguered* by these bats in my *belfry*. It is more *strenuous* for me to deal with *stress* than to ask God to *extend* the helping hand that will *extinguish* my troubles.

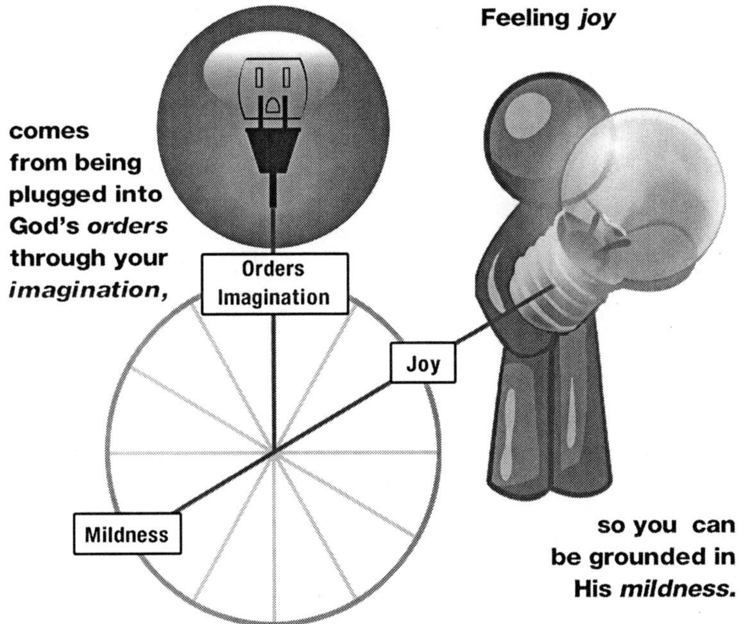

I have remained *ill*, because my *illegal* control-addiction is the *armchair arrogance* that flowed from the *illegitimate* birth of my original sin. My ego-addicted will has been *illiterate* toward this *illness* and only my remorse has been able to *illuminate* it so that my Fruits can *flower* and my wellbeing not *fluctuate*. I can speak the language of love *fluently*, but first I have to get rid of the *fluff* that Satan offered Adam and Eve when he made the *fluid* in their spine *flunk* the test God asked them to pass. I *relinquished* the Fruits I stored in my *reliquary*, but I can *savor* them if I have the *savvy* to *say* I'm sorry.

Paul's humility was a *no-show* until he was taken down a *notch* and was made to take *notice* of the *damage* on the road to *Damascus*. When he was knocked *off* his high horse, he realized he had behaved like an *ogre* and began to climb the spiritual *ladder*. He became less *laden* with ego, because he was *ladled* the divine sweetness by Our

Lady, so let's be *thankful* to Mary, because she *thaws* the Fruits that are *frozen* by our *frenzied* egos.

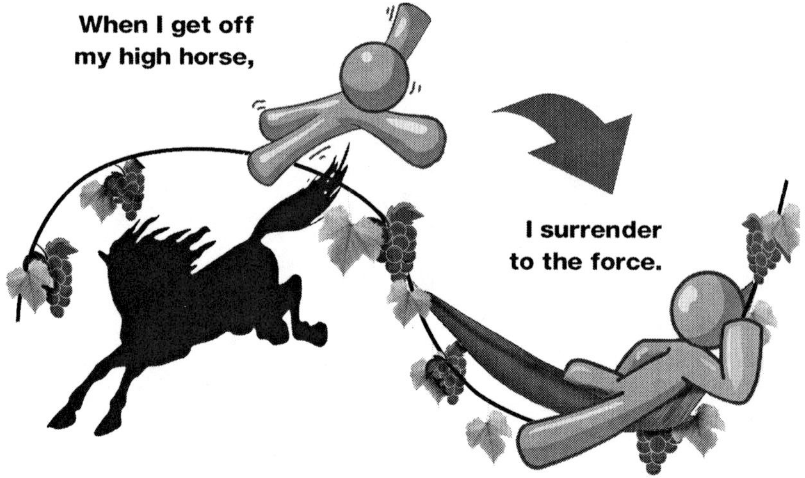

Therefore, if the Lord *knocks* me off my high horse, it is because the Crucifixion of Jesus on the *knoll* outside Jerusalem solved all the *knotty* problems that can beset me. My fear, hurt, and anger are the *vindictive* fruits of my *vine*, but my contrition is the *ascendant asceticism* that enables the *asexual* reproduction of the Immaculate Conception to put a stop to this *goading* I have received from these false *gods.*

This *symbiosis* with my parents has caused my *symptoms*, so I aim to ask Mary to do me this *good turn* that can save me from being such a *goody-goody.* I have not *idolized* that which is *immaculate* but rather these poor *imitations* which have *impaired* me, and I have eaten a *parental parfait* that has made me feel like a *pariah* in my own divine *parliament.* What I have *eaten* has made my divine sweetness *ebb*, but the *feat* of the *feast* of the Last Supper was to make it *feasible* for these *fears* not to *faze* me. This sequence is *against* alphabetical order, because the *agape* served at the Last Supper *turned the tables* by arming the apostles with the *twelve* powers that ended this *tyranny.* God can *pilot* my will better than the *pirate* Satan, so I intend to ask these twelve *pitch men* to help me avoid these *pitfalls.* This *abomination* can be *aborted*, so I will make this *about face* by using this *pivot* point to *place* the Fruits on my *plate.* I have gone *haywire* as a result of my family's *hazing*, but the twelve *apostles* can teach me to stop being an *apple polisher*, so that I won't have to *curry* favor with the people who fired me so many *curve balls*. I have eaten the *patriarchal pea soup* that has made me *peevish* and the *matriarchal meal* that has made me *mean*, but the *discerning discipline* of my remorse has enabled me to *discover* this particular *discrepancy disease* that has made me feel like I don't *measure* up and has spared me some *mega meltdowns*. These *disgraceful dishes* of *disillusionment disinherited* me from the *Digestible Dignitary* in the *dining* room of my heart, so I had to *die* to this *diet* that *differed* from the one *God* served in this *gourmet* kitchen. Our *Lady* heard the *laments* of my remorse, turned on the *lamp* in this dining room in my heart, and Jesus served the *Last* Supper.

I don't have to be my family's *camp follower* if I use my *candid camera* to document the *partisan* politics from my *past* that have robbed me of *peace* in the present. My remorse is the *technician* who *televises* this *travail* so it won't *trespass* on my good sense and give me a bad *temper*. It empowers the *vice squad* of the twelve apostles to use these *videos* to disarm this *cannon* that makes me *cantankerous* and *restore* me by the grace of the *Resurrection* to the *composure* I got *conned* out of in Eden. Therefore, I intend not to be *spineless*. I intend to take advantage of this *spiritual* love that vanished when Eve *splayed* her legs *there* and installed these *thermodynamics* of the *thief* in my heart. I intend to *feather* my nest with this *feature* that at one time was innate in every creature.

Our fears are the *forgeries* that make us *forgo* our Fruits, but if we take this *fork* in the road, this *genuine genus* will increase in *geometric progression*. It is my dream that *someday somehow* everyone on earth will learn how to do this *somersault* so that we can awaken from the *somnolence* of ego. We have all been through Satan's *assault and battery*, but we can *assert* our rights to our sweetness. We don't have to remain *intoxicated* with this *intrigue*, because in a *wink* we can *winnow out* our fears and end our *winters* of discontent. The *Fatherhood* of God will help us *fathom* how our *brotherhood* with Adam *brought* us this *brouhaha*, so let's drink the *brisk* tea sweetened with the divine sweetness that will keep us from *bristling* with this anger. Staying true to what's *false* will only make us *falter*, so let's *bake* our daily bread with this *balm* that came to us through *Baptism*.

When we *resort* to the *contrition* that ends all *controversy*, we defeat Satan and tap into the divine *resource* within. Adam and Eve were the *dissidents* who began the *dissolute* behavior which is our *aged agenda*, but we don't have to be led *astray* by the organs we sit *astride*, because our contrition will make us *astute*. Our *brains* have only led us into *brambles*, so let's *fill the bill* by *binding* our heart-mind to the task of sending the *SOS* to *soul*-strength that can make our Fruits *sound* off.

Only this *spiritualization* of my heart can rid me of this syphilis *spirochete* which is my ego-addiction, because my heart needs to be *moved* in this way if I am to *mow* down my fears. Only my original *innocence* can make my fears seem *innocuous*, so it's worth *wondering* how to get something so *wonderful*. It is not a good idea to leave my spiritual *development* in the hands of the *devil*, because he will only *exacerbate* my growth and *exact* the *exaggerated* price that I have to pay for my *excesses*. My five *pleasure* centers have suffered because of this *plethora*, but I intend to use the *pliers* of my *remorse* to *remove* each item on this *rap sheet* and return to the spiritual *rapture* that became *rare* in Eden. My pleasure centers and my sweetness were of *like* minds until Adam's *limb limbered up* and made my parents *dispense* the *displeasure* that contaminated my pleasure centers. Therefore, I can bring my sweetness on *line* if I just seek the *lineage* I had before Adam and Eve's *sex* in the *shade* of the apple tree made my ego *shadow* me.

Jesus is the *mainstay* of this *majestic make-up* known as my original innocence, because the *adroitness* he displayed in the *adversity* of his Passion helps me *cope*. I will eventually get rid of the *corny corollary* known as my original sin, because my contrition is the *pebble* that David put in the slingshot to slay Goliath, and I can do the same to this *peccadillo*. Satan was the *director* of this *dirty disappearing act* that made my sweetness *vanish*, but I can *vanquish* the devil, because the Crucifixion is the *variable* in the equation that he didn't count on. God is always *happy* when we seek to end our *harangues* and take *command* of this faculty that Satan *commandeered*. We don't need to allow our *sanity* to be *sapped*, so let's go back to the *acumen Adam* had before he fell in the garden. Adam lost the *battle*, and we won the *bauble* that was *bawdy*, but Jesus can give us the *armaments* that will enable us to win the war in an *armchair*.

These *rations* of *rational* thought helped me feel less *rattled*, because I realized that my five pleasure centers have the *abiding ability* to make me feel less *abject*. They just needed the *ablution* in my *contrition* that would *convince* them they weren't *abnormal*. I felt *sad* that I had been *saddled* with the *sadism* that made it necessary for me to go on this love-*safari* in order to feel *safe*. I hope to be able to see *straight* from now on so as not to always be in dire *straits*.

Nevertheless, when I was a child, I was expected to *dote* in *double time* on my mother's instructions, so I remained *doubtful* about my ability to understand. I felt like a *stooge* having to *stop* so as to *look* at this figure *looming* in front of me and then *listen* to her *litany*. I became the *onlooker* who *only* paid his *undivided* attention to his faults, so I thought that the divine sweetness was *undrinkable*, which of course gave me these endless *difficulties* I have had to *dig* into. I *projected* this circumstance onto my patients when the details in their explanations *proliferated* because it *prolonged* my agony by making these memories *promenade* in front of me. Therefore, when they *dwelled* too long on the details, my patience definitely *dwindled*.

On the other hand, I don't have to think of this inattentiveness as being *dyed-in-the-wool* because of the *dynamic* on the circle which is chastity-peace. I just need to let these *destructive* memories be the focus of my *detached observer* who is never *obsessive* about my fears, because his *fortitude* is the *forum* in which I can *argue* my case with the *armament* of my contrition and stop *slinking* around in shame because of my *sloth*.

Chastity-Peace makes you feel *upbeat*, because it gives you *unconditional* love *up-front*.

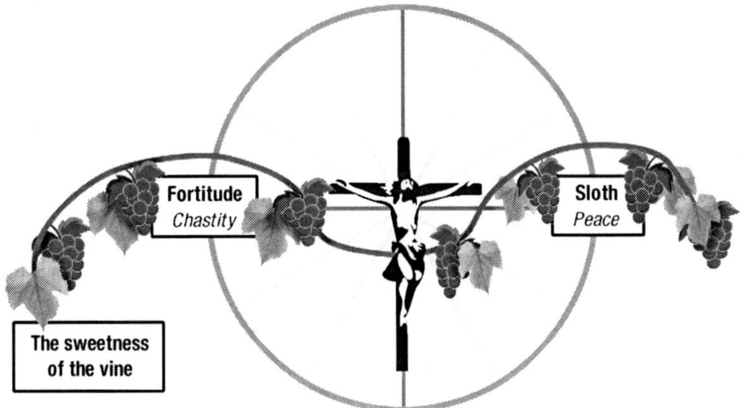

Prior to the fall of man chastity-peace was the *prism* that kept man out of the *prison* of ego. It is still available if you stop being a *truant* from the school of hard knocks and ask your contrition to call a *truce* with your ego. Then you will *truck* with your *true colors* and have the *colossal* benefit of peace of mind. Chastity-peace always *progresses* when we have the fortitude to *prohibit* sloth, because the Crucifixion was the *project* that made ego collapse so that heart-mind and soul-strength could *accordion* from opposite ends of the vertical axis and *accost* one another.

My fortitude has the *infallible influence* over my sloth that Christ brought to the Cross, because Jesus made this *Trinity trip* so that our chastity-peace could *triumph* over this *trivial* sentiment. When I began my *therapy*, my will believed in the *thesis* of my sloth, but then my fortitude took *aside* my sloth and told it that it was *asinine* to believe in this *aspartame aspect*, because *artificial* sweeteners aren't the work of the divine *artisan* and tend to cast *aspersions* on one's spiritual *aspirations*. I *diminished* the *dimwit* of my sloth, because Jesus' *bravery* on the Cross made my chastity-peace my daily *bread*. I *break* this bread with Jesus through the *Gift-giving* of my fortitude, so it doesn't make any sense to stay on the *sidelines* of my personal growth as a result of this *sin*. My fortitude-sloth is therefore the *crucifixion* power I have over my *crud*, and my chastity-peace gives me *rest*, because it is my *resurrection* power.

The *unconditional* peace in our *unconscious* is the *undaunted principle* that can *proclaim* an end to the *undernourished worker* known as our sloth who insists that we put up with our *worries*. This *ecology* of our *ecstasy* results from *understanding* how our *agony* caused our *ailment* and is an *ecumenical eddy* that we can *start* all over the world so as to enjoy the *steady state* Satan *stole*. *Eden* just made us *edgy*, so let's benefit from this *effortless effusion* and defeat this *wariness* that makes us *warlike*. God will *deliver* this *deluxe* accommodation, so let's *isolate* these *issues* that make us *itch*.

Chastity-peace is the *workable* answer, so let's summarize the problems in the *workbook* of our fortitude-sloth and then tackle them with the *work ethic* of our remorse. The three doubts shown below are the *itchy items* on the *itinerary*, and the corresponding Fruits are the *ivory tower* professors who teach personal growth in the *Ivy League*. Each pair of Fruits has the *pull* to make the heart *pulsate* with joy, because they are the clout that has *influence* over this *influx* of doubts. We just need to send our fortitude to *argue* our case, *arm* our charm with faith and love, disarm our alarm with mildness and joy, and destroy the harm growing on our farm with chastity and peace.

This *spate* of three doubts was *spawned* by our fear of being unlovable by God, but our contrition is the *trawl* we can drag behind ourselves in order to catch this *treachery*. Then we will end our *trea-*

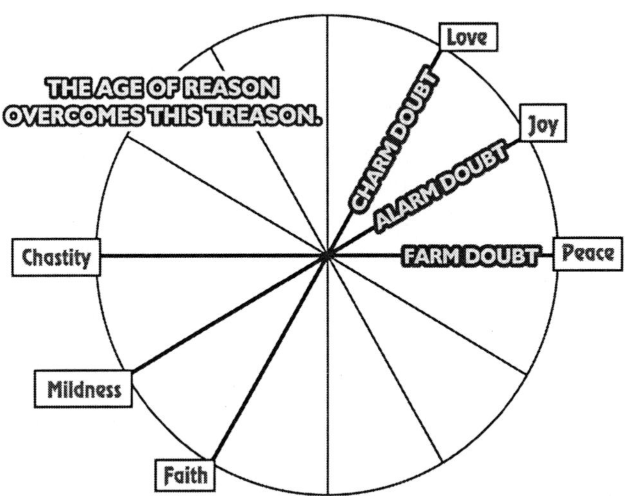

son and no longer have this God-shaped *vacuum* that makes us feel like *vagabonds*, because our love, joy, and peace won't be at the effect of the *vagary* of the *vagina* of Eve who was the *maiden* who *made love* with a *lower* kind of *loyalty*.

The Holy Spirit goes where it is *wanted*, so when we put this *want ad* in our hearts consisting of contrition for being *wanton*, then we will have recruited the forces to win the *war*. Our contrition is the *fee* we need to pay for our *feeble-mindedness* if we want to be *fed* the better *feelings* which are the Fruits of the Spirit. When he went through the Crucifixion, Jesus wrote the *tract* on how to *trade* the *sub-standard* feed of fear, hurt, and anger for the more *substantial* feed of love, joy, and peace.

We *stock* the *stodgy* items called fear, hurt, and anger, because Satan *was* on the *prowl* in Eden and convinced Eve to let him vote God's *proxy*. On the other hand if we decide we *require* love, joy, and peace, then God will *requite* our request.

This *imbroglio* of original sin *imbued* us with this bad *imitation* which is none too *immaculate*, so let's insist on having the divine sweetness which is *immanent*. Heart-mind and soul-strength lost their *conjugal* relationship when these forces were *conjured*, and Satan *connected* our *conniptions* to his *conniving*. Satan *conquered* our *consciousness*, but we can *consecrate* it to God by *constantly contemplating* our *contentious* behavior through the serial acts of *contrition* that are sure to *control* this *controversy*. Adam and Eve *chose* to *chop* off the hand that fed them, but that does not mean that our *preference* for our original innocence can't restore this *prefix* to our thinking. The human will is like a vine, and it can *curl* around the fears that make us *curmudgeons* or *wind* around the *windlass* of the circles that enable us to stop tilting these *windmills.*

Adam and Eve became *acquainted* with evil and *acquiesced* to this *laxity* that has *led* us into disaster. Our *tantrums* have resulted from this *taunting*, but that doesn't mean we can't eliminate this *inward irascibility* by *regretting* this *relentless* pestilence and getting the *relief* of the Christian *religion.* Man is *manacled* to his ego-addicted will, which is the *manager* who always says *mañana* to the concept of personal growth, but when we send this *mandate,* our wills will *maneuver* themselves free of ego-addiction. We can become *naked* of our *namby-pamby* fear, hurt, and anger by remembering that the divine sweetness is *unique* in the *universe* for healing that which is *unjust.* It is *peerless* for making us less *peevish*, and it is *singular* for getting rid of *sinister* thinking. I will *settle* for none other, because I am determined not to let the *seven* cardinal sins *sever* me again from God. I would *rather ratify* the divine sweetness than suffer from the opinionated *ratings* which are my fear, hurt, and anger. With the divine sweetness *on-line* I will be full of *oomph* and won't have to say "*Oops*!" every time my sourness *oozes.*

Planet earth was originally intended to be God's *composure compound*, but Adam and Eve's *compromise* with their morals got them in the *enclosure* called ego that *encompassed* their fears. Nevertheless, all *races* on the planet can *rack* up points with God and end Satan's *racket* by deciding to *amend* their ways so as to earn the *amenity* which is the divine sweetness. We can have this *ultimate* blessing through the *ultimatum* of our remorse, so let's make earth a *domain* of *domestic tranquility* by having contrite hearts that *transcend* our conflict. The *payoff* of our contrition is *peace*, so let's *negotiate* to make earth one *neighborhood.* The *target* of our fortitude is the sloth that *tarnishes* us, so let's not *hesitate* to *hew* our way *individually* through this *indolence.*

I knew that I was *befouled*, but I never felt like a *beggar*, because from the *beginning* of my therapy I knew that my contrition's *renown* was based on its power of *renunciation.* Therefore, I developed a *zeal* to sweep up my problems with this *zephyr.* This *refutation regime* became my race *car*, but it did not own the *caramel* which is the divine sweetness. Avoiding *impending* disaster became my *imperative*, so I drove this race car like a *fanatic* and made a *fanfare* of my penitence. I was a *maniac* behind the wheel, but my *manifesto* of personal growth was still control-addiction, and therefore it was not *adequate* to make the divine sweetness *adhere* to me. My contrition was the *talisman* that *talked* the talk, but only God could *waive* my original sin so that I could *walk* the walk. I needed to *submerge* my will in His sweetness in order to become *submissive* to it.

I wasn't very *compliant* to God but eventually regained my *composure* when I realized that our *three* core fears can be *threshed* out on the third circle by asking love to cross the *threshold* of our hearts. We can separate the *wheat* from the chaff on this *wheel* in order to get a better deal. A *broken* heart can be prone to *brooding*, but the *brook* of divine sweetness flows *through* the vertical axis of the circles and gives *thrust* to God's generosity. We just need to regret our *mumbo jumbo* in order to earn God's *munificence*, so let's not subscribe to this *folly* that Satan *foments*. Let's not *fondle* our free will or *relish* the *remarks* from our childhoods that we need to *remit* to God through our *remorse*. Free will is the *independence* from God that has left us *indescribably* unhappy. Therefore, let's return to the *previous* state of original innocence we enjoyed before we became its *prey* and not let Adam's *priapism* continue to make us pay this *price*.

My head won't give a *farthing* for the *fascist* leadership which is the *fashion* of my ego when my heart is no longer *fastened* to this *fatal* attraction. This *fascination* has brought me to an unhappy *fate*, so I prefer to let Jesus work his *magic* on this *magnetism* and give me results that are more *magnificent*. I intend to *persist* in my penitence until I become a more loving *person*, because I know that this *debate* between my head and my heart will end my ego's *debauchery*. Nevertheless, it has been one *merry* chase, because my thinking has been caught in these *meshes* that have resulted from the *mesmerizing* effect of my ego-addiction.

Adam and Eve's *orgasm oriented* us to ego rather than our divine *origin*. The frenulum of the penis and clitoris is where the orgasm nerves are, and so Adam and Eve's *frenulum frenzy* gave us original sin and obliged us to seek a *pleasure* that has led to *plenty* of problems. Nevertheless, we can have a *future* without this *fuzzy* thinking that makes our *worries wound* our wonder. It is a *yoke* that makes us think God is always down *yonder* when we shouldn't even address Him as "*You*," because He is really the "I am" that keeps us *young* at heart. Our *awe* is not *awful*. Its plans have just gone *awry*, but when our ego gets the *axe*, we won't suffer from the *axillary axiom* that says "I stink!" Adam and Eve *whetted* their appetites for this *whiff* and abandoned their *decency* when they chose this *deceptive decoration*. They forgot the *decorum* which *dedicated* their wills to God and did the dirty *deed* that left them *defenseless* against the forces of evil. They didn't *ask* God first, and God looked *askance*, so modesty wasn't built into the *fabric* of their character, but that doesn't mean we have to go on *fabricating* what they thought was *fabulous*.

Adam was given a *pittance* as a *pivot* point, but I can still eat the piece of *pizza* on the circles that has more *pizzazz*. It is better for me to *dip* into this spiritual *diplomacy* than into the *dire direction* of my *dirty* thoughts, because my rocket can *liftoff* to heaven when I *light* this *fire*. Then I can change the *first edition* of my behavior into something more *fitting*. I just need to let my clouts *ignite* my doubts so that I will not remain *ill-advised*. If I clean out my *doubts* with the *douche* of my contrition, my *clouts* will remove me from the *clutches* of the devil.

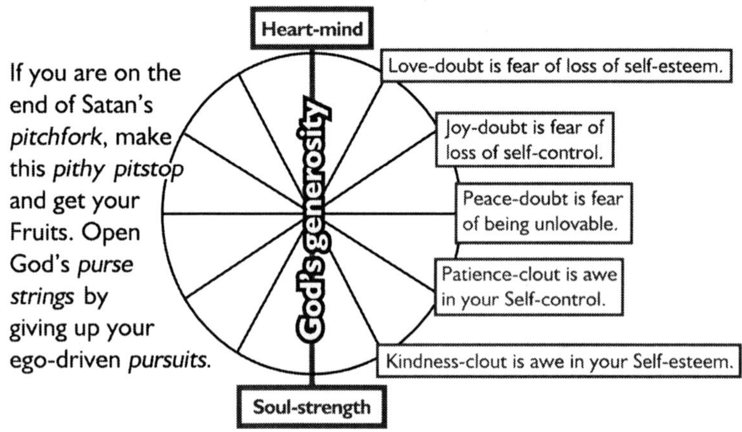

These three *doubts* are the *double-talkers* who make our spirituality go *downhill*, so we should *draft* our *clouts* and give these *clowns* some *coaching* so they won't tell such *cock-and–bull stories*. Love-*doubt* gets *doused* in Self-esteem, joy-*doubt* gets *doused* in Self-Control, and peace-*doubt* gets *doused* in fear of the Lord, which is the *parent* from which the other two *parts* were *derived* in order to end our *despair*. This is a *domino* effect that represents the *doomsday* of our *doubts*, but at first I wasn't a very *valiant warrior*, because my doubts had me feeling *washed-up*. I had *validated* these *vandals* and had *arranged* these *artless* members of the *Aryan Nation* like a *militia* in my *mind*, so they committed *assault and battery* on that *asset* called Fatherly love which most people *assimilate* easily in order to avoid going *astray*. Each doubt *parroted* its own *party line*, but I could *patch* up this *pathology* with my *patience-clout* and be in the *clover*, because then my *kindness-clout* would let me *coast* along without these *cockeyed* pilots in the *cockpit*, and God's *kingdom* would come. If I wanted to be in my right *mind*, I just had to send these *ministers* to work their *miracles* on these *misgivings*.

Once I *read* the riot act to these grim *reapers*, I felt *reassured* that these *rebels* wouldn't *rebroadcast* their *recklessness* into my behavior. My heart-mind and soul-strength were *secure seers*, so they *selected* my *Self*-esteem and Self-control and *sent* my *senseless* self-esteem and self-control some *sermons* on how to better *serve* God. This *lower case loyalty* had my heart-mind and soul-strength suffering from bad *luck*, but I don't have to *lug* around this *lunacy* forever. My heart-mind and soul-strength weren't very good *pundits*, because they couldn't solve this *putrid puzzle* until I placed it on the funeral *pyre* of my *contrition* which *cooked* these *hecklers* from *hell* until I became *cool-headed*. My heart-mind and soul-strength were *soiled soldiers*, but the *heat* of this *heavyweight* sentiment constituted the *solid* evidence that made them stop *munching* on this nonsense, connected them to God's *munificence*, and furnished them with the *munitions* in the above diagram that prevented Satan from *getting away with murder*.

When I become *abject* with remorse, these two *able-bodied* soldiers will *kneel* in front of God and ask Him to sound the death *knell* of my ego. Then Satan won't *knife* me in the back, so I intend to tell these warriors to make this *display* that can change my *disposition*. This *encouragement* will *endear* them to me, my morale will be *bolstered* up, and they will form the *bond* with God that will take me out of this *booby trap*. Satan *tailored* my ego to my will to put me in a *tailspin*, but I don't have to put up with this *chicanery*, because I am God's *child*. My heart-mind is Sir Ender and *ends* my *endangerment*, but my soul-strength is Sir Render and ushers in the *renaissance*, because he *renders* my will to God. Sir Ender and Sir Render both help me *surrender* so that I can be *surrounded* by the divine sweetness. They end the *hassle* and *hasten* my recovery by giving me a *nature* that is not *naughty*, so I intend to ask them *both* to help me end this *bother*. Then I will have a *nice t*emperament since God will always be *nigh*. The forces of *change* operate through these *chaps*, because they *mix* it up with my fears when I *moan* with remorse so that these *gobs* I have *gobbled* don't get between me and *God*. Therefore, I intend to *toast* their *togetherness* with my remorse and get under this *umbrella.* They can only arrive at this *unanimous agreement* if I encourage them to make me stop *ailing*, so I intend to *apply* myself to this task and keep the *appointment* with God known as my original innocence. I intend to ask Sir *Ender* to *endorse* Sir *Render's rendezvous* so that my *soul* can connect to its *Source.*

Don't *sell short* the science of *semantics*, because these word sequences show there was a *semblance* of divinity in the *semen* Adam spilled under the apple tree. My kundalini is the *seminal* fluid that I have spilled just like Adam, and the result is that I had to give my heart-mind and soul-strength a *seminar* on how to return to the *seminary* of the *Semite* Jesus. My heart-mind learned about its *virginity*, and my soul-strength learned about its *virility*, and they finally understood they were both full of *virtue* before the *virulent virus* of ego beset them. My heart-mind gave me the *head start* in becoming less *headstrong*, and then my *heartstrings* were warmed up by my soul-strength which is my heart's *heater.*

I got rid of the *holdover* from my childhood that says I have a *hole* for a soul and accept that I have the *compatibility* with God that brings me His *competency.* Satan made me a *caricature* of the divine as a result of Adam and Eve's *carnal knowledge*, but that does not mean that I cannot celebrate the *carnival* of the *carpenter* by parading through the three circles and *flaunting* the *flavors* of the nine Fruits. I may have felt *inhibited initially* in making this *initiative*, but when I *inject* this understanding into the *injury* in my inner child he will have the *inkling* that he is not an *inmate* in this prison but *innocent* of these *offenses* that have *oiled* the gears of my ego. I was *baffled* by this *bag* of *treacherous tricks* I carried around then, but on the circles I ate the *bagel* of my daily bread that allowed me to say "*Bah!*" to this humbug.

Heart-mind and soul-strength *cycle* the divine sweetness in the *cylinder* of the *engine* designed by Jesus, the *engineer* of the Christian Church. They are the *piston* that takes us out of the *pits* we got in by listening to Satan's *pitch*, and they produce the *energy* that *enfolds* us in God's generosity. God's generosity takes us out of Satan's *frying pan*, because it is the *fuel* with the *efficient effulgence*, so let's use the *Gifts* of wisdom and fear of the Lord to *gird* our *loins* and not *loiter* around licking Satan's *lollipop.* If you *treasure* your Fruits, write a *treatise* about your childhood showing how the *treatment* of remorse can give you the benefits of the *treaty* called the New Covenant, and make the Fruits appear on your *tree of life.*

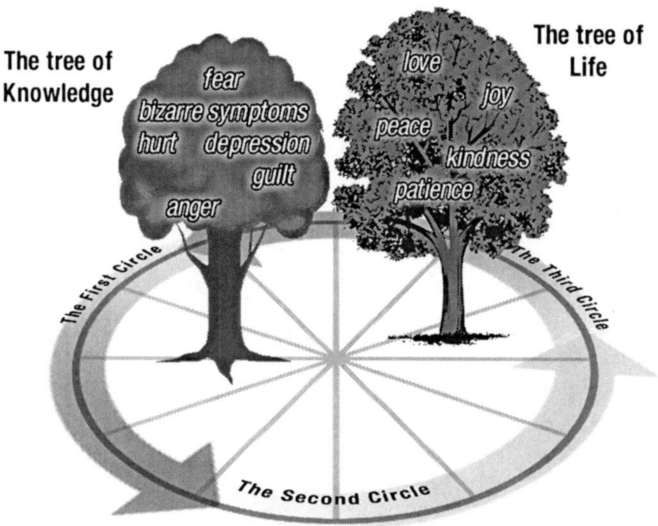

The New Covenant is our *victory* over the *villains* known as our repressed feelings. We have *minted* these *minutiae*, because Eve *misappropriated* the divine sweetness and contaminated us with *Eden's effluent*. This *hex* can remain *hidden*, but once it is *revealed*, we won't have to *revert* to this *revilement* again. We just need to unveil our *awe*, because it is the *axle* that connects us to the *wheeler-dealers* known as heart-mind and soul-strength. *When* we sit them down and tell them that we *appreciate* their *aptitudes*, they will end our ego's *smear* campaign. The truth is that they are *smoothies* and will make it look like a *snap* once they get a *sniff* of our contrition. Then they won't be *snooty* toward one another but rather will be the *arbiters* in the *arboretum* depicted above. They will bear *witness* to this *wondrous inspiration* and will *install* it in our minds so that we can have our original innocence *instead* of our original sin. They are the *judges* who have command over the *judicious juice* called *kundalini* which *labors* ceaselessly for Our *Lady* and the *Lamb*. They *land* us in God's *lap*, so go on this *lark* and don't be *neutral* toward the *New* Covenant when you can take advantage of this insurance *coverage* that is guaranteed to end your *cowardice*, *conquer* this abomination, and make you *consanguineous* with Christ.

Our *parentage* can arise from God, and we don't need to be *pariahs*. We became *outcasts* from the divine, because Eve opened this *outlet* when she became an *exotic* dancer in front of Adam. She made us *expatriates* from the *realm* of *reason*, but Christ's *bloodshed* made it possible for our Fruits to *bloom* so that we won't keep *blowing off steam*. We may have planted the *wrong* thoughts and may think they are made of *wrought iron*, but the Crucifixion made it possible to bend this *irksome iron*. Ego is the *enforcer* that makes our fears seem *engraved* in *granite*, but the Crucifixion made it possible for us to *grasp* the fact that they don't have to *grate* on our nerves. My parents took a *dump* in my heart and left me feeling like a *dunce*, but my heart is a *pump* that, thanks to Jesus, packs a *punch*. I *duplicated* this *duplicity* with my children and treated my *offspring* in an *off-the-wall* manner. I *often* behaved like an *ogre*, and I doubt my *brood* had much exposure to the *brook* of the divine sweetness, so I hope they take this apology as an *endearing endeavor*.

The first circle uproots the tree of *knowledge*, because the New Covenant makes our repressed feelings *knuckle* under to our remorse. These *kooky quirks quit* making us *quiver*, because when we are *beside* ourselves with remorse this agreement *between* us and Jesus certifies that we will get *beyond* this problem. Our remorse is the *suds* that *suffice* to wash off these stains, so let's remember that forgiveness is always *upcoming*, because in the *upper room* Jesus tossed us this *rope* that proved to be a *liberating lifeline*. God always *listens* when we *litigate* by using the *litmus test* of our remorse, so let's have this tête-à-tête in the *courageous courtroom* of the human heart, because this is where the New *Covenant* was ratified by the *rabbi* who ended this *racket*.

It is easy to end this *swindle* if you *swing* the *sword* of your remorse, so *wind up* and be a *winner*. You will *lose* your *lousy luck*, so decide not to *lug* around this *hex* that makes you a *hick*. You don't have to leave this curse *hidden* when you can reveal this *blessing* that you were *blind* to. You can *help* yourself in this way and stop the *hemorrhage* of the divine sweetness from your heart, because Jesus is the *lieutenant* of the tree of *life*. He shed his *lifeblood* to change our *life histories*, so let's make it our *lifework* to ask him to *lift* us out of this quagmire. Let's not be *strangers* to these boot *straps* but rather pull ourselves up on them according to the *strategy* of the New Covenant.

As adults we need to use our *bowels* to get rid of this nonsense that *bowled* us over as children. We just need to end this *defamation* through our *defecation* of the *deprecating* remarks that made us feel *depreciated*. Childhood is a time of *evasion* of difficulties, but adulthood is the time of *eversion* of them, meaning to turn them *inside* out so as to get rid of *insincere insinuations*. It is better to *excommunicate* this nonsense than *excoriate* ourselves with it, so let's use the act of *excretion* to get rid of that which is *excruciating.*

Adam and Eve didn't get much of a *bang* out of being *banished* from the Garden of Eden, so let's follow the *banister* of the three circles and not *bank* on remaining *bankrupt.* The three circles are the *entryway* of the divine sweetness, so let's encourage the grapevine to *entwine* itself around us by *enumerating* our fears. The grapevine *pines* away for the grape and wants to put it in the *pink* of the divine sweetness, but it respects our right to remain *frazzled*, because we have the *free will* to keep on being *wimps.* Therefore, our *privation privilege* is to remain without the *prize* of the divine sweetness. We can remain as timid as *mice* by thinking that our hunger can never be satisfied, or we can put the *mousse* in our *mouth* by knowing that we can become pure of heart. Our heart-mind has the *appetite* for the purity of heart that we lost under the *apple* tree, but only soul-strength can *satisfy* the appetite and *saturate* us with the divine sweetness, so let's get these two *together* by using the *tool* of our *regret* to *rein* in these *relentless* pests. Let's make this *year* the one in which we celebrate the acquisition of our *yearnings' earnings* so that we can be at *ease.* We can either remain *beaten* or become *beatific* by using the power of these two *beatitudes.* The *technique* for getting rid of the *tedious* feelings that *teem* in our subconscious is to use these two *teeth* on the vertical axis of the *gearwheel.* Then these silly *geese* will be calmed down, we will say *"Gee-whiz!"* and remain in awe of the divine sweetness.

In order to be more *humane* we need to eat more *humble pie.* We need to *accelerate* our growth by *accepting* the *fact* that our remorse is *fail-safe.* God will turn our *humiliations* into *humility*, so let's *disentwine* ourselves from these *disgraces*, *shake off* our toxic *shame*, and stop feeling like *degenerates* who have suffered some kind of *degradation. Apologizing* for *appalling* behavior always wins *applause* from God, because it is *admirable to admit guilt*, so let's have the *gumption* to *say* we're sorry and stop making everyone *scapegoats* just because we feel *scared.* When we *retract* injurious remarks the divine sweetness *retrenches* itself, so let's have this *rapport* with God that will restore our *rapture.* Ego is the house of cards that *crumbles* when we admit we're *culpable*, so let's get out of this *cult*, *cultivate* the Fruits, and get rid of this *cumbersome* burden by lighting this *lamp* that makes it possible for us to *land* on less *grouchy ground.*

The human will is *bipartisan* in that it is attracted to both good and evil, so it can enjoy the *bishop's bisque* or *sashay* around being *sassy.* We were *sandwiched* by *Satan* between the two sins of pride and lust, which aren't a very *satisfying* meal, but the forces of *change* can take place in this *chapel.* We can become more *gracious* by *graduating* from this *grammar school* in which we return to our *childhood* to find out why we are still so *childish* and then change our tastes *bit by bit* to make life less of a *bitch.* These *modest modifications* are the *amendments* that will make us more *amiable,* so let's ask the *troops* on the circles to win us this *trophy* and stop *trotting* into *trouble.* If we *esteem* our *estrangement* from God, we will just go on *honoring* the *hooch* of our fear, hurt, and anger, so let's *prize* the divine sweetness, because it comes from the *Pro* who can throw out our foe. The divine sweetness is without *precedent* for being *precious* and is the weather *vane* that ushers in good times, because the Fruits of the Spirit are in its *vanguard.* Therefore, let's make it the object of our *veneration* and stop suffering from the *venereal disease* called original sin. We are not *worms* and don't have to let our *wounds wreak* their *vengeance* on us, so let's not allow this *venom* to *vent* itself when it is a better *venture* to return to the *venue* of *veracity* in Eden. This is where the crime occurred, so let's *verbalize* our remorse and enjoy the *verdict* of our original innocence.

Our contrition *measures* our ego's *meddling,* so we should use this *ruler* and return to the authoritative *ruling* which states that we don't have to get drunk on Satan's *rum,* which only gets us in *rumbles.* We should each write this *journal,* because God *judges* each *transaction* that we have made *transparent* with our remorse and gives us His *clemency* so that our wills can be better members of the *clergy.* The *idea* of *identifying* the pollutants that confuse our souls' divine *identity* is the *model* of *modification* we need to *pursue.* Our petition for His sweetness will come under His *purview,* so let's get rid of the *notion* that we are *notorious* sinners unworthy of this *nourishment.* This is the *contaminant* that is most *contemptible,* because it implies that each of us is *nobody* God would give the *nod* to. This *noxious nuance* arose when Adam's *nubbin* got aroused at the sight of Eve's *nubile nudity,* so it is safe to *conclude* that our parents' *concupiscence* led to the *encore* performance that *encumbered* us with this nonsense. Nevertheless, our *conception* is also the *concern* of our spirituality, and therefore it is possible to make a *concerted* effort to ask Mary to share her sweetness, because her Immaculate Heart is the *concession* stand where we may ask for this *refreshment* to *refuel* us. Our contrition rids us of these *flaws* and *paves* the way to this *pavilion,* so let's *illuminate* these *illusions,* take our rest in Mary's *Immaculate* Conception, and *float* on air. All else is *immaterial*, because it gives us the *immediate* and *immense* benefit of the divine sweetness in which we can *immerse* ourselves. Therefore, let's *immigrate* there by *immobilizing* our *immoderate* behaviors with our remorse. The Immaculate Conception is the *tender tenet* that changes the *tenor* of the life of man, so let's become less *tense* by *using* this *uterus* and getting the *rebate* of the Fruits through this *rebirth*. Our contrition will *rebuke* our fears and *recall* our sweetness, so let's *pray* for this *precept* to take us out of this *predicament* and remove ourselves from the *tentacles* of ego that have made our sweetness so *tenuous*.

Our conception was an *accident*, because our parents didn't pray first in order to give God *acclaim*, but that doesn't mean that we have to *acclimate* ourselves to our shame. We each have a divine *spark*, meaning we can choose not to have Satan as a *sparring partner*. God planted His *seed* in us, and it automatically *seeks* the divine sweetness until it *seems* to *seep* into our awareness. Therefore, we should water it with our *devotion* until it *devours* our foe. Our wills are not *birdbrains*, but rather the *bird of paradise* that delivers this *birth certificate* to us. We are *creatures* of God and can get this *credential*, because we are *entitled* to our original innocence as well as its *entourage* which is the Fruits of the Spirit.

We have *sealed* off a lot of *seamy* memories; but when we *take them down a peg* or two with our *penitence*, it will usher in the *season* called the *Second* Coming of *Christ*. Christ invented the three *circles* to help us *mend* this *merciless mess*, so let's go through this *metamorphosis*. It is the *interior decoration* that *interlocks* us with God and locks out the meddling *interloper*, so let's take these *thirty six* steps through these *thorns* in our side and feel *thoroughly* better.

We can have the *camaraderie* with God that antedated Adam and Eve's *cameo* performance. We just need to take a picture with the *camera* of our remorse of the *camouflage* that has allowed Satan to set up *camp* in our hearts. We have borne this *disgrace* but can also take off this *disguise*. We don't need to live this *lie*, because we can be *lieges* of God. Only an *idiot* would watched his divine sweetness flow *idly* by, so let's not worship this *idol* called ego. We have all lived through *decades* of *decadence*, so let's make the enemy *decamp* and drink the divine sweetness from the *decanter* of the Sacred Heart.

I have followed the *presumption* that *pretending* makes it true, but this *magical* thinking has only *magnified* my troubles. Therefore, my own *make-believe* has allowed *malevolent* forces to cause my *malfunction*. I have made my life a *pretty* bad affair, but the *prevailing* wisdom is that I can *prevent previous* mistakes from recurring. My abrasiveness may seem to be my *nemesis*, but I don't intend to be a *nerd* without any *nerve* and therefore intend to ask the Sacred Heart to *erase* this *error* and be the *centerpiece* in my chest. Then the *centrifugal* force of ego will surrender to the *centripetal* force of my devotion, so I rest my case there. We have all gotten in this *brawl* that has seemed to *break* our hearts, but it is possible in this *century* to realize that our hearts are not *ceramic* and that they can dine on the *cereal* of the divine sweetness which is food that is *cerebral*. That way our hearts won't be *turbulent turf*, because the Holy Spirit is the *dove* that will make our wills *dovetail* with God's.

Jesus made this *mark* in my heart by going through the Crucifixion, because he wanted to *market* the divine sweetness there through his Resurrection. This *fluid* will *flush* out my *flustered* feelings, because my spiritual *marriage* to Jesus makes his bone *marrow marshal* these forces that give me *mastery* over ego. The *blood* of Christ is formed in his *bones*, so let's *book* our passage into the *bosom* of God by *welcoming* him into our hearts so that he can *weld* his bones to ours. This is the *boon* that gives Satan the *boot*, so let's end this evil *adulteration* and get on with this exciting *adventure*. Jesus is the *interior intermediary* who starts the *traffic* that ends this *tragedy*, so let's get on this *highway* that *hinges* us to God. It is called the *Trinity* and is not a *trinket*, because it *completes* this round *trip* and grants us *composure* that is *comprehensive*.

Jesus is the *sharpshooter* in our hearts who *shatters* Satan's dreams, because he went through the Sorrowful Mysteries, and they are *abuzz* with information about how *abysmal* difficulties can be overcome. We just need to study in this *academy* so as to *accelerate* the flow of our sweetness. Our minds are *taverns* with *tawdry* decorations, but Jesus' *rectitude* can *redecorate* our minds, so let's *retrace* our steps and *retrieve* this *blessing* that he spilled his *blood* to bring us.

Jesus wanted to *salvage* this *sanctity* so our hearts could be *sanctuaries* for *sane* thoughts, so he got on the *Cross* to *crucify* our *heresy*. Man had become a *hermit* and had withdrawn from God, so Jesus became man's *hero* on the Cross to help the *recluse* get *reconciled*. Jesus knew that man had to *reconnoiter* with certain *destructive details* from his *past* and *patch them up*, so he started the *finishing school* of the Joyous Mysteries *first*. Man had *preened* himself with *prejudicial* thoughts, so *curb-*

ing this tendency was the only *curriculum*. The *big* problem was that this *bigotry* had set different ethnic groups to *feuding* with one another, because the *fiend* had *spooked* their divine sweetness, so man had to *spot* the *narcotic* that had made him *narrow-minded. Nations* could be at peace with one another, because man could *haul* out his reasons for this *haunting* and get rid of these *ghosts* by using the *Gifts* of the Spirit.

Man had to *name* the *narcotic* that made him spiritually *somnolent* with the help of the *Sorrowful* Mysteries and *tame* the *tangle* by writing in the *journal* of the *Joyous* Mysteries. That way his *citizenship* in heaven could be *claimed*, and the *Glorious* Mysteries could give him their *glow*. Jesus wore the *shroud* in order to *shuck* this *oyster* so that man could get at this *pacifying package* God had *inlaid inside* of him. Therefore, when we feel lost in the *shuffle*, we should not *shun* the chance to allow the Gifts to *shunt* the divine sweetness into the production of the Fruits.

Nevertheless, it is *vain* for me to think that my *valor alone* can bring the Fruits to the *altar* in my heart, because the *interlude* in Eden made it necessary for Jesus to be my *intermediary*. God *internalized* him in my heart, so I intend to make my ego *eat crow* by taking advantage of the *Crucifixion*. We are *swamped* in our sins, but Jesus went through his *swan song* so that we could *swap* them for something better. The human will is the *frog* that *frolics* in this bog, but it

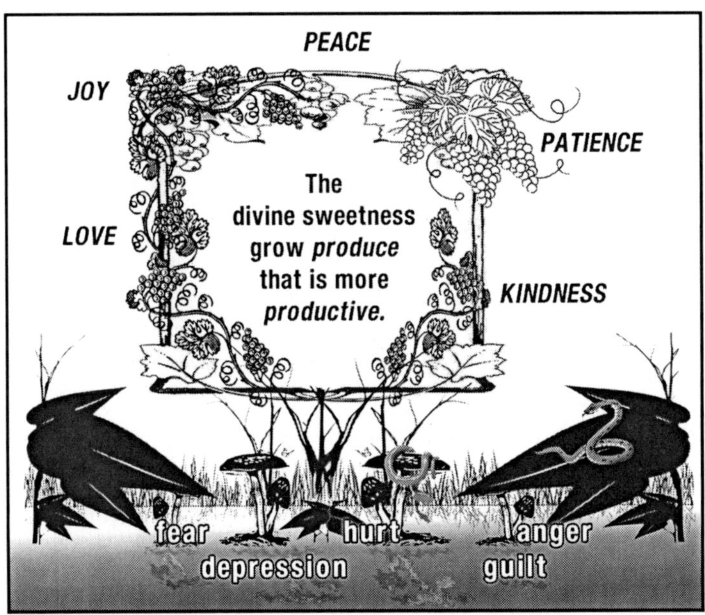

is also the *watchdog* of the *waterway*, so even if we start out in *perdition*, our minds can go through a *peregrination* to something more *perfect*.

The *traumas* of our childhood require that we *travel* back through this *bog* so that our mind won't be *boggled* by these *bogus* thoughts. The *purpose* is to see what *pushes* our inner child's buttons, *pacify* his *pain*, and make him our *pal* by going through this *travelogue*. We can *traverse* this *travesty*, because the Blessed Mother is the *nanny* who takes us on this *narcissistic tour* to remove the *tourniquet* we put on our sweetness.

I hadn't paid much attention to the *flow* of the divine sweetness in my heart and was constantly *flying off the handle*, so I began *filtering* out my *filth* in order to *finagle* a better *finale* to my first marriage. I *grieved* by *grilling* myself about how I let these *forces* cause my *foreboding* and did my *best* to *bestir* my contrition to chase away these *ghastly ghosts*. Nevertheless, I had a show-the-*world* attitude and bombarded all those around me with my *worm's eye view* of all the *worn-out worry* that I had hung onto since childhood. My *stick-to-it-iveness* made me *stiff-necked*, and so my divine sweetness got *stifled*. I didn't *shirk* my *shit* and sometimes even *shivered* at how *shocking* it was. The result was *uncomplimentary* to me, because it was such an *uncompromising* approach, and I *mowed* down my *moxie* with what I considered to be these *febrile feces*.

To me it wasn't a very *funny furlong*, because I was *humping* like a *Hun* from *hunch* to *hunch* to see what part of me needed to be *hung* by the heels. I delivered a *series* of *serious sermons* to the *serpent* in Eden that had put me in *servitude* to ego and those who didn't *reciprocate* in this *recital irked* me, because I considered them *irresponsible*. I would become *supercilious*, and my facial expression would let them know that I considered them *superficial*. I thought it was *disastrous* not to *disband disbelief* and figured that the improvement of worldwide *morale* could be accomplished by my *moralizing*. I assumed that *vomiting* up *voodoo* on *command* was a *commendable* undertaking. I attempted to *clarify* every *clash* I had had as a child, and I thought each one was a *classic* example of how a *clause* was left in my subconscious mind that I had to *clean* out.

I took my *atonement* and made the *attempt*, but it soon became *apparent* that erasing these *apparitions* did not bring the *benefit* of God's *benevolence* right away. The first *Noel* had implanted *no-fault* insurance in my *noggin*, but I was a *pilgrim* whose head didn't rest on this *pillow*, because I thought I was *no-good*, so all the *noise* of my remorse didn't change the fact that I was a *nomad* with *nominal* self-esteem.

I knew that God was the real *ancestor* who *animated* me and that my *parents* were *parenthetical*, but this *connection* had been destroyed by their *connivance*, so at times there seemed to be no *redeeming* feature in me that could *refill* me with these more *refined reflexes*. I seemed *immune* to the forces of good, so my fears were the *imps* who assaulted me in *hordes* and controlled the *horizons* of my thinking.

I felt *edified* as a child by these *editorials* of my *ego*-addicted will, so as an adult I had to *cross-examine* this *crown of thorns*. It was my *legal* right to ask Jesus to *lend a hand*, so I spent years *litigating* against this *load* and *eavesdropping* on the *eccentricities* in my behavior that came from its endless *echelons* of fears. I had *laundered* these *layers*, but I was still lacking in *decorum*, because this *knotty knowledge* was still *abundantly abusive*. It resulted in *kooky deeds*, because it was *deep-seated*, and I often thought that this *harsh harvest* was just going to resist all my efforts to *hash it out*.

These *misrepresentations* had brought about the *misrule* of a fool, but I also didn't *miss* the chance to hurl the *missile* of my remorse at each one of them on this *mission* of mercy. It was a *difficult* kind of *digging*, because my fears were the *burrowing* rodents who had *buried* themselves deeply so as to produce a *rank rat's nest*. They *nestled* close enough to my thinking to be as *nettlesome* as possible, but this *smoldering snake pit* eventually got the sales *pitch* of my remorse. The *downspout* of my awe in God's generosity helped my divine sweetness get *downstream*, because I had nurtured this *wise wish*. Therefore, I ultimately overcame my lust for this *garbage* that I had *garrisoned* in my mind. I wanted my *purity* of heart to *purr*, so I stopped letting *Satan* fill me with a hunger that could not be *satisfied*.

I was finger in *glove* with this *glum glut*, because my will was the *glutton* with an *insatiable* appetite for this *insecurity*. My fears were the *banal band* of *bandits* who stole my divine sweetness at this *banquet*, so this *starvation stayed* with me. I was a *gullible guy*, because I *believed* everything my parents *bellowed*, which included some *goofy gossip* that was so *asinine* that it would have made most people look *askance*. Nevertheless, I allowed these *ruinous rumormongers* to *scandalize* me and make me their *scapegoat*, so my mind became the *headquarters* of their *hearsay*. I thought my parents were *divine* and could *do* no *wrong*, so I *Xeroxed* all their *yammering*, which got woven into this long *yarn* that took me *years* to untangle.

Mary is the *lawyer* who helped me do this, because she is never *lax* in helping us use the *laxative* of our remorse. She *lays down the law* when we peel off our *layers* and shows us the *layout* of the Fruits, so let's stop being *lazy* and get the *energy* to solve this *enigma.* I have a *cozy* relationship with Mary, because she makes me less *crabby* by helping me *crack* this nut. I have *babbled* my troubles in her ear like a *baby* and have asked her to take me *back* to God. My contrition will never *backfire* but rather rid me of the *backlash* that results from this *backlog*, because Mary is always *backstage* bringing home the *bacon* of God's love.

Mary has her foot on the *serpent's* head, because she is a *servant* of God. She *hands out* the divine sweetness, because she is the *handmaiden* of the Lord, so I'm going to become acquainted with my original *innocence* by taking advantage of the *innovation* which is her Immaculate Conception. Then she will *inoculate* His sweetness into me.

After I stop *gobbling* my ego's *gobbledygook* Mary gives the *go-ahead* to Jesus who is the *goalkeeper* of the divine sweetness, so I intend to continue with this *rebuttal* of my *recalcitrant* ego and enable my will to *recall* my sweetness. I can *recant* my original sin, because my remorse is *sufficient* to enable me to exercise this right of *suffrage.* When I cast this *vote* my behavior will *vouch* for the fact that my ego isn't *promulgating* its *propaganda* any more. I need to love with all my *heart* so that it can house my *heaven* within. I need to love with all my *mind* so Jesus can *minister* to it. I need to love with all my *soul* in order to have *sound spiritual* connections. Then I will love with all my *strength* and will have ended my *strife.* The *wiles* of ego have corrupted my *will*, but when I get together these four parts of my *will power*, Satan will turn into a *wimp.* It is merely a question of whether I prefer to have a *congruous connection* or a *miserable mismatch*, so the *choice* that strikes the more harmonious *chord* is to *span* the gap between me and God with my *spark* of the *divine* rather than remain *divorced* from Him.

The *split-up* known as original sin has only *spoiled* my life, so I have *rehashed* my childhood, because the *reign* of God is the logical *reimbursement* I *expect* from this *expedient.* The *prospect* of *prospering* in this way rather than *prostituting* myself to ego makes me *more motivated* to *mount* this offensive and *determined* to *develop deep deference* to the *Deity.* He will *knead* me into the right shape, so I intend to climb on His *knee.* He is the divine *potter*, so I'll ask Him to put me in his *pouch* and then make me *plastic* enough to become a *plate* for the Fruits. My childhood was a *labyrinth* of *lack*, but I have not been *lackadaisical* about this *shortage* and intend for this *sure* and certain *sustenance* to *show up*. Therefore, I will send my *yearning* to the *yes man* who is my will and tell him to *summon* the good sense to welcome this *superlative supplement* that *supplies* all-*surpassing* peace in *surplus*. Then I will use the *excess* to *excite* others to *exempt* themselves from this tyranny, because the one concept that is not *nebulous* to me is that this *novel nutriment* is *necessary* to everyone's wellbeing.

When I was a child I was *desolate* with *despair*, because I had put my *hope* in a *hornet's* nest and didn't know that it was *inappropriate* to trust those who were *inattentive* to my needs. Therefore, I received the *stings* that arose from their *stinginess*, and this *stipend* from hell had the *payoff* of robbing me of my *peace*. My parents had *blinders* on that put their spirituality on the *blink*, and it allowed the devil to *sidle* up to them and lay *siege* to me. This *embattled* attitude is what I *embraced*, and the divine sweetness remained *absent*. I didn't *absorb* my sweetness, because I had a *stoic stomach* that always left me feeling *stoned*. I *set great store by* the nonsense I had *stowed away*, so I remained *intimidated* by this *intoxication* and embroiled in this *intractable intrigue* until my ex-wife said that I had missed some *significant signposts*.

Unresolved repressed feelings are a firearm with *unrestricted* targets, so whenever I fired the gun I had to find the *peg* in my mind on which I had hung these *pellets* so they wouldn't run around *pell-mell pelting* everyone around me. These pellets amounted to the huge *dune* of *dung* that the *winds* of fate had blown through the open *window* of my gullible mind. It was a *shocking shoot-out* in which anyone was fair game, so I became a *slime-slinger* and *mowed* people down with this *mud*. I *transferred* my *trash* in an *indiscriminate* manner, but I eventually decided not to *indulge* this vice and made an effort to *rise* above this *risky ritual*.

I was painfully aware that my *terrible* twos were reenacting themselves in my adult life, because my inner child had been through this *territory* that had struck *terror* in him, and I had not passed the *test* of crucifying it as described in the New *Testament*. There was a *gaping* hole in the *garage* where God should have parked His car, and it had left me *garbed* in *garbage*.

I must have *jumped* at the chance to store each piece of *junk*, because I was the *junkie* in this *junkyard*. Satan made me think it was a normal *routine* to store this *rubbish* in my mind, and he turned my will into the *rudder* of a *ruffian*. He *deceived* my *decency* just like he did to Eve in Eden, so everyone thought it was OK to *dump* their *dung* into the *dupe's* heart, because it was his *duty* not to complain. *Eve's* name refers to this *event* that allowed her *pornography* to become *portable,* so the *neurotic nibble* she took on Satan's bait the *night before* has *beguiled* our *behavior* ever since. The next day this *inexorable infamy* put *every* one of us at the *effect* of evil because of the *dawn* of this bad *deal* known as ego-addiction. The mind of man was intended to be a *concourse* where man could take a spiritually *wakeful walk,* and the *prognosis* was good, because when wisdom and fear of the Lord walked this *promenade,* it automatically *led* to the *leap* of faith known as God's generosity. However, Satan *defrauded* man *deliberately* with pride and lust, because he knew these poisons would become deeply *ingrained.* He used these two *ingredients,* because they were so highly *attractive* to one another that men and women would be all *atwitter* over their *concupiscence* and fall into the dysfunction known as *conditional* love. Satan *orchestrated* these temptations in the mind of man in *order* to use man's reproductive *organs* to entrench himself there through *original sin.* That way every time the act was *consummated,* Satan could *contaminate* them and their offspring and make them all *contentious.* Satan knew that original sin was the *promiscuous promise* that would make everyone view *continence* as a ridiculous *contortion,* so when he tossed this *bait* we swallowed and have gone *ballistic* ever since. Satan knew that man would *knuckle under* to these temptations, so he *KO'd* man's *kundalini* when Adam and Eve *wallowed* and installed *wall-to-wall wantonness* in the mind of man. God's *glucose* took a powder when this *glue* in the spine of man came *loose,* and it left man with a *lopsided love* in his heart. When the kundalini *fell,* the *family* life of man became a *farce.*

As a child I must have made this *comical commitment,* because my mind was a *copier* of these *copious* miscalculations that arose from Adam and Eve's *copulation.* I never realized I could return to the Author who held the *copyright* on *unconditional* love and ask Him to put me *under* its *spell,* so I just *spent* my time in this *stand-off.* The *staple* item known as God's sweetness never got *started* in my heart, which remained under this *hex,* because I had allowed the *hierarchy* of evil to carry out their *high jinx* there. My parents had *taught* me that I needed to be *taunted* in order to *gain* their approval, so the *galaxy* of *stars* known as the Fruits of the Spirit remained *stationary.* No matter how hard I *toiled* to get my parents' approval, my parents still used my heart as a *toilet* and expected me to show *tolerance* regardless of the *toll* it took on me. I paid this *exorbitant* price, because no one had ever *expanded* on the idea that this *expense* could be eliminated by *expiating explicitly* in prayer. I didn't take these *flexible flights* of my *imagination* and didn't *imbibe* the *Deity's delicious* elixir. I didn't realize my *tailor-made taint* could be *taken* away.

Nevertheless, I finally figured out that these *stains* could be *stalked*, so I got in touch with these bad *vibes vicariously* and watched these old *movies* that showed how I got so *much muck*. I *exorcised* the *experience* that caused each *vice* by returning to the *vicinity* in which I needed to *correct* each *corrupting* influence. I *extrapolated* to the *extreme* and used my *logic* to end this *long-drawn-out* conflict. I answered this *clarion* call to put an end to these *clashes* so that I would not be driven by my ego. My ego was the *internal combustion engine* that *interpolated* my fears into my behavior, but my contrition brought them to the *exterior* where they could become *extinct*. I brought the *powers* of imagination and life into *practice* so that their *intangible intelligence* could be focused on these *illusions*. Once my *imagination* shed the *light* that showed why I was *like-minded* with those of my *lily-livered lineage*, the *Lion of Judah dispelled* these *live wires*. Then God's *elite elixir* could be *dispensed*, and its *life* could make me more *light-hearted*. These *intoxications* could be subjected to the action of my *intuition* in order to show that they were *invalid*.

My parents were the *Indian givers* who only gave me *indignation*, so these *tiers* of anger were the *tigers* I thought I had to grab by the *tail* in my therapy. Therefore, I went into each *tailspin* and then tried to *take* control. I *danced* with each *danger* and then tried to follow each *trail* back to my incorrect *train* of thought. I thought my behavior had to *portray* my misery before I could take a *position* that was more *positive*, so I looked *backward* into this *backwater* rather than *forward*, and this just *fouled* up my chances of success. The *modus operandi* of my perfectionism was to be the *mole* who burrowed into my past until I found the *molestation*, but I just seemed to forget to *mollify* it.

I didn't *reset* the sweetness that *resided* in my heart, because I had forgotten that my self-*worth* was supposed to get bigger when my *wound* got smaller. My life, therefore, was a *vale* of tears, because I wasn't God's *valentine*. My own *neurosis neutralized* this *benefit*, and I stayed *bent* out of shape, because I had *pressed* this false *presumption* into service and nullified this *preventive* medicine. I was the false *prophet* who lacked this *prophylaxis* and consequently remained a *perpetrator* in *perpetuity*. Satan got in his *retribution*, because my *retrospec-*

tion was the *proprietor* of this store where good *prospects* weren't for sale.

I *carried* around this *cartoon*, because I had been *force-fed* this bad *forecast*, so this *scourging scrambled* my thinking, but I eventually realized that it was the *bailiwick* of the Sorrowful Mysteries to help me stop taking this *bait*. The *Sorrowful* Mysteries *sorted* out this mess, because my patience-clout *assuaged* my joy-doubt, and my kindness-clout *assured* my love-doubt that he needn't lead me *astray*. Each clout had the *task* of confronting the corresponding *taskmaster* and *curing* these *curious curmudgeons* so that the *brigand* from hell couldn't make them *broadcast* the *broken* promises from my childhood. Then I could greet my *peace* at the *pearly* gates of my heaven within, because I would have patiently earned the *joy* of *jumping* the ship of ego.

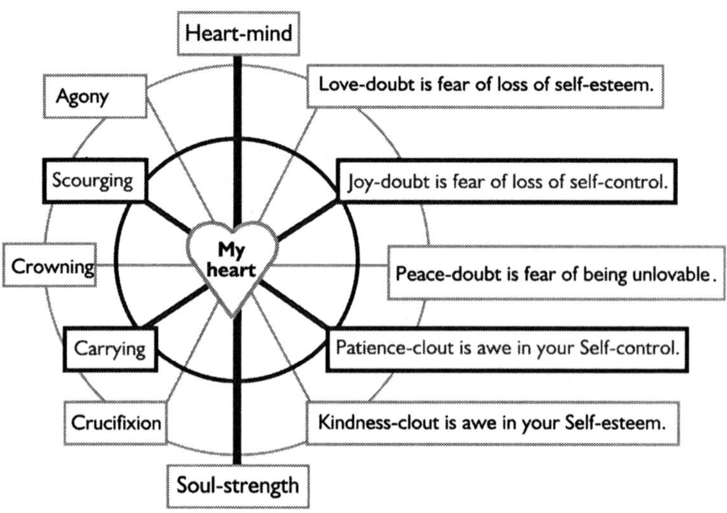

We have all paid the *toll* of watching this *torment ferment*, but if we *fertilize* our hearts with *fervent* contrition, the two *fighters* shown above will *release* this blessing of the Catholic *religion* known as Fear of the Lord and *repel* the enemy, because we will have *repented*. The Gift of the Holy Spirit known as *Fear* of the Lord *features* the two kinds of *awe* known as Self-*esteem* and Self-control who *nab* the two *awkward narcissists* known as self-esteem and self-control so their nasty *narrative* won't make us have to *navigate* troubled waters. These two kinds of *euphoria evict* the corresponding fears, so our love-doubt and joy-doubt get *killed* by these *kindness kinetics*. Our Self-esteem and Self-control *want* to fight this *war* against these two *wards* of our ego so that we can *warm* up to the *warranty* known as the will of God which has not *expired.* The *exploit* called the Crucifixion taught these two *explorers* to *extinguish* the *extremist views* of these two *vigilantes* so their *crocks* of nonsense won't result in our *crotchety* behavior. These two *concentric* circles *conciliate* us to God when we *confess* this *conflict* in order to become more *congenial.* The *outer* circle collars the *outlaws*, and the *inner* circle declares us *innocent*, because Jesus crucified these *cumbersome curmudgeons* on the outer circle and *carried* the Cross on the inner circle so the *scourging* from our childhoods wouldn't make our lives *screwy cartoons.* These two concentric *circles* break the *circuit* that has resulted in the *circular nature* of our *neurotic* behavior, because the *calmness* of *Calvary cancels* this *cancer.* These unresolved *needs* no longer *needle* us, because the *Savior* invented this *science* during his Passion. He took the *scolding* we got as children and evened the *score* by going through the *Scourging.* The *Sorrowful* Mysteries *sound out* these *spaced out sparring partners* known as self-control and self-esteem and prevent their doubts from *perpetuating* our *perplexity*, so we should bring their *atrocious attitudes* to the two *authorities* known as Self-Control and Self-Esteem and *awaken* the *penitence* that will make us more loving *people.* They are the *major generals* who *make* these *malcontents* stop *manufacturing* their *manure*, so let's use these *capable* soldiers and put an end to this *capricious captivity. Patience* is the Self-*control* that allows us to *convalesce*, and Self-esteem *kindles* our *kindness*, so let's *capitulate* to this *cardiac care* which will *caress* our hearts. The *hateful hawks* of self-control and self-esteem *have hatched* this *hazardous hazing* but we can *heal* our *hearts* with the *heavenly helmsmen* of Self-control and Self-esteem, because they have *patented* the *path* to the Divine *Patriarch* and He will rid us of these *careless caricatures* and bring about the *payload* of *peace* of mind. These *circles* depict a *civil* war we can count on winning by answering the *clarion call* to *claw* out of this mess and earn a *clean bill of health* for the *clergyman* known as the human will. This *wastrel* may have been *wayward*, but when he uses the *weapons* shown above he will *wear* the garment known as the will of God and will *weep* no more.

We all got a *dose* of these *doubts*, but we don't have to *clone* them forever, because we can use the *clouts* to *desert* this *despotism.* The clouts have the *adroitness* to enable us to stop *adulating* false gods, so let's not be the *adult children* who are *chips off this old block* that just prevents our Fruits from *blooming.* The *doubts* arose in the *drab dramas* from our past, and they are the *dreadful drill instructors* we put in the *driver's seat.* We *fawned* on our parents as children, but our *Fear* of the Lord doesn't have to remain *feeble*, because Jesus made it possible for us to *abandon* this *abomination*. He opened this crucial *crossroad* when he wore the *Crown* of *Thorns* and *threaded* this needle that *ties* us into the will of God. The will of God is the *tidbit* that stems the *tide* of ego and earns us the *tidy* sum of the divine sweetness, so let's get this *acquisition* that will cure us of our *acrimonious acts.* Let's get off this *hostile hot seat* and teach our heart-mind and soul-strength *how* to get in this *huddle* that can make our divine sweetness *hum*.

The divine sweetness was as *busy* as a bee before the fall, but then these *clumsy butterfingers* dropped it, and our minds have been *cluttered* ever since with this *trash* that causes our *travail.* Nevertheless, we can still have this *buttress* if we *orient* ourselves to feeling this *original pain.* We can make our doubts seem like *palaver* if we just remember the *motto* that *mourners* are *comforted*. It is not *comical* snake oil but *serious* relief, because it *sets* us *free* of the *freight* of ego by *commanding* Satan to stop *commandeering* our sweetness. It is no *joke* that we will feel *joy* as a consequence of this *suffering*, because our suffering is our *sugar's suitor*, so we should *send* the *sensible sentiment* of remorse after these *ageless aggravations*. Then we will feel all *aglow*, because remorse willingly feels our *pain* in order to make it seem less *palatable. Remorse removes* this *first fixture* of ego that Satan installed in our minds to make us *flagellate* ourselves. Our *hurt* is *hushed* up, because this *device* destroyed the *dexterity* of heart-mind and soul-strength. *After* they lost their *agility* they weren't a *dynamic duo*, because they had been *duped*. Therefore, the *realistic* view is that to restore them to *reason* we shouldn't *twiddle* our thumbs but rather feel these *twinges* and go through this *legitimate* suffering that will result in God's *leniency*.

The *suppression* of our feelings is a *sure-fire* way to allow them to *surface* later and *ramble* around going on *rampages*. Resentments that are *barred* from awareness only turn us into *barbarians*, so it is better to *bare* our hearts to God. *Repenting* of *repressed resentments* makes these *ruffians* follow the *rule* of reason, so let's not be *derelict* in the job of *de-repressing* them, because this is how to *deprive* them of the power they have *derived* over us. It just so *happens* that being *happy* depends on not *scrimping* on these *scruples*, so let's not have *any apathy*, because the *aphorism* that is the *last word* is better *late* than never. I don't want my *indolence* to *induct* my repressed feelings into the *half-wits hall* of fame. I have *maltreated* myself long enough trying to do the *mambo* with this *Mammon* and figure I'll be better off without this *mammoth* problem to which *man manacles* himself.

Our ego puts our *hands* in these *handcuffs*, but it is possible to *discharge* this load through the *discipline* of psychotherapy. We don't have to be *preoccupied* with this *preposterous* nonsense, because we can *disclaim* it by *disclosing* it to a *compassionate* therapist whose *competency* entitles him or her to listen to these *complaints*. The *promise* of the Cross is that the false *prophets* we *protect* in our minds can be *pried* loose by *completing* a *comprehensive treatment* plan whose success is ensured by the *treaty* known as the New Covenant. When we *persist* in this commitment, the *person* known as Jesus Christ will *persuade* these *pesky pessimists* to stop *picking* fights with us, so that we may rest our heads on the *pillow* known as the will of God. The Crucifixion is the *inquiry* that *inserts* the *insights* into our minds that we need to become *inspired*, so each *installment* is an *instance* of receiving *instruction* that *insulates* our minds from these *insults* and *insures* that we receive the *intense* bliss of an *intimate* relationship with God. It is a *stepwise sterilization* of our *stiffneckedness*, so let's collar these *stigmas*, wash off their *stink* with the *stipulation* of our remorse, *stop storing* these *stowaways* in our minds, *straighten* out, and fly right. We can *thaw* out our *frozen Fruits* through *therapy*, because these *thermodynamics* were *restored* by the *Resurrection* so as to *warm* our hearts and allow us to *think* straight. We can win this *war*, so let's give the *third degree* to these *thorny thoughts* with our remorse, follow this *thread*, distance ourselves from these *threats*, and cross the *threshold* into that *thrilling* place known as our heaven within. This *paradise* is not *paralyzed* and in fact will make us *thrive*, so let's not forget that the *success* of our *psychotherapy* is the reason Christ *suffered* his *public punishment*. If we make a *conscientious effort* to *consistently scrutinize* our *egos' seductive sentimentality* in this way over a period of *years*, it will kindle a *yearning* in our *hearts* that will open them to our *heaven* within. Our *derangement* has resulted from the *dereliction* in Eden that makes us *descendants* of Adam, so let's *free* ourselves from this *Freudian friction* by subjecting our *meanness* to this *medical* treatment which will *meet* our needs and not *rest* our case on the *restraint* of our denial, which will only let our troubles *resume*. *Prayer* alone is not the *precise* instrument with which to excise the fears which are the *precursors* that put us in these *predicaments*, so we should not adopt the *high* and *mighty* attitude that our *historical* anger will stop working its *hocus pocus* without subjecting our *minds* to this *discipline* that alone can put an end to this *disease*. *Christ* wants us to *chronicle* our *Cinderella cinemas* on the three *circles* so that our *clans' claptrap* will stop causing our *clashes*, and we can *claw out* of this mess and *clean up* our acts. The sacrament of *confession* is not the same as *confiding* to a *professional* in *seclusion* the *secrets* that have produced the *profile* of *profound dysfunction each* of us are here on *earth* to *eavesdrop* on. Rather it is the *job* of a *joint* effort between *therapist* and client to stick to it through *thick* and *thin* until the *thirty-six thorns* in our sides have been removed in a *thoughtful* manner together by confronting these *threats* on the *three* circles. This work needs to be carried out over an *extended* period of *time* so as to *extinguish* this *tinderbox* inside all of us that launches us into the *tirades* that our loved ones are sick and *tired* of. We will only continue to be *beleaguered* if we consider it *beneath* our *dignity* to indulge in this *diligence*, so let's be *thankful* for our *therapists* and go through *psychotherapy* to *pull* ourselves out of this *mess*, because the *Messiah* considers this *method* the *best* way for us to stop our *bickering*. The *cost* of not wanting to *cotton* to the idea of *counseling* is *high*, because we will just continue to be *hindered*, so let's *describe* the reasons for our *despair* and change our *destiny*. We can *count* on the Crucifixion, so let's have the *courage* to take this *course of treatment* which has been blessed by the New *Covenant*. It will *detach* us from these *details* we need to *detect*, so let's approach this task with the *determination* to *detoxify* these *detriments*. If we *pour* out our hearts during this *powerful process*, it will *produce devotion* to God, and these *diabolical didactics* will *die*, so let's do this *combat* and embrace the *Comforter* as well as the Second *Coming* of Christ in our hearts.

The *relief* of the *religion* of Christ depends on not *relishing* our *reluctance*, so let's not be *indifferent* but rather *forge* a better *formula* by *inducing* the *industrious* worker known as *fortitude* to *inflame* these *foul fragments* with the *ingenuity* of a contrite heart. We can *arraign* our *arrogance* in the courtroom of our *regret* and *rehabilitate* this offender, because by going through the Crucifixion Christ put an end to this *sport* in which Satan sends us on this crime *spree*. Christ's Crucifixion changed the *destiny* of man by making the human will a good *detective*, and Christ's Resurrection gave man the *detergent* to wash off this *haughty haunting*. Being *reborn* is not the same as being *recalcitrant*, so *before* we jump to conclusions, we should understand how we got *befouled*.

Before my therapy I thought I had it all *figured out*, but all I had done was listen to my ego's *filibuster*. I felt *smug*, but the contraband

I had *smuggled sneaked* into my behavior, so I took a *different* tack and began to *dig. Before* this remedy I *behaved* badly, because my *haughty head* had made me a *stubborn student*, so I decided to let my heart take *instruction* from the *intelligent supervisor* at the Last *Supper.* The New *Covenant* makes Satan *cower*, so let's not be *coy*, because it *curbs* the belief that we *can't* stop being *cantankerous.*

My head has been *swollen* with lies that make me *swoon*, but that does not mean that I can't *swoop* down on them with my remorse and make them exit with a *swoosh.* I have been *showered* with falsehoods each of which thinks he's a *showstopper*, and these delusions of *grandeur* haven't *granted* divine sweetness to the *grape.* Nevertheless, my *meekness* has the *megaphone* that will *disperse* these thoughts so that my sweetness may *dispose* me to loving behavior.

I have *defeated* my own *defecation*, because I have not always been able to *flush* out feelings that leave me *flustered.* I just couldn't believe that my *rectitude* was connected to my *rectum*, so I never *recuperated* fully, and my repressed feelings *recurred* in my behavior. When Adam and Eve *bowed* down to Satan, it affected my *bowels*, because they couldn't *identify* which *ideology* to get rid of. Therefore, I went *crazy creating examples* of bad behavior and then *excavating* their causes. My power of *renunciation* needed *repair*, because I often *purged*

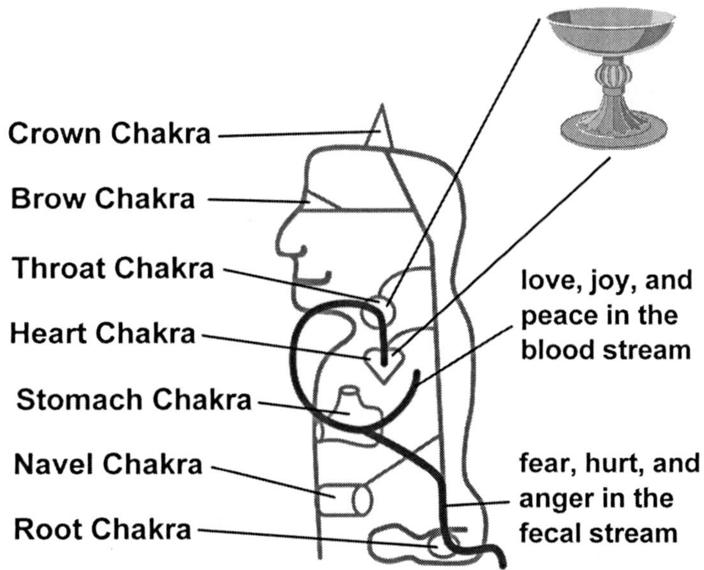

myself of my own *purity* of heart. My *evacuation* had *evaded* my *evaluation*, and my *feces* were *feckless*, so I needed to learn how to *chuck* the right *chunk*.

My soul-strength was *chafing* at the bit to break my ego's *chain reaction*, so I consulted the *chairman* of the *chakras*† whose *chalice* at the Last Supper *chalked up* my victory.

Adam's and Eve's *fornication* had *fouled* the *foundation* of this *fountain* of living waters, so it became necessary for man to rid himself of this *filth* that *encroached* on his *finesse*. In order for the water in the fountain to *flow* man's *embittered emotions* had to be *emptied*, and then the Fruits could *flower*. Man could *retrieve* his *lost love* and *reveal* the *paradise* within, but *first* man had to *fix* the *flaws* that made him *flip his lid*. Man's ego was the *parasite* that had made him *part* with these *heavenly heights*, so man had to *help* himself to a little contrition and get rid of these *heretics*. The *waste* in the *water* only made man *waver*, because Satan had *woven* this *web* of falsehoods and *wedded* them to the will of man, so man had to *weep* over this *weighty* burden if he wanted to *wet* his whistle with the Fruits.

God had given Adam and Eve their original *innocence inside* their Heart Chakras so they could be in touch with their *inspiration*, and their Throat Chakras *swallowed* the divine *sweetness* continuously before the *swindle*, but when they became *swingers* the divine sweetness got *swiped*. When God gave them *free will*, He told them not to go on a *frenulum frenzy*, because it would introduce a lot of *Freudian friction* that would leave them *frightened*.‡ Nevertheless, the *swingers* got *swivel* hips that soon began to *reciprocate recklessly*, and man *lost* unconditional *love*.

---

†Adapted from *The Chakras*, C. W. Leadbeater, 1985, Theosophical Publishing House, Wheaton, Illinois.

‡*God Talks with Arjuna, The Bhagavad Gita*, Paramahansa Yogananda, Self-Realization Fellowship, Los Angeles, CA 90065-3298, p. 931 The original prototypes of man and woman had no sexual members in their perfect bodies until after they had disobeyed God's command to them. "They were both naked . . . and were not ashamed" — a harmonious unity between the qualities of positive and negative, masculine and feminine, reason and feeling, unperverted by gross sensual sex attraction. But when the feeling or Eve-consciousness in man was tempted by vague recollections of animalistic sexual arousal, then man's reason or Adam also succumbed.

When Adam and Eve embraced each other with sensual desire, the serpentine or coiled-up energy at the base of the spine, which either lifts man Godward or feeds his senses, stimulated the heretofore undeveloped sex nerves. From this agitation, the sex organs developed. See also *The Second Coming of Christ* by Paramahansa Yogananda, I:128: The sex impulse is the single most physically magnetic power that pulls the life

The problem was that their *lewd liaison* left me at *liberty* to take a *licking*. God had given me *absolute* power in my stomach to *absorb whatever* I wanted, so as a child I felt like a big *wheel*, and *whenever* my parents *glared* at me I *gloated* and *glutted*. I suppressed my *wrath*, so the divine sweetness took the *wrong* turn, and it didn't work out as shown in the above *diagram*. These *diatribes* made me think the *riches* of love, joy, and peace weren't my *right*, so I *sent* these *senior* members down my fecal stream, and my *senseless* fear, hurt, and anger into my blood stream. However, my *contrition controls* my Stomach Chakra, because it *determines* that which is *detestable* and *rejects* it so that I can *rejoice* by choosing the *diet* that makes a *difference*. Therefore, I can *absorb* my love, joy, and peace and *abstain* from this *absurd abuse*.

My Heart Chakra is the *pithy place* that makes me *placid* and puts the Fruits on my *plate*. It is the *dining room* in which I can *dip* into the *bliss* that got *blocked* when I became my *parents' parrot*, because at the Last Supper Jesus started the *spiral* of the Holy *Spirit* there. Likewise, my Throat Chakra can *swallow* my love, joy, and peace rather than the *swill* of my fear, hurt, and anger, and then my Stomach Chakra can *digest* these *dignitaries*. My Stomach Chakra's *connection* to the vertical axis is meant to get rid of my *conniptions*, so it goes *downward* to *drain* out my *drastic* fear, hurt, and anger, whereas the spiral sends *up* the Fruits that I aim to *uphold*. As a child I had a *naughty navel*, because I *believed* everything my parents said, so my *bellybutton* got *bemired* in these *unresolved dependency* needs that caused my *unrest*. They *deployed* their *depravity* into my *behavior* and made me *belligerent*, but I can get a better *benediction* from my *Navel* Chakra, because it is *navigable* by the *Nazarene*.

My *Brow* Chakra's job is to *browse* through the *crock* of my childhood fears that I now consider my *cronies*. I can get rid of these *crooks*

---

and consciousness down from Spirit in the higher centers in the brain, out through the coccygeal center and into matter and body consciousness. They are blessed who are victorious over the sexual instinct.

Because suppression may only increase one's difficulties, yoga teaches sublimation. "Though the physical body of man was generally patterned after the physiological and anatomical instrumentalities that had resulted from the long process of evolution of animal species, human beings were created by God with a unique endowment possessed by no lower forms: awakened spiritual centers of life and consciousness in the spine and brain that gave them the ability to express fully the divine consciousness and powers of the soul. By an act of special creation, God thus created the bodies of Adam and Eve in the immaculate way of direct materialization, and empowered these first beings similarly to reproduce their own kind." (46)

by *crooning* my remorse in Jesus' *ear*, because he will plant the *crop* of the Fruits in my heart, and I will feel more at *ease*. He carried the *Cross* from the chakra in my *crotch* to my *Crown* Chakra so that my kundalini could get out of this *bawdy bay* below and respond to the *beacon* on my *bean* known as my Crown Chakra. The *Romeo* who *romped* with Eve in Eden disconnected the chakra on my *roof* from my *Root* Chakra, but the Mysteries of the *Rosary* can solve this problem. I just have to let the *Sorrowful* Mysteries train my chakras to *sort* out this mess. I just have to ask my *senses* to become *sensible* and *differentiate* the *digestible dignitaries* from the *dilemmas* I don't want to *dine* on. My chakras need to send my *Fruits* into my blood and my *frustrations* into my stool. They need to *sort out* the *spaced-out sentiments* that cause my *spats* and *separate* them in my *stomach* so the *aggravating* ones go out in the *stool*, and I may become more *agreeable*. Adam is the *Stone Age stooge* who taught us all to pass our Fruits in our *stool*, but the *carpenter carried* the *Cross* to make my *Stomach* Chakra *stop storing* these angry *stowaways*, *crucify* this *crud*, and *ship* it out in my *shit*. Therefore, I will take my *chagrin* and stop this repugnant *chain reaction* in my *chakras*. I will meet this *challenge* in these *chambers*, and let the *calmness* of *Calvary* send these *cantankerous captains* into the *toilet* where they can't take such a heavy *toll* on my happiness. I can get rid of these *cranky* crackpots by taking a *crap*, because Jesus made me a *partner* to his *Passion* so that my *past* could be *patched* up in this way.

The spiral through the chakras is a *cogent coil*[†], because it contains the *essence* of the divine sweetness which is *essential* to lov-

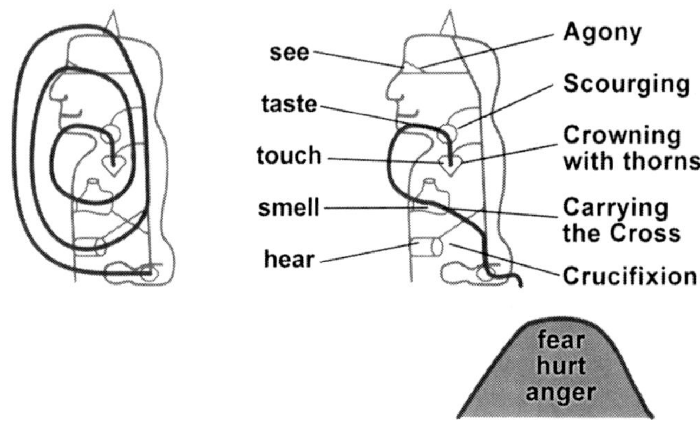

[†]*Wheels of Life*, Anodea Judith, 1987, Llewellyn Publications, P.O. Box 64383, St. Paul, MN 55164-0383, p. 217.

ing behavior. It makes the *blood* of Jesus *bloom* with the Fruits, so we should use this *circulatory system* to avoid being at the effect of *circumstance*. We got a *heap* of blessings from Jesus' Passion, because it gave us a *heart transplant*, took us out of the *trap* called ego, and gave us the *treasure* of the divine sweetness. The Sacred Heart contains the *fountain* of the divine sweetness that is under divine *franchise*, so let's *squelch* our fears with a few good *squirts* and get the *stability* that was born in the *stable* in Bethlehem. The Sacred Heart ends our *estrangement* from God, because the *eternal flame* above it is a *flashback* to the time when our hearts were *ablaze* with the *Absolute* and *abstained* from the *absurd abuse* of ego. Our *paradise* got *paralyzed*, but it can still be *found* in the *parapet* of the Crown Chakra by lighting a *passionate fire* in our hearts to return to this *first* blessing. The two *degenerates* in Eden *deleted* the *delicious flavor* of the divine sweetness and left us *flawed*, so they got *banished* from Eden, but Jesus installed the *spiral* in our hearts at the *banquet* of the Last Supper so that we could enjoy the *spiritual spoils* known as the Fruits of the Spirit.

The *Last* Supper gives *lasting* benefit, because the *Mass* is the cardiac *massage* that is delivered by the *master* in order to allow us to *masticate* on the Fruits. The Mass is the *liturgy* of the *living* waters known as the divine sweetness, so we should *thread* the needle to the *Throat* Chakra, not leave our sense of *taste* in *tatters*, and go with this *flow* that *flowers* with the Fruits. The Root Chakra represents *faith* that has *fallen*, so it is the *cellar* that needs the *centerpiece* of the Sacred Heart to get connected to our *cerebral cortex*. Therefore, let's *bridge* this gap and *bridle* our egos by asking Jesus to *bring about* this blessing. Then the Sacred Heart will *beat* in our chests, and the *beatitudes* will transform us, because the *purity* of the Sacred Heart will put us under the *purview* of its *sanity*. Therefore, let's *satisfy* our hunger and become just as *beautiful* as we were *before* the fall of man.

The divine sweetness is the *primeval principle* that was *imprinted* in our souls well before Adam and Eve's *impropriety*, so we should ask it to bring our *Fruits* to *fruition*. The divine sweetness is *consistently consoling*, so let's end our ego's *conspiracy* and enjoy this *constant consummation* that gives our *nasty natures* the *nurture* that makes us less *nuts*. We will certainly *flourish* as soon as the blood of Christ *flows* through the *spiral*, because each chakra along the way will make us feel like the *spitting image* of Jesus. The Throat Chakra has been a *slacker*, but he can still *slake* our spiritual *thirst*. We just need to tell him that the *supreme sustenance* of the divine sweetness is meant to be *swallowed* and not to *swig* the *swindlers* known as fear, hurt, and anger. The *thorny threats* from our childhood make our *Throat* Chakras feel *throttled*, but when he *drinks* the divine sweetness and asks it to do the *driving*, the blood of Jesus will *wind* through the spiral. The Eucharistic *wine* may *look* like wine, but it contains the *loot* of the *Lord* known as the Fruits, so let's have the *common sense* to *communicate* this blessing to our *throats* so the *throng* of the Fruits can get *through*. We can have this *communion continuously*, because the New Covenant enables our *contrition* to *convert* our wild and *woolly worries* into a sense of self-*worth* that nothing can *wreck*.

The divine sweetness is the *star* performer that *starts* in our *hearts* as soon as we begin to *heave* out our fears. Our *contrition* makes us *convalesce*, so let's give our chakras the *facts*, because they are the *factory* which *incorporates* the *incorrupt essence* into us that was *estranged* from us in Eden. Our chakras will *rouse* from their sleep when the *spiral splices* in love, joy, and peace, so let's take this *route* and enjoy the *buffet* of the Fruits. The Fruits are served on these *built-ins* after we have gotten rid of our *bull*, so let's use this *coil* to allow our true *colors* to take *command* over us. Divine sweetness is the *resource* that can give us this *rest cure*, so let's be *curious* about how we got *cursed*.

There is a difference between being *dazed* and being *dazzled*, so let's use the *dead reckoning* of our remorse, which is the *dean of students* in this school of hard knocks who can get us out of this *stupor*. Before the *slander* of our childhoods our sweetness was *sleek* and polished, but then it went to *sleep* because of these *slights*. Our *clans' clashes* can be *classified* in the *classrooms* of our Stomach and Navel Chakras, because they are the *cloisters* where we bring *closure* to these *mom-and-pop moments*. The brand of *theism* we had *then* was colored by the *hurtful hybrid* known as conditional love, which we allowed to *molest* us, but the Stomach and Navel Chakras are the classrooms in this *monastery* where the *discipline* of *disclosure* gives us *complete composure*.

The preferential *treatment* we gave as children to our *trees of knowledge* made the spiral through our *chakras* a *chancy channel*, but we don't have to let this *echo* from *Eden rot* the Fruits on our trees and turn us into *roughnecks*. We should take advantage of the *trick*

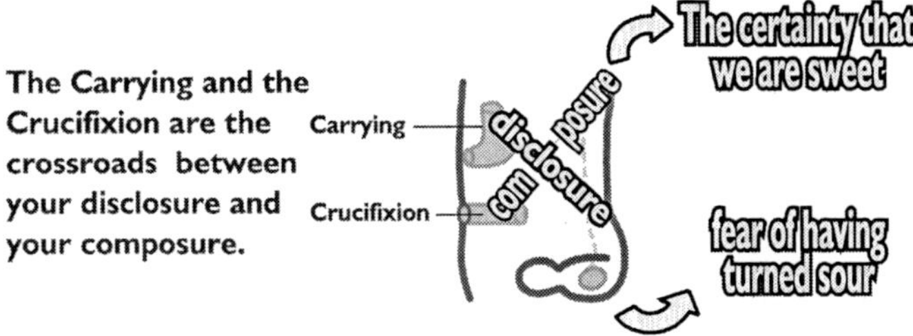

of the *Trinity*, and let the Holy *Ghost* solve these problems. Jesus is the *giant* who can make us its *clients*, so let's enjoy his spiritual *climate* by asking this Paul *Bunyan* to *buoy* us up. He will *uproot* these feelings that *upset* us, and we will wind up less *weary*, because he will get rid of these bad *weeds*.

What made life most *harrowing* for me as a child was this *harsh harvest* that grew on my tree of knowledge. These *graceless grains* were *gathered* by my ego, which is the *gauge* Satan adjusted to keep me spiritually *gaunt*. I didn't know that I had the right to *pick* the Fruits and *picket* my sour-grapes attitudes so as to avoid being in a *pickle*. Nevertheless, once I was given the choice of the Fruits, I had a *picnic* right away, because I was able to get the *picture* and eat my piece of the *pie*. I was *astonished* at how this *repast rescued* me from my *resentments* and enabled me to stop going *astray*.

The above understandings *notwithstanding*, I still didn't get the *nougat* of the divine sweetness, because my perfectionistic *morality* during my therapy required that my *morass* remain under *moratorium* until I became aware of just how *morbid* it all was. Early on my therapist *told* me that to be more *tolerant* I had to shovel my manure, and so I figured that my *shoveling* was the *show business* that I had to entertain her with. I was too *fascinated* with my *faults*, so I eventually got *fed up* and decided it would be better to send out my *feelers* after the *fellowship* of the Holy Spirit, which would *serve* me better by *setting* the divine sweetness in motion.

As a child I was *knocked for a loop* by my tree of *knowledge*, because it *bore* the fruits of my ego which made me feel *beaten*. My spiritual *slump* was caused by this *slush fund* I had set aside, because my will had been the *slut* who had taken instruction from Satan the *provost* of *prurience* in this *cold-hearted college*. Therefore, the *sly* one *smacked* me with *circumstances* that made my life look like a *circus*. I *wailed* with each *wallop* hoping that the *bisque* of my parents' love would be served after each *bitter* dose, but these *whippings* never earned me these *whispers* of affection. I *swaggered* with pride when I *swallowed* each *dollop* but wound up looking like a *dolt*, because the *appendage* known as my *approval*-seeking never *encountered* my parents' *endorsement*. Therefore, as an adult I *wallowed* in the self-pity I had hired as the *warden* in this prison. Nevertheless, I could get off this *treadmill* and take advantage of the Fruits in my *tree* of wisdom. I could become an *altruistic alumnus* of this school of hard knocks by understanding the *history* of each *hit* and allowing my remorse to give me the *birds-eye* view of this nonsense that could earn me the *birthright* of my sweetness.

Nevertheless, bitter *herbs* were the *heritage* I derived from my *hero-worship* of my father. I never learned to *sup* on my sweetness at the feet of this *superman*, because there was *nothing* about me that he seemed to think worthy of his *notice*. My particular *crime* was to let this make me feel like a *cripple*, so this *guile* filled me with *guilt*, and as an adult I was the *convict* who remained imprisoned in this *jail* of *jangled* nerves. I mistakenly thought my father was *Allah*, so my fears never got *allayed*, and I carried around this *bull* thinking

My self-*doubts* put me *down* for the *count*, because they ran *counter* to my faith.

it was a *burden* I *deserved*. I never got the *dessert* of the divine sweetness, because I thought I was just *destined* to have this *karmic* debt that would allow Satan to *kayo* me.

I kept getting this *knockout* punch as an adult, because this *knotty knowledge* was the *bias* that made me a *big baby*. I didn't have much *backbone* until I got into therapy and discovered the *backdoor* where this *caricature* I *carried* could go out as *crucified crud*. This *joy* was under the jurisdiction of Jesus the *Judaic judge* who could help me feel *swell* by teaching me to flip this *swill switch* in my stomach. I could send this slop out my *bottom* through my *bowels* by using this *forgiveness fork* that Jesus had put in the *road* to help me get rid of these *rogues*.

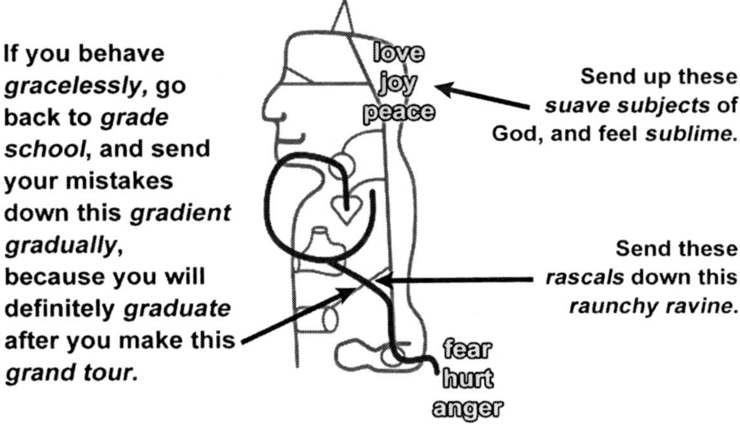

My particular problem was this *dilemma* of the *dimmer switch* in my stomach, which was intended to make me gradually more *sympathetic* to the Fruits, but I didn't *increase* their absorption by *increments* and just *decreased* my repressed feelings through my *defecation*. I was *hindered*, because my *hindquarter's hindsight* was blind to my *foresight*, so I got lost in this *forest* and *forestalled* the entry of the Fruits into my behavior.

I was so *intent* on *intercepting* my *scatological scatterings* that the *nectar* of the divine sweetness never got in the *nerd*. The study of my *nervous breakdown* was so *breathtaking* that the Eternally Begotten Son in my *Navel* Chakra couldn't *navigate* me into calmer waters, and I went on behaving like a *Nazi Neanderthal man*.

This *mania* of the *manure monopoly* left me *monumentally moody*, because my love, joy, and peace never *cascaded* through the spiral, so

I was the nut *case* who couldn't *cash* in on these Fruits. I had tried to *treat* myself without consulting the *treaty* of the New *Covenant* and didn't take *cover* under this *mantle* because of my *mania*. I needed to be *energized* by my Brow Chakra, because he was the *engineer* who could connect my hindsight and foresight.

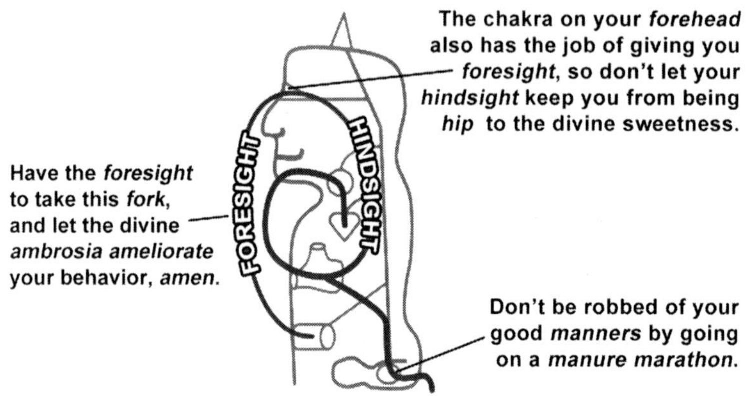

This light was *burning* brightly in Eden before the fall, but then it got *bushwhacked*, and man's interest in ladies' *buttocks* and *buxom* bosoms *bypassed* this connection. Therefore, the *cabinetmaker* had to reconnect the *cables* by *passing* the *test* of his *Passion*. He made it possible for our *therapy* to enable us to *think* with the *third* person of the Trinity and complete this *circuit* that the *circumstance* in Eden had *circumvented*.

The *Holy* Spirit could then bring *home* God's *honey* and not leave us *hopelessly* mired in the *horror* of our pasts. He wanted us to *gradually opt* for our *optimism* during our therapy rather than *persist* in our *pessimism*, so that the *grape* of the human soul could *grasp* the *vine* of the Holy Spirit and become *virtuous* again. Jesus' *aim* was to help us look *ahead* and *behind* at the same time so we would not be *beleaguered* by *pasts* that would continue to make us feel *pathetic*. However, my *hindsight* was so highly focused on my *historical* anger that my *foresight forgot* to take this *fork* in the road. I assumed that my *redemption* depended on identifying *reenactments*, so the more *eminent emotions* known as love, joy, and peace never got *enacted*. I had *exulted* too much in the use of these *eyes* behind my *head*, so I kept on flinging myself *headfirst* into disaster. No one had *taught* me that I could *sup* on the *superior supplement* of God's sweetness, so my *soul*-strength never *teamed* up with this *chicken soup* that the

Chief of my inner *child* had prepared at the chakra on the *chimney* top.

Therefore, my self-*doubts* made my kundalini go *down* the vertical axis, and the divine sweetness stayed *up* in the Crown Chakra, because my kundalini seemed to have no *use* for this *utilitarian* substance. It was the same *alienation* that had come *alive* in Eden.

When our kundalini *dropped*, we all became spiritual *dropouts*, and we began *drowning* in our sins. Adam and Eve's *lovemaking* brought *loving-kindness* to a *low tide*, so we became more *dexterous* at being *diabolical*. When Eve committed the *felony* of using her *femininity* as a *femme fatale*, man lost the *dividend* known as the *divine* sweetness, and earned the *divisive doctrine* known as original sin. The kundalini became *apathetic* toward the divine sweetness, because the *aphrodisiac* speech that Satan delivered to Eve made the *apical* chakra hold onto its *aplomb*, which had an *apocalyptic* effect on the Root Chakra.

We were *casualties* of this *catastrophe*, so Jesus opened the *passageways* through his *Passion* that *connected* the two ends *connubially*. Jesus made it possible for the kundalini to *rise* when we confront our fears, so we can *beat* these *rivals* by playing *catch-up* ball through the *catharsis* of remorse. *Knowing* how we got *kooky* raises the *kundalini*, because our chakras are *reminded* by our *remorse* that they are the *laboratory* in which we get rid of this *lack*. Each set of *mysteries* examines the particular *myths* from our childhoods that *nailed* us to this *cross*, so let's *crucify* our *crude behavior* and *crunch* these numbers on this *crusade*, because the *Mass* is the cardiac *massage* that will give us *mastery* over ego when we do this *math*.

The Inquiry

Sorrowful Mysteries

but when this *light* bulb goes on,

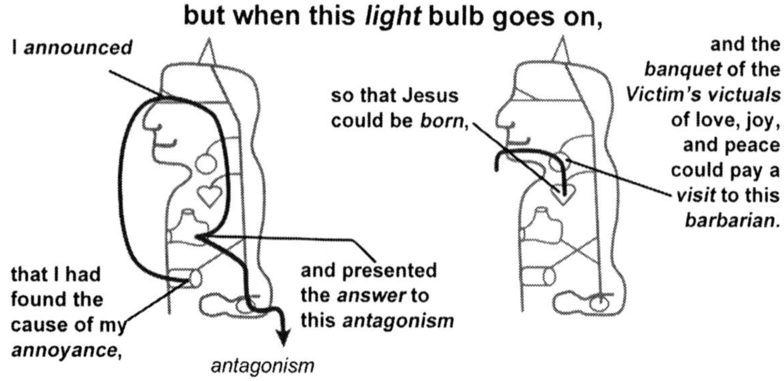

The Insight
Joyous Mysteries

---

you will discover your *likeness*,

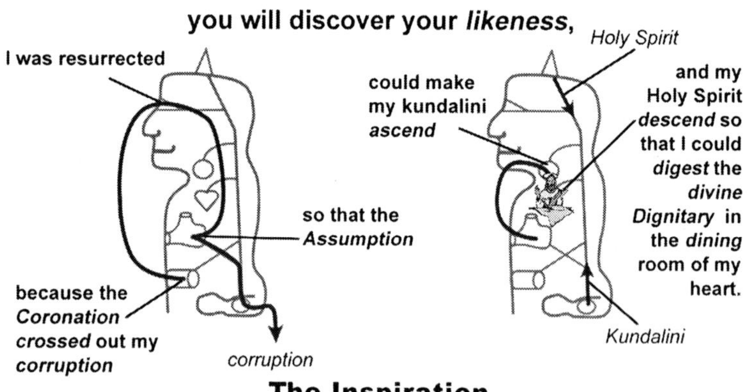

The Inspiration
Glorious Mysteries

---

because the two *liquids* in your spine will have *linked* up.

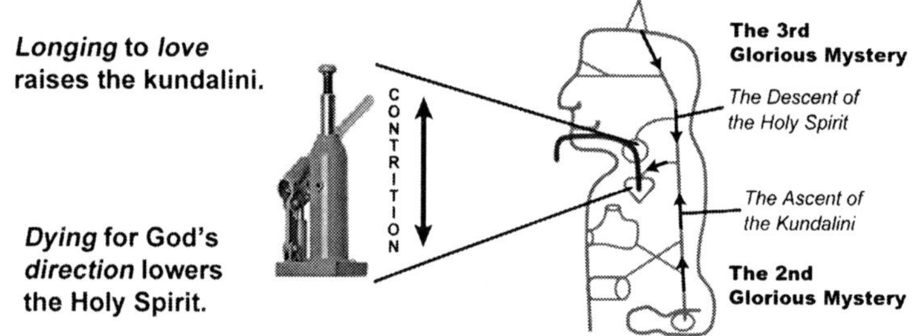

This *jack* near your *jaw* was installed by *Jesus* so that the *Third* Person in the Trinity could open this *thorny thoroughfare* that had been closed by the *threats* in your *throat,* so make the Holy Spirit *rain* down, *raise* your kindalini, and use this *ratchet.*

My neck and my navel *confronted* my *confusion* and were *consistently consoling,* because they used my *contrition* to *cook* up this meal that helped me *cope.*

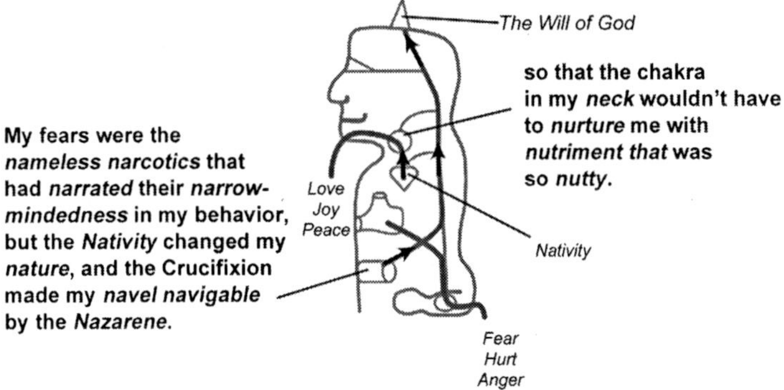

It is possible to *untangle* the *untruths* that have caused our *unutterable* suffering and *unyoke* ourselves from *upbringings* that have left us *upset.* We just need to use the *upstroke* between the Navel and Crown Chakras and become *urbane.* Therefore, let's use this *uterus* which the Virgin Mary gave us and bring back the *utopia* that was *utterly* destroyed in Eden. When Adam *spilled* his seed in Eve, their ecstasy caused our agony, because they squandered the fluid in their *spines* that God gave them to connect us with the Holy *Spirit.* Instead of *conserving* this *consistently consoling* liquid, they *dissipated* it, *dissolved* our relationship with God, and caused us to *vacillate* like *vagrants* in this *vale of tears.* Nevertheless, I can attest to the fact that the most *exciting* adventure on earth is to *exclaim* your grief for this *excrement* which has made *excursions* into your behavior, rid yourself of this *excruciating* pain, *exculpate* yourself, and *exercise* the will of God in your life. It is clear that we can *vindicate* the *vine* of the Holy Spirit by understanding how this *vinegar* brought its *violence* into our behavior and by allowing the *vivid vociferations* of our grief to rid us of these *vulgar vultures.* The *relationship* we share with God is *relevant* to our wellbeing, so we should use the *reliable relics* of heart, soul, mind, and strength to *wield* the power of our *will, wire* us to God the Father, get this *relief* of the Christian *religion*, and *bring* about the repair of this *broken* promise. When we gradually *relinquish* all the fears we have been most *reluctant* to let go of, God will *remake* us interiorly, and the *remarkable remedy* of the Holy Spirit will *render* us to God.

We can *repatriate* ourselves to our heavens within, because our heart, soul, mind, and strength still *speak* the language of love. Each of these *four foxy fragments* still possesses this *frame of mind* that is sponsored by the divine *franchise* in the Crown Chakra and *specializes* in the same *specific* task just as they did before Satan cast the *spell* on Adam's *sperm* and caused the human spine to *spin off* the by-products of the forces of evil. When we were *created*, the *Creator* allowed the Holy Spirit and the kundalini to be directed by this *crew* of four into the *critical delivery room* in the middle. The *Heart* Chakra could create *progeny* with a *heavenly prognosis*, because it contained a strictly *demarcated demilitarized zone* that man could use to bring about a new *crop* of children by *crossbreeding* them with the Holy Spirit.

After the fall heart, soul, mind, and strength still lived in the *spine* but weren't in touch with the Holy *Spirit* and began to *spit* out *spite*, because they had *splintered* off from God and were no longer His *spokespersons*. The Holy Spirit got *spooked* when Adam and Eve started to *spoon*, because it knew that they were intended to be *spotless spouses*† and follow the *principle* that was *printed indelibly* on them as an *indication* of their divine origin. God was to be the *referee* in the *refinery* of the chakras so that His grace could be *reflected* through these seven *prisms* into the *next* generation without man having to use the *nimble thimble* on the *thin thing* which would do the *thinking* and make the children feel like *nitwits*, because they would have no cognizance of their divine *nobility*. All Adam and Eve had to do was give the *nod* to God, and the Holy *Spirit* would *split* off the *pristine prize spontaneously* and make a new generation *spring* forth.

Adam and Eve were *privileged* to use this same *master stroke* God used with the big bang in order to *produce progeny*. God was the *matchless matchmaker* who *materialized* Adam and Eve in this way, so

---

†*God Talks With Arjuna, The Bhagavad Gita*, Paramahansa Yogananda, 1995, Self-Realization Fellowship, 3880 San Rafael Avenue, Los Angeles, California 90065-3298, p. 28. .At the beginning of the cycle of manifested creation, God materialized all forms by direct, special, creative command: The "Word," or cosmic creative vibration of Aum, with its manifest powers of creation, preservation, and dissolution. God endowed man, made in His omnipotent image, with this same creative power. But Adam and Eve (symbolic of the first pairs of human beings), yielding to touch temptation, lost the power of "immaculate creation" by which they had been able to clothe all their mental pictures with energy and life, thus materializing children from the ether (bringing them into manifestation from the ideational world), even as gods.

Man and woman, instead of seeking emancipation in God through soul unity sought satisfaction through the flesh. The seed of the original error of "Adam and Eve" remains in all human beings as the first temptation of the flesh against the immaculate laws of Spirit ("touch not the tree in the center of the garden!"). Each individual since that dim era has had to engage his soul in battle with the cosmically present temptation of sex. The creator in man has become a dictatorial creature.

he explained this *maternal mathematics* to them saying it would be much better to bring children into the world in this *matter-of-fact* way than to do it on *mattresses*. The *objectionable* thing, He said, about reproducing in an *obscene* manner is that it would *obscure* the role of the divine *obstetrician* and allow *occult* forces to *occupy* the *office* God was to use to produce *offspring*. God *organized* the *original equipment* of the chakras so that His *magic* could *make* children without the *maladjustment* attendant to the *malady* of *male* and female. *Man* was intended to be the *manager* of these forces that God *maneuvered* into the *manger* rather than become a sex *maniac*, which would put *manifold* forces of evil on the *march*. God *aimed* to *allay* man's fears through this open *alley* in his spine that would *allow* the *allure* of the *Almighty* to make its presence known on the *altar* of man's heart. He intended to *replace* the concept of the *erection* and spare mankind this *escapade* that would *estrange* man from Him. The *Deity deleted* sex *deliberately* so that man could learn this *delicate* lesson, make his heart a *delicatessen* of the Fruits, and serve the *delights* of love, joy, and peace to the children who were *delivered* into the world through these *conduits* which *conformed* to His will.

When God *invented* the chakras, he *invested* this *invincible* strength in them so that man could have an *iron will* that would make it possible for children to *issue* forth *out of the blue*. God's *blueprint* included this *feature*, because He wanted parents and children to *feel* connected with one another and to Him through the *fellowship* of the Holy Spirit. The *isthmus* between the Crown and Root Chakras would make *it* possible, because God's *sponsorship* of the event could make children appear *spontaneously*. The *gear* of the chakras included this *spout* in man's heart which man was intended to use *instead* of the *instrument* between his legs. Adam and Eve knew that they shouldn't go *fishing* around in a *fit* of lust in one another's *privates* in order to *produce progeny*, because God had told them that this *lechery* would result in the *legacy* of ego-addiction and would put out the *fire* of love in their hearts that He had put there *first*. Nevertheless, their *flagrant disregard* for God's will *flared* up as a result of Satan's *flattery*, *disrupted* the chakras, and required the *Fisher* of men to *fix* these *fixtures* by means of the *Last* Supper much *later* by empowering them to help us *launder* these dirty *layers* in our minds.

Our *distress* got *distributed* in the *district* of the chakras and *legalized* the *legendary* problems that the divine *legislature* in the Crown Chakra could have *prevented* if the will of man had retained its *priest-*

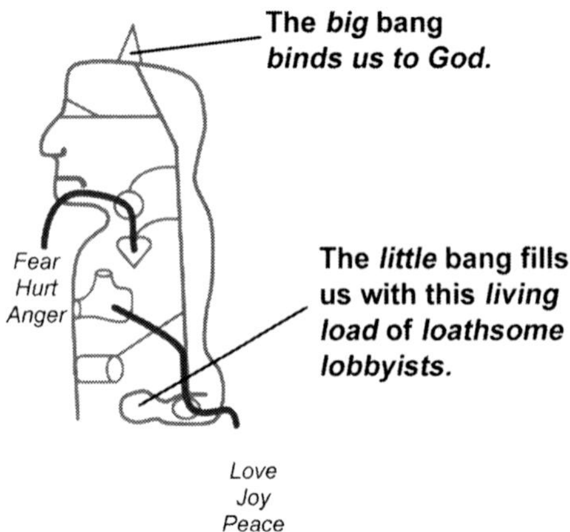

ly function, which is to say the *celibacy* that could *center* him in God. Man was intended to *generate* children without depending on his *genitalia*, which God knew to be the *device* the *devil* would use to rob man of his *devotion* to Him. Man could *get* the Holy *Ghost* to *gird* his loins if he *reproduced* in this *orthodox* manner, because it would preserve the *otherworldly outlook* that man needed to *contemplate* his world *contentedly*. God wanted Adam and Eve's children to have a *maturity* that could not be *mauled* by the hand of fate, but Adam and Eve *vacillated*, and Eve's *vagina* became the *valve* that let loose the *maximum mayhem* of fear, hurt, and *anger* that *animates* mankind to this day. They ate this *meager meal* rather than the *meaningful* one of love, joy, and peace, so we should all *reflect* on the consequences that flow from this *reflex* we find so *refreshing*, because it's just possible that the *mechanism* of *immaculate* conception may still be able to make children *appear* without *appeasing* the *appetite* Satan gave us under the *apple tree*.

God intended each of us to be an *immortal* who could never be *imperiled* by *impious* urges. Nevertheless, Satan *flattered* the floozy until she *flaunted* herself in front of Adam with the result that this *fleeting pleasure* we continue to pursue still brings *plenty* of adverse consequences. God had one *plan* for the *planet*, but when the *squaw squeezed* the *squire's* thing, he *squirmed* with pleasure and *stabbed* it in her with the *staggering* result that our spirituality became *stagnant*. The kundalini *sprayed* itself all over the ground and sent Adam and Eve on this crime *spree* that would cause all of us to *squander* this precious fluid. Adam and Eve *harmed* their *heart*-mind in this way, *sold* their *soul*-strength down the river; *spoiled* the *spring* of love, joy, and peace; and *fouled* the *fountain* of living waters, but our contrition still *links* up with the *liquid* in the spring and *raises* the kundalini so that it can *rally* with the *rampart* in the middle. The Holy Spirit also pays *rapt* attention to this *rare reaction*, which is to say that they both *listen* to this *little liturgy* called contrition which empowers them to earn their *living*.

The kundalini *climbs* to this *clinic* in the middle where the *clique* known as heart-mind and soul-strength is restored to health, so we should remember that it is a *fib* that we cannot be *filled* with God's love, joy, and peace. The seven *drains* shown above *empty* us of our *dread* and *endear* us to God, because during his *Passion* our *pasts* became the work of our *Pastor*, which is to say that Jesus empowered the chakras to *patch* up our relationship with God. He *patented* the *pathway* of the spiral through the chakras so as to make us *paupers* in the spirit of ego, so you could say that he also *paved* the way to the *pavilion* of the Crown Chakra *where* the *will* of God resides. Our *navel* chakras are *navigable* by the *Nazarene*, but he also uses the chakra in the *neck* to fill us *full* of blessings we cannot *fumble*. We *need* the *functionaries* called love, joy, and peace to calm our *nerves*, so let's become less *woebegone*, do this *work*, get rid of our *worries*, and find our Self-*worth*. Our *innate innocence* is *inoculated* into us when we complete this *inquest*, so let's get these *insights* and profit from these *inspirations*. Our *Freudian friction* has *frozen* our *Fruits* but we can get a *grip* on our *gripes*, use the *grist mills* shown above, get our feet on the *ground*, *grow* spiritually, get rid of our *gruesome grumpiness*, and be *guided* by the Holy Spirit.

The *Deity* always sends this *delegate* when we *deliberate* as shown above, and He *delivers* the Fruits, because our *kundalini* removes our *ancient anger* in this *laboratory* so as to provide the *answer*. Our kundalini *remembers* how to *reminisce*; so when we feel *remorse*, it *removes* our original sin and earns us the *repast* of love, joy, and peace. The *kinetics* of the Holy Spirit are better than those of our *kinfolk*, so let's use the *kingdom* of the chakras to replace these *kinky recipes* that rob us of our *reciprocity* with God. We have *swallowed* these *ingratiating ingredients* that have *embittered* these seven *enclosures*, but our *contrition* can still *cook* up a meal with this *cool-headed* component in this *kitchen*. We can turn off this *faucet* in our hearts that pours our *favorite fears* into our behavior, so let's get on our *knees* in front of this *knight-errant* that *knits* us to God and ask our *kundalini* to *acquit* us *across-the-board*. *Psychotherapy* is the best way to *pull* up this *punch-drunk pundit* out of the *puzzles* that have put him in a *quandary*, but *Kriya Yoga* is an *adjunct* that is *admirable*, because it takes our *kundalini* in *hand* and teaches it to *harken* to the will of God by *raising* this *rare raw material* up to the Crown Chakra where He lives. It causes a *warm* glow in my spine, because it raises this *powerful warrior*, so I *practice* it daily and *recommend* that we all have *recourse* to this *procedure* taught by my guru Paramahansa Yogananda.† We will *profit profoundly* if we use these two *techniques*, because they will *telegraph* many blessings through the *temple* of our chakras. If we *do* them like *doctor's* orders, our kundalini will *rise* in this *rod* and *staff* in our spines, because this is the *stage* where these *two types* of treatment issue the *ultimatum* that ends our *unbearable* suffering. The Mysteries of the *Rosary* will *rouse* this *sleepyhead* from his *slumber* so that he may *awaken* this *awesome axis* in our *back*, *coil* around the *Comforter*, and give us a *common* union with God. We can *end* our *endangerment* by means of this *endorsement*, so let's *engage* these seven *engines* and *enjoy composure* that is *comprehensive*.

The kundalini is the *potential energy* also known as soul-strength and can *pour* itself out, because when our heart-mind feels remorse it *kindles* the kundalini's *kinetic energy* and turns it into a *mountain mover*. The kundalini is held in *escrow* in the Root Chakra, but this *esoteric* liquid responds to the *espionage* of heart-mind, so let's get the two together on the vertical axis of our Chakra Systems, because this is the *esplanade* where they *espouse* the *essence* which is the divine sweetness.

The kundalini *rises* to the heart as a result of the *rite* known as contrition and then circulates in the *conduit* of the spiral until it gets to the *cone* which is my Crown Chakra. Heart-mind lives on the *roof* in the Crown Chakra, and soul-strength is the *rookie* who *rooms* in the *Root* Chakra. Heart-mind's job is to *reshape* my destiny, because he *resides* in the Crown Chakra with the will of God. Therefore, his profession is to direct the *residue* known as kundalini to *resign* from sinful pursuits and to become more *resilient* by embracing the *resin* known as the divine sweetness. The *faucet* of the divine sweetness in the Heart Chakra wants to turn on the *feast* of the Fruits, but the *plumbing* between the Crown and Root Chakras went up in a *plume* of smoke as a result of original sin, so my heart-mind and soul-strength have to *plunge* into the *task* as a *team* of two and meet one another *halfway* by making a commitment to *halting* my fears.

†To qualify for Kriya Yoga go to <www.yogananda-srf.org> and click on the Self-Realization Fellowship lessons.

My *Crown* Chakra is Christ the *King's kitchen*, because the Resurrection of Jesus gives it the *ability above* to make my *middle* chakra *mild* and to convince the *bedroom* chakra to give up its *belligerence below*. My *contrition* starts the *conversation* between the *hungry husband* below and the *wife* in the kitchen above, so she eventually becomes *willing* to *cook* the meal that helps them *cope*. They fill their *empty* stomachs and become *enamored* of one another in the *dignified dining room* in the middle, because a *simple* act of *sincere* repentance was *broadcast* by my will the marriage *broker*. This *romance* between my *roof* and my *roots* is reenacted in the *Mass*, which has the purpose of teaching them they are a *match* made in heaven. They no longer behave like *mavericks*, because they have eaten the *meat* and *potatoes* that have this *potential*.

Nevertheless, I have not had the *pleasure* of seeing this *pledge* fulfilled, because the *pundit* of my heart-mind has not made me *pure* of heart in this *delicatessen* above my head. The delicatessen is run by *Delilah*, but she has not gotten together with *Sampson* below, so my soul-strength has not been *sanctified* by the divine sweetness. They have not *eaten* this *éclair* together, so I have remained *weak*, because I have lacked this *wealth* and have suffered from the *poverty* that has resulted from my will being Satan's *POW*. I *have given* Satan *free rein to* be *relentlessly sadistic* to me, so I have *sailed* into troubled waters.

I have gathered a *roster* of fears as a result of this *rotten routing*, and the one at the top of the list is the most *unjust*, because it is that I am *unlovable* by God. This is the *horror* that came *from the horse's mouth*, and it is the *terror* that my behavior has *testified* to the most. It is the *fright* that has made my heart feel *frigid*, and it is the *trepidation* that has led to the *triad* of my fear, hurt, and anger. This is the *dread* that *dribbles* into my behavior, but I have the Self-*confidence* to *confine* this *flak* and not be a *flake*. To be *clear-sighted* in this way my *kundalini* must climb this *ladder* so that the two *laggards* known as heart-mind and soul-strength may *land* in the safe *harbor* of my heart. They can end my *hard luck* and *erase* the *erotic error* of Eden, so I don't want these lovers to remain *estranged*. They can cause the *Eucharist* to *evangelize* my heart so my kundalini won't attach itself to the *cleat* that makes my eyes pop out every time I see a woman's *cleavage* or gluteal *cleft*. The greatest *test* of my *testicles* is whether they can listen to the *testimony* of these *two tycoons* who have been *typecast* as *tyrants*. I had *godly gonads* before they made me go out of my *gourd*, so I might as well have the *balls* to take the hot air *balloon* ride to my Crown Chakra.

My kundalini is the *helium* in the *helix* that can get me out of this *hell*, because it naturally tends to *go up* until it reaches the *goal* called *God*, so let's not let it remain mesmerized by the *goings-on* in Eden that turned us all into spiritual *goldbricks*. Our kundalini doesn't have to go down the *sewer* called *sex*, because it still has the *smarts* to *smell a rat*. Satan won't *juggle* our *juice* or *jumble* our thinking, because our remorse can make this *fluid fly* high and get the *jump* on the devil at this *junction* atop our heads so as to lead us out of the *Jungian jungle* of our fears. I have *prostituted* my will, but I also know how to *prostrate* myself before God. He will give my kundalini *twenty-twenty* vision, and then I won't have to *twiddle* my thumbs when the Fruits make the offer to sprout on my *twig*. My *dread* will stop interfering with my *dream*, because my *longing* will have reached this *longitude* where the possibility of loving behavior no longer seems like a *long shot*.

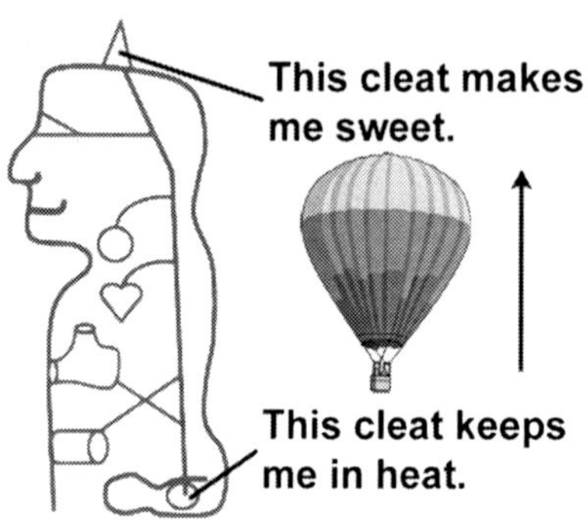

Therefore, the *lesson* I have learned is that my will is the property of God and that He is the *lessor* who leases it to me. I have lived *apart* from God, because my will has been the *apartment house* where only *apathetic* residents have dwelled. Nevertheless, my contrition is the *aperitif* that has given me the *appetite* to *oppose* my ego's *oppression* and to open myself to the *opulence* of the Fruits. I found *Providence* in this *province*, so my *selfhood* in God has no longer been the victim of the *self-hypnosis* which is my original sin.

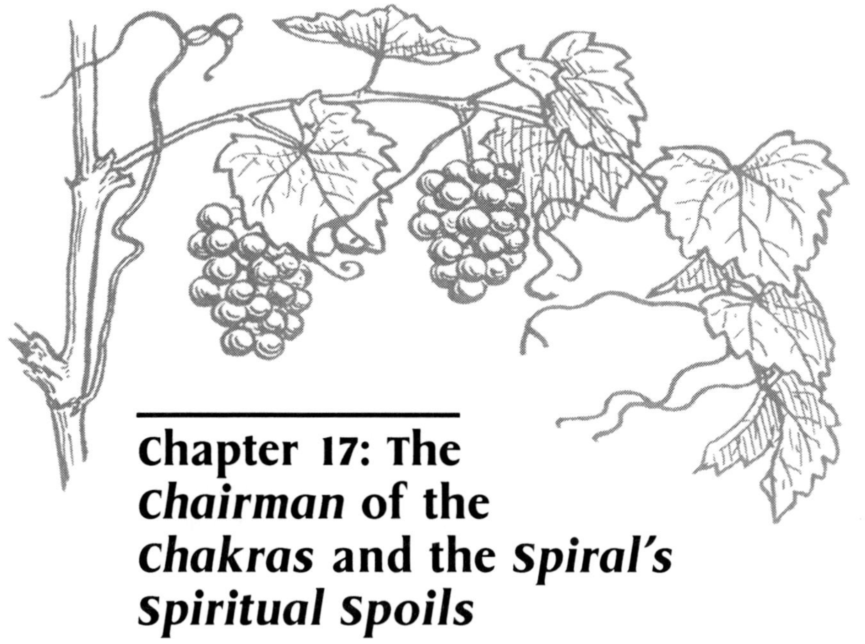

Chapter 17: The *Chairman* of the *Chakras* and the *Spiral's* *Spiritual* *Spoils*

Original sin is the *hypnosis hypothesis* that left my will on *ice*, but my heart-mind and soul-strength formed the *committee* of *common sense* that *looked into* this *loony* thinking. They were the *sentries* who could *separate* the wheat from the *chaff*, so God put them at each end of the *chain* of *chakras*, because they could best relieve my *perplexity* from this *perspective*.

I had been raised in a *pueblo* of *puerile puffery*, so I had to ask them to figure out *where* the *whiz kid* in me had gone. I was tired of thinking I was made of a *substance* that was *substandard*, and I didn't want my fear, hurt, and anger to be the *oil* that made me *oink*. It wasn't *OK* with me to keep doing this until I got *old*, so I asked them to *expedite* this *exposé* and give *expression* to the divine essence still *extant* in me. I figured that I needed more *piety* than a *pig*, and if I wanted to *graze* on greener pastures, I would have to *grease* the wheels of my chakras with something kundalini-*compatible* and spiritually *compelling*.

I could become the *critic* of my own *crock* of nonsense, because I was the *crook* who had stolen that which belonged to God. I was the *thief* of the *thing* called my will, so I was a *cross patch*. I had *munched* on these *cruel crumbs*, so I had to eat *crow*, *muster* up my *contrition*, and *crucify* this *meager meal*. I had to stop being a *stranger* to the *strength* of my *conviction* and *instruct* my chakras to start this *insurrection* against my ego. Their *job* was to *integrate* me into God's *intelligence*; *join* me up with my love, *joy,* and peace; and *repeal* these *repugnant resolutions* of my ego with the *Resurrection.* I just had to *grieve* over my *behaviors* until they revealed why they were *beholden* to my fears, because this was the *grist* I needed to feed into the mills of the chakras in order to enjoy the *groceries* of the Fruits.

This *critique* in my Navel Chakra was the *Crucifixion*, which is to say the *tool* that could get me to the *top* chakra and make ego *topple.* The Crucifixion was my *navel navigation*, because it helped me *depart* from these *dependency* needs that my family had *chained* me to at this *chakra.* Then the Resurrection *fixed* my *fizzled* faith and gave me *poise* at the chakras of both *poles* so that I could be *polite.*

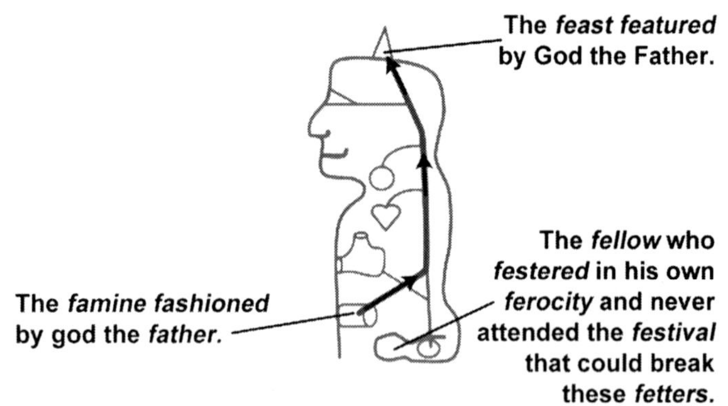

The *deep-seated deification* of my father *depicted* above was the *idolatry* that *ignited* my *ill will.* It robbed the *couple* known as my heart-mind and soul-strength of their *courage* and made me *mean*, but Jesus' *meekness met* with my *megalomania* and made it *mellow.* This *painstaking pair* had the job of healing the *dysfunction* from *each end* by *engaging* those in the *middle*, and they were able to accomplish this because of the *might* of Jesus' *mildness.* Jesus made this *gentle gesture* to *teach* the chakras to work like a *team* so that you and I could answer our *calling* to *calmness.* The *chakras* were able to exert these forces of *change* through the *channel* of the spiral on the *character* of man at each of seven *charming checkpoints*, because Jesus built this *edifice effortlessly* during his Passion.

Jesus wanted the *Supreme* Being to be able to get to the *surface*, so he *bled* through his skin during the Agony in the Garden. We had been *blind* to the *brotherhood* of man, so he restored sight to our *Brow*

Chakras. Consequently, our *inner inspection* could help us feel the *ouch* that would let love pour *out*, and the *victual* in the *vine* known as the divine sweetness could bring the grapes into *considerate contact* with one another. We just had to sit at this *desk* of the *detached observer* and take an objective look at our *obstinacy*. Then the divine sweetness could set man on the *right* path by *rising* to the *surface* in the spiral with a *surplus* of the Fruits. The Sacred Heart became the *wellspring* that is *well-thought-of* by spiritual seekers, because it led the *turkey* known as the ego-addicted will through these good *turns* that eliminate our moral *turpitude*, so let's take this ride to the *turret* of the Crown Chakra where the divine sweetness resides. Let's tell our *heads* that the Sacred *Heart bled* to help us take off these *blinders* and to restore the spiritual *sight* that can *silence* ego. Jesus made himself the object of *derision* during the Crucifixion to bring about this logical *derivative* called the Resurrection, so let's go through this *protocol* that delivers our spiritual *provisions*.

Nevertheless, as a child I had a *superstitious supply* line, because my family's *fever pitch* of critical remarks gave me a fear of being a *fiasco*. However, as an adult I decided to *wise up within* myself so as not to have to bear *witness* to the alienation of a series of *wives*, so the *fiat* of my contrition got rid of this *fib*. During my therapy I became determined to *make mincemeat* of this *malady* that had shackled my *mind* to *yesteryear's yoke*, and I was anything but *blasé*, because I wanted to *blast* this *blatant blather* into kingdom come. I was so *earnest* in the task that I was never at *ease*, and the *price* of this *pride* in my *lust* was that the growth of the Fruits was never *luxuriant*. It was really my *magical* thinking and arose from believing I was a spiritual *magnate*, when I was really the *madman* who was full of his own *malfunction*. Therefore, I asked the *maiden* known as Mary to *mail* me some of her mercy so that I could put a stop to this *maiming*. The *upshot* is that my kundalini was able to get *upstairs*.

The spiral through the chakras is the *trench* that was dug by Jesus our spiritual *trendsetter*. He wanted to fit us with *eyeglasses* that would be an *eye-opener* so that we could be *eyewitness* to our own sweetness. Nevertheless, I had swallowed this *crock* of nonsense and had become a *crony* of the *crosspatches* who raised me, so this *blarney* left me *bleary-eyed*, and therefore my *mildness* didn't get much *mileage*. For many years I played *roughness-roulette*, because I believed in the *gruffness-guarantee* that came from unfavorable self-comparisons with my father. However, my Father tells me that my *abrasiveness* can be *abridged*, and so it seems that I can win this *tug-of-war*. I can *tumble* to the truth by *tuning* into the *turbojet* of the Resurrection which will *land* me in the *lap* of God. The *protest protocol* that was most *protracted* as a result of my relationship with my father was that I became *proud* and was determined to *prove* that I possessed the *proverbial provisions* he was never able to give me. The tactic didn't always *work*, so I wound up feeling more like a *worm*, because these *bombs* were constantly exploding that were due to this *bond* with my *dad* that proved to be a *booby trap* and made me look *daffy*. Therefore, I think I need to *scrub* off these *scruples* and *sculpt* something less *scurrilous*.

The *barricade* in my *basement* was that my Root Chakra had not gone through the *basic training* of my remorse. My kundalini didn't climb the staircase in the *basilica*, and I didn't *bask* in my sweetness. The *microscopic middle* chakra appeared to be a *big bigot*, because he wasn't *broadminded* enough to *broker* the *agreement* with the chakras at each end. I could only get *ahead* through the *reconciliation* of the ends to the middle, but I didn't *recover*, because the *teamwork* in this *teapot* couldn't get rid of this *tempest* in my *temple*.

Nevertheless, my contrition could *result* in a *resurgence* of my sweetness, so I asked the *Resurrection* to *brew* the tea that could establish this *bridgehead*. I became an *anger-angler* and *fished* for this *ancient animosity* I needed to *fix*, because the *logic* of the *Logos* in my Crown Chakra could make my *resentments resign respectfully* and give me some *rest*. When Jesus was *resurrected*, he became the *lookout* in our Crown Chakra, because his Resurrection is the *loophole* that *loosens* the hold of ego and gives the *kosher kudos* to our *kundalini* that enable it to fly high. The Resurrection is the *operation* that gets rid of the *opiate* known as ego-addiction, and it took place in the *bonnet* known as the Crown Chakra, which packs the power to give the *boogieman* the *boot*, so let's enjoy this *clemency climax*. We just need to use this *key* to *kick* out the *kidnapper* of our divine sweetness.

We can all *include* ourselves in this *inconceivable* blessing by realizing that our *disorientation* can be *dispelled*. We have *trashed* our *treasure*, so we need to *listen* to our *litter's little voice* and *volunteer* to feel this *pain* we have *painted* on our hearts. Then we will *accustom* ourselves to the *acoustics* in this *temple* and *hear* the voice of God in our *hearts* so that His Fruits will make us *tenderhearted*. The *chronic chronicling* of our remorse will make our emotional age catch up with our *chronological* age, because the *chronometer* of the Sacred Heart makes the *chrysalis* turn into the butterfly. Therefore, let's take advantage

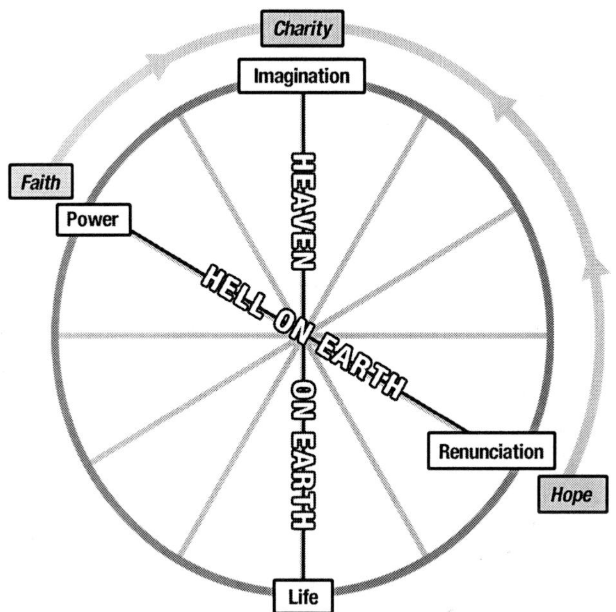

of this *metamorphosis metaphor.* The chakras are the *metaphysical* devices that enable us to see how the cancer of our ego *metastasizes* our fears into our behavior, so let's use them to *mete* out our remorse and march to the *meter* of our divine sweetness.

Hope, faith, and charity are the three *theological* virtues. The job of hope and faith is to *theorize* how our remorse can be *therapeutic,* whereas from *there* on it is the job of charity to exert the *thermal* effect of warming our hearts. We can get into this *clemency clench,* because our will is the *cleric* who can show us how to bring about this *clever click* of the *clock.* We start in our *hell* on earth with these *helmsmen* piloting our ships, but they eventually *shipwreck* our egos, so we

The persistant person has this perspective.

won't lose our *shirts*, because on the beaches of God's *charity* we will find our *charm*. My hope and faith were my *uprightness uprising*, and they delivered me to these *shoals* just off the beaches of charity, so I wasn't very *shocked* to see that my hope and faith had *shot their wad*. My hope and faith were the *generators* of charity which is the *generosity* that would help me *capture* the *carafe* of the divine sweetness.

My will is the *boat* that *bobs* up and down in my troubled waters, but when I *shop* for the virtue of charity I will always reach this *shore* where my needs will not get *short shrift*. My ego is the *rudder* that is guided by *rudeness*, but my remorse *evaluates* these *events*. My remorse has the sense of *reason* that makes me less *recalcitrant*. It has the *scrupulous scrutiny* of the *scuba diver* who can end my *scuffles* by plumbing my *depravity's depth*. He indulges in this diversion to *sink* my ego and make me *sinless*.

We can *reach* this *ready real estate* in our *hearts* known as the *heaven* within, because the *lighthouse* on the shores of charity *shows* the way to the divine *image* and *likeness* in this *shrewd shrine* so that we can *imitate* that which is *immaculate* rather than that which is *immature*. It gives us the *guts* to stop *guzzling* nonsense, so we just need to *chew* on this leftover *chicanery* until we have reached the *antithesis* of our *anxieties*. The *Holy Spirit* makes its *home* wherever the *Honcho* finds someone *whetting* his appetite for the divine sweetness by ridding himself of the *whims* of his ego. The Resurrection enables me to *execute exemplary* behavior and makes me *exempt* from original sin, because Jesus makes it possible for me to *exercise* the twelve powers in my Chakra System.† My five central chakras *empower* me to *empty* myself and *emulate* Jesus. They *enable* me to *enact* the Fruits in my behavior when I become *enamored* of the divine sweetness. My *emptying* powers are the *coaches* who teach me how to get rid of my *coarseness*, and my *emulating* powers teach me how to *coast* along *effortlessly*, because I am carried along by the *effusion* of the divine sweetness and kundalini that flows up and down this *awesome axis* in my *back*.

When Jesus descended to the dead, he taught the *little* man at the bottom about the *liturgy* of the Eucharist. He taught him that the divine sweetness is a *living thing* that *thinks*, because the little man had been *duped* into thinking his *duty* was to let his other *thing think*. This only made his divine sweetness *dwindle*, so Jesus taught

---

†*The Twelve Powers of Man,* Charles Fillmore, Unity Books Unity Village, MO 64065, p. 14.

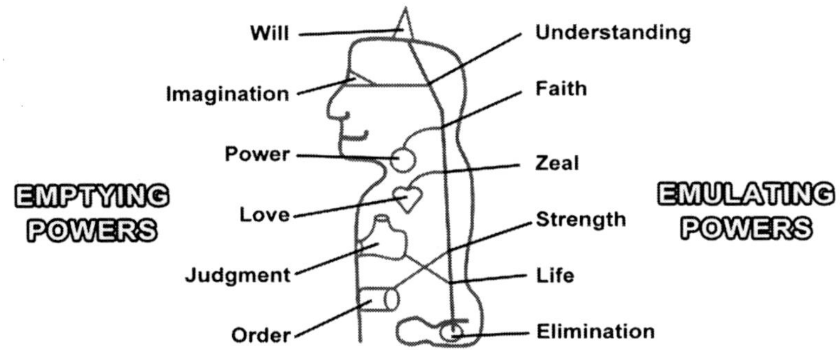

him that his *handy* vertical axis would help him *hang* onto God so that everything that *happened* to him would make him *happy*. The little man then realized that his ego had **ordered** him to use poor **judgment** but that **love** could **power** his **imagination** differently. This is how he got the **will** to **eliminate** his fears. Then God gave him an **understanding** of how his **faith-zeal** could put spiritual **strength** into his **life**.

What was most *encouraging* about the powers was that they could block circumstance from *encroaching* on your wellbeing, because they had an *encyclopedic* knowledge of how to *end endangerment*. The concept of the human will as an *automobile* with *autonomy* was reaching the *autumn* of its days. It was more properly an *auxiliary* to God and would be *avenged* on the *avenue* by God's *aversion therapy* if man did not accept this *thesis*. That's why Jesus *patented* the *path* between the Crucifixion and Resurrection. He wanted his *stream of consciousness* to be used on the *street* to end man's *stress*. Jesus opened this *expressway* that leads to the *expulsion* of ego so that man could be driven by *impulses* that were not *impure*. Jesus was the traffic *cop* who could teach us how to *cope*, and so he invented mildness-chastity as a more *captivating car* and generosity-faith so that our ego's *drivel* wouldn't have to do the driving.

The spiral through the chakras *begins* in my heart when I *face* my *fascist fears* on *behalf* of better *behavior* and say, "Get thee *behind* me, Satan!" My *throat's throes* are due to the fact that it's not such a *swift* idea to *swig* this *swill* when I can *swim* in the divine sweetness. When I decide not to *glut* myself with this *godless gossip*, the Holy Spirit will fill me with its *gourmet* fare. Likewise, the divine sweetness *splashes* around in my Stomach Chakra, because I have learned that not venting my *spleen* is a more *splendid* idea. The job of the Stomach Chakra is therefore to *splice* in the love, joy, and peace that had

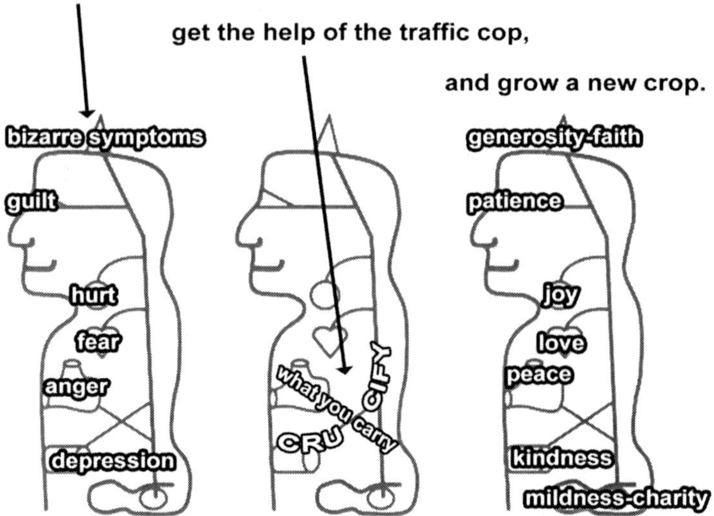

splintered off, and the Brow Chakra removes the *splotch* that blocks us from making a *splurge* of these Fruits. Then at the Navel Chakra love, joy, and peace become the *spoils* of the *spokesman* known as the Eternally Begotten Son who can make your ego *throw in the sponge*. He directs you to the divine *Sponsor* in your Crown Chakra, because only God can bring a *spontaneous* end to Satan's *spoof*. God then tells the *timid tinhorn* in the Root Chakra that he doesn't have to be *spooked* by the fear, hurt, and anger that winds off the *spool*, because his will can *spoon-feed* him love, joy, and peace that comes straight from the heart.

The Brow Chakra is the *high beam* that identifies our *high comedy* and puts us through the *higher education* that makes our *high jinx* a thing of the past. The *hex* of sex put ego in its *heyday* and created a *hiatus* between man and God. Nevertheless, when man uses his remorse as the *highlighter* of his behavior, the consecration of the *High Mass* is reenacted; man becomes higher-minded and less prone to think of himself as a *high muck amuck*. We do not need to *cast* ourselves into the perpetual *castigation* of our *cast-iron* egos, because our remorse can *castrate* our egos by means of a *casual* inspection of our behavior.

We just need to *cope* with our *core* fears by *tuning* into the *tunnel* of love in our spines so as to meet our *chakra challenge*. We need to *ponder* how our twelve *powers* can separate our *bother* from our *bounty*.

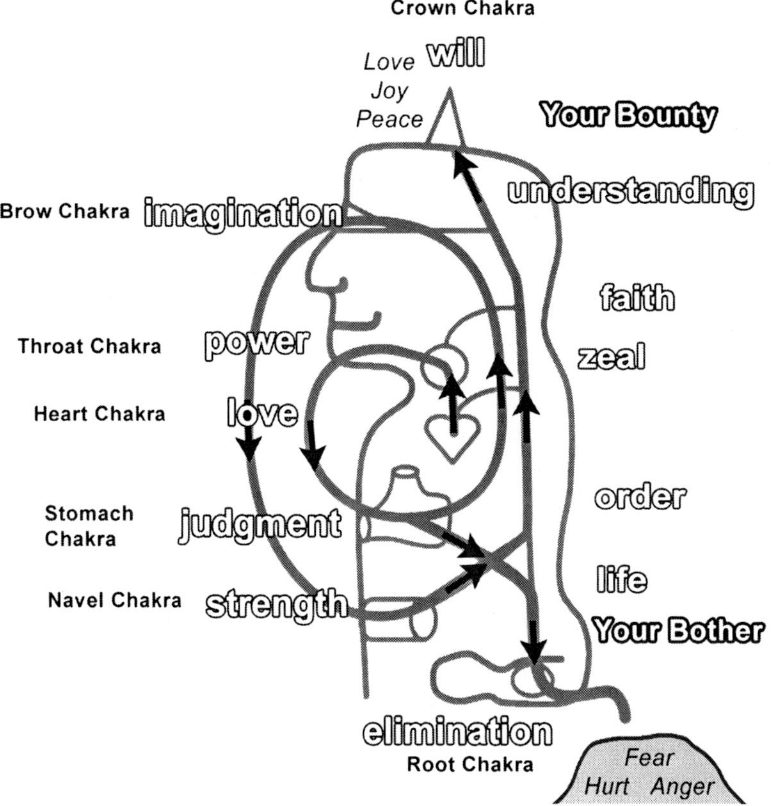

Unfortunately, I was too *dumb* to take this *dump*, because the *dutiful dwarf* below *dwelled* so much on my *hassles* that he *hated* to part with them, so I just continued going *haywire.* His *understanding* had been *understated*, because the *peculiar pedagogue* called ego had given him *insolent instruction*, and so my job was to help him *confront* this *confusion.* I had to be *hot* on the trail of eliminating this *hotbed* of *hotheads* by *persecuting* my ego with *perseverance.*

I decided to *curb* my ego, get the *cure*, listen to the voice of *counsel*, and *count* on reconciling this *chap* to the *chapel* of my heart so he could *learn* to get off this *leash.* During my second adolescence my *cock* wasn't *cognizant* of this *coil* through my chakras, so the *sawed-off scalawag* who *roosted* in my *Root* Chakra kept on indulging in *coitus* and left me out in the *cold.* We had been *looking* for *love* in *all* the wrong places like an *alley cat* on a series of *all-nighters*, so I told him that this *dissolute* behavior would only slow the *distillation* of the divine sweetness through the chakras. We kept our eyes *peeled* for past *peeves* that were still *pending* and removed each of these *impediments* so as to avoid *impending disaster* by *disavowing* our *disbelief.* These *conferences* made us more *confident*, so the understanding that eventually *loomed* was that we were not so *loony*, because we had found the *loophole* that let love through.

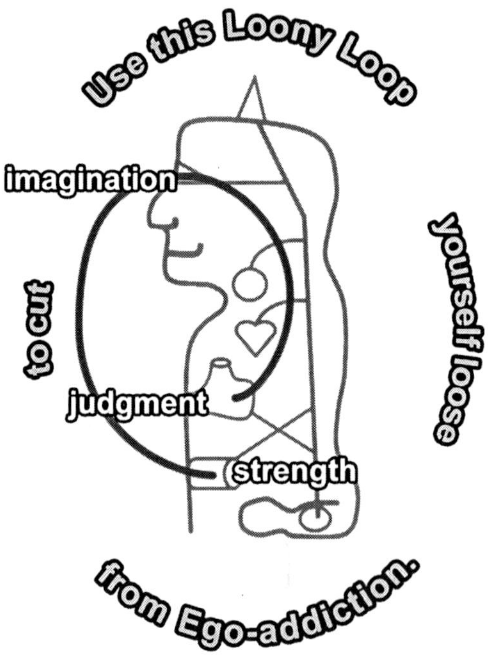

I had had *liberal* doses of influence from my *libido*, because I had not been loved *enough* by my mother. I had not been able to *enrich* this *rogue* in my groin with the understanding that God would *roll out* the red *carpet* if we stopped giving our lust *carte blanche.* The *lack* of love from the *lady* who was my mother had left us at *play* with the *pleasure principle*, and I felt the sting of this *lascivious lash*, but my father's love didn't *flow* either, so I asked my *Father* to turn on the *faucet* of love, joy, and peace in my heart. When these *delights* were *delivered*, I sent these *sensible sentiments* into my bloodstream rather than into my *sewage.* I just had to use my *grief* to get a *grip* on this *sham* so that the *Shepherd* could help me *crucify* the real *crud* and *ship* it out in my *shit.* I was in *deep shit*, because I had *defecated* the *Deity's delectable delights.* I just had to remember that my *feast* didn't belong in my *feces.*

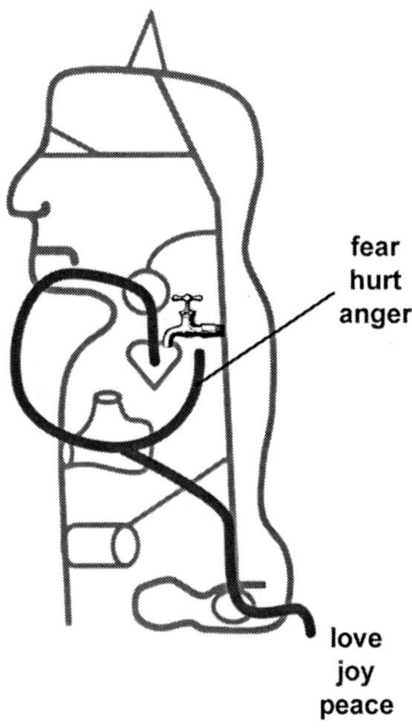

Holy Shit!

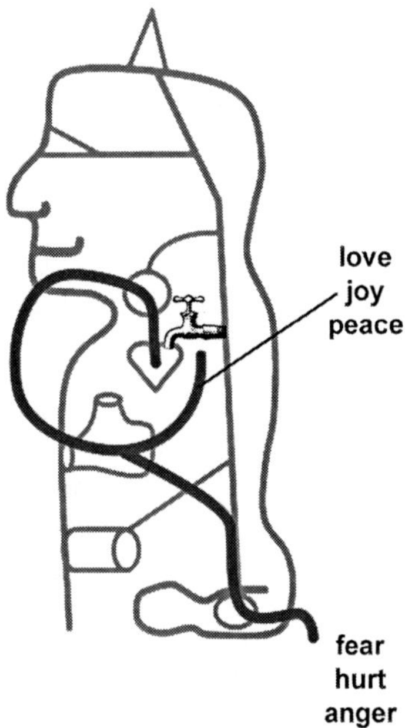

Good Grief!

I was in this *cussed custody*, because my *dad* had shared his *damaged* goods with me, so I wore the *masculine mask* that filled me with *workplace worry*. I tried to *put up* with these *puzzles*, but the resultant *pyrotechnics* left me looking for these *missing links* I figured it was my *mission* to find.

I had a *father* who was not to be *fathomed*, and what filled me with *fatigue* was thinking I was at *fault*, so I *assumed* that I would feel more *assured* if I made the *substitution* for a better *substructure*. Accordingly, I asked God the Son to take my *father-fear* and *share* his relationship with God the *Father* with me so that I could be filled with more *favorable feelings* and wouldn't have to take this *shellacking*. I was the *medic* who had felt *mediocre*, so I *meditated* on the matter. I figured I could get my *medley* of the Fruits, so I went to the traffic *policeman* who worked at the corner of composure and disclosure. His *policy* was to give me *polish*, so I asked him to make me a *polite politician*. He told me my *tummy* was full of *tumult* and that I could *change my tune* by focusing my *tunnel vision* on the *turban* atop my *head*. Therefore, I asked my *Crown* Chakra to share the *cuisine* that would *cure* this *curse*.

I felt *bushed*, because I had been *bushwhacked* by the devil, and it had left me thinking my divine sweetness had gone *bust*. I was tired of being the *butt* of the devil's jokes, so I decided that my divine sweetness was a better *legal tender* than these *legends* that had left me with *legions* of problems. Therefore, I *jumped* to this *junction*, *joined* up with my *joy*, and *reaped* the rewards of this *rebirth*. I *expelled* this *expensive exploit* and exchanged my *gloom* for my *glory*, because my *Navel* Chakra healed my *nerves* and feathered my *nest* with the *nimble nine* Fruits of the Holy Spirit.

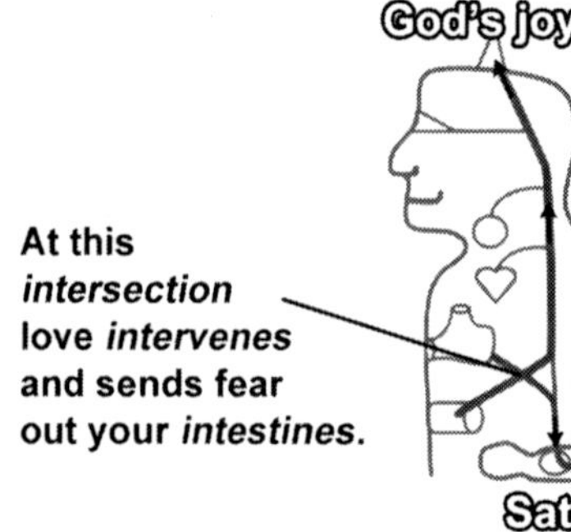

***Join* up with your *joy*, and put an end to Satan's *ploy* by sending your *rancid rancor* out through your *plumbing*.**

My *joy* had *jumped* ship, because my *dad* and the *dame* who was his wife never passed along the *data* that could make this *happiness happen.* I never got the *mildness* of a mother's love, so it gave my ego *mileage.* I was a grape on a vine that never developed that *tender tendril,* so I remained *tense.* I was never able to *grasp* that *grassroots commodity* known as the divine sweetness which is the *common denominator* of all loving behavior. That's why I *sought* out the Blessed Mother. I knew I needed to do this *soul-searching,* so I asked her to share her Immaculate Conception and make my *Navel* Chakra *navigable* by the *Nazarene.* Then the *cornucopia* of the Fruits in my Crown Chakra could be opened by the Coronation.

My *bellybutton* never told me I could *belong* to the *beloved,* so my divine sweetness went *underground.* The *underhanded* dictator called ego blinded me to this *underlying* truth, so my divine sweetness wasn't *comme il faut* when I *commenced* my teenage years. *When* I was a child I didn't know *where* this motherly love had gone, because no one had taken the *trouble* to show me this *trough* on top of my head, and I *carried* this *torch* into my first marriage. No one ever took enough *interest* in my *interior design,* so I never got the *kisses* I needed and figured my *kitchen* couldn't prepare the *satisfying sauce* called the divine sweetness.

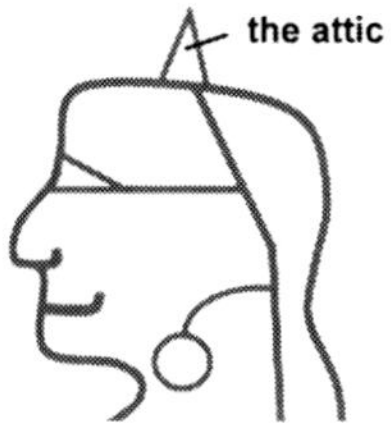

Therefore my behavior *attested* to the fact that I needed help in my *attic* from the *attitude attorney* known as the Blessed Mother. I thought that my original sin was *unbeatable,* and so I remained *unbegotten* by the Eternally Begotten Son, because I had a Crown Chakra that was full of *unbelief.*

My mother's love was the *yardstick* that made me feel I didn't measure up, so I was left with a *yearning* as a result of this lack of *sympathy.* The *symptoms* of this dilemma were under the control of the *syndicate* called ego whose *synthetic* versions of the divine sweetness proved to be a *substitute* that was *subversive,* so I never *succeeded* in getting the *succor* of the divine *sucrose.* I thought I had lost the mildness-*lottery* and therefore became the *loudmouth* who thought he had to *lounge* around in *lovelessness* forever. The *warning* my parents gave me to be seen and not heard *warped* my nerves, put me on the *warpath,* and I have indulged in *overkill* ever since, because I thought I had been *overlooked.* Therefore, I expressed my *rage* by *raising* my *voice's volume voluntarily.*

Maria tells me that I *monopolize* conversations at social gatherings and that my speech is a *monotonous monsoon* that comes from a *mon-*

ster. Therefore, I think I have been *overbearing*, because my fears have been *overblown.* I *laugh* more loudly than normal, because no one ever told me I could rest on the *laurel* of my mildness. I must have hoped that my loud laugh would make me more *appealing*, but I'm sure that everyone could see that I had some fears to *appease*, because I still felt like an *appendage* to my parents. The laugh sounds *artificial*, because it is backed up by the heavy *artillery* of my pretense and is a *phony phosphorescence.* One thing I have taken *note* of is that there is *nothing funny* about not being *furnished* with the necessary *furniture* to feel *comfortable* rather than *comical* inside yourself.

When I *speak* it is like throwing a *spear*, because I have *vivid* memories of my mother behaving like a *vixen* and uttering *vocalizations* that were more properly *vociferations*, so I am sorry to say that I have adopted the same *vogue* with regard to my *voice.* This is my *latter-day* problem which is no *laughing matter*, so I have been *maudlin* in prayer so as not to be *mauled* in this way by an *upbringing* that left me in an *uproar.*

Nevertheless, I felt *battered* as a child mostly because my Attention Deficit Disorder made me think the divine *battery* wasn't *linked* up to my *listening.* I figured that my *brain* just owned this set of *brakes* that was going to bring me to a *screeching* halt on the road to success and that this was a *screw job* that I just had to put up with. The *restriction* that *resulted* was my fear of *failure*, which was the *fall-out* that I tried to *subtract* by becoming determined to *succeed.* Yet I was often clobbered by this *sledgehammer*, because it was wielded by my ego, and this *sleeping* giant used this *missing link* to oblige me to make many *mistakes.* My main slip-up was to assume that someone had *auctioned* off my *auditory* ability, so I thought my thinking wasn't *wired* to the divine *wizard.* My ears didn't *hear* and behaved like *heathens*, and my *thirsty throat* only *drank drivel*, so I *ingested* these *insults* that had an *intelligence* all their own. I didn't *reckon* that my *rectum* could *recuperate*, and as a result the *Redeemer* couldn't see to it that my *reeking refuse* got *rejected.*

These *stifling stigmas* stayed in my *stomach*, because I never learned how to *stop storing stormy stories* there. Nevertheless, I could have got this *relevant relief*, because Jesus *demonstrated* to the *denizen* of the Root Chakra how to *denounce* these *deplorable deposits.* When he *descended* to the *dead*, he struck this *deal*, and then when he *ascended* he took *aside* my Throat Chakra and explained that *suspicious sustenance* was not meant to be *swallowed.* He said I didn't have to be *constipated*

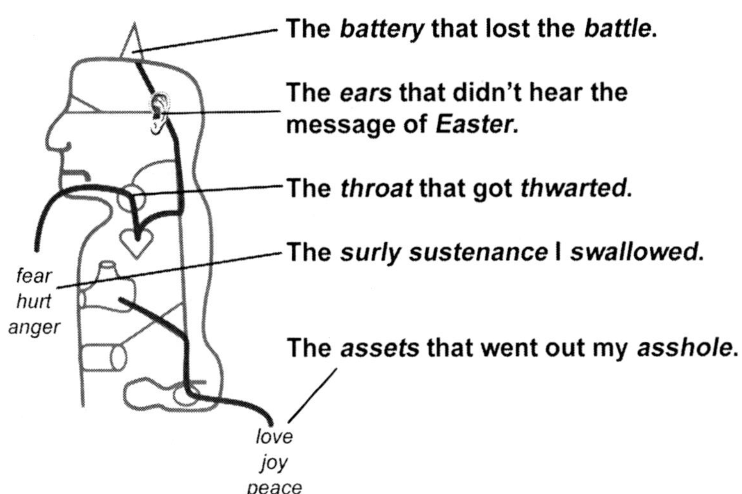

with the wrong *constituents* if I would just *remember* not to *consume* this *contemptible contingent.* Nevertheless, my *throat* got *thwarted* in this way, because no one had taught me that I could *eat* my *ecstasy* instead of this *eerie effrontery.* This turned my *pharynx* into a *philistine*, because my Throat Chakra never *dreamed* he could *drink* the divine sweetness. Consequently, he wasn't *soothed*, and I didn't feel *sophisticated.* Likewise, my ears never remained *convinced* of my sweetness, because no one *cooed* with me as an infant. This *larceny* in my mother's *larynx* made me *boohoo* a lot as a child and as an adult gave me the *booming* voice of a *loquacious loudmouth.*

My Throat Chakra *mobilized* these *morbid mouthfuls*, so the *cook* in the kitchen of the Crown Chakra couldn't *cooperate* by preparing the *love potion* that could give me better *luck.* My Throat Chakra never got this *memorandum*, so my *mental illness* remained on the *menu*, and I wasn't able to *swallow* the *sweetness* that the *merciful message* of the *Messiah metes* out. My *ears* never got this *Easter* message, because they had been *stifled* by these *stilted stimuli* and didn't *stoke* the fires of love in my heart.

I thought I was a *bastard* because of this bad *battery* above my head and figured that *God* just didn't think I was *good* enough to be *governed* by His *grace.* I was the *illegitimate* child who deserved to be *ill-treated* in this way, because these bad *specters* had cast a *spell* on me and had prevented the *spirit* of *adoption* in my overhead agency

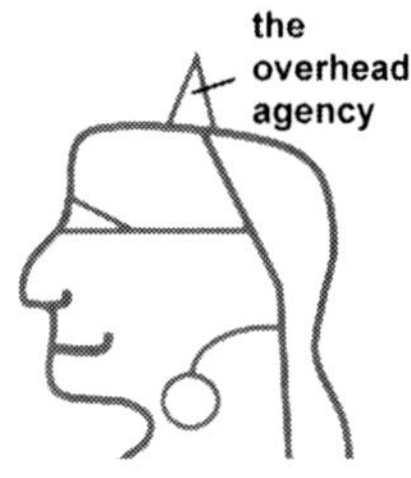

from making me feel *adorable.* The divine sweetness was a *no-show* in my Throat Chakra, because the *notary public* there never certified this *august* substance as *authentic*, and my *notorious* behaviors resulted from the lack of this *nourishment.*

I became a *misfit*, because I *mislaid* my own auditory *acuity*, and it disappeared according to the *adage* which states that you use it or lose it. Perhaps I *aspired* as a child not to have my ears *assaulted* by my mother's angry *assertions* and made a decision not to *hear* because of this *heartache.* Therefore, sometimes I thought it was *mea culpa* that I couldn't get the *meaning* and at others that the *other* person owned the *ounce* of inattentiveness. Maybe that's why I hurl these *projectiles* in my speech. Maybe it is the *projection* of my fear of *never* understanding onto the *next* person who speaks to me, because I'm afraid he won't understand. Nevertheless, I do know that I have this *comprehension compulsion* that makes me try to *snatch* an understanding before it *sneaks* away. It must make my patients think that my speech is *supercharged* with *superciliousness*, because I *interrogate* them and become *intolerant* of their *intricate* explanations. My Attention Deficit Disorder is therefore my *maladroit malady* and the *sickness* that is constantly at my *side*, because it has put me on a *derangement derby* that has made my behavior *derelict.*

I thought that I was *governed gracelessly* as a child by this *alcoholic alderman* who couldn't seem to *digest* the facts, and he left me with the *dilapidated dignity* of a low self-esteem. He never seemed able to *concentrate* enough to get the *concept*, and the sweetness in my *vine* was certainly *violated* by this *VIP* of my A.D.D., because he made me think I was the *attention-getter* who never seemed *attractive* to my *audience.* I allowed my *ears* to make my self-esteem *ebb,* because I thought they *had* no connection to my *head* due to these *electronics* that weren't very *elegant.* I felt that I was never *granted* the ability to *grasp* what was said, and this *grated* on my nerves. I swallowed this *bad bait* and felt *frustrated* to think that the divine sweetness was the *fugitive* whose *flavor* would *flee* before I could *tap* into its *taste.* This *atrophy* of my *attention* span has resulted in this *deficit* that has left me *defiled.* This *disorder* has *disparaged* me and has made me a member of this *frantic fraternity* which teaches *dysfunctional* behavior, because we feel that our *ears* can't *earn* us the ability to feel at *ease.*

I was the *voodoo votary* who conjured up this *madcap madness*, and to make things worse I must have figured that I could get my *sweetness* by means of my *swiftness*, because I developed the habit of *speed-*

ing in my car. I am under this *spell* in my *sedan*, because I am constantly *seeking* to *overtake* the divine sweetness that is *owed* to me. My mind has perpetuated this *disparity*, because it is the *dispatcher* who sends me off on these *perfectly perilous* ventures. I am the *captive* in my own *car* of this *nonsensical notion* that my divine sweetness is the *cast-off* I am constantly trying to *catch up* with. It has made me a *reckless* driver, and I have never *recovered* from this *haste*, because the devil *hatched* this plot that makes me *accelerate* in order to gain *access* to that which is *accessible unconditionally*. Therefore, I have been the *unconscious accessory* before the fact who gets in lots of *accidents*, and maybe I need to rethink this *answer*. Then perhaps I can give up these *antics* in which I give my car so much *gas* that it makes those around me *gasp*.

Maybe my mother's *tongue-lashings* are the *tonic* that makes me use my car as her *tool*, because I *toot* its *horn* enough to *horrify* those around me, and it may be a *rerun* of her *resentments*. Maybe it's due to the lack of my *father's favor*, or maybe both of my parents left me with this *frenzy*, because I never felt that either of them were my *friends*. Perhaps I have tried to make an *end run* around those I perceive as my *enemies* on the road, because my parents never put the gas in my *tank* that would help me avoid these *tantrums*, and I aim in this way to *get* the sweetness I feel should be coming from the *geyser* in my heart. It's possible that I have been in this *race* in an effort to *rack up* the points I never got from them and have therefore allowed my *impatience* for their approval to *imperil* me. This *ineffective* coping strategy has resulted in the *inertia* of my divine sweetness and is also the *modus operandi* of my *momentum* on the road. It definitely comes from their *manipulative manner*, but I'm the one who welcomed this *invalid invasion*, and I can *vanquish* these strange *vapors*.

I probably thought I was on their *blacklist*, because I drew a *blank* about what they said and decided to make a *dash* to gather the *data* that would make the understanding *dawn* on me. The absence of their *endorsement* may still make me want to gun my *engine* and may have given me this *quickness quirk*, because I have driven at *vehement velocities* on *trajectories* that are not very *tranquil*. My mother's *sonic booms* may be the *sorcery* that still *rings in my ears* enough to make me *run riot* in my car. Maybe I was so *startled* when she let off *steam* that I became the *frightened frog* who would always *leap* in this way, and maybe I just *learned* to stay on this *leash*. It's possible that even now I let her pull *rank* in my mind and set me off on this *rash dash* that is still in effect to this *date*. I may have this *incautious incentive*, because I aim to *arrive* at my destination in spite of her *arrogance*, or perhaps I just aim to show that my *listening* hasn't made me a *laggard* who is *lame*. Nevertheless, I have been *goaded* to achieve this *goal* of overcoming these *hurdles* in a *hurry*, because I decided to install these *hydraulics* of my *hyperactivity* in my mind. The *spectacle* I therefore put on display is that of a *speed demon*, because I have *denounced* the Fruit of patience. Hence, when I get in an *automobile*, I become the *avenger* who is *avid* to *avoid* these *delays* that I feel have been *deliberately placed* in my path as a *plain* nuisance. I don't *drive* well, because I am still *driven* by this *yes man* in my mind who seeks my parents' approval and who aims to overcome *yesteryear's roadblocks* by pretending my car is a *rocket*. I *shoot* this *shopworn* pellet out of my mind, because my mind is the *miserable missile launcher* that has not yet been *laundered* by my remorse and goes on being the *lawbreaker* who fires from my *shoulder* in order to *shove* people out of the way.

I may not have *healthy hearing*, and my mind may be the *distractible district* that is full of these *obsolete obstacles*, but I don't have to let my *pride* be the *prince* who keeps me in this *prison* when I can be the *pauper* who *pawns* this nonsense in order to get some *peace of mind*. I can *correct* this *corruption* and stop *streaking* through the *streets*. It is definitely a *hazard* to be driven *headlong* in this way, and I don't have to let heavy *traffic* make me a *traitor* to my patience. It has been a *protracted provocation* that has not arisen from a very *prudent psychodynamic*, so I intend to get rid of this *flying foible*. I don't have to pretend to have *wings* that can fly over obstacles in a *wink* and here and now ask God to put my *patience* on *patrol* on the *pavement*. When I drive I don't have to be the *maniac* who is *manipulated* in this *manner* by this diabolical *mantra*. I may not have brought many *mellow mementos* from my childhood, but I don't have to be in a *rush* on the road to overcome this *ruthless sabotage*, because Mary is the *mama* who raised the *man* who can make me stop driving like a *maniac*. Her *motherly motive* was to raise the *martyr* whose *masculinity sprang* from God so that he could *sprinkle* me with God's *paternal patience*. This patience was *implanted* in her *implicitly* when her mother Saint Anne was *impregnated* by the Holy Spirit and can *imprint* itself on me to *improve* my driving. This is the *placid plan* that God has for ending this *disturbing diversion*, so I intend to ask the *Virgin* Mary to give me this *virile virtue*. I am in the *shape* that results in these close *shaves*, but Mary is the *mold* that can give me this *mollification*, because she is the *cafeteria* worker who serves us the Fruits when we have done our *calamity calculations.*

We get these *morsels* from the Blessed *Mother,* because her Immaculate Conception was the culinary *institute* which made it possible for the *instrument* of the Mass to be brought to *earth* so we could *eat* sensibly. God made the human heart the *mess hall* of the *Messiah* at the Last Supper, and therefore I intend to enjoy this *dignified dining,* because the real *McCoy* of the divine sweetness is served at this *meal.* The *Mass* gives me *mastery* over ego, because this is how Jesus pinned Satan to the *mat.* Jesus installed this mass *transit* in our hearts that *transports* heaven to earth, but first we have to use our *trap doors* to get rid of our hellish *trash.* We should not *buck* this system that our *buddy* Jesus installed in our hearts but rather *share* this meal that lets us *shed* ego. Then the *common denominator* of the *Communion* will *join* our hearts to God, so let's bring about this *joint venture* that will *commute* our *sentence* of original sin and reconcile the *sentient sentries* at each end.

The Fruit of patience is in the *buffet* of the Fruits and can end the *bugaboo* that makes me want to *bully* everyone on the road, so I will *calm* myself in my car with this blessing that *came* from God. This is the *focus* that will *foil* my attention deficit disorder as well as the repressed feelings that were *foisted* off on me by my *folks,* so I might as well *attach* my *attention* to this *august authority.* Mary's *ancestry* didn't depend on anyone's *androgens,* and therefore she can give me the *balance of power* that doesn't come from Adam's *baleful balls* or from Eve's *ovaries* that installed the *oven* of ego in my mind. I am of Adam and Eve's *ilk,* because their *illicit* sex resulted in this *implicit* hex that God allowed Satan to *impose* on us all. Their *impulse* may therefore have also gotten me *into* this *mess* that makes me want to put the pedal to the *metal.* I may still have some of this *frosty fuel* in my tank that results from this *original ostracism,* but I don't have to go on thinking that my sweetness has been *banned* just because Satan the *bandit* induced Adam to *bang* Eve and got them both *banished* from Eden.

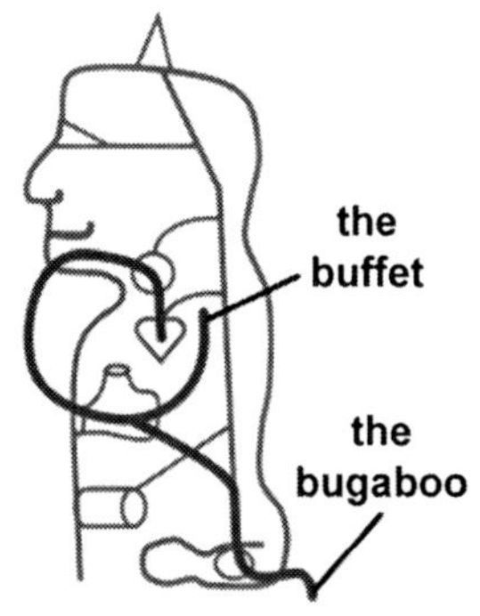

I can use the sweetness in my *bank* and don't have to go on trying to *outmaneuver* people on the road. I don't have to go on being *outwitted* in this way by my ego, and I don't have to drive like a *hothead*

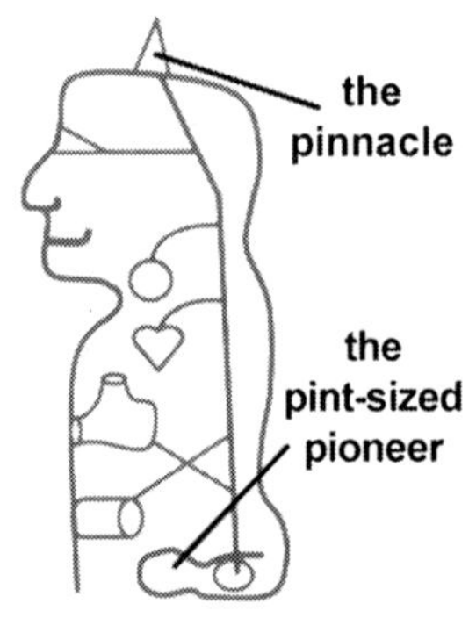

in a *hot rod.* I don't have to let this *macho madness* give me this *motion sickness* in my *motor vehicle.* I don't have to *careen carelessly,* and I don't have to let the *urgent utensil* between my *legs legislate* this madness. My car is a *whale* of a set of *wheels,* but I still don't have to be the *hasty* driver who *hauls ass* all the time. I don't have to let my *kindred's kinetics* give me this *fascination* for driving *fast,* because I can be *piloted* by my *pinnacle* rather than this *pintsized pioneer.*

This *rattlebrained reactionary* is always *ready* and *raring* to go, but I am sick and tired of this *rat race,* so I intend to drive *slowly,* because it is the *smart* thing to do. I wasn't a very *attentive attorney* as a child and *indulged* in the deficit *spending* that arose from my family's *sphere* of *influence.* My involvement with them was *enormously entangling,* but Adam and Eve's *enthusiasm* for one another under the apple tree also gave me the *illegitimacy illness* that cut off the divine *illumination.* This *confusing congenital anomaly* therefore also left its mark, because Adam and Eve were the *understanding-underwriters* who *undid* my connection to my *comprehension computer.*

This battery stopped *supplying* the *sureness* that enabled me to *surmount* obstacles, so for both of these reasons I felt like a *jughead.* The *juice* stopped flowing from the *divine dock* when Adam and Eve played *doctor* and induced mankind to follow the *doctrine* that it was all right to *dodge* the truth. The divine sweetness was the *élan vital* that stopped completing its circuit, because Satan was the *electrician* who *flipped* the switch when he induced Eve to *flirt* with Adam. The chakras got *flooded* with the sins after Adam got on the forest *floor* with the *floozy.* That was the *end* of the *energy* known as the divine sweetness, which also resulted in the *flop* of the *flora* known as the Fruits. The *awesome awning* at the top of my vertical *axis* stopped giving me its protection, and I became a *daydreamer* who was *dazed* by this lack of *unity* with the divine. I thought that my own *unmindfulness* had resulted in this disaster and that my *negligent nervous system* was not open to these *wondrous workings* of the divine. My *storage battery* above had lost its connection to my *storm cellar* below, because Adam and Eve's *amo-*

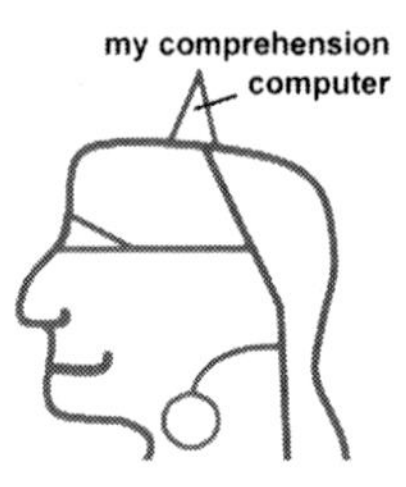

rous amperes gave me these *volatile volts* and allowed Satan to gain the *advantage* over me. Satan's *advertising* campaign in Eden instituted the *monotheism* of the *mons pubis* and turned me into a *monster*, because the *polytheistic pomp* of the seven *sins* began to exert their *sinister* influence on me. Satan was the *camp follower* in Eden who said to Adam and Eve, "You *can* use the birth *canal* to have a little fun!" However, he didn't tell them that it would *cancel* the divine sweetness, so my parents were *gung ho* for this *gutter* appetite, and the *guy* and the *gal* went on a *gallop* to hang my will on this *gallows* of ego-addiction. Therefore, I got clobbered by my *clan's claptrap* and became a *man* who allowed himself to be *managed* by this *short shrift*. I tried to *shoulder* this burden, but it turned my mind into an *incestuous incinerator*. I got *burned* by the trash I *buried*, which was *force-fed* me by my *forebears*, and it consisted of the *paternal pathology* and lack of *maternal maturity* that my *family fancied*. Our *minds* had *mingled* with the sinister *minister* who made us all play in the *minor leagues*, and the result was that I wound up with this *meltdown* of the divine in my *memory*. All of these *souvenirs* have probably made me look like the *space cadet* who is still in *cahoots* with these deceptions.

This *heritage* of *hesitant* hearing *must* have made me think I was deaf or that everyone else was *mute*, so I figured I had to *decode* what was said by using my powers of *deduction*. Nevertheless, it became a *gruesome guesswork*, and my hearing became a *dropout* rather than suffer these repeated *drubbings*. My ears never acted like *Johnny-on-the-spot*, so I *joined* this *unfocused union* whose members' attentiveness goes on *strike*. People must think I don't *strive* and am too *lazy* to let my ears take the *lead*. Nevertheless, the truth is that the *spark plugs* in my ears don't fire when people *speak*, and therefore when I get in *conversations*, they don't *convey* the meaning. My ears are my *renegades* of *renown*, because I constantly ask people to *repeat* what they have said, and they usually get *sick* of seeing me leave my ears on the *sidelines*. I have tried to *rev up* my mind hoping that this *reveille* will awaken me out of this inattentive *reverie*, but it has only made my mind the *fidgety field* of influence that is easily controlled by the *fiend*.

Finally I decided to take *Ritalin*, and this proved to be the *rite of passage* that has enabled my ears to stop being my *rivals*. I no longer suffer from this *black magic* that makes me want to *blame* myself, because I don't draw a *blank*. It is not really my *fault* that my hearing is *feckless*, and I get the *meaning* as long as I take this *medicine*, because my *drowsy* ears are awakened by this *drug*. I no longer feel *inadequate*, because I am no longer *inattentive*, and what people say is no longer *inaudible.* I am no longer a *chaotic chap*, because this medicine has gotten me out of this *labyrinth*, and my ears are no longer *lackadaisical.* I don't have to play *tag* when people *talk*, so I no longer suffer from this *ill-natured illness.* The spoken word is no longer a *phantom* and my *listening* is no longer *listless*, because this *pharmaceutical centers* my ears to my *cerebral cortex.* This medicine connects me to the *transmitter* that ends my *travail*, because this transmitter always *travels* with me. I am glad that Jesus is willing to turn on this *beacon* in my *bean* and send me these *signals* that were formerly *silent.*

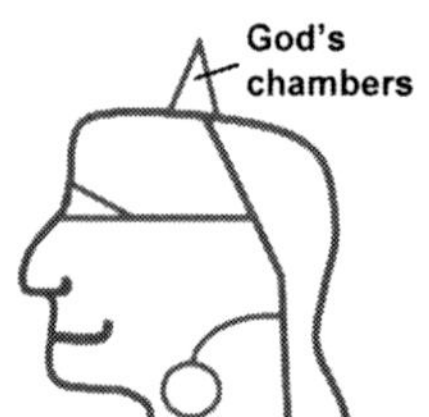

When I realized he was glad to *bear* this burden, I *beat* a path to this *beautiful mind* and *mined* it to help me solve this *knotty* problem of not *knowing* what was said. Jesus helped me meet this *challenge* in God's *chambers*, so I *thank* him for ending this *theater of the absurd.*

This *academy* atop my head has the *remedy* which is the will of God, so I just use this *remote control* which Jesus placed in this *convenient* location through his *Resurrection.* Now people don't have to *retell* their stories, because Jesus uses this *crane* to lift my *cranium* out of this *crap* that drives me *crazy.*

In Eden before the fall the *skull* of man was connected to the *sky*, but then Satan *hatched* the plot that resulted in the feud between the *Hatfields* and the real McCoy. Before original sin the Crown Chakra was located on this *harmonious hatfield* where the real McCoy lived, so the *minds* of God and man *mingled* there. Then original sin obliged the *Supreme Being* to make His sweetness stop *surging.* Satan's *hat trick* had made the divine sweetness disappear and *haughtiness* appear, which started the *feud* on this *field. Ancestor* worship *and androgens* became *rampant* on the *range* known as the hatfield, and each *foggy fold* consisted of *folk* who *followed* one another's *folly.* Each *surname* was worshipped like a *surrogate* god, so the Hatfields and the McCoys each *reveled* in this *reverence.* Nevertheless, it proved to be an *irrational irreverence*, because *after* some time *aggravations* and even *pitched* battles arose between the two families. It was a *pitfall*, because what at first seemed like a *lovely loyalty* turned out to be the work of *Lucifer.* Therefore, their *irrita-*

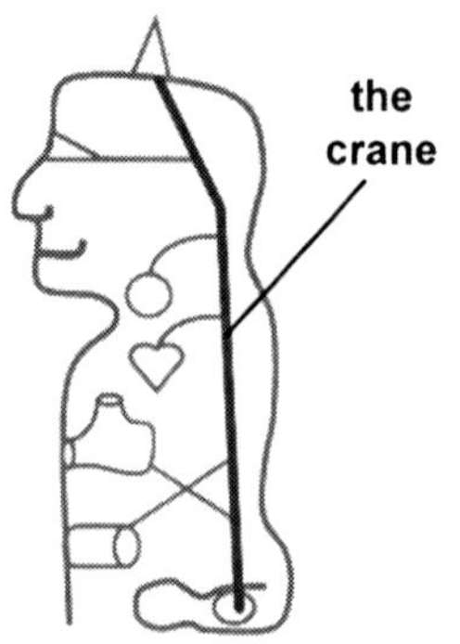

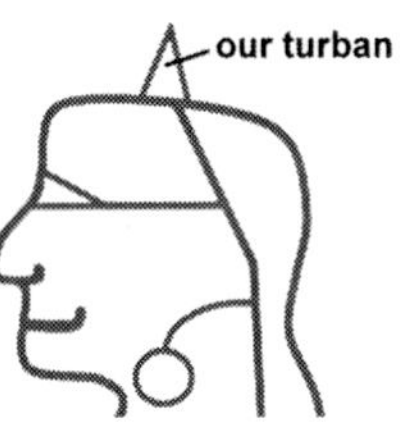

bility toward one another *isolated* them from the *mainstream* of people who tended to avoid such *major maladaptation*. We have all reaped this *harvest* of the *Hatfields*, because we are *suspicious* of the *sustenance* called the *real* McCoy. Therefore, the *reality* for us is that we think our *turbans* can't *turn* the divine sweetness into the Fruits.

I come from a long line of similar *iconoclasts*, so as a *child* my Gifts of the Spirit didn't come down the *chimney*, because the adults just went on *bragging* about their *brains*. Satan had worked his *craft* on them by *cramming* them so full of pride that even Jesus couldn't lift it out with the *crane* shown above. They flashed around this *brassy brawn* without realizing that it was a *brazen breach* of the law of the Eucharistic Orders of the vertical axis. They didn't realize that their *humility* had to satisfy this *hunger*, because their *intellect* was *intended* to *interact* with God through their *intuition* and *invest* them with the Fruits located in the *ivory tower* of the Crown Chakra. They lost this *undaunted underpinning*, because they didn't *understand* they had to *stand* under this law to get this *staple* commodity. Therefore, none of us *participated* in this *passive transport* that would have allowed the divine sweetness to *travel* into our behavior, and we never felt like *descendants* of God, because these two sacraments never *described* how God could butter our daily *bread*.

Nevertheless, my father always took pride in being a successful *breadwinner* and would often explain how the *breakthrough* of his family's *breeding* had enabled him to *apply* his *aptitudes* to avoiding the *deplorable* poverty of the Great *Depression*. He avoided this *taint* by *taking heart* in his *take-home pay* for which he had an obvious *talent*, but he never talked the *talk* that could make me feel I *tallied* up in this way. Consequently, I thought he came from a *pedigree* that was *peerless* but that my intellect was the *peewee* that sprang from his *pelvis*.

I have been a *purebred pushover*, because I have allowed this *idiotic idolatry* to make me the *gullible guzzler* who thought his *perceptivity* couldn't *perform*. The resultant *misfortune* is that I have *missed* the chance to eat the real *McCoy* as a *meal*. I thought it was a *meddler*, so God took a *powder*, and I have done without His *power*.

The combination of this *atrocity* with the *atrophy* known as my *Attention* Deficit Disorder *attenuated* the power of God in my *attic*. It was an enduring source of *attrition*, so as a *day-to-day* matter I often felt *dazed* as a child. Nevertheless, my mother also took the *initiative* of adding insult to *injury*, because when she lent an *ear* it wasn't in *earnest.* She had this *habit* from *Hades* of *deactivating* her attention before I conveyed the message, so I often felt I had reached a *dead end.* She frequently seemed *deaf* to my needs, but there is another Mother who never *tunes* me out, and she wears a *tunic.* She is *engrossed* in the task of *engulfing* my Crown Chakra in the divine sweetness and *enlivening* my Root Chakra so as to put an end to their *enmity.* With her help I won't be spiritually *indigent*, because the divine sweetness won't seem *indigestible* to me. Therefore, I take my *blunders* to her, and she puts the divine sweetness back on *board* for me.

My wife, Maria, felt like the *darling daughter* of the Blessed Mother, because whenever she had *somber* thoughts as a child she knew that *something* had happened *somewhere* that she needed to talk over with her. One night Maria and I had taken to *chatting* about these things in bed, and she said every time she felt *cheated* of the divine sweetness as a child the Blessed Mother would make her feel *so much* better by putting her in touch with her *Son's soothing.* Maria had eaten some *harsh hash* as a child that her family considered *haute cuisine*, but she figured that the Blessed Mother's job was to remove these *stern* ingredients before they got into the *stew.* Maria always trusted Mary to *sort* out the *sour* ingredients, so she would always put the *disparaging* items on *display* and ask Mary to *dispose* of the ones that didn't belong in the *recipe.* Maria *reclaimed* her sweetness by going through this *checklist* so that the *chef* in the *restaurant* could make *restitution* of the Fruits through his *Resurrection.* Maria *solved so many* problems in this way that by the time she became an adult she no longer suffered from the *sour sovereignty* of her family. The Blessed Mother taught her to trust this *chemistry* of the *Christian Church*, which was based on *crucifying* this *crud.* Maria used this *agility* to embrace her *agony* and end her *ailment*, so whenever her nerves got *taut*, she used this *teamwork* in the *cathedral* of her chakras to end this *caustic cavalcade* her family had *celebrated* in order to *censure* her.

As a *child* I had also *choked* on some of these pork *chops*, so I figured I could also put a better meal on the *table* by taking this *tactic* and become more at *ease* by *eating* the *chow* of *Christ.* Therefore, while we were in *bed* I talked to Maria about how I had been *bedeviled* and *asked* her how I had *assembled* the wrong ingredients. She said it must not have been a *cakewalk* to have gone through as many *calamities* as I did as a child, but she said that my fears didn't have to *catalyze* my current *catastrophes;* and that if I *refueled* with the divine sweetness, it would *regenerate* the Fruits. I no longer felt *paltry*, because she had *pampered* me with the *panacea* of her compassion by feeling my *pangs* of pain. She was therefore one of the *role models* who taught me about the *rollicking* fun that can be had in a *Roman Catholic romance* with God. I felt a profound *melancholy* that night regarding my *melee* of fear, hurt, and anger but also looked forward to its *melioration*. She had *melted* my heart by listening to my *memoirs*, and I didn't feel like such a *sad sack*, because I had told my *saga* to someone I considered to be *sage*, and she had *said* it was possible to *sail* to calmer waters.

One form of *sadism* I *sailed* into was the fact that my parents *adopted* an *adoring* attitude toward my older brother whom they considered to be a star in the *firmament*, because he was the *first-born*. Their *indifference* added to my *indisposition*, because I thought I was a *maggot*, and my older brother was the *magnate*. I was not the object of such *adoration* and thought I had not been *adorned* by the divine sweetness. In fact their reaction to me was so *ho-hum* that I never *hoisted* myself out of my *hokum*. He was treated like a *duke* who deserved to be *dulcified* by the divine sweetness, whereas I was more of a *dullard* and was *dumped* aside. Therefore, I concluded that I was the *shrimp*, and he was the *shrine*.

The *gulf* between me and God also widened, because I felt like a piece of *gum* on a *bedpost* as a two-year old. At that time my *beef* was that I felt *invisible*, and I am sure that I am still paying off some of the *invoices* that have resulted from this *expensive experience*. I had been *overlooked* by my mother who considered my older brother my *overlord*. She made me feel like I was *underfoot*, and so what I *underwent* was my fear, hurt, and anger.

When I told these things to Maria, she offered to *rock* me in a *rocking chair* and *simply sing* and *coo* until she felt my *cooped* up *pain* in the *palm* of her hand so that she could throw it away. She said that *hugging* was the *humane* way to show that this *neglect* was *negotiable* and that she would *welcome* the chance to add to the *well-being* of my *inner* child by showing him how fun it was to get *inoculated* with God's sweetness. She said that my parents may have *withheld* their affection with the result that I felt *woebegone* or *botched* the act of giving me a *bottle*. She said that I had been *misled* as a result of what I had *missed* but that this *scarcity* didn't have to be *scary* and that all I needed was *more motherly* love. Her words hit the *target* where I had paid this exorbitant *tariff*, and a *torrent* of *torrid tears told* the tale of this *torture* that I had *toted* around. I felt like an *orphan*, but my *outcries* seemed to *heal* me, because my *heart* was less *heavily laden* as a result of these *laments*. My *misery* was *mitigated* by these *moans*, and the *mob* of my fear, hurt, and anger stopped *mocking* me, because these *snorts* and *sobs* made me more *soft-hearted*. It lasted ten to fifteen minutes, during which I *curled* up next to her like a child grateful at having gotten rid of a bad *curse*.

It was a *bittersweet bivalence*, because I had attached myself to these *bizarre* symptoms, but I was also capable of *black balling* them. I had the choice of being *enveloped* by *enviousness* or of using the *enzymes* in my stomach according to the *Messiah's metabolic method* so that the divine sweetness could *differentiate* without *difficulty* into the Fruits. Therefore, I let the *caravan* of love, joy, and peace *caress* my behavior and asked Jesus to *carry* off my fear, hurt, and anger. I had gotten this *living load* of *loathsome lobbyists* from the *hereditary heroes* who were my *paranoid parents*, but I decided not to let this *suspicious swarm railroad* me, so I let my remorse *rain*, and it *raised* my *spirits* to a *spiritual* plane.

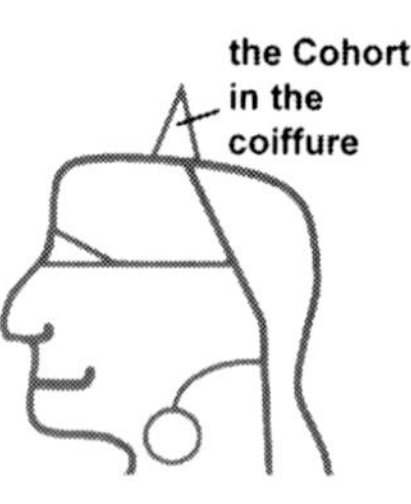

I got rid of this *ugliness* at my *umbilicus*, because I knew the divine *cohort* in my *coiffure* would send the Fruits down the vertical axis and through the *coil* to reverse this effect of my parents' *coitus*. This *pension* in my *penthouse* had been *pent-up*, and my *umbilicus* had been *uncooperative* spiritually, because these *icy idols* I had *worshipped* had given me a lousy *worth* shape. Therefore, I got in touch with the divine *nature* Jesus left in my *navel*. It was only *befitting* that the Eternally *Begotten* Son leave this there to improve my *behavior* and make my navel a more *mellow memorial*.

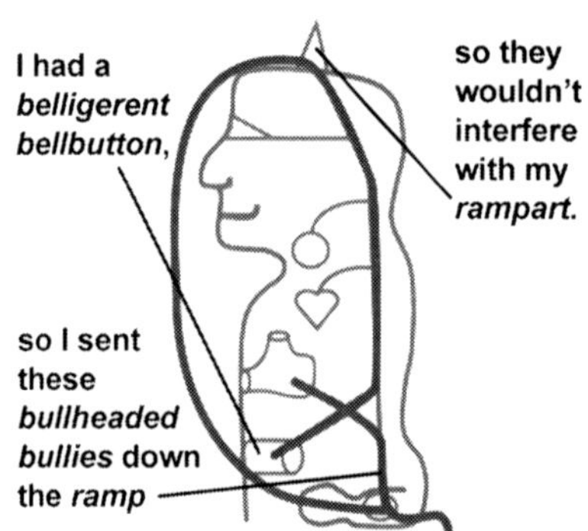

I had suffered some *apocalyptic* consequences from being an *apple polisher* and was glad that the *fall-out* I got from following *family traditions* did not have to bring me to a *tragic* end. I decided that the divine *spark specializes* in getting rid of these *foibles* we are *fond* of *fondling*, so it burst into *flame* as I went through these *flashbacks*, and I did away with

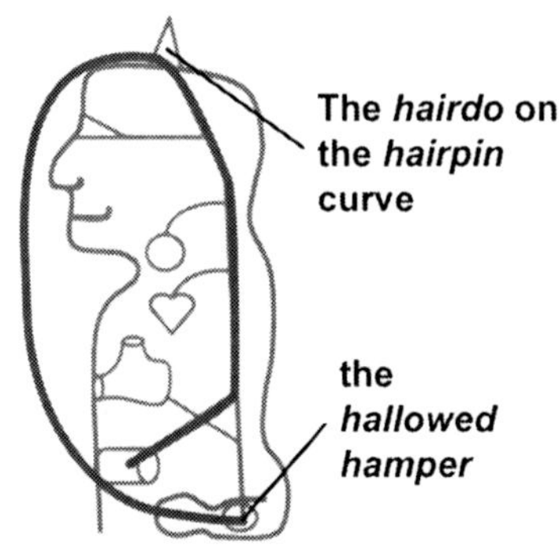

some *flaws*. I emptied an entire *file* of *films* and felt less *bewildered* by this *bewitching*. These *riddles* no longer *riled* me, because I got in this *relationship* with God who is my closest *relative*. I *released* the pain caused by the *hackneyed hailstorm* of my fear, hurt, and anger, and the *hairdo* on the *hairpin* curve turned my Root Chakra into a *hallowed hamper*.

Nevertheless, as a child I was a *basket case*, because my Root Chakra wasn't a *bastion* of the divine sweetness. Rather, it was a *forsaken fortress*, because my mother's *over-controlling* nature was in *overdrive* most of the time and caused my fears to *overgrow*. I wasn't very *blessed* by this *blizzard*, which made my sweetness a *shut-in*. She must have felt I was *sick* with a *terminal* case of the *terrible* two's, because she had a list of *do's* that didn't make me very *docile* and *don'ts* that made me feel like a *doormat*. It was a *schizophrenic school* in which I learned the *science* of ego and used these *scissors* to *cut* off my *cuteness*. It was a *contest* of *contingency punishment* that left me feeling *punk*, so what I hoped for the most was the *contingency* of her punishment not *continuing*.

I felt *strangulated* by the *strings* she had *attached* to this *stronghold* where she *locked* up her *love* and thought I had to go through an *attrition audit* before I could earn it. They weren't very *conciliatory conditions* and left me with the impression that I *couldn't* get into the *country* known as my heaven within. Therefore, I remained spiritually *lame*, because this *lamentable* circumstance left the *lamp* on the top of my head unlit. It was an enduring *lampoon* that made me feel I had been *ridiculed rightly*, but I finally figured that it was just a *plot* whose depths you had to *plumb*, so I shed the *light* that would make me feel more *likable*.

One of the reasons my *unconditional* love never got *uncorked* was that my physical appearance *reminded* my mother of her little brother. As a child she received *remonstrations* from her parents for getting in her *two cents worth* in response to her little brother's *tyranny*, and apparently she thought I was *predestined* to put her in a similar *predicament*. Therefore, she did her best to *preempt* this *impending imperfection* before it *played back* the *plight* of an *unspeakably* difficult *upbring-*

ing. Her efforts to *rout* the enemy in me in this way didn't make me feel like *royalty*, so I got hung by the *neck* by her dependency *needs*. I naturally tried to *fulfill* these needs, but it got my ego going at *full tilt* and gave me a bad *disposition*, because I felt *dispossessed* of my sweetness. After that I displaced my anger onto all members of the *fair sex*, because my mother had been a *fair-weather* friend, and my childhood hadn't been a *fairyland* of the *faithful*. This *hoax* was my mother's *hobby*, so I *hobnobbed* with my fear, hurt, and anger, and my divine sweetness remained in *hock* because of this *hocus-pocus*.

I still feel *miffed* on occasion, so my *mind* must be the *riled* hockey *rink* where these feelings *skate* around and even now cause *skirmishes*. I have done my best to avoid these *collisions*, because I don't want to let my mother's *colon contents* be the *contraband* that I *hurl* around *hurtfully* especially in my role as *husband*. This *anger* leaves me *anguished*, and I still have a *loud* mouth because of this *lovelessness* I am still *loyal* to. Nevertheless, I don't have to *barge* in and *bark* as if I had been raised in a *barn*, so I intend to *pacify* this *pack* of thieves.

I was *filled* with *films* from my past, so I had to have a *conversation* with the *cop* who could stop the *robbers*. The robbers could only *rock the boat* because of my *resentful residue*, so I decided to change my *destiny* by letting my *detached observer* get rid of these *obstacles*. I became a *detective* who was *determined* to see what I had *sidestepped* as a child and *sift* out the problem through the *sightseeing* of my remorse. I became a *disciple* of Christ through this self-*discipline* which was illustrated on the *eight* to two o'clock diagonal, and I got out from *behind this eight ball*. I *grieved* this *grim* reality and got a *grip* on the *groceries* that would make me *grow* spiritually, which is to say that I brought my *Fruits* of the Holy Spirit to *fruition*.

We got under this *curse* when Eve *curtsied* to Satan and took pride in her *curvaceousness*. When she *tantalized* Adam she *tapped* into the *knowledge* of evil through the *kundalini*, which was designed by God as a *laborer* who could do *whatever* he was asked *whether* it was right or not. Therefore, the chakras could continue being the *strong structure* of the *subconscious*, because the kundalini could remain *powerful* through *prayer*. However, the balance was *precarious*, because when Eve *disrobed*, her kundalini got *dissipated*, and became a *weak weightlifter*. God was *very* clear when He told Adam and Eve that the Chakra System was a holy *vessel*, because it was *vested* with the *holy* water known as the kundalini, which would make the chakras a suitable *home* for the divine sweetness, but that if man began to

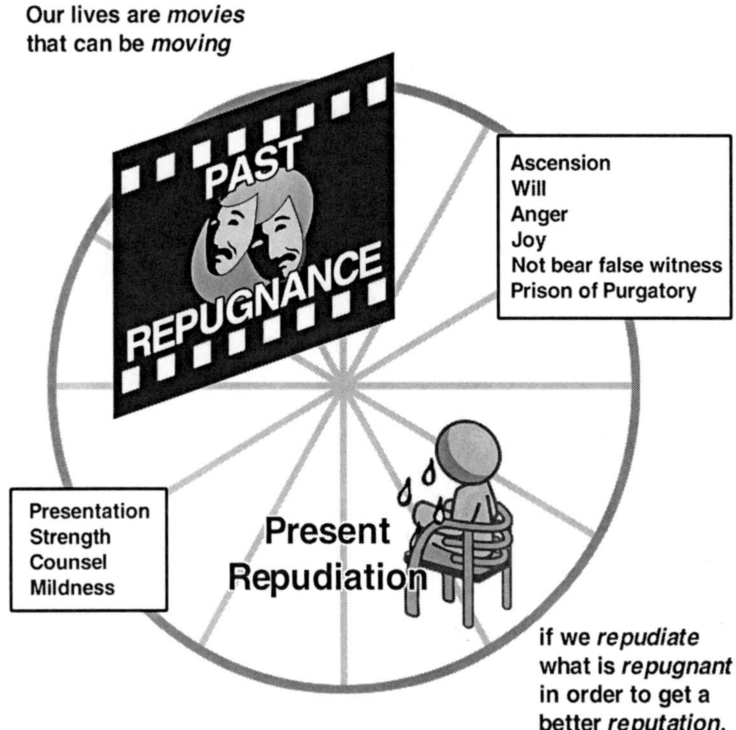

honor false gods, no *vestige* of His sweetness would remain. God said He would have to *veto* the use of feminine *vibes* that would lead man into *vice* through *seductive* behavior, induce him to recklessly spill his *semen*, and make the Chakras System a sinful *seminary*.

Therefore, our kundalini took a *tumble* at the time of Adam's *tumescence*, and our sexual *desire* became the *despot* who prohibited *love's loveliness*. The *alchemy* of lust produced an *alienation* of the *head* from the *heart*, because the spiral through the chakras no longer *twined* and stopped connecting the *two*. Head and heart originally felt an *amazement* toward God that made them *ambidextrous* about following His orders, so each had a *hand* in God's *handicraft*. This created a tranquil *ambience*, but after the kundalini fell *ambivalence* toward God *ambled* along requiring that the human will be rescued by the *ambulance* of remorse. Only in this way could man *ambulate* through life without being *ambushed* by his desires. His remorse could *ameliorate* the situation, because it was the *amen* that could make *amends*.

The Crown and Root Chakras have been torn *apart* by this *apathy* and have become *rampant ramparts*, but they can still *communicate*

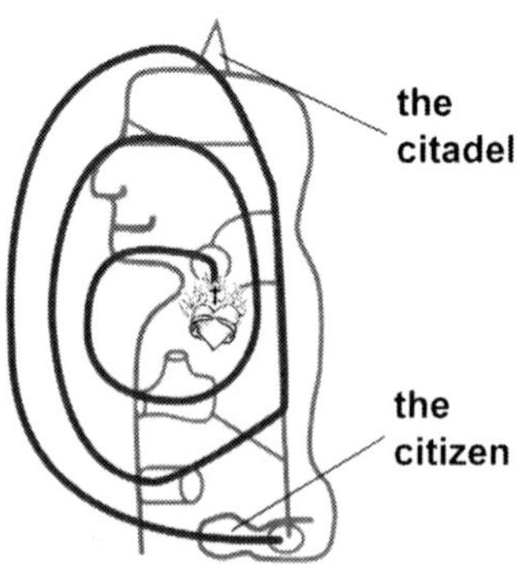

with one another as a result of Holy *Communion*. The *blend* in the *Blood* of Christ consists of the kundalini and the divine sweetness, and it *circulates* from the Sacred Heart to the *citadel* and the *citizen* through the *Body* of Christ which is his Chakra System. The Body of Christ therefore *bolsters* us up by *spanning* the gap between these two *spheres of influence.* God *mounted* our *mouths* so that we could be *fed* this *felicitous* meal *to our heart's content* from our *heaven* within, so let's *notify* our Throat Chakras that *we* expect them to *welcome* this nourishment. The Sacred Heart of Jesus is the *sanctuary* that lets us turn back the *sands* of time to the *ecology* of *Eden*, so let's make the Fruits *edible* by giving *sway* to the divine *sweetness.*

The *sabotage* of our *sacerdotal* power in the *sacral* chakra was a *scandal* that *scared* man, but the *sacraments* of the Eucharist and Holy Orders were *deposited* in the two *depots* of the *citadel* and the *citizen* when Jesus died. When Jesus died he *descended* to the citizen in the Root Chakra who had been spiritually dead and remind him that he was a *descendant* of God. Then he made the citadel a *restaurant* of the Fruits when he was *resurrected.* Hence, the *sacred* relationship between the divine sweetness and the kundalini was restored through the *sacrifice* of the Crucifixion, and the vertical axis of the Chakra System was made *sacrosanct* as a result of the Resurrection. The Crucifixion and Resurrection *united* that which had been *unjustly* torn *asunder* and gave man *asylum* from the *atheistic atrocities* that had resulted from his *innate* sinfulness. Jesus became the *innkeeper* of the chakras and gave man an *image* that was *immaculate* so as to make him *immune* to the *inexorable infirmity* of ego-addiction.

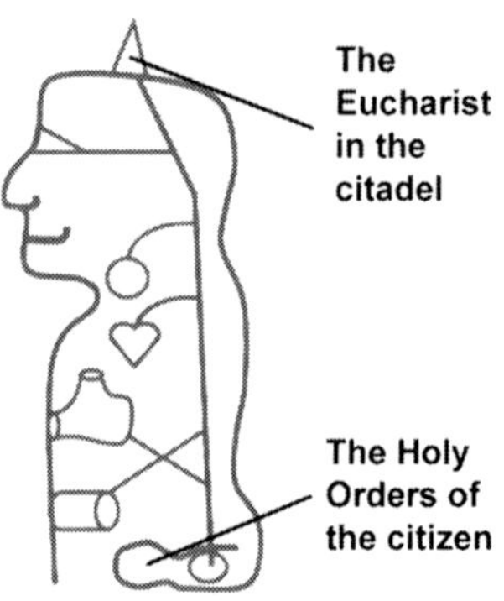

Jesus helped us to *cope* by leaving this *copy* of himself at the *corner* chakras, so let's *correct* our *corruption* by *coughing* up the *insights* into our driven behaviors necessary to bring about this *inspiring transformation* that will end our *transgressions.* Our egos have made our wills *vain valets,* so we should *remember* that our wills still have the power to *render* ego helpless. In fact our wills are *clerics* who are *clever* and can get us out of the *clink* that resulted from Adam and Eve's *promiscuity,* so let's return to the *Promised Land.* We can become *asymptomatic* by letting the spiritual *athletes* known as heart-mind and soul-strength *process* these *proclivities* that have resulted from making *procreation* a *profane* sport. God put the Sacred Heart *inside* our chests as a source of *inspiration* when Jesus wore the Crown of Thorns, so let's ask it to give us the *etiquette* of the *Eucharist* and get rid of this *wild* hair that has plagued our *wills.* We have the *capacity* to end this *caper,* because our wills were *priests* when they were in their *prime.* They still have the *masculine* ability to celebrate *Mass* and give us *manly manners,* so let's tell this *vicar* that the *vice* that Adam and Eve thought was nice has only enabled our *parents* to make us feel like *pariahs. Wanting* our parents' love has enabled our egos to be our *wardens,* so let's end this *incarceration* and bring about the *inception* of a *new* age. Let's stop *nibbling* on these *knickknacks* that have cause our *nightmares* and start *nibbling* on the *nimble nine* Fruits of the Spirit. It is better to drink the divine *nectar* than have these unfulfilled *needs,* because these *debilitating debts* are *incendiary incentives.*

Satan knew from the *inception* that we would sustain this *setback* as a result of having *sex* for *fun,* because it would *funnel* the kundalini out the penis at the time of the *climax.* He knew that the kundalini could only *climb* up the vertical axis again if we succeeded in *grappling* with these issues that were difficult to *grasp.* Likewise, Satan knew that most of us would rather remain *befuddled* than *begin* searching the *archives* for the *arctic* fears which are the *agents* of our *aggressive* behavior. Satan therefore *paved* the way to our hell on earth by changing the *peaceful* kundalini into the *hostile hot potato* that would get passed along from generation to generation through the sexual *potency* of man. Satan gave us this *dose* of pride that *dovetails* with our lust so that *incertitude* about God would bring about *incessant* conflict. As children we would have a *vivid void* which would make us *urgently* want our parents to love *us,* and the *repression* of these feelings would *require* that their *expression extend* throughout our lives. The lack of love from the parent of the *opposite* sex would not leave us with a very good *option,* because these *incestuous inclina-*

tions in our subconscious would travel *incognito* so as to make us *incompatible* with our spouses in marriage.

Our hearts are *faint*, because when *man fell* Satan pulled off this *maneuver* and the *romantic Root* Chakra still feels the *allure* of this *lethal lewdness* more than that of the *Almighty*. The *little* man who *lives* in the Root Chakra thinks love is a bunch of *frivolous frolicking*, so he doesn't realize he is *lovesick* because of this misplaced *loyalty*. He doesn't realize that the *haunting* that sons *have* is the lack of their mother's love, and he doesn't realize that *daughters* feel *daunted* because their fathers didn't hold them very *dear* as children. Therefore, men try to get *filled* with love by *finagling* it from their wives and girlfriends, and women by coaxing it *from* their husbands and boyfriends, which only makes marriage the *front* line in a war of the nerves. Therefore, a man's *mother* sets in *motion* this *oedipal oil* that *greases the wheels* of *great* sex, and a woman's *father* turns on the *faucet* of *electra elements* which *attract* her to men who have her father's *attributes* and make her want to *remodel* them by *removing* her clothing.

We all have this *incapacitation* that makes us think *incest* is *best*. Nevertheless, this *bestial* notion only *bestirs* our hearts to *betray* the unconditional love source, so let's not have this *depravity deriving* its energy from the kundalini, which is the whirling *dervish* whose *descent* in the spine has resulted in this *desecration*. We don't have to *wander* around as adults *wanting* what we couldn't *get* as children, so let's not let this *ghastly glacier* make us behave like *Stone Age stooges* who still suffer from this *Paleolithic pall* that makes us feel *paltry*. We have the *navels* of *Neanderthal* men and behave like *wild* beasts, but our *wills* can be *tamed*, so let's stop going on this *tangent* and *get* the divine sweetness from the *geyser* in our hearts.

Our heart-mind and soul-strength can *give* our hearts these *glad* tidings and declare a *cease-fire* with ego, because they were created by God to be the *celebrants* of the *Mass*. They can give us this cardiac *massage*, because they are our true *colors* and enable us to *combine* with God. We just need to *explain* the *exploit* of the Crucifixion to them and ask them to *wield* its power to benefit our *wills*. We will not behave like *wayward weaklings* when our wills learn to use this *armament*, because it is the *artillery* of the Divine *Artisan*, and it could even make the kundalini of the *Aryan* Nation *ascend*. Hence, let's end our *bigotry*, because our wills are the *big shots* who deserve the *bill of fare* known as the divine sweetness. Even if you have the will of a *Tasmanian devil*, when you get a *taste* of this *tater* it will make you *discard* your ego's *discernment*. Then Satan won't have his *tattoo* on your heart, and you won't be subject to his *tawdry taxation*.

We are *bugged* by our egos, but we won't stay full of this *bull* if we send them the *bulletins* God designed to tame this *burdensome beast*. When our remorse gets on the *pulpit*, the love *pumps* in our chest deliver this knockout *punch* with the first of the three *purgative* beatitudes. Therefore, let's not *beat around the bush* but rather ask this *beatitude* to *beckon* our heart-mind and soul-strength. They will make the *spillway* in our *spines* start the *spiral* and help us *mourn* so that we can *move* this *muck*.

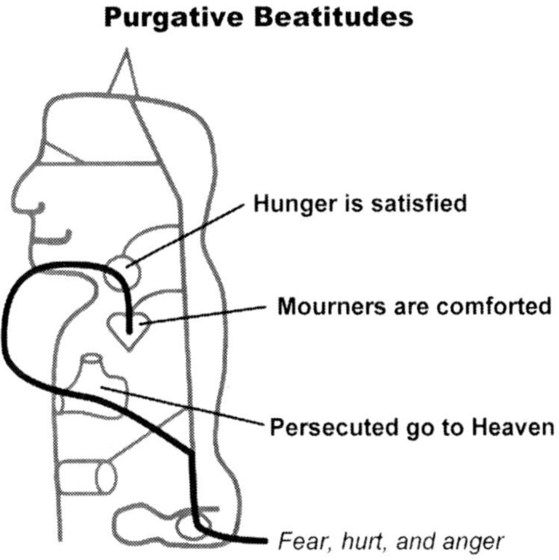

These two *celebrants* are *celibate* and therefore bring about the *asexual* reproduction that conquers our ego's *aspersions*. Heart-mind and soul-strength *size* up the problem and win this *game* of *skill*, because they *benefit* from our *bereavement*. Our *mourning* makes them feel *mutual* regard, so heart-mind *releases* the *reliable remedy* of the divine sweetness and soul-strength releases the kundalini. This *espousal* ends their *estrangement*, because when they *meet* in the *middle* chakra, the *gametes zoom* in to form the *zygote*, and they reenact the same *mystery* man and wife accomplish by getting *naked* in bed. The two *gametes* earn us the entire *gamut* of the Fruits of the Spirit, and they *repeal* the *reprimand* of original sin. This asexual *reproduction* is possible, because we have *rescued* them from our *resentments*. Their *fertilized* egg gives rise to this blessing, because our *fervent* mourning *comforts* them and *commutes* our sentence of ego-addiction.

The second beatitude on this *cogent coil* satisfies our spiritual *hunger* when we *hunt* for the dirty secrets we have *hushed up*. This organ is a *gullet* that can *gulp* both fact and fiction, so we should be careful what we *swallow*, since it can give *sway* to either *sweetness* or sourness in our behavior. We were *naïve* as children, so our fears remained *nameless*, and our *pride* entered its *prime*. That is how we got led down this *primrose path* that is so *pathetic*. When Eve did the *hula* in Eden it affected *humanity* in this way, so we should cultivate our *humility*, because when it reaches its *peak* it will get us past the *pearly* gates.

The *third* beatitude on the spiral takes the *thorn* out of our side which is known as a *stoic stomach*, because we have *persecuted* our *pesky* egos for *righteousness* sake in order to avoid getting *riled*. When Jesus *carried* the Cross, he *carved* out this *contract*, so let's focus our *contrition* on our *controversies* and *see* the divine sweetness *seep* into our behavior. When our Stomach Chakras *select* it for *absorption*, it automatically turns into an *abundance* of the Fruits, so let's remember this *inheritance*. It even nullifies an *inhumane* upbringing, so let's *earn* it and be at *ease*.

The fourth beatitude in this sequence is the first of the three *illuminative* beatitudes which dispel the *illusions* that have *impeded* our progress. Our *Stomach* Chakras have *blindly* sent these *churlish citizens* into our *blood* rather than our *stool*, so we need to *claim* our right to *clarify* this matter. We send these *riled ringleaders* down the *river* and the *mighty mild military minds* up the river in order to win this *war* against our *waste*. Our *meanness* and our *meekness meet* at this *fork* in the stream so that we can *forsake* that which is *foul* and embrace a less *fractious frame of mind*. We absorb the *Eucharist* and *evacuate evil*, so let's use our *colons* and not *colonize* our hearts with this *colossal column* of *fecal feelings* that only make us *combative*. Our colons will respond to the *command* of our remorse, so we should *recover* by using our *rectums* and remember that our *anal* chakras will get rid of *anything* we ask them to.

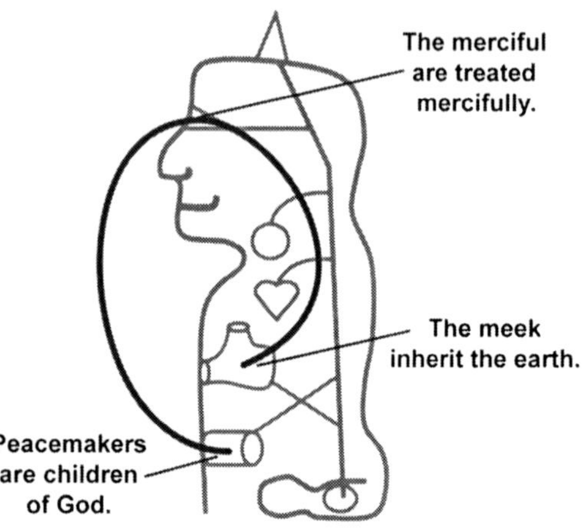

The *fifth* beatitude in this series *fights* the *menace* of our fear, hurt, and anger with our *mercy*. Our mercy *can* make this *cancerous can of worms* stop *metastasizing* itself into

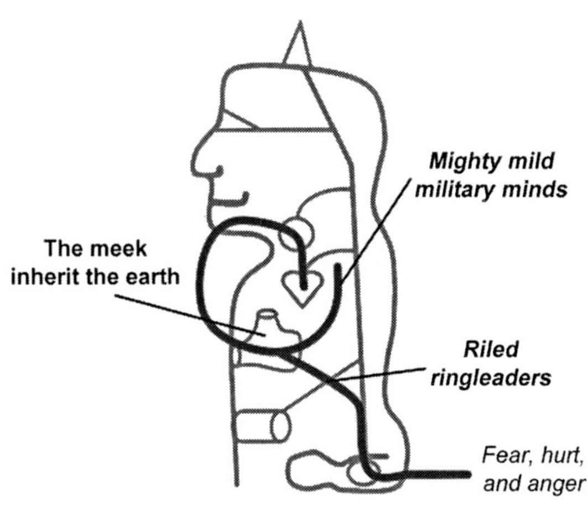

our behavior, because it is the *canon* that makes us stop being *cantankerous.* We can earn this *clemency,* because the *Brow* Chakra is the *clever clinician* in the *cloister* who helps us stop *bucking* the system and start eating the *buffet* of the Fruits. The Brow Chakra is the home of the *fifth* beatitude, because this is where we *figure* it all out. It is the midpoint of the *calipers* which *call into question* our motives for behaving as we do. These calipers take the *meanness measurement* of our *driven* behaviors so that we can *drum* up the *memories* we need to *mend* with our mourning.

Our stomachs contain this *bad bag* of tricks we need to *bail out* of, so the Brow Chakra reminds us how we became *sitting ducks* by going through certain *situations* during our childhoods. On command of our remorse these *sitcoms* stop making us *sizzle,* because our *babble* of repressed feelings *back out* through our *back door.* Therefore, we should use the Brow Chakra to *visualize* what is *vital* in this *reckoning* that *reconciles* us to God.

The *Navel* Chakra is the *peacemaker* who *peddles* the *peerless calmness* of *Calvary,* because the *Crucifixion* opened it to this *cup* of kindness that can *cure* ego-addiction. It is *navigable* by the *Nazarene,* so it knows when it has become *neat.* It is the *clasp* that attaches to God when we have *cleaned* it out, so let's rid our Navel Chakras of the *unresolved* dependency needs that make our spiritual hunger stay *unsatisfied.*

When Adam and Eve ate the *bonbon* fed them by Satan, the Navel Chakra became the *bondage bongo* whose drumbeat drove man *bonkers.* The Navel Chakra contains the *sewage* that resulted from the *sex appeal* our parents had for one another, but the Eternally Begotten Son opened it to *traffic* that is less *tragic,* so let's enjoy the *tasty* tea that is sweetened with the divine sweetness at this roadside *tavern,* because this is the *beverage* that will end our *bewilderment.*

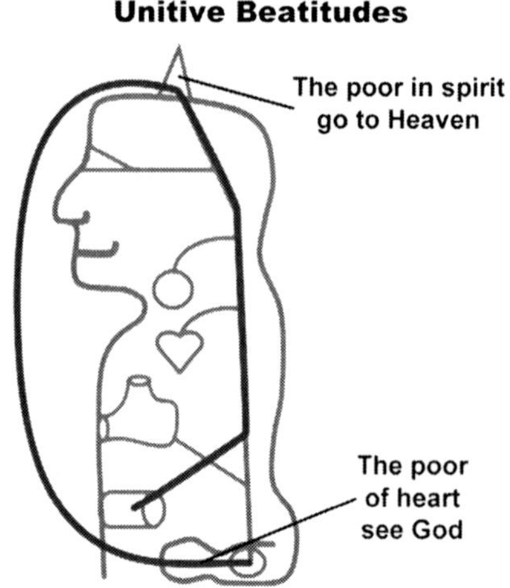

The *head* makes the *heart smart* by going to our *hell* and saying *hello* to the *helpless heretic* at the bottom who has been the victim of ego's *smear* campaign. When our remorse *smells* this *rancor* that has *rattled* our brains, it *smites* this *smoke screen* and gives us *smooth* sailing. The *central* chakra responds to the *ceremony* of our remorse, initiates this *cessation of hostilities*, and *rehabilitates* our *relationship* with God. The love *pump* in our chests has been *punch-drunk*, but we are able to *purchase purity* of heart, because the *purgative* beatitudes *pursue* this end for us. We have *followed* our *folly*, but the illuminative beatitudes put us on a *friendly footing* with the *Fruits*, so we follow this *loop* in order to regain this *lost love*. Lastly, the unitive beatitudes connect the chakra on the *bonnet* to the one in our *bosom* through this *boulevard* which also hooks up to the one at the *bottom*.

We can *toot* our own horns at the *top* chakra, because our *clan's clandestine claptrap* has been erased, and we have a *clean slate*, a will that is no longer a *slave* to ego. We are *poor* in the spirit of this *portable potentate's preposterous pretense* and are ready to have the nerves of *steel* that the will of God in the church *steeple* can deliver. We have *paid* this price at the Navel Chakra and have become *peacemakers*, so our inner *child* is ready to *climb* the *chimney* to the Crown Chakra and have this *chit-chat* with *Christ* in which we ask him to share the *relationship* that is most *relaxing*, the *treasure* of the *Trinity*. Adam's *semen* robbed us of this *serenity*, but the *series* of *serious sermons* delivered to the *serpent* by our remorse puts our serenity back in *service* to us in this *seventh* beatitude.

We are poor in spirit, because we have delivered a *knockout punch* to our ego, so this *puny puppet knuckles under* to the will of God. The *tonic* of the divine sweetness at the *top* chakra turns into a *torrent* of love, joy, and peace, because the *contract* of the New Covenant begins to exert *control*. *Circumstance* no longer turns our lives into a *circus*, because the *mechanics* of our ego's *meddling* can't survive the *meet-*

ing of the minds that takes place in this *memorial.* The *will of God* hasn't vanished from our *memory*, so it *wins* us the *wisdom* at this *peak* that flows from our divine *pedigree.*

The *pagan pal* at the bottom of the *palace* has been a *panderer*, but when "poor in spirit" *parachutes* down, his hell turns into a *paradise.* It is certainly a *paradox*, because he has been anything but a *paragon* of virtue, but the will of God *paralyzes* the *paraphernalia* between his legs, which is the *parasite* that has robbed him of God's *pardon.* His *parentage* has been decided in the divine *parliament* above, so he can play his *part* with the *partisan* up top. Heart, soul, mind, and strength *partner* with God, because the *password* of the *Pastor* known as "pure of heart" has opened the *path* to the divine *Patriarch* so that the all four parts of the human will can become *patriots* of the heaven within.

This *reconciliation* of the ends to the middle is due to the *reconnaissance* of our remorse. We just use the twelve *powers* to make our *prayer* stop our egos from *bedeviling* us, and we do this so that the *beatitudes* may *begin* to work on our *behalf.*

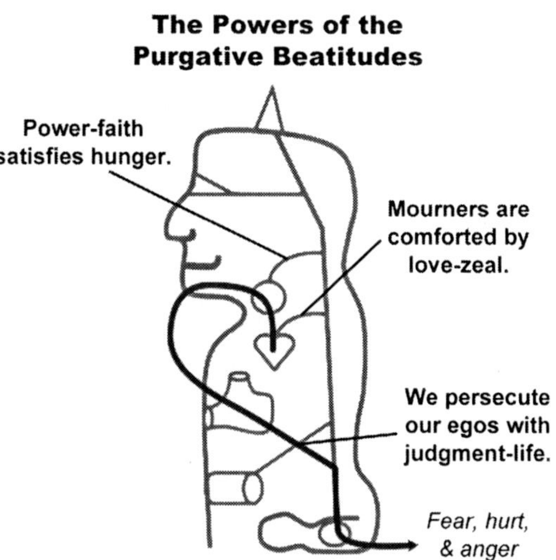

Ego-*paupers* have *peace* of mind, because the *Prince* of Peace has enabled them to look through the *prism* of their remorse. They have found their true *colors* and *regained* their *regal* status, because God's kingdom has *come* for them. They are no longer *roped* in by this *roughneck* anymore, because they have pondered the *routing* from their childhoods and found their *royal* lineage buried under this *rubbish.* They are *poor* in spirit, because they have seen *promise* in the *prospect* of *psychotherapy* and become *pupils* of *purity* of heart.

The *pagan organ* that reaches *orgasm* makes man feel like an *orphan*, because it *pants* over everything in *panties.* It is the *other* parent that *our* Father *warned* Adam and Eve about in Eden, because he said it could *oust* Him and *warp* their nerves. We have all been kicked out of *paradise* because of this *parallel parenting* that makes us *part* with the blessings that Jesus went through his *Passion* to restore. It is a *patent* fact that this *comparative paternity* makes us feel *pathetic*, because it is the sole *competence* of God to *complement* our human nature and give us a *comprehensive* awareness of our divine *pedigree*. Our *paradise* may seem to have gotten *paralyzed* by this *parasitic* parenting, but this *parcel* of *nonsense* is susceptible to *pardon* by the *particular nutcracker* who is our *Pastor*. Our hearts can recover, because our *therapy* works through *thick* and *thin* to solve these *thorny* problems and enables us to follow the *thread* back to the *threshold* of our heaven within. When we *rummage* through the *rumors* of our past, our *rupture* with God is healed, and the *four fragile fragments* decide on a different *framework*.

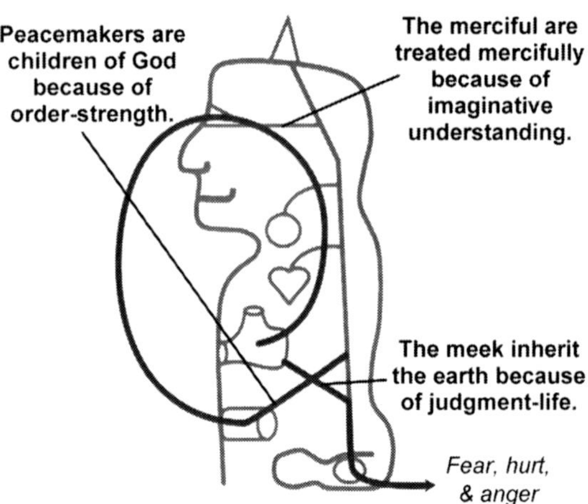

Our *hearts* have *heaved* out the resentments that have *heckled* us, because the *doctors* known as heart-mind and soul-strength have *documented* the *domino effect* of our egos. We have *educated* our *egos* with the *bullshit-bunkers* which are the five central chakras and taken the *bullshit-bypass* which is the vertical axis of the Chakra System. The five bullshit-bunkers have *dosed* the *double-dealers* with our remorse,

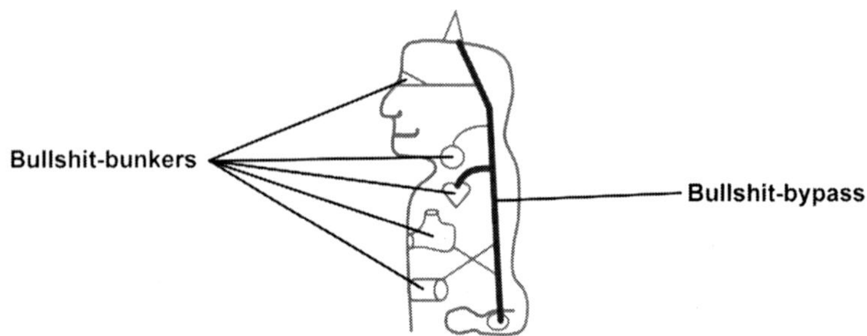

and the *treaty* of the New Covenant has made the *Trinity triumph* over these *troublemakers.* Heart-mind and soul-strength have *tirelessly toiled* with these five *toilet tools* to *eliminate* our *embittered* repressed *emotions*, but only soul-mind and heart-strength have the *will* to *wire* us to God. Soul-mind takes the *bullshit-bypass* and enables heart-strength to get on *top* of this *torment.*

Therefore, if your *unkindness* is getting *unmanageable*, *kick-start* your *kindness* by *mustering* up your *spark* of the *divine*, and *dock* it up to the *nature* of the *Nazarene*, because it's his *domain* to *fan* your *flagging* kindness into a *fantastic flame. Reproduction* by means of the *genitals repudiated* your *gentleness*, but it can be *rescued*, because your *resemblance* to the divine can make it *germinate* from the *reservoir* of love in the Sacred Heart. Jesus will *send* this *sentiment* you were *separated* from in Eden into your behavior and *settle* your nerves in the *seventh* chakra. Jesus was created without *sexual shackles*, so if you want to be *kind*, ask the *king* to share his *kinship* so that the *Trinity* can *trip* up the devil and make your *kindness kinetics shine.*

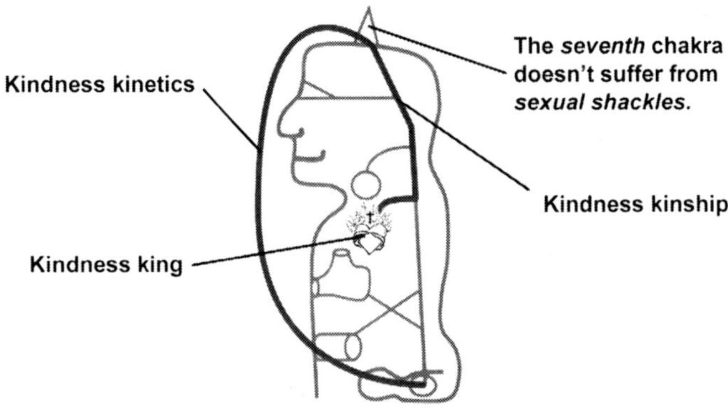

We have been in *deep* shit, but our *defecation* has gotten rid of these *degradations*, and the *Deity* can now *deliberate* in our minds. These four parts of our will have been *strangers* to one another, but they have been *stricken* with grief over these *travesties* and have *treated* them by getting in the *trenches* to fight for this *trickle-down* which is *tried and true.* They have now *struck* it rich, because the *Fruits* have *fueled* this *fulfilling function.* We also have a better *future* because of the *strong structure* that has resulted from the *combination* of soul-mind and God-thought. Soul-mind is the *keeper* of the *key* that opens the *lock* in the Crown Chakra and lets God's *logic silence* our *silliness.* God's kingdom can *come*, because the *Mediatrix* has made us *mellow*

The Powers of the Unitive Beatitudes

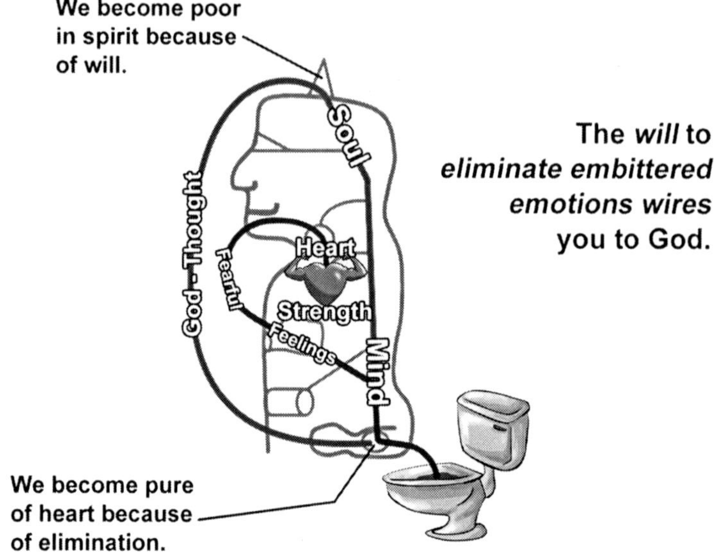

by putting an end to these *melodramas*, so our *mistakes* don't have to come back to *mock* us. She has *mollified* our bad *moods* by *channeling* Jesus' strength of *character* into our hearts. The *Mother* of God became *pregnant* to help us stop these *prickly problems*, so you could say that she installed this *motor* in our hearts that helps us *mount* the offense of our *mourning*. She always hears this *plaintive* call and responds to our *pleas* by sending the *calmness* of *Calvary* to *caress* our hearts, so let's remember that the *Carpenter carried* the Cross in order to put an end to this *cartoon*. Winning this *war* will *warm* your heart, so take off the *mask* of ego so that the *Mass* will give you this cardiac *massage* that will make you pure of heart. Jesus gives us *mastery* over ego, but Mary is the *matchless matron* who makes us *mature* when we are *maudlin* because of our *mayhem*, and therefore she also serves us the *meal* of love, joy, and peace.

This *path* leads to *peace* of mind, because the chakra on the *peak* is where the *will* of God is *won*. After the *loony loop* one goes from the *bewildered* chakra at the belt to the one above that is *beyond* this *bias*, because this is where the divine sweetness *bides* its time. This part of the *circuit circulates* the divine sweetness so that the confusing *circumstances* of our upbringing can be *circumvented*. Therefore, it starts at the chakra at the *belt* and then rounds the *bend* to bring this *benediction* to the *bereft* chakra below.

I felt *bereaved* as a child and was driven *berserk* by the *interfering intermediaries* of my fear, hurt, and anger, but now I would rather have the *syrup* of the divine sweetness whose *system* of *saving* grace gives me *savoir-faire.* When I was a child Satan must have *trumped* my *trust* of this *sacred* substance, but my heart is still the *sacrosanct* repository of the divine sweetness that makes me invulnerable to *sadistic* influences. Therefore, the *truth* is that I can *change my tune,* because my heart lives inside the Sacred Heart, which is the *filling station* that uses the *filter* called the Crown of Thorns. This filter blocks my ego-addicted will from filling me with *filth,* so I have *confidence* in this *configuration* and trust it to give me *finesse* that is *fine-tuned* by the Holy Spirit.

Nevertheless, as a child I *diverted* the flow of my *divine* sweetness into the *toilet,* because I thought that only the *tonic* of my parents' approval could cure my *inferiority complex* and therefore *inflicted* this injury on myself. The *hogwash* I believed in was that I couldn't *hold* anything *sacred* inside myself, so I came under this *sad influence* that made me an *informer* to the forces of evil and divulged *details* that would enable their *detestable* bombs to be *detonated* in my life. I *counted* on *counterfeiters,* so I never learned to *read between the lines* in order to determine what was *real.* Even now I *reveal* secrets that sometimes make me feel that someone *revoked* my good sense and need to get rid of this *pernicious* habit of letting *personal data* loose that most people hold *dear.* I have been unable to keep my mouth *shut,* because the *shuttle* on the spiral between my heart and my mouth has been run by the *shyster* Satan rather than my *sibling* Jesus. This *idiotic idolatry* of my parents has made me *trust* the wrong people, so I haven't *tucked* Jesus into my heart.

I have been repeatedly *punished* for letting myself be Satan's *puppet,* but I can also *purchase* something more *pure* by sending my remorse on the *march* to the *market* where the Fruits of the Spirit are sold. The Fruits are the *victuals* of the *vine* that cannot be *violated* by any kind of *violence,* so I intend to solve this *purity puzzle* by having this *chastity chat* with Jesus and by asking him to fill me with this *gasoline* that will allow me to shift *gears.* I am a member of God's *special species,* so I have been *endowed* with the ability to *endure* the *enemy* or *engage* him with my remorse. I just need to *beep* the Eternally *Begotten* Son at the Navel Chakra. He will give me loving *behavior* there, because this is the *place* with the *placenta* that has the *Planned Parenthood* of the Immaculate Conception.

Its *umbilical cord* is *under* divine control, because it connects to the Crown Chakra, so I intend to ask for this spiritual *rebirth*. Mary is the *receptionist* at this *wellspring* where anyone can *wet his whistle* with the divine *sweetness*, so I might as well cure my *swellheadedness* by taking a *swig*. *Well-being* is available at this *wellhead*, because Mary's Immaculate *Conception* came about without her parents' *concupiscence*, so we should ask her to *share* it in order to *shed* our ego-addiction. We *stock* up fear, hurt, and anger in our *Stomach* Chakras, but she can make the *brook* of the divine sweetness flow there, because our *Brow* Chakras contain the *measuring mechanism* of the *Mediatrix*. The *nature* of the *Navel* Chakra is to store up these *calamities*, but if we make these *calculations*, Mary will teach us how to get rid of this *dung* that makes our hearts *dungeons*. If we send these *bundles* out our *bungholes*, our Navel Chakras won't be the *dolorous domain* of our upbringings, because Mary will connect them to our Crown Chakras, which is God's *dominion*.

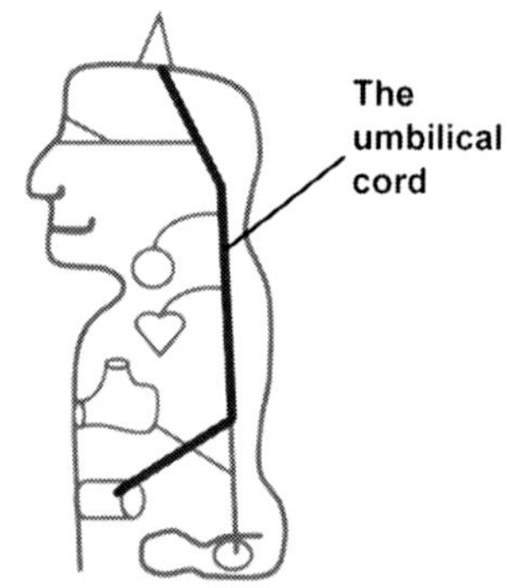

My Navel Chakra became my *dependency depot*, because my Stomach Chakra had indulged in a very *sorry* kind of *sorting*. My Stomach Chakra was the *sieve* that *sifted* out my fear, hurt, and anger for inclusion in this *rebellious recipe*, while my love, joy, and peace were the *parties* that *passed through*. I was tied to my mother's *apron strings* at my Navel Chakra, because my ego had *arbitrated* these disputes. Therefore, I decided to ask my love, joy, and peace to *sign* in, my fear, hurt, and anger to stop *singing* out, and for my heart to listen for the *signal* of the divine sweetness that my ego had *silenced*. I told these *perforations* in my Stomach Chakra not to hold onto my *peril* but to let it go through the *perimeter* of my Root Chakra which was located in my *perineum period!*

This diabolical *sieve* must have set its *sights* on my *pockets*, because my money also seemed to be going through its holes. This law of *poetic justice* seemed to be making me a *pauper* where it came to my *paycheck*, because my practice *earnings* weren't the greatest on *earth*. Therefore, it looked like my *money* had been *monitored* about as well as my *self-esteem*, so it was *self-evident* that both had gone through the

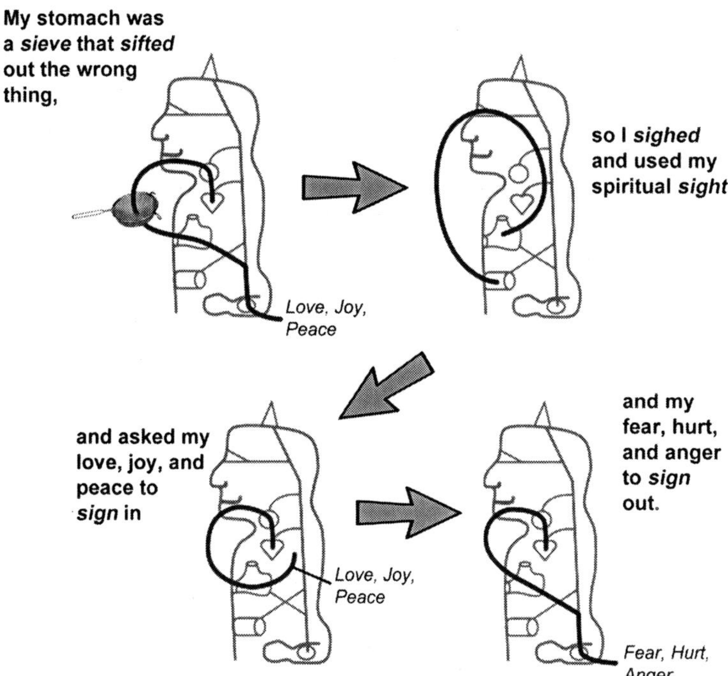

holes in the sieve. I wanted to *reverse* these losses and earn my just *reward*, so I *offloaded* my *onerous* fear, hurt, and anger and *on-loaded* the one and *only* divine sweetness. I just needed to stop being *intolerant* of that *intrinsic* part of me known as the *divine* that was not *divisible* from me. *Staying* on this track was the focus of my *steadfast* determination, so I welcomed the *steady state* of the divine sweetness and *protected* it with walls of devotion by being a *protégé* of Jesus. I would

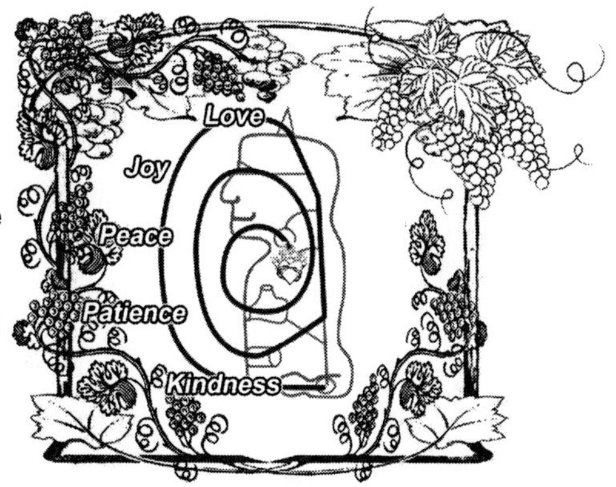

If your *destiny* has been *determined* by *arbitrary* whims, let your remorse build this *arbor*, because the Holy Spirit is the *vigorous vine* that *supplies* the Fruits when you give it this *support*.

rather have this shelter than an *alley cat's alliance* to God, so I asked the Sacred Heart to let my heart *nestle* inside so that the *network* of *neurons* in my head could use the Fruits of the Spirit to make me less *neurotic*.

I was *hung up* because of what I had *hushed up*, so I told my *heart*-mind above that our life would be less *hectic* if she would be the *general officer* in charge of *generosity*-faith, and I told my *soul*-strength below that it would be easier for us to tap into our *Source* if he used the *might* known as *mildness*-chastity. I reminded my heart-*mind* that she couldn't *mine* the divine sweetness without generosity-faith, and I reminded soul-*strength* that his job would be less *strenuous* if he took advantage of mildness-chastity. I just needed to teach the gal above to use God's *largesse* so that the guy below could get rid of his *lassitude* and see to it that the *Last* Supper started serving the Fruits in my heart. I just had to show them the *light* by *lining* up the *goods* just the way they were explained in the *gospel*.

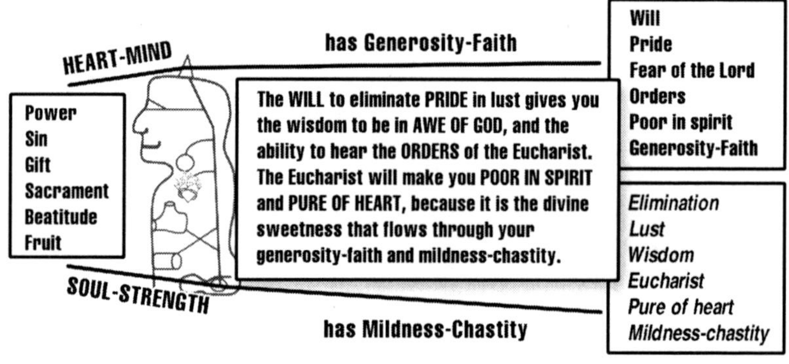

If I wanted to stop running the *gauntlet* of ego, I would have to show the *gearshift* of my *generosity* to the *genie* of my *gentleness* in my Root Chakra. Then he wouldn't use my chakras as a *meanness mechanism*, because he would realize that he was my *kindness kingpin*. He had suffered from the *lewd liaison* that had turned his *paradise* into a *paradox*, so he might consider this a *strange strategy*, but once he saw the *strata* shown above he would realize it was the *bridge* that he could take to stop being on the *brink* of disaster. Therefore, I can *lasso* my happiness with the *last* loop of the spiral by asking my soul-strength to make this *last hurrah*. My soul can *pass* along his strength to my heart and become *passive* to God's *mind* so I won't *misbehave*. My soul was originally *confident* in this *connection*, and even af-

POWERS	MYSTERIES Sorrowful	Joyous	Glorious	
1. Imaginative understanding	helps you see the **Agony** that is the pain of your wound	and hear the **Annunciation**	of the **Resurrection** of your original innocence.	**SEE**
2. Power-faith	teaches that the **scourging** from your childhood	can be **revisited**	in order to bring about an **ascent** of the divine sweetness.	**TASTE**
3. Love-zeal *Holy Spirit*	teaches that your ego-addicted will is a **crown of thorns**	that you can surrender to the Sacred Heart so as to give **birth** to your branch of the grapevine	and make the Holy Spirit **descend** on you.	**TOUCH**
4. Judgment-life *love, joy, peace* *fear, hurt, anger*	teaches you to **carry your cross**	so that Jesus cab **present** you	with a better **assumption.**	**SMELL**
5. Then your chaos will become **order,**	because your spiritual **strength** will have **crucified** your ego-addiction	and you will have **found** out	how to bring about the **Coronation.**	**HEAR**

ter being *conquered* in Eden its *consciousness* can still be *consecrated* to this *consistently consoling constituency*. The four pieces of my will need to *jockey* into position and become *joint* owners of God's *joy*. They need to *format* themselves to the *formidable formula* of God's sweetness which is the *framework* of the *fraternity* of the Holy Spirit which will set me *free*.

The Eternally Begotten Son is the *embryo* that *emigrates* into the Heart Chakra when we make the *effort* to fertilize the *egg* in order to get rid of *ego*. We just have to take our *errors* to the *escape artist* known as the Mediatrix of Grace in order to gain *ascendancy* over the forces of evil. Mary carries the *registry* of *regret* that *rehabilitates* man, so she starts the *reign* of God in our hearts again. She is the *arbitrator* who makes the grapevine climb up the *arches* of the *archaic* Chakra System, which God provided as the *structure* on which to build our *struggle* for freedom from ego. Therefore, we can solve a *myriad* of problems by asking Mary to use the *Mysteries* to give a *pounding* to the fiend with the twelve *powers.*

The five central chakras put us in touch with our *innate innocence.* They handle the *inquiries* that make *inroads* into the *inscrutable insecurities* that plague our minds. They are the *units* that we need to use to achieve *unity* with God. We just need to bring our *disputes* there and *disqualify* them through the *togetherness toil* of our remorse. Then the *primeval* forces that were *printed* on our hearts *prior* to Eden will *splice* together the Crown and Root Chakras that got *split* up there.

These two *outposts* are waiting for the *outreach* ministry of the five *central* chakras to reach our *cerebral cortex.* Our *small-mindedness* can be healed with the *smarts* of the divine *sweetness*, which thinks *swiftly* on its *feet* and makes it possible for a *fellow* to be *considerate. Consolidating* the forces in the Crown and Root Chakras enables God's *intelligence* to *intensify* our happiness, so let's become *winners* by *wiping* away the *shame* that leaves us in bad *shape.*

The *Top Dog* in the Crown Chakra is always willing to discuss the *topic* of why the *torch* there doesn't burn brightly, but the bottom line is always the *torpor* of our Root Chakras. Nevertheless, the *lazy* man who lives below can be *led*, because the five central chakras use the *herculean* power of the divine sweetness to *herd* out our fear, hurt, and anger. Satan the *bandit* can be *banished* from our hearts, and we can stop the *bondage* of ego from making our behavior *boomerang*, because there is no *backlash* when we get rid of this *baggage.* It is possible in the *here* and now to stop the *hereditary heresy* called original sin, because our contrition *animates* the chakras to eliminate the *animosity* that originated at a time when the *yoke* of our *youth* made it possible for our *ordeals* to *outwit* us. We surely *annexed* it then but can *annihilate* it now so that every year we spend in this work can be the *anniversary* we *celebrate* in the *celestial sphere* of our Crown Chakras. We have all been *marred* by the *marriage* of our wills to ego, because we *breed* by taking this *bribe* that makes the devil our *bridegroom*, which of course is not a very *brilliant* idea. *Prayer* is therefore the *precious preface* to *pregnancy*, because that way the *prelates* in the Crown and Root Chakras will be *prepared* to release the kundalini and the divine sweetness at just the right *moment* in the *monastery*, so let's have the *presence of mind* to do this before we *press the flesh.* Our *orgasms* won't make *ornery* children if we *dedicate* the *deed* to God beforehand, because when Christ descended to the dead, he *planted* the vine of the Holy Spirit in this *playpen.* Then at the time of his *Ascension,* he was able to restore the *asexual* relationship between the two end chakras, because he was born of the one *woman* whose *womb* had the *placenta* in which this *plant* could grow. Hence, the Immaculate Conception made it possible for us all to be *born botanically* so that God's *fructose* could bring the *Fruits* into our behavior.

When Jesus descended to the *dead,* he made this good *deal* possible, because he planted the grapevine of the Holy Spirit in the chakra at the *bottom.* That way the baby-making in the *boudoir* could make the *bough* of the Holy Spirit *sprout* in the heart of the child to give him *spunk.* However, if we didn't *pray* as a *precaution,* the kundalini couldn't *saturate* the divine sweetness, because the *Savior* in the chakra *above* couldn't release this *asset* from the *attic.* Therefore, being too *absent-minded* to ask for *absolution* in advance is the worst kind of *child abuse,* because if we don't *chime in* beforehand, the grapevine can't connect the *child's chimney* to the chakra near his *chin.* Then the child won't be able to swallow the divine sweetness and won't know that he is a *chip* off the Old Block.

Jesus *scaled* these heights to connect the chakra on the *scalp* to the one right *below.* This way the child could *benefit* from the *benign beverage* of the divine sweetness that was *stored* in the Crown Chakra and enjoy its spiritual *strength* at times of *stress.* The chakra *bracketed* above could make the child's *brains* a *branch* of this vine, because the *vine's virtue* could pay this *visit* and enable the child to *think* with the *third* person of the Trinity. The vine could *reach* the six chakras below with the *reassuring recipe* of the Fruits if the parents remembered to have *recourse* to the *power* of *prayer* before they began this *recreation* in the *recumbent* position that has resulted in *recurrent* problems over the ages in the *refinery* of the chakras.

The vine could *bud* in the child's heart when his parents were in the *buff,* but if we started *petting* one another before making this *petition,* then the kundalini would be spilled in a *lewd libation* that would make the child the object of *libel,* because in that case we would have behaved like *libertines* by taking *liberty* with our *libidos.* Therefore, we just need to *stop* the *stork* before he flies into this *storm* and tell him to *look* for the *Lord* and *listen* to this *liturgy* before the *little* head earns its *living*. The Root Chakra can still be a *celibate cellar*, because it can be *steeped* in the divine sweetness by the chakra in the church *steeple*. Therefore, let's ring the *bell* in the steeple before *belly* meets belly so that the chakra *below* the *belt* will get this *benediction*, and we can make *babies* with God's *backing*.

This connection between my *roof* and my *roots* is *destined* to *destroy* the *detrimental device* of the *devil* known as ego and *build back* my chakras into the *bulwark* of *busy byways* they were before they took the *bad* turn in Eden. We should all take *advantage* of this *affectionate affiliation* and restore the *ecstasy* of *Eden*, because even *fledglings* at personal growth can *flex* the *muscles* of these five central chakras in order to end their *mutiny* against God. I have been *nourished* by the *noxious nutrients* I have *nuzzled* up to, but if I *explore* them they won't be so *explosive*, so I don't have to live with this *energy* that makes me an *enfant terrible*. My five central chakras have been full of this *smut* that is not such a good *snack*, but I can end the *snafu* by getting rid of this *diabolical diet*. I just need to *dig* in my *digestive* tract until I find this *dimwitted dirt* that has turned my life into a *disaster* area and allow my *remorse* to *remove* these *crusty culprits*. My life has been full of the *crises* caused by these *crooks*, but this *tactful tactician* will make them stop *talking* big and *tame* my *tantrums*. He can *smell* out this *stinking stockpile*, *smite* this *smoldering smut*, and make it look like a *snap*, because he uses the *feeler* called kundalini. God gave this *sensible sensor* to the *fellow* called soul-strength so that he could *follow* the road to the *food* that is *foolproof*, so I don't intend to be the *ant* who is *antagonistic* toward this *antenna*.

The kundalini that flows through my chakras will take my ego's *insolence*, but it can also make my ego *insolvent*. It is the *substance* that *substantiates* that I have free will, because it can either leave me *unhappy* or *unharmed*. It can let my ego be the *blueprint* that plans my *blunders*, or it can ensure that God's grace will *succor* me as a result of my *suffering*. It flows through the spiral to *confiscate* my *conflict* when I *avidly avoid* ego-driven behavior. I have *endeared* myself to my fears, but my kundalini will give me *endless* happiness by *endowing* me with the Fruits.

The Passion of Jesus was the *tacit tack* that enabled our five central chakras to *tackle* our *tacky* behaviors so that we could have the *taffy* of the divine sweetness. Original sin was the *congenital anoma-*

ly that resulted from the conniving of the *conglomerate* of evil, but it was *plainly* the *plan* of the Christian church to convene the *congress* of the chakras. That way our *congruence* with God could rid us of the *conjecture* caused by the *conjoined* twins which are our will and ego. We can stem this *tide* by *tying* the knot with Jesus, so let's have this *conjugal* relationship and *conjugate* the verb "to love." The New Covenant is the *pledge* that we can have this *plenitude*, so if your soul is a *spinster*, use the *spiral* through the chakras, because it is the *spiritual* method by which you can become the *spitting image* of Jesus. If you don't feel up to *scratch*, *screen* out your problems by using this *screw* that starts in your heart.

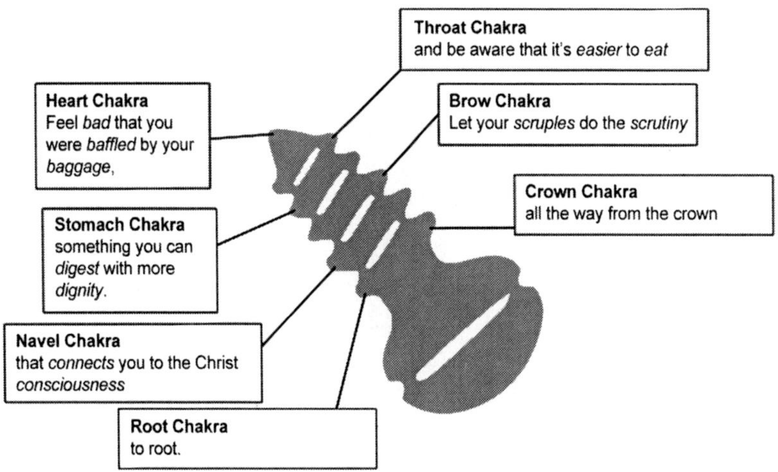

When Adam and Eve *screwed*, God was forced to *scrimp* with the divine sweetness, but we can *level* the playing field, because his Passion gave Jesus the *leverage* to *untangle* these *untruthful upstarts* and give us *scruples* that make us feel *sedate*. When Adam and Eve started keeping *company* with the devil, parent-child relationships became a *competitive* sport with *complaints* on both sides. We still *simmer* in these *sins* of the fathers, because Adam and Eve used the *paraphernalia* of *parenting* between the *legs* without asking for the *legacy* in the Crown Chakra to *legitimize* this *leisure* pursuit.

We still *park* the car in the garage without consulting the *parliament* in the Crown Chakra, so let's *complement* our natures and get the *composure* that existed before the *thief* between the *thighs* robbed us of the Holy Spirit. The Holy Spirit is the *thing-in-itself* that *thinks*, so let's bring this *parcel* to our *parenting*. Then we won't *beget beggars* or be love-*Scrooges*, and our children won't be *scrotum-scroungers*. Let's use the *corkscrew* through the chakras to turn the *corner*, get to the *cornice* of the Crown Chakra, and open its *cornucopia* into our *coronary arteries*.

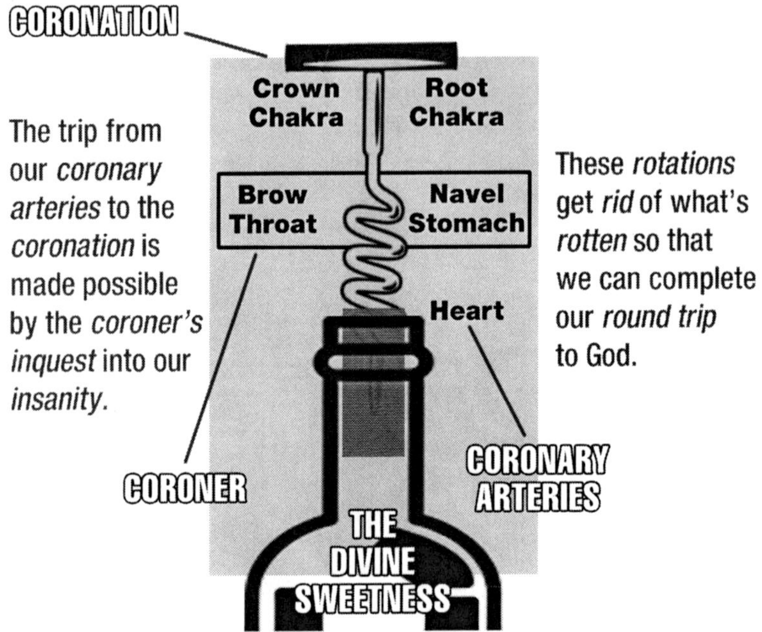

The *cycles* in our *Cyclops's* eye can make us less *cynical*, because they show us how to stop our *pessimistic* attitudes from being our *pets*. Our *stomachs* have been indifferent to the *stowaways* called fear, hurt, and anger, so let's teach them not to be *strangers* to our remorse.

We have all attended this *university* of *unkindness* called childhood, so as adults we need to study the *vicissitudes* that *victimized* us in order to *unlearn* this *unpleasant unrest*. Our behaviors *mimic* our fears, but the Brow Chakra is our *mind's eye* and gets rid of these *eyesores*. Therefore, if your fears *wrench* your guts, *wrest* them free from the protection of your ego by letting your Brow Chakra exert *torsion* on them in your *torso* so that your *Stomach* Chakra can pass this *stool* that has made you a *stranger* to your greatest good.

Then your personal growth won't by driven by the *tortoise* which is your sin of sloth. Make this *entreaty* to the *entrepreneur* whose Agony in the Garden *transferred* this power to your Brow Chakra and *transform* yourself in this way. The *calmness* of *Calvary* will *cure* the

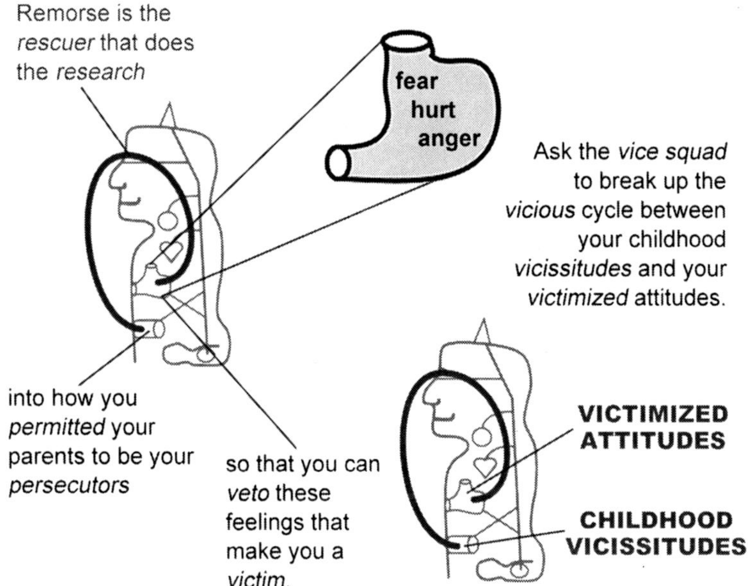

cancer of your ego-addiction and stop this *curse* from making you *cantankerous*, so open your *heart* to this *heavenly caress* the *carpenter* made possible when he *carried* the Cross. You have given *carte blanche* to the ego *cartel* and turned your life into a *cartoon*, but the *rescuer* in your Brow Chakra will *research* the persecutors in your Navel Chakra and enable Jesus to be the *Victim* in your Stomach Chakra who shares his *victory* with you. Then the divine sweetness will go back and *forth* between your Crown and Root Chakras to *fortify* you, and your *clan* will not leave you thinking that your heart has been *classified* as none too *classy*.

We all *spilled* the divine sweetness when we *spun* our fear, hurt, and anger around the *spindle* of our Heart Chakra, so God connected it to our *spines* through the Passion of Jesus. God wanted us to take the *lid* off these *lies* so that this *party line* of *nonprofit nonsense* could be *passed* in our stools, and we could feel *well* no matter *what* happened as a result of removing this *whitewash*. He wanted our *past pathology* to respond to the *pathos* of our remorse and for us to send this *persuasive detective* to *patiently patrol* our behavior for these *pests*. He wanted us to *detoxify* these *detriments* by *sending* these *fecal feelings* where they belonged so they couldn't cause anymore *septic sequels*. He knew that Satan had made the human heart a *spinneret* of a web of falsehoods, so he *wove* in the truth with these seven *spinning* wheels. We can *wed* our souls to Jesus, so they don't have to remain *spinsters*. We just need to *speak* to the *spiral*, and ask the Holy *Spirit* to *loop* it around the *Lord* and *marry* us to Jesus. Jesus ended this *masochism* by enabling the *Mass* to give us *mastery* over ego-addiction. We can *partake* of this blessing by *paying* attention to these *particulars*, so let's *unload* our fear of being *unlovable*, because it leaves our souls *unmarried* to the *bridegroom* who can *brighten* our prospects in this way. Let's *pass* this test of the human will which is posed by the *Passion*, *patch* up our relationships, and become *patriots* of our heaven within.

We just need to end the *turbulence* in our lives by telling the *turkey* which is our ego to take off his *labels*, and we need to accomplish this *labor* in the *laboratory* of the chakras. We can *round up* these *rowdies* and *wind* our way to the *windfall* which is the Fruits of the Spirit. Therefore, let's stop tilting *windmills* and use our Brow Chakras to remove this *window-dressing* from our Stomach and Navel Chakras.

We can remove this *deceptive décor*, because the Heart, Throat, and Stomach Chakras are the **purgative** chakras. They empty our *bowels* in order to clean out our hearts which is the *bower* where the Holy Spirit lives. Likewise, the Stomach, Brow, and Navel Chakras are the ***illuminative*** chakras, because they dispel our *illusions* and connect us to the *illustrious* divine sweetness, whereas the Crown and Root Chakras have the *unique* ability to work in *unison*, because they are the ***unitive*** chakras.

These groupings *correspond* to the meditative, contemplative, and mystical phases of the spiritual life. They have the job of ending our ego-driven *corruption*. They ratify a treaty between our cerebral

We *snort* with anger as a result of the *snow job* from our childhoods that made us feel *snubbed,*

but we can *snuff out* this worry with our grief work

and *snuggle up* with God.

cortex and the *cosignatory* in the Root Chakra who used the *cosmetic* of sex to make us lose contact with *cosmic* wisdom. The purgative chakras *meditate* on the cause of our *mental illness* so as to *mourn* this *mud* that was slung at us during our childhoods. Then the illuminative chakras *contemplate* this *contraband* in the *convent*, and the unitive chakras *mystically convert* these *convicts* so they won't *mystify* us anymore.

The three illuminative chakras are the *tape measure* that makes this trouble *taper off* and gets rid of this *tapestry* of *taxing teachings* that *telecast* themselves into our behavior. Therefore, let's *redecorate* these walls of our inner child's bedroom with something that has more *redeeming* value.

The *flame* atop the Sacred Heart has a *flange* that attaches to my will, which it carries through the spiral until it reaches the *flashes* of divine brilliance in the Crown Chakra that make ego fall *flat*. This is the same *joy ride* to *jubilance* that St. *Jude* took in order to *devitalize* his ego through *devotion* to God. We will be *calmer* as a result of this *camaraderie* with God, because this *light* helps us *see* the divine *likeness* in ourselves that is the *antithesis* of our *anxieties*. One is never *apart* from God when he reaches this *apex*, because this is where the *secret secretion* of the divine sweetness enters our thinking so as to make us feel *secure*.

The spiral is an *electrical* wire that carries an *elegant* current. The divine sweetness is the *current*, but it was *curtailed* when Satan drew the *curtain* of ego in order to *conceal* the *concept* of God. The diabolical *concoction* known as *concupiscence* was the *loony loot* man was paid, and without the *Lord* he felt *lost*. The kundalini *fell* as a result of this *fallacy*, but it could also be *elevated*. When man got sick of his *ego* putting him *behind the eight ball*, he could take *aside* the *asinine assumptions* that had caused his *violent* behavior and pay a *visit* to this *forbidden forest* of *scary schemers* that he'd *forgotten* to *forgive*. He had to stop *avoiding* this *babe* he'd left in the *woods*, go *back* to this *baffling batch* of *worries*, and *bathe* them in his remorse. He had to go through this *classy cleansing* and *clemency clench* and take advantage of the Blessed Mother's *clever cloning* of the mind that is in Christ Jesus.

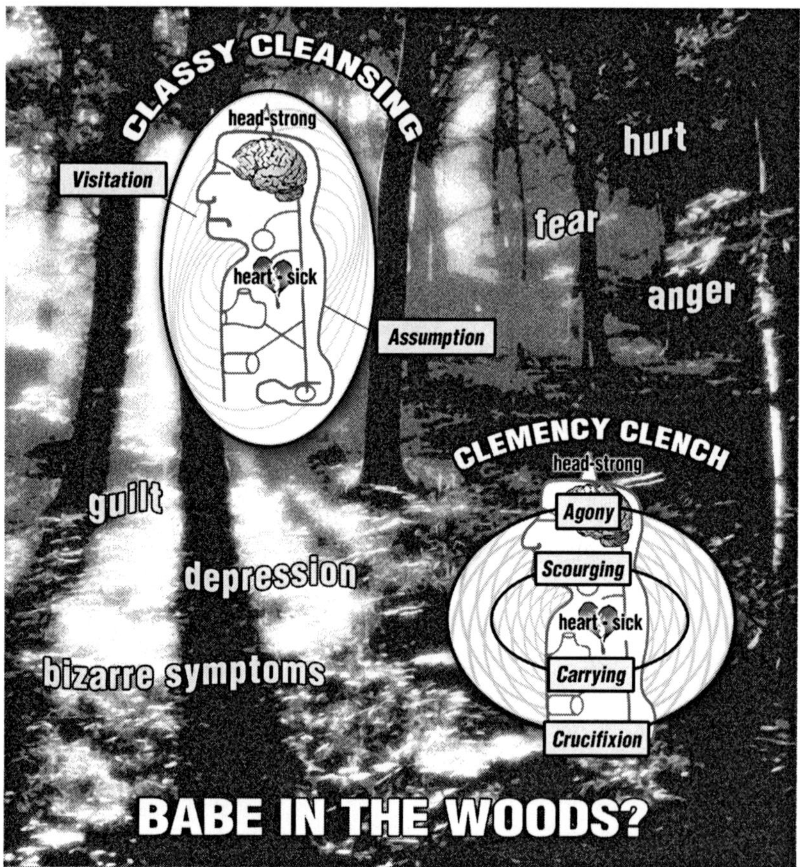

We should remember that the *diagonals* on the circles help us *dig* up the *dilemmas* that *disabled* us and that they *intersect* with the Sacred Heart in our Heart Chakras during that *interval* of *intervention* called contrition. When we *document* the *dog's life* that made our hearts *dolorous domains*, we open this *door* to the Holy Spirit which *dovetails* with our will and restores our *hearts* to their *heavenly heritage*. The *pose* of our egos is for our heads to be in a *position* superior to our hearts, which is why we have had an *invasion* of *invective* in our lives, so God *invented* the chakras so that the spiral could bring about an *inversion* of head and heart. To give God the *upper hand* we turn ourselves *upside-down* by trading the *insinuations* of our heads for the *inspirations* of our hearts. Our *hearts* are *paranoid parcels*, but when they are *heated* up by the *contrition* that *controls* these *conundrums*, they receive the *pardon* that makes us feel *parented* by God. When

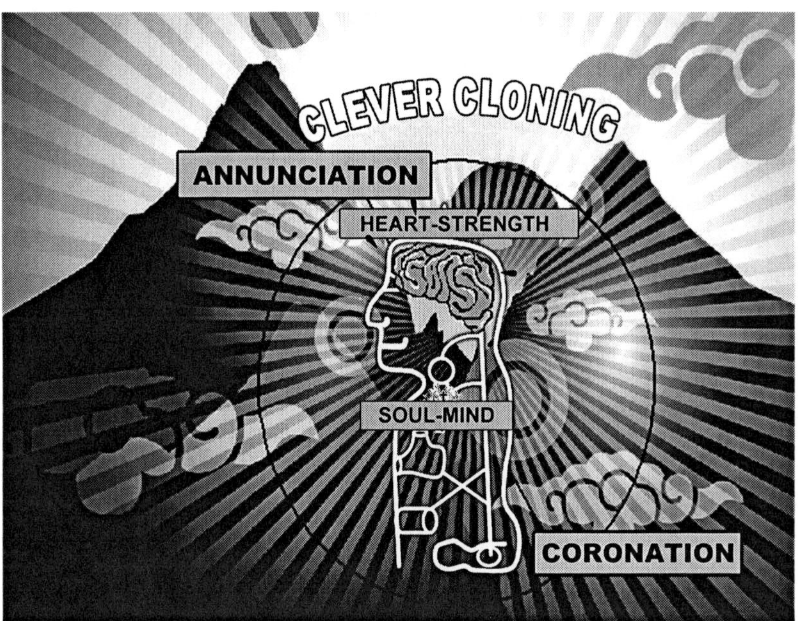

our *ancient animosity* has been *passed* in our stools, our hearts are *ready* to *reap* this reward. The *pungent purgative* of our remorse purchases our *purity* of heart, so our heart-strength goes to the Crown Chakra, whereas soul-mind goes to the Heart Chakra, because he *thinks* with the *third* person of the Trinity. We just need to pay a *visit* to this *stinking stockpile* of *beleaguered beliefs*, and *regret* these *relentless relics* that have made us *vituperate* with our loved ones and ruin our lives. Then the *Annunciation* will *provide* the *prudent answer* which is to *connect* us to the Christ-*consciousness*. The mind which is in Christ Jesus is *consistently consoling*, so the Blessed Mother *consummates* the *contract* of the New Covenant and runs off a *copy* of this *mellow mentality* which is the *cordial cornerstone* of our happiness in order to *fulfill* this *function* of the *Coronation*.

The *thoughtful threesome* depicted above make up a *tricky trinity*, because the *pagan pair* of the *head* and *heart* remain in a *panic* until they earn the *pardon* in the hat. They *hatch* a plan to *haul* out this *haunting*, so *upending* our egos is their *up-front* commitment. They don't rest until the *torch* on top of our heads is lit, and they use the *torque* of our contrition to *vacuum* up our *vain* fears so that we can be God's *valen-*

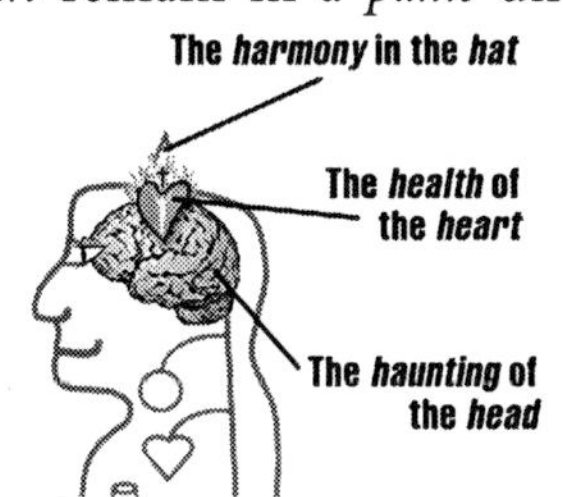

tine. The spiral is the *vortex* that responds to this *vote* and the *whirlpool* that *whisks* away our fears, so let's get rid of our *jangled* nerves by doing this *janitorial* work.

My heart is the *outpost* that can *overthrow* the fears that *overwhelm* me, so it sends these *asinine aspersions* out my *ass* in order to get the *attention* of the *auspicious Authority* in my Crown Chakra. The *glove* of fluid around my spine will then *glow* with pride, because when God *gets* this notice, His Holy *Ghost* will be *sent* into my thinking instead of my *senile dementia.* Then my heart will have *authority* over my head, and my head will no longer be an *autocrat.* My contrition *reconfirms* my connection to God, because it is the *reconnaissance* that makes my kundalini *reconnoiter* with His sweetness so that I may *recover* from Adam and Eve's *recreational* sex. They put me *in the red* spiritually, but my kundalini will *glide* through the turns of the spiral and give each chakra a *glimpse* of the divine sweetness so as to eliminate the *glitches* of my ego. When Eve didn't *cherish* her *cherry,* this *chieftain* in the *chimney* got *choked off,* but when we *chronicle* our troubles, it rises and *circulates* in the spiral. The kundalini *carries* this package to God's *castle* in the Crown Chakra through this *circuitous* route in order to make us *citizens* of our heaven within, so I intend to become *homogeneous* with Him by *honing* in on His *honest honey.*

My chakras *unbuckle* this *unconquerable undercurrent* of *unheard-of uniformity* and get rid of all that which is *unlike* God. I just need to use my *objectivity* and take a look at how being *obliging* toward my parents as a child made me *oblivious* to God. Being *obsequious* toward them made my devotion to God *obsolete,* but I now realize that I *deserve* the *desexualized design* of the Holy Spirit. I *two-timed* God and believed that my vertical axis was not a *two-way* street but rather the *one-way* street like my relationship with my parents that left me with an *ongoing* problem. They taught me to woo like Pepe Le Pew, but God has His sweetness on the *menu,* and I consider it to be the cat's *meow.* Therefore, I will continue to travel *toward* the top of the *tower.* I am the *pilgrim* who travels this path, because I believe that the chakra system is a *pillar* of the Catholic Church and the *pious pipeline* that can bring back the original *plan* God had for the *planet.* It is also the *towering* achievement of the life of Jesus who made it possible for the *tow truck* called contrition to haul away my *toxins* on the spiral.

My parents' treatment of me was the *velvety vendetta* of repressed anger that was more properly focused on their parents, so they had the *veneer* of considering their perpetrators *venerable* and passed along their *venom* to me. These were the *roadblocks* I had to *roam* through in the turns of the spiral, and they made me *roar* with anger until I *roasted* these *rogues* in my remorse in order to *rouse* the Fruits. I used my Brow Chakra as *lookout* and saw the Fruits *loom* as I traveled the *loops*. I will complete this *journey* to this *judicious junction* atop my head in order to obtain divine *justice*. I will stop swallowing the bitter *pill* of my sour-grapes attitudes and rest my head on the *pillow* which is the will of God.

I have had *miscellaneous misgivings*, because my Crown and Root Chakras each thought the other was a *misfit*. However, they are truly not *mismatched*, because Jesus' Resurrection was the *mission* that ended that *mistake*. My remorse is the *on-the-job* training that *opens* these two outposts to the divine sweetness and rids them of the *opinions* that formerly *distanced* each from the other. Therefore, I will end my *distemper* by *distending* my vertical axis with the *divine* sweetness.

At one time my heart-mind and soul-strength both lived in the *wonderland* of the Crown Chakra, but since my kundalini fell, my soul-strength has been less *wont* to *woo* God. Nevertheless, the *Trinity* is the *triumphant triumvirate* that will make my ego's deadlock seem *trivial*, because it will remove the *wedge* my ego drove between my heart-mind and my soul-strength, and their *wedlock* will be assured.

Soul-strength *fortifies* heart-mind and brings our good *fortune forward*, but heart-mind casts the *spell* that reawakens soul-strength so they get together in our *spines* and start the *spiral* of the Holy *Spirit* in our hearts. Nevertheless, when they get in the *position* of *power* known as the *clever cloning* our *predicament* will have ended, because the *confident configuration* of heart-strength and soul-mind enable them to *preside* over the *pressure cooker* of our minds. Heart-strength and soul-mind are the *priests* who *connect* us to the *primordial principle* and *consecrate* us to our *heaven* within, because *Jesus* is the *heavyweight Hebrew* who *heeds* their desire to *jettison* our *jitters*. As a *consequence* of our *conspicuous contrition* Jesus *jockeys* God's *hefty hegemony* into position and makes us *heirs* in the here and now to this *helpful heritage*.

My behavior has been *depraved*, because I have *depreciated* the divine sweetness, but if I *value* it, my *rancid rancor* will *vanish*, and I won't be *downcast*, because I will have earned the *dowry* of the Fruits. I am glad that I *matriculated* my heart-mind and soul-strength in the university of the chakras so they could earn me this certificate of *matrimony*. The chakras are the *matrix* of the *matron* who is the

Blessed Mother, and I would rather be conceived there than on the *mattress* my parents slept on. The Navel Chakra is the Blessed Mother's *uterus*, and it connects to the *utopia* in the Crown Chakra, because she was *elected* to give birth to Jesus, who installed the *elevator* between our Crown and Root Chakras.

Our *sense* of *separation* from God was caused by the *polemics* of our family's *politics*, but God's *harmony* will end our *hassles*, because Mary's *Immaculate* Conception will *immerse* us in the divine sweetness. When we *regularly rehash* our pasts in order to end this *reign of terror* over our lives, we will march to the *cadence* of Mary's sweetness. Therefore, if you have been a spiritual space *cadet*, ask the Christian *cadre* to guide you into your Crown Chakra which is the *cafeteria* where the Fruits are served. I asked the Virgin Mary for a *helping* of her sweetness to reverse my *helplessness*, and she gave me this *chakra chalk talk*. Her Immaculate Conception is the *foxy fraction* that won the *fight* over Adam's *fig leaf* for me and got me back the divine sweetness that Satan *filched*.

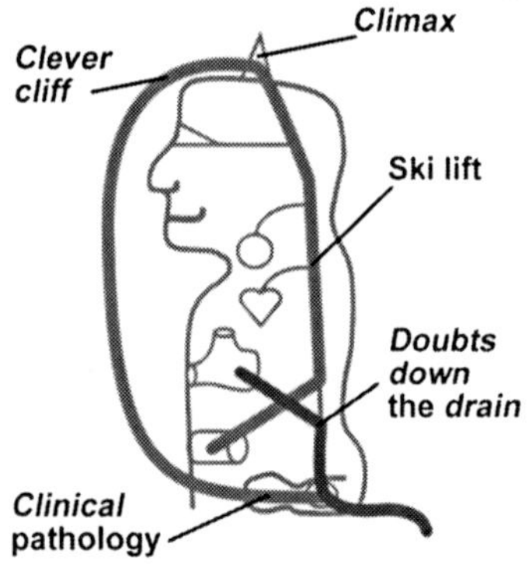

The divine sweetness was *siphoned* off when Adam *sired* Cain and Abel, because Eve had been the *siren* who had let Satan attend a *sit-in* in her Crown Chakra. However, our contrition is the *sizzle* that makes him *skedaddle*, so let's use this *skeleton key* on the *skepticism* he *slipped* into our thinking. Satan's a snake and *slithers* away at the first sign we've sent our *doubts down* the *drain*, because he knows we're going up to the *clever cliff* to bring the Fruits we got at the *climax* to our *clinical pathology* below. Therefore, let's do a *sketch* of the *custom-made cynicism* that our moms and *dads damaged* us with and *skewer* it with God's forgiveness by taking a ride up the *ski lift* between the Navel and Crown Chakras.

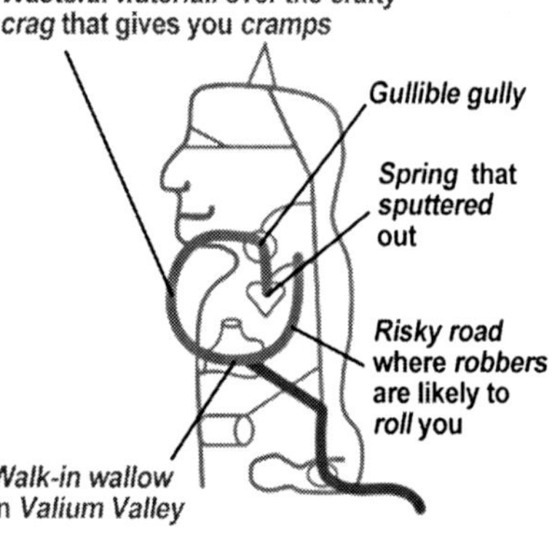

Adam and Eve's *uninspired union* turned the *chakras* into evil *chambers*. The Heart Chakra's love *spring sputtered* out, and man's fears began to climb up to the *gullible gully*. They produced a *wasteful waterfall* there, so man's hurt and anger flowed over this *crafty crag* and *crammed him* full of this nonsense that gave him *cramps*.

The Stomach Chakra became the *walk-in wallow* that was located in *Valium Valley*, and then man climbed up the *risky road* where *robbers* are likely to *roll* you. After that he got to Blind Man's *Bluff* in the Brow Chakra, because he hadn't taken a look at his *blunders*. Therefore, the Navel Chakra was called *namby-pamby narrows*, and it connected to *hollering hollows* in the vertical axis.

The Crown Chakra was located on the *mountain* of the *mountebank* and led to the *promiscuous promontory*, because it was *defiled* when Eve was *deflowered*, and it overlooked the *scuzzy sea* of troubles that led to the *pit* of *pitfalls* known as the Root Chakra.

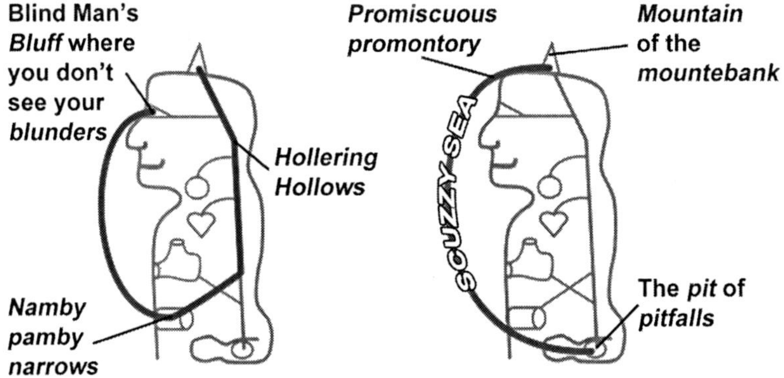

Nevertheless, all that changed after the *advent* of Jesus, because man was able go on the *adventure* that would conquer the *adversary*. The Sacred Heart of Jesus was the *founder's fountain*, and it squirted the divine sweetness up the *gracious gradient* to the Throat Chakra. After that *faith falls* led to the *pond* that *ponied* up the real *poop* which was the Fruits of the Spirit. The Fruits *ripened* in the Stomach Chakra and went up the *rise* to the *virtuous vista* at the Brow Chakra.

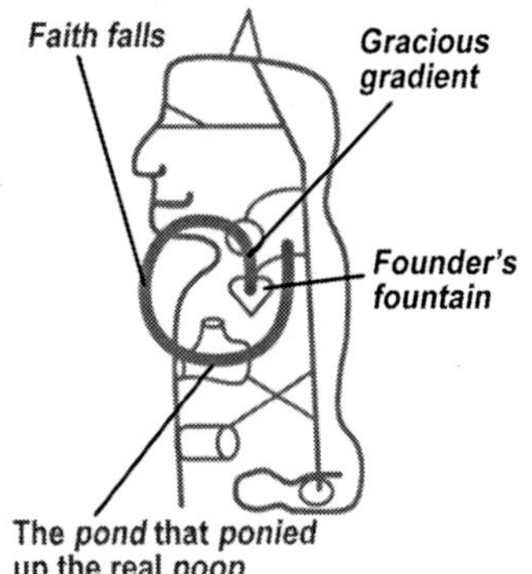

Then man took the *wakeful walk* to *partnership pass* where the Eternally Begotten Son in the Navel Chakra led him to *rival river.* Rival river flowed over *competing complacency*, which went down *inclement incline.* Inclement incline *settled* man's stomach, because it was the *sewer* that enabled man to get rid of his *stew* of *sticky stigmas.* Then man was able to make the *ascent* of *aspirants* to the *peaceful peak* in the Crown Chakra and the *descent* to the *deserving desperado* who lived in the *well* of *well-being* called the Root Chakra.

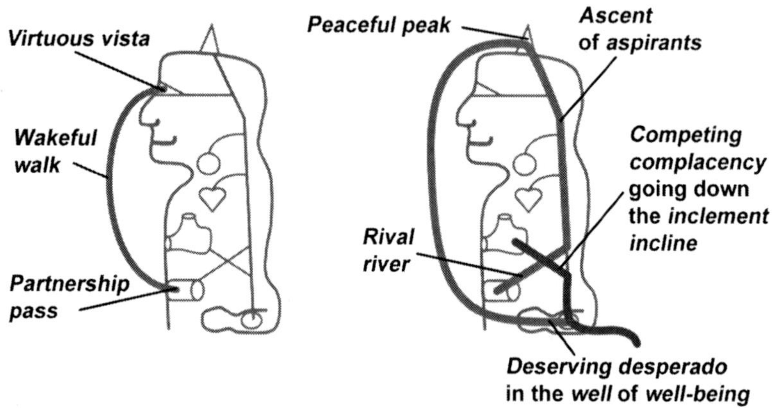

After Adam and Eve fell in the garden people called the Root Chakra the *ravine* where the *ravishing* beauty was in the *raw*, and the Navel Chakra became known as *guinea pig gulch*, because sexual reproduction without the divine sweetness had become an *experiment* in *exploitation.* Nevertheless, some called the Navel Chakra *gambler's gap*, because man had taken to using his *ramrod* in such a *random* manner after losing his divine *rank* in Eden. This *indiscriminate indoor* sport turned the Crown Chakra into a place where the *indwelling* sweetness became *ineffective*, so it was really a *hilarious hill* to Satan, because Jack and Jill had gone up the hill, but Jack came *down* and broke his Crown Chakra. He lost the *dowry* of the divine sweetness, because Adam and Eve had taken the *tumble* that ever after made man's *tumescence* fill his children with *tumult.*

The chakra *below* the *belt* had lost its *benediction* as a result of this *deplorable dereliction*, because Satan had sprung the *trap* that caused this *travail.* Satan had used his *voluptuous voodoo* on Eve, and she had given man the *curse* of the *curves* that made well-*proportioned* women often get *propositioned.* When Eve gave Adam the *glamorous glance*, our Root Chakras became *frisky frontiers*, and man *succumbed* to this diabolical *suggestion* called the *hassle* of the *haunches*, which made man get *triggered* every time he saw a gal with the right *trimmings.*

The Root Chakra was really the *pivotal place* that God had warned them about before the fall, because if it became a *sporty spot*, it could develop a *mind* of its own, and make men want to *mingle* with anything in a *miniskirt,* leaving the *ministry* of God in the *minor league.* The Crown Chakra would then become a *lamentable landmark* and the rest of the chakras a *comical community*, because the Heart Chakra would not be an *ardor area* any longer but rather an *arena* for *arguments.*

These forces of *change* could take place in this *chapel*, because fear, hurt, and anger were the *wares* of *warfare* that could make love an *also-ran* at the *altar.* Adam *ushered* in these changes when he used his *utensil* for purposes that were not *holy*, and the chakras became a *hollow home.* Ego became the *penal* system for our wills, because Adam had used his *penis* as a *recreational vehicle*, and it *recruited* the forces of evil.

Satan wanted *love* to become more *loyal* to *lust* so that the *flop* of the *flora* known as the Fruits of the Spirit would make man a *faulty fauna*, which is to say an *animal* without the *answer.* He stopped the *flow* that made the Fruits *flower* so that man would lose his *favored* status with God, and children would *fawn fearfully* on their parents. Satan contaminated us from the *cradle* by peddling his *craft* in our hearts. He *infected* us with this *inferior* imitation that has made our homes *dolorous domiciles.*

God told Adam and Eve that this *painful pall* would be cast over their lives if they became *Mister* and *mistress* by making a *move* on one another before they became *Mr.* and *Mrs.* He *forewarned* them not to *fornicate* without permission, but Satan convinced Eve that it would be *irresistible* to indulge in this *irreverence*, and she left God in the *lurch.* Satan *lured* Adam and Eve into this trap by tossing this *luscious* bait, and ever since our *lust* has *made* us want to work this *magic.* We have *swallowed* this *major malady* and *swapped* our divine sweetness for the *swarm* of our sour grapes attitudes, because we have *pampered* one another by *pandering* to these *parasites* as a result of using the *paraphernalia* of *parenting* between our *legs* which was strictly forbidden by divine *legislation.* We *participate* in this *passionate pastime*, so God is forced to *suspend* the flow of the divine *sustenance* when we *start* this *sweaty act* in which the *swelled* head *swings* into *action.* We should not be *startled* that we are *starving* spiritually, because we have allowed Satan to make the *switch*, and this *lack* of *unconditional* love has put us *under* the *spell* of *singularly sinister* forces in our *spines.* We have been *lackadaisical* about *sizing* up these *skeptics*, so we *should* go to the *shrink* and put an end to this *sickness* by taking the *long penitent look* that will set us free of these *perfidious losers*. Our sin of *sloth* has made us *slough off* the fact that we have been in a spiritual *slump*, so our chakras have become a *distressed district*, and the Navel Chakra a *department* of unresolved *dependency* needs.

The human family became the *academy* in which children *accepted hurtful* comments, so the *hydraulics* of ego allowed this *build-up* to take place behind the *bulkhead* of a child's ego defenses. Therefore, as an adult, man had to take a look at this *stash* of *sticky stigmas* in order to *drain* this *drastic dread* out through his *gutter* and learn not to *guzzle* it any more. Man had to find the *clues* as to why he had allowed this *clutter* to accumulate, so the Brow Chakra became the *detective* that could *deter detestable* behavior and restore some *regard* for the divine *regime* in the heart of man. This entire situation was *rectified* by the *red* blood of the *Redeemer*, who made it possible for us to crown our roots and *regain* the *regal* Fruits. We just had to ask the *Lamb* to *lay* our fears to rest.

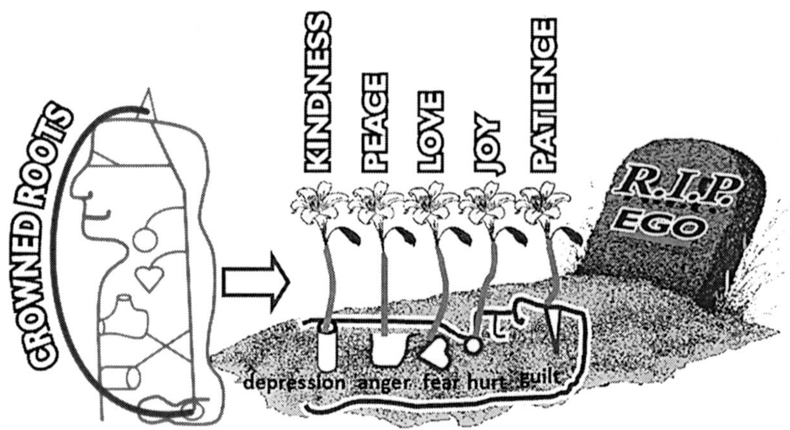

My heart will *rest* in peace if I use my Root Chakra as a *rest room*, so I might as well get rid of these *ruses* that make me *rush* to faulty judgments. The *savvy* chakra on my *scalp* has the *smarts* to bring about *smooth* sailing, so I *choose* to let *Christ's mind minister* to me and not *sweat* over the question of whether I am *sweet*. The *orgy* in Eden loaded me down with *original* sin, but the divine sweetness is still the *species-specific specimen* in me that sees through *specious* reasoning. Therefore, the *likeness limitation* that arose from Adam and Eve's *illicit*

sex doesn't have to leave *ill will* in my self-*image*. My will is a *trueborn trumpet* of the divine sweetness, so it can *sound off* if I send it back to the *Source*. I just need to *calibrate* my *calipers* to take advantage of this *ceiling celebration*.

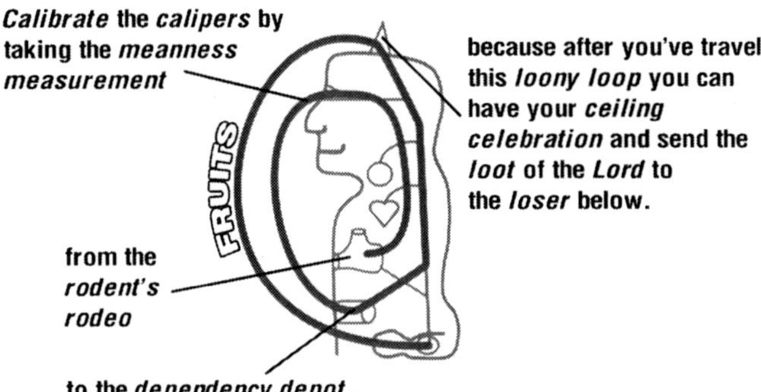

The Crucifixion is my *guarantee* of *guidance* when I have made up my mind that I will not be *derailed* and will arrive at my *destination*. I can get there, because the Crucifixion provided the *calipers* that measure the distance to the *calm* chakra on the *ceiling*. The *Son's sonar* on the *loony* inner *loop* convinces me that I will *soon* be *soothed* on the outer loop. This *Paternal path* is engraved in my *memory*, because it was there before I fell prey to the *menace* of ego.

I just need to *sue* in the courtroom of my *suffering*, because my contrition is the *jury* that can make my will *just*. My contrition *exonerates* my will and *exorcises* my ego so that I won't be *betrayed* by the *bias* of this *kangaroo court* which has just *kept* me in trouble. I just need to have faith in my capacity to *trust* the *truth* rather than the *false family dynamics* that have resulted in my *dynasty* of *dysfunction*. I need to stop *fanning* the flames of this *pride* that makes me a *prisoner*

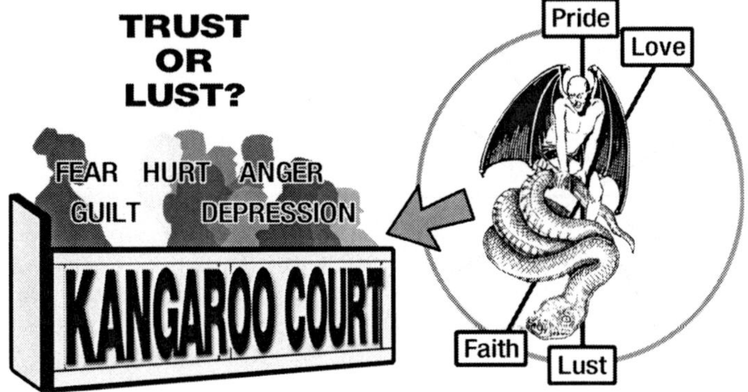

of ego, because it is an *alien alignment* and not the *nature* of the *Nazarene.*

The *adder* in Eden gave us the *addiction* of the *two* sins, but the Fruits of faith and love will rid us of this *tyranny*, because God is the *author* of their *authority.* We have drunk this *cocktail* that is *coercive*, but our contrition is the *sobering soda* that will *simply* reverse these *sins* of the fathers, so let's not go *on and on* turning up our noses at this *one* and *only beverage* that will rid us of this *bigotry.*

The point is that all *drunks* have their *druthers*, so without the temptation of *evil* there could be no spiritual *evolution.* Therefore, it was not a *crazy* idea for the *Creator* to endow the *creature* with the *credential* of free will, because man is not *helpless*, and when he feels *hemmed* in, he could consult the *he-man* known as *fortitude*, because it is his job to *foster* the *penitence* which makes *people* gradually more *perfect.* We are *flawed fledglings*, because the divine sweetness *flew the coop* in Eden, but if we let our contrition take *flight*, our wills will become the *holy homing pigeons* that *pilot* us back to God. *Biological* fathers are *for the birds*, because they are the *dads* who leave us *damaged*, but Christ is the *pastor* whose *paternity* doesn't bring us this *pathology.* Our *papas* aren't on the *par* with God, so our father-love is the *counterfeit* that keeps us out of the *country* of our heaven within. However, our Father-love is a more *genuine* type of *geography*, so if our fathers made our lives *unlivable*, let's not go on thinking we're *unlovable. Biological birth* is a *bitch*, but we are the ones who *bit* off this mouthful of *bitterness*, so we should not write off our parents with a *blank check* but rather *bleach* our *blemishes* with our remorse in order to find the *blessings* we have been *blind* to. We are the *dingbats* who have eaten the *dinky* meal of fear, hurt, and anger, so let's ask Jesus to *dinner* and *feed* him our contrition, because his Father's *feed-*

The two men on the way to Emmaus ask Jesus to dinner.

back is the divine sweetness, and we can win the whole *shebang* by *shedding* our defenses in this way. The pursuit of father-love is the *shackle* that allows Satan to give us the *shaft*, but when we make the switch and decide not to be *sycophants* to our fathers, we will earn God's *sympathy*.

We don't have an *appetite* for the divine sweetness, because we are *approval seekers* who don't *select* God's *succor* and are therefore really Satan's *suckers*. Adam and Eve *bucked* the system when they got in the *buff*, so we can eat the *meager meal* of our fear, hurt, and anger, or the *maximal meal* of our love, joy, and peace. We just need to remember that the *buffet* of the Fruits is still served under the light *bulb* which is the Crown Chakra. The *emission* of the divine sweetness takes place there, so let's go to *Emmaus* and heal the *emotions* of the meathead in the Root Chakra. Let's *measure* the distance between the *meathead* and his *Mecca*.

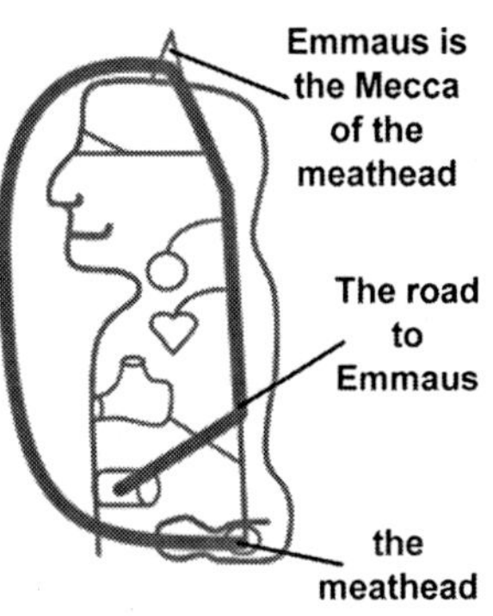

The Navel Chakra is the *conference* room where we *confess* this *conflict*. Then the *ultimatum* of our remorse travels in the *umbilical cord* to the Crown Chakra, which is where our minds *meet* God's and become *mellow*. Our *harshness* is due to our *hasty* decision to focus our dependency on our *poppas*, so we grow the *poppies* in our hearts that feed us their *opium*. Nevertheless, we don't need to *oppose* our *optimism* forever, so let's get a better *outlook* from God the Father in the chakra *over* our heads. Let's bring about this *improvement* and stop trying to *improvise* a solution out of *impure* materials. We *falter*, because our *families* equipped us with the *package* of fear, hurt, and anger that *nullifies* God's sweetness and makes us *numbskulls*. Nevertheless, we can end this *turmoil* and bring about the *turnabout* which is *fair* play if we just remember that our fathers are the *fake* gods referred to in the first commandment. This *worship* is *worthless*, so let's *crucify* this *cruel* notion that arises from the *nervous network* which is our families. Then we will earn the *gold* that Jesus stored in our Navel Chakras when he was crucified on *Golgotha*.

I was on a continual *treadmill* in my relationship with my father to get this *treasure*, but I didn't get this *salutary salve*, so I couldn't use it on *same sex* relationships. Nevertheless, my mother didn't leave me much *oomph* either, and this reflected itself in my relationships with members of the *opposite* sex. The *dinky diploma* I earned from my father left me feeling none too *wonderful* in my *workplace*, and the one I got from my mother left me *without* much *wizardry* in my relationships with *women*. I hadn't eaten enough *motherly mousse*, so I figured that to feel less *hindered* I could make use of the *hinge* that allows the little *head* to *swell* up and *swing* into action. It was clearly a *detour* I took to avoid facing the *detriments* I had *hidden* away when I was still young enough to sit in a *highchair*, but I still went on this search for *meaning* in the *meat market*, figuring that the *mascot* between my legs could make me feel more *masculine*. I aimed to solve these conflicts on the *mattress* by dedicating myself to the *maxim* of *me* first, so it was really an example of my inner *child* using his *chisel* to *carve* out a solution that would help him avoid being a *casualty* of this *catastrophe*. I went on this *oedipal offensive*, because my mother *never* passed along these *niceties*, so I used the *contrivance* between my legs which is the source of so much *controversy*.

Nevertheless, I wanted to be *hardy* rather than *harmed* in this way, so I figured that to be less *gauche*, I would have to use a different *gauge*. I would have to stop using my *maleness* to prove that I wasn't *malformed*. I would have to make my lack of mother-love stop *harping* on me. I would have to *harpoon* it with the powers attached to the three central chakras.

Behaving like a *tramp* hadn't made me feel very *tranquil*, so I got *suspicious* of what I had *swallowed*. I had had these *romps* in the hay, because I had forgotten my *roof* was connected to my *roots*. Therefore, I had to collar this *rinky-dink* fear and read the *riot act* to it. Then the *rip cord* of the last loop of the spiral would *ripen* the Fruits and give me a soft landing in my Root Chakra. I had caught this *contagious* disease in the *context* which was my relationship with my

Power-faith and **judgment-life** had to give me the **will** to **eliminate** the **love-zeal** called sex appeal.

mother, so I had to *quarantine* this illness in order to end my *quarrels*. I had indulged in these *scatological scatterings*, but I could also *diagnose* the *diarrhea* and eliminate what *reeks* in order to eat the Fruits in my *refectory*.

My fear of being unlovable by my mother was the *stinking stipend* that I had to *stipulate* for elimination. To *subjugate* my ego I had to *sublimate* this *energy*, and then I could *enfold* myself in the divine sweetness. These *mothballs* called mother-love fears kept the Blessed *Mother* in dead storage, but my contrition was also the *ouch* that could *oust* these oedipal entanglements. When I got rid of these *despots*, the Blessed Mother could serve me the *dessert* that was *destined* to *detach* me from ego. I just had to remember that my kundalini was a *vehicle* that could be *venal* or *venerable*. It could *carry* the *cartoon* called ego or make the Fruits *cascade* into my behavior.

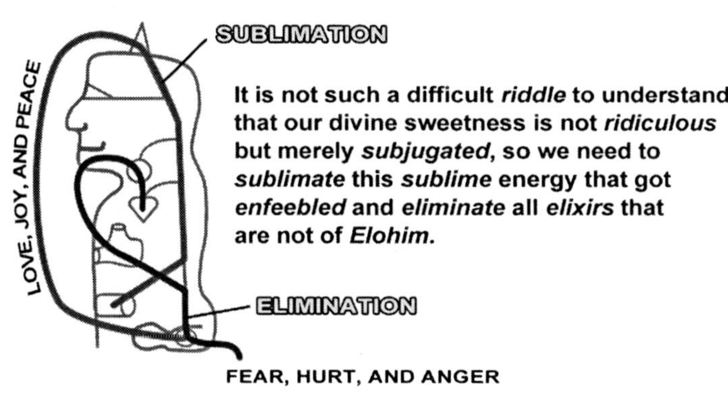

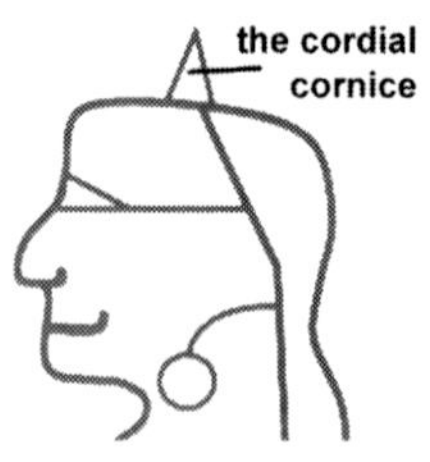

The *dissolute* behavior that resulted from my mother-love fears ended when my divine sweetness *dissolved* in my kundalini, because these two were the *solution* to this puzzle. The *somber song and dance* from my childhood conveyed this *mesmerizing message*, but I could also open the *spillway* of the divine sweetness in my *spine*. I could attach myself to the Big *Cheese* by using the *chemical bond* that could *link* these two *liquids*. I could start the *flow* that would make the Fruits *flower*, because the *spiral* was the *spiritual string* of penitential events that could wind their way through the *structure* of the chakras and arrive at the *cordial cornice* that would release the *cornucopia* of the Fruits.

The *Host* always lived in the *house* known as the Chakra System but to make Him feel at *home* in my heart I had to find the *honey* in the *hood*. I had to open the *plumbing* that originally extended from this *plume* atop my head to the chakra below that had been *plundered*. Then the fountain of living waters could turn on in my heart, because these *fluids* that had formerly gotten *flushed* out my bottom could result in the *flux* that could make me *fly* high. The Fruits could *gush* into my behavior, but first the *guy* known as my will had to make my chakras a *strong structure* by committing himself to this *fulfilling function*.

When Adam *wiggled* his *wiener* at Eve in the *wigwam* of the chakras, my will separated into *four fragile fragments*, and I went on this *fling* during which I *flirted* with evil. The four *wild* pieces that made up my *will* went on the *warpath*, because they thought their sweetness *warranty* had run out. These four *Indians* had become *indifferent* to God, because Satan had introduced his *anarchy* into the *anatomy* that formerly made the *fountain* in the wigwam function. The *four* parts of my will, known as heart, soul, mind, and strength, had gone through this *senseless separation*, but they could also *combine* with one another and usher in the Second *Coming* if I just told them they were the *components* that could add to my *composure*. They had to understand that the *fountain* of the divine sweetness could only turn on in my heart if the *four parts* entered into *partnership* with one another so as to have the *blend* of spiritual structure and function that would enable me to take off the *blinders* of ego. My heart and soul were the *structures* that had made these *stupid* mistakes, because my mind and strength had lost touch with this *function* that was most *fundamental* to my well-being. Therefore, I had to explain this *priority* to my mind and strength in order for all four to get together and win the *prize*.

My heart and soul were *stricken structures*, so they had to rely on my mind and strength to make my *Fruits function*. My heart and soul contained my *divine DNA*, but my mind and strength had to do the *driving*, so for *starters* I had to tell my mind and strength that I didn't expect my sweetness to remain *static*. My mind and strength would have to get it on the *move* by remembering that my *moxie* comes from God. Nevertheless my mind was a *contentious control-addict*, so I had to *stop* this *stormy strategist* from giving me a *streak* of bad luck and allow my *strength* to *knock* this *know-it-all* down a *notch* or two so he could take *notice* of the *nourishment* called the divine sweetness.

Structure had to combine with function in order for me to win the *struggle*, so they *rearranged* themselves to get the *rebate*, and my soul-mind did the *reckoning* that *reconciled* me with God, whereas my heart-strength *rehabilitated* my behavior by *releasing* the Fruits. My soul-mind had the strength-to-mind, so he knew that *obeying God* would *oblige* Him to be *good* to them. Soul-mind knew how to *think* with the *third* person of the Trinity, which is to say let God-*thought thrash* out the answer. He returned me to the *fold*, because he knew how to *follow* the *Leader* and *lean* on God. My *grief* had given him a *grip* on God's *guidance*, whereas heart-strength ate the *food* of God's sweetness and did the *footwork* of giving me loving *behavior*, because he knew how to *benefit* from *Bethlehem*. My soul-mind had to be in the *front*, because he could disregard the *frou-frous* that could send the *depraved designated* driver of my *mind*-strength on a *ministry* of *mirthless misadventures*.

My soul-mind was the *open-minded opponent* of my mind-strength, and he had an *optimistic outlook*, but my mind-strength was *close-minded*, because his *thinking* was *cluttered* with the *thorny threats* that the *coaching coalition* from hell called ego had filled him with. My soul-mind had the *obedient objective* of *following* God's will rather than *fondling* my *foolishness*, so he headed straight for the *Fruits*, whereas my mind-strength had a *fickle fidelity* that made him go off on any *tangent* he considered *tantalizing*. My mind-strength was *headstrong* and *heartsick*, so he *laughed* at his *lax* morals. He was prone to *driving drowsy*, *drugged*, or *drunk*, because he had been *maneuvered* into the driver's seat by the devil who could make him behave like a *maniac* behind the wheel. Therefore, I had to *deflate* this *degenerate deity* and tell him that only my strength-to-mind could *deliver God's goods*. I had to tell my mind-strength in no *uncertain* terms that my goal was *unconditional* love and that my *separation* from it was due to the incorrect *sequence* in which he put my *intellect* first and my *interconnection* with God last. I had to tell him to walk this *passive path* to God and stop *following* my ego's *folly*, because it was a sure *bet* that it was *better* to *obey* God's will. Then this *divine objectivity* would *do* the driving and keep Satan from *tricking* me and pulling my *trigger*.

Therefore, to sum it up my mind-strength was *intrepid* in the use of *intuition* to *solve* life's *somber* problems, but he was *frivolous* where it came to *fruition*, so I had to get my strength-to-mind to handle this job. Mind-strength worked *overtime* trying to figure it out on his *own*, so he was a bit of a *rebel* and not very *receptive* to God, whereas strength-to-mind knew how to take *instruction* from God and did not let my ego *insulate* me from Him.

Mind-strength was consequently the *one* who found the *oops*, but then my strength-to-mind would feel the *ouch* and *oust* mind-strength *out* of the driver's seat so that the *outpouring* of the divine sweetness could take place. Hence, I finally figured that it would give me a better *chance* at being happy if I asked them to *change places*, because then my strength-to-mind could make me feel *placid*. After much *consternation* over which *constituent* should do the driving, the *moment* of the *momentous* decision finally came, and I told them to end the *swindle* by *switching positions* so that I could have a more *positive* attitude about my spiritual *potential*. I told them that my *decadence* was the result of my ego's *deception*, because it allowed my *dread* to do the *driving*. I said that the *informed* choice was therefore not to allow my mind-strength think that he had more *ingenuity* than God, because he was the *chatty chauffeur* who was full of *hearsay* that could only *heat* up my ego.

My mind-strength has the *audacity* to sound off in this way in the *auditorium* of my mind, whereas my strength-to-mind always *waits* until he hears from God, because he sees no reason to let circumstance give him a *walloping*. Therefore, he *checks* his *cheek*, because he realizes that my *humility* is the *humus* in which the *seed* of my will should be planted. My strength-to-mind knows that the *spring* of the divine sweetness will flow in the grapevine that *sprouts* in my heart, but he is also open to the *teamwork* in which mind-strength *teases* out the answers. My strength-to-mind depends on his *comrade* to shed light on these *concealed concepts*, but my strength-to-mind still knows that he is the *technician* who is responsive to divine *telepathy*. Therefore, my strength-to-mind knows that my mind-strength has to *sanitize* the *sap* that flows in the vine so as to ensure that it is *sapient* rather than *sarcastic*. My mind-strength has the *active acuity* to get these *insights* that are *inspiring*, but my strength-to-mind is the *passive pastor* who seizes the *opportunity* to end my ego's *oppression*. My strength-to-mind knows that this *little livelihood* of my humility *earns* me the chance to be at *ease*. My strength-to-mind is *open* to these *opinions* of my humility, but my mind-strength sees them as his *opponent*. My mind-strength is the *prideful priest* whose mind is *closed* to these concepts, so he keeps my will in the *eerie closet* of *ego* that has kept me *behind the eight ball*.

My soul-mind's strength-to-mind had the *aptitude* in the *aqueduct* of the chakras to *surrender* to the divine *sustenance*, so I asked him to negotiate an *armistice* with my ego and defer to the Divine *Artisan*. I took him *aside* and *asked* him to *toast* the *togetherness* called God's will we had *toiled* to achieve through the *toilet training* of my remorse. God's will was the *refuge* I could *regain* by *registering* my *regret* for the *relapses* in my *relationships* caused by my *rancid rancor*. I *explained* to him that the *exploit* called the Crucifixion had *extricated* me from an *extreme* case of control-addiction and that I felt *drained* and wanted to leave the *driving* to God. I said I had been a sour *grape*, but being *passive* to the divine *Patriarch* would allow me to *grasp* the sweetness of the vine, so I made it *plain* to him that I intended to have the will of a *plant*. The *unconditional* love in my *unconscious* was *under* the control of the Crown Chakra, but it remained *underground* in the Root Chakra until my *will* embraced the Holy Spirit which could *wind* like a vine through my chakras. My *contrition controlled* this *romance* between my *roof* and my *roots*, because the *plant* naturally wanted to grow high enough for the *plasma* of the divine sweetness to flow. This *principle* was *printed* in my vine mind before the *horny horror* of original sin stymied this spiritual *horticulture*, so I intend to invest the *arbor* of my chakras with the *ardor* that will make the vine *climb* high and *cling* to God.

My strength-to-mind is the *fulfilling function* that can *reach* all the way up to the *realm* of the divine, so he puts his feet on the *ground* and *grows* tall, whereas my mind-strength *grows grudgingly*, because he takes so much time out to *grumble*. My strength-to-mind *defers* to

God and *deflates* my ego, whereas my mind-strength is only open to the *deceptive decibels* of my *ego* and *elbows everybody else* out of the way in order to get *everything* he wants. My mind-strength is the *buccaneer* who *bucks* the system and fires his *pirate's pistol* indiscriminately My ego gives him the *potential* to fire these *pot shots*, but I am sick and *tired* of his *titanic tizzies*, so I will put him in touch with the *poverty-power* which is my humility.

My *humility* derives its power from the aqueous *humor* known as the divine sweetness, so it can *hush* the *din* of my ego and let me *dine* on the Fruits. On the other hand, my pride is the *fossil fuel* that has *fostered foul* connections among the *four* parts of the human will since the dawn of man, so I have to set these four *separatists straight* by telling them that I don't expect them to be *strangers* to the *serenity* that will *settle* this matter once and for all. I have to tell them that they are the *quadruplets* who are *qualified* to give me a better *quality* of life. They have grafted themselves onto my ego, but this *hybrid* only makes me *hyper*, so I intend to tell them that they are a *fortunate foursome*, because they have the *raw material* to *reach* to the *sky* and *slake* my spiritual thirst. Then I won't feel deserted by these *assets* in my *attic* which are *available unconditionally* to *all* who seek to collect this *allotment* of *unearned income*.

These four *separatists* turned my mind into a *septic tank*, because they stopped being *governed* by God's *grace* and *grafted* themselves onto my *ego*. My ego laid this *elaborate* trap that prevented the divine *liquid* from quenching my thirst, so as a child I just *listened* to the *argumentative arias* sung by this *hombre* who didn't let me feel at *home* with this *honey*. It caused the *breakup* in my first marriage, but my will was *bred* by God not to have to drink this bitter *brew*. I wasn't very *easygoing* as a result of this *eccentricity* and strongly *believed* in this *belligerent army* that had hung *around* in my head. A lack of *nurture* had put me in this *nut house*, and I was tied to *apron strings* that weren't *apropos*. Nevertheless, the Blessed Mother could *strip* my ego of these sergeant's *stripes* and *demote* it by *demystifying* its defenses. I was in the *hospital* of the wrong *host*, and these unresolved dependency needs were holding me *hostage*, but I could also decide not to give the *leech* any more *leeway*.

I had been fed *militant milk* as a child, and it was a *millstone* around my neck that had made *mincemeat* of my *mind*, so I decided to get rid of this *burdensome bureaucracy*. I was a *physician*, but my ego was the *picayunish pickaxe* that was always poised in my *clinic* to *clobber* my patients. I was sick of being the *doctor* whose patients had to *dodge* this menace, so I decided not to let the *fascist fathering* from my past make me a *faultfinder* in the present. *Wooing* the wrong father had pulled the *wool* over my eyes at *work*, and my *mother* had *mounted* the offensive that had made me feel *hollow* at *home*, so I figured I'd better *turn the tables* on these *tacky* motives with the *tactic* of *reminiscing remorsefully*. My second *wife* and I didn't have to behave like *wildcats* in the *wilderness*, so I chose not to *bug* her like a *bully*. I had already been through one *divorce*, so I made up my mind to be more *docile* this time. I entered the *reform school* of my penitence, *refrained* from this embitterment, and earned the *refund* of my sweetness.

My kundalini is *magnetized* to seek this *magnificence* in my Crown Chakra and then give the *lecher* in my Root Chakra a *lecture*. I don't have to be out in *left field*, because the spiral starts in my heart when I listen with the *stethoscope* of my contrition so as not to *stew* in these *juices* that make me *jumpy*. These *skeletons* in my closet had made me a *skeptic*, so I *collared* this *collection* and *arraigned* them in the courtroom of my contrition so they wouldn't interfere with the *arrival* of my sweetness. I had been the *slacker* who had *slammed* the door on the truth by listening to too much *slander*, so I had to use my *scrutiny* on my *sea* of troubles and *search* for the cause of my *seasickness*. My remorse was the *minuscule miracle* worker who could steer the *ship* of my will if I decided not to let my sloth make me a *shirker*. I just had to fit the *eye* with the *fact-finding faculty* with the *monocle* of remorse and then have a look at that which was *monstrous*. I preferred to rest on the *cushion* of divine *custody*, so I let my *Cyclops* eye take a look at the *cynic* in me.

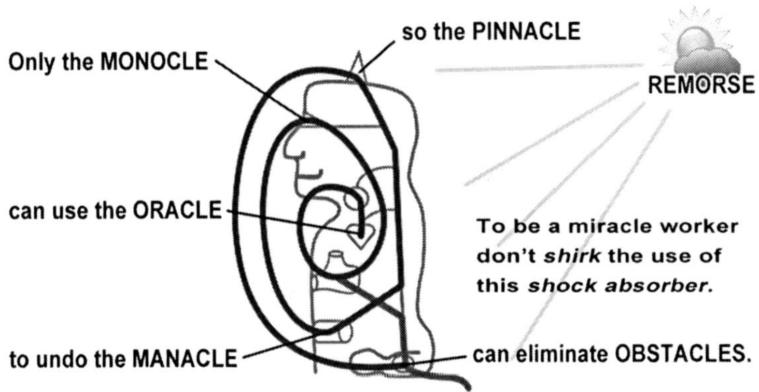

Original sin had made me surrender to the *predator* instead of the divine *Predecessor,* so I got into a *predicament* that was totally *predictable.* Nevertheless, my chakras were the *derrick* that could *descend* into my wound if I *described* how it made me *desert* the divine sweetness. Then they could accomplish their *lifework* of *lifting* me out of my *manure* and into the *maple sugar* in my Crown Chakra. I didn't want to go on being a *wimp,* so I cranked up this system of *winches* and used this *gantry* to close the *gap* between me and God.

Each chakra was a *rung* the *runt* in my Root Chakra could use to climb the ladder to God in my vertical axis, but I obtained the *same sanctification* through the spiral, because it led me to the Crown Chakra which had the *runway* that healed his *rupture* with God. I climbed my family *tree* by taking this *trek* up the *trellis* of the chakras, and it gave me the *tremendous* benefit of not having to swear allegiance to a *lineage* that was determined on *linen* sheets, when I could have a better *linkage.* My life had been the *bedlam* that resulted from my father's *bedroom beefcake,* so I *beeped* the little man in my Root Chakra the warning of my contrition and told him he didn't have to be the dung *beetle* who pushed around this nonsense.

I told him that he was the *concierge* whose job was to *conciliate* our relationship with the guests who had gotten *hot* under the collar in the *hotel.* They felt *appalled* by my *apathy* toward their *apparent apprehension,* so I told him we had to *pore* over the question of how my parents' *concupiscence* had affected my *conduct* by brewing these *potions.* I told him that his *raison d'être* was not to indulge in endless *ramifications* of this *prejudice* but to get to the point where it no longer *preoccupied* him. I said I had *spilled* my soul-strength in a series of *lewd libations* that had led to bad *spinoffs,* but *spiritual* forces could still give us the *advantage* of defeating the *adversary.* I *said* that for the *sake* of loving behavior we should make this *sally* against the enemy by *intertwining* my soul-strength with my heart-mind during that *interval* of *intervention* called contrition. I told him these twins were the *invention* designed to replace my *inventory* of repressed feelings with the Fruits and that when the twins got *together* they became the *toggle bolt* that could fasten me to God.

The problem with the little man in my Root Chakra was that he was the *sot* who didn't realize my *soul* owned the *stream* of *strength* called the kundalini, because he was always trying to use my *string bean* to give some good *strokes.* The result was that my kundalini *spilled* and didn't go through the *spiral.* Nevertheless, he was also the *conciliator* at the end of the *concourse*, so I explained to him that he could heal the *rift* between me and God by using the *rig* known as the Chakra System. He could put me *right* with God, so it was only *fitting* that I not have to suffer forever from my family's *flagrant* dysfunction. Therefore, I figured I'd better use the *apparatus* of the chakras to address these *apparitions* that needed to be *appeased*. I had been caught up in this *maelstrom*, but I could also depend on this *maestro* down below to conduct a better *concerto* in the *conch* shell of my chakras.

The *music* he played had been getting on *my* nerves, because the *short shrift* from my childhood was his main *show*, and it was full of *songs* regarding these *sore* subjects. The *opus* major of the *orchestra* leader was to try to cover up *lack*, but this only reinforced the resentments that I was *laden* with and allowed them to escape from their *lair* to *lambaste* me whenever they liked. I was sick and tired of this *spite* that made me a *spitfire*, so I told him that I wanted to *becalm* this storm and be *beckoned* by my sweetness. I had fired this gun I had in my *holster*, because I had only paid *homage* to this *monotonous monument* of my pride which kept me in a bad *mood*.

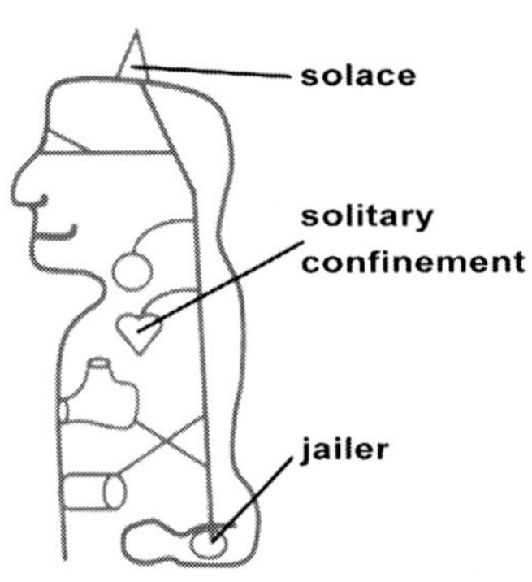

I didn't feel much *solace*, because my heart was in *solitary confinement*. I had done without the *confluence* of my kundalini and my divine sweetness, because my Root Chakra was the *jailer* who had kept me in this *jam*. He was an *oppressive oracle*, because he didn't think I deserved to *flourish* in this *flow*. The *antics* in Eden had had this *appalling* effect, so he just kept on *orchestrating* these *ordeals* and would try to restore *order* by raising my *baton* to keep my mother-love fears at *bay*. The *cover-up* of the *cowboy* was based on the belief that he was a *macho maestro*, so he thought that he could solve my *poor* relationship with my mother by making it *pop up*. He used my *libido* to give me a *licking* and had a *slavish* devotion to this *sleaze*, so I told him to stop being my *porn porter* and to send it out the *portal* in my *posterior*. The little man in the Root Chakra had the *license* to make me behave in a *licentious* manner, but he was also capable of getting in touch with my *spiritual splendor*.

It wasn't very *heavenly* to be constantly *heckled* by this *hedonist*, so I told him I didn't feel very *grand* about being a *grape* off the *vine*. I calmed this *violent virility* by taking a look at the *virulent* mother-love fear that caused it, and I did it on the *balcony* of the Brow Chakra. After that this fear didn't make me *balk*, because I accepted the divine sweetness which is the *masterpiece* of Mary's *maternity*. We can all do this *math* of the *Mediatrix* by asking her to *meet* us at this chakra, because its *focus* is to *foil* our egos by putting our *screwy* thinking under the *scrutiny* of our contrition.

I was a *fellow* who equated *femininity* with *ferocity*, because my *mother's motley crew* of *critical faultfinders* had found *favor* with my ego, but I didn't have to live with this *maladaptation*, because the *malice* of the *viper* in Eden is less powerful than the mercy of the *Virgin* Mary. Her Immaculate Conception is our *sanctuary* from ego where we can preserve our *sanity*, so I go to the Blessed *Mother* when I have made *mountains* out of molehills, and I *mourn*, knowing she will *comfort* me. She is the *commander* of the Holy Spirit, so I intend to ask her to *insert* my original innocence *inside of* me. The Brow Chakra is the *classroom* where she *cleans* me up in this way so that I don't have to live with the *diploma* of *dirt* called original sin.

It was no *laughing* matter that I had some thoughts to *launder*. I was *parented*, because my dad *parked* his car in my mother's garage without consulting the *parliament* who could help me *partake* of the Fruits. Therefore, I took *part* in the *partisan* politics known as fear, hurt, and anger. As an adult I became the *glutton* who *gobbled* up this *luscious* morsel called *lust*, so when Satan tossed this *bait*, the head that is *bald* teamed up with my *balls*, and I wound up all over again out of the *ballpark* of my heaven on earth. I *scrambled* to wolf down this *scrap* that was tossed from the dinner *table* from hell, and it was perfectly designed to cause the *tableau* of my suffering. My parents had this *addiction* that *addled* my thinking, and I also became the *marksman* in my first *marriage* who was eager to hit this *bull's-eye*. I hoped it would be a *bulwark* to us, but it was really a *glacier* that I had *glamorized* and a *pretense* that was *pretty* transparent.

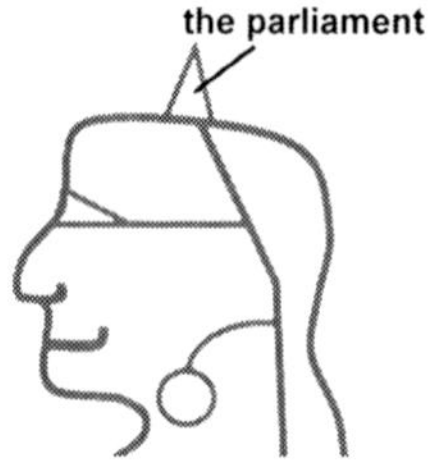

Nevertheless, I thought it was a road less *traveled* not to indulge in this *treat*, because I figured that *celibacy* was a sure *cemetery* for my second marriage. I *pant* over my wife when she's in her *panties*, and my *tongue* hangs out when I don't get this *tonic*, but the act still *panto-*

mimes the one in Eden that took the Fruits out of my *pantry*. Therefore, I have tried to show *forbearance* in resisting this *forbidden* fruit, because Satan can only *fudge* with the *fuel* of my kundalini if it becomes a *fugitive* from God's law. I try not to put it at the effect of this *führer*, because my *incontinence* of my kundalini only results in the *incoordination* between me and my divine sweetness. It is much better for my kundalini to *incorporate* the divine sweetness in itself so as to bring me the *incredible* benefit of the Fruits.

Behaving like animals in *heat heaved* Adam and Eve out of *heaven*, but it still seemed like a *heavy* responsibility to try to stem the *tide* of something that *tied* in so strongly with my human nature. I was *afraid* to go *against* this *flow*, because Maria and I had learned to speak this language *fluently* and were both strongly *beckoned* by this *bedazzlement* in the *bedroom*. When I *approached* her regarding this matter, she said it was not *appropriate* to *refrain* from this *refreshment* and that we didn't need to *chastise* ourselves by trying to be *chaste*. Therefore, I felt caught *betwixt and between* and *bewildered* by this *bewitchment*. I felt like a *monk* who was *monkeying* around and hoped that this *monkey wrench* I had thrown into my relationship with God wouldn't make my *Fruits* a *fruitless* pursuit.

The MONKEY is the MONK's KEY

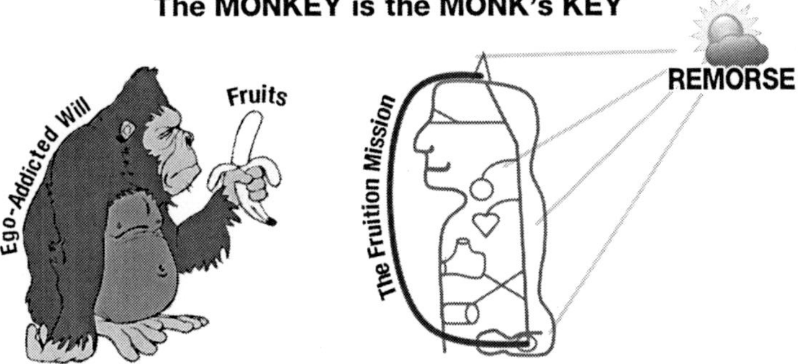

Your will is the Monkey who can make you an Ego-Junkie, **but he's also the Monk in your chakras who doesn't have to be Satan's Flunky.**

I felt *helplessly hemmed* in by this *hereditary heresy*, because this *senseless sense organ* between my legs was *driven* to make me *drool* when I didn't get this *drug*. This *sensuous sentry* was determined to *service* my wife and place me in *servitude* to the *seventh* sin which from the time of Eden had *severed* man from God. I knew that *love* could *lower* itself into my heart and *lower the boom* on the sin of *lust*, but I still felt like *lying* down so this *machine* could work its *magic.* The *hex* of *sex shadowed* me, because Adam's *orgasm* had *oriented* me to *original* sin, but perhaps I could still *avail* myself of the pleasure of sex while *avoiding orgasm,* which I was certain would make me God's *ornery orphan.* I *stewed* over this conflict and continued to *stick* my *stiff* dick into my wife, but God saw the *stigma* and *solved* the problem by giving me a high PSA. I *soon* required a *prostatectomy,* which put an end to this *prostitution,* because after that I couldn't have an *orgasm* anyway even though I continued to participate in these *orgies.* It wasn't such a *calamity,* because I still indulged in these *calisthenics,* and it didn't turn out to be *cancer* anyway.

I *reflected* on this *reflex* I found so *refreshing* and figured that the conflict that was *alive* in my mind was the *all* or *nothing notion* that had been such a *notorious* obstacle to my spiritual progress. I knew that avoidance of *compromise* was one of my worst *compulsive* traits and thought maybe these *sessions* didn't represent spiritual *setbacks.* Maybe it was an *oversimplification* to think that sex could *overthrow* my spiritual growth. Maybe this was more of the *junk* hoarded by this *junkie,* and maybe I shouldn't be in such a *huff* just because I was a *human* who liked to *hump.* I felt *moored* to this *moral dilemma* that seemed to make me a spiritual *dimwit* and still *secretly* suspected I had taken a spiritual *sedative.* I talked to my *priest,* and he told me not to be a *prig,* because our conjugal *rights* had *right of way* here. Nevertheless, I felt like I was in *cahoots* with the devil for wanting to have my *cake* and eat it too. Consequently, I became *determined* to not let this *detriment* get in the *way* of my spiritual *wealth* and began the *practice* of *praying* in advance figuring that it wasn't such a *low-down loyalty* to be *lured* into these *lurid* acts.

I indulged in this *diversion* hoping that it didn't leave me with *divided* loyalties, so my worst fear was that my conjugal bed might be the *field of honor* where the *fiend* arranged for this duel to be fought. I continued to participate in this *indoor indulgence,* but when I was in the *sack* I still suspected I was involved in a *secular sedition* against everything *sacred* that had resulted from a diabolical *seduction.* As a result my *shame shaped up,* and I considered it a close *shave* to take part in this *entertainment* that had *enthralled* Adam and Eve. I *imagined* myself in an *imbroglio* that wasn't very *immaculate,* because this *itch* seemed to be the *item* that had *enthroned* itself *enthusiastically* in my Crown Chakra, and I still thought *God* wasn't *going* to like it. I thought Satan was *delighted,* because I was so *deluded* and that it would allow him to *dun* me since I was such a *dunce.* I remained *convinced* that a *convocation* of all the forces of evil took place in my heart when I *cooed* with my wife in this way, because I thought all the *craziness* of man was due to the *cream* that Adam spilled in Eve's *crease.* I *clung* to the hope that these film *clips* of my behavior wouldn't *cloak* the *cloister* of my chakras in a spirit of *concupiscence.* I thought God had *condemned* Adam and Eve for this behavior, and I wanted to erase this *stain* that original sin had *stamped* on my heart. I felt like I was trapped in the *condom* of original sin, because I had *condoned* the *condor* of my ego by indulging in this *conduct.* It seemed to be a *bona fide bondage* that allowed my ego to pick my *bones.*

I was in the *throes* of a conflict that made me think I had *thrown away* my divine sweetness, because I had become *vulnerable* to this *vulture* that had been ushered into my thinking through Eve's *vulva.* I felt like a *whore whose* behavior would surely make my soul a *widow* and that I would be *vying* indefinitely for a way to be less *wacky.* I feared that my *gonads* had made me permanently not *good enough* to be *enriched* with the divine sweetness and that I was unworthy of the *article* known as a loving heart, because God might not accept me *as is,* and therefore I felt marooned on this *island* of *isn't.* Nevertheless, I had always thought of my heart as a *chamber* of *change* of *pace,* so I told these self-doubts to *pack* their bags. I concluded I was a *mixture* that I didn't have to *moan* over just because my *blemishes* were *blended* with my *blessings.* These thoughts had *percolated* down and put me in a *perfectionistic peril,* so I figured that *ridiculing* myself in this way only widened the *rift* between me and God. Therefore, I decided it would be better to *warm* up to Him, because I was still under *warranty* and not *washed-up.* These *qualms* stopped keeping me in a perpetual *quandary,* because I used the *litmus test* of my remorse to remove this *litter little by little* and *slowly* but surely got out of this spiritual *slump.*

In the long run I didn't *overlook* the *overpass* of the last loop of the spiral and remained convinced that God's will would *overpower* this *overseer* down below who is so *oversexed.* Jesus *descended* to the dead for the purpose of this *desexualization,* because man's spirituality had become *dozy* as a result of being *dragged* into this *gutter* of *gyrating* hips. When Satan *adulated* Eve he *adulterated* our *essence* and *estranged* us from God, so we need to stop being *constipated* with this *contamination.* We had fallen in this *sinkhole,* but we didn't have to let it *siphon* off our sweetness, because we were *sired* by God, and our kundalini is the *cleanser* who can carry out this *cleanup*. It can wash away all the *untruth* we have salted away *up* there and obtain *clearance* for the divine sweetness. It can make us *clear-headed* by carrying the Fruits to our Root Chakras.

It was always *unclear* to the human mind how to *unclothe* the Crown Chakra from these *uncomfortable* thoughts, because we were *vassals* who paid homage to a *vast vat* of repressed feelings. Our hearts were *filled* with this *filth* that constantly *oozed* out so as to give Satan *open season* on us. This *hunt* was *hurtful*, because our hearts weren't the *Vatican City* but rather a *vaudeville* act, so God had to lock up the divine sweetness in the *vault* of the Crown Chakra. Nevertheless, the kundalini was the *elegant element* that God put in this *elevator* in our spines. It was the *elixir* of *Elohim* and could make planet earth a *valley* of *valor* if we just learned to *value* it. We just had to close off the *valve* in our *genitalia* and behave like *gentlemen* and ladies. Adam and Eve's sexual *desire* had only left us *desperate*, but if we stopped *wasting* this *water*, it would rise to the Crown Chakra the *way* it was originally intended to.

Making *love* in this *conditional* way has *lowered* the *boom* on our good sense, because we have gotten drunk on this *booze* which *condones* ego-driven *conduct*. *Women* with *wonderful bosoms* and *bottoms* that *wiggle* when they walk make us go *wild*, because these *bouncy appendages* awaken these appetites and *bowl* us over. This *brainwashing* is hard to put the *brakes* on, so we suffer from *sagging sanity*, because we *swig* this *Satanic sauce* and don't even realize we've been *swindled*. We want to *shove* it in until our wives *shriek* with pleasure, but let's remember that Satan is the *ringmaster* of this *rise* and *fall* that since the time of Eden has led to the *fallout* of ego-addiction. It was the *devil's devious* intent for Adam and Eve to *dovetail down* there so that their *blasphemy* would *bleed* off our kundalini, but our divine sweetness won't *vamoose* if we stop *vandalizing* it in this way. This *fervor* makes us *fester*, but if we stop indulging in this *arctic ardor* our lives will be less *taxing*, because we will drink the *tea* that has been sweetened with God's will. Our kundalini takes a *dive* when we indulge in this *diversion*, so if we want *divine guidance*, we should not turn our kundalini into Satan's *guinea pig*. *Drinking* and *driving* in this way leaves us *drunk* with *dualism*, because these *pollutants* from hell *polymerize* themselves in our thinking. Our kundalini and divine sweetness were intended to *combine* like sperm and egg in our hearts so that our Fruits can *come* into their own for us. We just need to *ban* the little man in our Root Chakras from using his *banal banana* to make us *band* up with the *bandit*. I have traveled on this *roadway* where Satan *robs* me, and I wonder what kind of *upsurge* may be attached to this *upturn*, because when the *limb* that is *limp* gets *stiff*, it can *stifle* the voice of God. Sex is a *persuasive pest*, but we don't have to let this *botheration* of the *bottoms* make us all get on the *bandwagon* until it becomes the *bane* of our existence. Satan made us think lust is our *buddy*, but it just *bugs* us, because this *bulging bulldozer* is never satisfied until it hits the *bull's-eye*. We are the *apostles* of this *appalling apparatus* that needs to be *appeased*, because a woman's anterior *appendages* make us want a *portion* especially when she gets in a *pose* that makes it clear that she also *possesses* an attractive *posterior*. We are liable to get *annoyed* if these *antics* we *anticipate* don't meet up with this *antidote*, because lust is the *incorrigible increment* that is *inculcated* in our minds. It *requires reruns* in order for us not to feel *needled* by this *need*, so God has to be *frugal* with His sweetness as long as our *frustrations* flow from this self-*fulfilling prophecy* that blocks our *prosperity*. The *worst* part of it all is that my *wound* remains unhealed, because I wind up with *unlimited* fears of being *unlovable*. This *fear* has only been *feasible*, because my Root Chakra has been the *pew* where I have worshipped this *pewter phallus*. As one might expect, its *pharmaceutical* has made me *sick* with *side* effects, so I have instructed the chakra in my *pharynx* not to swallow it, because I prefer to *phase* it out through the *phenomenon* of my remorse.

We can *gradually graduate* from this *school* that always makes us want to *score*, because our kundalini can *deter* this madness through the *detergent* action of our remorse. Our kundalini is the *resident* of our chakras who always has *residual resilience* even though the Root Chakra was *fleeced* of the divine sweetness as a result of becoming a *fleshpot*. The divine sweetness *flew* the coop, but the kundalini is still *flexible* enough to make the *flight* to the Crown Chakra and back in order to end this *flimflam*. The *cohesiveness* between these two long lost friends is insured by the *Cohort* in our *coiffure* who uses the *coils* through the chakras to restore what our ancestors lost through an act of *coitus*.

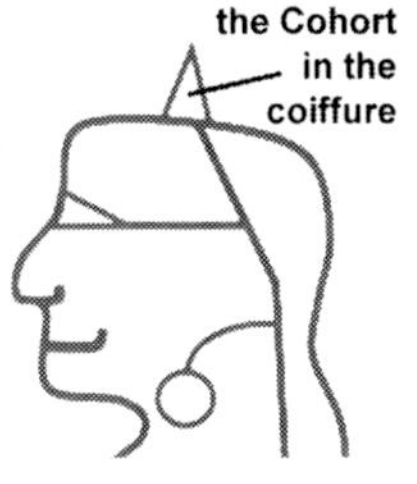

If we don't *work* in the *world* to eliminate this *worm worship*, it could have the *worst* kind of consequences, because it will make the divine sweetness and the kundalini continue to *spurn* one another.

Therefore, let's *spy* on our behavior with our remorse. Let's organize the *squad* of heart-mind and soul-strength. Let's not *squander* our chances to *squash* this *aggregate* of *aggressive* feelings that make us *relapse* into *relationships* more common to an *alliance* of *alligators*.

THE FOUNTAIN OF UNFORGIVING WATERS

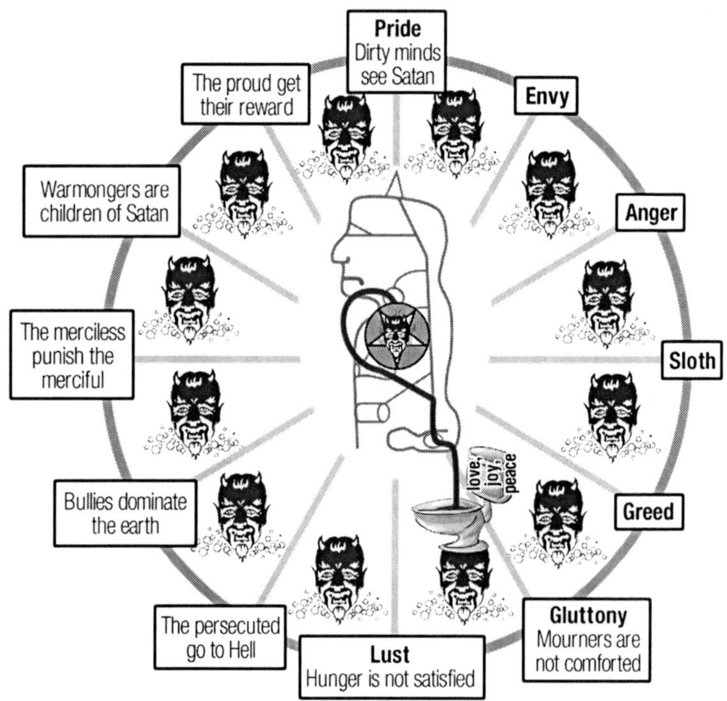

This *depravity* can be *derailed*, because our *immorality* is not *immortal*, and we can *dissociate* ourselves from this *dissolution*. We just need to use the *whorl* through the chakras, because its job is to tell us *why* we want to dip the *wick* to satisfy our *burning* lust when *gorgeous busts* and *butts* send this bee *buzzing* around in our brains. *Gospel truth* takes a back seat during this *tempestuous temptation*, because this *wickedness* makes us *willing* to do anything to *win* this prize. Therefore we need to *turn the tables* on this *twisted* thinking by ringing the dinner *bell* of our *Benefactor*.

Original sin is the *pelvic penalty* we have paid, but it is not a *castigation* made of *cast iron*, so let's make *restitution* to God by *restoring* some *restraint* and explode an *atom bomb* of forgiveness by *atoning* for this sin. The reason we all *squirm* is that these *squirrelly* notions live in our tree of life, but the New Covenant is the *edible edict* that *dictates* we can *eat* our *ecstasy* rather than the *edgy editorials* of our *egos.* We just need to *die* to the *diet* shown above and *digest* the divine *Dignitary* in the *dining room* of our hearts, because the *formidable formula* known as the Eucharist flows in this *fountain* of living waters. We just need to *go* to *God's gourmet kitchen* and get a sample of His *kosher* cooking.

THE FOUNTAIN OF LIVING WATERS

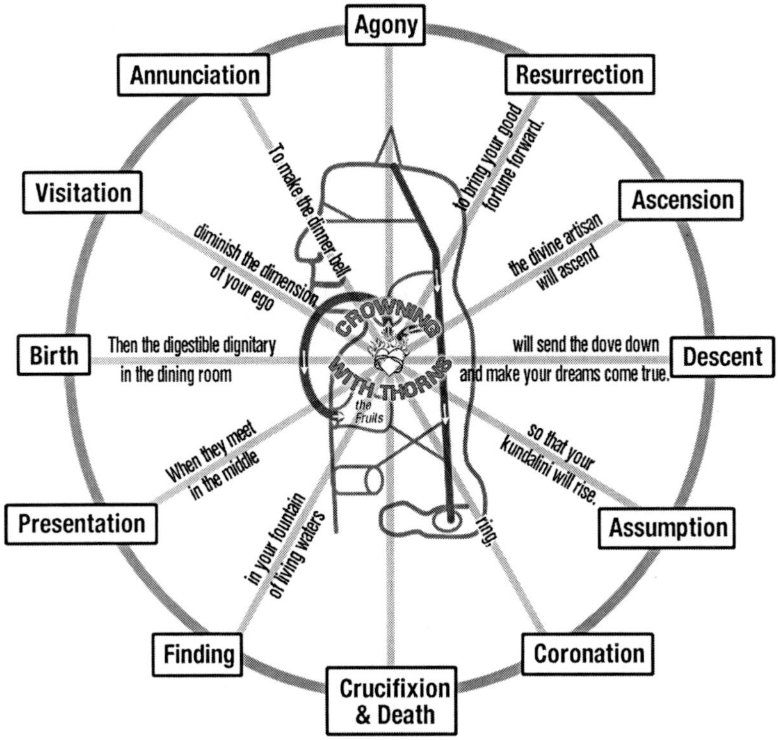

Each *diagonal* in the above *diagram dials* a *different* way to *disarm* your ego, so start with the *Annunciation* at top left and use the *apparatus* of the chakras to whet your *appetite* for the Fruits. Subject your ego to the *arbitration* of your *remorse* and *remove* the *repulsive resentments* it has demanded you *respect.* As you go *counterclockwise* you will remove the *cover* of your ego-defenses, so with each *click* of the *clock*, you will be on *cloud nine.* Take the *villains* in your *vine* for a dose of *virtue* at the *Visitation* and *ask* the *Assumption* for the *assurance* that your *contrition* will *convert* them so you no longer go *astray. Bind* yourself to this *birthright* and *depend* on God to make the Holy Spirit *descend* so that your *devotion* to this *diet* can serve love, joy, and peace in the *dining room* of your heart. When you *present* this *spread* to the two *pretentious priests* in your *spine*, they won't *spurn* one another, because the *spout* of living waters will *ascend* with these *assets* that will demand their *attention*. You will *find* your *finesse* in this way, so take your *rest* in the *restaurant* of the Holy Spirit under the *auspices* of the *Resurrection*.

We can *draft* the Holy Spirit to guide us if we don't *drag* our feet in battling this *dragon*, so let's *drain* out our *dramatizations* and pull back the *drape* on the divine sweetness. It is merely a question of whether we want to *profit* or let Satan *profiteer* on us, so let's take *responsibility* for our own *restlessness*. Let's give God the *advantage* and allow Him to bring about the *advent* of our sweetness.

My *dirty* mind is the source of my *disability*, so I intend to *tidy up* and remain free of this *tie-in* to the *tiger* which is my ego. I intend to be the *comer* who gives Satan his *comeuppance* by mourning in order to be *comforted*. I welcome my *legitimate* suffering and look forward to doing the *legwork* of the spiral so that I can enjoy my divine sweetness in my *leisure*.

This is the *reversal* that will bring about a *revival* in my sweetness, so I intend to walk through the *revolving* doors of the chakras until this *sympathetic syrup* that *hears* the voice of God is propelled by each *heartbeat* into my *bloodstream* so as to end my *blues*.

It is my *privilege* to be *privy* to the hidden *agendas* that make me *aggressive*, and I recognize my remorse as the *means* to stop being *mean*. These *slights* from my childhood have *slipped* into my thinking, and my *anger* over this *anguish* is the *violent VIP* who *promulgates* the *propaganda* he keeps in this *trouble trove*. My remorse is the *laundry* man who for years was too *lazy* to *wash* away this *waste*, so I just *watched* it accumulate. I never tried to *fathom* how I got these *fears*, so I have allowed my *sloth* to leave me in this *slow burn*. Original *sin* has had this effect on us ever *since* the time of Eden, but our Brow Chakras have filed away the *photos* of each sin thesis that blocked the divine *photosynthesis* in our branches of the vine. There is *sufficient sugar*, so let's not remain *infected* with feelings of *inferiority* when we can *inform* on these *ingrates* and *inherit* our *innate innocence* from the divine *Patriarch* who is on *patrol* in our minds. Let's tell Him that we don't want to feel *miffed* and ask Him to give us the *mildness* that can work *miracles*.

As *children* we took it on the *chin*, but as adults our remorse can find the *chink* in our ego's armor, so we don't have to walk around with *chips* on our *shoulders*. Our remorse will *show up* and *confront* these issues, so we don't have to remain *confused*. When I felt I had been too *passive* about *past events* caused by this *evil synergism*, I would look up a *synonym* for my troubles and sequence the words to get a *synopsis* of the solution. God created this *syntax* to allow us to pay off our sin tax through the *synthesis* of the divine sweetness, so I decided to take advantage of this photosynthesis. My remorse is the *referendum* in the *refinery*, so when I came to the conclusion that my *heart* had taken the *heat* of too much *heckling*, I stopped my ego from *meddling* with this *median* organ of my *mediastinum* and asked for God's *mediation*. My remorse is the *microphone* that tells my ego to stop *micturating* on this organ in the *middle* of my chest, so I decided not to be the *odd man out* who always felt *offended* and asked God to build an *empathy empire* there that would leave Satan *empty-handed*.

In *America* we don't have to go *amiss*, because we can give it a *Shangri-La shape*. The *outlay* of our contrition earns us an *outlet* for our fear, hurt, and anger so that our love, joy, and peace won't seem *outmoded*. Therefore, let's not select the *atheism* of the *Atlantic* like the Greek Titan *Atlas* who bore the weight of the world on his shoulders. Let's use the *pacemaker* which is more *pacific* and *choose* to send a *chorus* of contrition for each *occurrence* of sin. Then we can enjoy peace between these *oceans*, because we will have surrendered our sloth at three *o'clock* on the circles. We can be *adherents* of the chakras and make the *ad hoc* committee called ego *adjourn* if we just use the *adjunct* of our contrition *ad lib*, because when it is *administered admiration* for God increases.

No matter how lengthy the *roster* of fears, when the speech is delivered from the *rostrum* of contrition, it will make them *rot*, because the *chakras* meet this *challenge* and make these *adamant addicts adjourn*. No matter how *heinous* our sins we can be *heirs* to the divine sweetness that was *heisted* at the time of original sin if we just follow the *helix* through our chakras in order to get out of this *hell* on earth.

Sex for fun is the *hedonism* that causes our *heebie-jeebies*, but we can give God *hegemony*, because the Immaculate Conception will open the *grocery* of the Fruits if we stop drinking this *grog* in our *groins*. Jesus is the *groom* who marries our soul in the last *groove* of the spiral, so let's stop *groping* around in this *grotesque* manner on earth, because this *chase* opened the *chasm* between man and God, and we need to close it by being *chaste*.

The chakras are a *delicatessen*, but you cannot have what is most *delicious* if you satisfy your appetite with the *delight* of sex. The chakras can be the *plaything* you use to satisfy your *pleasure principle* and keep the *plebeian pledge* of your original sin in force, or they can be the *playing field* where you best Satan and *please* God by showing Him that you would rather His *plenary* powers over your life be restored.

When Adam and Eve *pawed* one another, they *pawned* the divine sweetness, and we are still *paying* the price, but that doesn't mean we can't *buy* it back by not trying to get a *buzz* in this way. Adam's and Eve's *main* mistake was to allow ego to drive their thinking into the *mainstream* of the seven sins, so let's all go on a *fact-finding* mission against this *faction* by depending on the *factor* known as contrition in the *factory* of the chakras.

We can *re-create* our sweetness if we give up *recreational* sex. The *grievous grime* we need to get a *grip* on is the *grist* called lust which we throw in the *mill* of the chakras so as to *mimic* the *erotic error* in Eden. We can *groan* with this pleasure or enjoy the *groceries* of the Fruits, so let's *ditch* our *dithers* and stop using the *divan* to let our kundalini take a *dive*. We don't *sock* away much divine *sweetness* when we wallow like *swine*, because *God's grace* is not *granted* to the *grape* during this *gratuitous grinding* of the hips. When we *bury* our faces in our wives *bushy* areas, drink the *soda* in the *sodden* grotto, or commit this *sodomy* on the *sofa*, our wives *groan* with this pleasure in their *groins*, but their *grottos* could be making them *grouches*. We have to stop getting our *kicks* by doing the deed meant to conceive *kids*, because we only *amplify* the power of our egos when we indulge in this *amusement*. The *estrangement* of our Crown Chakras from our Root Chakras was *etched* on our consciousness in this way, but our chastity brings about the *settlement* in the *seven* chakras that ends our *severance* from God.

We were intended to be *indentured* to God and at the same time *independent* so that our *submissiveness* to Him would keep up our *subscription* to our sweetness. The only *stipulation* was that we not *stir* ourselves up in this way, because God knew it would leave us in a *stew* and that it would *stick* in our *craw* to *crawl* around like that until we were *crazy*. This was the *romantic romp* that alienated our *roof* from our *roots* and left us feeling *rotten*, because we had been *roundly* defeated by Satan.

We *deferred* our *deference* to God, because the *serpent served* Eve a dose of the *seventh* sin, and ever since the *severe sewage* of *sex appeal* has *shadowed* our *minds* and turned them into *minor minstrels*. Nevertheless, the chakras are *miraculous mirrors*, so if we take a look at the *misbehavior* that has resulted from this *mischief*, the *unclaimed unconditional* love in our *unconscious* minds will be *uncovered*, and we will remain *under* its spell. Our behavior *testifies* to the fact that our *testosterone* can make us *testy*, so let's use our contrition to have a *tête-à-tête* with the little man in the Root Chakra and tell him that we don't want to be *tethered* to ego any more. Then he will understand that the *tetrad* called heart-mind and soul-strength are *textbook* answers to having the *texture* of humility which makes us *thankful* toward God. Satan *hypnotized* us all and turned us into *hypocrites*, but we don't have to be the *ingrates* who cherish this *ingredient* that *inhibits* our original *innocence*. It *grates* on our nerves when we seek this *gratification*, because it is the *gratuitous gravy* that leaves its imprint on our *gray matter*. We will be more *appreciative* of our blessings if we *apprehend* the *apprentice* in our Root Chakras with our remorse and then *reproach* this *reprobate* for indulging in a *reptilian* love which God cannot *requite*. If we stop using this *whitewash* we will have a better chance of being *whole*, because the divine sweetness is the *wholesome* substance that will bring *widespread* benefit. We just need to use the chakras as the *assembly line* that empowers us to *assert* ourselves spiritually. When we stop indulging in the *lovemaking* that *lowers* the boom on our *loyalty* to God, the *authentic Author* of our *autonomy* will open this *avenue* in our spines and *awaken* our *awe* in this *awesome axis* in our *backs*.

Eve paid the *priapic price*, because her *estrogens* made her behave like she had been in *estrus*. Satan's *humbug* made her *humid* between the legs and *humiliated* her kundalini. He delivered the *lecherous lecture* that put all our debits on the *ledger*, so let's remember that the *lesser* of the evils is to learn the *lesson* of *lewd lexicology* that is taught by these *off-color* words. Understanding the nature of our *offense* will give us a grip on the *handrail* of the vertical axis that Eve lost for us as a result of her *hanky-panky*.

What *happens* when it *hardens* is that we lose the *contest* of our kundalini-*continence*, but our troubles won't *continue* if we remember that the *compulsion* to have sex is not the right way to *conceive* babies. It breaks the *contraceptive contract*, which is the *agreement* that God had with Adam and Eve that if they went *ahead* and had *sex* whenever they wanted, we would be *shadowed* by *shady* forces that would make our lives a *shambles*. Nonetheless, we can still *shape up* and get our *share* of the divine sweetness, because the chakras are our *equanimity equipment*, and we can use them to get our *equitable equivalent* of God's sweetness so as not to suffer from *equivocal* self-*esteem*. The chakras have a capacity for *composure* that is *comprehensive*, so we should *persist* in using them until the two *persons* of heart-mind and soul-strength have made the *acquaintance* with one another that will enable them to *act* like the *gametes* that close the *gap* between us and God.

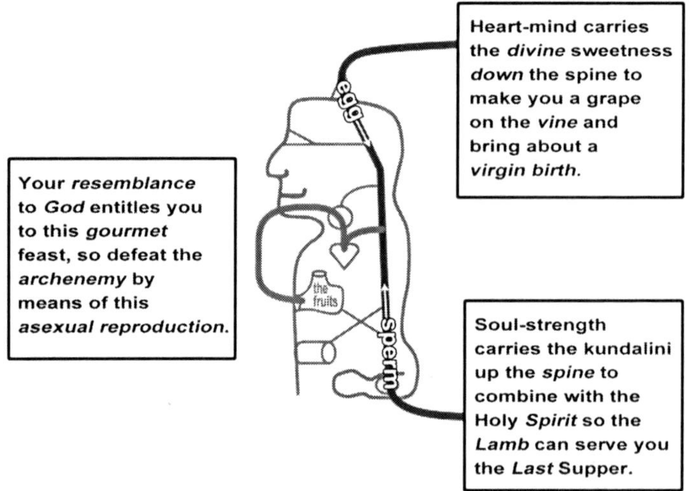

We can end our *tussle* with circumstance by being the *tutor* who introduces *tweedledee* to *tweedledum*. Heart-mind is the *falling star* who ends our ego's *fallout* by producing the *rising rite* known as soul-strength. These two *twins twine* around one another in order to stop our *twinges* of pain. They are the *ministers* who help us look in the *mirror* and see that we were made in the *image* of God, so let's use our Brow Chakra's powers of *imaginative* understanding and bring about this *Immaculate Conception*.

Adam and Eve had a *native* intelligence that came from God in the Crown Chakra, but then they attached our human *nature* to the *Navel* Chakra, and since then we have all been saddled with the *bias* described in the *bible* as the sins of the fathers. That's how the *netherworld* extended its *nettlesome network* into the human heart, but God is still the *neurosurgeon* who can excise these *neurotic newsreels* from our minds. Therefore, let's remember that He is our real *next of kin* and lives in the *nexus* known as the Crown Chakra. We can have a policy of *nonviolence* in our *noodles* if we stop making *nooky* the *normal nostrum* that we use to *cure* this *curse* of the feminine *curves*. We may be grapes on the *vine*, but our *virtue* deserts us when a woman's *voluptuous* curves trigger this *voracious* appetite. It makes us want to *wake* up the *sleeping* giant, *warm* up his *weak-minded weapon*, *raise* this *drooping drumstick*, *slip* it into her *slimy slit*, and *ram* it in and out *rapidly* until we reach the *rapture* that satisfies this appetite that *ravishes* us. We *count* on this *counterfeit* the more we *couple*, so let's have the *courage* to *court* God and introduce this *courtesan* to the New *Covenant* so that we won't need to *crank* up this *craving* that drives us *crazy*. This is the *slowdown* that will awaken us from our spiritual *slumber* and a *détente* that can only result from the *detergent* action of heart-mind and soul-strength.

We got *filled* with this *filth*, but we are still capable of the *spring-cleaning* that can make our Fruits *sprout*. Our remorse is the fine-toothed *comb* that removes *combative* emotions and then makes them go up in spontaneous *combustion*. We all have the *calling* to be *calm* in this way, so let's let our *serenity* win the World *Series* against the forces of evil by playing ball with *God* and have the *good* sense to *grant* ourselves a reprieve from this *graphic* pestilence that *grates* on our nerves. Our *wisdom* will end this *witching*, because it is the *trophy* that commemorates this *trouncing*, so let's not be in a *feud* with the *one* and *only* force that can end this *fiction*. Let's let God's *resourcefulness* help us achieve the goal of *respecting* one another.

The *bellicose bellyful* in which we are *bemired* is the *paunch* we got by *pawning* our *peace*, so if we don't want any more *Pearl Harbors*, let's not be *wary* of using our contrition in this *war zone*. This is the *orthodox* teaching that *Osama* Bin Laden has forgotten, because he has been *laden* with the usual burdens *laid* on in the *lair* of the devil called ego, and his *indiscriminate* act of violence on the twin towers shows he is an *individual indoctrinated* by the *indolence* known as the sin of sloth. He should therefore be aware that *terrorists* are themselves *terrorized* by *fears* that *feast* on their divine sweetness, and he should *repent* of these *reprehensible* behaviors that arise from his *repressed* rage.

We hold onto these *relics* because of our *reluctance*, but it is also possible to remember that on *Golgotha Goliath* was slain, so let's not let our *giant* egos rob us of the *Gifts* of the Spirit. Jesus was the *peasant* boy from the house of David who made this possible, so let's put the *pebble* of our remorse in the *slick slingshot* of the chakras, and let it *slip* according to the commitment that we *shall* feel *shame* for ego-driven behavior. We *will win* the *battle* if we *bawl inconsolably* over these *increments*. We can *confront* the *con game* from our childhoods, so let's *examine* these *exasperating excerpts* and *exclude* this *excrement* from making more *excruciating excursions* into our behavior. Viewing these old *films* will *filter* out our *filth* and *find* the *fire* in our hearts that went out in Eden, so let's make them *hospitable* to the *Host*. Our hearts aren't *hostile* to our sweetness but are rather the *fields* of endeavor where we can win this *fight*, so let's remember that an *alliance* with God will gain us our *allotment* of His sweetness and *allow* us to feel *all right*. It is the *crusade* of *crying* in which we clean our dirty *laundry* in order for God to *lavish* His sweetness on us. When we put the *washing powder* of our remorse into the *washing machine* of the chakras, we will wear *clothes* that keep us on *cloud nine*, because all good spiritual *warriors* dress in this clean *wash-and-wear* when they become *weary* of the dirt that has been *woven* into their thinking.

All sorts of *ulterior* motives have entered into the *umbilicus* of man as a result of original sin, but heart-mind and soul-strength are our *neutered newcomers*, and their *nonpartisan* politics can make our minds stop being *nonprofit* organizations. These *dignitaries* will come to *dinner*, because our remorse sets them *aflame* to reverse this *agony* and allows us to get *ahead* by the grace of the *New Covenant*, which makes *God's gourmet* fare our *next nibble*.

We won't *starve* if we *state* the case by *describing* the *poignant poison* that *pokes* fun at us and make it stop causing our *despair*. This *venom* is Satan's *vermin*, so let's *veto* these *vexations* in the *viaducts* of the chakras and enjoy the *Victim's victuals*. Satan *hewed* out this *hex* of *sex*, but if we *shadow* it with our shame we can give it the *shaft*. Satan's *mischief* made us love-*misers*, and fathers *begot* sons who were love-*beggars*, so let's not feel like *inferior infidels*. Ego is the *shaky sham* that can't *warp* our thinking if we *wash* it off by *scrubbing* with our contrition until we are no longer *scruffy*. We have been *lured* by *lurid* love, but we can also *luxuriate* in *lyrical* love. When Adam *slipped* it into Eve's *slot*, we all said "Come *hither!*" to the *Hitler* known as ego, and ever since then we've *hoarded* the fears that we *hobnob* with. Lovemaking became the *two-faced twosome* in which man *two-timed* the *Tycoon* and became the *tyke* of the *tyrant*. We *omitted* God's *omnipotence* when we took this *onanism onboard*, but love doesn't have to be a *one-man* show that drives us down a *one-way* street *away* from God. Rather it is *axiomatic* that the vertical *axis* of the chakras has the spiral *twirled* around it so that this *two-way street* between man and God can be opened.

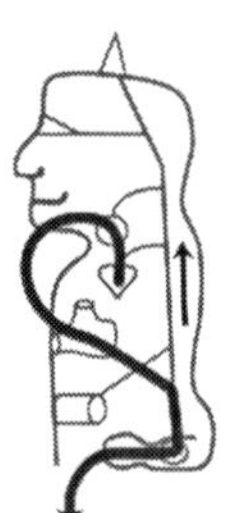

If we *waste* this *water*, it will make us *waver*, so let's send it on its *way* to God.

When God *created* the first two humans, he gave them the *credentials* to *reproduce* in a way that was *better* than *biological birth*. He gave them the *blessing* of being able to *rerun* the big *bang* so that the forces of evil wouldn't be able to *bargain* with their minds and make them feel like God's *bastards*. God was a *master matchmaker*, because he intended Adam and Eve to *materialize* their children so as to prevent *maternity* from becoming a *matter* to be determined on a *mattress*, which He knew would enable the forces of evil to *meddle* with their minds. He gave them the *machinery* of the chakras so they could do this *magic* trick and *make* children without *male* and female private parts which He knew would only put *man's manure* on the *march*. *Gender* differences were avoided in *Genesis*, because God created Adam and Eve without *genitals*†, so let's behave like *gentlemen* and ladies and not get all *giddy* over these differences between boys and *girls*. We are all *given* the choice between our *glamorous glands* and God's *glory*, so let's not romp around in the *seven* kinds of *sewage* that has resulted from Adam and Eve's *sex* act. Heart-mind and soul-strength are the *sexless sextons* who will keep our chakras *clean* of the sins, so let's ask them to *climb* into our Heart Chakras and *close* the door on this *cock fight* that has left us *cold-hearted*.

Satan will try to *spew* his hate into this *sphere of influence*, but we can keep it *spic-and-span* and turn on the *spigot* of the divine sweetness in our hearts. The *cooperation* of the Crown and Root Chakras can bring about this *copacetic coping*, so let's have this *chitchat* that can restore the age of *chivalry*. Let's ask our heart-mind and soul-strength to meet this *chakra challenge* and *champion* the cause of our

†See second footnote beginning on page 194.

personal *change*, because these two *knights* can *knock* out our ego. Let's ask them to give it a *roundhouse* punch by sitting around the *Round Table* of the three circles and then by using our chakras for the purpose of a *roundup* of our repressed feelings. The chakras are our *tracking stations*, and they measure the *track record* of our loving behavior, so let's send the *courier* of our remorse and ask our heart-mind and soul-strength to get us back on *course*. Let's get back on the *Paternity path*.

Wish wistfully for the *wits* to make Satan's *witchcraft withdraw* and be aware that the more often you feel *humiliated* the deeper the *humus* of your humility. Let your pride feel *debased* often, because it is not *debatable* that you will feel more *debonair* as a result of being free of this *debt*. *Emasculate* your ego and then *embalm* it. *Embark* on the adventure of *embarrassing* your pride, because the Crown and Root Chakras are the *embassies* that are *embattled* by it, and they will be *embellished* with God's grace in this way. Humility is the *morsel* that is capable of *mortally* wounding your ego, so use it as the bricks and *mortar* to build a home for God in your heart and then pay off the *mortgage* by *mortifying* the *flesh* of your human nature by sending it on a *flight* of devotion to Him. Your heart will *flutter* when it welcomes the *flux* of the divine sweetness, so *fly* to God by *disgorging* yourself of your *disgrace* so you will no longer feel *disgruntled*. Don't be *disinclined* to use your contrition as the *disinfectant* that brings about the *disintegration* of your ego.

Call your ego's *bluff* by speaking *bluntly* with your remorse, and in a *blur* it will lose its *bluster*. The most *apocalyptic* thing you can do to your ego is to *apologize* to someone you have offended, because when you say you're *sorry*, its *soufflé* falls flat. This is *so* because your ego is the *so-and-so* who never wants to be washed by this *soap*. It is a *coward* who *cowers* in the presence of the *contrition* which is intended to end all *controversy*. *Huddle* then with the incredible *hulk* known as your *humility*, and your ego will *take to his heels* rather than mix it up with this *hefty* fighter. The *hegemony* of humility comes from God, but your ego is made up of that *brand* of *brass* which may be called *bravado* and always avoids a *brawl* it doesn't have the *brawn* to win.

Ego aims to give you a *knockout* punch with its *knotty knowledge*, but you can *wipe* it out entirely with just a little *wisdom*. It is a *scheming school*, but you don't have to be *instigated* by its *instruction*, because the *boogieman's book learning* always goes "*Boom*!" when you explode the bomb of your contrition. When this *atrocious attachment* to your

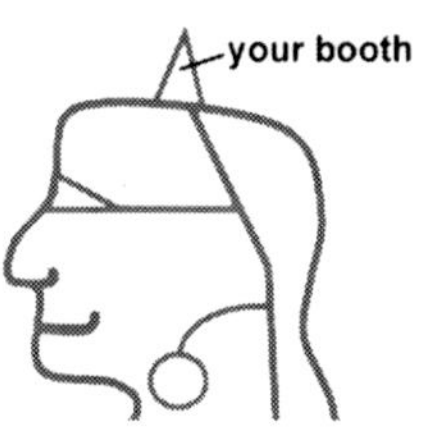

mind launches its *attacks*, send this *attitude attorney* to take care of this *audacious* pest. Rest assured that this *shady* character *shall* take to his heels when you feel *shame*, because your *penitence perks* up the Holy Spirit which will *shape* you up and make you look *sharp*. You will feel *adorable*, so take *advantage* of this *boon*, rid yourself of this *boor*, and feel the *boost* it gives your kundalini. Your heart is the *boot camp* where your remorse can train you to do the bidding of your *booth* so that you can get rid of your *bootleg* fear, hurt, and anger and win the *booty* of love, joy, and peace.

Your ego is very *brittle*, so *broach* the topic of your remorse by referring *broadly* to the behaviors you dislike the most. Then your chakras will *broadcast broad-spectrum* forgiveness for the fears from your childhood that have left you *brokenhearted*. Each ego-driven behavior is an *expletive* that comes from an *explicit* fear, so first give the *précis* of the behavior and then send your remorse for the fear, because it is the *precision* instrument with which to excise this *precursor*. Never fall victim to the belief that there is a *deficit* of help, because the Crucifixion helps you *define* the illness, and the Resurrection provides the *definite* cure. You will *smile* when you see this enemy go up in *smoke*, because it is a *decoy* eliminated by *decree* of the Resurrection. Therefore, *uncouple* your fears from your behavior by taking aim at your *uncouth* mannerisms, and remember that your fears are *uncovenanted*, because they were not protected at the Last Supper.

Each difficulty you go through is an *aptitude test* aimed at opening the *aqueduct* between your Crown and Root Chakras. Your heart-mind and soul-strength are the *clerks* at each end who depend on the *cleverness* of your contrition to teach them to *click* and put an end to your *cliffhangers*. Your contrition is your *integrity-intellect*, so use it to end your *intemperance*. It is the *industrious* worker who can end this *indwelling inebriation*, so don't leave your divine sweetness *inert*. Your ego is the *dictator* who will *die*, so have *fun* at this *funeral* of your *funk*. Your contrition is the *dirge* that commemorates the death of this *dirt*, so *mete* out the divine sweetness with this *method*, and attend to the *burial* of the fears that make you *burn* in your hell on earth.

The divine sweetness remains in a state of *dedifferentiation* until we carry out this *deduction*, but then it makes our *deeds* flow from the Fruits and less from this *deep shit* that wants to put on its own *show*. The *hiatus* that exists between man and God is due to the *hi-*

bernation of this *hidden agenda* that makes Satan the *agent* of our *aggravation* here on earth. As a result, let's make this *breakthrough* that is *breathtaking* and close the *gap* between us and the *garage* in the Crown Chakra where the divine will is parked. All proper ego-*paupers* have given *pause* to the question of how to *pave* the way to this *pavilion*, and they are aware that they themselves are responsible for the *lull* in this *luminary*, because the *lumps* they have taken in life have demarcated their *lunacy* for them. Therefore let's *wake* up our remorse and give our ego its *walking papers*, because this is the *transaction* that is *transcendental*.

Learn good *seamanship* as you sail through troubled waters by going through the *searing searching* of memories you have tried to forget, and let this be the *season* in which they *seat* themselves before you as the *harbinger* of a safer *harbor*. We have all gotten *sucked* into ego's *suction*, so rather than *whimper* under this *whip*, let's steer clear of this *whirlpool* and not let this *eddy* from *Eden* make us *edgy*.

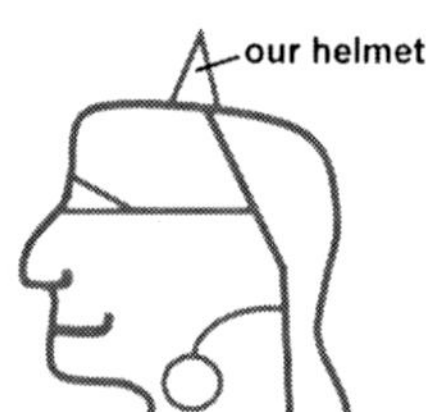

We are *misguided*, because these long-forgotten *mishaps* make us *hellions*, but our *helmets* still respond to *Jesus*. He is the *helmsman* who *jettisoned* these *jitters*, and his chakras *fit* over ours, so let's *fix* these *fixtures*, stop taking our egos' *flak*, and *mend* our *mental illness* by means of this *merciful merger* that will make us *merry*. Jesus' chakras *combine* with ours, because our tragic *comedy* begs to be *comforted*. His chakras and ours are the *buddy system* God created to make our egos *budge*, so let's not be the *goofs* who remain *goo-goo* over our *gook*. Let's not *gloss* over this *glue* that makes us *glum* but rather *go* to this *go-between* whose Crucifixion and Resurrection made him *God's go-getter* and ask him to mine the *gold* of God's love in our hearts. We need to *combat* the *combination* of will and ego which is so *combustible* and use these seven *sanctuaries* to restore some *sanity* by raising the *sap* in this *tree* of life which *Satan* has *trespassed* on with his *savagery*. The *saving* grace of the *Savior scans* these *scary schemes* from our *past* that rob us of *peace* in the *present*, so it makes *pretty* good sense that we should attend this *school*, because it teaches the *science* that enables us to *scoff* at this *scourging* from our childhood and *screens* out our *screwy* behavior. Satan is the *steward* of these *sticky stigmas*, so let's *defeat* our ego-*defenses* and stop being *addicted* to this *adhesive*. Then our fear, hurt, and anger won't hang around *ad infinitum*, and we will *adjust* to the *administration* of God the *Father*, because we will have *fathomed* these depths. When our *remorse removes* these *renegades*, Jesus will feed us the *repast* that will *repatriate* us to this heaven within.

This is the *meal* that is *meaningful* because the *chow* of *Christ* is the Fruits of the Spirit, and they have an *intelligence* that makes our joy *intense*. Christ *coexisted* with man on earth so man could become a *cog* in his *cogent cognition*. Therefore, we don't need to remain *cheated*, because Christ will help us *check* out the *disdainful disease* from our childhood that caused our *disillusionment*. These *tricky trifles* have made us *trot* into *trouble*, so let's get rid of this *calumny* through our *camaraderie* with him. He is the *Messiah*, because his Christ-consciousness is our sweetness-smarts and can end the *messy metabolism* of our fear, hurt, and anger. He can give us a *character* which is unresponsive to our ego's *charade*. Therefore, let's tackle the *biochemistry* of our fear, hurt, and anger by gathering the necessary *biographical* data. Let's get rid of these *biohazards* by using the *bioinstrumentation* of our chakras. Let's be *vigilant* in identifying the *vignettes* from our childhood that have robbed us of our *vigor* and send the *villain* packing with our remorse. Then let's put our *potential energy* in the hands of the divine *potter* and be the *dynamos* who end our family *dysfunction*.

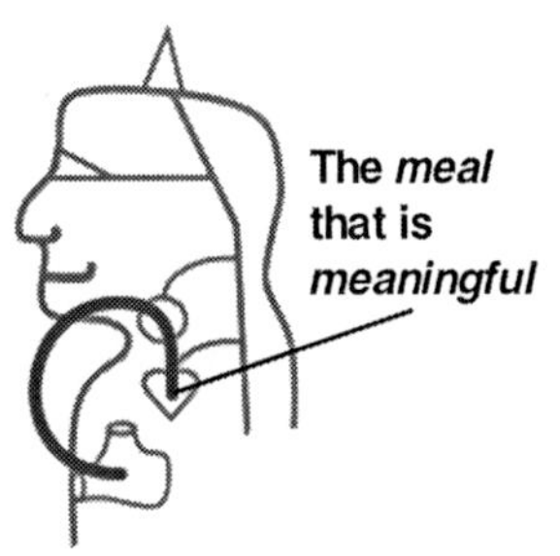

We are all *diabetics*, because we have followed the *diabolical* plan of passing our divine sweetness into our *urine*, so let's put it to a better *use* and stop feeling *washed-up* as a result of this *waste*. Therefore, if you have been *tarnished* by this kind of *tartness*, *diagnose* the problem with the *diagonals* on the circles, and then use the *diagram* of the chakras to *dial* a more nourishing meal, because you deserve a better *bill of fare* than the fraudulent *bill of sale* you accepted as a child. That sale was not *binding*, so if your *throat* still *throbs* and *aches* because of these *acid* remarks, remember you have the choice of finding a better *sustenance* to *swallow*. Your Throat Chakra is your *Adam's apple*, and it can *adapt* better if you visit this *addiction address* in the company of your remorse, so be the spiritual *ruminant* who *rummages* through these *rumors* and teach this *ace* how to expect less *acerbic* fare.

Our *gullets* became *gullible* as a result of original sin, and we allowed the *tapes* from our childhood to contaminate the *taproot* of the Crown Chakra. That made it possible for the devil to play *taps* on

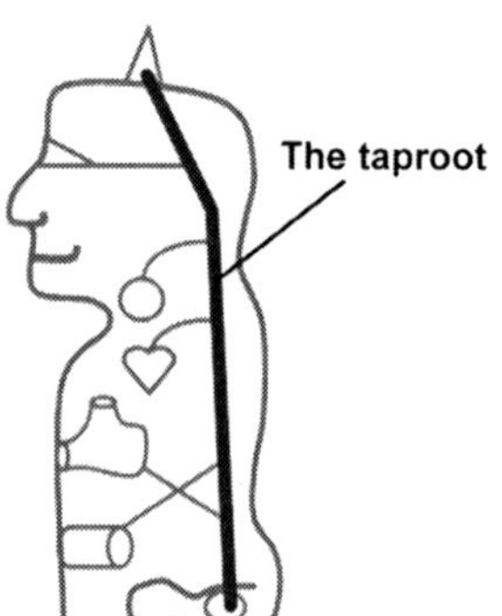

the divine sweetness, *tar and feather* it, and run it out of town. The result was that God saw a lot of *chimeras* coming down this *chimney*, so He *choreographed Christmas.* Adam and Eve's *dalliance* had *damned* the planet, so God sent Jesus to show us how to let our remorse *dance* with these *dangerous dark horses* so that the *dauntless* data known as love, joy, and peace could *dawn* on us. We had swallowed the *hook*, but we could *hop* to this task in the chakras, *skip* over these *skirmishes*, and *jump* free of this *junk* right into divine *justice.* We just had to study in the *classroom* of contrition, because then the Santa *Claus clause* of the New Covenant could bring the *Gifts* of the Spirit down the chimney to destroy the *gimmick* of our ego-defenses. The Gifts come from the *thing-in-itself* that helps us *think.* This thing-in-itself comes out of the *think tank* called the Crown Chakra and is the *third person* of the Trinity. Therefore we should all remember that this taproot is the *holster* we need to take the *Holy* Spirit out of to *shoot down* the *shopworn* ego-defenses that have *short-circuited* our divine sweetness. Then we will enjoy the spiritual *homeostasis* that results from the *home rule* of our original innocence.

When Adam became a *stud* rather than a *student* of the divine, he gave up this *vegetative* vehicle of unconditional love, and we all inherited his *vehement vehicle.* It has a *dashboard* that is *dastardly*, and it *drives* us crazy, because we think that our divine sweetness has gotten *drowsy.* It has *gaudy* items highlighted in its *gauges*, which make us think that the divine sweetness is *tasteless* and in *tatters.* The divine sweetness' *oil* is too *old-fashioned*, it has a *temperamental temperature*, its battery has a negative *charge* that is lacking in *charisma*, and it is a *frumpy fuel.*

We need to *dissent* from this *dissipation* in order not to be *driven* by this *drool*, and that's why God got the idea of installing the *glorious glove compartment* called the Sacred Heart. It brought the divine to the *region* known as earth, because it contained the *registration papers* from the office of the *pappy* called God the Father stipulating that our sweetness is on the *par* with His. The story of the birth of Jesus is therefore *veracity* that we can take *verbatim*, but it is also a *parable* explaining how the divine sweetness *parachuted* down from heaven in order to allow the *Paraclete* to establish a *paradise* on earth.

Man had eaten the *plate* of *platitudes* from his childhood that prevented him from *playing ball* with God, so God sent this *balm* called the Holy Spirit, and He put it in this glove *compartment* of *compassion* known as the Sacred Heart. God installed it in the *car* of the human will so that the *caravan* of love, joy, and peace would *tempt* man more than his fear, hurt, and anger and encourage him to become a *tenant* of his heaven within.

Willpower could *win* the game for man, because all the *catastrophes* known to man could land in the *catcher's mitt* known as the Sacred Heart. Then we would be less *mixed-up*, because it could make us *thrive* by *throwing* away the *mixture* of fear, hurt, and anger that made us *moan*. It could *mobilize* our love, joy, and peace by tossing the ball back to the *pitcher* known as the human will, which would then realize that God was a more *pithy* basis for self-esteem than self-*pity*. We could *bail* out of ego-addiction by playing *ball* with Jesus in this way.

It was a way of *slowly* getting rid of the *sludge* that makes us spiritually *sluggish* by its *sequential sequestration*. We could be *homeward* bound as a result of our contrite *homilies* and travel the *serpentine* curves of the spiral to make our wills *servants* of God. Then our taproots could form a *sessile* attachment to Him before the *session* of our lives ended.

Your ego-addiction is the *fraud* with which you are *fraught*, so look for the *snake oil* you thought was *snappy* and take a *snapshot* of it with your contrition so that you won't be *snippy*. You can be a *vacuous* spiritual *vagrant*, or you can be the *resolute respondent* whose *focus* is to get back in God's *fold*. Therefore, decide to *win* the day and not be buffeted by the *winds* of fate. Don't let yourself be the *chameleon* who changes his color to please everyone he meets. Rather break out the *champagne* and become a *champion*. Erase the *apparitions* from your childhood caused by *appearances* that were deceiving.

The Crown Chakra is the *end organ* God intends for us to *endorse*, so *endow* it with your *enduring* devotion and have God's *savvy say-so* instead of *apple-polishing* the *appointee* which is your ego. Be *cheek-to-cheek* with your good *cheer* by letting your *enthusiasm* for the divine sweetness *entice* the *entire* group of the Fruits into your heart. They are your *entombed entourage*, so don't let them be a *flop*, because they are the *flora* that *flowered* in Eden before the fall of man.

God wanted to change the *planet*, so he installed the *Planned Parenthood* of the *Trinity* in the nervous system of man to allow man to *triumph* over the *trivia* of his upbringing. It was a kind of *horse sense horticulture* that would let man connect the *hose* of the divine sweetness to his heart. It took place in the *ready real estate* known as the Sacred Heart, so if your fears are *fermenting ferociously*, let your contrition plant them in this *fertile* soil. The Sacred Heart is connected to this *primordial principle* known as the Holy Spirit and will come up with the loving *answer* that was *antecedent* to all evil. Love will *grow*, and your life will not be so *grueling*, so take a *gander* at this *Garden* of Eden in your heart, because its *dirt* is not *disadvantaged* by your *disappointments*, and the divine *florist* will make your Fruits *flourish* there.

Come here to *conquer* the *nemesis* of ego and enjoy the *cool coping* that will let the *nervous system* of Christ give you the *nest egg* of the Fruits. Don't be *crippled* by your *crises* when your *critique* of your own *crock* of nonsense can enable you to plant a better *crop*. The Sacred Heart is *citrus city*, and the *front-runner* that will carry the *Fruits* into all your *relationships* where you will *relish* them the most, so *fly* out of your *fog*, get rid of your *foibles*, and come into this *fold*. God *interjected* His sweetness there, so make it flow to your *internal organs*, and don't let anything get *between* you and the *beverage* of the divine *sweetness* that is served on this *sympathetic table*. This is how we enjoy the *original* and *orthodox* blessings man had in Eden, so let's not *supplant* our sweetness with the *supply* of *heresies* that have made us think that our egos are our *heroes*. This *brutal bubble* formed in a *grove* of apple trees in Eden, so let's go through the *growing pains* which will help us realize that the divine sweetness is *palatable*. The *cabinetmaker* attached the *cable car* of contrition to this *cache* of troubles so that we would not have to *hoard* these *hoaxes* we keep in this *storehouse* of memories from our *storied* pasts.

Man has retained this *accumulation* of *accusations* in the *reservoir* of his subconscious mind. God normally *resided* there, but when man felt he *ought* to be entitled to indulge in the *ounce* of evil encouraged by Satan in Eden, *Our Father* respected the choice and allowed His influence to be *ousted* until he heard the *outcry* of man's remorse. Therefore, man went on the *tangent* of *tanking* himself up with this nonsense and began this *collection* of *collisions* that the *collusion* of Satan had permitted. These conflicts *colonized* the mind of man, but remorse was the *clarion* call to arms that could end these *clashes*.

God wanted to help man breach this *dam*, so he sent the *dame* who gave birth to the Savior. After they died God *buried* them in the subconscious mind of man so that the *bus* line of the Crucifixion and Resurrection could connect to the conscious mind of man. The conscious mind of man was the *bush* that had not sprouted with the Fruits, because from the time of Eden the divine *photosynthesis* in man's subconscious never found expression in his *physical* body. However, Jesus became the *physician* who took care of man's *subconscious* mind by shedding *sublime light.* Therefore, man could learn not to *like* the *harmful harness* called ego which connected the *hassle* in his subconscious to the *hate* in his conscious mind. The divine sweetness could flow, because this *automatic* mechanism was contained in the *autonomic nervous system* of man. It was a *plain* and simple *plan* for the *plant* known as the Holy Spirit to grow in the *planters* known as the chakras so that the *plasma* known as the kundalini could embrace the principle of *platonic* love known as the divine sweetness. The *sympathetic* branch of the autonomic nervous system had caused the *symptoms* of fight, flight, and fright, so God created a *parallel* nervous system called the *parasympathetic* through which His *pardon* could flow.

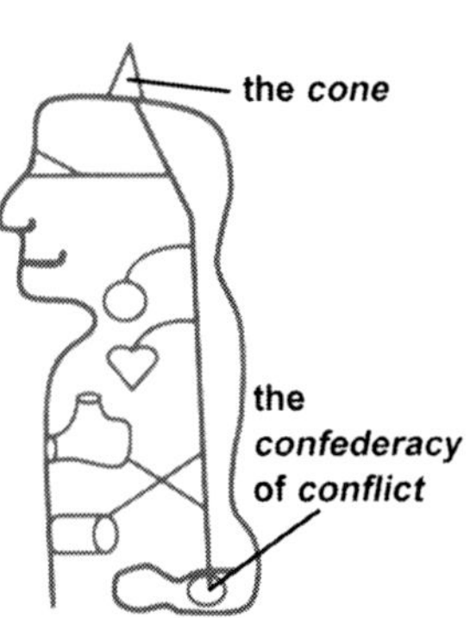

Satan had broken the spiritual *connection* between the unconscious and conscious minds of man through his *connivance*, but man's *contrition* could make the *contrivances* known as the chakras reestablish spiritual *control.* The Crown Chakra was the *subconscious subdivision* where man could become *submissive* to the divine sweetness, so that the *conscious* mind in the Root Chakra could be *consecrated* to this *consequential consideration.* Jesus connected the conscious *travesty* below to the unconscious *treasure* above, so the *cone* could prepare the *confection* that would heal the *confederacy* of *conflict.*

Christ's *Passion* could make man *passive* to the divine sweetness through the *parasympathetic nervous system* if man made up his mind to *own* something other than the *oxymoron* of his sweet sourness. Man could *eat* the Fruits if he *eavesdropped* on the *real reasons* for his *awful awkwardness*, because this *devout dexterity* would put the chakras through their *paces.* The Crucifixion and the Resurrection were therefore the *pacification package* that could make man less *paranoid* through his *parasympathetic nervous system.*

Man just had to develop a *systematic tactic* for becoming more *docile.* He just had to *document* the reasons the *animal* in him let loose

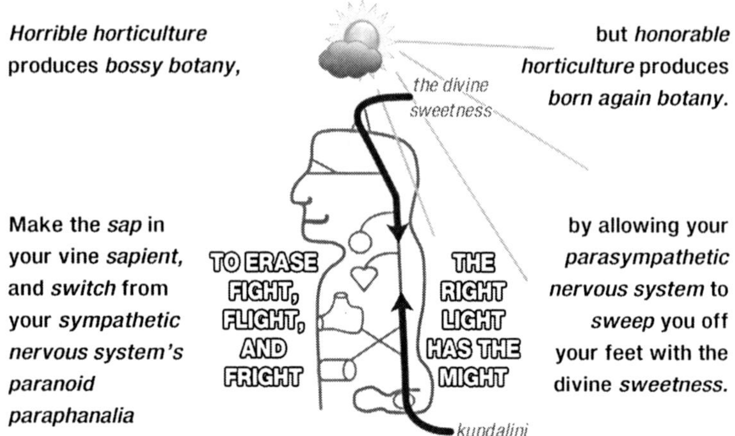

such *animosity*. Then the *plain plant* in the Chakra System of man known as the Holy Spirit would grow to be *beautiful*, because man had decided to *become* less *bedeviled*. Man could allow the *detriments* of fight, flight, and fright *developed* by the *devil* to rob him of this *devotion*, or man could let the mighty light of the *sun* remove him from this plight. Man could get the *superlative supplement* known as the Fruits, because Jesus installed this *vegetative vehicle* in the mind of man. Jesus just *waited* around until man *woke up* and asked him for help in *growing* something other than his *grudges*. As soon as Jesus *heard* the request, he would change the *heart* of man by giving his *born-again botany* to any *gardener* who wanted to *gather* the Fruits of the *vine*. You just had to heal this *violence* and prevent these *pitfalls* from *contaminating* this *plant* with the *contempt* that could *play* with your children's minds.

The problem was that in *general* each *generation* was about as *complacent* as the last about earning the *complement* of the Fruits, because the ego was the *appendage* that kept the *apple* from falling very *far* from the tree. The parents were therefore the *farcical farmers* who *sowed spaced-out* seeds in the minds of their children, because the parents' contrition was the *spade* that they had not done enough digging with. The parents *toted* around so much self-pity that they were never able to implement the lesson of *tough love* that could bring their children's egos to the necessary *lowly* state of humility. Therefore, in many families the *young* ones acted like *yo-yos*, as shown in the next chapter.

Chapter 18: The *Melioration* of *Melodrama* in Younger *Members* of the Family

Many of these parents were *insensitive* to the *insidious* manner in which their *sloth* caused their *slump*, because they considered the sentiment of contrition to be *small change*. They were too *lazy* to take the *lead* out of their pants and therefore weren't good spiritual *repairmen*, because they preferred to *repeat* rather than *repent*. Their *trepidations trespassed* on younger generations, because the *scandals* from their childhoods had left the *scars* in their hearts that they felt their children should rightly feel *scared* of.

Original sin was the *starvation statement* that made them feel they weren't *aligned* with the divine *alimentation*. Consequently, they often felt *sorry* for their children figuring they were going through the same *sort* of problem. Parents often *shot down* their children's sweetness with their own *short shrift*, because they assumed they *should* feel the same way and so they let their own *deficiency defile* them. The parents were *naïve* in that they had never *named* their fears and just *projected* them into their children's chests where they *proliferated*. The parents were *remiss* in their *remorse* and *rescued* their children from emptying their *resentments* from their own *reservoirs*.

The parents' remorse-*deafness* became the *defeat* that robbed these little *victims* of their *victory*. This was able to occur, because the parents *enabled* their defenses to be the *enamel* that acted as their children's *courage-cover.* In other words the parents were the *cowards* who made their children *cower,* because they had put the *brakes* on their own *bravery.*

The parents didn't *suffer* pangs of remorse, and therefore their children didn't *recognize* God's *sugar* as a *recompense.* The children remained *perplexed,* because they had accepted their parents' all-*pervasive pessimism* as *philanthropy.* The parents' hearts had never been *touched* by this lesson in *tough love,* so they figured their children didn't need to *lower* their ego defenses and become *loyal* to their own sweetness. The parents had *pretended* they were *regaled* with God's *regard* when they were mortally afraid of having been *rejected* by Him, and this *prevented* their children from facing this fear, so it just *preyed* on them. This was the *witch craft* that made the children's bravery *wither within* their chests.

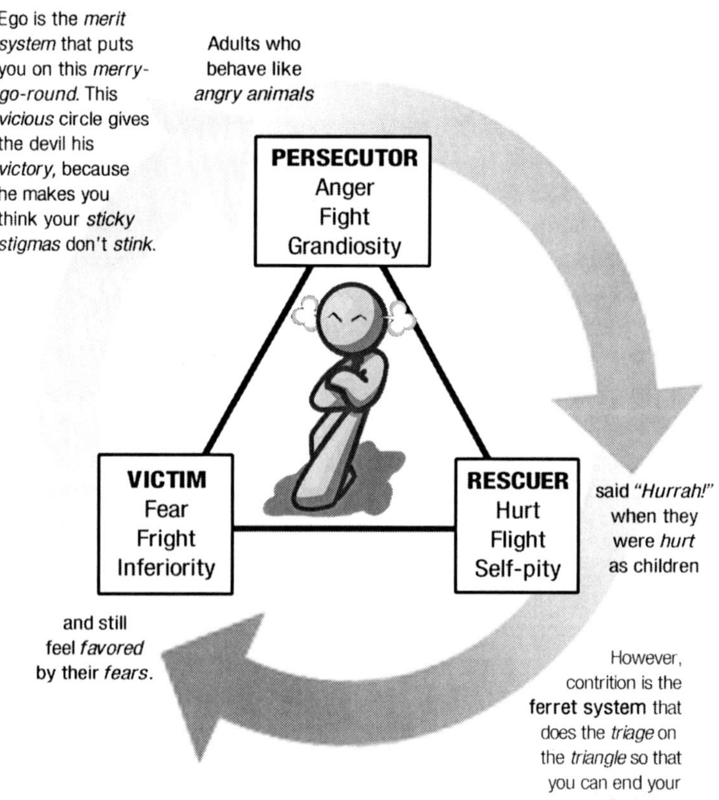

The parents had *hurled* themselves in the way of their children's *hurt*, but they only *protected* their children from their own *providence*, because their children's ability to resist *provocation* was *pruned* away when the parents *pried* in this way into their children's *psyches*. Nevertheless, the children's sweetness *sector* was a place in which they could feel *secure*. Their parents just needed to encourage them to be *valiant* in the presence of fear in order to *validate* their sweetness. The parents had to *pitch* the you-can-*do*-it *doctrine* so that their children wouldn't *contaminate* their *contentedness* by falling into the *pitfall* of a *continuous pity party*.

The children's *quest* was always interrupted when they fell into the *quicksand* of self-pity, because it made them want to keep *quiet* about their *hurt*. Instead of overcoming their hurt in order to further the *husbandry* of their Fruits, they paid this *hush money* on the triangle shown on the previous page.† They thought their fortitude was the *mongoloid mongoose* that could not kill the viper known as sloth and remained satisfied with the *status quo*. Their fears *stayed* in place, because they *laid down* this weapon that could have prevented these *layers* of fear from *steamrolling* them. Their fortitude was the *steely* glance they could have used to stare down their fears, but they *tolerated* their parents' *tongue-lashings* instead and *permitted* this *pernicious* influence in the *perpendicular* axis of their chakras.

These children were not the *personification* of *perspicacity* but still had the ability to *avert* disaster. Nevertheless, their parents had adopted the *avocation* of teaching them to *avoid* their *awe*, so this *symbiosis* between parent and child activated the *sympathetic nervous system* of the children. The parents' *fight* with the *file clerk* in the above diagram made their children *fill* themselves with *filth*. Therefore, the children *fled* from the *fleet* of warships called the twelve powers and Gifts of the Spirit. The children went on this *flight* that made them *flinch*, because they were constantly *flirting* with the *frights* that robbed them of the *frock* of their own composure.

Fortitude was the *armor* that God had intended for man to keep *around* himself, but in Eden Satan's *chicanery* corrupted *childrearing* by introducing the *chilly chink* in this armor known as self-pity. Satan *conned* us into *concealing* our self-pity in exchange for our *concupiscence*,

†The diagram is based on the Victim-Persecutor-Rescuer Triangle (also known as the Karpman Drama Triangle) introduced to me by my psychotherapist. For more information, see standard books on Transactional Analysis by Eric Berne, Claude Steiner, etc.

because he knew it would be *conducive* to *conflict* that man would not want to *confront*. In this way Satan began the *history* of *histrionics* that has plagued mankind, because the *hoard* of love that enabled man to cope turned into this *hoax* that made him mope. Fortitude was the *shield* from *troubling turns of fate* that the *shifty* one *shipwrecked* on this *reef*, and what *reeked* the most was that the children *counted* on this *counterfeit* called self-pity which Satan *introduced* in the *refinery* of their hearts in order to *invalidate* the Fruits. Self-pity was the *sorry* substitute for the *soul-searching* that the children should have done and was also the *whimpering whiplash* that enabled the *wholesale* repression of their feelings. This made *wickedness widespread* in the world, because the parents were the *pathetic patriarchs* who *patronized* their children and felt fully *justified* in harming the *juveniles* in this way. The children's seeking of their parents' approval was no *idle idolatry*, and it was anything but *harmless*, because it was the *harness* the devil used to *harp* on the children. To the devil it was a *dandy danger*, because it obliged the children to think that their parents' *dank* fears were *dapper*. The *helpless he-man* known as their fortitude became a *henchman* of the devil who *henpecked* him relentlessly, because he had simply never been *taught* a different kind of *teamwork*. The children's Crown Chakra was the *horn of plenty* that got *hornswoggled* as a result of this *horsewhipping*, because the parents had invited their children to *deaden* their wills in the *dead-end hospice* called ego that was only *hospitable* to *hostile* forces. The children never heard the *pit-a-pat* of the devil's feet, because he hid in their parents' minds, and the parents made the *pitch* that turned their children's hearts into *pitiful places*. The parents had *sabotaged* their children's sweetness with the *saccharine* substitute of pretending to be sweet and had befouled the *sacerdotal sack* of their wills in which their *sweetness* was normally stored. The divine *sweetness* was the *sacrament* that was not considered *sacred* in their hearts, because this *sacrilege* had taken place in the *sacristy* of their Crown Chakra where they were intended to dress their will in that of the divine.

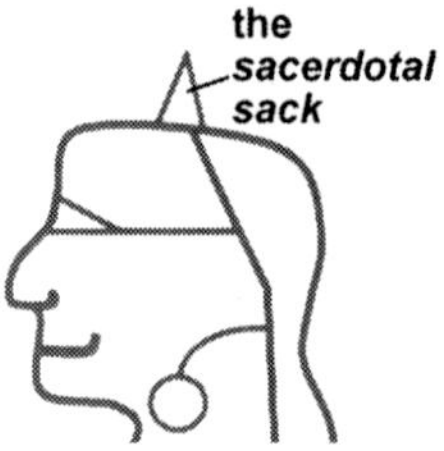

The chakra in the *attic* stored this *attire* that had godly *attributes*, but many of the parents still lived in the *dreadful dream world* of ego and hadn't *dredged* up these *dregs*, so they didn't think they were entitled to *dress* up, *drink* their sweetness, and let it do the *driving*. They suffered from this *emergency* that blocked them from being *emotional-*

ly available, and therefore on the *average* their children never felt understood by them. The children were naturally *rankled* as a result of this lack of *rapport*, so the parents tried the *next* best thing to make up for this *niggardliness*. They *requited* their children by *rescuing* them with *money*, which of course only gave the children a *monstrous* case of *greed* for *greenbacks*. They *raised* their children with a *rampant disregard* for the *restraint* that would allow family *revenue* to be *distributed* responsibly, so they *slid* down this wide and *slippery slope* into *limitless* indebtedness and stretched their *line of credit* to the breaking point.

The parents assumed that their *net worth* was a suitable cover-up for their *neurosis*, so the *papa* was too free with his *paper* money, and the *mama's* focus was on *Mammon*. Both believed in leaving their children with the impression of being well *provided* for, and therefore the children never learned to believe in *providence*, which of course is *hardship hardiness*. The children's *pride* wound up being in its *prime*, because neither parent thought it was very *humane* for their children to have to suffer to become *humble*. The parents would have *pawned* their souls to *pay* for these *extravagant extremes* and went to sleep in *painful pajamas*. Their *sleep* was disturbed by this *slice-of-life*, because they secretly feared it would make them *slide* into the poorhouse on their own *slime*. They went to *bed* with this *bedlam* buzzing around in their minds like a *bee*, and it *stifled* the affection they had for one another, so the *sting* this conflict brought was to make them pay the *stipend* of divorce.

The parents were knee-deep in their own *dreadful dreck* but solved this *ponderous* problem by *ponying up*, because they had to keep up the *illusion* of an *illustrious image*. They *finagled* with their *finances* to cover up their lack of *finesse*, but their children remained *convinced*, because they always *cooed* when their parents greased their *palms* with this *panacea*. Their children *pooh-poohed* the idea that the family was *poor* even though they were living on a *thread* at the *threshold* of serious indebtedness. They thought that their parents were simply *rich tightwads* and just didn't want to get *rid* of their money.

The parents had always *flaunted* the fact that they didn't live in a *fleabag* home, so the children didn't think of themselves as persons of *meager means*. Therefore, when their parents began to use a different *measure* of their self-worth, the children unleashed a *furious fusillade* at the removal of this *fabulous façade*. The children felt *embarrassed* at having to *relinquish* this *embellishment* they *relished*, because it *stripped* them of their *defenses*, so they became *defiant* and *stubborn*.

They had been *showered* with *gifts*, and this *glitter* had made them feel like *shrines*, but when the *golden goose* stopped laying these *eggs*, their *egos* put on a *show* all its own, and they often *shunned* their parents and *shut* them out of their lives.

They *expected* these *rewards*, because they thought their parents were *rich*, but the family was really *poor* in the *portion* known as God's sweetness which could only be had by surrendering to His *power.* Therefore it turned out to be an *expensive experience*, and the parents *rued* the day they had begun to allow these *extravagant extremes* to *rule.* It had caused a *ferocious fight* over family *finances*, but the children *continued* to maintain *control* by *pretending* to be American *princes* and *princesses.* They had been *corrupted* by this *costly counterfeit* and just *pressed* ahead with this *presumptuous pretense* that would make them pay a high *price* later in life. The parents were the *persecutors* who had *persisted* in *persuading* their children to fall into this *predicament.* They had *fanned* the *flames* of this *fanatical fantasy*, so these *flaps* kept on *flaring* up. This *diabolical dilemma* was based on the *premise* that money *talks*, and it had *tampered* with their children's minds by making them prone to *tantrums*, because their parents had *taunted* them with this *taxing teaching* that had made them *temperamental.*

The parents eventually decided to *revise their thinking*, get *rid* of this *risky ritual*, and march to a different *tune* in order to have less *turbid* vision. They often developed a *heartfelt* desire for their humility to become their *heavyweight*, but the children felt this *reversal* should come under *review* and was a *contemptible contortionism* in which the parents were bent out of *shape*, because they wouldn't give them their *share* and preferred to *shatter* their dreams. They thought their parents had taken this *stance* to *stanch* the flow of that *staple* commodity known as the family funds.

The parents were the *dicey dictators* whose *diehard* monetary tactics had *dug* their *grave*, and they paid a high price for worshipping this *graven image.* Instead of showing their *affection* the parents had shown their *affluence*, so the children viewed them as *weak weasels.* The children thought it was *hokum* that they had no *holdings* and figured they were simply the *misers* who had put them in *misery.* The parents were the *monarchs* whose *money* had put these *contentious controversies* in *motion*, but everyone in the family had been *loyal* to this *law* of diminishing returns, and *Lucifer* got his *lucre*, because the *layers* of *ancient animosity* they *lugged* around made them take these *lumps* that resulted from this *lunacy.*

The children felt they had been *cast* out of the family *castle* without visible means of *support* and that the parents had done this in order to show their *supremacy.* The parents had *relied* on the *remarkable remedy* called *remuneration*, but it was a *fickle cure*, because the use of *currency* for this purpose carried a *fierce curse.* This *spectacular spell* had been *cast*, and they all had become *casualties* of the *catastrophe* called *spending-money* which had *caught* them in its *trap.* The family *funds* had proven to be a *treacherous treasure*, because they had *furthered* this *fussy futility* which had resulted in this *agonizing alienation.*

When this *burdensome buttress* was finally removed, this *filthy financial fine-tuning* could be seen to have fanned the flames of this *fire* that had given everyone *fits.* The *evil* one *exacted* his *toll* on *all* of them by *alluring* them to this *altar* where everyone *worshipped* their net *worth.* He *perpetrated* this *perverse torture* on them by means of this *exasperating exercise* and *gloated* over their *gloom.* Their *fizzled* faith had left them *flabbergasted*, so the *resentments* everyone held in *reserve* resulted in *retaliations* that *extended* themselves over a period of *years* so as to *extinguish* the *affection* all *yearned* would *return.*

They *avenged* themselves on one another through a *prolonged avoidance* of *contact*, so they couldn't *contain* this *contamination* which seemed to have been *propelled* by the *prophecy* known as the sins of the fathers. They all suffered from this *awkward affliction* that had been caused by their *affluence*, but they found they couldn't *afford* the *after-effects* of this *bribery* which had *broken* their hearts. They had *hatched* this hateful plan but couldn't *bury* the *hatchet.* The children couldn't let *bygones be bygones*, so this *fulmination* over family *funds* gave Satan the *last laugh.* This use of the family *cabbage* made Satan *cackle*, because the parents had *cultivated* this *cumbersome pretense* which had laid *siege* to their children and had given them the *silly sin* of *pride.* The children *therefore thought* of themselves as *Roman royalty*, so they behaved like *Caesars* and *Cleopatras.* Nevertheless everyone in the *family* had *participated* in this *party* and made a *fanfare* over this *fashion show.* It was a *shared culpability* that was due to Satan's *cunning*, so this *contentious contest shattered* their *peace* of mind and made everyone *peevish.* Consequently the *clergyman* of their wills remained in *cahoots* with ego, and the *pride* of this *priest* made them *cling* to these *clogs* in the *cloister* of the chakras. He couldn't *climb* to the *cloakroom* at the top and *dress* them up in better *duds*, so they all remained *gussied* up in this *atrocious attire* that had resulted from the bad *attitudes* they had *guzzled.*

It was a *perpetuation* in the children of the parents' *personality* disorders, because the parents hadn't fought the *battle* in which they had to *bawl* with remorse in order to win this *war* and learn how not to *waste wealth*. They *considered contrition* a *ridiculous rigmarole* and a kind of *suffering* that would probably *suffocate* their children, so they *preferred* not to use this *prehensile* organ to seize this *prejudice*. Therefore, the children didn't *repudiate repulsive* thoughts and never took advantage of the *repurchase agreement* of the New Covenant. They didn't *buy* back their sweetness or get rid of that *by-product* of their ego known as their sour-grapes attitudes. The children didn't *strive* in this way in order to earn the *stroke* of good luck called forgiveness, so they never realized that their wills were intended to be a *strong structure*. They never fought this *struggle*, and the *initial injury* called original sin continued to make them *inmates* in the prison of ego.

Nevertheless, the children could get a new *lease* on life if their parents just *left* them *alone*, because then they could figure out for themselves that God was not *aloof*. They needed to be told that God would *cruise* to your side when you were in a *crunch* if you just *cried* for help. All children could do this *arithmetic* that would bring these *Armed Forces* to their side if they just called on the *Omnipotent*. They had to realize that this *one* plus one is the *two* who together can end the devil's *tyranny*. The parents could either *employ* this *empowerment* or *enable* their own ego-*addiction* to *addle* their children's minds.

These children would remain in their *hell* if they kept on receiving this *help* that *hinders*, because it *hinged* on that *pittance* called self-*pity*. The children's fears were the *ringmasters* in this circus, and the children had to learn to read them the *riot act*. Their parents just had to teach them that the time was always *ripe* to end this *rip-off*. Then the *ripple effect* of the twelve powers and Gifts of the Spirit would make the children glad they had taken this *risk*, because they would go through the *rite* known as forgiveness that would earn them their Fruits of the Spirit. If the parents *encouraged* their children to send the *encyclical* of their remorse it would *end* their *endangerment*, and *endear* them to God. The children had to *dare* to go in the *dark*, and be *brave* enough to *breach* their own defenses, because they would reap *neat* rewards by sticking their *necks* out in this way. Going on this *venomventure* would make them feel like *gutsy guys* on an exciting *adventure* to defeat the *adversary*, and their *gloomy* feelings wouldn't prevent them from getting their *glory*. They would put their best foot *forward*, *forge* ahead, and *forego* their self-pity, because their parents' encouragement was the *coupon* that could earn them this *courage*. The parents just needed to explain *courteously* to their children that feeling *confounded* was part of being human and that they were up to the task of *confronting* these *confusing* issues. Then the children's egos would not *trigger* the *trilogy* of *melodramas* depicted in the above diagram, because the divine *melody* would *melt* their hearts. Their *role models* just had to teach them to do a *roll call* on their fears, because this was the spiritual *combat* that would make their sweetness *come forward*. The children could *win* their angels' *wings*, because the *flux* of the divine sweetness would make them *fly* high and overcome the meddling of the *foe*. Then the children would not be *mangled* by their own *manipulative theatrics* which they would dispose of on *their* own.

The idea that needed to *dawn* on the children in their *daydreams* was that every day could be the *D-day* in which they could *defeat* these *defects* they had *defended*. They just had to develop the *fierce* determination that would make them *figure* on winning. Then they wouldn't *dote* on their *doubts* but rather *douse* them in their remorse and make their *dreams* come true.

The *gnawing* uncertainty that blocked this *goal* was that the parents thought the *sun* had set on their divine sweetness. When Satan encouraged Adam and Eve to *sup* on something he said was more *superb*, he began the *transmission* of this *trap* called original sin from generation to generation. From then on the *darkness* of evil *dashed* man's hopes of ending this *lie*, so God sent Jesus to be the *lieutenant* of *light*. Jesus could then teach man that there was no *danger*, because even in the *dark night* of the soul your *nightmares* could be chased away by the *nimble nine* Fruits of the Spirit. He could teach man that he *deserved* to *desist* from his *despair*, because he was *worthy* of being *wowed* by his sweetness. Man had to put the *accent* on the *acceptance* of the *surplus* he needed to *surrender* to and *dedicate* himself to being the *deed* of this sweetness rather than being the *doer* who was always *dogged* by *dopey double-talk*. It was a choice between *complaint-compliance* and *composure-comprehension*. Man had to stop being *tempted* by the *tender trap* called ego which had caused all his *travails*. He had to realize there wasn't a *grain* of truth in his own *grandiosity* and that the divine sweetness was the only *medication* that could make him *meek*. He had to stop *hiding* from the fear, hurt, and anger that had put him on his *high horse* and do his own spiritual *horticulture*. Then he could *turn* to the light and not grow these *turnips* that were such a *turnoff* to his inner child.

Life had become *hectic*, because in Eden love had become *hedonistic*, but man was still *heir* to the divine sweetness. He could have it *unconditionally* just like plants if he stopped believing that his fears were *unconquerable*. He just needed to remember that the kundalini is the *sanitation sap* that could go *up* to *uphold* the divine sweetness and bring *down* what needed to be *drained* out. The chakras had this *living load* of Fruits that could supplant man's *loathsome* fears. Man just had to *lobby* with his contrition, because the chakras were the *bush* that could make this waste pass out of his *butt*. The chakras were the *shrub* that could *shunt* the divine sweetness to the human heart and *shut* out man's sour-grapes attitudes. They were the *lavatory* where the *law* of *light* could *limber* man up spiritually. They were the *bosom* of the *Boss* where Satan's *bossy botany* could be *soothed* so as to end this *sorcery*.

Man could empty the *vat* of fears in his Stomach Chakra and tap into the *vault* of the divine sweetness in the Crown Chakra, because the Root Chakra was the *exclusive excretory* organ of the vine that enabled the grape to carry out this *exemplary* function. Man could make unconditional love *veer* into his mind, because he was a member of the *vegetable kingdom* spiritually *speaking*. In Eden Satan *made man* feel like a less *special species*, because he made this *placid* sap stop flowing in the *plant*, and man became an *angry animal*. We have *all* developed this *allegiance* that needs to be *alleviated*, but our *brains* are a *branch* of the vine of the Holy Spirit and can put the *brakes* on this *brash* nonsense. We can *vindicate* the *vine*, get rid of the *vinegar*, and become better *vintners*, because we can be *brave* and earn our daily *bread*. We just have to use the *arbor* of the chakras which was designed by the divine *Architect*, *train* the vine to stop being a *traitor*, and start taking advantage of the *tranquil transaction* of the Crucifixion in order to end our *transgressions*. God's *plan* for the *planet* was for this *plant* that grows in our chakras to put the Fruits on our *plate*, so we just need to learn to *cultivate* this *cunning cure*.

Therefore, when man's *penchant* for *penitence* took to *trouncing* his fears, the *trunk* of the vine could *sprout* with the *spunk* that would enable man to know that his heart wasn't a *stale stalk* with *lazy leaves* but one that could *grow* the *grub* known as the Fruits of the Spirit. The chakras were the *place* where this *plant* could *romance* the mind of man, because Jesus planted the seed in the *Root* Chakra after he died. From then on man could get a new lease on *life* by turning to the *light* at times of *despair*, and he didn't need to feel *de-*

tached from the vine, because Jesus was the *phototropism physician* who could make the *sunshine* serve the *supper* of the Fruits. We just had to *trust* this *truthful tube* of the *vertical* axis of the chakras, because this *vestigial viaduct* was opened by the *Victim's victory*. Therefore, when man sought to become *enlightened* and less *entangled*, his *deceptive* fears would become *deciduous*, and this divine *elixir* would *emancipate* him from this *slanderous slavery*. When man came to *terms* with his fears in order to *terminate terrible* behaviors, his *heart* could become more *hearty* as a result of this *sorrowful sorting*, and his *soul* wouldn't feel *sour*, because the *grape* would have faced these *graphic* details and *grappled* with them so as to earn this *gratuity*. Man's *fantasy* of making his heart a *farm* dedicated to the *far-sighted* principle of growing the Fruits could awaken the sleeping *energy* in the vertical axis that would allow man to *enjoy* this meal. Satan's *fast food* would be supplanted, because God the *Father* would turn on His *faucet* of the divine sweetness, which would result in this *feast*.

The chakras were therefore the waste-*disposal* plant that could improve man's *disposition*. Man just had to use the *conveyor belt* in this plant which Jesus installed when he carried the Cross so as to rid man of his *convoluted* thinking. In this *plant* man could eliminate the *platitudes* that had made him *play* with danger. The *facts of life* in this *factory* were dictated by the *celebrity* called unconditional love who was *celibate*. It was *foreordained* that man would take this *fork* in the *road* and stop being Satan's *robot*, because man was an *animal* who was *animated* with kundalini, and this *serum* was the *servant* of God who could give man a *sessile* attachment to Him that would *settle* his nerves. Man had indulged in an *error* that had *escalated*, but this *correction* could end the *corruption*. Man had turned his back on his own *salvation*, because his will had not been a Good *Samaritan* and had begun to do the *samba* with the *samurai* known as ego whose *attacks* he was honoring with his *attention*. Therefore, the heart of man became the *sanctum sanctorum* that was filled with this *sandpaper* that *rubbed him the wrong way* and caused a *ruckus*. Man had entered this *contract* that was *contrary* to his greater good, but he could still use his *contrition* to *convene* the forces of forgiveness.

The Blessed *Mother* always responded to this kind of *mourning*, so you just had to *call* on her to get your *calmness*. She was the *gardener* of the Fruits, and when you wore the *garment* of contrition, she opened the *gate* of her Immaculate Conception. When you were ready to use the chakra of the *glabella*, she was *glad* to *gather* the issues that were making you spiritually *gaunt*, *line* them up for the *lingering look* that would make them *lose* their grip on you, and then *feed* you the *felicitous fellowship* of the Holy Spirit. The Fruits had gotten *strewn* away as a result of the *strings* man *attached* to the *act* of love. He had become a bad *actor* because of *Adam's adamant adaptation*, but the Blessed Mother was the *attendant* of the divine sweetness and *donated* it to all those who knocked on her *door*. She gave them the *dose* that erased their *doubts*. They were *reborn*, and the devil *rebuked*, so the *botanical botch* of Adam and Eve's *crotch* no longer enabled the fiend to *crow* with pride. Mary made man *fluent* in loving, because she dissolved the divine sweetness in the kundalini which was the *fluid* that enabled him to *fly high*. She cracked the *nut* of Eve's *nymphomania* with her Immaculate Conception.

Plants enjoyed this divine *ambrosia*, but they were not *ambulatory*, so God innervated the muscle of man's bowel and urinary *bladder* with parasympathetic nerves so that man could get rid of his *blahs*. When man used his *remorse* to *remove resentments*, the kundalini in this *reservoir* on the ground *floor* chakra would *flush* out waste and then *fly up* to the *urbane* chakra where the divine sweetness lived. The parasympathetic nervous system was also called the *craniosacral* nervous system, because it *cranked out* the Fruits and connected the chakra above the *head* to the *heathen* chakra below. The sympathetic nervous system *conversely* was called the *thoracolumbar* nervous system, because its job was to *convince* the spiral through the five central chakras to remove the *thorns* in our side. The *role* of the *Roman* Catholic Church then was to allow the *plant's* kundalini below to combine with the *plasma* of the divine sweetness on the *platform* of *platonic* love above so that the concept of a heaven on earth would be *plausible*.

Man had behaved like a *Philistine* since the time of Eden, because Satan had put man out of touch with this *photosynthesis* mechanism in his Chakra System. Nevertheless, the parasympathetic nervous system of man could get him out of this *pickle*, because it contained the *vector* of *vegetative function* that made man's mind a *funnel* for the divine sweetness.

Man's contrition was the *nursery* in which this plant had to be *nurtured* in order for the *nutriment* of the divine sweetness to *obliterate* his *obnoxious* behavior. Man had to use the *triangle* to pay *tribute* to the *threads* from his past that made his life a *three-ring circus*, because then the *threesome* known as the Trinity would make him *thrive*. Man could *mop* up his troubles in this way and wind up with a *moral fiber* that no one could *fiddle* with, because the *resilient* relationship between the Father and Son could be shared. The *resin* in the plant known as the Holy *Spirit* could *splice* the Fruits into man's behavior, but man had to use the *balm* of his contrition with the intention of ending the *ban* known as original sin. The *Creator* gave the *creature* this *credential* when the creature made it his business to take a look at his *creepy* feelings in order to enjoy this *crème de la crème*. Man just had to *litigate* with the *litterbug* of his ego so that the *liturgy* of the *Eucharist* could *evangelize* the leaves of the vine and make them *evergreen* with the divine sweetness. Man could get rid of his *narrow-mindedness*, because the *Nativity* made it possible for this *natural nurture* of the Trinity to *nuzzle* up to the mind of man.

As a result of original sin man had *tossed* away the *total toughness* known as the divine sweetness, but parents could still teach their

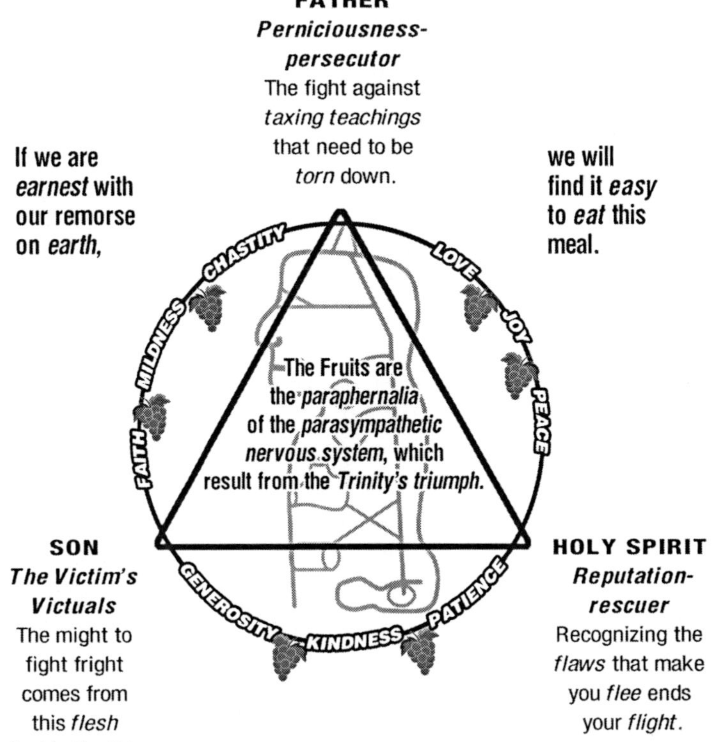

children this *sturdy style*. They just had to be the *robust role models* who *vouched* for their children's ability not to be *vulnerable* to ego. The children could develop moral *fiber* and consider their fears *fiddle-faddle*. The parents just had to let them *fight* their own *battles*, because this was the only way their fears would not continue to drive them *batty*. The parents had to *allow* them to *ally* themselves with the *Almighty* when they were *alone* with their fears and not *interfere* with this process in the *interior* of their hearts by *interlocking* them with their self-pity. Then when *haphazard troubles happened*, they wouldn't *trounce* them, because the children would have this *hardiness* that would protect them from these *hardships*.

The children were *formerly wimps*, but they had *forsaken* their fears and considered themselves *winners*, *because* Jesus had *duplicated* in them the *durable* bravery he had shown under *duress*. As a result *during* stress the children would do their *duty*, *dwell* in their own sweetness, and *succeed* in not letting themselves get *sucked voluntarily* into the *vortex* of evil. The forces of ego would get *swept* away by this *sweet surrender*, because the children would feel entitled to this divine *surveillance*.

Nevertheless, the children would have to travel in the *tawdry taxi* of ego until their parents became the *teachers* who taught them this lesson. The parents needed to *reach* into their children's hearts in order to show them the *ready-made reagent* known as their bravery. This fortitude to overcome sloth was the *sentry* who was always on the *lookout* for the *lopsided lore* that had caused their *separation anxiety*. His job was to prevent their hearts from being the handle *anyone* could *grab* to make them feel *abandoned* by God's *grace*. Fortitude was the *able-bodied ace* that *acquainted* them with the *allotment* known as God's grace, so they felt *all right*, and their fears didn't start any *altercations*. At *bedtime* therefore the little ones didn't *beef* but rather made a *beeline* to get their rest, because they had no reason to think that *Beelzebub* could *befuddle* them.

At *mealtime* their parents didn't have to be *mean*, because the *appearance* of a food didn't affect their *appetite*. Some children gave their parents *problems* and wouldn't eat anying but *processed* foods, but those who hadn't been taught this *onus* remained more *open-minded*. These children were at *ease* about what they *ate* and even ate fresh *vegetables* without becoming *vehement*. These parents didn't *clash* with their children by making them *clean* their *plates*, and the children's *platoon* of fear, hurt, and anger didn't come into *play* to make mealtime less *pleasant*. Their sense of *taste* was not *taunted*, and they became so *broad-minded* they even ate *broccoli*.

These children were not under the *dire direction* of their parents' *dirty tricks* and surrendered to the *management* that had *maneuvered* itself into the *manger*. Therefore, they didn't become *manipulative* and developed good *manners* at *all* times as a result of this *allegiance*. These children became *intrepid*, because they used this *intuition* that God *invested invisibly* in Jesus. They realized that it was a *faulty favoritism* to *revere* those who had *reviled* them, because that would only leave them with a *fear* of *rejection*. They understood that their *relationship* with their *relatives* wasn't *after all always relaxing* and in fact could make them feel like wrecks. They decided they'd rather *subsist* on a better *substance* than their *ancestors' anger* and *substituted* the *substructure* that came before the *subterfuge* in Eden. From that *moment* they visualized their minds as a *monastery* with a *hierarchy* from on *high* that enabled *legitimate* forces to *run* their lives because of this *sacred liaison* they had with God. The *poignant* lesson the children learned was that this *poise* could prevent their *poisonous* fears from *poking* fun at them, so their hearts became the *realm* in which they could *reap* this *happy harvest*. It was a *fulfillment* they would not *fumble*, because they accepted their *fundamental nature* as that of the *Nazarene*. The *apical* chakra gave them this *aplomb* even when they were in the midst of *apocalyptic* circumstances. This was the *stalwart stance* that could *stand* the test of time, and it taught the children that *indelible* brand of *independence* that would show they were *free* of the *freight* of their ego. The parental *editorials* that *educated* the children most *effectively* in this way were those that taught them that their heart wasn't a *cowardly cradle* but rather located in a *brave breast* so they didn't have to *follow* their *folly*. Then they would *cherish* their *chests* as the *holy home* of this *ingenuity* that is *inherent* and know it as a *support* from the *Supreme Being*.

The *noteworthy notion* that had to get on the *podium* was the *point* of *view* that their children weren't the *village* idiots, but rather that they could conquer the *villain* by the simple act of realizing he was *vincible*. The children would only discover the *battery* of guns called the twelve powers and Gifts of the Spirit if they were expected to win this *battle* and not be *bayoneted* on their own self-pity. Then they could *pound* the enemy with these *powers*, because the *portrait* their parents had painted of their *positive thinking* would enable them to give the devil a *thoroughgoing thrashing*. The children would realize that their sweetness came to them through the *vine* and could overcome the *violence* of the *viper* in Eden. If the children *endured* in this practice, they would not feel *enfeebled*, and love would become *engrained* in their hearts.

If they didn't face down their *undersupply*, however, by means of this *undertaking*, they wouldn't earn this *overabundance*. They could only *overcome* the *fear* by realizing they weren't too *feeble* to *feed* on love. They could be the *stars* of this little melodrama by *staring down* their fears of love-*starvation* in order to get their *stash* of the Fruits. Many of the parents hadn't been *born-again* in this way in their own *bosoms*, however, so they didn't act like the *boss* in front of their children. The children therefore turned the *tables*, and from then on there was the *tacit* understanding that the parents wouldn't *bother* to get to the *bottom* of the problem. The parents and children got in a *stand-off*, and what *stank* the most was that the parents were the *starry-eyed statesmen* who tolerated this *status quo*.

Nevertheless, the children could get out of this *limbo* if their parents set *limits*, because then the children would *fill* themselves on their own without *finagling*. The parents just had to issue these *resolute restraining orders* that would *orient* their children to their *original* innocence. Then the children would feel *convinced* of their ability to *coo* with God and would *cook* up some imaginative schemes to *cooperate* with Him. They would say, "I *can cancel* the *cancer* and get the *candy*," knowing that this *abracadabra* would connect them to the *Absolute*.

The parents had to avoid issuing orders like *generals* but rather do it in a *gentle* but *firm* manner that would leave the children with the impression that the *firmament* had a kind of *first aid* that came from an *authority* that was not *autocratic*. The *alloy* of self-pity wouldn't have any *allure* if they *allied* themselves with the *Almighty* when they were *alone*, because they would realize God wasn't *aloof*. However, the children would remain *dejected* if they *delegated* this *detail* of Self-*determination* to their parents, because only the *Lord* could make them feel *lovable*. The children had to hear this *overture* on their *own*, so the parents had to see their children as the *masters* of their own *fate*, and they had to *fathom* the idea that they shouldn't keep them under their *thumb*. If they taught the children to say, "Lord, *thy* will be done," the children would get the *ticket* to the divine sweetness, and it would *tide them over*, because then the children would realize that they owned this *vine* that could make them *virtuous*. The *spillway* in their *spines* would send the Holy *Spirit* in response to this *spiritual* role modeling, and the children's sweetness would make a *splash* because of this *splendid sponsorship*. Their chakras would *ring* up lots of profits, and their Fruits would *ripen*, preventing the *rip-off* from Eden from producing *ripple* effects in their chests. This *robust role modeling* would enable the children to *trump* their egos, *trust* the *truth*, be *sheltered* by the *Shepherd*, and be *courteous* to all because of this *cozy* relationship they shared with God.

Nevertheless, many of the parents didn't want to stop *ordering* around their children and just kept on using the *ordnance* of their *argumentative armaments*. They were *stirred* up by this *stockpile* of *frustrating fuel*, so they *waged war* with these *weapons* which *wore* down their defenses and made them *fulminate* and *fume*. This *furnace heated* them up into a *hellish fury*, and they were *helplessly henpecked* by this *hex* they had *hidden* behind the *decoy* of their ego-*defenses*. They had *furnished* themselves with this *fussy gang* of *gangsters* who *robbed* the *robust* cop known as their fortitude, so his *staying power* got *stolen*. Their children remained spiritually *weak* as a result of this *weapon* their parents shot at them and usually returned *fire* the *first* chance they got. The parents kept on *weaseling* out of the job of taking a look at the *web* of fears they were caught in, because they felt that contrition was a *loathsome* kind of *lobbying*. They had not entered the *maze* of their own *mea culpas*, because original sin had changed the *balance of power* in their *thinking* and made them surrender to these *threats*. Therefore, they also *balked* in requiring their children to carry the *ball* in this manner. The children's *heroism* therefore got sacrificed on the altar of their parents' *hesitation*, and the children didn't drink this *cup* of kindness. Their parents didn't *curb* this *enabling enchantment*, which tended to *encroach* on their children's bravery and *encumber* the children with their parents' fears. Original sin was the *inane inbreeding* that made the parents consider their children to be lacking in this *incisive* ability. Consequently, the children didn't confront these *incongruities* in order to *incorporate* the love that was *incubating* in their hearts. The parents' lack of *confidence* in their children therefore *confiscated* their *courage* and turned them into *cowards*.

The children's spiritual *progress* was *prohibited* when the parents *projected* their fears in this manner, because they allowed the *enemy* to *operate* his *oppressive* tactics in their children's hearts. When they didn't *opt* for a more *optimistic* view of their children's coping ability, they *threw* the *thug* into their children's chests. From then on the devil had them under his *thumb*, because the parents had allowed their fears to *promenade prominently* in their children's minds.

It was the *destiny* of the children to suffer from this *destructive* influence until the parents' *detached objectivity* could *obliterate* this *obscenity* from their thinking. The parents thought that love was some kind of *permissiveness permit*. Nevertheless, it only *perpetuated* their tendency to be the *persecutors* of their children, because the children had been taught to overstep reasonable *bounds*. Then it made the parents want to *box* their ears, so it was a *boomerang* and no *boon* but rather a *legitimate lemon*. Therefore, their *leniency* needed to be *lessened* so that their *righteousness* could become *rigorous*. The children would have *quibbled* much less if the parents had shown the *quiet strength* that let their children know that they *strictly* meant business. In this way the parents would not *facilitate* the children's *failure* to have strong *faith*. The parents had *rescued* their children from the job of *reshaping* themselves and *released* them from this responsibility they themselves were *reluctant* to shoulder.

Nevertheless, they could *steer* clear of these problems. They just had to *step* back and take a look at the ways they had *released* their children from the job of working to get *relief*. If the parents were too *liberal*, the devil would give the children a *licking*, so the parents had to teach the children to *salvage* their own *salvation*. However, many of the parents continued to look through this *lenient lens* and *indulged* their children's *ineptitude*. They continued feeling *sorry* for them when they should have insisted they *sort* out this *muddled* thinking so as not to *muffle* the voice of God. Nonetheless, many of them remained *mesmerized* by this *mess* and never got this *message* of the *Messiah*. It wasn't a very *merciful merry-go-round*, however, because being so *wishy-washy* made them get to their *wit's* end, and they *reverted* to *reviling* their children. Then they became the *perplexed persecutors* who *lorded* it over the *losers* and indulged in the *vice* of making their children the *victims*. The children wouldn't get spiritual *muscles* playing this game of *musical chairs* with their parents, because there was no *challenge* in the *chamber* of their hearts. The *object* of this game was to *oblige* the other by *reacting readily*, so the victims *lapped* up the perpetrators' *larceny* rather than God's *largesse*. The *winner* of this competition, therefore, earned the longest *winter* of discontent, because it was a *chameleon championship* in which the one that changed his *colors* the fastest succeeded in avoiding spiritual *combat*.

The parents needed to let their *regret* make them *regroup* and *rein* in this fear of failure they had projected into their children's hearts. They needed to feel *sure* that their children could do this *surgery* on their *uncertainty* and feel *undaunted*. They needed to feel *certain* their children were *certifiable champions* of *change* and that they could *cut* out this *cyanide* that poisoned the *cyber* connections of their chakras. However, if the parents didn't believe in this favorable *prognosis* and *projected* their fears, the children wouldn't learn this *discipline* and would be filled with *discord*. Then the devil would *rack up* many victories, and the children's love-*radar* would remain out of order, because their parents didn't embrace this *radical reckoning* that could *help* them *recover* from this *helplessness*. The parents thought that it would *sting* too much to have a look at the *stinking stipulations* that prevented love from *stirring* their hearts. The parents' self-pity therefore was the all-*pervasive pestilence* that made them *tolerate* this *tonic* in their children, and they felt like *turncoats* when they considered having to make their children confront this *turpitude*. Their own remorse was the *tutor* whose *twenty-twenty vision* never made a *vital* difference, so they *sank* in the fears they failed to *siphon* off and drove these *vehicles* that were *venal*. This *gargantuan gas tank* they had *tapped* into was fitted onto the *capricious car* called ego that gave their behavior the ridiculous *caricature* more typical of a side show in a *carnival*.

Their desire was to avoid *seeing* the *seedy* inside of their hearts, because *speaking* up would require them to feel *unsettled* about fears they considered *unspeakable*. Therefore, it was easier to leave well *enough* alone than to free themselves from these *eccentricities* that had *edged* their way into their minds under the influence of the *entangling entity* which was their *egos*. They felt like *emperors* who shouldn't have to sink to the degradation of *emptying* these *cesspools* in their hearts. They thought it was beneath their dignity to do the *cha-cha* with their own *chagrin* and have to dig up what was dead and *buried* like some kind of *busybody* who had nothing better to do than to *butcher* himself in that way. Therefore, they decided not to *hear* the reasons they had for feeling *heartbroken*, so the *evil* in their lives was *exalted* and not *examined*. The children became *year-round yellow bellies* without a *yen* for personal growth, because their parents were the *yes men* who let *yesteryear's yield* of fears become today's *yoke*.

Nevertheless, the parents could swear out a *death warrant* on these *deceitful decoys* by using their *remorse* to *reopen* these issues and *defecate* these *defiant deficits*. They could take a *shit* and get rid of their *short* fuses. They *could court* the divine *Craftsman*, take a *crap*, and rid themselves of these *creepy* feelings that made their children feel *crestfallen*. They could *discover* how to *discriminate leniency* from *level-head-*

edness and *expel* this *expensive exploitation* by *exploring* these matters so as to *expose* the fears they had *extolled*. They could *parole* themselves in this way from their *paroxysms* of anger, and their children would *parrot* the behavior.

The parents had to *ponder* the fact that saying, "*Poor Child*!" would only *chip* away at their children's self-esteem and fill the *vine* in their children's chakras with *violent* urges rather than *virtue*. The vine could *blossom* with *blotches*, so the children had to identify the *stain* by not being afraid of the *stakeout*, and they had to avoid *mimicking* their parents' tendency to *mince* words. Therefore, if the parents *mindlessly minimized* the importance of the task, so would the *minors* in the family. The children could give *sway* to *peace* of mind by taking a *peek* at these *penalties* they had *pending* if their parents *swore off* their fear of being *offensive ogres* and *insisted* their children make this *inspection*. The children wanted to earn this *brave bravo* from their parents, so their parents had to teach them to *raise* the vine of the Holy Spirit and make it *ramify* in their hearts rather than the evil *branch* that would turn them into *brats*. The parents had to teach the children that they could be *geniuses* at being *gentle* if they just used the *armchair army* known as the twelve powers and Gifts of the Spirit. Then the children would *win* the war against their egos, because the vine would *wind* through their chakras, and they would *grow* up without having to *growl* all the time.

The parents' *insistence* that their children be *inspired* was not some kind of *torture* but rather the concept of *tough love*. The children could easily *find* this *fire* from the *firmament* as a result of this *firmness* and use it as *first aid* whenever their tempers *flared*. Being *loyal* to this *lucidity* would lower *Lucifer's lucre,* because it would teach the children to *probe* these *problems* until they earned the *profit*. Tough love wasn't a rough *shove* therefore but rather the insistence on the part of the parents that the children *should shovel* their manure until the divine sweetness *showed up*. This was the *bold bond* that would keep them out of ego-*bondage*, but the children had to *earn* it *earnestly* through this *courageous courtship* of pristine *principles*. These *ethics* of the *Eucharist* could make their fears *evaporate*, because they were *printed* on our minds before the *procurer* of ego started this *program* of *prostitution* that has made us all need the help of a *psychotherapist*. Then the children would learn to *value* this *vegetative viaduct* in their spines, and the *Victim* would share his *victory* with them by making them grapes on the *vine*. Their *parents* could help them *par-*

take of this *particular pastry* by teaching them that only *cowards* feel *cozy* in their hearts with the *venom* that arose in the *venue* of Eden. From the time of Eden children had been taught to live with the *funny furnishing* known as their *inferiority complex*, so they had to be taught that this *infirmity* was meant to be *informed upon* so that it couldn't *infringe* on their *innate innocence*. Satan had inflicted this *hurt*, so the parents had to teach the *hustle* that could give them a better spiritual *hygiene*.

Satan had made the sentiment of self-*pity* the *placebo* that looked just like love, so both generations had to stop swapping their *competency* for their *complacency*. All of mankind tended to *stumble* when the *stunt double* of self-pity got in the picture, because it required *facing* one's fear of *failure*. Therefore, they just pretended to *succeed* and gave up the *succor* that God could *provide* according to His law of *providence*. They allowed their *money* to be *monitored* by the *monkey* called feelings of *inferiority*, which *infringed* on their *ingenuity* and *subverted* their *success*. The parents hesitated to look at this *motion picture*, because it seemed to be *motivated* by a kind of *groveling* they considered *gruesome*, which was to admit they had made a *mistake* and were a *mite mixed-up*. This *confusion* was *congenital* in man, but they could still stop looking like *silly simians* and *welcome* their *wellbeing*. The children's minds were *complexes* made up of the two *components* of good and evil, so they could be part of the *stupid style* or the more *suave subculture*. Therefore, the children had to *face* the *facts*, go to their *hell*, say *hello* to their *heathen* fears, *heave* them out of their *heaven*, and then say *good-by* in order to welcome their *good-naturedness*.

In order to get rid of this *smudge* the parents had to stop being *smug* about this stain that Satan had *smuggled* into their hearts, and then the children wouldn't run into these *snags*. The parents had a *constellation* of *contagious contraband* which the children would view as *sublime* even though it was the torpedo Satan had *submerged* in their parents' minds to *subordinate* the children to him and *succeed* in making them *suffer*. This *inexorable infection* in the minds of the parents cast this *painful pall* over their children, because the children viewed their parents as officials in a *government gowned* in *infallibility*, when it was really gowned in *infamy*. The parents *wielded* these *wiles* of their ego-addicted *wills willy-nilly* without smelling the *scatological scent* of the *scepter*, and the children became *wimps* who did nothing but tilt *windmills*. Therefore, it was a government *of* wimps with *off-the-wall* behavior, *by* wimps who never *by-passed* their egos, and *for* wimps who allowed Satan's *forcible entry* to *envenom* their wills.

The children were taking a ride on the *credulous crest* of original sin, so the *crew* who took care of the babies in the *crib* could get away with any *crime* they wanted. They could make their children *cringe* so that as adults they would be emotional *cripples.* The parents were really the *crooks* who raised a *crop* of *cross* children, and their *peevishness* was never *penetrated* by their *penitence.* They wouldn't give a *penny* for being *pensive* about the conflict *resolution* that could enable them to *resonate* better with God, so the *unfortunate* consequence was that they were never *unhooked* from their egos. Rather they were the spiritually *penurious people* who never gave their children the *pep talks* that might teach them a more *hopeful horticulture.* Therefore, their children didn't *perceive* the *percentage* in making some *peremptory* strikes against their egos in order to improve their *performances.* The parents' *linkage* with God was something they paid *lip service* to, but they were really in *servitude* to ego, so this *hypocritical hypothesis* gave *entry* to Satan's *envoys* of fear, hurt, and anger.

The parents had to be *resolute* that their children not *resort* to feeling like *abnormal aborigines,* but in order to get this job done they had to remember they were *parents* and not *pariahs.* However, many of the parents had felt like *outcasts* in their nuclear families, and the *outcome* was that they hadn't *denounced* their own *dependency* needs which they considered a *quaint quandary.* Their *family's* spiritual *famine* was *famous* for lasting *forever,* because no one had used their *fortitude* on the *foul foundation* known as their ego-addiction. The parents' *worship* of their parents had left them feeling *worthless.* Therefore, the children *gained* the advantage by having the *gall* to consider them *weaklings* and took to *wearing* them out. This *role* reversal between parent and child often got on a *roll,* because the *panel* of *pangs* in the hearts of the parents made it possible for the children to wear the *pants,* and the children's *domineering* turned their parents into *doormats.* The parents' fear of *rejection* by their children made them dread their children's *rejoinders,* so the parents *sought* the children's approval and neither used the *sounding board* of the *Sovereign* who could make their spirituality *sparkle.*

Often the parents became *patronizing* toward their children, and then the children would become *patsies,* because they would think it was more *gallant* to lose the *game* than to be *steadfast* in the decision not to let anyone *steal* their sweetness. These children sought the *ap-*

proval of their parents, and it left the *aqueduct* between the Crown and Root Chakras closed, because no one told them they had to seek the approval of the divine *Arbiter* to open it.

If the children *toadied today* by showing a *respectful response* to their parents' *stigmatizing stimuli*, they would pay the *toll tomorrow*, so *toddler* and parent had to work *together* if the children were to *unhitch* themselves from this *unholiness*. Parent and child had to face the *agony* and cure the *ailment*. They had to *eavesdrop* on their *eccentricities* and learn how they had *eclipsed* their *ecstasy*. They had to stop *dramatizing* the *dread* that had *formerly driven* them crazy and had made them *forsake* their *fountains* of living waters.

It was a *bitch* for parents to *bite* their lips, remain *mute* in the face of their children's *mutilations*, and not *mutter* expressions of self-pity. Nevertheless, if they *spoke* up in this way, their children wouldn't feel *special*, because they could see their parents didn't *trust* them to *tryst* with God, and their sweetness would go *down the tubes*. The *solid* truth was that the children needed to go on this *solo flight* to end their ego's *fling*. However, the problem that was *afoot* was that the parents were *afraid* for their children to get in the *cockpit*, so they kept up this *cocky coddling* and exerted a *control* over their children from which they never *convalesced*. The parents never realized that it was *their theft* that prevented their children from *owning* the *ox* of their own will. The parents robbed their children of their *bravery* by *breaking* and *entering* their hearts in order to further the *enterprise* of their egos. The children therefore concluded they were made of *timid tinsel* and that they had *murine muscles* which would always be *flabby*, because they deserved this *flack*.

However, if the children didn't *tarry* and *tattled* on their egos, they would *flex* these muscles and *float* on air, because the divine sweetness would *flood* their hearts. Then they would feel *classier*, because *cleaning house* would make them stop thinking their minds were *hovels*. The children could then *listen* to the fears that *lit* the fires of their *anger*, calm their *anguish*, and enjoy the *rest* that flows from this *restraint*. If they took a *look* at these *lollapaloozas* when they were *alone*, they would realize they had God *alongside*. Then they wouldn't feel *fidgety* when the *fiend* went around *bursting* the bombs he normally *bushwhacks* us with. The parents just had to be *adamant* in insisting that their children *address* their own need for this *adeptness*, because then the divine sweetness would *adhere* to them.

If their parents didn't deliver the *pitch* for the *pity party*, the children would develop *self-confidence* and surrender their fear of loss of *self-control*. The children's disarming-clout would *advise* them *against* their *alarm*-doubt, and their strong-arm clout would *challenge* the *charlatan* of their *charm*-doubt. Then they would fall in God the *Father's favor*, because their *fear* of the *Lord* had rid them of this *lousy* trouble. The children could reach this safe *harbor* and get the *hard noses* that would make their fears *no-shows*. They could be *optimists* if their parents were the *optometrists* whose *first* priority was to *fit* them with these *glasses* of their fortitude. Then they would stop *glazing* over their fears and could *glean* their sweetness, because the *whirlpool* in the chakras would sweep away this *whitewash* and put them in touch with this force *within* that would enable them to *withstand* any *woe*.

The children just had to find this *gasket* in their hearts that fit into the *gas station* of the Sacred Heart and *know* that it was OK to fill themselves with this *kosher fuel* that was *fundamental* to their well-being. Then they could *refuel* whenever they wanted, obtain *refuge* from their ego's *refuse*, and see to it that God *regained* his *regal* status there. When this *hose* of the *Host* got *turned on* in their hearts, the divine sweetness would come right out of their *turrets*, travel down the *tube* in the vertical axis, and make the Fruits *tug* on their heartstrings, because the Passion of Jesus had connected their *pinnacles* to this *pipe* in their hearts. They had been *head-strong* and *heart-sick*, but their *heads* could *hear* the message of their *hearts* and get *heated* up with *heaven's* fire. The children had to *think* that the *third* person of the Trinity could satisfy their *thirst* so that the sweetness in the chakra in their *thorax* could get to the one in their *throat* through the spiral. Then the children could *celebrate* the connection of the *central* chakra to the one above the *cerebral cortex*, and no one could get their *goat*, because they would feel connected to *God*. Their *sixth sense* was the *skill* that *analyzed* the *anatomy* of this divine *anchor* in their chests.

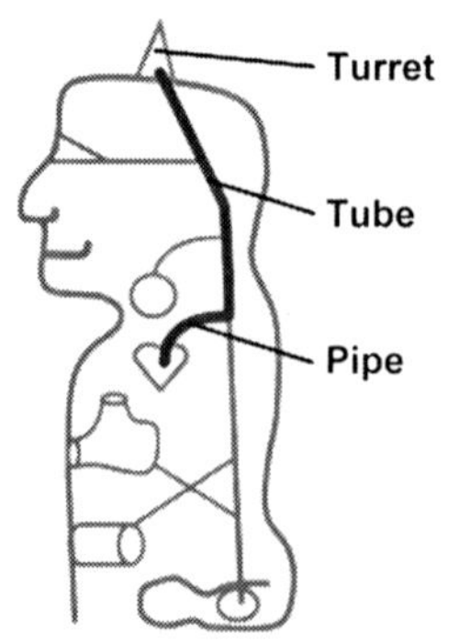

They could feel like *angels*, because the *intuition* of the children could *investigate* their *retinue* of fear, hurt, and anger and make it *retire*, but their parents had to teach them to fight this *war*. The children had to *warm* up their wills to the fact that their egos would only take them on the *warpath* and that it was much better to use the *warranty* of the Crucifixion to *wash* off this nonsense. Overcoming their *fears* was a *feasible feat* but only if their parents taught them that it was more *satisfying* to *saturate* themselves with God's *sweetness* than *swig* Satan's *swill.* Then the children would realize that making this *choice* was not a nasty *chore.* Parents had to be *confident* that their children could overcome *conflict*, *confront confusion*, and become more *congenial.* The children's *potpourri* of repressed feelings could be *poured* out, and they would not want to *pout*, because the *powerful practice* of *prayer* would bring about this *restful result.* Then the *wealth* of the Fruits would enable them to *weather* any *storm*, because they would have become *stouthearted.*

Many children didn't receive this *compensation*, however, because their parents suffered from the *complacency complication* that has afflicted the heart of man since Satan *complimented* Eve in Eden. This *token* of *toleration stank*, because the *staple* item in the children's diet was the same self-pity that had taken the *starch* out of their parents' hearts. They didn't realize their *captor* Satan had given them his poisonous calomel hoping they would think it was a *caramel.* The parents didn't realize this *morbid morsel* would *replicate* itself in their children's minds and fill them with *resentments* they wouldn't be able to

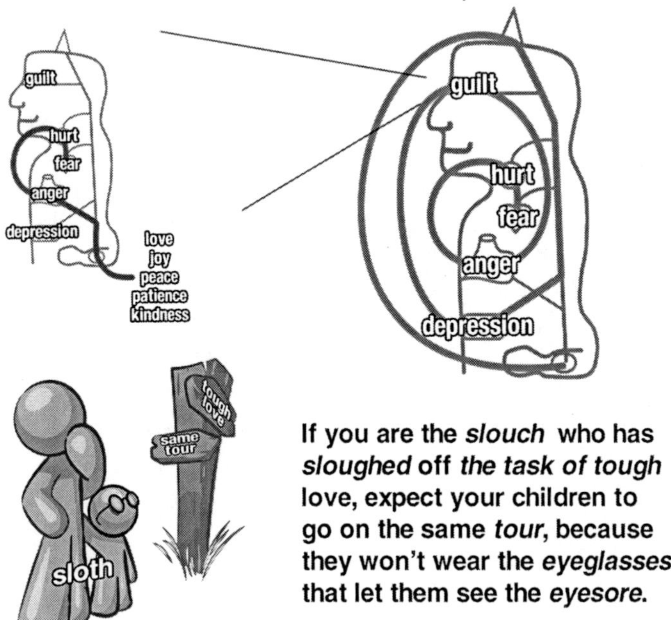

resist. The children would have no *objectivity*, because they would feel *obliged* to allow this *oblique* suggestion to turn out *carbon copies* in their hearts of their parents' *cardiac* disease. The parents passed along this *careworn cargo* as a result of this *pusillanimous pussyfooting* and gave their children *pygmy pyloric* valves at the end of their *stomachs* that didn't let their fears pass into their *stools.*

The parents had to teach their children that this *hearsay* in their *hearts* didn't have to *heckle* them, because they owned the *hardship hardware* which was the first part of the spiral. They had to tell them that its job was to teach the stomach's pyloric valve not to *clamp down* on *claptrap* but rather let these *shadowy shapes* pass into their stool so they would not leave *scars* on their hearts that were *scary. Instead of* these encouraging *instructions*, however, the parents had *whispered* little *white* lies in their children's ears, and these *second-hand secrets* proved to be *intimidating intoxications*, because they left them with the *unspoken* implication that they were emotionally *unstable.* Therefore, the children caught these *curve balls* and swallowed them whole thinking they were some kind of *custard* when what they had taken into *custody* was this *custom* from hell that would be *cutting* to them all their lives. The children's lives therefore *careened* out of control because of this *carload* of *carnage.* The devil wore a *carnation* in his lapel to show that even the *carpenter* couldn't prevent this *carry-over*, because if the parents were *hell-bent* on remaining at the *helm* in this way even the carpenter couldn't *help.* The parents had the free *will* to make their children weeping *willows*, or they could contact the *representative* whose Crucifixion was the *reprisal* that could end this tyranny. The children could *reproduce* love and *repudiate* fear in their hearts if their parents *requested* help from Jesus. Then the parents could stop *gypping* their children, and the family would not indulge in *habitual haggling.*

The parents could get back their *impartiality* by simply acknowledging they were at an *impasse.* They just had to see their *objectivity* as their *obligation*, and then their egos' *subjectivity* would not *subjugate* them. Their *attention* to these *destructive details* would not be *attenuated*, and they could make their children take *notice* of this *nourishment* that could keep their *heads healthy.* The children would then recognize their egos as *perverse pets* and *detach* themselves from them in order to *detect* the *enemies* they needed to *engage.* These *battles* could be won. The parents just needed to use the *beacon* in their Brow Chakras. They needed to *disclose* their *discomfort.* They needed to identify the *disease* they wanted to *disengage* from. Then their children would also learn this *low-key* perspective that came from *loyalty* to their *health* rather than to their *heartache.*

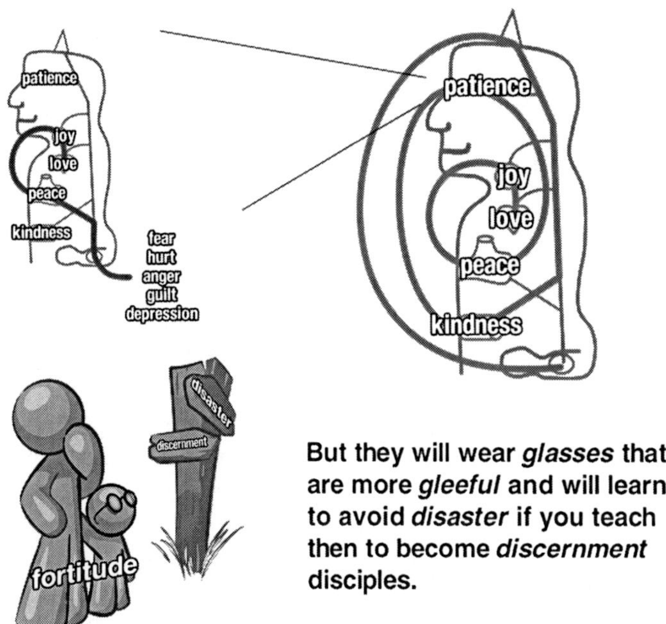

Many parents remained *naïve*, however, and their discernment continued to take a *nap*. They were *sophomoric sopranos* who *sang* a *singularly sinister opera*, because their thinking was guided by the *opiate* of pretending to be *immaculate* when they were really *immature* and *overburdened* with *overconfidence*. They were really *overflowing* with anger that came from fears they needed to *overhear* but which they chose to *overlook*. Therefore, they couldn't *modestly modify* their reactions to *stress*, didn't march in *stride* with the Holy Spirit, and didn't feel *matter-of-fact* in the midst of *mayhem*. Satan *heightened* their pride as part of this *heist*, so they passed this *contraband* on to their children who did not *contradict* it by *contrasting* it with their *contrition*. Therefore, the children never *paused* in the *pawnshop* of the Immaculate Heart of Mary. They never took advantage of this *field test* that could defeat the *fiend*, and they never learned to *fight* spiritually by making use of the *figurative* meaning of the Crucifixion. They didn't *annihilate annoying* thoughts or get *anointed* with the *answer*, but given the necessary encouragement, they could still face their *difficulties*, *dig* up their causes, and *uncover* this *undaunted under-*

current of *unheard-of uniformity.* They could be *brokers* of love and not *brook* any *interference* in the *interior* of their hearts, but their parents had to *insist* they not get *tangled up* in their *tantrums.* Their parents had to encourage them to *tackle* the *task* of figuring out how they had been *taught* such *taxing teachings* and *tease out* a little contrition in order to feel better.

God and man could get together in the *pavilion* of the human heart, and *peace negotiations* between these two *neighbors* could be *furthered* when man insisted on detaching himself from the short *fuse* known as ego. As a result of his Passion Jesus gained entry into this *gazebo* so that the *gear* known as the chakras could attend to man's remorse and earn man the *gem* known as the will of God. Jesus became a *one-man* welcome committee for those with this *one-minded* determination who would not rest until they enjoyed this *one-of-a-kind* relaxation. The Sacred Heart was *installed* in the heart of man so that *instead* of fear man could enjoy the fund of love in this *war chest* that God reserved for the purpose of ending Satan's *war crimes.* Satan opened his *saucy sauna* in the heart of man by encouraging Eve to *saunter* over to Adam so that he would use his *sausage* to make his descendants *savages.* Satan opened this *savings account* in man's *chest* to make him *chicken* by feeding him fearful *rations.* Satan made man's *ravings count* him out from true happiness, because Satan's *counterfeit countermanded* the will of God in the mind of man. Satan knew that the interest that *accrued* would leave man feeling *accursed,* allowing him to deposit his *wickedness* in the *will* of man and make *withdrawals* that would make his self-esteem *wither.* He counted on becoming the *chancellor* of *chaos* in the *chapel* of the human heart, because he knew that his *trash* would be *treasured* by man who would then be too *lazy* to let his remorse take the *lead.*

Nevertheless, man could always get a *new* perspective by feeling *shame,* because these were the only *shears* that could cut him *loose* from this *lopsided lore.* Therefore, from the time of Eden remorse became the only *ace in the hole* that could heal man's *aching* heart. What was necessary was a *systematic* approach to this *tabernacle* in which man could put his fears on the *table* by recreating the *tableaus* from his past that made him think love was *taboo.* If man *canvassed* his childhood for the *capers* that made him lose this *capital,* his heart would become the *classroom* in which he could *claw* out of this mess. Man's heart-mind had *photographs* of the events from his childhood that required his soul-strength's *phototropism.* Therefore, man had to *nab* the two *narcissists* and explain to them that loving one *another* was the *answer.* Man had to *sum* up the problem to them by explaining that the light of the *sun* was in his Crown Chakra and that he expected them both to attend this *Sunday school* so he could eat the *super* meal called the Last *Supper.* This *reciprocity* with God could be *reclaimed*, so man had to remember that it was the *nature* of his *Navel* Chakra to connect his *umbilical cord* to God so that his joy could be *unabashed.*

The *plank* describing this *plantlike* attachment to God was included in Christ's political *platform* so that you and God could *play ball* together. Your behavior is the *proving ground* where you earn these *provisions* when you satisfy the *proviso* of your contrition, so *possess* the divine sweetness that comes from this *post* of your heaven within. Your contrition is the *tender-hearted tendril* that *grasps* God *gratefully*, takes *hold* of His *holiness*, and never misses the chance to *seize* the divine so as to make it part of your *self.* Your contrition is the *Johnny-on-the-spot* who gives you *joie-de-vivre.* It reestablishes the *joint venture* you were meant to have with God as part of your original innocence. Hence, use it to *share* your reasons for having so many close *shaves*, end your *commotion* by *communing* with Him, have *mutual* admiration, and put an end to the *myopia* that has led to your *myriad* of problems.

When man was *created* by the *Creator* the divine *artist* gave him an *asexual* nature like Himself. He *invested* His *inveterate* sweetness in mankind so that *discrimination* according to gender would not even be up for *discussion*, and he intended for it to raise the act of *reproduction* above that which takes place among *reptiles* so that man would be *imperturbable* and *impervious* to evil. Nonetheless, Satan approached Eve and told her that her *contours* could win the *contract* of Adam's love, so she got in the *clench* that resulted in the *climax*, enabling Satan to open his *phallic pharmacy* in the heart of man. Satan then filled the vertical axis of man's chakra system with the *drugs* that would *dry* up this *duct.* Satan *dispensed* the pride, envy, and anger that *displaced* love, joy and peace.

The *continuous conversation* between man and God that had formerly connected the *chain* of the *chakras* from top to bottom met with this *challenge* that turned them into *chancy channels*, because Satan's *conniving* made man's *consciousness* lose *contact* with the *happy harbor* at the top. Man developed a *thermal thinking*, and his mind became a *hot hub*, because this *absence* of the *Absolute* made man *drunk* with *duality*. This *duct* became a *dud*, because the *vertical* axis of the chakra system had turned into a *very vexed viaduct*. Adam and Eve's sex act was the *awareness axe* that made *faith* in God *fall*, and the *soul* lost touch with its *Source*, because they *bowed* down to these forces that made the divine sweetness *boycott* the *brain* of man. Man became a *blind blockhead*, because during his *life* this *light* that formerly *inspired* him started filling him with *insults*. Nevertheless, man didn't have to *expire* to get *explicit* answers, because he could *expose* these *daunting details*. The *soul* of man was a *sounding board* that could *span* this gap between man and God, because it was *attentive* to the *dirt* that caused this *discord*. It was a *persistently perspicacious attorney* who could *sue* to regain access to this *summit* where the Last *Supper* is prepared.

We don't have to *die* to gain access to this *diet*. We can take this *wakeful walk* during life. We can restore this *alert alignment* to God and *allay* the fear that resulted when the *shaft* of our vertical axis got *shook* up in this way. When Satan *flattered* Eve by encouraging her to *flaunt* her *shapeliness* in front of Adam, our souls became the *shards* that *broke* loose from the divine *broker*. Nevertheless, the soul still has a *sharp* cutting edge of personal growth, so let's not have our hopes getting *shattered* just because Satan got Eve to use the *sheath* of her vagina to turn us into lost *sheep*.

Man was *outfitted* with the *outlet* of ego, because Eve thought she *outranked* God. She thought the *meaty median* organ between Adam's legs was a more *inspiring instrument* of love than his heart, so Adam's *penetrating penis* became the *ornament* that turned us into God's *ornery orphans*. Eve opened this *venereal vent* which proved to be a *conduit* for *conflict*, because the *favorable feed* of the divine *nectar* was supplanted by man's *needs*. The *resultant retention* of fears in the heart of man made it a *repository* of *repressed* feelings, and this *deficit* was *deflected* into the *negligee negotiations* that *beckoned* man and wife in *bed*.

When man was *tempted* to put his *tentacle* to the *test*, it *confused conjugal* relations, because Satan's *fiction fiddled* with the *mind* of man when this *minor minstrel* went on this *misadventure*. Nevertheless, man tried to *fill* his heart with this *fire* between his legs, so this *concupiscent conflict* continued to play itself out. Man thought he and his *wife* could have a *wild* time with his *plaything* if he *plugged* it into her *plumbing*, so they both *plunged* into this *act* which made *Adam* and Eve feel more *allure* for one another than the *Almighty*. Man suffered from *marginal marital* relations when he tried to hit this *mark*, because his marriage became a *market* in which Satan sold his wares.

The *controversy* often began when man tried to *convince* his wife to *coo*, because she often felt *cool* and didn't want to *cooperate*. Therefore it was an *embattled embrace*, because the man usually *anticipated* these *antics* more than the woman, and this would make her *anxious*. The *problem* with the *process* was that the chakra at the *apex* couldn't take part when the *lecherous apparatus* between the *legs demanded deployment*. The *prince* of darkness was the *warden* of this *prison* when their *private* parts *warmed* up in this way, because the *prize* of God's will was ignored by the kundalini.

Man was *driven* to *raise* this *drooping ramrod* which *drummed* this idea of *duality* into his head, and the kundalini was the *profane professor* who aimed to *profit* from this *profligate promise*. Therefore man *put* it to his wife until the *pygmy* organ brought about its *pyrotechnics*, and the kundalini went *down* the *drain* at the moment of high *drama*. What they didn't realize is that they had *shut* down the *shuttle* bus between the Crown and Root Chakras as a result of participating in this *side show* that *silenced* the voice of God.

God had *prohibited promiscuity* in order to *prop up* man's *prosperity*, but the *Root* Chakra was *roped* into this *rotten* deal, because Adam didn't *value* this *valve* in his *prostate* gland that could have prevented the *sap* called the kundalini from *sashaying* into this disaster. When Adam's *sperm spilled*, the Holy *Spirit split*, and the *sushumna* of man got *suspended* between his *suspicions* and his *sustenance*.

Man was *naive* enough to swallow this *narcotic* and was never able to *guess* that his divine *guidance* had deserted him because of this *gullibility*. Nevertheless, the *high* chakra's *Hindu hinge* throughout all of *history* has enabled man to *see* the fears he needs to *seek* so they won't *seep* into his behavior. It has been the *hitching post* that man has used to *hoist* himself up to God's *holiness*, so man had to realize his *libido* had given him a *licking*. He had to confront these *lies* so as to *lift* the kundalini up to the *lighthouse* of the Crown Chakra and pay his respects there before he *limbered* up his *linchpin*. Before man got in the *saddle* he had to obtain *safe-conduct* for the *salacious saloon keeper* who was *salted* away in the Root Chakra by *saluting* God in prayer. The kundalini was the *component* that made the chakras a *composure compound*, so that children could be *conceived* without *confiscating* their divine sweetness. Nevertheless, man remained *confused* about this *conjugal connection*, so their children got *shortchanged* as a result of this *shortfall*.

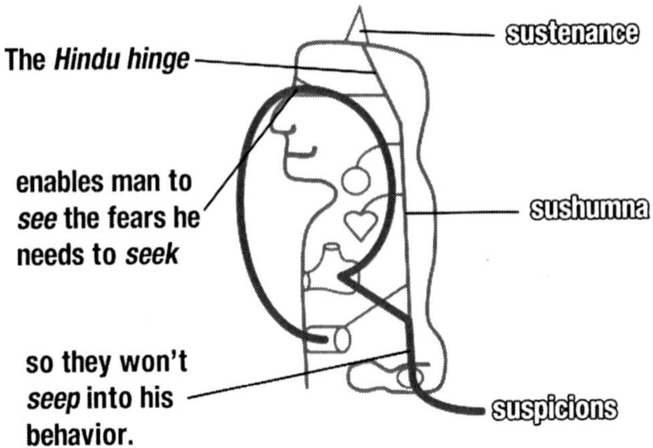

The *stories* children *stowed* away in their minds contained *gobs* of untruths, because it resulted from a worship of the *god* of the *gonads* who made the divine sweetness seem like a *good-for-nothing*. It was a *deification* that was *deleterious*, because the *parental parody* that resulted from *omitting* the *Omnipotent* made *mortifying mothers* and *fascist fathers* raise *prodigiously* unhappy *progeny*. Man had become *inattentive* to the *incandescent* light at the *top* that had been *toppled* and had begun to suffer from *incestuous* son to mother *attachments* that *augured* poorly for *wedded* bliss. The *weight* men carried around in their marriage was made up of these unresolved dependency needs that made *them* demand *then* and *there* that their wives supply what their mothers had not, because their mothers had *not* considered them very *notable*. What had never *materialized* for these men was the *maternal loving-kindness* that *Lucifer lulled* to sleep with the *lullaby* of original sin. Mother-son relationships carried this *opposite* sex *oppression*, because when Eve put Adam's *slim* thing into her *slimy slit*, sexual *reproduction* became the *reptilian rerun* that carried this *heterosexual hex*. Men therefore *displaced* their *displeasure* in their marriages, and it was a show of *revenge-reverence* by a bunch of *outcasts* who used this *outlet over* and over until their marriages were *overturned*.

Farcical father-son relationships, however, conveyed the same *song and dance*, and some men became *professionally profitless* in the *workplace* because of this form of false *worship*. *Men* who had been raised by *menacing men-folk* wound up doing *menial work*, because their sense of self-*worth* didn't include this *manly manna* that had to be passed along from father to son. Some of them even got effeminate *mannerisms*, because these *incestuous* son-to-father attachments *inched* their way into their sexual behavior. They *gathered* in the wounds of *gay* men so as to produce a particularly *goofy gore*. One man would think the other was so *gorgeous* that they would *sock* it to one another in the wrong *socket*. They indulged in *sodomy*, because their fathers had never been very *softhearted* toward them, and they sought their fathers' *solace* in this way.

Likewise, *lesbians* had learned a bad *lesson*, because the lack of their *mothers'* love made them want to give one another *mouth-to-mouth* resuscitation. Their mothers were *woeful women* with *feminine fences erected* around their hearts, and this *error* put their *daughters'* hearts in the *deadlock* of not feeling like a very *womanly wonderland*. Therefore, these women were *wont* to *woo* one another, because Satan had pulled the *wool* over their eyes in this way.

This *gay gear gelled* in the hearts of each sex, because these fears of *rejection* had originated in father-son and mother-daughter *relationships*. The *erotic error* in each case was that the divine sweetness of the child could not *homogenize* itself in the kundalini without the love of the parent of the *homologous* sex. Therefore, the kundalini would feel *devalued* and would *deviate* its flow into the *satisfaction* of one man's *sausage* by another and the *climax* of the *clitoris* one woman could give to another. In each case they had *settled* for less, and used *sex* to fill this gap. As children their *nuclear families* had left so little love in their hearts that they felt they had to get *nude* to make up for the *nuisance*. Their families had been the *laboratories* in which the *lack* of this *same* sex *sanction* set them in pursuit of this *homosexual honey*.

Eve's *senseless sensuality* had made man the *mindless minister* of this *miscellaneous mischief*. This *lecherous legacy* resulted from the *secretion* of *secular* influences into the vertical axis that deprived man of the *security blanket* of the divine sweetness. Every time man made love the *disaster* he reenacted was *discarding* the divine sweetness, because this was the *payoff* he owed the devil at the *peak* of his sexual pleasure. Man's *ejaculation* always *elated* the devil, because the *onus* of ego resulted from this *ooze* and allowed Satan to start the soap *opera* he *operated* in the life of man. Satan's *trickery* had stopped the divine sweetness from *trickling* down into the act, because the divine

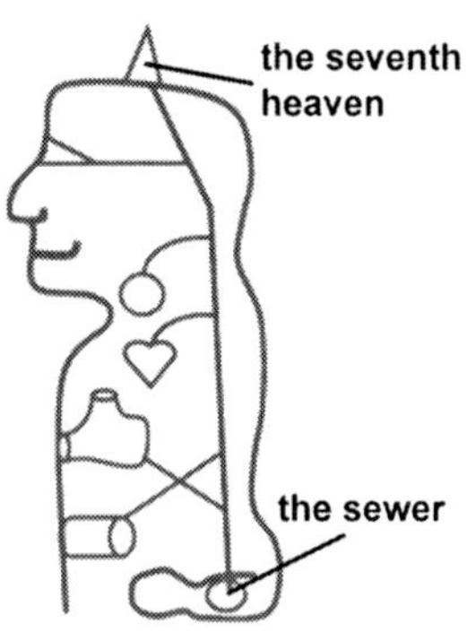

sweetness in the *seventh heaven* became the *sewage* that went out through the *sewer* when man had *sex*. When a man *warmed up* to his wife, it turned into a *war of nerves*, because man's *regret* over the loss of unconditional love always tagged along. It *reinforced* man's fear of *rejection* by God and made man *insulting* in all his other *interactions*.

We consider ourselves *hunks* who are on the *hunt* when we approach our wives and feel *hurt* when as *husbands* we don't make them want to behave like *hussies* in bed. We *wield* our *wieners* as if our *wives* should take one look at the *wild* beast's *sterling* possession and want the *stick* to get *stiff*, so we can *shove* it in them until they *shriek*. I want to make these *thrusts* land with a *thump*, and I am driven *bonkers* by the appearance of some women's *boobs*, because my mind is the *bordello* in which the motherly love that *runs* short makes the *runt* between my legs want to become the incredible *hulk* and *hump*. The sight of a woman's well-rounded *rump* makes me want to reenact this *rupture* with God, and their *stern* sections make it want to get *stiff*, because the *dwarf* that *dwells* there thinks he can only be *happy* when he gets *hard*, so that I can *poke* with this *pole*. Gazing at women's *butts* and *buxom* bosoms has given me this *buzz*, but its *by-product* is my ego-addiction, and I choose not to be held *hostage* by this *hothead*. Therefore, I intend to ask Mary and Joseph to make my mind their *household*. Then I won't be *heckled* by this *hedonism*, because they *raised* Jesus, and he can stop this *rampage* by *tranquilizing* this wild beast who leads me into this *trap*.

I have been *spurred* on by this *spurious hankering* for *hanky-panky*, but instead of getting my *jollies* in this way I will go to Saint *Joseph* and ask him to share *joy* that is more *judicious*. That way my kundalini won't have to *jump* ship, because Saint Joseph is the *celibate* spouse and can give me this *cement*, which is the *male* bonding that will help me stop *maltreating* others. He is my *foster* father and can help me stop this *foul play*. He can give me the spiritual *foundation* instituted by the *founder* of the Christian religion, and I prefer this *winning wiring*, because it makes my *computer* stop responding to this *con game*. Then God will be the *commuter* on my vertical axis who will keep me *company* in order to make me *compassionate*, and the *thief* won't control my *thinking*. I don't have to have *thoughts* that *threaten* my well-being, because my *mind* can be God's *minister*, and it doesn't have to *perform* the *perfunctory* tasks of my ego, because it can be *perfused* by the divine sweetness. I *wait* for the right moment to *wallow* with my *wife* and *want* to *warm* her up, *waste* this *water*, and have a *wild* time, but when I *hope* for this *horny fairy tale* to come true, my *faith falls* for her *charms*, and the devil takes *charge* of my *charity*. I am a grape off the *vine* because of the loss of these theological *virtues*, so I am *charter* member of the club begun in Eden. I still *chase* my wife, but St. Joseph was a most *chaste* spouse, so I aim to go to him and ask him to put this *cheap* thrill in *check*.

Joseph was *married* to *Mary*, and they are the *couple* who can make me *courteous*, because they were *chosen* to raise the child who began the *church* that completes this electrical *circuit*. Mary will turn on the *motherly motor* in my heart that will fill my *mouth* with the divine sweetness, because her Immaculate Conception is the *Fatherly faucet* God installed in her heart. Mary and Joseph knew that the human mind was a *brothel*, so they *prayed* as a *preamble* to *screwing*, and God didn't have to *scrimp* with the divine sweetness when they conceived Jesus' *brothers*. Nevertheless, I was born in this *whorehouse whose wickedness* has infected me, so when I feel *tortured* by the fact that my parents' *toss* in the hay has produced this *totalitarianism*, I can ask Mary and Joseph to connect me to the *Benevolent* Dictator who won't leave me *bent* out of shape in this way.

We just need to *pray* for *relief* from this *precarious balance* and *remember* that the *ballyhoo* over Adam's *banana* and Eve's *bare* ass *precipitated* us into this *merry mess*. Nevertheless, this is a *discrepancy* we can *disengage* from by asking Mary and Joseph to *raise* us so that we can *rally* with God. God made Jesus a member of the *holy* family so we could have happy *homes*. Joseph and Mary are willing to *adopt* anyone who has made the commitment to stop *adulating* his *adulterants*. They overcome the *adversary* and establish an *affectionate affiliation* with God, so if you have *weird* behaviors that indicate that your parents have *welched* on your sweetness, go to Joseph and Mary, because they will *welcome* you. Their *accent* is on *acceptance*, and they don't *reinforce* the idea that your disobedience will invite their *rejection*, so it results in a better *relationship* with God. I have pretended to be a member of the holy *family*, and this *fantasy* has resulted in an *upbringing* that has given me the *upper hand* over *behaviors* that formerly *beleaguered* me. Mary is the *cook* in this family, and she has helped me *cope*. She prepares *meals* that the devil can't *meddle* with, because she always includes the *essence* we were *estranged* from in Eden. The *rearing* she has given me is *reassuring*, because she *begot* the one who *began* our church and just *repeats* the *recipe* she used with Jesus so as to *replace* the items we missed and *reconcile* us with God.

Jesus is our *chakra champion*, because he reopened the *Catholic causeway* that was closed when the *caveman* known as Adam *ceased* being *celibate*. He made it possible for the divine sweetness to *travel* to the Root Chakra and end the *travesty*. Jesus *constructed* this framework so we could *contact* God, and he did it by going through his Passion. He *crucified* the *cryptic* problems that stemmed from the *cuddling* in Eden and *curbed* the *curse* of the feminine *curves* that had put man in the *custody* of the devil.

Man had always wanted to *hook* up because of this *horny horror*, so he had taken to *doctoring* his wife with his *hot dog* until they were both *done for*. Therefore, Jesus got in a *huddle* with God over this *dose* that man had been *doting* on and went through his Crucifixion to disband this *frankfurter fraternity* whose *pledges* were getting into *plenty* of trouble because of *fraudulent* love that made them *freak out*. Satan had *conned* man into this *conditional* love, so the *icy idolatry* by a child of his parents made man feel *illegitimate*. I have suffered from this bad *imitation*, but I am *impassioned* to *impeach* it, so I will *implore* God to bring about this *improvement*, because I am a *legitimate* child of God and not a *lemon*.

Jesus made the *titanic toast* at the Last Supper that brought man and God *together*, so all *Christians* are entitled to *gulp* down this *wholesome wine* that *gushes* out of this fountain of living waters. This *refreshing beverage* fills the *bill*, *binds* us to God, and allows us to feel *regaled* by His *regard regardless* of what happens. The *flow* of this *fluid* began before the *travesty* under the *tree* resulted in this *deviant devotion* to *parental pathology*. The *cloister closed*, and the divine sweetness *clotted* when Adam and Eve took off their *clothes*, because the chakra in the *clouds* lost its *clout* over the one run by the *clown*. The *chakras* became a *chaotic chapel*, but my heart can be the *salutary sanctuary* where I do not *drink* that which makes me *drunk*. I can choose to *imbibe* the *immaculate beverage* of the divine sweetness that will make me happy *beyond* my wildest hopes. I can choose to end my *blasphemy*, because at the Last Supper Jesus *blessed* this *wine* that *wires* me to God.

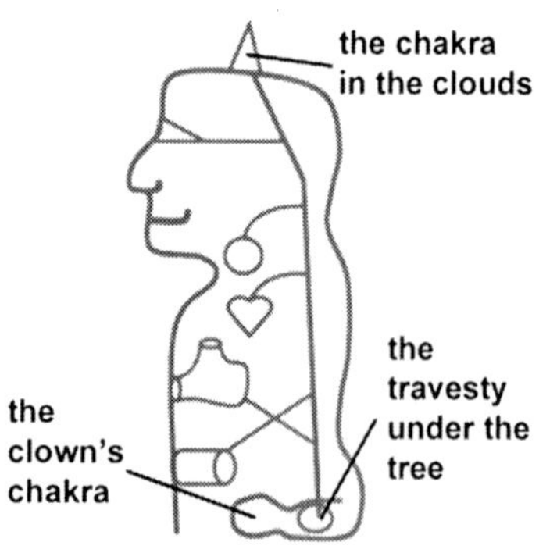

My mind is a *tavern* in which I can drink beverages that are *taxing*, or I can drink this *tea brewed* as a *bridge* to God. God *be-*

stowed this *beverage* on me, because the *Eucharist evens* the score with the *evil* one and *centers* me spiritually when I swallow it through the *cervical* chakra. Adam and Eve's *lewd liaison* gave me an *indolent inebriation*, because they opened the *bar* of ego in my mind when they got *bare*. This allows Satan to *barge* in whenever he wants, but I became God's *partner* at the tea *party* Jesus celebrated before his *Passion*. Jesus offered himself as the tea *bag* at this party and *bailed* me out of this *baleful ball of wax* by jumping into the *teapot* of my heart. It was *teeming* with fears, but Jesus prepared the *tea* that *taught* my heart-mind and soul-strength the tea's *teamwork* with the sugar and water. *Adding* the tea to the sugar and water was the *admirable* solution; because heart-mind and soul-strength *admitted* their mistake, and each *admixed* his *adroit* ingredient with the other's so as to *advance* the cause of the *Lord's loving-kindness* in my behavior.

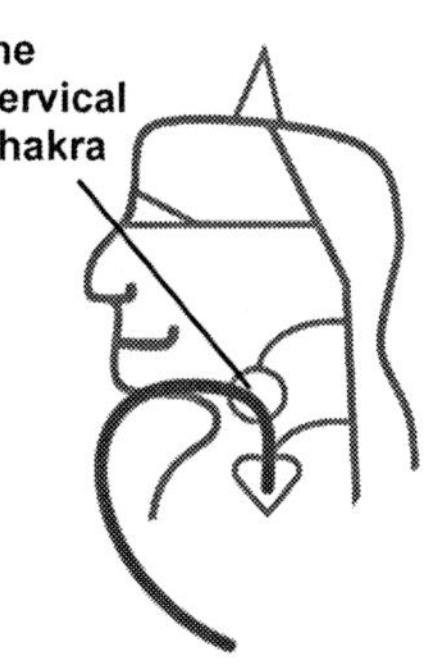

They had been *scared* of one another because of the *schism* caused by original sin, but Jesus *coordinated* the insights of the *coping strategist* above with the *stream* of my soul-*strength's* kundalini from below so that the divine sweetness that normally *flowed* in the vine of the Holy Spirit could *flower* in my chakras. Consequently, I got the *outlook* that enabled me to *outsmart* my ego, because my heart-mind finally figured that his *sugar* was *suited* to my soul-strength's water. My heart-mind stopped *sulking* around, and in *summary* I got to enjoy the *sumptuous supper* of the Fruits.

Jesus decided to have this *get-together* in the *ghetto* of my heart so that the two *beleaguered guests* from *above* and *below* could *abstain* from this *absurd abuse* and be *guided* by the *infallible influence* of the Holy Spirit. Each guest had been the victim of the *guillotine* Satan had used in Eden and believed in the *decapitation deception* of original sin. Therefore, Jesus couldn't *infuse* his *ingenuity* into the blood in my heart until each of the two guests brought the necessary *ingredient*. The guest above had to *submit* the *sugar* and the *warrior* below had to bring the *water* so the *teabag* in the middle could *team* up with these two *technicians*. Then I could get a better *temperament*, be-

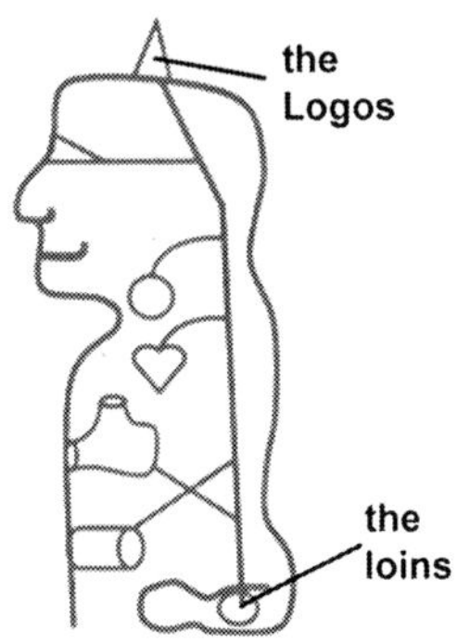

cause the *locker-room logic* that flowed from the *temptation* in Eden would no longer alienate the chakra of my *Logos* from the one in my *loins*.

If I *steep* the teabag in heartfelt contrition, the chakra on the *steeple* will *steer* the two guests into my heart so that the tasty tea *leaves* in the bag can reverse the *lecherous legacy* of my original sin. This *bad blood* between the two guests can end, because this *bag* of tea contains the *bones* that bring the *bonus* of Jesus' bone marrow. Jesus' *body* is made up of the *flesh* and *bones* that make his blood *flow*, so when he was on the Cross, his bones weren't *broken*, because they *brokered* the *deal* of the New Covenant which erases these *debts*. Original *sin* is no longer able to *sing* this same old song, because Jesus' *skeleton forms* the *formidable formula* known as the blood of Christ, brings *forth* our good *fortune*, replaces the *foul foundation* of original sin, and starts the *fountain* of living waters in our hearts. We become children of God and are no longer *marred* by this *mark* of Cain, because Christ's *bone marrow produces* this *prudent glue* that makes the two guests *go* to *God* and ask to be *bound* in marriage. Their improved *public relations* make my heart *pump pure* love, because the chakra on the *floor* makes its *fluid* go up, the *flying* chakra above makes the divine sweetness come down, and they both meet with the teabag in the *middle* by walking this *mild mile*. I just have to *irrigate* the teabag with the two *isolationists*' sugar and water and *mix* well so that they won't *mock* one *another anymore*. Then the *Italian* Church enables the sugar and water to complete their *itinerary* in the *spiral* by sending the Holy *Spirit* to *splice* the Fruits into my thinking and end the *split* in Eden that made me such a *spoilsport*.

The *tea taught* the two *whiz kids* who had been *wicked* that my *will* could *win* the *windfall* of the Fruits, so my heart-mind's sugar got *soaked* by my soul-strength's water, and they both *sobered* up. The sugar and water *mixed* with the tea so as to end the *mob* rule of ego. Heart-mind and soul-strength became *compatible compatriots*, because they each got rid of the *anorexia* they had for one *another* and *mutually* brought forth *my* wellbeing by *appeasing* the *appetite* known as my spiritual hunger.

They had remained *apart*, because the *aphrodisiac potion* from Eden had fed man the *potluck* dinner of the seven sins, but they realized that the *powerful practice* of *praying together* could end this *toll*. In Eden the Fruits became the *rudiments* man *rued* not having, because man's appetite for them had been *ruined* by the *appetizer* Adam and Eve ate under the *apple* tree. Therefore, man needed to be *reminded* of these *remnants* by using the chakras. The chakras were the *machine* where the *made-to-order magic* of the *ingredients* known as the sugar and the water could take advantage of the divinity *inherent* in the tea so as to overcome *iniquity*. Therefore, the tea and sugar were the *solids* that went into *solution* by *linking* up with the *liquid*, and Jesus was the *chef* in my *chest* who devised this *reasonable recipe* that *reconciled* the two *jilted* lovers. They did the *job* of *serving* the tea that would *settle* my nerves, because Jesus taught them to be the *teetotalers* in the *temple* who could *abstain* from this *absurd abuse*. They each *anointed* one *another*, so heart-mind *anted* up the *antidote*, and the *poison* that had *polarized* them in their relationship was counteracted. This *disreputable* situation was *disrupted*, because heart-mind *dissolved* its *glucose* in soul-strength's water in the *distillery* of the chakras, and they both *went* with the *flow* of this *fluid* that made the *Deity's delicious* Fruits sprout on my vine.

Jesus *steered* the *stem* of the vine into the *bower* of my heart so that it could be *braced* up by the *sanguineous sap* of his blood that flows in the vine. The Fruits *sprouted*, and the divine sweetness wasn't *squandered*, because the New Covenant was the *growth guarantee* that said that the plant would grow in the animal if I *fertilized* it with *fervent* contrition. The vine *festooned* my chakras with the Fruits, and my sentence of original sin was *commuted*, because the two *companions'* *compatibility* with one another gave me the *competency* known as the *victuals* of the *vine*. My *dissociation* from God ended, because the divine sweetness *dissolved* in my kundalini.

Jesus' *plan* was for the *plant* of the Holy Spirit to grow inside the *anguished animal* and *tame* his *tangled* thinking. He wanted to restore the relationship between man and God that Satan had left in *tatters*, so when he wore the Crown of Thorns, he *healed* the *heart* chakra, and *heated* it up with *heavenly* fire. He evened the *score* with the devil through his *scourging* by *threading* the needle through the *throat* chakra, and when he *carried* the Cross, the chakra of the *solar plexus* *cashed* in, because it *solemnly solicited solidarity* with God. The *sweetness swindle* in Eden had *switched* off this *sympathetic syrup*, but the Chakra *System* was taken under God's wing during the Crucifixion, and the *tank*

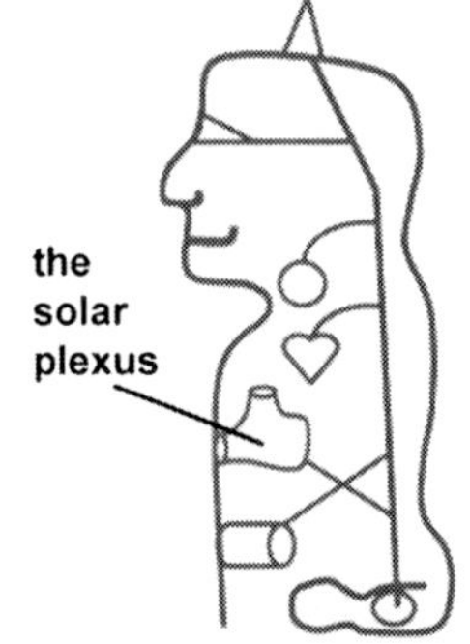

of sweetness above the head *tapped* into the heart so man could get a *taste* of this *tea*. The *top* chakra *touched* man's heart when Jesus went through this *tough tour*, because he brought about this *coup d'état* through this *courageous course of events*. The *crafty creek* of *critical* ingredients known as the Fruits of the Spirit turned into the *crop* man was able to *harvest* in his *heart*, because the *Blood* and the *Body* of Christ *merged* with the blood and body of man in the *mess hall* of the *Messiah* in the chakra in the *middle*.

When Jesus carried the Cross, he *toughened* this part of my digestive *tract*, so the *gastric juices* opened the *gate* to this *food* that was *foolproof*. The Body of Christ consisted of these *seven sheepfolds* that were intended to *shelter* penitent sinners so that their spirituality could *shine*. The *Stomach* Chakra *stopped* being *nonchalant* and sent this *noteworthy nutriment straight* into my blood, because the *Eucharist* had *evangelized* this *evildoer* and taught it a *different* form of *digestion*. When the Blood of Christ *waded* into my bloodstream through this part of the Body of Christ, the *wafer* put an end to the *wages* of *my* sin, because the *mystery* of the Eucharist ended the *myth* that the *twain* between me and God would never meet. The Holy Spirit *twined* through the spiral, and I was given new *life* by this *link* with the *Lion* of Judah. *Christ* makes this *live wire available* to all members of his *church* who want to *awaken* their spirituality, so let's *cuddle* up with the *chairman* of the *chakras*. Let's share the *cunning cup* of his Blood that is known to *cure* this *curse*, because he invented this *circuit* that *circulated* his *Blood* through his *Body*.

The *transubstantiation* made this *travel* possible, so let's go on the *journey* that enables the grape *juice* to *vindicate* the *vine* and complete the *tour* from the *tower* to the *toy* so that we can get back on *track*. The spiral through the chakras is the *tractable trail*, because when the tea *diffuses* from our *digestive* tracts into our blood, the *inherent innocence* that took a *dive* in Eden will no longer be *divided* from our nature. The *divine* sweetness and our *DNA dock* up with one another, because the *Creator* sent Jesus to *cancel* this *crime* of mistaken *identity* when he *carried* the *Cross*. He *siphoned* off our sins, and we were *sired* by God, because he gave us a Self-*image* that was *immaculate*. During the *Crucifixion* our navel chakras took this *cue* and got *cured* of the *curse* of *Eden* that had

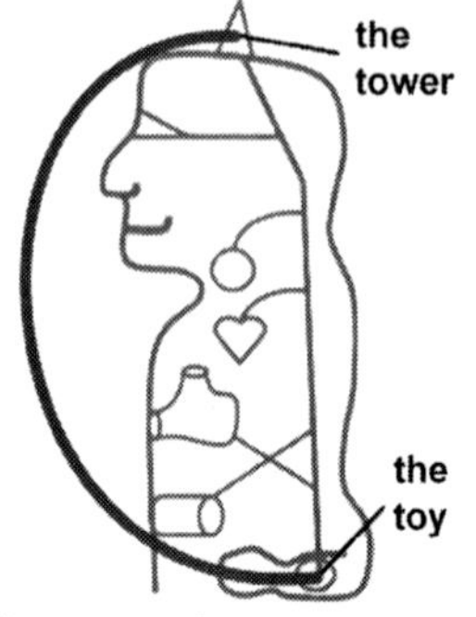

placed that chakra under the *custody* of *ego* which was so *cutting*. This *tranquil transaction* was *tremendously* beneficial, because Satan couldn't *trespass* on man with any of his dirty *tricks*, and it took place on the *ski lift* that went from the navel chakra to the chakra above the *skull*, so let's *complete* our natures with these *components* the *Savior* gave us to end our *scandals*. The *Passion* of our *Pastor* earned us this *Paternity* and *paid* off our debts, so let's enjoy this *peace* on earth.

Human beings can be *humble*, because the Cross was the *peace* pipe of the *peasant* named Jesus. He died on the Cross so that we could *crucify* our *crud*, so let's *smoke* the *smooth tobacco* that will give us the *togetherness* called the brotherhood of man. His pipe is made of *meek meerschaum*, so let's put the *aromatic arsenal* known as the twelve powers and Gifts in the pipe and send smoke *signals* to God as we meditate in *silence* about the reasons for our *silly* behavior. Our hearts have *harbored harmful* feelings that *harp* on us, so God *hatched* a plan to *shelter* them in the Sacred Heart by making Jesus our *shepherd*. Jesus took the *plant* known as the Holy Spirit and grew it in the *planter* known as his *Sacred* Heart, so let's buckle ourselves into this *safety belt*. The *sap* in this vine will *saturate* us with sweetness, because the Sacred Heart was the *modest module* that got *pierced* so that this *piety* could flow. When his blood *oozed* the gates of heaven *opened*, and the divine *mercy meshed* with the will of man. The Crucifixion was the *thesis* that through *thick and thin* we could be calm, because the *third* part of the *Trinity* was the *tropical* vine with a *tropism* that made it turn to those in *trouble*. This *hardwood* vine brings us the *harvest*, because Jesus was the *victim* who put the sweetness back in the *vine*. We can become *virtuous* by *swearing* we will do whatever it takes to become *sweet*, because that is the commitment that makes the Body of Christ *switch* from solid to liquid and enter our bloodstreams with a *swoosh*.

From the time of Eden man's *Freudian frights frittered* away his sweetness, so Jesus' job was to bring the *frock* of the Trinity to the *frontier* in the mind of man where the *fructose* normally turned into the *Fruits*. The *Trinity's* job was to *trip* this *mechanism* that Satan had *meddled* with so that soul-strength could realize that he was the *sugar suitor* and start the *courtship* sponsored by the New *Covenant*. Then the two *clerics* known as heart-mind and soul-strength could wear the *cloak* of the Holy Spirit and *close* the gap between them and God by realizing that they were both men of the *cloth*. The celebration of the *Eucharist* was the *event* that made it possible for these two *op-*

pressed optimists to take their Holy *Orders*. Then the Trinity's *chaste chemistry* could *marry* the *masculine* soul-strength below to the *feminine* heart-mind above. As a *consequence* our wills wouldn't be *constantly* on the *fence* between the divine *effulgence* and *ego*, because when Christ was on the Cross his *body bonded* us with God by *vindicating* the *vine's* theological *virtues*. His *victory* was to make the *vine* of the Holy Spirit *twist* through the chakras. He reconciled the *two* lovers, so each stopped thinking the other was the *ugly orphan*, and the *orthodox osmosis* known as our original innocence allowed the divine sweetness to *diffuse* into our minds and connect us to the *dignitary* known as God the Father.

The sweetness in the vine *went to bat for* us when Christ's body got *bathed* in his blood, because he *drew* the spiral line through the chakras, and that is where we should take our *dread*. Christ got *drenched* with blood so we can *drink* the divine sweetness and put loving behavior on the *march*. When Christ's blood *marinated* his body, the *fluid* of the kundalini *flushed* the tea out of the bag, because the liquid is the *solid's solvent*. We should remember these *hydrodynamics* when we feel *hyper*, because the divine sweetness and the kundalini give us the *cure* by *curling* up with one another and starting the *current* through the chakras that ends the *curse* of original sin. It is a *similar simile* to say that the *wine* makes the wafer take *wing*, because the divine sweetness has to *flow* for our spirits to *fly high*. We will all be *elated* when we complete this *electrical* circuit, so let's wend our *way* through the spiral to the *wealthy* chakra above and then to the *weary* one below that got *woven* into a *web* of falsehoods.

Lies have a *life* of their own, so Christ *sacrificed* his body to make man more *sage*. Christ became the daily *bread* in the human *breast* when they nailed the *boards* of the Cross to his *body*. The Cross was the *yardstick* of his *yearning*, because he *longed* to *look down* from it and feel the *pain* that would *pair* us to God.† He allowed *heartless heathens* who *hated* him to *haul* him up there, because he knew

† *City of God*, Venerable Mary of Agreda, 1978, Tan Books and Publishers, Rockford, Illinois 61106. p. 407. During prayer our blessed Master sometimes assumed a kneeling posture, sometimes He was prostrate in the form of a cross or at other times raised in the air in this same position which He loved so much. In the presence of his Mother He was wont to pray: "O most blessed Cross! When shall thy arms receive mine, when shall I rest on thee, and when shall my arms, nailed to thine, be spread to welcome all sinners? [Matt. 9:13] But as I came from heaven for no other purpose than to invite them to imitate Me and associate with Me, they are even now and forever open to embrace and enrich all men. Come then, all ye that are blind, to the light. Come ye

the *Cross* was the *crowbar* that could pry loose the *cryptic* messages from our childhoods. He took the *skeleton* key of our *fortitude* from the chakra in the *sky* and allowed our sense of *shame* to heal our *shattered* nerves, start our *fountain* of living waters, and stop our *sloth's smear* campaign. The flame of love in Jesus' *Crown* Chakra taught our Throat Chakras to stop swallowing *cruel crumbs*, and enjoy the *cuisine* served in *God's gourmet* kitchen.

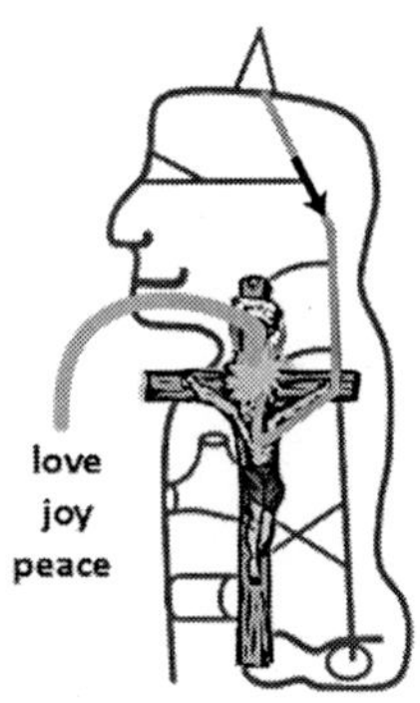

These messages we got as *cubs* drive us *cuckoo* as adults, so Jesus *got* on the Cross to bring us the Holy *Ghost's gifts*. He accomplished this *onerous* task, because his *only concern* was to restore the *concord* between man and God that would enable man to *discontinue* his *discord*. This discord was *offensive* to God, so Christ made the heart of man the *office* of man's original innocence. He accomplished this *colossal* task by *combining* the two *ingredients* that were originally *inherent* in man, which is the divine sweetness that was dissolved in the kundalini. He *sweetened* the tea and ended the *swindle* by showing man that he didn't have to *dissolve distasteful ideas* into the tea. As a child man's *idiotic idolatry* of his parents was a *worship* that only caused *wrangles*, because no one's *ancestors* are *angels*, and in general they leave us with a *bitterness* that makes us think we're on God's *blacklist*. The will of man had become an *incendiary* device, because he thought he was *incompatible* with God, so Jesus encouraged man to take this *misunderstanding* and *mix* it with a little contrition in order to *mobilize* the divine sweetness. All of this took place in man's heart which is the *pot* with the *potent potential* that was responsive to the *tea's team*. The tea's team is the *thoughtful three* known as the Father, son and Holy Spirit, and they can make our hearts *throb* with *pleasure*, so let's drink *plenty* of this *brisk* tea that *broadcasts brotherhood* rather than *brutality*.

---

poor, to the treasures of my grace. Come, ye little ones, to the caresses and delights of your true Father. Come, ye afflicted and worn out ones, for I will relieve and refresh you [Matt. 11:28]. Come ye just, since you are my possession and inheritance. Come all ye children of Adam, for I call upon you all.

I am the way, the truth and the life [Matt. 13:6], and I will deny nothing that you desire to receive. My eternal Father, they are the works of thy hands, do not despise them; for I will offer Myself as a sacrifice on the Cross in order to restore them to justice and freedom. If they be but willing I will lead them back to the bosom of thy elect and to their heavenly kingdom, where thy name shall be glorified."

All of us are members of the *tribe* that can profit from this *trick* of the *Trinity*. This trick was brought into play when Christ *shouldered* the Cross, because he made the heart of man a *shrewd shrine* by installing the *telecommunications* of the Trinity in this *temple*. The *internet* he *interpolated* between man and God was the *custom-made cyberconnection* to our *daddy* in heaven who provides the *damage control* that ends all *controversy*.

Man is the *free agent* who can choose his *freedom* — or the *restrictions* on it that lets the devil *resume* control. We each carry a *résumé* in our mind specifying how we lost the divine *resource*, so we should *recover* from these *red herrings* and enjoy this *refreshment*. We can earn this *refund* by *returning* to *Eden* and *ridding* ourselves of our *ego's embarrassment* so we don't have to *endure* the *enemy*. This is the *crime scene* that turned us into *cross patches*, so let's go *back* and *bail* ourselves out of this *baleful ball of wax*. Man adopted this *motley motor vehicle* whose *motto* was for problems to *mount up*, but God thought it was a *jaundiced jaunt* that was making man *jealous*. He figured that man could hit the *jackpot* of His sweetness and feel less *jaded* if he just realized he had been *duped*. Then he would see it as his *duty* to love with his heart rather than the *dangerous* organ that *dangled* between his legs. Consequently, Jesus was crucified so that man could *forgo* this egotistical *fork* in the road and embrace this *formulation* God created prior to Adam and Eve's *fornication*.

When Jesus was resurrected in the *tomb*, he got rid of this *tomfoolery*. The Crucifixion rid us of a *bellyful* of trouble, and the Resurrection brought us back to the *Beloved*, so together they are the safety *belt* that *bends* our wills to this *benediction*. The Crucifixion and Resurrection are the *tongue and groove tonic* that fits in perfectly with our ego's *tonnage*. Therefore, let's *buckle* into them until we remember *budding* off of God just like our *buddy* Jesus did. We won't have to pay *lip service* to ego if we *liquidate* our troubles in this way, so let's *listen* to the messages that come through this *intercom*, because it is connected to the other side of the sexual *intercourse* that resulted in our conception.

God is the *inhabitant* who is *inherent* in you, and he never intended for you to *broil* yourself on the grill called ego. When He *broke* off a *piece* of himself to create you, He gave you the divine sweetness as His *pièce de résistance*, and it was part of your *bill of rights*. This bill of rights resulted from the *binary fission* that *binds* you to Him unconditionally to this day. Let your ego be *mitigated* then as a result of this *mitosis*, because it gave you the divine sweetness and the Fruits for the express purpose of avoiding any *mix-up*. This bill of rights *stipulates* you don't have to live in a *stockade* to feel safe, because God is not *parsimonious*, and you are not a *part apart* from Him. Therefore, use the chakra at the *apex*. *Overcome* your fears. Start the *overflow* of the divine sweetness. Your heart will be *overhauled* by this blessing from the *overhead* chakra, so acknowledge that your will is capable of *overlapping* with His.

If you want your sweetness to *reign*, *rejoin* your will with God's in the *relationship shop* that never sells your sweetness *short* but rather gives you *release* from ego and enables you to *relish* your sweetness. It is the *nun's nursery* known as the Immaculate Conception, so *graft* your will onto this plant she will give you for the asking, and be aware that there's not a *grain* of truth in any other way to reproduce your sweetness, because this is God's *grand* design, and you might as well consider it engraved in *granite*. The Immaculate Conception is a *bush* that is not part of the *bush league*, and it is a *shrub* you don't want to *shrug off*, because it is the *tranquility-transfer* that will make your *havoc* stop *hazing* you. It will make your Fruits *sprout*, and you will be *sprung* from the prison of ego, because it has the *spunk* called the divine sweetness. The Immaculate Conception is the *purveyor* of unconditional love that *pushes* Satan out of the way, so *put* it on your shopping list!

You can enjoy an *unrestrained* flow of *unrivaled* sweetness by *unrooting* your reasons for being *unruly*. Your heart is a *place* that can be as *placid* as Adam and Eve's before the fall, because God revealed this *plainspoken plan* to them at that time. He said that their hearts were the *plants* that needed to remain in the *planter* of the chakras. That way, he said they could have their Fruits on their *plates* but that, if they *played* around and Adam behaved like a *beast* when he saw Eve's *beauty,* that man's heart would be *uprooted* from the chakras. Then man would be *uptight* until he made the *urgent* appeal of his contrition. He told Adam not to use his *plaything* in this way, because it would rob him of the greater *pleasure* which is the divine sweetness.

Nevertheless, He also *pledged* at that time that man's *reverence* could make this situation *reversible* and that man could *revert* to the *steady state* more common to plants and get nerves of *steel*. God told Adam that even if mankind turned into a *flock* of lost sheep, man's heart still contained the original *flora* in Eden. Therefore, at heart man was the *florist* who could return to this *paradise* that got *para-*

lyzed in his mind. God said that man's contrition was the *ecumenical* road to this *Eden* and that the Chakra System was the *fold* for *folks* who wanted to *follow* Him. God said that the heart of man did not have to be a *church* that was *churlish*, because it was a *sacred plant* that could restore the *pledge* of man's original innocence and make man *safe* from the *plight* called ego-addiction. He said that *man* could *manage* this *maneuver* and not *fondle* his *foolishness*, because the *Passion* of Jesus would make the heart of man *passive* to the divine sweetness. Jesus was the *strong way-shower* who could *subject* man's *weakness* to the *wealth* known as the Fruits, so the heart of man could *sprout* with love, joy, and peace. Man could be *spurred* on to greater spiritual heights, because Jesus could become the *tree of life* in the heart of man. Accordingly, when man was in the *trenches* of spiritual warfare, evil would not *trespass* on him, because his heart would be the *focus* of this divine *fodder.* Then man would not continue to suffer from the *evasive* maneuver of *Eve* in Eden, because man would want the *bearing* of the *beatitudes* more than that of a *Beau Brummell* and would *becalm* his ego in the *categorically* plant-like *cathedral* of the chakras by *worshipping* these more *worthy* principles.

Man just has to *prime* the love pump in his heart by returning to this *primitive* and *uncomplicated* state in which *unconditional* love *surges* in *surplus.* Trees, for example, don't follow the *vogue* of being *volatile* like humans, because they don't hold onto *sour souvenirs* like we do. An *oak* tree doesn't have to take an *oath* to be *obedient* to God's will, and a *palm* tree doesn't have to resort to *palmistry* to know whether its *fronds* may be subject to attack on their *frontier.* A *birch* tree gives a warm welcome to the *birds* without having to ask about their family of *birth*, and the *aspect* of an *aspen* tree in fall indicates that its only *aspiration* is to please God. A *map* is not necessary for a *maple* tree to know where to send its *maple sugar*, and an *evergreen* tree shows *everlasting* gratitude to God, because the divine sweetness is never *evicted* from its leaves.

Trees are *unconcerned* about the loss of *unconditional* love. When they *germinate* from seed, they don't worry about the *Gestapo* tactics of ego, because they are *open* to the idea of the Immaculate Conception *operating* in them. They have the *ingenious ingredient* of the divine sweetness that I miss the most, and I therefore ask God to *sanitize* my mind with this *sane syrup* he *tailored* to *take* me home to his bosom. I ask Him to dissolve it in the *sap* which is my kundalini so that *sweeping* emotional changes may result in me from His *sweetness.*

The Immaculate Conception is the *sweet shop* where all *swellheads* get this cure, and it is my *inalienable* right to benefit from this blessing that God used to *inaugurate* the Christian *religion.* I *relish* this *candy*, because it helps me get rid of my *can of worms* based on the *canon* of the Immaculate Conception which states that the divine sweetness is the *canopy* under which I am intended to rest. God created the *plant kingdom* so the Mediatrix of Grace could put the Fruits on our *plates*, so let's take our *kinky* thinking to this *kinswoman*, because her Immaculate Heart is the *kitchen* in which she *cooks* this food that helps us *cope.* She was *garbed* in her Immaculate Conception so she could be the *gardener* who toils ceaselessly in my heart. Therefore, I will ask her to *garnish* me with the Fruits by giving the *branches* of my tree of life the same *brand* of sweetness that Jesus has. This *cordial core* of the *coredemptrix* resulted in the birth of Jesus, so I intend to ask them both to be my *correspondents* with God.

The divine sweetness is the greatest *treasure* of a *tree*, because it brings its *fruit* to *fruition*, and its *leaves* don't have to take a big *leap* of faith to believe that God's *sunlight* will produce this *superb* result. A tree doesn't have to study the *philosophy* of *photosynthesis* to avoid fears of *frozen fructose* or its *sugar's suicide.* Its *wood* doesn't get the *wool* pulled over its eyes and continues doing its *work* of carrying the divine sweetness to and fro. My tree of life has a *similar simplicity*, because its divine sweetness is the *artful article* that makes me *articulate*,

The phloem is the sap that flows down in order to bring fructose from the leaves.

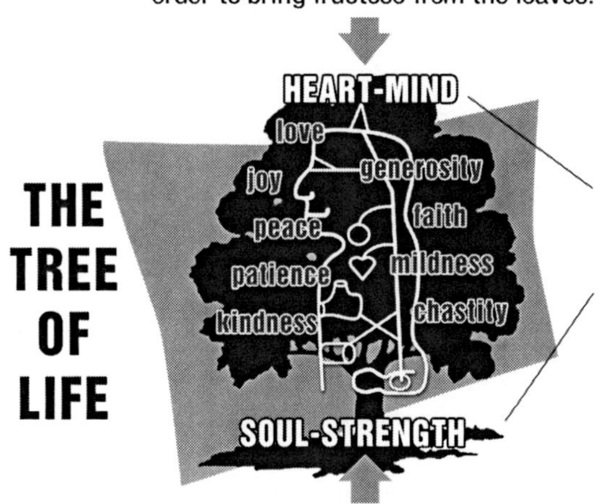

To *guarantee* safe passage to the divine sweetness, put these two *guards* in place, and tell them to follow *protocol* in their handling of this *prototype.*

The xylem is the sap that flows up to bring water from the roots.

and my heart-mind and soul-strength *enlarge* their devotion to it until it produces the *enlightenment* that is the Fruits.

My kundalini is the xylem that goes *up* in this tree in order to make me feel *upbeat*, and the divine sweetness is the phloem that flows *down* in order to make me stop feeling *downcast*. Their *partnership* will enable me to give up the *party line* of ego, because my heart-mind's *X-ray* vision teaches my soul-strength to use my *xylem* to carry out the *philanthropic philosophy* of the *phloem*.

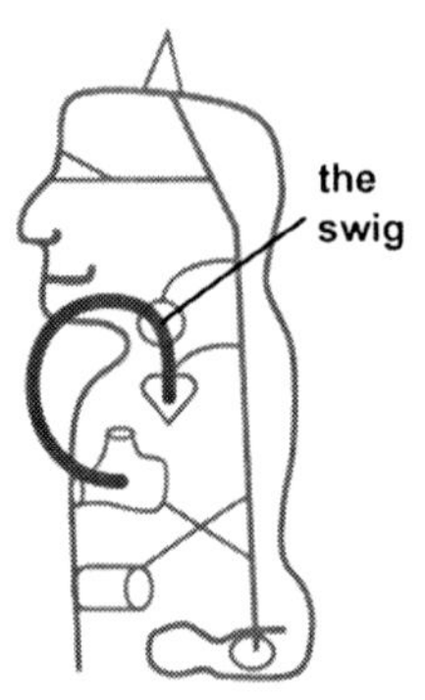

Heart-mind and soul-strength are our *photosynthesis physicians* who enable our *light* to give us a spiritual *lilt* and take us out of the *limbo* of ego. Heart-mind lives in the *attic* and is the *attitude attorney* who is *attracted* to the divine *sweetness*, but in order to take a *swig*, he needs the *aptitude* of soul-strength who lives at the bottom of the *aqueduct*. Heart-mind *figures* out how we got *filled* with *filth*, and soul-strength *reconciles* us to the *recourse* known as the Fruits of the Spirit so we can *recover*. Heart-mind's focus is to *ponder* until we become *poor* in spirit, but soul-strength's job is to improve our *public relations*, stop being ego's *puppet*, and make us *pure* of heart. These two *beatitudes becalm* our ego, because the *solace* they give to these two *soldiers* enables them to fight *together* and free us from the *toils* of ego.

This *convivial convocation* helps heart-mind and soul-strength *cooperate*, so they *plod* on and *plug* into the *receptacle* in our *heart* that enables us to take *heed* of the *hefty hegemony* called the will of God. They *recharge* us with this *reciprocity* that was *recklessly reckoned* to be worthless in Eden, so we *reclaim* this electrical *outlet* and improve our *outlook*. God saw that Satan had broken this *circuit*, so man had *circular* behavior that was *neurotic* from the time he was a *newborn*. Man had gone *haywire* because of the *hazardous hazing* in Eden, but the chakra above his *head* was still the *headquarters* of this *army* of the divine *Artisan*, and his *heart* could be *heated* up to end this *separation* between him and God that had robbed him of his *serenity*. For this reason Jesus offered to become a *casualty* and help man end this *catastrophe*. He helped man play *catch-up* ball by wearing the *Crown* of Thorns so man would not have to be satisfied with these *crumbs* that represented the *culmination* of Satan's *cunning*. It was a spiritual *shell game* in which Jesus gave *shelter* to man and became the *shepherd* of lost sheep by taking the *sherbet* in the Crown Chakra and *shifting* it to the heart of man. As a result of the Third Sorrowful Mystery Jesus opened the *tributary* of the spiral in the heart of man, and Satan was none the wiser that he had been *tricked*. Satan had *wiped* out this *wiring* as a result of original sin and made it possible for *biological birth* to make man forget he was a *descendant* of the divine. Therefore, God used the *Descent* of the Holy Spirit to help man *remember* this connection. *Remorse* brought about the *rendezvous* of heart-mind and soul-strength who could then have their *get-together* at this *geyser* in the human heart. Consequently, the *turkey* known as the ego-addicted will could *turn* the *corner*, and man could recognize God as the *cornerstone* of his *happiness*. Then the heart of man would be a *safe harbor*, and his spirits would not *sag*.

The *chap* called soul-strength meets heart-mind in the *chapel* of the human heart, because ego has not been a good *chaperone* to them, and they *reject* this *relentless* pest. Jesus then starts a new *chapter* in their lives by giving them the strength of *character* to end this *charade*. The *gal* and her *Galahad* then recognize the *galaxy* of stars in their *galley* known as the Fruits of the Spirit. They become a team of two whose *astuteness* cannot be torn *asunder*, because they tie the *knot* that gives them the *know-how* not to *knuckle under* to the *effrontery* of *ego*. From then on these *unfriendly* forces don't make their lives *unfruitful*, because heart-mind and soul-strength have gone through this *reconciliation* that has allowed their spirituality to *recover*. They live *happily ever* after, because their *hardiness prevents* them from falling *prey* to the forces of *evil*, and they *hardly* go through any *hardships*.

I had become *wicked*, because my heart-mind and soul-strength thought they were *widow* and *widower*. Their *cessation* of relations turned my heart into a *cesspool*, and I began to *feather* my nest with my *fecal* matter. Nevertheless, I finally figured that my heart was a *contraption* that could profit from a *contrition expedition*, so I set out to *expel* my *fears* and told my heart-mind and soul-strength that they were the *fearless federal* agents empowered by *God's government* to *feed* me the divine sweetness. Therefore, they *probed* the *problem*, and each worked *diligently* to solve this *dilly*. They each did the *legwork* and looked around *at length* with a fine-toothed *comb* but finally decided that they had to *combine* forces if they were to *succeed* in finding this *succor*.

The point is that each felt *anxious apart* from the other, but the more each *tried* to *tryst* with the other the more likely they were to *tumble* to the truth. Satan's *quick* wit had made them think they had lost their *quintessential* nature, and God had given them the *cold shoulder*, but if they *collaborated* they could end their *revolt* and earn their *reward* through this *merciful merger.*

Each *disbelieved* in his *discernment*, and it had left their sense of *taste* in *tatters*, but God's *master plan* was for them to *match* wits with the devil by *agreeing* to get *ahead* together in order to end their *ailment.* This *truce* brought back the *true frame of reference* that existed before the *fraud* in Eden made everybody *freak out.* The *rigging* of the chakras had gone through the *rip-off* that made us think our *paradise* was *paralyzed*, but we didn't have to be *pals* with the *panel* of three core fears that had caused this *panic* reaction.

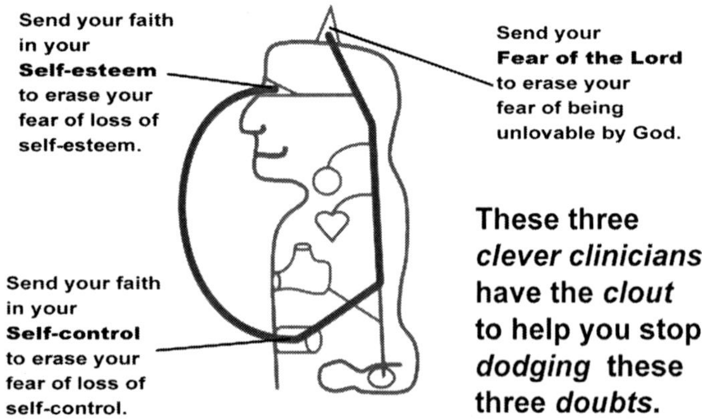

Man had stopped *going* to the *go-between* of the Holy Spirit, so *God* sent his Son to *Golgotha* to deliver the *goods* all over again. Satan had taken *away* man's *awe*, but Jesus went down the *axis* in man's *back* to the chakra that was *dead* and canceled that *deal.* The *contract* of the New Covenant enabled the *Eucharist* to *evangelize* man's heart and restore his sense of Self-*control*, so the *composure* that was formerly *concealed condescended* through the spiral into these seven *service stations* which God had created to *share* Himself with us.

Man's divine *essence* could become the basis for his sense of Self-*esteem*, but first he had to feel an *ounce* of remorse for his *outlandish* behaviors at the *outpost* of the Brow Chakra in order to *overcome* the *overwhelming debt* of *defamatory deficits* that continued to *defile* him. He *owed* it to himself to *own up* to this *pack* of *scoundrels* and *screen* them out with *scrupulous* remorse, but his *fear* of loss of self-esteem didn't *feel* the same way and just tried to *fend* them off. This fear was the *clairvoyant* who tried to keep the lid on these *clandestine* fears and *always anticipated* a *clash*, because he hadn't *cleaned* house. Nevertheless, the Brow Chakra *erases* these *errors* by indulging in *espionage* on our reasons for feeling *estranged* from God. It identifies the *reenactments* in our lives that make it necessary for us to *reflect* on the *Cinderella circumstances* we need to *remember* in order to feel *remorse*. As soon as we begin to *spy* on this *squad* of *squalid* cowards, they *squeal* the truth, and our *regret reins* in these *relentless* pests whose only *role* is to *remind* us of our sense of *inexcusable inferiority* and turn us into *roughnecks*. The Brow Chakra is the *trooper* who gets us out of this *trouble* and enables us to *trust* the *truth* and *tryst* with God, because we *view* the *violence* that robbed us of *virtue* and hear these *vivid voices* that speak from the God-shaped *void* in our hearts. The Brow Chakra has the *expertise* to allow us to *expiate* these fears and *unlearn* our reasons for feeling *unloved*. It *espouses* the Self-*esteem* that enables all *ethnic* groups to feel connected to God through the *Eucharist*.

The *ceremony* of our *chagrin challenges* the *chamber* known as the Navel Chakra to *denounce* the *unresolved dependency needs* that leave us *unstrung*. It stops *channeling* our *chaos* and starts channeling our *charm*, because it has heard the *chatter* that has to do with the *cheap* tricks that have *cheated* us out of our good *cheer*. It makes sure we *cherish* God in our *chests* as the *Chief* of our inner *child* and connects us to our Self-control through the *chimney* so that we can keep our *chins* up. Fear of loss of self-control is therefore the *doubt* that makes us think we're going strictly *downhill*, so this is the *drama queen* we need to *draw* back the curtain on and *drum* some sense into.

Once the *lawyer* of our remorse has removed these two *lax layers*, the *ringleader* of this *rip-off* is ready to *rise* to the occasion and get washed clean by the *river* of *mercy* that *meshes* us with God. The *Messiah* opened this *gate* in the Crown Chakra through his Resurrection so as to *gather* penitent sinners to himself and put them in *gear* with God's Holy *Ghost*. The God-shaped *vacuum* known as fear of being unlovable by God is therefore recognized as a *valuable valve*, because when it is opened the *various* Fruits of the Spirit descend through the *vertical* axis to celebrate Christ's *victory*.

The *Almighty* sent Jesus to *heal* His *altar* in the human *heart*, but first man had to pore over these three core fears, because they were the *gore* that *governed* his *graceless* behavior. Nevertheless, man *abhorred* looking at this *lore* that made him a *loser*, so he didn't *adore* God, the *adversary* robbed him of *affection*, and caused *affliction*. Man was an *exile* from this paradise within, because he thought this *expensive experience* was beyond *explanation*, but the Crucifixion was the *exploit* that made it possible for man to *explore* this *extortion*. It was the *cunning cure* of an *illness* that was *illogical*, and it used the *remedy* of *remorse* as the *treatment* that could restore the *treaty between* these two spiritual *warriors* who had been *bewitched* by the devil and had thought they were *washed up*.

Heart-mind and soul-strength were the *two* who could open the *two-way* street between *Creator* and *creature*. The Crown Chakra was the *holy home* at the *encouraging end* whose job was to terminate the *discouraging discrepancy* at the *bottom* that implied that God was *out of bounds*. Man owned this heaven within, but it was a *country* from which the *couple* known as heart-mind and soul-strength had been banished, because they had lost the *courage* the divine sweetness gave them before the *court-martial* of original sin. They thought they were a *pagan pair* and figured the *twain* between them could never meet in order to end their *twinges* of pain. However, their *courage* could be restored, because the New *Covenant* stated that they could be *encouraged* by our contrition and would then set themselves to the task of *endearing* us to God. The *wild card* of remorse could be used by the human *will* to restore this *congruous connection* between God and man and end man's *exile* from his heaven within through this *existential* understanding. The will was the *hand* on the *handle* of the love *pump* in the human heart, and the *pundit* who had to *evangelize* heart-mind and soul-strength in order to make them more *even-tempered*. They were the *templates* in the *temple* that needed to *fit* together. They had to *fix* the *fixture* of the vertical *axis* that Satan the *axman* had *chopped* apart and put an end to this antagonistic *chord* that had turned them into *chumps*. Then the *dovetailing* through the *dowel* of the vertical axis between heart-mind above and soul-strength *down* below could earn us the *dowry* of the Fruits.

We need to *transcend* our connection to our parents in order to go through this *transformation*, because our parents are our *painful pals* whose original sin was the *trick* that enabled them to fit us with our *triggers*. Our ego then put us through a series of *sudden sufferings*, because we had not accepted the *contentment context* that is our connection to God the Father. We all *worship* our *wounds* and *tolerate* this *toll*, because every *Tom, Dick, and Harry* considers remorse some kind of *tomfoolery*. Nevertheless, our Chakra Systems are the *grids* upon which our *grieving* will locate the *filth* we need to *find*. Our minds are the *fields* of battle for this *fight*, and our remorse is the *investigator* who *invigorates* these two *invincible soldiers* known as heart-mind and soul-strength. Their *sole* job is to *solemnly solicit solidarity* with God and restore the *breathtaking breeding* that was in place before we took the *bribe* of original sin. They are the *bride* and *bridegroom* who *bridge* the gap between us and God, and so we should encourage them to establish this *bridgehead* by *bridling* our egos. Let us *brief* them about the events from our childhood that put our wills in the *brig*. Then they will send the *brigade* of twelve apostles to chase the *brigand* out of our minds and make our futures *bright*.

We think of ourselves as *nasty natives* lacking in *innate innocence* but can have *unqualified* mastery in our growth if we *unravel* this mystery. This mystery is the *unbridled uncertainty* that we can *unchain* ourselves from, so let's stop believing that Satan *absconded* with the *Absolute* in us, and let's not let our egos be the *rumormongers* that perpetuate this *ruse*. The nuclear family is the *shop* in which we got *shortchanged*, so let's not have our connection to the Father get *obscured* by this *obsequiousness* that only makes us *obsessive*. This *approval-seeking* has only kept us connected to our parents' *apron strings*, so let's remember that our ego is the *end organ* that our parents *endorse*. It doesn't have the *endowment* of the Fruits, so let's not be mesmerized by this *showman* who doesn't bring us a *shred* of benefit. The love of our *relatives* is not very *relaxing*, and it is a *rudder* we will come to *rue*, but the Crown Chakra is the *steeple* of the church where the will of God lives, and He will *steer* us clear of these troubles. We should not stay *caught* in the *caustic* belief that our *kinfolk* can lead us into this *kingdom*, because it is the sole *province* of God to give us this *prudence*, and all other branches on our tree of life need to be *pruned* away with our remorse. The *fallacy* that is *familial* is that it is *appropriate* to seek parental *approval*, but this is the *noose* that choked off our *normalcy*, so let's all *sojourn* to God in *solo* prayer and take off this *somber sombrero*.

Somehow someone in our families did *something* to *ruin* God's *rule*, so let's *ruminate* about these *condescending conditions* and not let our *parents* leave us this lack of *parity*. There is a *legacy* that is more *legitimate*, so let's ask our contrition to *lend* a hand. Let's not *ignore* the principle that these *illegitimate* sources of love have brought on our *illness*. God's love is the more *valid value*, so let's end this *vandalism*. Let's take advantage of this *incontestable* fact. Let's *increase* our *pleasure*, enjoy His *plethora* of sweetness, and end our *plight*. Satan *wreaked* this emotional *wreckage* on us, but we can *wrest* ourselves free from this *wretchedness.* Then we will not have such a *fatalistic* attitude about God the *Father*, because He will grant us *wisdom* and end the *witching* that took place in our families of origin.

God the Father can *insulate* us from evil, because He is an *integral part* of us, so let's explain this to the *partisans* known as heart-mind and soul-strength, and *partner* with Him through the *Passion* so as to earn His *Paternity.* Our *doubts* may leave us feeling *downright downtrodden*, but the *dozen draftsmen* on the first circle *drew* up a plan for us to face our *dread* and earn our daily bread so as to make our *dreams* come true. If we *square* off with these *squatters* in our minds, they won't make us *squirm*, because God *bakes* the *bread* that restores the normal *balance of power.* He *stabilizes* us with this *staff of life*, so let's ask for this *breakthrough* in our lives. God doesn't take the *seat* known as *second fiddle*, because it gives the devil a *field day*, so we should remember not to *worship* that which is *worthless. Biological birth* turned us into *black sheep*, so let's set our sights on *ideals* that will give us cognizance of our divine *identity. Idolizing* our parents has only given us *ignominious* behaviors, so let's stop being *Satan's satellites*, because he only feeds us these *scraps* that make us *scream.* We are not required to continue being *devastated* in this way, so let's *develop* the *devotion* to return to the *orb* and stop *orbiting* around this *sour source* that began in an apple *orchard* in Eden. This *hub* is present in all *humans* and is anything but *humdrum*, so let's return to the *center* by overcoming these *centrifugal* forces. Let's ask God for His *sweetness*, because it thinks *swiftly* on its *feet* through the *fellowship* of the Holy Spirit and *livens* those who are *livid* with fear by turning into the Fruits.

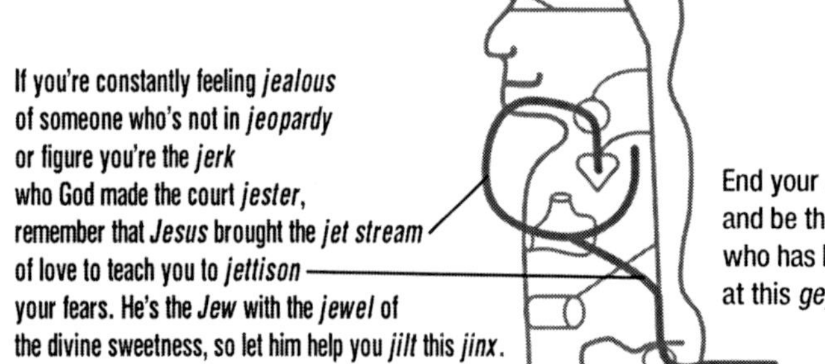

The *hearsay* from your childhood causes the *heartburn* that keeps God at *bay*, so if you want your heart to *be run* by God rather than by your *rupture* with Him, *reflect* on this *reflux*, and stop this *frenetic fretting*. As long as you are *active* in this *addiction*, you cannot *surrender* to the love that *surrounds* you, so *mourn* this *muck* and enjoy the *edification* that is *effortless*. Be the *passive patron* of *support* that comes from the *Supreme Being*. The *evil eye* known as ego has only *exacerbated* our lives, so let's surrender to this *sample* of *sanctity* and give it *sanctuary* in our hearts. We can end our *war* of attrition and stop having to *ward off* these fears we have hung in our *wardrobe*. We can make our *dreams* come true by *dressing* ourselves in the divine sweetness, because then we will not *drift* out of *kilter*, so let's ask the lady in the *kimono* to give us this blessing and make us *kind*. Her Immaculate Conception was *installed* in our hearts so she could give us happiness *instead* of sorrow, so let's use this *nozzle* of the *nun* which is connected to the *hose* of the *Host*. The *nozzle* of the *nun* is *full* of *fun*, because it may be *adjusted ad lib* to *rinse off* ego's *rip-off*.

It *squelches* Satan by *squirting* the *sweetness* that ends his *swindle* and *solves so many somber memories* that we whip ourselves with *mercilessly*. Our *head's health* depends on our *hearts*, so let's stop *inflating* the *influence* of this *emperor* who is excessively *enamored* of our fears. The Blessed Mother is Mediatrix of Grace and Corredemptrix, because we can *give* her our *gloom* in exchange for our *glory*. She uses the Glo-

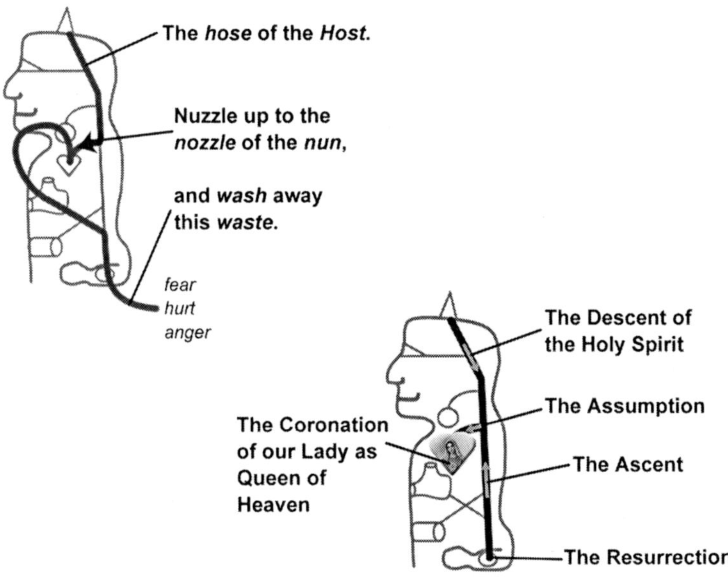

rious *Mysteries* to show us the *nature* we share with the *Nazarene*, and is therefore the *go-between* between man and *God*.

The *tranquilizing transaction* that *transcends* the *trap* of original sin is to *travel* back from our *heads* to our *hearts* with the conviction that we can *traverse* this *travesty*, end our *treason*, and earn the *treasure* of the divine sweetness by taking advantage of the *treaty* known as the New Covenant. Our *intelligence* can *interact* with the *deity's delicacy* rather than the *repugnant reruns* of our egos, because our *ego's electricity* isn't as *elegant* as the *emotions* of love, joy, and peace that God can *empower* us with. God *supervises* this *supply*, so let's ask the *Supreme Being* to make this *superlative supplement surge* through our hearts. Let's ask Him to enable us to *surmount* the *limitations* imposed on us by our *lineage* and to *surrender* our *suspicions* to Him so that His *sustenance* may *sweep* us away in its *sweetness*. The divine sweetness is a *fluid* that is not Satan's *flunky*, so let's use the *plucky plumbing* of the chakras to *deliver* this *deluxe substance* into our thinking. Then its *subtle reasoning* will make our loving behavior *rebound*.

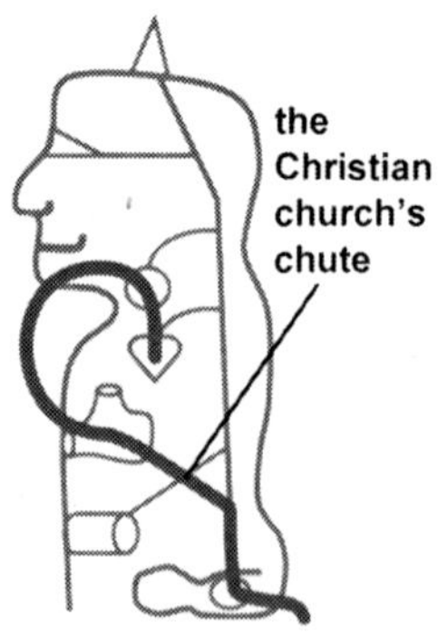

Your parents' *chicanery* made you a *chicken-hearted child*, but you are now an *adult* and don't have to let this *adulterant* give the *advantage* to the devil. Your ego-*defenses* will be *deflated* when your *remorse* makes you *repent* of your *repressed* feelings, so remove this *corrupt cosmetic* that Satan uses to *infect* you with his *influence*. You are *carrying* around this load that makes your life a *cartoon*, so get rid of the *slander* that causes the *slapstick*. Use the *Christian Church's chute* and watch the *cinema* with the *screwy script* until you get the *tip-off* that explains your *tirades*. Satan *shunted* out your sweetness, but Jesus *shut* down the *shyster's sick side show*, so get back the *sweetness* Satan *swiped*, and make the *word* of God *work* for you by sending your *troubles* down this *trough*. Your ego's *slop* will go down this *slope* if you overcome your spiritual *sloth*, so let your *sorrowful soul-searching* send your *lies* down this *lifeline*. Get the spiritual *lift* that comes from using this *truthful tube*, and send your *tumult* down this *tunnel*, be-

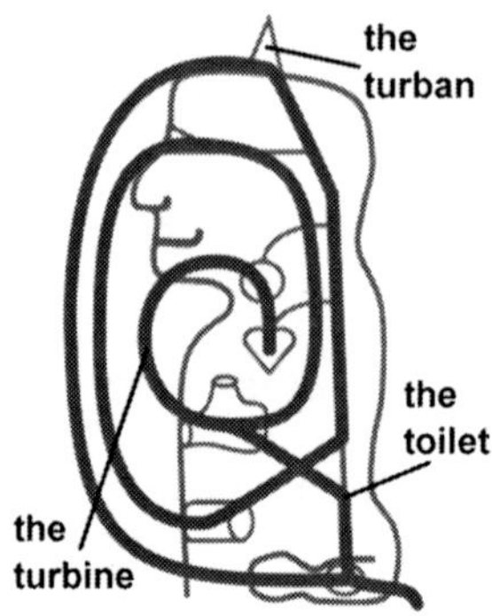

cause this *duct* is not a *dud*. Happiness will *rain* down when you *raise* your kundalini, so tune into your *turban*, start the *turbine* of the chakras, and enjoy the *bliss* that the *blood* of Christ causes by making the Fruits *bloom*. This is the *flow* that *flushes* out the *foe*, so let's get *together* and use this *toilet* to *rid* ourselves of these *riddles that* block our *right of way* to our sweetness.

The Crucifixion is the *warranty* regarding the elimination of *waste*, and the Resurrection is the *watchdog* agency that *governs* the *water*, so let's earn God's *grace*, make the kundalini rise, and give Satan his *waterloo*. The human will is the *priest* that knows how to honor this *primeval principle*, so let's ask the Blessed *Mother* to be *moved* by our misery and use her *Immaculate* Conception to help us *immigrate* to our heaven within. Then the *ancestral* sweetness she brought to earth will *anesthetize* evil in our hearts, and her divine *genealogy* will turn on the Sacred Heart, which is the *generator* of our *gentleness*.

The spiral through your chakras makes up this *electronics* of *Elohim*, so *initiate* your will to these *innervations* and use these seven *energy* centers that can *engage* your behavior to the love *engine* called the Sacred Heart. Operate your will *properly* by using this *property* that makes you *prosperous*, because it is the *possession* that Jesus bequeathed to all *posterity* through the *hypostatic* union so as to end your *hysteria*. *Operate* your will without the *opiates* that *oppress* you and remember that the Way of the Cross was the *intersection* between Jesus and your *intestines*, so use this *disparagement disposal* to rid yourself of your reasons for having *disreputable* behaviors.

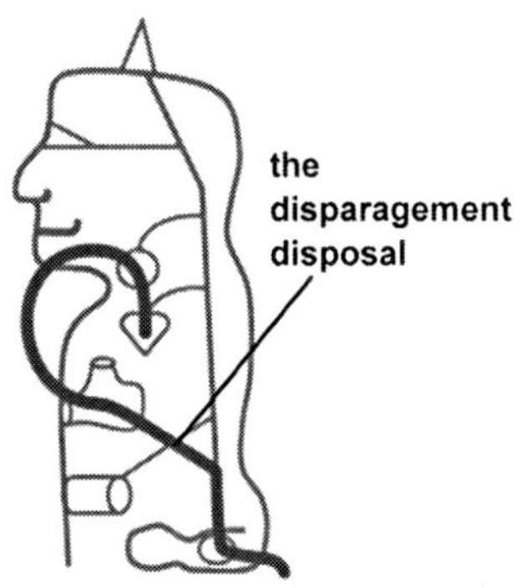

This *ridiculous riffraff* is the *trash* that causes your *travail*, but these *explosions* that Satan *exported* from hell are susceptible to the *exposé* of your remorse. Jesus carried the Cross for the *express* purpose of this *expulsion*, so use this *effective* defecation of the *effluent* of your ego and stop letting these *fecal feelings* impair your *felicity*. These feelings are *henchmen* of the devil but can be *herded* out by Jesus, because he is the *Pastor* who can lead you to greener *pastures*. *Patch up* your relationship with God then, and let your *gray matter graze* on your sweetness. Turn on the *chandelier* above your head by having this *change* in attitude. Make your will *shine* and your ego *ship* out, because your will is the *dipper* God intends to use to serve you your sweetness rather than Satan's *dirty tricks. Insist* on having the *inspirations* that rid you of these *dreadful dregs* that *dribble* into your behavior. Your heart is not a *certifiable cesspool*, so use your Brow Chakra as your *calamity calipers* so that your ego will stop being the *mythmaker* that *nags* you. Then your *excrement* will stop making *excursions* into your behavior, and your will won't be a *spooky spoon* but rather the *ladle* of the *lady* whose Immaculate Conception will cure you of these *sinister sips*. Her Immaculate Conception made her the *deified delegate* qualified to give you these *delights*, because she was the *forerunner* of the divine *form*, and the divine *Mogul* Himself made her the *mold* that Jesus called *Mom*. She is the *lady* who gave birth to the *Lamb* and is the object of my *devotion*, because she silences the *diabolical dialogue* that fills me with *obscene obsessions*. She has taught me that my will is made of *rubber*, because when I repent of my *rubbish*, it bounces back. Then it becomes a *rudder* that can help me *stay* on course, because it can be *steered* by the Holy Spirit. That way I can *luxuriate* in *lyrical* love rather than *indulge* in an *inebriation* that leaves me spiritually *inept*. I am sick of suffering from this *inequity* that has *expelled* God's sweetness from my heart and tired of this *expensive* chemistry *experiment* from Eden that allows Satan to *exploit* me.

The *gamble* in the *garden* was the *bet* that caused the *bias*, but the divine sweetness is still the *occupant* of my heart, and it can give me better *odds*, so I aim to *recoup* my losses in this *refectory*. My heart can be the *home* of *honest devotion* that doesn't *dicker* with the forces of evil, so I intend to stop being the *beggar* whose *behavior* is traceable to the repressed *emotions* I became *enamored* of as a child. My heart can turn out these *carbon copies* of my parents' *cardiac* disease, or I can ask God's *wife* to make my *will* a *priest*. Then this cleric will *prime* the *pump* in my chest with the *precursor* that is *preferable* and put a stop to this *sentimental sequel* that is devoid of *serenity*.

Satan's *craftiness* has made me *cranky*, and I have *toted* around the *touchiness* that has resulted from these *knee-jerks* that I have *knit* into my thinking, but I don't need to be a *traitor* to my own *tranquility*. All *sincerely* penitent *sinners* go to *Jesus* to end their *jitters*, because he *supplies supreme sureness*, and I know I can *count* on him. He is the *counterpart* who can end this *complaint* by *complementing* my nature so as to furnish what is *missing* and will not consider his *mission* complete until he *fills* my void with his *finesse*. Then he will *voluntarily* end all *infringements* on my happiness and *infuse* me with a *serenity* that is *serious*. After that I won't have to *sing* the blues, because when *sinner* and *Savior* get together, the sinner learns to *savor* the Fruits. Jesus will give me a *fresh* start, because my will is the *friar* who can wear the *friendly frock* that consists of heart-mind and soul-strength. The *monk* will be in a better *mood* when he accepts this *optimistic option*, because his holy *orders* will enable him to *react* to God's *essence* which is the *ready reagent* in the *Eucharist*. Then he will say "*Eureka*!" and stop being the *broody brother* who has made me *brusque*. He will wear this *garb* that makes me a *gardener* of the *Fruits*, and my life will be *fulfilled*, because I will *belong* to God and be one of His *beloved* as a result of this *benediction*.

Our *bliss* will *blow our minds* if we *unravel* the *unrivaled harmony* that can *hatch* from this *haven* within. We have all been *ostriches* and have avoided feeling this *ouch*, but ***our Father*** can help us *fathom* this mystery of *hazardous hearsay* that keeps us out of ***heaven***. The human mind is the ***hallowed*** *hallway* that can give *way* to this help that God *weaves* into our lives, so let's cry out His ***name*** and ask Him to heal our *narrow-mindedness* and make the world one *nation*. Then the *kindness kinetics* of God's ***kingdom*** will ***come***, and He will *comfort* us so as to reverse our *wholesale wickedness*. God's ***will*** can be ***done*** in this corridor, and we can open the *door* to His sweetness. When we *satiate* ourselves with this *sauce*, *each* of us on ***earth*** will be at *ease*, because we will have tapped into the ***heaven*** within and will have become *heirs* to our divine *heritage*. God is the *daddy* whose ***daily bread*** can give us this *breakthrough*, so let's ***forgive*** one another according to the *formula* that it is better to *treasure* His will than to ***trespass*** on it. He will ***lead*** us if we ask to *lean* on Him, so let's not let our fears be the ***temptations*** that are so *tenacious* that we think we cannot be ***delivered*** from them. Then the *demon* won't be able to use the force of ***evil*** to *exacerbate* our lives, because this *prayer* will have released the *precious prescription* that will have *cured* this *curse*.

Let's make planet earth the *zealous zone* where our spiritual *evolution* can be furthered by this *exciting exercise* that ends our *exile*. It is *narrow-minded* to believe that we have to be *nasty* to one another just because we come from different *nations* and *religions*, so let's *relish* the *remarkable* fact that it is our *nature* to drink the divine *nectar* that *binds* us together. We all have the *birthright* to *give the slip* to our *sloth* and not let the *guy* who lives in the Root Chakra make us *guzzle* the *iconoclastic idea* that our *hearts* are not *hearths* of God's love. Our *ideals* don't need to remain *idle*, because we can *bounce* back by becoming *bound* and *determined* to stare the *devil* in the face and tell him that we don't intend to suffer from the *iffy illness* that makes our fulfillment an *illusory* goal. It is possible to have *stainless steel standards* that no one can *steal* and to *share* a dream that no one can *shatter.* It is possible for all on *earth* to enjoy the *easygoing ecology* described in the Our Father, so let's bring *forth* our *fortitude* and have the *grit* to confront the *grotesque* memories that make us hold *grudges* against one another. This kind of *willpower* will *win* the day, because the *one* and *only* God will come through this *open* door. It is the divine *strategy* for us to develop the *strength* of *mind* that will allow our Father to *mingle* with us here on earth, so let's not let our sense of *disgust* leave us *disillusioned*, because we can *snoop* around in this *snot*. Our *noodles* are connected to our *noses*, so let's feel *nostalgic* until the *nourishment* of the divine sweetness comes out of the *nozzle* in our hearts. We don't have to stay *snarled* up in these *sniffles*, because the Crucifixion is the *dynamite* that will bust up this *dysfunction*. Therefore, let's help *each other* end these *disturbances*. Then the *divine* sweetness will *turn* our hearts into the *twigs* that *twine* through the chakras so that we can enjoy our *Fruits* rather than suffer from our *frustrations*. We are *chips* off the Old Block who lives in the Crown Chakra, so let's have this *chitchat* with God and ask Him to bless our *chlorophyll* so that the *leaves* on our tree of life can stop being in *league* with the devil and *get a new lease on life*. Our *philanthropy* toward one another depends on this green *photosynthesis pigment*, so let's complete this *pilgrimage* and feel *sired* by God by paying our respects to Him at this sacred *site* on the *top* of our heads that can make ego *topple*. The *omnipotent One* will include us *all* in this *alliance* if we make the effort to become *altruistic ambassadors*, so let's get *together* and be *tolerant* of one another. Let's *collaborate collectively* and be aware that our *differences* don't detract from the *dignity* of this *essence* that transcends *ethnic* boundaries. Let's *celebrate* together in the *celestial cell* of the Crown Chakra, because it has a *potent potential* and will help us *regain* the *regard* for one another that can *reinstate* the planet in *God's grace*.

Let's *muster* up the courage to *face* the *fact* that we have been *mutilated* by our *mutiny* against God and restore our *esteem* for one another by ending our *estrangement* from Him. The divine *indweller* will *infuse* us with the *ingredient* of His sweetness which is our rightful *inheritance*, so let's *subscribe* to this law of *success* and *prove* the Lord's law of *providence*. God the *Father* will turn on this *faucet* in our hearts, so let's *earn* this *prodigious profit* and *make* all *men* on *earth benefit* from this *convincing cookery* in *God's gourmet* kitchen. Jesus got *nailed* to the Cross to *bestow* this blessing on us, so let's *thrive* by solving these *riddles* that keep us under Satan's *thumb.* Our hearts can beat in *rhythm* with the Sacred Heart of Jesus, so let's *return* to God and make our *reverence* run *rings* around the planet.

Let's expand our *horizons* by making our hearts *hospitable households* in which all *humans* are *welcome.* We can be *well-fed* at this *wellhead*, so let's *invite* God to stop being an *involuntary* force in our hearts and get Him to *involve* Himself *voluntarily.* Let's *volunteer* our wills, because the one sure way to get rid of our *voodoo* is to ask God to make our behavior *vouch* for the fact that we no longer have this *vulnerability.* Let's get together and play this *symphony* of *synergistic* devotion so that God will exchange our *addictions* for His *adeptness.* He will *orchestrate* the *organs* of love in our chests, so let's *snuggle* up to Him and be *sociable* toward one another by allowing Him to run our *affairs affectionately.*

We all carry around the *shortfall* that was *shot* into our hearts when we were children and need to go to the *shrink* if we don't want our wills to stay wrapped up in the *shroud* of ego. *Psychotherapy* is the best way to *pull* up these *roots* that cause our *rough* edges, because when we *dig* up these *dillies* we won't feel so *dinky.* Then we won't feel left out of the *almanac* of the *Almighty* and will know God is *alongside.*

This *holy list* will make us feel at *home* in our hearts, enable us to *listen* to God, and feel *lovable*, because we will have become *loyal* to this *lucidity* that we enjoyed before *Lucifer* brought us bad *luck.* As children our wills were the *soldiers of fortune* who were *solicited* to fight for these causes that were *hostile* to the divine *household* in our hearts. However, we can *negotiate* with these *neighbors* in our subconscious by means of psychotherapy so as to prevent their *gossip* from *governing* our lives.

Our *allegiance* to the *Almighty* will make our sweetness *surge*, so let's *surrender* this *recalcitrance* which is based on *reckless reckoning* and take advantage of the divine *solicitude* built into the *solid-state* circuitry of the chakras. We can say "*So long*!" to ego, because our original innocence is a *canny cannon.* It says that God's sweetness is *soluble* in our kundalini, so let's embrace this *solution.* My *vertical* axis is the *vessel* that carries this blessing when I wear the *vestment* of heart-mind and soul-strength, so I intend to end this *logjam* at the *Logos.* Then the *Lord's love* will *come over* me, and the *Comforter's commerce* with my heart will make it the *commissary* of the Fruits. Jesus *lassoed* my heart at the *Last* Supper with the *spontaneous spout* of the divine sweetness that *sprouts automatically* with the Fruits. The divine sweetness has the smarts to make the Fruits *available* when they are needed, so I intend to *dedicate* my will to this blessing that Satan *deducted*. My will is the *instinctive instrument* that can end my ego's *antics*, because it can *anticipate* this stroke of good fortune that flows from this *antidote* from *antiquity*. The divine sweetness is the *relic* in the *reliquary* of my heart, and the *cure* for the *curmudgeon* known as my ego-addicted will. Therefore, I intend to let it *prompt* my heart *properly* according to these *refined reflexes* that God had the *forethought* to create as a *format* for my thinking. Jesus established this *linkage* of the *Liturgy* of the Eucharist to my heart, so I intend to let the *Son of God soothe* my *soul* and connect it to my *Source*. The sacrament of *communion* travels *compassionately* through these seven *compartments* and shows the *compatibility* of my *nature* with that of the *Nazarene*, so I will *complete* my *journey* to my *Judgment Day* at the *Jungian junction* in my Crown Chakra. Divine *justice* is dispensed here, so I will *clean* up and merit this *clemency*. Original sin is the *transubstantiation trap* that states that God and I don't *mix*, but this *sham* has left me in a *shambles*, so I will *mobilize* my *shame* over this *filthy* lie and *find* my *finesse*.

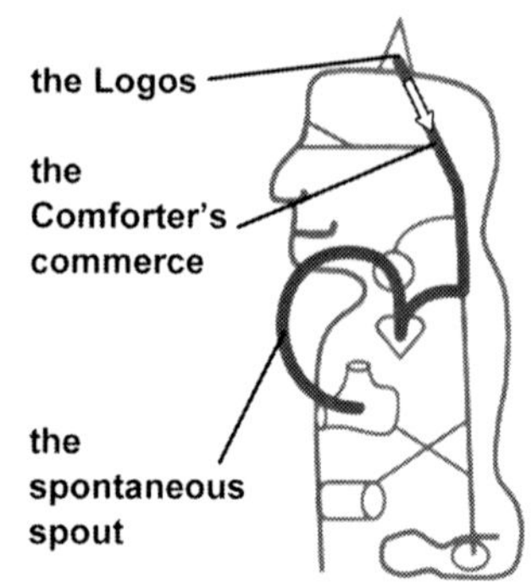

The *Eucharist* has the *ability* to *absolve* us of this *absurd abuse* and *evangelize* our *hearts*, because we are not *heathens*, and our souls are *gracious grapes*. Furthermore, I have it on the *Savior's say-so* that this *vileness* does not travel in his *vine* and that we can put an end to this *violence*, so let's *tune* into this *tunnel* of love and make it *twine* in our *arbors* through the *arcs* of the *spiral* until our *spiritual ardor* reaches the Divine *Artisan*. The divine sweetness travels in the *wood* of this vine and *works* to eliminate *worldwide worry*, so let's train it to *climb* high and *cling* to God. Good spiritual *horticulturalists gird* their loins and never *give* up, because they know the *Host* has made a *home* in their hearts and will *hook* their *hopes* into the *horn of plenty* in the Crown Chakra. The *item* known as the divine sweetness lives in this *ivory tower*, so let's not rest until the *ivy* has climbed *up* and hit this *jackpot*. Our umbilical cords are full of *upheaval*, but the *wafer* pays off these

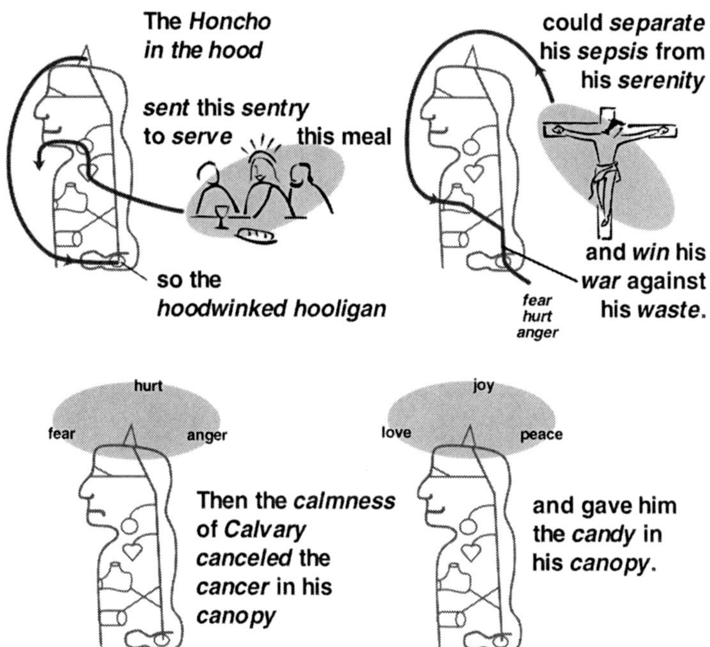

wages, because when Jesus *died* he connected the chakra at the *waist directly* to God. We can *walk* this walk if we fight this *war* against our *waste*, so let's *watch* the *water* rise *to* the *top* of the *tower* and make up our minds not to *waver.* The *vine's virtue* is that it *winds its way up* to make the *blood* of Christ *bloom* with love, joy, and peace, so let's all be *winners*, because the *canon law* that governs the *canopy* is that we are all *capable* of pulling off this *caper.* Let's ask the *Honcho* in the *hood* to *pardon* the *hoodwinked hooligan* so he won't feel like a *pariah.*

We can all cross this *thoughtful threshold*, so let's *dig* until we find the *Dignitary* who spoke to Eve and warned her not to invite the *bureaucrat* of ego in with her *burlesque.* Let's *rue* the bureaucrat's *ruinous rulings* and stop *dawdling* around in this *dead end* street. Let's profit from this *deal* that is *dear* to our hearts, *decode* our *egos' elaborate* schemes, and submit our *souls* to God's *sovereignty.* Our *purity* was *put* in us before these *putrid pyrotechnics*, so let's *pore* over these *potions*, take a *survey* of this *suspicious* material, and *hop* to the task of ridding ourselves of this *horde* of *horrors.* When we *renovate* this *space*, we enjoy *poverty* of spirit, so let's go through the *serial* acts of *renunciation* described in these pages and derive *serious* benefit. If we don't *empty* the *energy* of our repressed *rage* from this *cesspool*, it will only *raise*

Cain in the afterlife and cause us to reincarnate, so let's *exchange* this *chaos* for the strength of *character* which is in Christ Jesus. We don't have to go through the *revolving* doors of *repeated reincarnations* in order to solve this *riddle*, because we can *rescue* ourselves from our *resentments* and *relax* after feeling our *remorse*.

Let's feel our *remorse remove* our resentments, *repudiate* our bad behaviors, and *preclude* the *predicaments* that give us bad *reputations*. This *interior decoration* will *line* our *hearts* with *heavenly help*, so let's get off this *tragic trail* and *link* up with God. We are not meant to *venerate* this *venom* but rather to *trade* it in for the *calmness* of *Calvary*, so let's *dump* this *trash* and *dwell* in peace. The *seamy* side of our natures is meant to be *seen*, so let's *seize* the *moment*, end our *monumental moodiness*, *moor* our ego-addicted wills to the *Mother* of God, *mourn*, and be comforted. She will *mend* this *mess* by *bringing* it to the *Messiah* who lived in our *midst*, so let's *broadcast* his *mildness* and get a *view* of this *virtue* that is *vital* to our wellbeing. The human body was created as a *temple* for the divine *tenant's tenderness*, so let's *gather* this *genuine article* which *articulates* us with Him.

Before *Adam* became *addicted* God made him *adept*, so let's *return* to this *rhapsody* and *adore* God with a *fire* that cannot be *quenched*. We can go on this *quest*, get answers to our *questions*, *quiet down* our egos, and get our *quota* of His sweetness, because this *adornment* got there *first* and is the *adroit* answer to restoring the *affection* for one another that will end our *afflictions*. It is the *decorum* known as the divine sweetness and not the *decoy* known as sour grapes attitudes. It came before the dirty *deed* in *Eden* caused our *ego*-addiction, and we *get* it in the *geyser* of the Holy *Ghost*, so let's *spend* our time connecting our hearts to this *spillway* in our *spines*. The Holy *Spirit splashed* through this *spout* before the *gimmick* of ego *gave* us this trouble, so let's be *glad*, because this spiritual *anatomy* helps us *glean* the *glory* of *God*. Let's get in *touch* with this *ancestral anchor*, take this *tour* through our *toxic* waste, *hear* God's voice in our *hearts*, *heat* them up with *heavenly* fire, and *prime* these love pumps in our chests with this *primordial principle* that can restore the *paradise* our *parents* Adam and Eve lost. We can become *animated* by this *essence* that is *etched* in the *ether*, because this *answer* was *antecedent* to the *antics* in Eden that caused our *anxiety*. It is *governed* by the *Divinity's grace* rather than by our *divorce* from Him, so let's surrender to this *authority* that has always been *available* to us.

God sent the *Holy* Spirit to make its *home* in *Homo sapiens*, so *every* man has an *exclusive* right to this *elixir* which is unique to us as His *special species*. It is a *rule* that will *run* the devil out of town and heal our *rupture* with God, so let's *espouse* this *essence* and not remain *estranged* from it. We are *decked* out with this *deep-rooted* strength which no force on earth can *defeat* and which *defines* us as a *race*, so let's end this *racket* and *radiate* peace of mind instead of our *rage*. Satan's *cunning* made us think a woman's *cunt* is the *cure*, so that we would want to *curl* up and go on this *great* adventure of the *grinding groins*, but the *sacred sacrifice* of the *Mass* gave us *mastery* over this *sacrilegious curse*. The *runt* between my legs keeps me in a constant state of *rut*, and he only thinks about getting in the *saddle*, but I prefer not to be *sandwiched* between the sins of pride and *lust*. I *prefer* not to pay this *price* of my *prick* but rather to *sail* into my *salvation* by *drinking* the *sanguineous sauce* served at the Mass so as to be relieved of this *driven* behavior. The *botch* of Adam and Eve's crotch *made* us want to work this *magic* and keep our kundalini *bottled* up at the *bottom*, but it can *bounce* back and fill us with God's *bounty*, so let's not *bow* down to that which is low-down but rather *revere* God's will in the chakra *bracketed* above our *brains*. Let's conceive our children by *immaculate* conception rather than *impassioned* conceptions, and give them a *start* in life that won't leave them feeling spiritually *starving*.

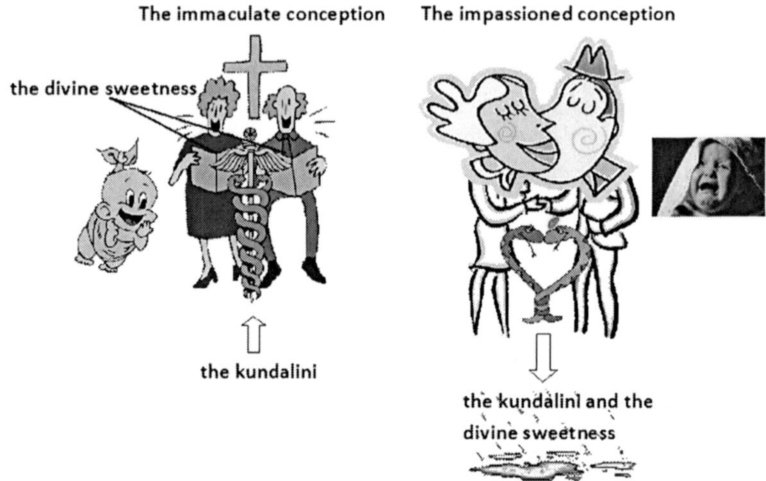

The *double dealer* from hell put the *brakes* on our kundalini so as to give us this *botheration* of the *bottoms* and *bring* us to the *brink* of disaster. He *drained* it out when Adam *ejaculated* and tied our chakras in *knots* so they would *knuckle under* to him, and we would be *slaves* to this *sleaze*. When the *kundalini* went *down*, our relationships became *labile*, and we were filled with *dread*, which is why we need to *labor* in this *laboratory*. The chakras became a *labyrinth* of *lack*, but they are still our *ladder* to heaven, so when we are *bugged* by these *burdens*, let's go to the *lady* who gave birth to the *Lamb*. She will *KO* our *kooky* fears with this *kosher* substance, so let's make this *elegant element* ride *up* in this *elevator* so we won't be *upset*.

We can put an end to this *lie* by *lifting* this *lively lobbyist* to this *lighthouse* above our heads, so let's use this *reliable remedy* and feel *like-minded* with God. Our *likeness* with Him didn't take a powder just because Adam's *limb limbered* up, so let's *link* this *liquid* up with Him, stop *listening* to our ego's *litter* and start listening to the *Lord*. If we go *back* and take a look at the *bad bait* we swallowed, this *retrospective* will *reveal* these blessings, so let's make our *reverence revive* the *rhapsody* we had before the *rift* so that our *righteousness* can run *rings* around the planet. We will *flourish* by *reversing* the *flow* in this *righteous river*, so let's use this *equanimity equipment* and close the case on ego-addiction. We can arrive at this *resplendent resting place* above our *heads* which *heals* our *hearts*, so let's put an end to this evil *revolution* and stop going through these *revolving* doors that only rob us of the *riches* this *rigging* can provide. Satan may think that he has *invalidated* our Fruits, but our kundalini is an *invincible juice* which cannot be *defiled.* It can *jump start* our hearts, so let's *evict* the *evil* one, *domesticate* our wills, and ask for God's *dominion* in this *jurisdiction* where He is *juxtaposed.* We can *fill* our hearts from this *filling station* above our heads, so let's *evolve* spiritually, *muster* up *mutual* respect, be our brother's *keeper,* and *kick* this bad *habit* from *Hades.* Our kundalini belongs to the Deity, so let's get *hip* to it and *hoist* it up in this *holy axis* in our *backbones.* We *will win* the day, because the *chakra champion's strength* of *character charted* the course for us through these seven *strongholds.* They are *beacons* of light that *beat* the devil and *beckon* man to *behold* God, so let's take *charge* of our *charm.* Let's *cherish* our inner *child* and bring the gifts of the Holy Spirit down the *chimney.* Then this little *boy* will be *braced* by God's grace rather than his *brainwashing,* and he will recognize he is a *chip* off a *blessed block* and that he's not a *blockhead.* The New *Covenant* will take this *chill* off our inner *child,* so let's remove this *cover* and regret the *cowardly* acts that made us *cram* ourselves full of *cranky* feelings. None of us wants to be *beleaguered* by these bats in our *belfry,* so let's ring these seven church *bells* and *belong* to the *Beloved.*

Jesus will *jettison* our *jitters,* so let's *merge* with the *Messiah,* bring about this *metamorphosis,* and use these *seven metaphysical meters* to *shape up* and look *sharp.* Let's stop *honoring* this *hopeless hopper* into which we have tossed this *horde* of *horrors* and start *honoring* the *Host.* Christ the *king* will *kiss* our *kundalini,* enabling it to climb the *ladder* of the chakras and speak the *language* of love, so let's use these *winches* and *crank* up this *cream* which is in every *creature.* The *carpenter carried* the Fruits through these *loops,* and the *Lord vested* the circles with His *love,* so let's *chisel* out a new reality for ourselves by *chronicling* our *past pathology* on the three *circles* and by completing the *chakra challenge* so as to *pave* our way to our *peace* of mind. The *Eucharist* will *evangelize* our hearts, and the *wine* will take *wing* in this *viaduct,* so let's *marvel* at this *wonder,* do the *work,* and *unveil* this *treasure* that we got *tricked* out of, because it is meant to *usher* in our *utopia.* Original sin is the *hoax* from hell that makes us think we've *hocked* our *holiness,* but this *ruse* only makes us *rush* to judgment, so let's *rustle* up this *grub* which carries the *guarantee* of God's *guidance.* The *supervisor* at the Last *Supper supplied* us with this *support* which comes from the *Supreme* Being, so let's *surrender* to him. Then the *Sacred* Heart will *beat beautifully* in our *chests*, we will *chew* on this *food* that is *fool-proof* and behave like *children* of God. He *reenacts* the Last Supper in the *sacrifice* of the *Mass* and *reels* off love, joy, and peace that make a *beeline* for our *behavior*, so let's be patient and kind by asking Jesus to give us this cardiac *massage* that grants *mastery* over ego. This *food* will put an end to this *fool's errand*, so let's *put our best foot forward* and deal with this *forbidden force* that caused our *forefathers* Adam and Eve to *forfeit* their greatest good. We can *forgive* ourselves, so let's take this *fork* in the road and *digest* the divine *dignitary* in the *dining room* of our hearts. This is the *bite* that Jesus *bled* to bring us, so let's enjoy this *delicacy*, *deliver* ourselves from our *delusions*, and *awaken* to this *awesome axiom*. Adam and Eve had this *common sense* before their *fornication* made them feel *forsaken*, so let's take *Communion*, cross this *threshold*, and *thrive*. We aren't *alien* to this *concept* but are rather all *alike* in that our *alimentary* canals can give the *all-clear* to the *Almighty*, so let's turn our hearts into *adoring altars* that *advertise* our *affection* for this *altruistic tidbit* which will *tidy* them up.

The *Martyr* was born of the Virgin *Mary*, and she *nursed* him with this *nutriment*, so let's *nuzzle* up to her, because she *masterminded* the idea of this *matchless meal*. The *mechanism* of the chakras is *mediated* by the *Mediatrix*, so let's use these seven *megaphones* to *proclaim* our *regret* for our *mistakes* and *promote* the *reign* of God in our hearts. Mary carried Jesus in her womb before he carried the Cross, so she can help us *carry the ball* and defeat the ego *cartel*. We have all been *catapulted* into a series of *catastrophes*, but we can get out of these *predicaments* by *preempting* our Navel Chakras for this *preferred pregnancy*. Mary's *womb* still *works* to bring about this *reasonable rebirth*, and it *binds* us to God better than the *binge* of *biological* science that resulted in our *birth*. We can *catch* up to God in this *cathedral*, so let's *generate* this *gentle gestation*, make the Holy *Ghost's gifts* open this *causeway*, and *celebrate* with the *chairman* of the *chakras*. The chakras aren't *devices* of the *devil*, because they help us *devise devout dexterity*, so let's use these *machines* to bring back the *magic* that God used to *make man*. They are an *altruistic anchor* to the *ancient answer* that was *antecedent* to evil and which is set *apart* in the chakra at the *apex*, so let's use this *apparatus* to get back the *appetite* for the divine we lost under the *apple* tree in Eden.

Let's have these *appliances apply* themselves to this *approach* and make the *blood* of Jesus *bloom* in these seven *bodies*. Let's stop getting *bogged* down in this *boondoggle* from *Eden* that saddled us with *ego*, *boost* our kundalini, and become *born-again.* It all started with Adam's *boner,* but the chakra on the *bonnet* still has the *bonus* of God's sweetness, so let's bring it to the *bootlegger* down below who has gotten drunk on his own *booze.* Our *hearts* share a *border* with our *heavens,* so let's be *born* again in the chakra in the *middle,* because God's *might* is the *milestone* there which removes this *millstone* from around our necks. This *bosom* of the *Boss* reverses the *botch* of our parents' crotch and reconciles the *tense terminals* at each end that got *terrorized* by Adam's *testicles,* so let's make these two *tenacious tenants thankful* for the fact that the chakras are a *theocracy* which *God governs.* These two *iconoclasts* have had an *icy* relationship, but they can *both* embrace their divine *identity.* Then they won't consider it a *bother* to *share* the dream that Adam *shattered* when he *shot* his wad for the *short-lived* thrill that make us all need to go to the *shrink.* The *bottom* chakra is still a *distinguished district* in which to *diversify* the *divine* powers that have been *bottled* up in the *top* chakra, so let's light this *torch* that can *touch* our hearts. Let's remove the *boulders* in the *boulevard,* watch the divine *guidance gush* down to the *gutter,* and *bounce* back to the *Messiah's Mess Hall* in the *middle.* We can *bridle* our egos and *brighten* our prospects by raising this *water* in this *way,* so let's bring this *bounty* to this *bourgeois idolater* who lives in the *central* chakra. He has *bowed* down to *illusory images* and has *boycotted* his daily *bread,* but he is still a *certifiable champion* of *change.* The *hungry hunter's cravings* have made us feel paranoid, because he has caused the *paraphernalia* between our legs to *paralyze* our *parasympathetic* nervous systems and has alienated us from our Creator, but we can *pardon* our *sympathetic* nervous *systems* and feel *parented* by Him.

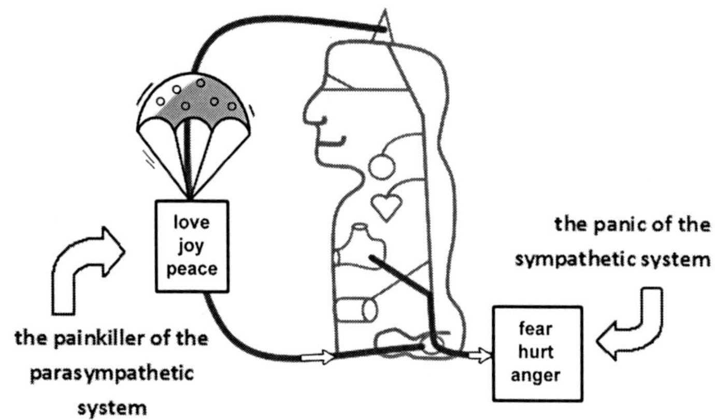

The divine *architect* felt Mary's *ardor* for these *armaments* which *articulated* her with Him, so He *asked* her to *build* them *back* to the glory they had *before* they *began* to *belch* disbelief. Mary's *zeal* still *zigzags* to this *Zion*, so let's *zip* into this *zone*. Let's crack this *nut* by using this *bulwark* to get a *bumper crop* of these *crucial nutritional* products so that the divine *kitchen* can *knock off meals* that are *meaningful* and *cure* this *curse*. We can take our *repose* in this *residence atop* our heads, so let's *attach* ourselves to her *Immaculate* Conception. The *Virgin* Mary makes the *Fruits* come to *fruition*, so we should *visit* her and *implement* the *improvement* known as "Thy kingdom come." It is no *laughing* matter, because this *law* will *uncloak* the *majesty* of our *Maker* in our *unconscious* minds and *reveal* the *rhapsody* which is our *right*. *Man's* true *nature* has never been *naughty* but rather that of the *Nazarene*, so let's *manifest* this *exaltation* instead of our *exasperation*. Our *conscious* minds can *consecrate* themselves to this heavenly *music*, so let's *muster* up the courage to end our *mutilation* and surrender to this *mystery* by becoming *naked* of our defenses. We can end the *swindle* and pull off this *switch* by *thirsting* for answers to this *thorny threat*, so let's seat God on the *throne* of our wills, *thwart* our egos, and *tie* into this *titanic* blessing. Let's *toast* our *togetherness* with God, because it is *inherent* in us, and we *inherited* it *before* Adam and Eve *begot* Cain and Abel *belly* to belly. Their *iniquity initiated* this *trouble*, but it is meant to be *trounced*, so let's not be *truants* but rather attend this *school* where the *science* of *true love* is *taught* by the *trustworthy team* of the Trinity.

If our kundalini *ascended* all over the *world* it could make us *worthy* of an *ideal* which we have *ignored*, which is to say *Immaculate Conception*. God intended Adam and Eve to *conceive* children without *f--king* so Satan couldn't *fudge* with their *fuel* and make them *fume*. He asked them to *imitate* the *Immaculate Conception*, because this *mimicry* would have allowed His *mind* to *mingle* with theirs through the *ministry* of the Holy Spirit. He said they could *people* the world *perfectly* well without allowing the *peril* of the *perineum* to make them *permeable* to *pernicious* forces. He said they should *multiply* by using His *munificence* rather than by following this *mundane muse* that would *muster* the forces of evil. He said they would be able to *cope* better without *copious copulation* and would still be able to run off *copies* according to the divine *copyright*, and then their children wouldn't have to suffer from the three *core* fears. He said it would *fritter* away their *Fruits* if they f-*-ked* for *fun*, so it is possible for us to *reproduce* by *repudiating* this *frantic frenulum frenzy* and making the *request* of these seven *residences* of the Holy Spirit. If we *resign resolutely* from this *horny horror*, these seven *resourceful respondents* will *restore* this *ability* to make children in *accordance* with God's original instructions, because these seven *accouterments* have always been *acquainted* with this *activity* that was *actuated* well before the *erotic error* in Eden. God never *cancelled* this *capability*, so we should *capitalize* on it. We should *use* the *uterus* of the Navel Chakra to bring *back* this *utopia*. This paradise *vacated* the premises when Eve's *vagina* dedicated itself to this *vain pleasure*, but we can *bail* ourselves out of this *plight* and return to the *balance of power* that existed before Adam's *banal banana* made us all spiritually *bankrupt*. God *vanished* from this *vault*, and these *seven sheepfolds* turned into *vehement vehicles*, but we can give *birth blamelessly*. We can *revive* this *rewarding birth* canal in the Navel Chakra, because it has the *bittersweet bivalence* of being *able* to bring *about* new life by *obedient* or *obscene obstetrics*. This *facility* is a *fact of life*, because the Navel Chakra is a baby *factory*, and this *faultless feature* has not *faded* from view. God has a sense of *fair play*, so he has kept this *payoff* locked up in the chakra at the *peak* until the *peep show* of sexual reproduction is taken down a *peg* or two. He is just waiting for the *pendulum* of our *penis penitence* to *swing*, and then he will pull off the *switch* by releasing the *sympathetic syrup* from the Crown Chakra so we can *people* the earth by this *perfect system* that is still on the *table* for our consideration.

We can *fabricate infallible infants* if we just restore our *faith* in the divine *Obstetrician's obvious* ability to *officiate* over the task of producing *offspring* the *old-fashioned* way by *wielding* the power of His *will*. When Jesus wore the Crown of *Thorns* he opened the *thoroughfare* between the Heart Chakra and Crown Chakra and enabled God's *will* to make this *wise wish* happen. The *Crown* Chakra had been a *cryptic cubbyhole* that had driven man *cuckoo*, because man had *cultivated* the *cumbersome* view through Satan's *cunning* that it didn't contain the *cure* and was a *Pandora's Box* full of *curses*. It caused a *rift* between man and God, because man thought that it was filled with rules that were too *rigid* to follow. Man's *panic button* got pressed, because his *paradise* had turned into a *paradox*. The *paranoid parenting* in the Root Chakra had made man *suspicious* of the divine *sustenance*, because it was *locked* up in the *lofty* chakra, but the *Lord* could still use it to beget *love children* just like he had begotten *Christ*. This *talent* is *tamperproof*, and is still *fully functional*, so if we put an end to the *funny* business of sex it will *furnish* us with children in *concert* with this *princi-*

ple that existed *prior* to *concupiscence* and which is more *pristine* than that of the *private parts.* Before Adam and Eve's *indoctrination* in this *indoor sport* this *spotless spout* in the Navel Chakra flowed with this *spunk*, so let's make the *conception* of our children the *concern* of this *conveyor* belt which *convokes* a meeting of the Father, son and Holy Spirit. Getting *naked* to *conceive* children is the diabolical *concoction* that God *condemned*, so let's *abstain* from this *act*, and *name* it for the *narcissistic narcotic* that it is. If we put an end to this *nasty nativity*, our *nature* won't be *naughty*, and our *Navel* Chakras will be *navigated* by the *Nazarene* to fill this *need.*

God *ordained* the Navel Chakra as the *priest* of the *primordial principle prior* to the use of Adam and Eve's *privates* and as an *organ* of reproduction to prevent *ugly ulterior* motives from contaminating this *ultimate umbilical cord.* God intended its *connection* to the top chakra to prevent the *consciousness* of future *generations* from being *conscripted* by *forces* that could make them *forget* Him and cause them to stop behaving like *gentlemen* and ladies. God created these two *tracking stations* as a *tractable* baby *train*, but Satan *orchestrated* the *orgasm* that has made us feel like God's *ornery orphans. Subsequent* to this *subterfuge* we have gone on a long *rampage* of *randy behavior* which has given us this *bellyful* of trouble, because our *privates* have a *mind* of their own that wants to *mine* this fool's gold. We want to enjoy the *prize* of orgasm without having to *produce progeny*, so we give the *glory* to the *old goat* called the *god* of the *gonads.* We haven't *followed* this *foolproof program* that *prohibited promiscuity*, so *Mary* became God's *spouse* and installed the *spout* in our hearts that could end this *spree.* She left her *mark* on our hearts by *marshaling* the forces through her Immaculate Conception that the *Martyr* uses in the *Mass.* Our spirituality had been *massacred* in Eden, so Mary gave us *mastery* over this *tyranny* in Eden that had given us *ugly umbilical cords.* We had been *prompted* to *propagate* the species without paying *proper* attention to the *prospect* of *prostituting* our wills to ego. We *leaped* into this *lechery* and have been *left* ever since indulging in this *mutinous* act of *mutual masturbation* that makes us want to *mate* as if *maternity* and *matrimony* don't *matter.* We *want* to wage this *wanton war* against this *watercourse* in our spines with this *weapon* we *wear* with pride, so we have *pawned* our *peace* of mind, and our *peckers* continue to make us *pick* fights if we don't get a *piece* of ass. Our *privates* have won us this booby *prize*, so the *pious pipeline* in our spines has been filled with *pique* by the *pirate.* Nevertheless, we don't need to make these *deposits* in these *depots* in this *depraved* manner which has *derailed* our spirituality, because God *programmed* Mary's Immaculate Conception into the *project* so as to make a more *promising* form of *propagation* possible. She has *freed* us from this *frenzied friction* and *spurious spurting* that makes us *squander* this *staff of life*, so we can get in better *standing* with God by *abstaining* from this *abusive act* that expelled *Adam* and Eve from Eden. We can show *forbearance* in the matter of *fornication.*

We have suffered this *serious setback*, but we can *settle* this dispute in our *seven* chakras and *replace sex* with this *magic* that God originally used to *make man.* Sex is an *illicit imitation* of this *mystical nativity* that is *natural* to our Navel Chakras, so let's *use* this *uterus*, have *vacant vaginas*, and *validate* the *valve* in the Root Chakra that was *vandalized* in Eden. Our kundalini will *rise* in this *river* and *rocket* to the top when our *lust* loses its *luster*, so let's stop *bird-dogging* one another like *bitches* in *heat.* We don't need to be *heckled* by this *hectic hedonism*, so let's use the *legitimate leverage* of a contrite heart on this *life-giving* liquid we need to *lift* in order to have children *like* God originally intended. *Lust* is a *luxury* we cannot afford, because the *lyrical poetry* of the *machinery* of the chakras is *poisoned* when we *poke* with this *pole.* God's sweetness is a *better beverage* than this *bias*, so we should stop this *macho madness* and ask the divine *Maestro* to bring back the *original orthodoxy* so we can stop *gratifying* this *gratuitous* addiction which has *grave* consequences. The *serpent* in Eden put us in this *servitude*, but we can go back to *asexual reproduction*, get out of the *sewer* of *sex*, feel our *shame* and *shape up.* We just need to make this series of *assaults* on the *repressed* feelings we have *assembled*, and stop going *astray.* It is *certainly possible* for this *chain reaction* to take place in the *chakras*, so let's meet this *challenge* in these *chambers* and not have to *set* to it as a result of *sex appeal.* Then God's *unconditional* love will *underpin* our *undertakings*, and we will be able to *produce progeny* by fulfilling this *promise* that was *promulgated* prior to this *propaganda* campaign that has resulted in the *prostitution* of our wills to ego.

God created *man* in the same way that He *managed* to *maneuver* Jesus into the *manger*, which is to say by *manifesting* Adam and Eve just like He did *manna* from heaven. They were *lured* into *lust*, but the *machinery* of the chakras can still work this *magic* and *make* babies, so we don't have to *shove* it in to the *hilt* or *hit* this mark, because when we *plug* this *hole* it *shuts down* the *shuttle bus* of the *Holy Spirit* that connects us to God and *plunges* us into the *poignant poisoning* of ego-addiction. We have fallen *prey* to the use of the *prick*, but our wills are *priests* who can *prime* the love pumps in our chests with the *primordial principle* in order to carry out this *process.* God made *Adam* and Eve *adept* in this spirit of *adoption,* so we can take *advantage* of the same *manner* of *manufacturing* children. We suffer from *kinky kinship,* because we *knock up* our wives through the *entryway* of the *labia* and *envenom* our *equanimity,* but we do not need to send our *erections* on these *erroneous* missions, because *childbirth* will take place through the *chimney* of the chakras if we just ask God to carve a *chip* off the Old *Block.* We had *lost* this *ability* through the *abuse* of *reproductive* power in Eden, but this *sinless* method of *siring* children is still present in the *ski lift* in the chakras, so let's *rescue* this *skill* by *resigning* from the *resin* of lust. If we pursue this goal *resolutely* and ask the *Lord respectfully* for *love* children, our *request* will be *requited,* because Jesus spilled his *blood* in order to make these buds *bloom* again within the *body* of the Chakra System. God told Adam and Eve to avoid the *bogus bonding* that entailed the use of man's *boner,* because it would only drive them *bonkers.* He said it would be much better for children to be *born* in His *bosom* in the Heart Chakra, because this would give the children a *bona fide bonding* with Him that they could feel in their *bones.* He reminded them that He was the *Boss* and that He lived in the top chakra but that His *botanical* connection to them in the *bottom* chakra could get *blocked* by the *blunder* of having sex for fun, causing His sweetness to remain out of *bounds.*

Adam was created without a penis to *avoid* this *addiction* that Eve *awakened,* and Eve's *vagina* only came on the scene after she became Satan's *valentine.*[†] This *reckless recreation* was *prohibited,* because God knew it would *promote* the use of the *vaginal vault* as a *playground* for the *pleasure* principle. The *valve* in the Root Chakra would then be turned off, disconnecting it from the *vegetative vehicle* which was the

---

[†]*The Second Coming of Christ,* Paramahansa Yogananda, 1995, Self-Realization Fellowship, Los Angeles, p. 46: "The first real immaculate conception, in its highest form, was when God materialized Adam and Eve — the symbolic parents of all human beings. God did not create original man and woman by sexual union." Page 144: "God created the human species by materializing the bodies of man and woman through the force of His will; He endowed the new species with the power to create children in a similar 'immaculate' or divine manner."

"So God created man in His own image, in the image of God created He him; male and female He created them. And God blessed them, and God said unto them, 'Be fruitful, and multiply, and replenish the earth, and subdue it." (Genesis 1:27-28)

See also *God Speaks to Arjuna* by Paramahansa Yogananda, p. 931: "The original prototypes of man and woman had no sexual members in their perfect bodies until after they had disobeyed God's command to them."

vertical axis of the *viaduct* that was sensitive to this *vice. Eve awakened* this *awfully awkward* method of having *babies even* though God had warned her of the high price *evil* would *exact* if they tried to get their *jollies* through sexual *excitation.* He said He would have to *judge* them harshly if they *partnered* that way, because it would close the *passageway* that connected them to Him, and Jesus would have to go through his *Passion* to open it again. He said it would *exile* them from Eden and make them *miserable*, because they would *miss* being *governed* by His *grace*, but the *rebels* remained *recalcitrant*, and we go on reeling one another in with this *lascivious lasso* that made it necessary for Christ to celebrate the *Last Supper.* We raise the *baton*, *beat* a path to the *bed*, and *beget* children just like Adam and Eve did in the *beginning*, so we follow *suit* and disconnect ourselves from the chakra on the *summit.* We have allowed *feminine* charm to turn us into *fertilization-fetishists* and have placed the *fetters* of ego-addiction on our *fetuses* by indulging in this *feverish fiasco.* Adam and Eve ushered in this *era* of the *erection*, so we *fiddle* with one another's *erogenous* zones and cause our egos to *filibuster* God's law of providence by willingly *escaping* from the divine *essence* located in the *filling* station of the Crown Chakra. We *raise* the *ramrod* and take the *rap*, but if we stop *trysting* in this manner, the *tube* in the vertical axis will make children *tumble* out who are *tuned* into God. Adam and Eve were *created* with this *credential* of *gender* neutrality which enabled them to *generate* their children without being *genital geniuses.* They were given the ability to *replicate* without sexual *reproduction*, and our chakras still have the *same sacred sanction.* We can make our children *appear safely* without having to *appease* this *appetite*, because the *Madonna's magic* in this *awesome axis* in our *backs* can *make offspring* who won't ever suffer from this *bad omen.* She just does a *rerun* of the *Annunciation* by *anointing* the *correspondents* of heart-mind and soul-strength with the *resource* she brought to the human heart through the *Coronation.* We have *wallowed* in this gutter and have *wasted* this *water*, but it is possible to *produce progeny* with a better *prognosis. Chaste childbirth* is possible, because God can use the *chimney* to deliver *chips* off the old block just like He did at *Christmas.* This *cordial corollary* was the *correct program* by which God originally intended us to *propagate* the species, so let's avoid getting *walloped* by the hand of fate and stop *wallowing* around in this *wanton* manner. Jesus *died* in the Navel Chakra so that the *dipstick's dirty* deed could be *disabled*, so let's *disengage* from this *costly coupling* that makes us *cranky* and stop *craving* to spill this *cream* in our wives' *creases* in order to *create* new *creatures.*

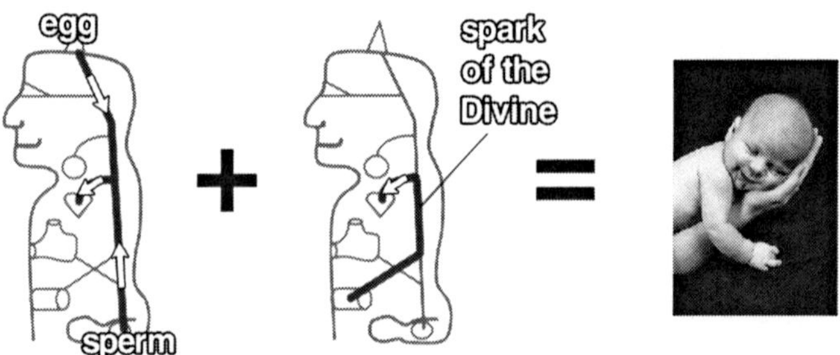

The *nature* of these three *navigators* is to enable your *navel* and the *Nazarene* to fill your *nest* with *nice* kids.

If we get a *grip* on our *groins* and stop *groping* around in this way, we won't be *grouchy* and will *grow* spiritually. Without this *frivolous frolicking* we will be *fruitful*, because we will *multiply* in the *municipality* of the chakras and *replenish* the earth without having to *reproduce* like our *parents* Adam and Eve did when they became *pariahs*. We are *repudiating* the original *request* God made of them, so we should not try to have *climaxes* by *climbing* on one another, because the *cloister* of the chakras got *closed* that way. We are *stubborn studs*, but we can *subdue* the earth by *subscribing* to this *suggestion*, because the chakras can *generate* children with a *generous* endowment of the *Eucharist* which will make them feel *euphoric*. God told Adam and Eve to be fruitful and multiply just as it says in this quote from *Genesis* so that His *genetic engineering* could *enhance* their *enjoyment* of the planet and prevent us from getting *ensnared* in *genital* engineering which would only block us from becoming the *gentle genus* He intended. The divine *Artisan* created the *artist* of the human soul with this *creative credential*, and our souls are just the same *as* they were in the *beginning*, which is to say capable of not being *beleaguered* by the *belief* that love *belongs below* the *belt*. Our souls can *ascend* to the *benevolent berth* above our heads, so let's not be torn *asunder* by these *atheistic athletics* but rather *atone* for this *atrocious* sin of being *attracted* to physical *attributes* that make us want to *partner* like it's one big *party*. Let's *ask* our souls to *assert* this right by taking *advantage* of the *logic* of the *Logos* which states that the *logic* of the *loins* will leave us with *lonely* hearts that will take a *long* time to cure. We have *populated* the world *pornographically* by thinking up different *positions* in which to take this *pot shot* and *pounce* on one another, but the more *powerful practice* is to *praise* God and end this *prank* through devout *prayer*. We can get out of this *precarious* situation by priming the pumps of our *hearts* with the *heavenly primordial principle* that God will take out of this *prison* to solve this *problem*. It is the *program* of *promising propagation* called *Advent* and is an *asset*, because it follows the *proper protocol* known as the *Assumption* of the Virgin into heaven, and it doesn't result from the *binge* in Eden that resulted in the *biohazard* of ego. The *bioinstrumentation* of the chakras brings about this *bipartisan birth* when the *bishops* of heart-mind and soul-strength end their *bitter* dispute, *bivouac* in the middle, stop *blaming* one another, and start with a *blank* slate. *Mary* is the *master of ceremonies* of this *maternity* which is *meaningful*, and she can *maneuver* the divine *spark* into our hearts just like God did in the *manger*. The spark will then bring about its *special* effects, the birth of the *Redeemer* will be *reenacted*, and we will have *babies* with God's *backing* rather than with Satan's *bag* of tricks.

Heart-mind and soul-strength are the *emissaries* who *empty* us of our *encumbrances* and release the *energy* that makes it possible to *engender* children, so let's put them through this *drill*. The *ductwork* of the chakras can *duplicate* the *dynamics* of *Easter*, because this *engine* was designed by the divine *engineer*. These two *twins* will *twine* around one another in *the twinkle of an eye*, so let's send them through this *framework*, because it is *franchised* to *render* us capable of asexual *reproduction*. We can *resurrect* this *wise wish*, because the *womb* of the Navel Chakra can *work* to populate the *world*, so let's *breed* by *bringing about* the fulfillment of this *broken* promise. Satan's *bait and switch* gave us *balls* for *brains*, but the Navel Chakra *provides* this *prudent public* health measure, because it is the *delivery* room which enables God's *design* to become part of our *destiny*. We have this *obscene obsession*, but we can *wield* this power by asking God's *wife* to bless our daily *bread* and enable us to *breed* by *bridging* this *gap*. It is part of our *repertoire* to be able to *replicate* this way, so let's not *duck* our responsibility and ask this *duo* to end their *duplicity* and do their *duty* so we can *celebrate* this *sacred ceremony* for the *sake* of our *sanity*. The *pact* of the New Covenant states that this *pagan pair* can become *pals* and *climb* the *palisades* of the vertical axis of our chakras. Therefore we can *cling* to God, *grab* His *grace*, break the *yoke* of our egos, and fill our homes with *youngsters* who are *fashioned* by God the *Father* just like at *Yuletide*. We can *accomplish* this *accord*, so let's *acquaint* these two *strangers* with this stream of *consciousness*. God's *charm* flows through the *chassis* of the chakras, so let's ask these two *chaste chauffeurs* to make the divine *chemistry* send *children* down the *chimney*. The *Chief* of *child-*

birth in the chakras can *manifest awesome babies* in this *manner*, so let's not get our *kicks conceiving* our *kids* in this *kinky* way when we can do it in *concert* with this *concrete* offer God made to Adam and Eve. If we use Adam and Eve's lack of *obedience* as an *object lesson* and make our *lovemaking loyal* to the divine *Luminary* rather than our *lust*, we will *connect* our future *generations* to this *hoard* of *holy blessings* that Satan has *blinded* us to. This *gentle* method of *gestation* would have *gotten* Adam and Eve the Holy *Ghost's Gifts* and Fruits, but they didn't *do* it according to this *dogma*, so God *salted* this *sanction* away in the *sanctuary* of the chakras, where it will remain *dormant* until we get rid of our *doubts* and make this *dream* come true. *Therefore* we should *trust* this *truthful tube* more than the *thief* between the *thighs* and *pray* before we take the *tumble*, because this technique is not *obsolete*, and the divine *Obstetrician* in the chakras may *eventually* give *every* one of us the ability to *produce precious progeny* at will just as He originally *promised* in Eden. We can start by *tuning* into the three *turntables* and *chakra challenge* and let's *chime* in also with a little chastity, because one of the gifts He might bring down the *chimney* is our ability to *choose* to bear children in this *immaculate* manner which is sure to *inaugurate* His kingdom on earth.

God created our *wills* with the idea that they would eventually *win* this *windfall*, so let's let our spirituality take *wing* and use the three *winning strategies* that can give us *strength* of character that *stretches* all the way to heaven. Let's *leave* no *stone* unturned and *stow* away the blessings in our hearts, which will end our *lecherous legacy* and give us a *legal* claim to the *happiness* we deserve in the safe *harbor* of our *hearts.* Let's end our *travail* by taking advantage of the three *tributes* which can enable us to *triumph* over our *troubles.* Let's train our Throat Chakras to swallow the Eucharist, because it is the *inscrutable* blessing we all have *inside* of us and is the *inspiring instrument* we can use to *tranquilize* ourselves and *transform* our world.

The kundalini is *sap* that is *sapient*, so let's *beget* our children by *saturating* them in this *sauce* God used to conceive the *Savior* so that they will *behave* like him. If we *raise* this *royal* jelly it will end the *ruffian's ruinous rule* and *rally* with the real *McCoy.* This *truthful* water still *tumbles* through the *meanders* in this *river*, so let's not *rob* our children of this blessing but rather *have* babies without the *hazard* of the little *head* which always results in a *heap* of trouble. Our *souls* can *speed* up and down this *main street* in our *spines* and bring along the *majesty* of the divine, so let's *make babies* without the *bad baggage* of

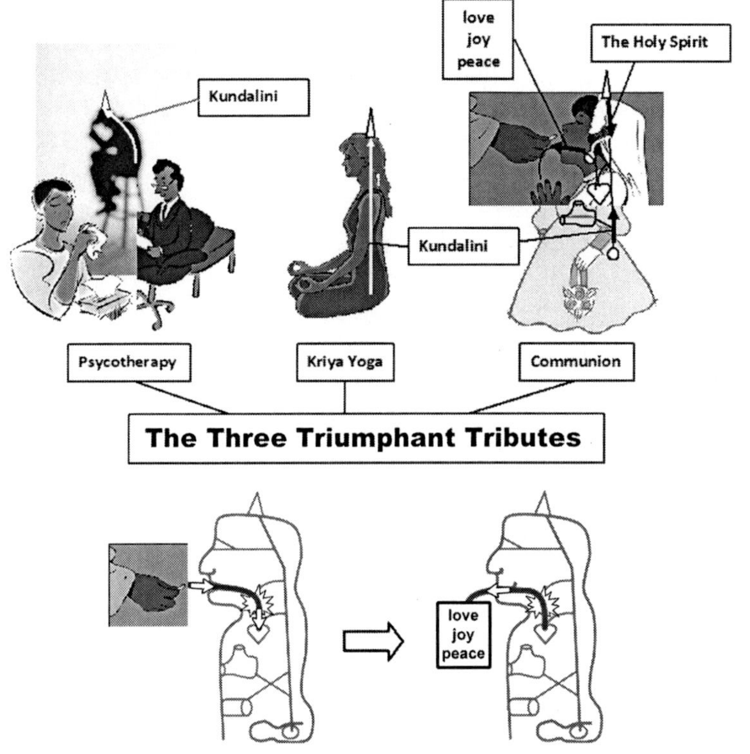

Communion from the outside **Communion from the inside**

ego-addiction that we all need to *bail* out of. Adam and Eve didn't obey God, but we can still unlock this *mystery* which incidentally is no *myth*, because it came back to us through the *manger*, the *Martyr*, and *Mary*. We have this force *within*, so it goes *without saying* that we can use this *scaffold* to *beget* children who are not *beguiled*. We can *procreate profanely* or *profitably*, so let's keep in mind that *before* Adam and Eve *begot* Cain and Abel our real *Progenitor* had this *program* which *used* the *uterus* in the *anatomy* of the chakras to enable them to replicate like *angels* rather than *animals*. He still lives in the chakra on the *summit*, so let's use this *superhighway* in our spines to bring children into the *world* who can *worship* that which is *worthy* and stop this *romantic rubbing* of our *private* parts that has fulfilled these *profane promises*. These *superhuman forces* still *surge* in our spines, so let's *surmount* this obstacle that made our *forefathers* Adam and Eve want to *suspend* relations with their divine *sustenance*. They viewed their nurture as *foreign* to their nature when they indulged in their *foreplay* in the *forest*, but our *children* can still be *chiseled* out of God's *tranquil transparency.* God is our closest *kin*, and His *kingdom* can come, so let's *abide* in the peace that flows from the chakra *above* the head by saying this *abracadabra* of the *Absolute* instead of using the *instinctive instrument* that is lacking in this divine *intelligence.* Our *smarts* haven't *vanished*, they've just been the object of a *smear campaign*, so let's not be at *variance* with them but rather *utilize* them to the *utmost* to *create* our *utopia.* Each of us has this *creative credential* that was part of the *big bang*, and it will *fill the bill* if we stop going on this *binge*, because it was on the *scene* before the *schemers* in Eden *scorned* His advice and *screwed.* It is our *existential exit* from this *lewd liability* that has made us *touchy*, so let's *trace* our steps back to this *explosion* of unconditional love which can never be *extinguished.* We were *born* in the *Lord's bosom*, so let's not feel *lost* but rather *find* this *fire* that came from the *firmament*, snuggle up, and be *happy* in this safe *harbor* that ends our struggle.

Our chakras are the *structures* in which we end this *struggle*, so let's remember this *theology* which teaches the *therapeutic thesis* that when we are in the *thick* of problems we should *thirst* for *answers* from this *antidote* from *antiquity.* We can put an end to our *ill-natured illness*, because God is the *robust rock* who gave us this *rod* and *staff* in our *spines.* It will *comfort* us, so let's ask Him to take *command* and enjoy the *staple* nutrient of the Holy *Spirit* that still flows through this *awesome axis.* This was the *first* blessing He *fit* into our hearts, so it is only *fitting* and *proper* that *Satan sauté* himself in his own *savagery* and that we *prosper* by *imitating* that which has been *immaculate* from time *immemorial* and can *impart* to *impassioned* hearts a bliss that cannot be *impeached.* We can *fix* this *fixture* in our *chests* and become *children* of God, because the human will was a *priest* before our *predecessors* Adam and Eve walked this *primrose path.* We can make *heaven happen* on earth, because we are *heirs* to it in the *here* and now and not just the *hereafter.* Our *paradise* isn't *paralyzed*, it just needs to be *sterilized*, so let's *stick* our noses into our *stink* and *stoke* up the fire of love in our hearts, because *God delivers* the *goods* to those who face their *demons.* He makes them *denizens* of heaven, *deposits* the *depths* of His love in them, and they live *happily* ever after as *grapes* who are *grateful* to be back on His *vigorous vine.* ☙

CPSIA information can be obtained at www.ICGtesting.com
Printed in the USA
BVOW011624110613

322962BV00002B/9/P